Money and Its Laws

Also from Westphalia Press
westphaliapress.org

Money and Its Laws

Embracing a History of
Monetary Theories and
A History of the Currencies of
the United States

---

by
Henry V. Poor

WESTPHALIA PRESS
An imprint of Policy Studies Organization

Westphalia Press
An imprint of Policy Studies Organization
1527 New Hampshire Ave., NW
Washington, D.C. 20036
info@ipsonet.org

ISBN-13: 978-1-63391-707-1
ISBN-10: 1-63391-707-X

Cover design by Jeffrey Barnes:
jbarnesbook.design

Daniel Gutierrez-Sandoval, Executive Director
PSO and Westphalia Press

Updated material and comments on this edition
can be found at the Westphalia Press website:
www.westphaliapress.org

MONEY AND ITS LAWS:

EMBRACING

A HISTORY OF MONETARY THEORIES,

AND

A HISTORY OF THE CURRENCIES OF THE UNITED STATES.

BY

HENRY V. POOR.

He knoweth not the law who knoweth not the reason thereof.
LORD CHIEF JUSTICE COKE.

———•———

NEW YORK:

H. V. AND H. W. POOR,

68 BROADWAY.

LONDON: HENRY S. KING AND CO., 65 CORNHILL.

1877.

Cambridge:
Press of John Wilson & Son.

TO

GEORGE S. COE,

PRESIDENT OF THE AMERICAN EXCHANGE BANK, AND CHAIRMAN OF THE

NEW YORK CLEARING HOUSE ASSOCIATION,

IN TOKEN OF ESTEEM FOR HIS CHARACTER, AND IN ACKNOWLEDGMENT OF HIS

EARNEST AND INTELLIGENT LABORS FOR THE REFORMATION OF

OUR CURRENCY,

THIS WORK IS RESPECTFULLY INSCRIBED.

PREFACE.

In the following pages the subject of Money has been treated as coming within the range of the exact sciences; the conclusions being assumed to be in the nature of demonstrations. That they wholly contradict those laid down in the books, which have been accepted as fundamental truths for more than two thousand years, is due to the fact that a subject which could only be made to yield to rigid analysis has been treated after the manner of Aristotle and the Schools. Although the laws of Money are assumed to be sufficiently laid down in the first part of the work, the writer, from the universal prevalence of erroneous opinions, has lost no opportunity of illustrating them in the discussions which follow. If he have not in all cases clearly established the connection between his conclusions and premises, the reason will, he believes, be found in the fact that he has not, with all his efforts, yet been able entirely to emancipate himself from the methods of the Economists and Schoolmen.

Brookline, Mass., 1877.

TABLE OF CONTENTS.

THE LAWS OF MONEY.

	Page
The desire to possess gold and silver an original instinct stronger than that felt for any other kind of property.	1
This universal desire renders them the universal equivalent — MONEY	2
The grounds of this preference, their beauty and the uses to which they can be applied.	2
Other qualities fitting them to serve as money	2
Illustration of the uniformity of their value (note)	2
From their durability they become the reserves of society	2
Illustrations of their value as reserves (note)	3
Errors in monetary science have arisen chiefly from overlooking their universal attractiveness	3
Necessity to social and material progress of some article or articles for which a supreme preference is felt	4
Demanded in exchange for all other articles, and in discharge of all contracts	5
Their value ABSOLUTE; depending upon cost alone	6
That of all other articles RELATIVE; depending upon cost and demand	6
Their value being absolute, they are the STANDARDS of all other values	6
Standards of value and media of exchange the same things	6
Misleading influence of the term "medium of exchange" (note)	6
Prime factors in the creation of wealth and in social progress	6
Always in demand at INTEREST as the basis of reproduction	7
The demand for capital increases as natural laws are unfolded	8
The importance of the precious metals vastly increased by interest, paid in kind, on loans of them	8
Such loans transfer the actual possession of capital from the owner to the borrower	8
They become in this way the highest guarantees for the peace and order of society	8
Provision for the future to be made only by contracts payable in them, with interest payable in kind	9
Without them, there could have been neither civilization nor continuity of history	9
Contracts in them authenticated by written instruments	9
Hence the origin of paper money	10
Exchanges must be made at the standard, but may be made without the actual intervention of the precious metals	10
Their use always barter	10

viii   TABLE OF CONTENTS.

Their use as money double barter 10
Importance of avoiding their actual intervention in exchanges 10
The manner in which this is effected 11
Sketch of history of coinage (note) 11
Bills of exchange 11
Their use in commerce between distant communities dispenses with that of
    a corresponding amount of coin 13
Not presently due 13
Currencies between communities widely separated 13
The mode in which they serve as such 13
Based upon or symbolize merchandise, and retired by its use 14
Producers of merchandise the drawers of bills 14
The holders of bills entitled to the specific thing drawn against 14
Bills not adapted to serve as local currencies 14
Such currencies required to be of every denomination, and payable presently,
    as they do not secure to their holder specific articles of merchandise . . 14
Cannot, like bills of exchange, be issued by producers 14
To be issued by parties possessing capital, and not subject to the risks of
    production and trade 15
Issued in great part by BANKS 15
Description of the mode of their issue 16
Banks do not pay out capital in making their loans 16
These are made by an exchange of their notes, presently due, for the bills of
    their customers, due at a future day 16
Retired in the payment of the bills in the discount of which they are issued 17
Makers of bills virtually undertake to retire the notes issued in their dis-
    count 17
All these operations based upon merchandise 17
The instruments by which they are conducted paper money — CURRENCY . 17
So long as they represent merchandise their movement regular and au-
    tomatic, and they are retired without the intervention of coin 17
No distinction made by the public between currencies where there are
    several issuers 18
Banks discharge obligations arising between themselves by mutual offset . 18
Only balances arising between them payable in coin 18
Bills and notes of Banks differ chiefly in time of payment 18
Interest paid by the borrower on all issues of currency 19
Currency the equivalent of capital to the borrower 19
The effect of currency to reduce prices 19
Coin reserves of Banks 20
These never to be made the basis of loans 20
Bear only a small ratio to the amount of loans 20
Hence a change in their amount followed by a far greater one in the amount
    of currency 20
Profit of Banks 21
Advantages of a currency issued by them in reducing prices 21
All merchandise entering into consumption should be symbolized 24
Amount of symbolic currency in Great Britain 24
Reserves, their proper amount, and how maintained 25
Deposits, how they arise 27
No difference but in form between notes, and checks drawn against deposits 29
Necessity of division of labor in distribution as in production 29
Cumulative symbols representing the same merchandise 30

Currencies, like bills of exchange, only instruments arising in production
and distribution 31
Distinction between capitalists and Banks 31
The manner in which banking capital may be provided 32
/This always in the hands of the public till Banks go into liquidation . . . 33
Bills proper to be discounted 33
Effect of discounting accommodation bills 33
Inflation and contraction which result 34
Disastrous consequences 35
Of the discount of bills given in the purchase of real property 36
Of the discount of bills given in the purchase of securities 38
Cause of the failure of Banks based upon real estate or securities 38
No bills to be discounted but those given for merchandise entering into con-
sumption 38
That a currency may be convertible, the means therefor must be provided
previous to its issue 39
Of the discount of bills given in the purchase of merchandise not in demand
for consumption 39
Short bills only to be discounted 40
Banks by discounting bills not properly based responsible for all the great
fluctuations in production and trade 41
Disastrous moral effects of fictitious currencies 42
Limited functions of governments in the matter of symbolic currencies . . 42
Should forbid the discount of bills not based upon merchandise and having
more than four months to run 43
Or such as will not mature within the time required for the distribution to
consumers of the merchandise they represent 43
Governments can never issue a convertible currency, nor one that is not at a
discount from the standard of coin 43
Wide difference between currencies issued by governments and by Banks . 44
The former never issued in the discount of bills 44
All government currencies the representatives of debt, not of capital . . . 44
Governments the only parties to retire the currencies issued by them . . 45
They are made legal tender as the only means by which they can be got
into circulation 45
Their issue always favorably received 45
Symbolic currencies measure the means of consumption of a people . . . 46
Disastrous effects of a currency that does not symbolize capital 47
Further difference between government and Bank currencies 47
Interest always paid Banks on loans of their currencies 47
Never paid on the issue of currencies by governments 47
All government currencies in their depreciation involve a loss greater than
interest on their amount 48
Why governments cannot issue convertible currencies 50
Constant and excessive fluctuations the law of all government currencies . 52
They reduce all business operations to the hazards of chance 52
The great problem of society distribution, not production 53
A flexible currency a representative currency 54
A government currency never flexible, as it bears no relation to the means
of consumption 55
The value of all currencies depends upon their quality, not quantity . . . 56
Unlike measures of weight and extension, money, as the measure of value,
passes in every exchange 56

A currency of government notes never issued for the purpose of facilitating
exchanges 57
Always a forced loan 57
Always superfluous 57
Their price their real or estimated value 57
Their value never affected by the number of exchanges taking place 57
Wholly dependent upon the credit of the issuer 58
Usually repudiated 58
Symbolic money simply the record of transactions 59
The propriety of its issue shown by its return in the payment of the bills in
the discount of which it was issued 59
Every possessor of merchandise competent to issue a convertible currency . 59
The greater part of the currencies to be issued locally 59
Convertible currencies will never circulate far from the place of their
issue 59
Erroneous assumptions in reference to money 60
Methods followed in the investigation of its laws those of the Schoolmen   61
Their exposure and refutation the necessary condition of progress in mone-
tary science 61

HISTORY OF MONETARY THEORIES.

ARISTOTLE, 350 B.C.

The source of all monetary theories 62
Acquisitions according, and opposed, to nature 62
Acquisition of money unnatural 63
Money devised from the necessity of its use 63
Money not wealth 63
Money-getting a servile art 64
Object of all acquisition two-fold 65
One for its own sake 65
The other for use in the family 65
The former justly censurable ; the latter commendable 65
Usury — money born of money — most contrary to nature 65
Falseness of Aristotle's method 65
His definitions of money pure assumptions 65
Solved all questions by dialectics 65
His successors the Schoolmen and Political Economists 65
The unscientific character of his mind 65
Childishness and absurdity of his illustrations 66
The great obstacle in the way of all progress 66
Complete failure of the Aristotelian method (Whewell) 68
Bacon in reference to (note) 68
The legitimate founder of the Schoolmen (Whewell) 69
Becomes an authority with the Church 70
Methods of the two the same 70
Each alike fatal to scientific progress 70
Emancipation from either could come only from the new races 70
Bacon the first to teach the proper method of scientific investigation . . . 70

Difference between his method and that of Aristotle 70
Emancipation of the exact sciences from the Aristotelian methods. . . . 71
In the moral, the methods of the Schoolmen still prevail 71
No considerable progress made in any but Law (note) 71
Unlawfulness of usury first attacked by Bentham 73
Money not yet emancipated from the teachings of Aristotle 73
Permanence of theories in themselves wholly absurd (note) 73

JOHN LOCKE.

The first writer calling for notice after Aristotle 74
Reasons for the discussion of money by him 74
Metallic currency in England in 1696 74
   Disastrous consequences of its debasement (Macaulay) 75
   Its reformation proposed 77
   Opposition headed by Lowndes 78
His proposition for lowering the standard 78
Locke called upon to refute him 78
Standard value of the coinage to be maintained 79
Government to assume the loss 79
   The people for a time without a currency (Macaulay) 80
The inconvenience and distress 80

JOHN LAW.

"Money and Trade Considered," 1700 82
His object to supply Scotland with capital 82
   The value of gold and silver their value in barter 82
   They acquire additional value from their use as money 82
The first proposition correct 83
The last not 83
   Objection to gold and silver as money 83
   Perishable goods better fitted to serve as such 83
His assumptions opposed to the fact 84
Adam Smith greatly indebted to Law 84
   Proposition for a Land Bank 85
   Its impracticability 86
Suits his principles to his necessities 86
   "Money not the value for which goods are exchanged, but the value by
     which they are exchanged" 86
   Land better than silver as a basis of currency 87
   Money for domestic exchanges may differ from that used in foreign
     exchanges 87
These propositions opposed to the fact 87
Goes to France, and founds a Bank based upon coin 88
For a time eminently successful 88
Holds that its issues might be made the basis of industrial enterprises . . 89
His Bank becomes an instrument of the government 89
Its disastrous failure 89
The Mississippi scheme 89

DAVID HUME.

"Essays, Moral, Political and Literary," 1752 89
Value no necessary attribute of money 89

Money a thing of no importance 90
Its value imaginary 90
An imaginary value no value 91
Hume's plan for debasing the currency 94
His untrustworthiness shown by it 94
Prices reduced by reducing the amount of the currency 95
Prices increased by reducing the currency 95
Money is in ratio to products exchanged 95
Paper money displaces a corresponding amount of coin 95
Does not displace a corresponding amount of coin 97
His views upon money wholly erroneous 98
His ignorance, and indifference to truth 98
The anomalous character of the Bank of England 98
Its success due to the practical sense of its managers 99
(For Bank of England, see *infra*, p. 183.)

ADAM SMITH.

"Wealth of Nations," 1776 99
Assumes to construct an universal science 99
Buckle's account of his plan 99
Adopts the deductive method 100
Invention of money consequent upon division of labor 101
Any substance may be used therefor 101
Divisibility of the material the most important attribute 102
Coinage an essential attribute of money 102
Invention of money impossible 103
Its use preceded division of labor 103
The universal equivalent is money 105
Labor, as an abstract notion, the real measure of values ; coin, the apparent measure 107
The measure of value a palpable object 108
Further illustration of this subject 108
Corn a better measure of value than coin 109
Perpetual rents should be made in corn 110
Fluctuates more from year to year : less from age to age 110
The money or coin price the one by which transactions are made . . . 110
The universal preference for the precious metals renders them money . . 110
The convenient, the natural medium of exchange 110
Contradictions in which Smith involved himself 111
Puerility of his illustrations and arguments 112
The price of every commodity resolves itself into wages, profit, and rent 112
The gross and neat revenue of society 113
The expense of maintaining its fixed capital no part of its neat revenue 113
The expense of maintaining its circulating capital may form a part of its neat revenue 113
Its circulating capital divided into four parts, — money, provisions, materials, and finished work. 113
Money is the only one the maintenance of which can occasion any diminution in the neat revenue 114
It forms no part of either the gross or neat revenue 114
It is the wheel of circulation, not the thing circulated 114
Smith's elements of price and classifications of property arbitrary and absurd 115

Money the highest form of finished work 115
The legal division into "real" and "personal" the only proper one . . . 115
Defect of Smith and the Economists in overlooking interest as an element
    in price 115
The expense of maintaining all kinds of property is in ratio to its cost . . 115
Money essential to the value of all other commodities 116
Need not be actively employed to be productive 117
Groundlessness and absurdity of Smith's assumptions and conclusions . . 118
    Distinction between real and nominal prices 119
    A person's income is not the money he receives 119
Absurdity of such distinctions 120
    Paper money a substitute for metallic money 121
    That of Banks and bankers "seems" to be the best 121
    Advantages of such substitution 121
    Mode of its issue 121
    It circulates upon the credit of the issuer 121
    Only occasionally returns for redemption 121
    Reserves necessary to be held 121
The word "seems" illustrative of Smith's method 122
Wholly failed to comprehend the nature of paper money 122
All notes issued return regularly for redemption 128
If good bills only be discounted, the notes return in their payment . . . 123
    Manner in which paper money may be substituted for coin 123
    An amount of coin equal to the issue liberated from use 123
    The channels of circulation will only hold a certain quantity of money . 123
    If there be too much, they will overflow 124
    The available capital of a country increased by the amount issued . . . 124
Mode of issue of a symbolic currency 124
Never issued in the manner supposed by Smith 124
A growth, not an improvisation 125
Its issue no increase of the relative amount of money 125
The channels of circulation never overflow 125
The holders of money never send it abroad as the condition of using it as
    capital 125
Exported in consequence of previous expenditures 126
Smith wholly misconceived the object and effect of paper money 126
    Provision, material, and finished work, the only things that can set indus-
        try in motion 126
    Money neither of these 126
    Wages do not consist of money 126
    Money only a small, and always the most unproductive part of a nation's
        capital 126
Money material for the reason that it is always going into the arts . . . 127
Capital, as it can always be loaned at interest 127
The chief thing to set industry in motion 127
All kinds of capital necessary to the operations of society equally valuable
    and equally productive 127
    The proportion of money to the merchandise circulated by it 128
    The advantage of substituting paper for gold 128
Proper limit of paper money the amount of merchandise to be symbolized . 128
Tendency of all commercial countries to symbolize their products 129
Paper money (unless legal tender) cannot be substituted for coin 129
The greater the amount of paper, the greater that of coin 129

Advantages resulting from the use of the former 129
The amount of paper money can never exceed that of the coin it displaces 129
All excess immediately drawn in coin 129
Absurdity of such assumptions 130
Disproved by reference to the currencies of England and Scotland. . . . 130
Paper money used in foreign as in domestic commerce 132
Only the excess of paper money issued returns to the issuer 132
The coin liberated will go abroad 132
Increased cost of maintaining excessive issues 132
There can be no excess of symbolic money 133
All regularly returns for redemption 133
The amount of notes issued has nothing to do with their return 133
A currency not symbolic is in excess to its whole amount. 133
Cost of maintaining a currency in ratio to its amount 134
The advances that Banks may make to merchants never to exceed the
    amount of coin which would otherwise be in circulation 135
Advances to be made to merchants only as the representatives of manu-
    facturers. 135
To equal the amount of merchandise entering into consumption 135
Paper money does not supersede, but supplements the use of coin 136
A community will "absorb" all the money it can get 136
The promptness in payment of merchants would show that an excess of
    currency had not been issued 136
Such promptness for a time rather a proof of excessive issues 137
All reserves, and all gold and silver used as currency, dead stock . . . 138
The object of banking to convert this dead stock into active capital . . 138
Paper money a wagon-way through the air 138
Increase of money increases the price of commodities 138
The quantity of paper money added to the circulation, always to equal
    the amount of coin taken from it 138
Absurdity of these propositions 138
Gold and silver as money never dead stock 188

"The principles of the Commercial or Mercantile System " 139
The assumed science of Political Economy a modern one 139
The Greeks, though addicted to commerce, seldom speculated upon subjects
    coming within the range of the economic sciences 140
The Romans never a commercial or manufacturing people 140
The overthrow of the Empire by the Northern races 140
Commerce and trade highly regarded by the latter 140
Freedom the necessary condition and result of the commercial spirit . . . 140
Contempt of the Greeks and Romans for the useful industries 140
Illustration from Aristotle 141
Disastrous influence of his teachings 141
Contrast between the old and new races 142
High estimation placed by the latter on gold and silver 142
These could only be acquired by commerce 142
Efforts to acquire them seconded by legislation 142
Hence the rise of the so-called "Mercantile System" 142
The error not in the importance attached to them, but in the modes in which
    they were sought to be acquired 142
These in harmony with the spirit of the age. 143
Usury everywhere held in detestation and forbidden 143

Sketch of the history of usury (note) 143
   Principles of the Mercantile System. 144
   1st, That wealth consisted in gold and silver. . . : 144
   2d, That these can be brought into a country having no mines, only by a
      favorable "Balance of Trade" 144
   Hence it became the great object of Political Economy to increase expor-
      tations and diminish importations 144
      1st, By restraints upon the importation of such articles as could be pro-
         duced at home 147
      2d, By restraints upon importations from countries with which trade
         was considered disadvantageous 147
   Exportations to be encouraged, —
      1st, By drawbacks 147
      2d, By bounties 147
      3d, By treaties of commerce 147
      4th, By planting of colonies 147
   The six preceding provisions the means for increasing the "Balance of
      Trade" 147
Smith's opposition to the Mercantile System, —
From the inadequacy of its object 147
From the inadequacy of the means to their object 147
   Argument against the Mercantile System 147
   The precious metals not wealth 147
   The idea that they were arose from the double function of money . . . 147
   Illustration of this distinction . . . . : 148
Money the measure of value and money the instrument of commerce, the
   same 149
A person rich in proportion to the amount he holds 150
Money an instrument of commerce by reason of its value 150
Absurdity of Smith's propositions and conclusions 151
A sale of goods for money an exchange of equal values 152
Absurdity in asserting the universal object of acquisition to possess no
   value 154
Doctrines of Smith and the Economists in reference to "Balance of Trade"
   the necessary sequence of those held by them in reference to the
   value of money 154
Would not allow that to be an object of commerce which was not even a
   subject of commerce 154
Importance of an equilibrium of the precious metals the world over . . . 156
How this is to be maintained 157
Illustrated by the action of the Bank of England 157
Governments incompetent to control the movements of the precious metals 158
The Bank competent . . . . •. . . 158
Its action a triumphant vindication of the correctness of the doctrine of
   "Balance of Trade" 158
Free-trade and Protection 158
Smith assumed to have demonstrated the superiority of the former . . . 158
No such demonstration possible 158
The opposing doctrines not the result of natural laws, but of conditions . . 159
Those possessed of superior capital and skill, Free-traders 159
Those lacking and seeking to acquire them, Protectionists 159
The same parties Free-Traders in one country and Protectionists in
   another 160

The age of Protection, the heroic one 160
That of Free-Trade, one of realization or enjoyment 160
Free-Trade constantly gaining at the expense of Protection 161
The question as at present treated, insoluble 162
Smith had the same contempt for merchants and manufacturers as Plato
    and Aristotle 162
  "The sneaking arts of underling tradesmen erected into maxims for the
    conduct of a great empire." 162
  "The mean rapacity and monopolizing spirit of merchants and manu-
    facturers" 162
  "The capricious ambition of kings and ministers not more fatal to the
    repose of Europe" 163
Untruthfulness of such assertions 163
Merchants always the champions of commercial and political freedom . . 163
  Merchants the authors of the spirit of protection and monopoly . . . 164
  Teach the doctrine of buying in the dearest, and selling in the cheapest
    markets 165
  "Their interested sophistry has confounded the common sense of man-
    kind" 165
  Their interest directly opposed to that of the great body of the people . 165
If these assertions be true, the greater the freedom of trade, the greater the
    monopoly 165
"The sneaking arts of underling tradesmen" have made England what
    she is 166
Absurdity of his tirade 166
Wholly ignored moral laws as the chief factors in civilization 167
  The heresies of country gentlemen taught them by merchants 167
Smith incapable of conducting a scientific discussion 168
Wholly unfitted for the work he undertook 168
His ignorance and want of method 169
Cause of his influence 169
The great obstacle to progress in the subjects upon which he wrote . . . 170
Whatever vigor and originality he possessed wholly lost in his followers . 170

DUGALD STEWART.

"Lectures on Political Economy" 171
One of the most distinguished disciples of Smith 171
Reduces Smith's statements to precise and logical terms 171
  Agrees with him as to the invention of money, but denies value to be a
    useful attribute of it 171
  Were England insulated, her currency might as well be paper as coin . 172
  Value complicates the theory of money 172
Stewart, in denying all value to money, more logical than Smith 172
Absurdity of his conclusion drawn from an assumed insulation of Eng-
    land 174
His argument puerile to the last degree 175
  Divisibility the attribute fitting gold and silver to serve as money . . . 176
  Coins render ideas of value more precise than mathematical statements . 176
If value be no attribute of money, then divisibility is of no importance . . 177
  Rapidity of circulation 178
  Illustration: money employed at the siege of Tournay 178
Absurdity of the illustration 178

The value of money is in ratio to the rapidity of its circulation 180
Money possesses no more activity than any other kind of property . . . 180
Stewart a striking example of the weakness and folly of the Schoolmen . 181

BANK OF ENGLAND — THE BULLION REPORT, 1810.

Suspension of the Bank of England 182
Historical sketch of the Bank 183
Its organization in 1694 183
Its nature and functions 183
Act of 1708 making it the manager and regulator of the currency 184
Authorized to issue notes to any amount 184
No other association having more than six members to issue notes . . . 185
Beneficent influence of the Bank 185
The foundation of England's commercial and manufacturing supremacy . 185
Sketch of early banking in England 186
Private and country Banks 186
Issue of notes a right at common law 187
Number of country and private Banks in operation from 1809 to 1832, in-
    clusive (note) 189
Extent of their operations (note) 189
Operations of the Bank of England from 1814 to 1832, inclusive (note) . . 190
Amount of commercial bills under discount at the Bank, from 1795 to 1813,
    inclusive (note) 190
Forbidden by its charter to make loans to government 191
Loans made in violation of this law 191
Parliamentary authority sought for such loans 192
Mr. Pitt secures such authority, but without limit as to amount 192
Controls the whole monetary power of the kingdom 192
The tremendous struggle in which he was engaged 192
Financial condition of England at the time 192
The necessities of Mr. Pitt impair the ability of the Bank to loan to mer-
    chants 192
Great distress the result 192
The Bank remonstrates 192
Mr. Pitt promises compliance 193
Means of the Bank steadily reduced 193
Mr. Pitt's operations from 1794 to 1797 194
The bullion of the Bank, on the 21st of February, 1797, reduced to
    £1,272,000 196
It appeals to the government 196
Forbidden on February 25, 1797, to continue to pay specie 196
Provisions of the Act of Restriction 197
Rapid recovery of the Bank after suspension 197
Signifies, in 1799, its willingness to resume payment 198
Act of Restriction continued by the government 198
Bank-notes remain at the par of gold till June, 1800 198
Statement showing the value of gold from 1797 to 1821, inclusive (note) . 199
The high premium on gold in 1809 causes great alarm 199
Committee of the House of Commons to inquire into its causes 199
Report of the Committee 200
    When the Bank was upon a specie basis, it regulated its issues by the
        price of gold and the state of the exchanges 200

If at any time the proper limit was incautiously exceeded, the excess
    returned for coin 200
The suspension of specie payments exempted the Bank from such
    check . . . . ˗ 201
The assumption of the Bank, that there could be no excess of issue so
    long as it was made in the discount of short bills representing real
    transactions, denied 201
Not the excess alone, but all the issues of the Bank speedily return for
    redemption 202
The excess acts upon the exchanges only through its effects 202
Mode in which it does act upon them 202
So long as specie payments are maintained, no difference in value between
    the notes of the Banks and gold 202
The Committee simply follow Smith in making the question of currency one
    of quantity, not of quality 202
Number of days during which the bank-notes remain in circulation (note) . 203
Years might elapse before excess of issue would be felt in the exchanges . 203
The issues of the Bank, properly made, never in excess 203
To regulate issues, after suspension, by reference to exchanges, would be to
    make none whatever . . . . . . ; 204
The proposition of the Committee an absurdity on its face 204
During suspension, the bills of the Bank could be paid only in its own
    notes 204
The requirement of the Committee would have left the country wholly
    without a currency 204
The rule acted upon by the Bank vindicated by the result 204
Adopted the only possible course open to it 204
Gave the country, for a considerable time, a symbolic currency equal to its
    wants, and of the value of coin 204
Saved it from ruin 204
Error of the Bank in not seeing that suspension removed the real check to
    overissues 205
After suspension its reserves its own notes 205
Great wisdom and ability with which it was managed 205
Ignorance, and narrow scope of inquiry, of the Committee 205
Economists never able to master the reason why the Bank recovered so
    speedily (note) 206
Distinction between " an advance of capital to merchants, and an addition
    of currency to the general mass of circulation " 207
No limit to the former but the inability to find good borrowers 207
When the advances become circulation, the general mass of currency
    inflated, and diminished in value 207
The amount of such currency permanently outstanding increases in
    ratio to the loans that are made 208
Notes representing capital the same in character till they are taken in . . 208
All issued fall alike into the channels of circulation, and all alike return to
    the Bank for redemption 208
Assumptions of the Committee wholly groundless 208
The currency of a country bears no fixed proportion to the quantity of com-
    modities 209
Its effectiveness depends upon the quickness of its circulation 209
Contrivances by which the same quantity may be made to do an increased
    amount of work 209

The currency inflated, and the remedy convertibility 209
Money no more active than other kinds of capital 210
If the assumption of the Committee be correct, then money is not capital . 211
No meaning can be attached to the phrase "rapidity of circulation" . . . 211
Quantity of money always in ratio to the exchanges 211
No difference in principle between bank-notes and other instruments of ex-
    change 211
Resolutions accompanying the report of the Committee rejected 212
Adoption of the counter resolutions of Mr. Vansittart 212
Lord Stanhope's bill 212
High price of gold due to excess of issues by the Bank 213
No reduction in their amount would have increased their price, unless it had
    increased their value 213
The great question, the proper manner of issue, never considered by the
    Committee 213
The report failed to establish a single principle in monetary science . . . 214
Placed on still firmer foundations the greatest of all its errors. 214

Henry Thornton.

"An Inquiry into the Nature and Effect of the Public Credit of Great Brit-
    ain," 1802 · 214
No distinction between business and fictitious paper as the basis of cur-
    rency 215
Difference between real and fictitious bills shown by the different effects of
    the currencies based upon them 215
Lord King (note) 215
"Thoughts on the Restriction of Specie Payments by the Bank of Eng-
    land," 1803 (note) 215
Of little value but in keeping alive the opposition to the Restriction Act (note) 215

William Huskisson.

"Question concerning the Depreciation of our Currency : " a vindication of
    the Bullion Report 216
Distinction between metallic and paper money 216
The latter circulates not by its value, but by confidence or authority . . 216
Value no more a necessary attribute of money than of a foot-rule . . . 216
Neither confidence nor authority can create values 217
A foot-rule not, like money, receivable in exchange for the articles it
    measures 217
If paper money be depreciated, the metallic money in circulation will also
    be depreciated in reference to bullion 218
A repetition of Lowndes' argument refuted by Locke 219
Singular confusion into which Huskisson fell in reference to money . . . 220

David Ricardo.

"The Principles of Political Economy and Taxation," 1817 221
Ricardo the central figure of the new school of Economists, as Smith of the
    old 221
As wanting in ideas as Smith in method and in knowledge of affairs . . . 221
Pushes Smith's doctrine, that value is not a necessary attribute of money,
    to its logical result 221
Value not an attribute of money 222

It circulates by virtue of the insignia of government 222
Convertibility only useful in preventing an excess 222
The insignia of government cannot create values 223
Convertibility a very inadequate test of the propriety of issue 224
Government should be the issuer of currency 226
The saving effected thereby 226
Government greatly the loser by issuing money 227
Ricardo's doctrines of Free-Trade 228
Prices controlled by the least favored, not by the most favored, producers 228
His assumptions wholly opposed to the fact 229
His doctrine of rent the sequence of that of prices 229
His plan for an economical and secure currency 230
To be made equal to coin by a provision of bullion 230
No bullion to be used, from the inconvenience of reaching it 231
Puerility of his scheme 232
Eminently practical as a man of affairs 232
Discharged of all sense the moment he took up his pen 232

THE BANK OF ENGLAND.

Price of bullion from 1813 to 1819 233
Act of Parliament of 1819 requiring the Bank to resume 234
Provision made for resumption 234
The Bank resumes May 1, 1821 235
Its condition, 1817-25 235
Great inflation of the currency, and rise of prices 236
Commercial crisis of 1826 236
List of speculative enterprises brought upon the money market (note) . . 237
Extent of the speculative mania 238
Run upon the Bank 238
Saved from suspension by the discovery of a package of notes 238
Action of the government 238
Communication addressed by Lord Liverpool to the Bank 238
Evil of an excessive issue of paper money 239
The remedy an improvement of the country paper 239
Evil not caused by small notes 239
The Bank of England to give up its exclusive privileges, and establish
branch Banks 240
Country Banks to be allowed to increase the number of their partners . 240
Lord Liverpool's plan adopted 241
Committee of the House of 1832 upon the extension of the Bank Charter . 242
Matters to which its attention was directed 242
Whether there should be one or several issuers of the currency 243
If only one, should that be the Bank of England ? 243
What checks to be provided to secure a proper management of Banks
of Issue 243
No conclusions reported by the Committee 243
Its labors consisted chiefly in the examination of experts, —
Mr. Loyd (Lord Overstone) 243
Mr. Ward 244
Mr. Norman 244
Mr. Tooke 245
Mr. Grote 245
Mr. Glyn 246
Mr. Gurney 246

Testimony of the experts opposed to every principle on which currency is based 247
Involved the subject in still greater obscurity and error 248
Evidence of the representatives of joint-stock Banks 252
These Banks successfully compete with that of England 252
The latter a great disturbing element in financial affairs 253
Its action corrected and neutralized by that of the joint-stock Banks . . . 254
The latter the great issuers of the currency 254
Management of the Bank 254
Evidence of J. Horsley Palmer, President, and other Directors 254
    Its issues not based upon bills, but upon government securities 254
    Discount of bills left to Banks and bankers 254
    Rule of the Bank to hold coin and bullion equalling in amount one-third its liabilities 255
    The currency then even or full 255
    Starting with this amount, all fluctuations left to take care of themselves 256
    An outflow of bullion to be left to work its own cure 256
    If excessive, the Bank might regulate its issues by reference to the exchanges 256
Condition of the Bank, Feb. 29, 1832 (note) 257
Vicious system of management 257
Government securities not the proper basis of loans 258
Cannot be made available in case of panic 258
If its assets were in bills, their payment would return its notes without effort on its part 259
State of the exchanges an inadequate rule for its action 259
The action of the Bank should prevent adverse exchanges 260
The rule adopted by the Bank fails to work 260
Gradual reduction of its reserves 260
Mr. Palmer undertakes to account for the failure of the rule 261
"The Causes and Consequences of the Pressure in the Money Market," 1837 261
    Increase of joint-stock Banks 261
    Their excessive issues create a demand for coin 261
    The Bank compelled to supply the demand 264
    It did not reduce its issues, for the reason that the demand was domestic, not foreign 264
    When the exchanges were even or favorable, it supplied all the currency wanted 264
    Hence the condition in which it was placed 266
    Existence of joint-stock banks incompatible with that of the Bank of England 267
Inadequacy of his explanation 267
The Bank governed by no rules 267
Its reserves to have reference to domestic as well as to foreign trade . . . 269
Its issues the cause of an unfavorable state of the exchanges 270
Made when they are even or favorable 270
A large amount of gold in the Bank evidence of a depressed condition of production and trade 271
Never to be made the basis of loans 271
Extraordinary demands upon the Bank in 1837 272
Its efforts to meet them only serve to postpone the crisis 272
Reply of Mr. Loyd (Lord Overstone) to Mr. Palmer 274

"Reflections Suggested by a Perusal of the Pamphlet of Mr. J. Horsley
    Palmer," 1837 274
"The Bank acts in two capacities: as a manager of the circulation, and
    as a body performing the ordinary functions of a banking con-
    cern" 274
These two functions wholly distinct 275
As a manager of the currency, the rule stated by Mr. Palmer perfectly
    correct 275
Wholly impracticable when applied to the regulation of its conduct as a
    banking concern 275
As an issuer of currency, it can keep the amount of its securities uniform   275
Cannot, as a banking concern 275
The amount of its circulation to be represented by a fixed amount of
    securities, and by the bullion it holds 275
By such means only can a currency be obtained varying in amount as it
    would have varied had it been metallic 276
The Bank to be separated into two departments 276
It now unites two wholly incompatible functions 277
It leaves the issue of currency to parties incompetent to their duties . . 277
Disturbing influence of joint-stock Banks 277
Distinction between Banks of issue and Banks of deposit 277
The process of inflation and contraction 277
Remedy, the strengthening of the monopoly of the central issuer . . . 278
Issue of circulation to be subject to the supervision of a Committee
    appointed by government 279
Partial recovery of the Bank in 1837 279
Drain of coin in 1838 279
Reserves reduced, 31st of August, 1839, to £2,424,000 279
The Bank applies to the Bank of France for aid 279
Causes of the disasters of 1839 280
Committee of the House appointed to consider the subject of Banks of Issue   281
Mr. Loyd (Lord Overstone) before the Committee 281
Distinction between notes and deposits 281
Notes money, deposits not 282
Money, coin and notes of Banks 282
The value of bank-notes regulated by precisely the same laws which regu-
    late the value of coin 282
The former the common medium of exchange, in all transactions, at all
    times, and in all places, and that too in endless succession . . . 282
Deposits possess no such attributes 282
Deposits, business worked; notes, the means by which they are worked . 283
Lord Overstone the real author of the act of 1844 283
Summary of his argument 285
His ideas of money wholly borrowed from Adam Smith 286
No difference in principle between the several forms of paper money . . . 288
Had no conception of the nature of symbolic money 288
The incoherency and absurdity of his statements and illustrations 289
The extension of the Charter of the Bank 289
Sir Robert Peel at the head of the government 289
His argument on bringing in the bill 289
A natural distinction between the notes and deposits of Banks 290
Notes affect the exchanges, deposits do not 290
Currencies of Ireland and Scotland 290

Notes and deposits to be dealt with upon different principles 291
His argument a refinement upon Lord Overstone's distinction 291
Example of the United States against plurality of issue 292
Supported by Sir Charles Wood (Lord Halifax) 292
By Mr. Goulburn, Chancellor of the Exchequer 292
Their ignorance of banking systems of the United States 293
An account of these systems 293
The "Suffolk system" of New England 294
Provisions of the Act of 1844 296
Its effect to create two Banks of issue 298
The issues of one legal-tender, receivable for the revenues, and supported by
    all the specie of the Bank 298
Those of the other have no support but its bills 299
No considerable amount of reserves needed by the former 299
To be held by the department whose issues have no extraordinary support 299
No immediate effect produced by the Act 300
Rise and progress of the railways of the kingdom 300
Vast sums invested in them in 1845 and 1846 300
Failure of the potato crop in Ireland 300
Financial operations of the country in 1845–46 300
Drain upon the Bank in 1846 301
Becomes excessive in 1847 301
Suspension of the Act of 1844 301
The panic confined to the issues of the banking department 302
Parliament called together 302
Speech of the Chancellor of the Exchequer 302
    During the panic, the Bank discounted all bills offered 303
    Restoration of affairs upon the suspension of the Act 303
Speech of Sir Robert Peel 304
    The Act of 1844 failed to prevent a financial crisis 304
    Secured the convertibility of the notes 305
The Bank held responsible for the suspensions of 1847, 1857, and 1866 . . 305
The public, not itself, to determine the amount of its issues 305
Has no discretion but to discount all bills coming within its rules 305
The advantages assumed for the Act wholly imaginary 306
Committees of Parliament of 1848 307
Lord Overstone again examined 307
    The Act "has verified every principle upon which it was established" . 307
    "It failed, however, from two accidents." 308
Committees of Parliament upon the Bank 308
Immense extent, and futility of their labors 308
Absurdity of forbidding depositors to be paid in kind 309
Note issue a monopoly in England 310
Folly of the restriction 310
Suspension of the Act approved by the officers of the Bank 311
Cause of the failure of the Bank 311

THOMAS TOOKE.

Before the Committee of 1840 313
    The amount of circulating medium the effect, not the cause, of inflation
        of prices 314
    A convertible currency cannot be inflated 314
    An inconvertible currency, not issued in excess, cannot 314

Money has two functions,— one as an instrument of exchange, the other
    as the subject of contracts for future payments 815
Value essential only in the latter 316
Tooke never mastered a single principle in monetary science 316
His poverty in ideas and style 317

James R. McCulloch.

Epitomizes all the speculations and conclusions of the Economists . . . 318
    Gold can be raised to any pitch of value, by limiting its quantity . . . 318
    Debased coins may be made to circulate at their nominal value 319
    The most valueless substances may be made to circulate as money . . 319
Impossible to control the movements of coin 320
To raise its value in reference to itself 321
Or to cause valueless articles to circulate 322
    The solvency of issuers has no influence over the value of paper money . 322
    It circulates for the reason that it is legal tender, and for the reason that
        a circulating medium is indispensable 322
    How an inconvertible currency may be maintained at the value of coin . 323
The price of paper money measured by its value 323
    High cost of gold and silver an objection to their use as money 324
    A cheaper money should be "fabricated" 325
    Paper the most eligible material therefor 325
The high cost of gold and silver the reason of their use 325
Every one seeks to convert that which he has to sell into higher forms of
    value 325
The whole effort of nature in the same direction 325
The principles of the Economists incompatible with the existence of society 325
    Supports the Act of 1844 326
    Opposes plurality of issue from the example of the United States . . . 326
    His incredible ignorance and assumption 326
Scotch Economists and metaphysicians wanting in the reasoning faculty . 327
The cause 328
Practical sense of the nation 329
Close resemblance to the Puritan emigrants to the United States 329

John Stuart Mill.

"Political Economy" 330
The text-book in most common use 330
Its author the great light in modern economy 330
    Money becomes such from habit 330
    The habit begets the illusion that money is wealth in a peculiar sense . . 330
    It is not money with which things are purchased 330
    No one's income derived from the precious metals 330
    The farmer converts his products into money, in order to "leave the
        laborer more leisure for work, and the landlord for being idle" . . 330
    "No more insignificant thing, intrinsically, in the economy of society
        than money 331
    "It is a machine for doing quickly and commodiously what could be
        done, though less quickly and commodiously, without it." 331
Mill's description of the nature and functions of money borrowed from
    Adam Smith 331
The use of gold and silver as money proves them to be capital in a peculiar
    sense 331

When one lends, the money is not the capital loaned 332
The fallacy that the lending of money is the lending of capital 332
"Money, the medium of exchange, not the capital that is passed from
    hand to hand through that medium" 332
Increase of the gold and silver of a community, no increase of its capital 332
Money, when used as such, always used as capital 333
The lending of money the lending of capital 333
The capital of a community in ratio to its money 333
The value of money inversely as its quantity multiplied by the rapidity
    of its circulation 334
If payments be increased, money must be increased, or the rapidity of
    circulation of that in use must be increased 335
Otherwise prices must fall 335
Money no greater rapidity of circulation than other kinds of merchandise . 337
"Neither bank-notes, bills, nor checks act upon prices" 337
"Credit, not the form and mode in which it is given, the operating
    cause" 393
Credits cannot act upon prices, unless they take a form which can be con-
    verted into money 339
Inconvertible currencies 341
The material of a currency a matter of convention 341
The objection to the use of worthless substances as currency, the diffi-
    culty in regulating their amount 341
What determines the value of an inconvertible currency? 341
Value no necessary attribute 341
Will be maintained at the par of coin, if it do not exceed the amount
    of the latter it has displaced 342
Exerts precisely the influence of a convertible currency, if not issued in
    excess 342
Importance of uniformity in the amount of currency 342
The precious metals selected from the uniformity of their supply . . . 342
Inconvertible money in excess when not exchangeable for equal nominal
    amounts of coin 343
The difficulty of regulating its quantity the only, but a sufficient, reason
    against its use 343
No currency not presently due equal in value to the capital it represents
    in hand 344
The difference between convertible and inconvertible currencies 344
The material and value of money do not depend upon convention . . . 345
Inconvertible paper money equivalent to the creation of capital 346
It liberates from use a corresponding amount of coin 347
Illustration of this argument 347
Fallacy of such assumptions 347
A convertible currency cannot inflate prices 350
Convertible currencies often inflate prices enormously 351
Agrees with Tooke, that paper money does not act upon prices 352
Opposed to plurality of issue 354
Attaches very little importance to notes of Banks 354
They have the power, however, of completely superseding metallic money 354
The issue of money should be for the benefit of the public 355
How government might issue it 355
Mr. Mill a most striking example of unwarranted assumption and imbecility 355
Reason of his failure, and that of his school 355

Their total misconception of the principles of the science of Political
    Economy. 355
Morality a necessary condition of material welfare 356
Example of the Hebrew race 356
Necessity of a higher law than morality 356
This to be found in the teachings of Christ 356
Christianity secular as it is religious 356
Importance of subjecting ethnic religions to its rules 356
Lesson taught by the history of the Seven United Provinces 358
Their vast wealth and prosperity 358
Inquiries as to the cause, addressed by the Stadtholder to the leading mer-
    chants of the country 360
    Their answer 360
    The causes threefold : physical, moral, and adventitious 360
    These stated in detail 360
The highest material welfare the result of the highest moral conditions . . 361
Where the latter exist, the Political Economist wholly superfluous . . . 362

H. D. MACLEOD.

Extracts from his work on banking 363
    " Money does not represent commodities at all, but only debt." 364
    ".Where there is no debt, there is no currency." 364
    " Among all civilized nations, gold and silver bullion is the representative
        of debt." 365
    " It would be perfectly possible to make a yard of broadcloth or a Dutch
        cheese the representative of debt and the measure of value." . . 365
The extravagance of Mr. Macleod's assertions their own answer 366
    An inconvertible currency may be maintained at par, if the quantity be
        no greater than that of a convertible one 366
    Issued in proper amounts so long as it can be converted into equal nom-
        inal amounts of coin 367

JAMES W. GILBART.
" The Principles and Practice of Banking " 368
A striking example of success as a banker, and entire ignorance of the
    principles of money 368
    Examined before the House Committee of 1840 368
    " Bankers in issuing their notes make no reference to the quantity of gold
        in the country." 368
    " The circulation of private bankers cannot be issued in excess." . . . 368
    " The country circulation under checks ; the Bank of England circulation
        is not." 369
    The notes of private Banks do not affect the rates of interest or the
        exchanges 369
    The notes of the Bank of England do 369
The notes of private Banks and the Bank of England precisely the same in
    kind, and, in ratio to their amounts, the same in effect 370
    Gold and silver to be demonetized in case of a war, as a means of retaining
        them in the country 372
Fallacy of this assumption 373
    Banking capital may be raised by an issue of notes 374
In providing a banking capital, makes no distinction between substance and
    fiction 375

HENRY FAWCETT.

"Manual of Political Economy" 375
Adopts Adam Smith's theories upon money 376
   Effect produced by paper money upon prices 376
   The economy of its use 376
   If the number of exchanges increase, the amount of currency remaining
      the same, prices will rise 376
   Prices depend upon the quantity of money in circulation 377
   If commodities increase, and money remain stationary, prices must fall . 377
   If money increase, and commodities remain stationary, prices will rise . 377
Paper money circulates by virtue of representing merchandise, not coin . . 378
Discharged by the consumption of its constituent 378
Notes in circulation do not displace coin from circulation 379
The economy of their use results from their supplementing other modes of
   distribution 879
Inadequacy of Mr. Fawcett's theory of the effect of money upon prices . . 380
Makes no discrimination between different kinds of money 380
Paper money, not symbolic, raises prices 381
That which is symbolic reduces them 381
Advantages of a symbolic currency 381
Money always to be in ratio to the number of exchanges 381
The nature of credits 381
A restatement of the subject 381
The credits that affect prices are those that are turned into money . . . 382
The proper basis of issues 382
   Inconvertible currencies may be maintained at par, if their amount be
      limited to the necessities for their use 383
   Illustration of the case of the United States in the War of the Rebellion . 383
The value of all currencies their price 384
Only repeats the prevailing monetary theories 385

W. STANLEY JEVONS.

"Money and the Mechanism of Exchange" 885
   Description of the nature of money 385
Absurdity of his description 886
   The State may issue the currency 387
   Fourteen series of methods for the issue of paper money 388
   An inconvertible currency may be made to circulate at par 388
   Legal-tender paper money 389
   Issue of notes analogous to the highest function of coinage 390
Quoted for the purpose of illustrating the present condition of monetary
   science 391
Introductory Lecture at the opening of the University of London for the
   Session of 1876–77 391
   Hundredth anniversary of the publication of the "Wealth of Nations" . 391
   Discouraging picture of the condition of economic science 391
   Disgust in which its teachers are held 392
   Breaking up of the old orthodox school of Economists 392
   Respect for the names of Ricardo and Mill no longer able to preserve
      unanimity 392
   Chaotic state of the science 393
   The new school 393

M. de Laveleye 393
Mr. Jevons's address proof of the extremity to which the old school is
    reduced 396
Political Economy a mathematical science 397
" The laws of supply and demand, and all the phenomena of value, may
    be investigated algebraically, and illustrated geometrically.". . . 397
Effeteness of the English school 399

BONAMY PRICE.

" Principles of Currency " 399
    " The doctrines of merchants and bankers have subdued the whole land " 399
    " Difference which separates the man of science from the man of practice " 399
    " No science has suffered so severely from the hands of the practical man
        as Political Economy " 399
    " The more he is engaged in affairs, the more mysterious his rules for
        the acquisition of wealth " 400
His method monopoly 400
His teachings adopted by every civilized country 400
Culminated in the famous Mercantile Theory 400
Cause of the decline of political science . . . ' 400
The truths of Political Economy have made no permanent lodgement in
    the public mind 401
The incredible absurdity that gold is wealth 402
Great bankers dominate men of science 403
Their methods preferred to those of the Economists 403
How checks arise, and their nature 404
How bank-notes arise, and their nature 405
Price an illustration of what is taught as Political Economy 406
Merchants, in holding gold to be capital, deny the fundamental principles
    of the Economists 407
Hence the hatred felt toward them by the latter 407
The incredible absurdity of Price's statements and illustrations 407

CONTINENTAL WRITERS. (note.)

Jean Baptiste Say (note) 408
" Treatise on Political Economy " (note) 408
Chevalier (note) 408
Wolowski (note) 408

AMERICAN POLITICAL ECONOMISTS.

Only repeat what they find in the books 408

FRANCIS BOWEN.

" American Political Economy." 409
    Money a contrivance for diminishing the friction of exchange 409
    Its value dependent on rapidity of circulation 410
    Reduced to a formula 410
Reductio ad absurdum from his illustration 411
    Money only a hypothetical or abstract medium of exchange 413
    Difference between bank currency and inconvertible paper 414
    The latter liable to be issued in excess ; the former not 414
His work only a restatement of Mill and McCulloch 415
Mischievous effect of such teachings 415

Professorships of Political Economy should be suppressed, or put into
    commission 415
Manner in which it is still taught in Harvard University (note) 415

WILLIAM G. SUMNER.

"History of American Currency " 416
    The Report of the Bullion Committee solves the whole subject of money . 416
    No condition expressed by the term " Balance of Trade " 416
    "Exploded by Quesnay a century ago, and gibbeted in the Bullion
        Report " 416
    " The fallacy is in the word ' balance ' " 417
    " If it means equilibrium, it regulates itself " 417
    " If it means remainder, it is a mere myth " 417
    The doctrines of the Report 417
    The value of an inconvertible currency depends upon its amount . . . 417
    When gold is at a premium, paper is redundant 417
Balance of trade a veritable fact 420
His " inferior " currency 421
Only repeats the stale theories and illustrations of the Economists 421

A. R. PERRY.

" Elements of Political Economy " 422
    Extracts from his works 422

DAVID A. WELLS. (note.)

" The Cremation Theory of Specie Resumption," 1875 (note) 424
An example of the manner in which the subject is popularly treated . . . 424

Objects of the second part of this work 425
The science in its present form the work of Aristotle 426
Discussed from his time to our own after the manner of the Schoolmen . 426
Most striking example in history of the permanence of erroneous opinions . 426
The whole question turns on whether value be an essential attribute of
    money 426
That conceded, it becomes a question in the exact sciences 426
The appeal to the empirical has fully sustained the conclusions of induc-
    tion 427

CURRENCY AND BANKING IN THE UNITED STATES.

Character of the revolutionary government 429
Did not possess the power of taxation 429
An issue of notes the obvious mode for providing for the prosecution of the
    war 429
Such currencies previously resorted to by the States 429
Their issue always popular 429
First Continental Congress, May 10, 1775 429
The New York delegates suggest the issue of notes 429

First issue of $3,000,000, June 22d, 1775 430
Form of notes 430
Continued Issues 431
Apportioned among the States (note) 431
Early decline in their value 431
Efforts to sustain their price 432
Further issues and increased decline 434
Attempt to arrest the decline 435
Robert Morris (note) 435
Order of Congress that the notes pass at their nominal value 436
Washington invested with dictatorial powers 437
Great strait to which the cause of the patriots was reduced 437
Committees of safety 437
Futility of their efforts 438
Amount of notes issued up to the close of 1776 438
Tariffs of prices 438
The notes counterfeited 439
Mission of Franklin to France 439
French loans 439
Capture of Burgoyne 439
Alliance with France, Feb. 6th, 1778 439
Further issues of notes 439
Depressed condition of the country 441
Continued decline of the notes 441
Addresses of Congress to the people 441
Varying fortunes of the war 442
Further issues, and decline in value of the notes 442
Committee of Congress on Finance appointed 442
Recommends a repeal of the law making the notes the equivalent of gold . 443
Rapid decline in their value 443
Demoralizing effect of their use 443
   How Washington regarded them 443
Apparent imbecility of the Revolutionary Government 444
Antagonistic elements in the nation 444
Massachusetts and Virginia 445
The notes still counterfeited 446
The issues of May 22, 1777, and April 11, 1778, called in 446
Consequent suffering 446
Hucksters and forestallers 447
Monopolies of money and merchandise always the effect of a legal-tender
   currency 448
Notes issued in 1778 448
Wretched condition of the nation 449
Mutiny in the army 450
Incompetency and imbecility of the enemy 450
Subjection of the colonies impossible 450
Unsuccessful attempt by Congress to call in its notes, Jan. 1, 1779, followed
   by new issues 451
Popular discontent 451
Committees of safety to regulate prices 451
Attempts to prevent the circulation of coin 453
Their utter failure 453
Continued issues and decline of notes 454

Address of Congress to the people 454
Attempt to demonstrate the ability of the country to discharge all its obli-
    gations 454
Amount of the public debt (note) 455
Statement of expenditures for 1778 (note) 455
Washington declines to receive the notes 455
Letter to the President of Congress 456
Excessive depreciation of the notes at the close of 1779 457
Statement of the amount issued (note) 457
Unsuccessful attempt by Congress to call them in 457
Proposal for a reissue at the rate of 1 to 20 of the old 457
The new no better received than the old 457
Josiah Quincy (note) 458
Pelatiah Webster (note) 458
Value of the notes falls to 500 to 1 of specie 459
Cessation of issue 459
Demonetization of the notes 459
Reappearance of specie 459
Mischievous effect of the government currency 460
Testimony of contemporaneous writers 460
French loan 461
Appointment of Robert Morris as Financier-General 461
Association of the citizens of Philadelphia, June 17, 1780, to aid the opera-
    tions of the government 462
They organize a "Bank" 462
Measure approved by Congress 462
Gouverneur Morris and Hamilton in reference to the Bank (note) 463
Bank of North America incorporated, Dec. 31, 1781 464
First adequate attempt to issue a symbolic currency in America 464
Valuable services rendered to the government 465
Establishment of peace 465
Disorganized condition of the country 465
Local jealousies and rivalries 466
General Washington in reference to them 466

Adoption of the Constitution 467
Formation of the Federal Government 467
Alexander Hamilton Secretary of the Treasury 468
Measures proposed 468
1st. Payment of the debts contracted during the late war 468
2d. Provision for the charges of the government by imposts on foreign
    merchandise 469
3d. Provision of a symbolic currency by means of a Bank 469
Debts of the old government assumed, and mode of their payment . . . 469
Opposition to these measures 469
Chiefly directed against the Bank 469
Ground of this objection, — government not one of paramount powers . . 470
Country divided geographically 470
Jefferson opposed to the Bank 470
Act creating it approved by Washington, Feb. 25, 1791 470
The Constitution an attempt to fuse into one two distinct nations . . . 471
The South could not commit herself to the guidance of ideas 471
Could take nothing on trust 471

Could derive no advantage from provisions designed to promote the general
    welfare 471
The Bank opposed as a political rather than a financial measure 472
Its charter 472
Branches 473
The Act a masterpiece of its kind 473
The existence of the Bank the brightest period in American financial
    history 475
State Banks 475
Continued hostility of Jefferson to a government of paramount powers . . 475
The Alien and Sedition Laws his opportunity 476
Virginia and Kentucky Resolutions of 1798–99 476
Illustrations of his opinions upon the nature and powers of our government 477
    The State and Federal Governments co-ordinate branches of the same
        government 478
    Hostility to the Constitution of the United States 478
    To the Supreme Court . . . . : 479
    Rebellion the corrective of oppression 479
Complete triumph of his ideas in his election, 1800 480
His views accepted as the authoritative construction of the Constitution up
    to 1860 480
The theory of government based upon them 480
The Rebellion a practical application of them 480
His overthrow a revolution in the literature as in the politics of the country 481
Mr. Bancroft asserts him to be the author of all the centralizing tendencies
    of our government 481
Untruthfulness with which the history of this country has been written . . 481
Alarm created by the Resolutions of 1798 481
Washington to Patrick Henry 482
Charter of the Bank expired March 4, 1811 483
Its extension refused 483
War of 1812 484
The Banks of the country suspend payment in 1814 484
Enormous increase of State Banks 484
Amount of notes outstanding in 1811 and in 1816 484
Excessive number of Banks created in Pennsylvania (note) 484
Great decline in value of the bank-notes 484
Necessity for a new Bank 485
Recommended by Mr. Madison 485
Second Bank of the United States chartered April 10, 1816 485
Its influence in restoring specie payments 486
Measures taken by it 486
Continued creation of new Banks 487
Disasters which followed 487
Illustrated in the case of Kentucky 487
Gradual recovery of the country 487
Connection of other countries with the financial condition of our own . . 488
The year 1826 memorable for commercial disasters both in this country and
    in England 488
The cause excessive issues of paper money 488
General Jackson's first Annual Message declares the Bank unconstitutional 489
The message received with surprise and indignation 489
Referred to the Committee of Ways and Means 489
Report of the Committee 490

Report of the Committee upon the Bank 490
The questions considered 490
The constitutionality of the Bank 490
Its expediency 490
The expediency of founding a Bank upon the credit and revenues of
the government 490
Constitutionality of the Banks established by the uniform concurrence of
all departments of the government 490
Founded by the framers of the Constitution 491
The second Bank recommended by Madison 491
Mr. Jefferson approves a bill creating a branch Bank 491
The most distinguished Republicans (Democrats) in favor of the Bank . 491
Great use of the Bank to the Government 493
Both great political parties in favor of its constitutionality 493
Supreme Court unanimous in its favor 493
The question of constitutionality forever set at rest 493
The Bank "necessary and proper" to carry into effect the power granted 494
May be created as an incident thereto 494
Its creation one of the lowest attributes of sovereign power 494
Not a question of metallic or paper currency 494
But of a paper currency subject to proper control 494
Immense number of State Banks to fill the place of the first Bank . . 494
Great excess and depreciation of the currency 495
Effect upon the revenues 495
Tendency of the currency to the level of the least valuable 496
Amount of currency in circulation in 1816 496
Great reduction which followed 496
Losses arising from its use 497
Uniform value of the currency furnished by the United States Bank . . 497
Its success in securing resumption of State Banks 499
Obstacles to resumption 499
Dangers apprehended from the Bank imaginary 500
Objections to the use of State Banks by the government 501
Importance of continuing the Bank 501
Evils certain to flow from its discontinuance 501
Summary of the Report 502
It only increased Jackson's hostility to the Bank 502
The second Bank opposed on the same grounds as the first 503
The revival of the old parties at the close of Monroe's administration . . 504
John Quincy Adams defeated for a second term 504
Causes of his defeat 504
Sketch of the revival of parties 505
The doctrine of strict construction 505
Denies to government the powers necessary to its existence 506
Effect upon the welfare and morality of the people 506
Finally overthrown by the party of progress and freedom 506
Continued warfare upon the Bank 507
Mr. Madison asserts its constitutionality 507
Judicial and legislative precedents the rule of interpretation 507
No other rule compatible with the existence of government 508
General Jackson's reply 508
The will or opinion of each department of government its rule 509
Jefferson denied to government the powers necessary for its existence . . 509

Jackson inaugurated the reign of anarchy and barbarism 509
Jackson in relation to the secession of South Carolina (note) 509
   Subscribes fully to the doctrines of secession 510
Identity of his political principles with those of Calhoun 510
Mr. Gallatin in reference to the Bank 510
   The disasters following the expiration of the first Bank 511
   The State Banks incompetent to furnish an uniform currency 511
   No progress made toward resumption till the creation of the Bank . . 512
   Services rendered by it to the State Banks 512
   Resumption impossible without it 512
   Manner in which its operations were conducted 513
Jackson denounces the Bank as incompatible with the liberties of the
   country 514
   As an engine to undermine its free institutions 514
   To control the amount of its circulating medium 514
   The "money power" perfected its schemes of oppression by the creation
     of the United States Bank 514
   Sought to regulate the value of all the labor and property of the country 515
   Waged ruthless and unsparing war upon the people 515
   Impoverished and ruined whole cities and communities 515
   "No nation but the freemen of the United States could have come out
     victorious in such a contest" 515
   The difficulty in the way of fighting the "moneyed power" 515
   The mischief arising from its control over the currency 516
   The arts and strength of the "moneyed power" . . . . · 516
   "My humble efforts to restore the constitutional currency of gold and
     silver" 516
General Jackson's attack on the Bank the first attempt in this country to
   array labor against capital 516
His prodigious untruthfulness and falsifications of history 517
Manufacturers and merchants, the managers of Banks, the great upholders
   of free institutions 517
The success of Jackson's attack upon the Bank illustrates that of Jeffer-
   son's upon Hamilton 517
Hamilton saw the necessity of a strong government 517
For opposing license was declared an enemy of civil liberty 517
The War of the Rebellion an overthrow of Jackson and Jefferson . . . 517
A full vindication of Hamilton 517
Gave him his first opportunity to be heard 517
Reversal of the judgment of the nation 518
Who were the dangerous classes at the epoch of Jackson ? 518
Who were the upholders of political and commercial freedom ? 518
Liberal and upright management of the Bank 519
Such management the necessary condition of success 520
Memorializes Congress for an extension of its charter 521
This extended by Congress 521
Vetoed by Jackson 521
Condition of the Bank at the time 521
Consequences of the refusal to extend its charter 521
Rapid increase of State Banks 522
Their capital and note circulation in 1834 523
Removal of deposits from the United States to State Banks 523
Disasters and distress which followed 523

Reasons for General Jackson's attack on the Bank 524
Its refusal to allow him to control its patronage (note) 524
Refusal to cash his drafts 524
His brutal treatment of the New York Committee 525
Rapid increase of State Banks 527
Their number, capital, and circulation in 1837 527
The delirium of extravagance which followed 527
Speculation seizes upon the public lands 527
Enormous purchases of these 527
Sought to be checked by the Specie Circular 527
Purchases of public lands from 1829 to 1847 inclusive (note) 528
Great accumulations in the public treasury 528
These divided among the people 529
Drain upon the Banks 529
They suspend specie payment 529
Their suspension and resumption 530
Enormous contraction the condition of resumption 531
Enormous increase of imports consequent upon the inflation 531
Excessive decrease as the condition of resumption 531
Disastrous effects of Jackson's attempt to "reform the currency" upon
        the moral and material condition of the country 532
"Came to Washington to lift American legislation out of the forms of Eng-
        lish legislation and to place our laws on currency in harmony with
        the principles of the Republic" (note) 532
Illustration of his purpose in the case of Sam Houston 533
The latter assaults a member of Congress for words spoken in debate . . 533
His defence 533
Declared guilty of a breach of privilege of the House 534
Mulcted in the sum of $500 534
Fine remitted, and pardoned by Jackson 534
The latter approved of the assault 534
The Bank receives a charter from the State of Pennsylvania 535
Enormous price paid for its charter 535
Does not resume with the New York Banks 535
Reasons of its president, Mr. Biddle, for not resuming 535
  The credit system on its final trial 535
  To attempt to resume would be to place the Bank in the power of the
        government 535
  Must sustain the Banks of the States 536
Absurdity of his reasons 536
The weakness of the Bank the reason for not resuming 536
The effect, upon Mr. Biddle, of his quarrel with General Jackson 536
Becomes incompetent to the management of the Bank 537
The Bank resumes in 1838 537
Suspends again in 1839 537
Resumes in 1841 537
Finally suspends February 1, 1841 537
Causes of its disastrous failure 537

Banking in Mississippi 538
An illustration of the times 538
The Planters' and Union Bank 538
Rapid increase of Banks 539

Amount of their capital and loans (note) 539
The explosion which followed 540
The State defaults in the payment of interest 540
Appeal of the holders of these bonds 540
The State repudiates 540
Report of a Committee of the Legislature 541
    Repudiators equally honorable with "Washington, Jefferson, Madison,
        Hancock, and Franklin" 541
Repudiation vindicated in Congress by Jacob Thompson 541
    His speech on the occasion 542
Persistent action of the Bondholders 544
Bonds declared, by the courts of the State, to be legal obligations . . . 544
The question of their payment referred to the "people" 544
Vote against their payment 544

Sketch of Banking in the several States 544
In Massachusetts 545
In New York 545
In Ohio 547
In Indiana 549
State Bank of Indiana 550
Banking in Michigan 551
In Illinois and Wisconsin 552

Action of the government upon the suspension of specie payments in 1837 . 552
Abandons its paternal function of regulating the currency 552
The effect of its interference 553
Separates itself wholly from the Banks 553
All the revenues to be collected and disbursed in coin 553
Establishment of the Independent Treasury 553
Third Bank chartered by Congress 553
Vetoed by the President 553
The process of resumption 554
Great contraction of the currency 554
Resumption not finally accomplished till 1843 554
Increase of Banks in 1847 and 1848 555
Great expansion of their operations 555
They suspend payment in 1857 555
Their rapid recovery 556
Their condition in 1860 556

Election of Mr. Lincoln to the Presidency 556
Outbreak of the civil war 556
Financial condition of the government 556
The Banks unite to sustain the government 556
Account of their operations 556
    Those of New York, Philadelphia, and Boston combine 557
    Their capital and coin reserves 557
    Undertake to supply the government with $150,000,000 557
    Urge Mr. Chase, Secretary of the Treasury, to draw upon them in the
        ordinary course of business 558
    Independent Treasury modified for this purpose 558
    Mr. Chase refuses to accede to their request 558

Demands to be paid in coin. 558
Success of their operations till he entered the field with his own notes . 559
The Banks receive them to sustain the credit of the government . . . 559
Their reserves drawn in proportion to the amount issued 559
They remonstrate against the issue of government notes 559
Mr. Chase persists in their issue 559
The Banks, in consequence, compelled to suspend. 560
Their error in yielding to Mr. Chase 561
Résumé of the above 562
The war might have been carried on by bank paper the equivalent of gold 562
Ignorance and perversity of Mr. Chase 564
His object not money, but political advancement. 565
The folly of his attempt to issue demand notes. 567
The suspension of the Banks a precautionary measure. 568
Decline in value of the government notes 568
Disastrous consequences of Mr. Chase's conduct 568
The dilemma of the government on the suspension of the Banks 569
Mr. Chase's Second Annual Report. 569
    The expenditures of government $1,250,000 daily 570
    Could not borrow coin on the credit of the government 570
    Could not borrow bank-notes on better terms than coin 570
    If borrowed, they would speedily become worthless 570
    The alternative legal-tender government notes 570
    Urges their issue 571
    " A wise expedient for the present time, and an occasional expedient in
        the future " 572
    Their constitutionality asserted by the Supreme Court of the State of
        New York 572
Résumé of his argument 572
Draws the bill for the second issue of notes. 573
Their decline in value and rise of gold. 575
    Mr. Chase denies the issues of the United States to be the cause . . . 575
    Or the currency to be inflated 575
The currency inflated equal to the whole amount of government notes . . 576
Suspensions of Banks unconnected with governments always temporary . 577
They speedily resume, as a matter of self-protection. 577
The public enforce resumption for a similar reason 577
Mr. Chase becomes Chief Justice of the Supreme Court of the United
    States. 577
    Declares the legal-tender notes to be unconstitutional 577
    Denies that he ever suggested their issue 578
Absurd untruthfulness of this statement 578
Advantage of a currency of bank over one of government notes 578
The former circulate at their value 578
The value of the latter can never be ascertained 578
Criminality involved in their issue 579
Mr. Chase's scheme for a system of National Banks 579
    The circulation of the Bank, January 1, 1860, $202,000,767 579
    " The whole of this circulation constitutes a loan, without interest, from
        the people to the Banks " 579
    " The advantages of the loan to be transferred from the people to the
        government " 580
State Banks unconstitutional 580

Government should interpose to provide a suitable currency 580
Circulation of Banks in inverse ratio to their solvency 580
Value dependent upon the laws of thirty-four States and the character of
    sixteen hundred institutions 580
Two modes for the reformation of the currency 580
    First : an issue of government notes . . . . . . : 580
    Second : The creation of a system of Banks, their circulation to be
        secured by a deposit of government bonds 581
The second mode the preferable one 581
Bank-notes a credit currency 581
Mr. Chase's misstatement of history 582
The constitutionality of State Banks never questioned. 582
The constitution always invoked by demagogues 582
Invoked by Jackson against the United States Bank 582
By Mr. Chase against State Banks 582
The circulation of Banks not a loan from the people without interest . . 583
Its value not dependent upon the laws of thirty-four States 583
The greatest amount of circulation not furnished by the weakest Banks . 583
Credit circulation never desirable 583
Absurdity of Mr. Chase's notions in reference to paper money 584
His *rôle* that of General Jackson. 584
Carries his scheme for a system of National Banks 585
Its consequences 585

How the currency is to be restored 585
Government notes to give place to a Symbolic Currency 585
This to be furnished by parties possessed of capital 586
A convertible currency can never be issued by a government. 586
Can be issued only as the representative of capital 586
Failure of Mr. Chase's attempt 587
A currency issued by government in amount sufficient for the collection and
    disbursement of the revenues would circulate at only a small discount 588
Would circulate at par by bearing interest at a low rate 588
Objections to the issue of such a currency 588
That used by governments as well as by the public to be symbolic . . . 588
Balances only, dischargeable in coin 589
Preparation for resumption will create large balances in our favor 589
A Bank of the United States an essential condition of resumption 590
Such a Bank might be immediately created. 590
Its reserves to be the coin in the Independent Treasury 590
By its means the government, and individuals as far as they were able,
    might immediately resume 590
The currency to be in great measure supplied by local institutions . . . 591
A National Bank indispensable to its uniformity in value and amount . . 591
The government notes to be demonetized as the condition of resumption . 593
To be funded, not paid in coin 594
The funding will take place only when money is plenty 594
Their discharge in coin impracticable 595
Funding to be followed by the repeal of tax on notes of State Banks. . . 596
The National Bank to be allowed to reclaim the securities and issue notes
    without special provision for their payment 596
Amount of securities held by the National Banks 597
Probable amount of liabilities of the Banks upon resumption 597

The note holders to be left to take care of themselves 597
Incapacity of government officials to deal with the subject 598
Security for bank-notes injurious to the public 598
The New England and New York systems compared 599
The losses arising from the use of Banks not due to their circulation . . . 600
All safety-fund systems radically vicious 601
Their capital loaned to the government 602
The National Banks to be allowed to reclaim their bonds 602
Plan of Mr. Sherman, Secretary of the Treasury, for resumption 603
   Not called upon to decide who is to issue our paper money 603
   Nor whether it is to be plain or legal-tender notes 603
   Government notes secured by bonds "the currency of the future" . . 603
   Resumption will increase the amount of currency in circulation 603
   Vast amount of notes hoarded 603
   United States notes to be receivable in the customs revenues 604
   To form the reserves of the Banks 604
   Resumption will vastly increase the amount of the circulation 604
   Confidence established, no one will want coin for notes 605
   Amount of coin necessary for resumption . . . . '. . . 605
Absurdity of Mr. Sherman's propositions 605
The question of issuer the first to be decided 606
None but legal-tender notes can be maintained in circulation 606
Notes convertible into bonds of no greater value than the bonds 606
Mr. Sherman's "currency of the future" the worst possible currency . . 607
The currency to be enormously reduced as a condition of resumption . . 608
Government notes to be wholly retired 608
Never to be receivable in the revenues 608
Never to form the reserves of Banks 609
Always to be at a discount 609
Confidence no substitute for capital 609
Absurdity of the statement that notes are now hoarded 610
Probable amount of currency in circulation upon resumption 610
Proper method of resumption 611
Apprehension of moneyed monopolies, with a single issuer of currency,
   groundless 611
Interests of Banks always in harmony with those of the public 612
Necessity of a National Bank to the South 612
The object of this work not to lay down systems, but to demonstrate the
   laws of money 613

APPENDIX.

THE QUESTION OF A DOUBLE STANDARD 614
All currencies of equal cost to the receiver 614
The question of kind that of convenience 614
Gold more convenient than silver from its higher relative value 614
The former the currency of nations with which we deal 614
Importance of adopting a similar standard 614
The adoption of a double, would result in a single standard, — that of silver 615
A silver standard would be a debased, for the reason that it would be an
   exceptional, one 616
Its adoption would entail great inconvenience and loss upon the nation . . 616
The question not even open for discussion 616

The standard of value not the instrument by which the exchanges are
  effected 616
METHOD OF RESUMPTION — AMOUNT OF COIN REQUIRED 617
  1st, Provision of a United States Bank 617
  2d, Return to the National Banks of their securities 617
  3d, Their demonetization, except in the discharge of outstanding contracts 617
  4th, Retirement of the government notes by refunding 617
Government never to issue its notes to serve as money 617
If it use paper money, it must use that of Banks 617
Must connect its operations with those of the people 617
The Independent Treasury to be abolished 618
The theory upon which this institution was based 618
Injustice of compelling creditors to receive the notes at their nominal value 619
Injustice of compelling debtors to pay debts at their nominal value . . . 619
The value or price at which the outstanding notes are to be retired . . . 620
That at which they were used 620
How such value is to be ascertained 620
Government not chargeable with bad faith in retiring its notes at less than
  their nominal value 620
Notes payable at the pleasure of government possess no determinable value 620
The funding of the notes necessary to establish their value 621
The advantage of retiring the notes by funding instead of by payment . . 621
Payment would immediately retire the notes 621
Funding would leave them in circulation till the new currency appeared . 621
Amount of coin to be held by the Banks upon resumption 621
Amount to be held by the public 621
The public to hold reserves as well as Banks 622
How the necessary amount of coin could be provided 622
Danger of proceeding too rapidly in the process of resumption 623

THE LAWS OF MONEY.

THE first lump of gold or silver dug from the earth, as soon as its beauty and uses were displayed, became the object of universal admiration; each beholder sought to become its owner by exchanging therefor such articles of merchandise or property as he possessed, not necessary to his immediate wants.

This preference expressed nothing less than an instinct or sentiment common to mankind. In the earliest periods of which history or tradition gives any account, and which are far anterior to any possible concert or agreement between different peoples, the precious metals sustained precisely the relation to the nature and wants of man that they do to-day. They have had, through all time, the same importance in the arts. They always served as money in trade, and have always been esteemed the most desirable of all kinds of property to hold. Their owner has always been able to command whatever a people possessed, whether civilized or savage, among whom he might happen to be cast. No other articles of property have a similar power; for, with the exception of the precious metals, what is highly prized by one is often little valued by another; but in the desire for gold and silver, in this *auri sacra fames*, all nations and races, barbarous and civilized, Asiatic, African, European and American, meet on the same plane. To all they have an attractiveness equal in durability and intensity; and among all, they have rendered those who possessed them masters of the property and services of those who did not.[1]

---

[1] The Book of Genesis, which is among the earliest records which have come down to us, and which describes the very infancy of the Hebrew race, speaks of the precious metals as articles of established use and value from the very beginning of their chronology; that is, from the creation of the world.

Articles for which such an universal preference was felt, based alike upon their beauty and utility, necessarily became, by virtue of such preference, the highest form of capital, the universal equivalent — MONEY; for the reason that every person possessed of any other kind of merchandise or property not required for his own present use or consumption, has always sought to exchange it therefor, from the certainty of being able, by its means, to obtain whatever he might wish to acquire. Of all objects those are most prized that minister in the highest degree to our sense of beauty. The value of gold and silver often sinks into insignificance compared with that of a diamond, or of some exquisite piece of painting or sculpture; but the latter values are exceptional and local, and have none of the attributes of universality and uniformity which gold and silver have maintained with equal intensity from the dawn of civilization to the present hour.[1]

The qualities, other than these named, which gold and silver possess which fit them to serve as money, are their durability; their divisibility without diminishing their value; the capacity of each piece, however minute, to receive an impress, denoting its quantity, and, consequently its value; and the uniformity of their cost and supply. No other articles whatever, for the want of similar qualities, are fitted to become money, no matter how great may be their relative or positive value.

It is the durability of the precious metals which has secured

"And a river went out of Eden to water the garden, and from thence it parted and became into four heads. The name of the first is Pison; that is it which compasseth the whole land of Havilah, where there is gold: and the gold of that land is good." — Genesis, ii.: 10, 11, 12.

[1] If a Greek, who lived 2,500 years ago, could revisit the world, the only articles which he could bring with him which would have the same value and significance they possessed in his lifetime, would be gold and silver, either in the form of coin, or of ornaments wrought from them. His coat of mail, his polished arms, the implements of his industries, his household goods, — whatever constituted his wealth, or ministered to his comforts or his tastes, — all, with the exception of his gold and silver, would have long since been mingled in common dust. His language might be wholly unintelligible, but with the coins in his pocket, still retaining their wonderful beauty of design and workmanship, which might have been paid out to him directly from the mint, and with which he might have traded and travelled, in the infancy of Greece, — he could start upon a tour around the world, with a certainty that they would be received without question, at a value determined by their cost, at every public house, caravansary, railroad and steamboat office, and supply every want in his long journey of 25,000 miles.

to them no small part of the esteem in which they have always been held. They resist all action of the elements, and are absolutely indestructible when at rest. As the demand for them has always existed with equal uniformity and force, their durability fits them to become, in a preëminent manner, *reserves* in which the earnings and means of every member of society, no matter how humble, can be treasured up for all future time. Possessing them, he is at once raised above the possibility of want; and by the ease with which they can be transported or concealed, is enabled to secure a degree of independence and immunity from want, without which, in many countries, life itself might become wholly intolerable.[1]

It is in overlooking the original and universal attractiveness which the precious metals have for the race that nearly all the errors in monetary science have arisen. " Gold and silver," it is urged, " cannot feed, clothe, or shelter us ; they cannot even help in any way to sustain life. How idle, then, to claim a greater value for them than for articles which can!" There is no doubt that in extreme cases a person would part with untold gold for a morsel of bread, a cup of water, or a plank to save from drowning ; but all such examples are exceptions, not rules. When famine or want threatens, or when political or social disturbances make men distrustful of the future, their

---

[1] The precious metals possessed, in many respects, a far greater importance in ancient than in modern times, and among Eastern than Western nations. So long as no considerable progress was made in the arts, they necessarily served as the materials with which were fabricated, in a great measure, articles of ornament or luxury. The Eastern races have never been able, like the Western, to oppose an effectual resistance to the tyranny and exaction of their rulers ; and most pitiable would have been their condition had there not been some form of property, the possession of which could be effectually concealed, its value in the mean time remaining unimpaired. Their whole history has been one of oppression on one side and of arts to foil it on the other. "The Rajahs," says Mr. Scrafton, in his tract upon the government of Hindostan, "never allow their subjects to rise above mediocrity. The Mohammedan governors look upon the growing riches of their subjects as a boy on a bird's nest; they eye their progress with impatience, and come with a spoiler's hand and ravish the fruits of their labors. To counteract this, the Gentoos bury their money under ground ; and often with such secrecy as not to trust even their own children with the knowledge of it; and it is amazing what they will suffer rather than betray it. Their tyrants use all manner of corporal punishments, but that often fails ; for with a resentment prevailing over the love of life, they frequently rip up their bowels, or poison themselves, and carry their secret to the grave. The sums lost in this manner in some measure account why the silver in India does not appear to increase, though there are such quantities continually coming into it and none going out."

first care is to lay in abundant stores, not of food and clothing, but of gold and silver, assured that with these, they can never be long in want of other articles, whatever may happen.

Without some article or articles, for which a supreme preference was felt, there could have been no adequate motive to industry; for without them, industry could have produced nothing beyond the food, clothing and shelter necessary to sustain life upon its lowest plane. There cannot, in the nature of things, be a continued or superior preference for food over clothing. Each is indispensable in its way; but a person possessed of one is not necessarily nearer any article of merchandise or property he may wish to acquire, than if he possessed the other. With either, he could only reach such article by the exchange therefor of that which he possessed. Exchanges made in this manner involve, as a rule, labor and expense greater in amount than the value of the article sought for, after it is acquired. So long, therefore, as a people have no other mode of disposing of their products, but by the exchange of one article of consumption for another, they will produce only such as they can directly consume. They will necessarily remain barbarous or savage; and every civilized society accustomed to the use of the precious metals as money, in ceasing to use them as such, inevitably tends to that condition of barbarism from which, with almost infinite toil, it has so slowly arisen.

The first step, therefore, necessary to be taken by a person possessed of property other than gold and silver, in order to reach by means of it, some other article, was to convert it into them. Such conversion is itself an act of barter; for gold and silver are merchandise equally with food and clothing: but it is the only act of barter which is certain, by one further exchange, to secure to the seller what he may wish to obtain. A person possessed of food will not necessarily have any adequate motive to exchange it for clothing, for such exchange might not advance him a single step toward the object of desire. No prudent man ever thinks of exchanging his stock of merchandise for one of other kinds, because that which he possesses does not happen to be in active demand. If it be made up of articles indispensable for consumption, he will hold it till a demand arises. He will rest assured that, sooner or later, some one will take it off his hands at some price, to be paid in money. He may lose by holding ; but he might incur a greater loss by any attempt to sell or exchange it for merchandise other than that which he wished to secure or consume, as he would be in the same dilemma in the latter case as in the former. Such an exchange, if made at all, would have to be at the estimated value of his merchandise in money, leaving him as far from a sale for cash as before the exchange was made.

If without the precious metals there could be no exchanges but in kind, still less could there be division of labor, upon which every thing deserving the name of wealth is based, and without which only the rudest fabrics can be produced. Division of labor is possible only where the laborer or workman can be paid in some article which he may not produce, but by means of which he can by direct exchange, reach any other article he may wish to acquire. If it were possible to exchange a skin for a quarter of venison, it is not possible that a person who polishes and fits the main-spring of a watch should have that which, in itself, would be received in payment for food and shelter.

All sales of merchandise, therefore, before commerce could assume any considerable dimensions, were, from the very nature of things, made payable in the precious metals. For the same reason, all contracts arising from such sales, or for labor or service, to be executed presently or in the future, were held to be payable in them, whether or not they contained such provision, not only for the purpose of securing to the party to be paid that by which he could reach by direct exchange any other article of property, but for the purpose of defining the extent of liability to be incurred on either side. If a person were to receive 1,000 bushels of wheat at the expiration of ten years, he could form no idea of what it would realize to him till it was received and sold for coin. If he were to receive $1,000 in coin in ten years, he would know its value as well when the contract was made as when it was to be executed. Its value would be the same, or very nearly the same, at either period. The wheat might not have one-half, or it might have double, the value when it was to be paid, that it had when the contract for its payment was made. Neither buyer nor seller, therefore, could with any safety enter, nor would either as a rule, enter into contracts not presently to mature, that were not to be discharged in coin.

As the precious metals are always in demand at the cost of their production, their value is ABSOLUTE; depending upon one condition, — cost. That of all other articles is relative, depending upon two conditions, — demand and cost. From absence of demand, their value, either in the precious metals or in other articles, may not equal one-half their cost. In all transactions the former pass at their absolute value. As all other articles must take the form of the precious metals, or of that which possesses a value equivalent thereto, before they can be made available to their owners; and must be accepted in exchange, at their absolute value in gold and silver, the latter must be the STANDARD of value by which that of all other articles is measured. As they are money by virtue of their value, they are standards of value by virtue of the same attribute. When they pass as money, the standard, as well as the instrument of exchange, passes in the same article, by the same act. The thing itself, unlike a foot-rule or pound weight, is the standard, — the measure of value. Other measures, those of extent or quantity, do not pass in the sale of that which they measure. The value of such measures has no relation whatever to that of the articles measured. But money, the medium of exchange,[1] and money the measure or standard of value, are identical things. The words that express them are, in the strictest sense, synonymous terms.

From what has preceded, the transcendent importance of the precious metals in the development and progress of society will be at once appreciated. They are the instruments, and the only ones, by virtue of their being the highest form of capital, the universal equivalents, which render possible the very first step towards a higher life. They are the foundation upon which rests the vast superstructure of civilized society.

---

[1] The term, "medium of exchange," is one of recent origin, growing out of the use of paper money, from which the idea of value has become in great measure dissociated. So long as exchanges were effected in kind, — one article of consumption being exchanged for another, — each were equally "media of exchange." The term, as ordinarily used, is one of the great stumbling blocks in the way of a proper elucidation or understanding of the subject of money. It is one of Bacon's "Idols of the Market."

Without them there could have been no exchanges, no wealth, no government, no institutions, no history; nothing but the eternal iteration of savage or barbarous existence. The moment they are disused, society is without any adequate standard by which the value of its industries can be measured. Without them, utter chaos would at once take the place of the order which now conducts to prosperous ends the industry of every laborer, — whether he be a cotton-spinner in England, a farmer raising wheat on the banks of the Missouri, a cultivator of tea in China, a grower of rice on the banks of the Ganges or the Nile, or of sugar in Brazil, — and awards to each an exact compensation, measured by a common standard, for the value of his contribution to the general stock from which all are fed and sustained. With them, a people, consuming the products of another, have no need to inquire what those of their own industries will bring in the countries from which their imports are to be made, but only what their own products are worth in the precious metals, at their own doors. By their means, at the close of each day, the most unlettered, equally with the most intelligent and learned, can measure exactly the value of his industries, and apply the necessary corrective, should it be found that they had not been properly directed or sufficiently remunerative. As without such standards there could be neither industry, wealth, nor civilization, the inference is irresistible that the universal demand for the precious metals at their cost, and the uniformity of their supply, are, equally with moral laws, part of God's providence with man.

As gold and silver are capital as well as money, and are always in demand to serve as the basis of reproduction, either by their conversion into forms other than that of coin, or in exchange for food, implements, and the like, every one possessed of them, where governments are sufficiently strong to enforce the fulfilment of contracts, will seek to loan whatever he may have in excess of his own immediate wants, for the income they will yield. The opportunity for loaning them at usury does not depend, as is too often supposed, upon the necessities of governments or individuals for capital for their ordinary expenditures, but upon the uses to which they can be profitably applied. The greater the progress made in knowledge, and in the arts and sciences; the more perfect

the means of production and distribution, the greater must
be the disproportion of capital to the demand that must exist
for it ; the more powerful the motives to industry and toil,
and the higher the rates of interest which borrowers can afford
to pay.   From the material progress that has been made within
the last fifty years, a significance and value have been given to
capital never before known.   That it must steadily increase
in importance rests upon the fact that God is Infinite and man
finite.   The mission of man is to unfold His laws, and render
them the instruments in promoting his own welfare.   The
greater his progress, the wider the field spread out before him.
Every step he takes becomes an incentive and an aid to the
next.   The more he achieves in any direction, the stronger
the motive and the greater the power for new acquisitions.
Every new discovery is a fresh demand for capital.   I need
only refer to the vast sums now called for, for the purpose of
utilizing the discoveries which the present generation has
made in electricity, and the almost infinite sums yet required
for the full development of that mighty force upon which
seem to rest all the phenomena of the universe.

When loans of the precious metals could be safely made at
usury, a principle or element of almost infinite value and power
was introduced into human affairs.   With gold and silver to
serve as the instruments of exchange, the means of acquisition
were for the first time given to the race.   By loans of them,
with interest payable in kind, its acquisitions could be treasured up, and be made to bear fruit for all coming time.   Until
interest could be obtained for their use, every person retained
whatever he acquired, in his possession, until forced by his
necessities to part with them.   So soon as they could be safely
loaned, no one would keep the possession of an amount greater
than that required for his immediate wants.   Thenceforth the
whole face of society was changed.   Order and good government were the conditions necessary to induce the possessors of
capital to loan it, for they were the only conditions under
which the borrowers could prosecute their industries in a
manner which would enable them to repay their loans.   Order
and good government, consequently, have in modern times
been the work of the industrial and commercial classes.   The
moral well-being of mankind rests upon its material well-being.
In the promotion of both, the precious metals, with loans of

them at usury, stand forth as the prime and paramount
factors.

With loans of the precious metals at interest, their possessor
could not only make provision for himself, and for his .family
after his decease, but he could found institutions for the culture of learning, of art, of science, or for the support of some
charity, — provisions that should suffer no abatement, but
secure the same results one hundred or one thousand years
after his death, as during his lifetime and under his own supervision. In other words, he could invest himself, as it were,
with the attributes of immortality. He could make no such
provisions by dedicating thereto great stores of food and clothing. All such articles are speedily perishable, so that with an
abundance of both, unless exchanged for gold and silver, their
possessor might presently come to want. No permanent
foundation, therefore, can be made, resting upon such kinds of
property. Should such an attempt be made, no one could ever
be found who would receive them on loans, agreeing to pay
for their use interest *in kind*, — to pay, for example, six bushels
of wheat, annually, for a loan of one hundred bushels. He
would not run the risk of the fluctuations in its value ; or he
might wish to change his residence to countries or districts,
from which the cost of sending wheat to the place of payment
might exceed many times its value. It is impossible, therefore, that there should be any other final solvents of transactions but the precious metals, while human nature is what it
is. No commercial people ever have adopted, nor will they
ever voluntarily adopt, standards of value other than those
Providentially appointed. If other standards are ever used,
it is only because governments interpose to set aside natural
laws. But all such attempts prove in the end utterly futile ;
for no government can long compel the people to act in direct
violation of their highest interests. However great the departure, the natural standards will always be returned to ; but
often, unfortunately, not until both government and people
are involved in common ruin.

As soon as any considerable progress had been made in commerce and trade, contracts to pay money would be authenticated
by convenient and proper instruments. The transfer of these
would operate to transfer that which they represented. With
the progress of social order, some of these instruments, for

greater convenience, would be made payable to their possessor
or bearer, and would transfer, by mere delivery, their constituents.   In this way, bills of exchange representing merchandise;
promissory notes; and, later, notes of banks and bankers
payable on demand to bearer, came into use.

While exchanges of property must always be made at the
standard of the precious metals, it by no means follows that
they may not be made without their actual intervention.
Their use is always an act of barter, in which equivalents in
value are mutually exchanged.   There is no generic distinction whatever, between an exchange in which a barrel of
flour is given for a hat, and one in which ten gold dollars are
given for it.   The first may be termed *simple* barter, as
articles which each party may produce are directly exchanged.
But the use of gold and silver involves two exchanges before
a party possessing merchandise can reach that which he may
wish to acquire, — the exchange, for example, of the barrel of
flour for ten gold dollars, and the exchange of ten gold dollars
for the hat.   The latter process, therefore, may be termed
double barter; for in it a third agent, or factor, has to be
present, which is not, in the function it performs or in the
manner in which it is used at the moment, the subject of
consumption.

When the vast magnitude of the transactions now taking
place is considered, the importance of eliminating from them
an agent or factor having a value equal to the articles exchanged will be readily appreciated.   The value of the merchandise moving between Great Britain and the United States
equals many hundreds of millions annually.   Were the precious metals required to move between them as currency, in
equal volume, the interest on so vast a sum would have to be
added to the price of the merchandise to be paid by the consumer.   To this would have to be added the loss by attrition,
estimated as high as one per cent annually; and the cost of its
transportation which would equal many millions every year.
But such burdens might be by no means the greatest of those
resulting from an attempt to effect all the exchanges of property by the use of a metallic currency.   The hope of seizing it in
transit would cover every sea with pirates, from whose vigilance
none could escape, and whom no punishment would deter.

Instead of sailing singly, a large number of vessels would have to go in company, convoyed by powerful ships of war. Were all the payments within the same community to be made in it, a file of porters, guarded by soldiers, would be required by every great merchant where an office-boy now suffices. Had no mode been devised of effecting exchanges but by the actual intervention of the precious metals, commerce and trade would not have reached one-tenth their present colossal proportions.

The manner in which the use of gold and silver are discharged from transactions between nations, and between communities widely separated, comes within the experience of almost every man of affairs. An importer in the city of New York does not accompany his order upon a manufacturer in England with the corresponding amount of coin, * but buys of

---

* Coinage — by means of which pieces of metal receive an impress denoting their weight and fineness, consequently their value, and which has been adopted by all civilized nations — is of comparatively recent origin. No traces of it have been found among the remains of Assyrian or Egyptian art; and Egyptian civilization, running through periods far greater than those which measure the life of subsequent nations, had begun to decline before coinage was used. Among all the ancient nations, including the Hebrews and Phœnicians, as well as the Assyrians and Egyptians, the precious metals passed by weight. When Abraham weighed out at Ephron the silver which he had named in the audience of the sons of Heth, — "four hundred shekels of silver, current money with the merchant," — he undoubtedly used scales and denominations of weight common to the whole East. The language indicates as thorough a familiarity with the use of money as does that used in financial newspaper articles of the present day. So Joseph gave to Benjamin "three hundred pieces of silver." These pieces were undoubtedly of very nearly equal weight, — consequently of value. The word *piece* had a significance precisely similar to that which we attach to the word dollar.

The invention of coinage has been usually ascribed to Pheidon, who reigned about 750 B.C., in the island of Ægina, a dependency of Argos, and at that time one of the greatest commercial emporiums of Greece. Previous to its invention, the form in which the precious metals were used as money was that of pins, or wires, silver being the metal chiefly employed. Of these, a certain number made a conventional handful, or *drachma*. This form was gradually exchanged for that of solid pieces, or wedges, which may be considered as a step toward coinage. To secure pieces of uniform value, coinage was properly made a function of government, its insignia or stamp being the proper guaranty for the value of the coins uttered. The Æginian scale, as it was termed, was adopted in Peloponnesus, in all the Dorian States, in Bœotia, Thessaly, Macedonia, and throughout Northern Greece. Another scale, however, soon arose, called the Euboeic, which was adopted in Athens, and in the Ionic States generally, as well as in Eubœa. Their denominations were the same, — 100 drachmas to the mina, and 60 minæ to the talent, — but the value, by weight, of the scale of the latter to the former was as six to five.

a neighbor shipping breadstuffs to that country a bill drawn against such shipment, paying the value of such bill or shipment in the local currency of the city, at the standard of coin, and sends it forward in the place of so much money. The English manufacturer collects the proceeds of the same in the local currency of that country, and credits his New York customer with the amount. The use of such bill, in the manner described, obviates that of a corresponding amount of capital in the form of money. Proceedings reciprocally the same are had by an English importer of American produce. In this way, by the use of bills, merchandise is offset against merchandise, and payments are made thereby as effectually as if made in money. If the exports of the two countries, the one to the other, were the same in value, no money — coin, or bullion — would move in the operations between them, no matter how great their magnitude. It would only move when there was a want of bills, and consequently of merchandise, to make good the deficit of those kinds which are the ordinary subjects of consumption. The balance arising on either side would be a debt for which the creditor, for the reasons already described, would receive nothing but gold and silver, — the highest form

From Greece coinage was first introduced into Egypt, by the successors of Alexander the Great, about 300 B.C. It was not until about 150 B.C. that Antiochus gave permission to Simon Maccabæus to coin money " with his own stamp." This is the first instance of coinage among the Hebrews. Through the Greek colonies, which were numerous along the shores of the Mediterranean, the art was gradually diffused throughout the then known world. As coinage gradually came into universal use ; as every nation, as well as almost every community of any considerable importance, had its mint, — a vast number and variety of coins were issued ; and as the impress they received commemorated events, or symbolized ideas or sentiments, and as great numbers have come down to us, they have proved of almost inestimable value in illustrating ancient history and life.

While all communities and nations have entertained a similar sentiment in reference to the desirableness or value of the precious metals — a sentiment which transcends all agreement or concert between them — they no sooner came to the subordinate matter of *coinage* than they were as wide apart as the poles. Nothing could be more convenient than a coinage common to all nations ; yet nothing can be more dissimilar than the denominations of their money. It does not seem probable that they will ever be any better agreed in this matter than now. If money, as all writers have claimed, be an *invention*, why was not a common standard of coinage invented at the same time ? That all nations are agreed upon the value of money, and none upon the forms or denominations to be used, although uniformity in this respect is a matter of very great importance, is of itself sufficient evidence that the value of the metals from which it is coined, rests upon a law far higher than the convenience of their use as media of exchange.

of capital. All balances arising in commerce, the world over, are held to be payable in the same manner. Every transaction, therefore, is upon the basis of coin, as to value, even when it does not interpose, and all balances have to be actually paid in it, or in promises to pay it, coupled with an agreement to pay interest for any forbearance of present payment.

The exchanges, therefore, between communities widely separated are now in great measure effected, not by the use of the precious metals, but by symbols, or evidences, of merchandise moving between them. Such symbols, or evidences, serve as money equally with coin. They perform in the exchange of merchandise precisely the functions of coin. A bill, for example, drawn by a competent party in San Francisco against a shipment of breadstuffs to Hamburg, is purchased by a merchant or banker in the former city for remittance to New York in place of a corresponding amount of coin. The New York merchant or banker credits his San Francisco customer with the amount as so much coin, and sells the bill to a party having a payment to make in Manchester, England. From Manchester it is again purchased for remittance, as cash, to London. From London it is remitted to Paris, whence it is sent for collection to its place of payment. In the mean time, it has served, by virtue of what it represented, in the hands of each holder, all the functions of coin which, but for such bill, would have had to follow in equal amount, in its track. The actual price at which the bill would be taken, in the place of coin, at the several places in which it was used, would be greater or less than its nominal value, depending upon the state of exchanges, and the time it had to run, — interest being always charged, or deducted, for such time.

Bills of exchange, consequently, serve as money between communities widely separated, for the reason that their transfer operates as the transfer of that which they represent. It is plain to see that their use is the only mode by which the value of exports could be made immediately available. Without them, such exports would be so much dead capital till they were delivered to the purchasers or consumers, and the proceeds of the same collected and paid over. By means of them, by their sale, the exporter of merchandise can, as soon as they are drawn, convert the value of that which they represent into money. A currency of bills, therefore, is in a normal and healthy condition — is perfectly adapted to its objects, when every shipment has its proper representative; in other words, when the currency of commerce equals the merchandise of commerce, as a corresponding amount of coin or bullion is thereby discharged from use. There could be no inflation so long as the currency issued was symbolic, as it would always be retired when the merchandise symbolized was delivered for consumption.

It is to be observed that, although the currency described is always drawn payable absolutely in coin, and usually without referring to that which it represents, yet it is always understood that, ordinarily, little other provision is made for its payment than by its constituent. It is a currency based, not upon coin or bullion, but upon merchandise. This fact is so obvious that it is referred to here only as tending to illustrate the subject of local currencies, which though resting, like those of bills, on merchandise for their solvency, are removed one step farther than bills from that which they represent, and are consequently somewhat more difficult of explanation than a currency in the form of bills.

It is sufficiently evident that bills of exchange drawn against the sale or shipments of merchandise in gross, are not adapted to serve as local currencies. They are too large in amount, and are not as a rule presently due. They are drawn, in theory, upon such time as will be required for the delivery of that which they represent to purchasers, or consumers, and the collection of their proceeds. Local currencies are presently due, because the merchandise they represent is always assumed to be immediately deliverable to the consumer. A bill of exchange, with the bill of lading which usually accompanies it, entitles the holder to the possession of the merchandise represented, or to the proceeds of the same. He has the right of possession to the specific thing, which is usually sufficient security against loss. For whatever may be sustained he has the right of reclamation upon the drawer as soon as its amount can be ascertained. Local currencies — notes of banks — do not entitle their holder to receive any specific article, or the proceeds of the same, corresponding in value. If the holders of merchandise will not accept them on its sale as money, then the right of immediate reclamation must exist against their makers and for their whole amount.

As the makers of bills, which serve as currency, are the producers of the merchandise which such bills represent, it would seem at first sight that they could supply a currency adapted to a local or domestic trade, by an issue of notes or certificates of various denominations, payable on demand to bearer, in the articles which they produce or hold, or in default thereof, in coin. Should all producers or holders of merchandise issue such notes or certificates, their bearers could hardly fail, either by presenting them, or by exchanging them for such as might be held by other parties, to reach any article of which they might stand in need. So far as they could be so used, they would serve all the purposes of a currency of coin. The fact, however, that the holders of such notes or certificates would be subject to the risk of the continued solvency of their makers, who would as a rule have the whole of their means invested in their various industries, would so discredit them that they would never be taken in any considerable amounts. If, however, other parties not subject to the risk which always attends production and trade, and possessed of adequate capital either in coin, or merchandise (the equivalent in value of coin, and in demand for consumption;) or in bills given for such merchandise on its way to the consumer; should issue their notes or certificates, payable on demand, to an amount equal to the means possessed by them in either form, — agreeing to hold a sufficient amount of coin, in reserve, for the payment of any reclamations that might be made, they would be taken, by all persons desirous of becoming possessed of the merchandise they represented, in exchange for what they had to sell, as readily as coin, so long as confidence was felt that they represented that which they purported to represent. The sole use of coin, as money, is to reach some other article of property of equal value. If it can be reached more conveniently by other means than by the use of coin, that of the latter will, of course, be dispensed with. The most convenient methods in this, as in all transactions, will, in the end, always have the preference.

Almost all domestic or local exchanges are now effected by the use of notes and credits issued in the manner described. The makers of such notes are usually Banks, and associations of capitalists; although every party possessed of merchandise entering into consumption, or of bills of parties given for such merchandise, is entirely competent to issue instruments for its distribution. The modes of issue of the notes or credits of Banks, and the conditions necessary to secure at all times their return without the withdrawal of any considerable amount of the reserves held to meet reclamations, — in other words, to preserve their value at all times at the standard of coin, — will be most readily shown by tracing from the outset the operations of one of these institutions.

A Bank — the capital of which, on commencing business, may be assumed to consist of one million dollars paid up wholly in coin, does not, in discounting bills, or in making its loans, pay out its coin, but issues its notes, or gives credit on its books to be drawn in its notes or in coin, at the pleasure of the holder, and which till drawn are termed deposits ; holding, in the mean time, its coin as a reserve to redeem such notes and credits as may be presented for payment. If it paid out coin in making its loans, no adequate advantage would be gained to its stockholders or to the public from its organization ; for coin could be loaned as well without as with a Bank. The very object of the Bank, in making its loans in the manner described, is to provide instruments of exchange and distribution other than coin, and thereby obviate its use. It is here assumed that the bills to be discounted were given for, and represent, merchandise having a value equal to their nominal amounts. As they would be paid by its sale and the collection of the proceeds, they would, in the hands of their holders, have a corresponding value, — a value equal to that of coin, — subject, of course, to the risks which attend all commercial transactions. The notes and credits issued would have a similar value, as the Bank would undertake to appropriate the proceeds of that which the bills represented for their payment. The process of discount consists of a mutual exchange of obligations. As those of the Bank would be discharged to the extent that its notes and credits were taken in, it would receive them in payment of its bills equally with coin. The holders of merchandise, therefore, would receive them equally with coin in its sale, as they would pay their bills equally with coin. As they would be accepted in the sale of merchandise equally with coin, they would be taken by the public, the consumers of merchandise, equally with coin. As the object of all currencies, no matter the form or materials of which they may be composed, is to reach by their exchange some other article or articles, the holders of the notes and credits of a Bank would have no adequate motive to exchange, nor would they exchange them for coin, to be used as currency, so long as they would perform, as currency, all the functions of coin. Producers, consequently, in whose favor the bills were discounted, would, from the greater convenience of their use, prefer to receive in their discount, notes and credits to coin, as they could pay them out equally with coin in the purchase of labor and material, in the prosecution of their industries, to the very parties who would be the consumers of the merchandise which they had produced and put upon the market. As fast as such merchandise was consumed, the notes and credits issued would come into the possession of the parties who had been its holders (the makers of the bills), to be used by them in their payment. The obligation created on either side, when the bills were discounted, would in this way be cancelled by mutual offset; but not until merchandise, equal in value, had been fully distributed for consumption.

The pivot upon which all these operations turn is merchandise. That provided, the instruments which represent it, and which entitle their holder to a corresponding amount of the same in value, or to the proceeds of the same, and which, by their transfer, transfer that which they represent, ARE PAPER MONEY — CURRENCY. As soon as they are issued, their movement commences automatically in their appropriate spheres, and continues until they have accomplished their circuit and work. It is merchandise that calls them into being; it is merchandise that gives them their value; it is merchandise that gives them their impulse; and it is merchandise that, by its purchase for consumption, returns them to those who issue them, not to be reissued but in the making of new loans. So far as merchandise is provided, they proceed noiselessly and beneficently in their proper orbits. So far as it is not provided, their course is as erratic and destructive as would be that of the planets, without the guidance and control of that central mass around which they now so harmoniously move.

All local currencies, therefore, are based, not on gold and silver coin, but on merchandise, for which they serve, in the place of coin, as instruments of distribution. Coin is itself money, and needs no symbol for its transfer or distribution. Except a small quantity by way of change, the precious metals are no longer used as currency. They are held and used chiefly as reserves for the discharge of such paper currencies as are not discharged by merchandise in manner described.

As the Bank, in the payment of its bills, would make no distinction between the notes and credits issued, — that is, as it would receive, in payment of bills given for breadstuffs, notes and credits issued in the discount of bills given for iron, — so the holders of merchandise, who would be the makers of its bills, would receive its notes and credits without any reference to the kind of merchandise for which the bills discounted were given. In the same way, if the merchandise of a community were symbolized by the issues of several Banks, such issues would be received on the same terms by its holders ; for the reason that each Bank would receive for the payment of its bills the notes and credits of the other Banks (provided they were of good standing) equally with its own. Whatever the notes or credits, therefore, that any person might hold, they would be directly exchangeable for any article that might have been symbolized, or which he might wish to obtain. In the settlements that would frequently, and in places where there were several Banks would daily be made, each Bank would have to take in all its notes and credits that might be held by other Banks. These settlements would be made by offsetting, as far as they would go, the notes and credits of other Banks which each might hold against those of its own held by them. The balances arising, after the notes and credits of other Banks held by any one Bank had been exhausted would, like all debts, have to be discharged in coin, as the only kind of capital which, as in the case of a balance arising in foreign trade, the party would accept in whose favor it might be found, or which the delinquent would have to offer.

The process of discount consists, as already shown, of a mutual exchange of promises payable by their terms in coin, — of the notes and credits of Banks for merchants' bills. The latter are payable, in theory, upon such time as will suffice for the distribution of the merchandise for which they were given, and the collection of its proceeds. The former are payable presently, as they are assumed to represent merchandise fitted and accessible for immediate consumption ; and in order that, if their holders desire, they may be used at any moment in the purchase of the same. They are payable by their terms in coin, that their holders, if they cannot by their direct exchange obtain that of which they are in search, may at once convert them into that form of merchandise, gold and silver, which have at all times the same value, and by means of which their holders are always certain, by direct exchange, to obtain that which they wish to acquire; or which they can safely hold, if they do not wish to convert them immediately into merchandise. The moment they are converted into gold and silver, their full value is treasured up for future use, placing their holder beyond all possible risk of loss. That the notes and credits of a Bank will not be received for merchandise at their nominal value, at all times, is evidence that they have been issued upon inadequate security, and that the safety of their holder requires their immediate conversion into coin.

As Banks guaranty the immediate convertibility of their issues into merchandise or into coin, possessing the means therefor either in their reserves in coin (which all Banks must maintain), or in the merchandise which the bills they have discounted represent, and which, whoever may have its possession, is to be esteemed a fund especially set apart for their payment, and consequently for the redemption of the notes and credits issued in their discount, they treat all such issues as the equivalent of coin; and charge the same rate of interest on loans made by their means, that they would charge on loans of an equal amount of coin. The borrowers are assumed to be producers; for only such are entitled to borrow at Bank by an issue of symbols, which anticipate to them the collection of the proceeds of merchandise which they have put upon the market. The interest they pay in the discount of the bills taken in its sale is charged to the purchasers, and is finally paid by consumers as a part of the cost of distribution. It properly makes an element in price; as, without the symbols issued by the Banks, the cost of distribution, and with it, price, would be greatly increased, by the use of a metallic in place of a paper currency. Consumers in fact are the parties chiefly benefited by a symbolic currency, as the object and effect of all such currencies are to simplify and cheapen distribution. While Banks derive a profit from their circulation, they can derive one only so long as they conduct their operations prop-

erly, and in harmony with the general welfare ; only so long
as they issue instruments against merchandise actually in demand for consumption.   The return to them of their notes and
credits, automatically, is the proper test, and the only one, of
competent management.

As the liabilities of a Bank are in ratio to the amount of its
discounts, and as it must, for its own safety, maintain reserves
to take in such of its liabilities as are not returned to it in the
payment of its bills, it follows that as its reserves are drawn, it
must reduce its discounts, — in other words, its interest-bearing securities, — in a far greater degree.   If, for example, a Bank
having reserves in coin equalling $1,000,000 could safely have
a discount line of $5,000,000, it would, if its reserves were re-
duced to $500,000, have to reduce its discounts to $2,500,000.
If its reserves were wholly drawn, the Bank would have to
replenish them, or suspend operations altogether.

The preceding statement fully explains the effect of the
addition to, or the withdrawal from the reserves of Banks, of a
comparatively small amount of specie.   In countries like Great
Britain or the United States (the currency of the latter being
on a specie basis), nearly all additions to their specie go immediately into the Banks, increasing their reserves in an equal
degree.   These immediately proceed to increase their issues,
somewhat in like ratio.   So long as they discount nothing but
legitimate paper, their position may not be immediately compromised.   All sudden additions of the means of expenditure,
however, will necessarily lead to over-consumption, to wasteful-
ness, and to enterprises in advance, or beyond the wants, of
the community in which they are undertaken.   On the other
hand, the withdrawal of the reserves of Banks, provided such
withdrawal be permanent, compels them to reduce their
issues in five-fold ratio to the amount of such withdrawal, reducing the available means of the public in a like degree.
Their operations are never in simple, but in far greater, ratio
to the amount of specie they hold ; hence, unless they are adequately managed, the movements of specie (which is always
in a state of ebb and flow), are certain to keep the public in a
condition of chronic excitement and agitation, from the constant variations in the amounts of paper money.   At one time
there will be a plethora of it ; at another not a dollar is to be

had. Banks, therefore, which when properly conducted are most efficient agents in promoting the public welfare, are, when mismanaged, the greatest of curses. Those who conduct them should early learn the lesson not to hasten to increase their discounts, for the reason that they are in possession of an unusual amount of coin ; nor to refuse them, whenever there is a slight decrease in their reserves. They ought always to bear in mind that such additions may be only temporary, and that loans made upon them may soon have to be taken in. They may also rest assured that so long as their loans are properly made, all coin that may be drawn from them is certain to be speedily returned by the necessary operations of the laws of trade.

The profits of a Bank are in the ratio that its interest-bearing securities exceed the capital required in its operations, and the cost of management. If a Bank, for example, with $1,000,000 of capital, — that is, with $1,000,000 of reserves in the form of coin, — discounts bills to the amount of $5,000,000, bearing interest at the rate of 6 per cent, it will be in receipt of an annual income of $300,000. Out of this it has to deduct interest on its reserves, say $60,000 ; expense of management, $70,000 ; losses averaging, say $50,000 annually, — the total being $180,000. The amount remaining for dividends in such a case would equal $120,000 ; or 12 per cent annually on the capital employed. The above figures are, of course, used only by way of illustration. It is certain, however, that the profits of well-conducted Banks exceed considerably the ordinary rates of interest. They deal with capital in its highest and most complete form, and their profits will always be in the same form.

It is often asked, " If the borrowers at a Bank pay interest on the whole amount of its loans, that is, on the whole amount of notes and credits issued, — what is the advantage of such a currency over one of coin, — of capital ? " One advantage is the greater convenience of a paper over a metallic currency ; a convenience often so great that, could a currency of coin be furnished without charge, borrowers would prefer a currency of symbols at the rates ordinarily paid for its use. A person having a remittance to make from New York to London always prefers a bill for this purpose, from the safety and economy of its transmission over that of coin. In local currencies, symbols are preferable to coin in by far the greater number of transactions. Were gold and silver required to be present in all exchanges, the amount necessary therefor, provided the volume of such exchanges remained undiminished, would be more than ten-fold greater than that in the world. As they would rise in price from the increased demand, the stimulus given to their production would be so great as to increase their cost probably five-fold. As their value increased, the cost, risk, and inconvenience attending their use as currency would be so great that production and trade would be reduced somewhat in ratio to their increase in cost. With such increase in cost, the value of all articles made from them, whether of use or ornament, would increase in like ratio, with consequences most detrimental to the moral as well as the physical wellbeing of society ; for the cultivation of the sense and love of beauty, to which the precious metals so largely minister, is among the most powerful means of promoting the well-being of the race.

No opinion or theory is more generally entertained than that the effect of symbolic currencies is to raise and sustain prices. Such an effect is constantly urged as the strongest argument in their favor. If such were their effect, they would be the greatest of evils, instead of being, as they are, among the most beneficent agents in promoting the general welfare. Whatever reduces the cost of distribution must reduce prices, as competition is always certain to reduce the profits of production very nearly to the ordinary rates of interest. As prices are reduced, however, consumption increases ; so that the aggregate amount of profits of a manufacturer, for example, may, for a time, be largely increased from increased production, the rate of profit remaining the same ; or his aggregate profits may be largely increased, the rate being reduced, by the increased amount produced. He might be able to sell twenty-five per cent cheaper on an order for $100,000 of merchandise, than on one for $10,000. The commerce of such a country as the United States has resulted in a great measure from a reduction in the cost of distribution. Previous to the opening of the Erie Canal, the cost of transporting a ton of wheat from Buffalo to the city of New York equalled $100.

That article, consequently, throughout the greater portion of the Mississippi Valley, had no exportable value whatever. As the people living in it could not export their products, they could not purchase those of the eastern States. The construction of that great work at once opened a market to an immense area, enabling a farmer in central Ohio to sell his wheat at $1.00 the bushel, or at three times its former price. The canal, at the same time, so reduced the cost of transportation that he could purchase largely of the fabrics of the eastern States, which had, from cost of transportation of his products, been far beyond his reach. With the canal, he could sell at higher and buy at far lower rates. So with the eastern manufacturer. Previous to the opening of the canal, he had to pay $3.00 the bushel for wheat. That work reduced the price, to him, to $1.50. At the same time, from the reduced costs of transportation, new and extensive markets were opened for his products. He could sell a much greater amount than formerly; and probably, at the outset, at equal and perhaps better rates. Both farmer, and manufacturer were thus mutually and equally benefited, but the benefit was mainly in the reduced prices at which each could purchase the products of the other. If the profits of each on the sale of their own products were increased, say ten per cent, in consequence of the reduction in the cost of transportation and of the markets opened by the canal, each would pay, say, fifty per cent less for what each purchased of the other. If in the end, the rate of their respective profits was not increased, each would make a very large saving at the reduced rate at which each would buy the products of the other. Canals and railroads supersede the old highways, for the reason that by their means merchandise can be the more cheaply and conveniently moved from producer to consumer. Symbolic currencies supersede metallic ones for reasons precisely similar. The question is the relative economy of the two. As the former reduce costs, they must reduce price. As cost, however, is reduced, increased consumption may for a time have the effect of increasing the rate of profits of the producer; but such effect can be only temporary, for competition, as already shown, will be certain in the end to reduce them very nearly to the ordinary rates of interest.

It follows, from what has preceded, that as merchandise can be distributed much more conveniently and at much less cost by a currency of symbols than by one of coin, it should, so far as it enters into consumption, be symbolized; or, to state the matter in another form, — as a certain time is always required for distribution of merchandise for consumption, all sales in gross should be made upon a corresponding credit as to time, in order, by the evidences of such sale, to lay the foundation for the issue of currency as the instrument of its distribution. A currency is ideally perfect when its nominal value equals that of merchandise to be distributed, for the reason that its use discharges from a similar one an equal amount of capital, — of coin. As bills of exchange anticipate, to their drawers, the value of that which they represent, so local currencies anticipate to producers the sale and collection of the proceeds of that which they have put upon the market. But for such currencies, if they carried on their industries in full volume, they would be compelled to provide an equal additional amount of capital, either by accumulating or borrowing it. Should the merchandise entering into consumption be symbolized to the full extent of every dollar of its value, there could be no inflation; the symbols could never exceed the value of that entering into consumption, as those which every one might happen to hold would only equal the value of the contribution he had made to the common stock, and as they would be returned by their use to the party issuing them, not to be reissued except in making other loans.[1]

[1] Mr. Inglis Palgrave in his "Notes on Banking in Great Britain," estimates the amount of Inland Mercantile Bills made in each quarter of 1870–71, to equal £677,776,000. The average time in which they were drawn was a little less than four months. He estimates the amount of Foreign Bills drawn on England for 1871 to equal £507,400,000; the amount of Bills drawn in England on other countries to equal £73,500,000; and the amount of Foreign Bills negotiated in England to equal £30,700,000: the aggregate of such Bills being £611,600,000. He estimates the immediate liabilities of the Banks and Bankers of the United Kingdom, including the circulation of the Bank of England, — that is, the total paper currency, — to equal £560,000,000. Of this sum only about £43,000,000 is in the form of notes. The aggregate of note circulation was made up as follows: —

Circulating notes of Bank of England			£24,000,000
„	„	Private and Joint Stock Banks about .	6,000,000
„	„	Scottish Banks	6,100,000
„	„	Irish „	7,500,000
			£43,600,000

The amount of the currency in the form of deposits exceeded £500,000,000. As the currency arises from the discount of Bills, and as the Bills in existence

As already remarked, the notes and credits of a Bank, so long as they represented merchandise, would serve as the instruments of its distribution, and would return to it, automatically, in the payment of its bills. So long, consequently, would its reserves remain intact in its vaults. It would, however, from the importunities of borrowers, or from want of proper caution in making its loans, be constantly liable to discount bills which either did not represent merchandise, or which did not represent such as was in demand for consumption. To an equal extent it would have to pay out, in the redemption of its notes and credits, a corresponding amount of coin. It would not unfrequently turn out that bills apparently the most legitimate would not be paid from causes which could not have been foreseen, or which could not have been avoided. It is to meet such contingencies or unforeseen calls that every Bank must, as already shown, retain reserves in coin; and in value, it is here assumed, equal at least to twenty per cent of its liabilities: that is, with $5,000,000 of notes and credits outstanding, it should maintain in its vaults at least $1,000,000 in coin. This coin, in fact, is the fund or capital which is to guaranty its undertaking that all its issues shall have a function or value equal to that of coin. They would have, as already shown, an equal value, provided the bills, in the discount of which they were issued, represented merchandise entering into consumption, and having a value in coin equal to their nominal amount. So long as they represented such values, there would be no adequate motive to draw them in coin. So far as they did not represent such merchandise, they would be speedily drawn in coin. Suppose a Bank, with reserves in coin of $1,000,000, to discount ninety-day bills given for merchandise to the amount of $5,000,000; and, thereafter, to discount additional bills having three years to run, to the amount of $1,000,000: all the notes and credits issued would be returned to it at the same time. Those issued in the discount of the bills given for merchandise, would be returned to it in their payment. To take in the notes and credits

at any one time are wholly retired within periods of four months, the whole amount of currency afloat is wholly retired three times each year, — its place being supplied by new issues in the discount of new Bills. Both Bills and currency are simply a record of the movement of merchandise, and are retired by its consumption.

issued in the discount of the three-year bills, the Bank would
have to pay out a corresponding amount of specie; that is, the
whole of its reserves, — its cash capital. Its means or assets
would then consist of bills having two years and nine months
to run. Such bills might be valuable, and by their conversion
into coin might, in the end, provide new reserves; but till they
were provided from such, or from some other source, the Bank
would have to suspend operations altogether; for the moment
it was understood that it was without reserves or means to
make good the losses which it was likely to sustain, no one
would exchange good bills for its notes and credits. It would
be regarded as in the light of a merchant, who not only required credit for the goods purchased, but for his rents, and
for the ordinary expenses incurred by him in the prosecution
of his business.

The bills of a Bank, so long as they represent merchandise
having a value in coin equal to their nominal amount, will not
only return to it the notes and credits issued in their discount,
but they will provide for the return to it of such portion of its
reserves as may, from whatever cause, have been drawn. If
they equalled $1,000,000, and one half be drawn on an equal
amount of notes and credits, an equal amount of its bills, for
the want of a corresponding amount of currency, would have
to be paid in coin. A Bank, however, as a rule, has nothing
to fear so long as the makers of its bills are solvent. Of
course, I am not speaking of periods in which confidence is so
far shaken that the holders of the notes and credits demand
the specie for their own real or fancied security. In such case,
the Bank must suspend; as its own liabilities are payable on
demand, while the greater part of those of the public to it are
payable at a future day. A Bank, to be always prepared to
take in instantly all its liabilities, would be compelled to maintain on hand, at all times, coin equal to their whole amount.
In such case, no motive would exist for its organization, and no
provision would be made for the distribution of merchandise
by any currency but one of coin. No provision can be made
by a Bank of issue for the instant discharge of all its liabilities; and there is no necessity for such provision, so long
as it conducts its business properly, — that is, so long as its
bills represent that kind of merchandise which will give proper
employment, in its distribution, to the currency it issues.

Such merchandise must be reached and utilized by means of a currency of some kind; and one of notes and credits will be preferred for this purpose, so long as it will secure to their holders the same amount of merchandise as an equal amount of a currency of coin.

As a rule, therefore, a Bank has little to fear from the withdrawal of its reserves, so long as its bills represent an adequate value of merchandise. It can, however, never be sufficiently informed upon this point. In case of a demand for coin, it should, as a matter of precaution, immediately reduce its line of discounts. The payment of its bills, which must continue, would not only take in its liabilities, but would contract the volume of currency to an equal degree. Money would at once be in active demand; rates of interest would be advanced; illegitimate operations of all kinds would be checked: and, if the latter were the cause of demand for specie, the proper remedy would be immediately applied, and the currency rendered so far symbolic that an excessive demand for coin would soon cease. A return flow would be certain to set in, and would soon bring back to the Bank all the specie drawn from it, and perhaps a much larger amount from the liquidations resulting from the disturbances which had been created.

For a considerable time after Banks were established, the currency issued by them consisted chiefly of their notes, for the reason that borrowers, kept their money in their own strong boxes, in their places of business. As the inconvenience and risk of loss attending the use and care of notes would be similar in kind, if not equal in degree, to that attending the use and care of coin, borrowers, for their greater convenience and safety, would gradually come into the habit of leaving undrawn and on deposit, such portions of their loans as were not required for immediate use. Other parties coming into possession of notes beyond their immediate wants would, for similar reasons, deposit them in Bank, to be drawn or transferred at pleasure by checks. The Banks in this way would not only become the holders of reserves of parties engaged in industrial operations, (for the latter must, equally with Banks, maintain reserves bearing a certain ratio to their liabilities), but of the unemployed money, whether coin or currency, of the community in which they were situated. To the extent of the deposits representing the proceeds of undrawn loans, or of the proceeds of such as had been drawn and returned to it, and which were likely to remain undrawn, a corresponding amount of merchandise would be without the appropriate means for distribution, and for such want would be unavailable both to the producers and the public. In a community in which the notes and credits of Banks had been used as currency, the precious metals could not be immediately provided to make good the sudden withdrawal of the former. They could only be provided by a sale of merchandise, which in the case supposed, for want of currency in some form, might be impossible. In ratio therefore, as the proceeds of loans were not drawn, or as the notes issued were returned to them on deposit, the Banks could discount new bills in manner described. The notes and credits issued in the discount of new bills would be used in the payment of the old ones first falling due ; and, as these again returned to the Banks, they would again be reissued, so that the currency at all times would tend to approximate the amount of merchandise entering into consumption. The Banks could therefore increase their loans, and with them their interest-bearing securities, and their profits, in ratio to the amount of their deposits that were likely to be permanent. These, in fact, would represent a corresponding amount of capital for which its owners, the depositors, had no immediate use, and of which, until wanted by them, they would allow the Banks to have the benefit. The amount so held in such countries as the United States and Great Britain is enormous, as every individual, no matter how small his means, will always seek to hold a portion of them in reserve, and as reserves must be held, and permanently, by all parties engaged in industrial and commercial operations in ratio to their magnitude. In this way, through the action of the Banks, all the capital of a community unemployed by its owners, and proper to be symbolized, is rendered available for consumption and production. In no other way than that described could it be made available. At the same time, but for the use by the Banks of the capital for which its owners had no immediate use, there could be no adequate motive to their establishment; as they could not on loans of their own means, their expenses being deducted, make a profit equal to the ordinary rates of interest.

From what has preceded, it will be seen that there is no difference whatever, but in form, between notes and checks as currency. Each (except deposits made in coin) springs from similar transactions, — the discount of bills. It always lies with the party in whose favor loans are made to say in what form he will avail himself of their proceeds, — whether in the notes of a Bank, or in credits on its books to be transferred by checks, or to be drawn by means of them in notes or coin. As notes and credits in the form of deposits arise from similar transactions, and as they are convertible the one into the other, and each equally into coin, at the pleasure of the holder or owner, the absolute identity of the two, in principle, is a matter of demonstration, — for " two things that equal a third equal each other." Writers, however, upon the subject of currency have without exception, I believe, made a radical distinction between notes and checks. Such a distinction, although utterly and wholly fanciful, has been one of the chief reasons why so little progress has been made in taking the subject of money out of the category of dialectics, and out of the methods of Schoolmen, and in subjecting it to that process of scientific analysis, without which it is impossible that any considerable progress in its solution should be made.

All modern Banks, therefore, are equally Banks of circulation whatever the form in which their loans are made. The tendency of checks to supersede notes arises simply from the greater convenience and safety of their use. They not only avoid the possibility of loss, but they are often of great value in serving as records of the character or nature of the transactions in which they are used.

It has already been shown that division of labor is not only the condition of all accumulations worthy of the name, but of all excellence in the articles produced. Not only may a single article pass through a dozen different hands before it is fitted for the market, but it may pass through as many more after it has received its final touch, before it reaches the consumer. Division of labor, consequently, is just as important, and may be carried to an equal extent, in distribution as in production. It is not for the interest of the producer or of the public, that he should attempt the distribution of his products. All his capital and all his attention and skill should be devoted to two objects, — economy of production and excellence in quality. He cannot

go in search of the consumers, or of those who purchase for the
retail trade; nor can he spare the time necessary to ascertain
their means or wants. All such matters are properly left to
another class — to merchants — who have functions in distribution as distinct and important as are those of the manufacturer in production. The latter, producing perhaps only one
article, if he undertook its distribution might have to wait days
or weeks before he could find a party in want of it. Such
operations would be simply *barter.* The merchant, on the other
hand, has the goods of all producers in his stock, and can
supply the want of all applicants. He is in position to know
their wants, and can keep producers equally informed with himself. But for the merchant, — who by his purchases notifies
them of the condition of the markets, of the styles and kinds
of goods in demand, producers would be without any adequate
guide whatever, and by an unwise direction of their industries
might wholly ruin themselves in the course of a very few days
or weeks. So, wholesale merchants sell very largely through
brokers, who look up customers, and ascertain their wants and
means. The greater the division of labor in distribution, the
more economically is it accomplished. The amount saved is
so much deducted from the price to be paid by consumers, who
reap nearly all the advantages resulting from decreased cost
either of production or distribution.

As all banking currencies are instruments arising out of, or
in, the sale and distribution to consumers of merchandise
it may happen that several sets of symbols issued against
the same merchandise may be in existence at the same time.
Suppose the bills of a New York merchant, given in the purchase
of 1,000 bales of cotton, to be discounted by the issue of currency
equal to its value. The merchant may presently sell the same
cotton, taking the bills of a manufacturer therefor. These he
may procure to be discounted. In this way, a currency may
be created equalling twice or thrice the value of the merchandise upon which it is based. In such cases, however, only an
amount of the currency equalling the value of the cotton first
sold will, as a rule, enter into circulation. The first seller, the
producer, may draw from the Bank which discounted the bills
given for his crop the whole amount of their proceeds. The
merchant who procured the discount of the second set of bills

will, as a rule, hold their proceeds on deposit to meet the bills given by him. The deposits growing out of such bills do not become currency, nor do they act upon prices unless the Bank makes loans upon them in the manner described. In periods of great confidence, or when a speculative feeling prevails, deposits, no matter how they may have arisen, may be loaned upon to an extent to create an excess of currency, — that is, a currency which has no adequate constituent, — a currency that is duplicated upon the same merchandise. The temptations to make loans upon deposits, which may not represent loanable capital, is a sufficient reason why Banks should never allow interest upon them. If interest be allowed, loans must be made upon them to save Banks from loss. If they do not represent loanable capital, such loans inflate the currency in an equal degree, for which in the end the Banks must pay the appropriate penalty, in the loss, as will hereafter be shown, of a corresponding amount of their reserves.

A wide distinction is always to be made between capitalists and parties engaged in the active operations of production and trade. The former seek to part with — to invest — their capital for the income or interest it will yield. The latter must always have their capital in hand for the prosecution of their various avocations. To part with it is to give up business altogether. In this respect Banks, bankers, manufacturers, and merchants, — in fact all engaged in production and distribution, — are similarly placed. Each has his proper function or department in the great co-partnership which embraces every employment and every pursuit. The capital which each is required to possess is that necessary to carry forward his particular business or calling, and to meet the losses likely to be incurred. A commission merchant, although he may become responsible for all the merchandise passing through his hands, has only a qualified interest in it. He may with a capital of $100,000 be turning merchandise and incurring liabilities to the amount of $1,000,000, or ten times greater than his whole means. There is no more propriety in his paying cash for the merchandise he distributes, than that the railroad should own the merchandise it transports. All that is required of either, by way of capital, is an amount necessary to carry on their operations including the losses they may suffer. The means for the payment by the merchant of his bills, or the greater part of them, must be provided by the sale of the merchandise for which they were given. So with Banks. They deal in bills given for merchandise, not by paying out their capital, but by issuing their own obligations. Their capitals are the reserves which are always to be held to meet losses and extraordinary calls, and are never to be permanently parted with. If made the basis of loans, they would have to discharge the notes and credits that were issued against them. If they are drawn to any considerable extent, their loss must immediately be made good, or the Banks must reduce their operations so that there may be a proper relation between their liabilities and their cash means. Every person and every institution engaged in production and distribution seek not only to retain their capital but to increase it to the utmost extent, as they can enlarge their operations, not in simple but in geometric ratio, to the means they possess,—increasing their profits in like ratio; for their profits are not so much made upon the capital they may own, as upon the whole volume of their transactions.

It will be observed that while the reserves of Banks must be in the form of coin, the reserves of the public may be in the currency issued by them. As the former undertake to supply currency, they must supply it in whatever form it may be required.

Although a Bank must always maintain reserves in coin bearing a certain ratio to its liabilities, it may commence operations with its capital paid in almost wholly in bills. It is usually so paid, or in checks upon other Banks. The merchandise represented by the new bills discounted would give full employment to the notes and credits that might be issued, while the payment which could be demanded, in coin, of those which constituted its capital, would supply all the reserves that might be required. The amount collected for this purpose might be all the capital, in the form of coin or merchandise, ever in its actual possession, till its affairs were wound up. In such case, its whole capital might be returned to it in coin. Its capital represented by its bills, less the amount collected in coin to serve as reserves, would remain in the hands of its borrowers, and at interest, pending and after its organization, as before. As the possession of capital is always assumed to carry with it an obligation to pay interest, every person and every institution, Banks especially, always seek to hold as little as possible, in order to have as much out at interest as possible.

As the capital of a Bank, less its reserves, would always remain in the hands of the public, it would be constantly moving from one producer to another, and be constantly taking new forms. Suppose a bill, which made up a portion of its capital, to represent 1,000 barrels of flour. The notes and credits issued against it, which in this instance would be the discount by the Bank of its own bill, might be used in the purchase, for consumption, of this flour, which would speedily reappear in other forms of merchandise — say cotton goods — which would soon be represented by bills, to be discounted in manner described, their constituent to reappear, like the flour, in some other form. In this way, the capital of the Banks represented by bills is constantly employed in the various industrial operations of the community, and is constantly changing hands and taking new forms. Its return to the Banks in the form of coin — and it must be returned in this form, if at all — would be evidence of such a cessation of demand for merchandise, or such a disturbance of industries, that it could not be profitably employed, — that borrowers could no longer afford to pay interest for its use.

Currency, in whatever form, is the instrument of expenditure. The degree of the latter, as a rule, is always in ratio to the amount of the former. From the credit attached, and very properly, to currencies, they are usually received, on their issue, at their nominal value in coin. So far, however, as they were not symbolic, — that is, so far as they did not represent merchandise, the instruments of expenditure would be in excess of the means, and an inflation of prices would be the necessary result. If, for example, the products of a community entering constantly into consumption equalled $50,000,000, and if such products were represented by an issue of notes and credits — of currency — to an equal amount, business would remain, as far as the currency was concerned, in a normal and healthy condition. The reserves in coin maintained in such case would equal, say, $10,000,000. Suppose the Banks to increase their loans and issues to $60,000,000 by discounting, in addition to bills rep-

resenting merchandise, accommodation bills to the amount of
$10,000,000. The excess of issue, if confidence were felt in it,
would be as readily accepted by the parties to whom it might
be paid, and by the holders of merchandise, as that which was
symbolic. As there would in the mean time be no corresponding increase of merchandise, prices would rise in ratio to the
increase of the instruments of expenditure. That already produced, the proper subjects of consumption and which would
have sufficed for five months, will now suffice for only four.
To meet the increased demand, additional importations would
be made, and an unhealthy stimulus given to production of
all kinds. New schemes would be set on foot involving large
outlays, but being uncalled for by any permanent ability to
consume their products, would rest upon no solid foundation;
while extravagance and thriftlessness would be encouraged
just in ratio as the instruments of expenditure were to be had
without labor, or without any adequate consideration being
given therefor.

For a time, every thing would wear the appearance of great
prosperity. All who might happen to have merchandise would,
by its rise, become suddenly rich. But when the accommodation bills matured, their makers would have nothing to pay
with. These were made, not in the purchase of merchandise
for its distribution to consumers, but for the purpose of supplying it to their makers for consumption. The holders of that
which had been produced would, from its rise in price, come into
possession of the whole or the greater part of the currency which
had been issued upon accommodation, as well as upon commercial bills. Upon the maturity of their own they would,
consequently, be creditors of the Banks to the amount of
$10,000,000 of notes and credits in excess of the sums due on
their bills, — that is, to the whole amount issued on the accommodation paper, — and would draw the amount in coin, as
balances due them. If the Banks, in discounting the accommodation bills, had increased their reserves in ratio of one of
coin to five of liabilities, they would, after the notes and credits
issued in discounting such paper had been taken in, have only
$2,000,000 of coin reserves left. In such case, they would be
compelled to reduce the line of their discounts to $10,000,000;
or they would have to provide new reserves to the amount of
$8,000,000 in order to supply to the public its accustomed

amount of currency. Till these were provided, they could not make loans exceeding $10,000,000 in amount (their reserves being only $2,000,000), in place of the $60,000,000 in circulation previous to the taking in of the notes and credits issued in the discount of the accommodation bills. For a time, therefore, the community would be almost wholly without the instruments or means for effecting their exchanges. Production and trade would be brought instantly to a complete stand-still. No debts of any kind could be paid. In the excitement and panic that would be certain to follow, a run would be immediately made upon the Banks for the $2,000,000 of reserves still remaining in their vaults. Their immediate suspension would be the necessary result.

The condition of affairs, in the case supposed, would be greatly aggravated for the reason that, with the increase of currency from $50,000,000 to $60,000,000, prices would not only have been greatly inflated, but production greatly stimulated at a correspondingly high cost. When the reverse came, those who had conducted their operations in the most careful manner, if they had continued them at all, would be as fatally involved as the most improvident and reckless. Merchandise which had been produced at even ordinary rates could not be sold at any price; so that the bills of the Bank, which were considered as perfectly safe and legitimate when taken, would be almost as valueless as the accommodation bills, the discount of which had produced all the ruin and bankruptcy described.

It may be asked, " Will not the parties who, in the case supposed, drew the reserves of the Banks on notes and credits issued in the discount of accommodation bills, and who received them in the advanced prices charged for their merchandise, deposit them in the Banks to serve as additional reserves in their operations; and if so, why may not the Banks keep up their usual line of discounts of good paper?" The answer is obvious: the stimulus given to consumption due to the increase of currency on accommodation bills will have caused a large increase of consumption of foreign goods which will have to be paid for in coin. So far, the specie drawn would go out of the country. Such portion of it as had been drawn and retained in the Banks would be used by the depositors as reserves for their own operations, which would always be increased in ratio to the increase of their means. These reserves would, at all times, be subject to their necessities; they might be wholly drawn at any moment. In such case the Banks would find themselves in the dilemma already described. Every institution and every person engaged in business, must maintain reserves in ratio to the magnitude of their operations. They are to make good their own losses. Those of one party should never be held to make up for those of another. If reserves are lost from any cause, they must be made good, either out of fresh capital, or by reducing liabilities,. so that the proper ratio may be preserved.

An inflation and contraction precisely similar, with similar results, would as necessarily follow the discount of bills given in the purchase of real estate as of accommodation paper. Purchases made in this manner would be in a great measure speculative, both on the part of buyer and seller. A seller who wanted to reinvest his means in property similar to that sold would never take bills therefor, leaving the title of the property sold in the possession of the purchaser. Should the bills given as the purchase money be discounted, the proceeds would, as a rule be used to meet the personal expenditures of the seller; or he would enter upon, or would lend them to a party entering upon, some enterprise in which they would be speedily paid out for material and labor. In such case, there would be a corresponding inflation in prices from a corresponding increase of the instruments over the means of expenditure. In order that the bills might be paid, the property for which they were given would have to be sold previous to their maturity. Bills given for merchandise are paid because the consumption of that which they represent is absolutely necessary to sustain life, and must consequently be taken and paid for before they will mature. Real estate, on the other hand cannot, like merchandise, be eaten, drunk, nor worn; nor is its ownership at all necessary to its use. As it cannot be consumed, its sale never can be forced without danger of excessive loss. This depends upon laws wholly different from those which govern sales of personal property. Real property may be active, as the phrase is; or months or years may elapse before that for which the bills discounted were given could be sold without involving a heavy loss.

Merchandise in demand for consumption, on the contrary, can always be moved, in almost unlimited quantities, by a slight concession in price. Capitalists will be always ready to purchase, if they can by so doing make a commission or profit on the operation only slightly exceeding the usual rates of interest, well knowing that consumption will speedily take it off their hands. Sales of real estate, on the other hand, depend upon so many contingencies, that the manager of a Bank who should discount bills given for it, leaving the property they represented in the hands of the purchaser; or in fact should discount them, taking a mortgage on the property for which they were given, would be esteemed as fit only for the madhouse.

But even if the bills given in the purchase of such kind of property were paid, their discount would, as a rule, involve the same losses, and in the end, to the same parties, as if they were not. The same inflation, with the same advance in prices, would be the result, with a corresponding excess of expenditure, and production at a correspondingly high cost. Their payment would contract the currency in an equal degree. The discount of similar bills might postpone such contraction; but the time would speedily come when the holders of real property would either refuse to sell at any price, taking bills in payment; or the Banks would refuse to discount bills given for it for fear that, the fact becoming known, their credit would be so far impaired that the notes and credits issued by them would be immediately demanded in coin, instead of being held and used as currency. As soon as they ceased to discount such bills the currency would be permanently contracted in an equal degree, with all the consequences which have been described. With a fall of prices, bills given for merchandise could not be paid. A still further contraction would be the result. In this way, contraction might follow contraction till the operations of production and trade became involved in almost hopeless embarrassment. It is notorious that speculations in real estate have been among the most potent causes of those financial revulsions which periodically sweep over such countries as the United States, where the greatest inducements always exist to engage in such operations, from the constant appreciation in value of such property from the rapid increase of the country in population and wealth.

Similar remarks apply with almost equal force to the discount of bills given in the purchase of securities, such as bonds of government, or of corporate bodies of one kind or another. Such securities, like real property, can be neither eaten, drunk, nor worn. A currency issued on bills given in their discount could, as a rule, be returned to the Banks by their makers only by the sale, before their maturity, of the securities for which they were given. In this, as in all other cases, that which is symbolized must discharge the symbol, or must be used for its discharge. If it could not be sold, the bills would not be paid. If sold at a loss, the Bank would have to bear the loss, even if the proceeds of the sale were paid over to it. If not paid, the currency which had been inflated in their discount would be contracted to an equal degree. If paid, either no similar bills would be made, — for it is hardly possible that any one possessed of securities would sell them at their market value, taking in payment bills of purchasers, — or the Bank would soon come to its senses, and refuse wholly to discount such bills. If no new ones of the kind were made, the currency after having been inflated would be contracted in an equal degree, with all the consequences that have been described, greater or less in severity according to the amount of illegitimate paper discounted.

From what has preceded, the reason of the failure of all Banks, the capital or reserves of which have consisted of real estate or securities, will have been made sufficiently evident. All currencies, to be accepted as such, must be instruments representing and serving for the distribution of merchandise. If they will not secure to their holder merchandise, the equivalent in value of coin, they will always be immediately drawn, or attempted to be drawn, in coin. The holder of a note issued by a real-estate Bank does not want that which it represents, but merchandise, or, in the absence of merchandise, coin. Such a Bank has neither. Should it seek to discount nothing but business paper, an impossible supposition (for all such Banks are got up to supply the lack of business paper, — that is, of merchandise, the basis of business paper), no one would take its notes and credits to any considerable extent, as it would be seen by all that no proper provision had been made to carry forward its operations, or to meet the losses to which it would be subjected. Such Banks, therefore, from the very nature of things, have never been able to make even the first successful start. The moment they have attempted to issue notes and credits as currency, these have always been presented for immediate redemption in coin. As they can pay neither merchandise nor coin, they have no other alternative but to go into immediate liquidation.

That a currency may at all times be convertible, the means for its redemption must always be provided previous to its issue, not by the Bank, but by the public, the producers of merchandise. With such provision, the currency from the moment of its issue would take care of itself. The attempt to make such provision after issue would be certain to defeat itself. When merchandise is provided, the necessities of consumers compel them to purchase it, piece by piece, for consumption. Their necessities and purchases will have the effect to maintain its price, so as to render it adequate to the discharge of the currency issued against it. But neither real estate nor securities can be taken for consumption, piece by piece ; they must be sold in gross, or not at all. A proposition, or a necessity, for the sale of a large amount of either would be naturally met by the public, by a combination not to purchase except at very low rates, or by a shyness growing out of an apprehension that sales in large amounts would necessarily tend to bring down prices by creating a disturbance in the money market. The result would be that property symbolized at a fair value would not, under the peremptory sales that would be necessary, bring half that at which it was symbolized : the loss sustained by the Bank in its first operations would be usually sufficient to drive it into liquidation. The world has seen no end to attempts to establish Banks upon capital other than coin and merchandise ; but all such, without exception, have proved disastrous failures.

For similar reasons, bills given for merchandise not in demand for consumption are no better subjects for discount than bills given in the purchase of real estate or securities. Such merchandise, since it could not be sold, would not retire the notes and credits issued in the discount of the bills representing it. These would have to be taken in by paying out the corresponding amount of coin. It is in the discount of notes given for unsalable merchandise that Banks make by far the greater part of their losses. Where the demand for their products is not active, producers, as a means of tempting purchasers, offer longer credits. Merchants will often buy on six months' credit, when they would by no means buy on a credit of three, well knowing that within the shorter time they could not make their payments out of the merchandise purchased. They hope, however, to be able to turn their purchases within the longer period, and so take the risk. If merchants take long paper, Banks are tempted to do the same by a concession in the rate of discount. In the mean time, producers, being supplied with means, push their industries without any reference to the condition of the market, and daily add to the stock of unsalable goods already pressing upon it. As they increase their stocks, they again tempt purchasers by giving still longer credits; and tempt the Banks to discount the new bills by increasing the rates paid. Producers will always keep at work so long as they can find the means of doing so. As the bills so discounted will not mature till a long time after the notes and credits issued in their discount will have been returned to them for redemption, the Banks must take in the latter by paying out a corresponding amount of their reserves. As they must maintain these in ratio, it is here assumed, of one of the former to five of liabilities, they must reduce the line of their discounts in like ratio, or must cease discounting till new reserves are provided equal in amount to those drawn. In either case, the currency must for a time at least be contracted, and prices must suffer a corresponding decline. As soon as it was seen that the market was a falling one, no one would purchase at all, or only sparingly, or at greatly reduced prices, or at those far below the cost of production. As goods could not be sold, a very considerable portion of the long paper discounted could not be paid. With every failure in their payment, the means of Banks would be still further exhausted; so that no considerable time would elapse, before the holders of their notes and credits, seeing that they did not represent merchandise adequate for their redemption, would for their own security rush to the Banks, and demand to be paid in coin. Their immediate suspension, as in the instances already given, would be the necessary result.

No Bank, as a rule, will discount what is known or suspected to be accommodation paper. It is impossible that serious losses should not result from its discount. On the other hand, while it well knows that it should discount only such bills as were given for merchandise, it may be wholly unable to form a correct opinion as to its salableness, or market value. The only rule, in such case, that can protect it from loss is that which forbids the discount of any bills having a longer time to run than that necessary for the distribution for consumption of the merchandise represented by them. If Banks will not discount long paper, merchants cannot take it to any considerable extent. The merchant is to be trusted that the price he contracts to pay shall not exceed the current rate at the time. Should he purchase, say on three months, and should prices soon after show a tendency to fall, he will not add to his stock till he sees how he is coming out with that already on hand. The decline which may be suffered before his bills will mature will hardly ever be sufficient to sweep away the reserves which every careful business man is assumed to maintain. Till these are exhausted the Banks cannot suffer. His declining to purchase is timely notice to producers that the market is already overstocked. If purchasers will not buy, producers can get no bills for discount; and, if they cannot, they must of necessity reduce their production in ratio to the falling off of the demand.

From what has preceded, it will be seen that, as in such countries as the United States and Great Britain Banks and bankers supply almost all the instruments of consumption, they are directly responsible for the greater part of the fluctuations that are constantly taking place in production and trade, and for those great financial revulsions which from time to time sweep over them with such disastrous effects. There can be no considerable fluctuations in price or values, with a metallic currency, as in all operations equivalents are exchanged at the value of coin. There are no commercial crises in Turkey, and rarely in France, where most of the dealings are in a currency of metals, — of capital. The money in circulation is itself a proper subject of expenditure. A paper currency on the other hand, while it may serve as the instrument, may by no means represent the proper subjects of expenditure. As it is the instrument of expenditure, — as it serves to the party issuing it all the functions of capital, so far as it can be made to circulate at all, — there is at all times the strongest possible motive to needy, improvident, or dishonest parties for its issue. Such temptation is the weak point in all symbolic currencies, and is the one, of all others, to be especially guarded against.

While there is the strongest temptation for the issue of paper money without the provision of adequate means for its redemption, there will always be a plenty of parties to take, at some figure, what they consider of doubtful value, or perhaps worthless, from a confidence in their own cleverness in palming it off, at a higher rate than that for which they took it, upon others more credulous or less informed than themselves. They flatter themselves that they shall never "get stuck" with it, as the phrase is. It is here that the moral, or rather the immoral, side of a fictitious or fraudulent currency comes in. Its possession always carries with it the suggestion of fraud, of swindling some other person out of a sum equal to a portion of its nominal value. The most worthless of currencies are as attractive in form, and promise as solemnly to pay coin, as the most valuable. Those who deal in them, therefore, start with their case more than half made out. As most currencies are good, they have seldom much difficulty in persuading those upon whom they wish to impose them that those they hold are equally so. The wild-cat currencies of the Western States, which were issued in such abundance some forty years ago, could never have got into circulation but from a belief, on the part of those who took them, that they could shove them off upon somebody else without loss to themselves. Where a currency is a fraud, almost every act of the community using it is tainted with fraud. Of all agencies at work in society, a fictitious currency, or one that is made irredeemable by law, is the most potent in sapping alike its moral sense and its material welfare.

From what has preceded, it will be seen that the functions of governments in the matter of currencies are extremely limited. A metallic currency derives its value wholly (except in some countries in which a slight charge for coinage is made) from the cost of the metals that compose it. The stamp of government is affixed as evidence that each piece, of similar denomination, contains an equal quantity of pure metal. Coinage is an attribute of the supreme power, for the same reason as is the establishment of a uniform system of weights and measures. It often has no property in the metals it coins, and has no more to do with their value than it has with the value of the material out of which are made the weights and measures it establishes. If the quantity of pure metal in a coin is increased or reduced, from whatever cause, the value of the coin is increased or reduced in an equal degree, its denomination meanwhile remaining the same.

Its functions in the creation of a symbolic currency are, if possible, still less important than in the creation of a metallic one. It neither provides the means for its conversion, nor does it affix its stamp to the materials of which it is composed. All it can properly do is to add its sanction to laws, not of its own enacting, but arising out of the operations of production and trade. It has been shown that a symbolic currency represents merchandise, and is discharged by its purchase for consumption; that so long as it is symbolic, it must, as a rule, be discharged in this manner, and without the intervention of coin. In creating a Bank, therefore, the government, as the custodian of the public welfare, need make hardly any other provision than to forbid the issue of currency except in the discount of bills given in the purchase of merchandise, and maturing within four months; or within the time required for its distribution to its consumers. The amount of reserves to be maintained, the next most important matter, must as a rule, be left to the discretion of its managers.

As governments are never possessed of merchandise or coin for the purpose of making loans, they can never issue a currency convertible at the pleasure of the holder, nor one that is not at a discount from the standard of coin. The currency they issue, therefore, is wholly different in kind from that issued by Banks. As already shown, the process of issue of the latter consists of a mutual exchange of obligations, — of their notes and credits for the bills of their customers. The parties to whom the notes and credits are issued are the producers of merchandise. Such notes and credits represent such merchandise, and are convertible on demand into it, or into coin, at the option of the holder. The makers of the bills discounted are the purchasers of the same for distribution. Although the Banks are the only parties that undertake, in terms, to convert their notes and credits into coin, the makers of their bills contract to pay to them a corresponding amount of coin; or, what is equivalent thereto, a corresponding amount of notes and credits. They are consequently the parties that are to retire such notes and credits, or provide the means therefor. All that the Banks have to attend to is to see that they discount nothing but good bills. This done, they need give themselves no further concern. All the burden of taking care of their notes and credits falls upon the makers of such bills. The producers of merchandise, as endorsers of the bills, also guaranty the undertaking of their makers. So long, therefore, as the Banks discount only solvent bills, their notes and credits are returned to them automatically in manner already described, leaving the whole, or the greater portion, of their reserves undrawn. The consumption of the merchandise represented by such bills, or by the notes and credits issued in their discount, does not ordinarily imply impoverishment or waste. Consumption is the necessary condition of production. Laborers, to work, must be sheltered, fed, and clothed. That which has been consumed is constantly reappearing in new forms. So long, therefore, as the industries of a people are properly conducted, production will always be in ratio to consumption. The greater their consumption, the greater their production and wealth. The currencies issued by the Banks are simply the instruments of distribution for consumption of that which they represent, which is to provide the means for their retirement. Such merchandise seldom or never comes into their hands. It goes directly from the producer to the wholesale merchant; and from the latter to the retailer, by whom it is broken up to suit the wants or means of his customers. If it went into the possession of the Banks, it would have to be handed over immediately to the merchants, as the former have none of the means or facilities for its distribution.

Currencies issued by governments, unlike those of Banks, are always issued, not in exchange for bills which their makers are to pay, and by their payment retire the currency issued, but for merchandise, not for its distribution to the public, but for its profitless consumption, usually in military operations. Such merchandise is never made the basis of reproduction. Every government or people, consequently, by whom it is issued is just so much the poorer therefor. The issuer is the only party that undertakes to retire it. The means therefor, if provided at all, can only be provided in the future, and by taxation. It can never be presently retired. It would never have been issued had the means for its retirement been provided previous to its issue. It is always the last confession of imbecility or exhaustion. As it cannot be presently paid, it must always be at a discount from the standard of coin, which is capital in hand, and as capital in hand must be more valuable than capital to be received at a future day.

A currency issued by government is made legal tender in the payment of debts as the necessary condition of its circulation. The effect of this provision is to cause its notes to be received as money at their estimated value, otherwise they would no more have the attributes of money than any other form of debt, or than merchandise. Their value is greatest when first issued, as they are always assumed to be a temporary expedient, and soon to be retired by their payment. Such an expectation alone might for a time maintain their value very nearly at par with coin. They will have a value equal to that of coin to all parties in debt at the time, as they will pay their debts equally with coin. A market, consequently, is at once created for them equal, or very nearly equal, to the whole amount of merchandise held for consumption, as such merchandise is usually purchased and held on credit. They decline rapidly in value so soon as it is seen that they are not likely to be speedily paid, and as contracts existing at the time of their issue are discharged. The consideration of those subsequently entered into will have reference to the real value of the notes, which is measured by the time that, in public estimation, is to elapse, before they are retired by payment. The effect of the legal tender clause is to cause them to circulate as money at their estimated value, whatever this may be. If they become valueless, — that is, if in public opinion they are never to be paid, either from the inability or indisposition of their issuers, — the clause ceases to have any force or effect whatever.

While the issue of a currency of legal tender notes is a most direct and efficient expedient on the part of government for raising money, no act can at the outset be better received;

for it seems equivalent to the creation of capital equal to the
whole amount issued. It is capital to every one in debt and
holding merchandise or property. Government must accept
the effect of its own act. When it issues legal-tender notes it
is the great consumer, and must pay an advance equal to the
amount of the instruments of consumption — money — with
which it enters the market. The demand which it creates
may suddenly double the value, in paper, of all the merchandise upon it. The holders of such property become suddenly
rich. They can pay their debts and have a large surplus left.
The indebted classes, consequently, always eagerly welcome a
currency of the kind. The creditor classes — the capitalists
— seem, at the same time, to be benefited rather than injured,
as some time usually elapses before the currency suffers any
considerable degree of depreciation ; as the debts owing them
are more readily paid, and as whatever they possess is largely
advanced in price, and apparently in value. The delusion on
all sides is increased from a real addition to the means of consumption, the greater part of the metallic currency previously
in circulation, or held as reserves by Banks and bankers. All
this becomes available for consumption, and, as it is no longer
needed at home, it is speedily sent abroad in the importation
of merchandise of one kind or another, but largely of luxuries
to gratify an already pampered appetite. A currency of capital
— of coin — will never circulate alongside of a currency of
debt to which is given the legal competency of coin. Of the
two methods, or instruments, the least valuable will always
have the preference. No fact in reference to money is more
universally recognized than this. In the abundant supply
of capital, as well as of the instruments of expenditure, it would
not be singular if even the coolest and most sagacious heads
should come to regard such abundance and activity as the
evidence of a genuine prosperity, and should lose themselves
in the general delirium.

It has been shown that a symbolic currency is always an
accurate measure or test of the ability of a people to consume.
Such a currency, or the capital represented by it, can always
be made the basis of reproduction of an equal or of even a
greater amount of merchandise, as production should, and
always does, in a healthy condition of industries, exceed con-

sumption. Such an excess is the test of the prosperity and progress of society. The fruit tree, or the field, should always realize a larger sum than that expended in its culture. But a currency issued by government is no measure or test of ability of the people to consume. It is the evidence of a want of such ability, — of the waste or loss of a corresponding amount of capital. As it is however treated as capital, it is made the basis of vast industrial and commercial undertakings, the products of which there is no ability on the part of the public to consume. Utter failure and disappointment are the inevitable results. The condition of the United States, to-day, is a striking illustration of the effect of the use of a currency of debt as capital. There is a great abundance of products of all kinds, but no demand for them, even at rates far below cost. All are sellers, — none buyers. Utter stagnation prevails in all the departments of commerce and trade. No one dares to purchase in excess of his immediate wants, as he has no means of telling whether there will be any market for what he buys. The amount of money in circulation is no test. It is not capital for exportation, nor does it represent capital for domestic consumption. In the general stagnation which prevails, money flows to the centres; but no one, in the face of losses which stare at him on every hand, dares to use it in any industry whatever. He fears to lend it, for the reason that the borrower may be no better able to employ it than himself. He sees no solution of the condition of things; nor is there any, but for government to allow the people to provide themselves with a currency which is capital, or the representative of capital. Till this is done, there not only can be no permanent recovery, but the community must become more and more exhausted, and less able, when permitted either by the retirement of the currency, by its payment, or by repudiation, to resume their industries upon any thing like the scale of the past.

It has been seen that borrowers at Banks always pay interest on their loans. Although this is paid in the first place by producers in the discount of bills received by them in the sale of their merchandise, the amount is added to the price at which it is sold to be paid in the end by the consumers. The latter must pay the total cost, which includes distribution as well as production. If they fully understood the process of distribu-

tion by symbols, they would more readily pay interest charged
for their use than for the use of a corresponding amount of
coin, as they would see that by their means merchandise would
come to them at a lower rate than by the use of a currency of
coin.   Such symbols, as they represent capital, are its equivalent in the hands of every holder ; and, as already observed, the
possession or the right to the possession of capital always
carries with it the obligation to pay interest on the value of
the same.   But a government receives no interest on the currency it issues, for the reason that it does not represent, nor
does it entitle the holder to, capital (except, perhaps, in the
doubtful contingency of its ultimate payment).   Such a currency is the exact opposite, in every particular, to that issued
by Banks.   No one ever questions the propriety of a demand
by the latter for interest on their issues.   The borrower, if he
choose, could require to be paid the proceeds of his loans in
gold or silver, — in capital in hand, — as well as in notes and
credits.   If he take the latter, it is for his own convenience.
But no act could be regarded as more absurd than for a government to demand interest on its issues of currency, even
from those to whom, in consequence of owing debts, it
would in their payment, be equally valuable with a corresponding amount of coin ; for the reason that, as no time could be
agreed upon for its retirement, no basis was established upon
which interest could be calculated.   It is fifteen years since the
legal-tender notes of the United States were issued.   Assuming
that they will be paid by January 1, 1879, the interest upon
them at six per cent, had it been demanded at their issue, would
have exceeded their whole nominal value!   Loans made by
Banks are for certain periods.   The amount, therefore, paid for
the use of their currency can be exactly determined when it
is issued.   No more striking illustration can be given of the
radical difference betwen the two currencies than that interest
is always payable upon one, and never upon the other.

That which has preceded sufficiently disposes of the assumption of all writers (without exception, I believe) upon the
subject of money, that a currency of notes issued by government saves to it, and consequently to the people, in relief
from taxation, a sum equal to the interest on its amount.
Such an assumption is an absurdity for the reason that in-

terest arises from the possession of capital, and has nothing to do with the character of the parties to whom it is loaned. Governments no more than individuals can borrow, nor did a government ever attempt to borrow without agreeing to pay interest. By seeking to avoid its payment it only increases the rate from the discredit attached to such an act. If bills discounted at Bank do not in terms bear interest, it is for the reason that the amount agreed upon is included in the principal sum, to be deducted from the amount paid the borrower. Suppose government to attempt to borrow, at the same time, on bonds bearing no interest, and upon bonds bearing interest at the rate of six per cent annually. In the latter case it would receive an equivalent both for the principal and interest which were contracted to be paid. This might be a sum equal to the par value of the bonds; the interest to be paid being the equivalent for the use of the sum loaned. In the former case, interest for the time the bonds had to run would be deducted from the amount to be received or paid in their purchase. If the bonds were made payable, in say sixteen years, and if perfect confidence were felt that they would be paid when due, the government might receive, in their sale, a sum equal to that which, at interest at a high rate, say ten per cent, (for no one would lend at the same rate on non-interest bearing as on interest bearing bonds) would produce a sum equal to their par value. People in dealing with governments, as well as with each other, deal, or assume that they are dealing, in values, — in realities, not in shams or fictions.

Governments not only pay a higher rate of interest on non-interest bearing than on interest bearing securities, but they suffer from the use of the former as money a loss far greater than the excess of interest paid, in the increased price of every thing they have to purchase. By the time the United States had issued its notes to the amount of $400,000,000, — a sum about equalling the coin and Bank notes in circulation in the country at the outbreak of the rebellion, — the prices of merchandise and labor of all kinds were, from the effect of such issue, fully doubled. Assuming the amount paid in such purchases, by the Federal as well as the State governments and municipal bodies, to equal $3,000,000,000 after the notes were issued, the excess of payments growing out of their use in the prosecution of the war over values received, measured by the standard of coin, was fully $1,500,000,000. This vast sum is a part of the penalty which the people paid, or contracted to pay, for the use of a legal-tender currency.

As Banks are seen to maintain in circulation notes and credits largely in excess of the specie they hold, why, it is asked, may not a government, — that of the United States, for example, — with reserves in coin equalling $50,000,000, maintain in circulation notes to the amount of $250,000,000?

All currencies, no matter their kind, circulate only at their value. Were a Bank, holding $50,000 in coin, to issue notes to the amount of $250,000, making no other provision for their payment, they would circulate, if at all, only at their actual — that is, at 20 per cent of their nominal — value. That they circulated at their par value would be due to the fact, that, in addition to the coin held by the Bank, estimated to equal one-fifth of its liabilities, it held bills, speedily to mature, exceeding the amount of the latter. The payment of its bills would retire its liabilities, leaving its coin untouched in its vaults. Its issues would not inflate prices, as each would have its proper constituent. They might be taken in a dozen times without the movement of a dollar of its reserves. These would be drawn only to take in such notes as were not retired by its bills; the process having already been fully described. That the amount of its circulation appeared to be uniform would be due to the fact, that, as the old disappeared, new symbols would be issued, in equal amount, to represent new creations of merchandise.

Currencies issued by governments, so far as they resemble those of Banks, obey a similar law. If a government should issue notes to the amount of $250,000,000, providing only $50,000,000 for their payment, they would be worth only 20 per cent of their nominal value. If they circulated at all, it would be at their value. If a government, in the case supposed, should hold, in addition to its coin, good bills to be speedily paid, representing merchandise, and equal in amount to its notes, these, like those of a Bank, would pass at their nominal value from the provision made for their payment. As they would return to it without drawing its coin, it might, were it possessed of new bills representing merchandise, make new issues; so that its notes would appear to be uniform in amount, and to remain permanently in circulation, although constantly appearing and disappearing. They would circulate by virtue of the merchandise represented by its bills, and not, as is commonly supposed, by virtue of the coin held by it. They would no more than symbolic currencies of Banks inflate prices. So far, the action of Banks and of a government would be precisely similar, and attended by similar results.

The action of Banks and of governments in the matter of currency is never similar. Governments can never issue convertible currencies. Banks can maintain in circulation none other. That of the latter must represent capital, or cease to circulate: they must always be presently payable. Government currencies are always issued to supply the lack of capital, never as instruments for loaning it. As a government issuing them can never pay presently, it never makes them payable presently. Their value, consequently, depends on the provision to be made for them at some future day. As plain notes, whatever their value, can never be gotten into circulation as money, the notes of governments are always made legal tender, — that is, a competency is given them to discharge contracts at their nominal value. This attribute gives them, to those in debt and to holders of merchandise, a value, for a time, nearly equal to that of coin; and is one of sufficient potency to drive coin out of circulation, which plain notes can never do. The value of legal-tender notes, whatever it may be, can never equal the value of coin, as they possess only one attribute of coin, — capacity to discharge contracts. They cannot be used in the arts; they cannot discharge foreign balances; they cannot serve as the general reserves of society. They cannot equal the value of coin for the reason that they are, to their whole extent, instruments in excess of the means of expenditure. Their price necessarily declines, at least in ratio to their amount, even if perfect confidence be felt in their ultimate payment. There is, on account of their issue, no less, but always a far greater amount of other kinds of currency in circulation. As they do not represent merchandise, they are superfluous to their whole amount. As they are "lawful money," they immediately flow into the banks; increasing their reserves, and with them their issues, in far greater ratio. As these have no greater value than their representative, they become depreciated in ratio to the whole amount of currency for which they form the reserves.

Even with a currency of government notes, its warmest advocates always seek to place all their transactions on the basis of coin. They will never take such notes at any price but at their value, or their supposed value, in coin. To be consistent, they should always receive them at their par value equally with coin. To do this, a person would be no better than a lunatic. In every sale, it is sought to convert that which is sold into something that shall have a more uniform and universal value, — into that which will, at cost, when desired, secure to the holder the possession of any and all other kinds of property. No one at the present day can cut himself off from the world. He must consume the products of every part of it. He must have his means in that form which will pay for the articles he consumes, wherever they are purchased. He is compelled to keep this fact constantly in view; and if any intermediary process is to be gone through in the sale of his products, he will take good care that that which he receives shall have the value of coin. The degree of his ability to do this measures that of his thrift or success. A currency of government notes is certain to defeat the purpose which every person has always uppermost in his mind, which is to maintain all his transactions on a specie basis. With all his vigilance and skill, it is impossible but that he should constantly be making losses in taking them. They are always fluctuating in price, often excessively, from causes which he can never foresee, and which he is powerless to control. The only way by which he can hope to escape loss from such fluctuations is to demand, in notes, more for what he has to sell than it is worth in coin; so that, if they fall in value, he may still escape loss. But the purchaser who buys to sell again may be equally subject to the risk of loss, from a rise in price of the currency. If that rises in price, merchandise necessarily falls equally in price. He consequently must add to the price of that which he holds, as his guarantee against loss. It is in this way that the transactions of society become, under a government currency, mere gambling operations, — mere chances at hazard, — always involving a risk of loss, and inevitably sapping in a most insidious manner the moral sense of the community. For the reasons stated, prices of all kinds of merchandise are maintained at extravagant figures, so long as money or currency can be had to carry it.

The time will inevitably come, however, in which holders will be forced to sell, from the inability or indisposition of the public to purchase, and a break will be made which will carry prices far below what they would have been in coin, under a currency of symbols.

It is always to be remembered that the great problem of society is distribution, not production. There is hardly a member of it that could not double his products, could he find a market for them. He has only to extend and quicken his industries, to add additional belts to the shaft already in motion. His difficulty comes in the attempt to reach consumers who may perhaps be on the opposite side of the globe. As the slightest break in his machinery will arrest his industries, so the slightest defect or interruption in the process of distribution may shut him off from his markets altogether. The former he may readily repair; the latter is far beyond his reach. A rumor that the relations between two European powers are no longer friendly may cause an American merchant engaged in the China trade to stop his shipments to that country till he can see what is to be the issue. Should a war break out, and his ventures be in foreign bottoms, he may be threatened with the loss of them. The rates of insurance may rise excessively; or the money market may become so disturbed that future shipments may involve a loss where previous ones, at the same rate as to cost, had realized a profit. So, in every community, events are always occurring to interfere with the process of distribution. Its instruments may be supplied by a Bank which may become insolvent, and its issues lose their whole power. A corresponding amount of merchandise, consequently, will be left without the means of distribution, and will fall largely in value. Its fall will affect the whole market. If it be of a perishable nature, it may, if the consumers cannot be readily reached, become wholly valueless. A great merchant may fail, and the machinery he set in motion and directed come to a sudden stop. If others cannot be readily reached to fill his place, the merchandise which he held may have to be thrown upon the market at half its cost. The moment, therefore, that one goes from the process of production to that of distribution, he steps from the firm land upon an uncertain sea. Whether the inherent difficulty be greater in one case than the other, it is certain that losses arise much more frequently from defective or inadequate methods of distribution than of production. Theoretically, the power of people to consume should equal their power to produce. That the actual power to consume does not equal the theoretical power may be owing, in part, to the want of a proper balance, or equilibrium, in production. In the latter, however, the best methods will almost always be used. No one would assume to be a manufacturer without putting machinery into a building which he might erect; while nothing is more common than a currency discharged of all representative value. Such a currency is the great disturbing element in distribution, and none so much so as one issued by a government. That it, without a dollar at its command, can issue bills to serve in exchanges between nations is too absurd for belief; yet it is really no more absurd for it to issue such bills than to issue its notes to serve as currency in domestic trade. If its bills issued for use in foreign exchanges were treated as capital, as possessing a value in coin equal to their nominal amount, it would not be long before the trade in which they were used would become so involved in confusion, and the loss of all parties to it so excessive, that all foreign commerce would come to a stand, not to move again till the fictitious bills had been got rid of, and new and adequate ones had taken their place. So with domestic trade. The issue and use of the notes of government, representing nothing but debt, would in the end produce results precisely similar to those following the use of fictitious bills. The transactions for which they were used, resting on no adequate foundation, would never produce the results predicated of them; and no great length of time would elapse before the affairs of the community would become so involved, and such losses would be suffered, as in great measure to arrest all business operations. If it were free to act in reference to its interests, it would speedily rid itself of the mischievous instruments, and substitute adequate ones in their place. Till such substitution was made, no real amendment or relief would be possible.

The great call, and apparent necessity, in countries where the currency is one of government notes, and consequently irredeemable, is for a flexible currency, — one always adapted to the demand. At periods when the crops are being moved, a great deal more currency is required than at others. Why, it is asked, should it not be made to correspond, in amount, to the transactions that are taking place, instead of being fixed at an unvarying sum? and governments issuing it are always importuned, whenever there is a great stringency, to interpose and increase the amount, and relieve a pressure so detrimental to all.

As already shown, a symbolic currency rises and falls in amount with the value of the merchandise symbolized. If the value of wheat received at Chicago for shipment to the Eastern markets for the present year (1877) be double that received for the same purpose in 1876, bills twice in number, or amount, will be drawn the present year over those drawn the year previous. The currency of bills in both years must correspond to the amount, in value, of the exports. The currency issued by · the Banks in discounting such bills would equal their nominal value, or that of the merchandise they represented. The local instruments, consequently, would correspond to the means of consumption. If, on the other hand, the crop of wheat exported from Chicago the present year equals only one-half that exported in 1876, only one-half the bills in number, or amount, will be drawn the present, as were drawn the previous, year. As a necessary consequence, only one-half the amount of local currency will be created. In either case the currency would have, in the highest degree, the attribute of flexibility, as it would correspond perfectly to the amount of merchandise to be moved. No small amount of inconvenience and suffering might result from a great falling off in value of the exports, and a corresponding reduction in the volume of the currency; but no one would venture to suggest that the latter was in any way in fault, or that there was any method of relief but better prices or better crops.

As already shown, a currency of government notes differs wholly in kind from one based upon merchandise. As it bears no relation to the means of the community upon which it is imposed, it is justly chargeable with a want of flexibility. An increase in its amount to meet an extraordinary call, or stringency, only serves to increase the degree of its inflexibility. With every increase of issue prices rise, so that the currency, relatively, is no more abundant for such increase. In a very short time, prices of all kinds of property are adjusted to the new level. With every increase of the currency, however, the resources of the people are diminished in like ratio, increasing in like degree the difficulty that those in debt, and from whom the clamor of inflexibility always comes, find in borrowing capital, or the notes in circulation, which are capital to their possessor to the amount of their market value. The meaning of inflexibility, consequently, is a lack of capital. The demand for flexibility is only a demand for a greater quantity of capital; or that which, at some price, will serve as capital: with every additional issue the demand necessarily increases in intensity, from the increased impoverishment of the community that has been suffered.

As the value of currencies has been held by all writers to depend upon their quantity, the remedy proposed, to restore their value when depreciated, has been to reduce their amount; or to cease issuing till the increase in number or magnitude of the exchanges, due to an increase of production, shall not only give full employment to the amount in circulation, but require an additional quantity. Such is a necessary conclusion from premises which assume value, either intrinsic or representative, to be no necessary attribute of money. In illustration, it is said that if there are too many yardsticks in a community, a part of them must remain in abeyance till the increase, in the number of yards to be measured, will give employment to all. The price, which has been depreciated from an excess in number, will then rise so as to equal cost.

It has been shown that the value of money is the quality or attribute which measures the value of other things; that, unlike the yardstick, it always, when used, passes in exchange for the value of that which it measures. Yardsticks and weights do not measure values, but space or quantity. Neither do we say that one place is so many dollars distant from another, or that a coat is worth so many yardsticks. Yet it would be just as absurd for government to measure space by dollars, and values by yardsticks, as to declare that its notes, payable at a future day without interest, shall have a value equal to that of coin. Governments cannot change or avoid the operations of natural laws. It would be mere *brutum fulmen* for them to declare that, after a certain period, equal quantities of copper and gold should have the same price. That of each will always be regulated by its value, real or estimated. Government notes bear no relation to the amount of capital of a community, nor will they ever bear any relation to such amount. They will be just as much out of place ten years after, as on the day in which they were issued. No increase of exchanges will increase their value. They are never issued in the outset with a view of facilitating exchanges, but always as a forced loan. They are always suggested by the necessities of government. There never was any other ground for their issue. No community ever lacked the means of exchange that possessed the proper subjects of exchange, — merchandise in demand for consumption. These will give their possessors all the money — gold and silver — they are entitled to for any purpose. In highly civilized countries only a small amount of these metals is used as currency, exchanges being in great measure effected by the use of symbols. A currency of government notes, therefore, is always superfluous. An increase of exchanges twenty-fold, within the period during which they are in circulation, will no more increase their value than it will raise the price of other articles above their value. The price of a currency issued by Banks is always regulated by its value. If from any cause it is depreciated twenty-five per cent, an increase in the number of exchanges will not exert the least influence in increasing its value. If a metallic currency is debased, it will be taken only at the value of the pure metal it contains. No increase of exchanges will exert the slightest influence over its price. The media of exchange are the things exchanged; they mutually measure the value of each other, whether they be coin or merchandise. The idea, therefore, so commonly entertained, that a currency of government notes can be increased in price, can be absorbed, as the phrase is, so as to raise their value to the par of coin by increase in the number of exchanges, is one of the most preposterous and absurd ever entertained. Strange to say, no opinion has a stronger hold upon the public mind.

As the ability of an issuer of notes to convert them depends largely upon their quantity, such quantity becomes a most important element in their price. If a government like the United States should issue $1,000,000 of its notes, these might maintain their value very nearly at par from the ability of the government to redeem them at any moment, and a belief that they would be speedily redeemed. If, in place of $1,000,000, $100,000,000 were issued, the good faith of the government might begin to be questioned. If the amount should become excessive, the decline in their price would become excessive, in spite of the strongest assertion on the part of the government that its promises would be faithfully kept. When the want of ability or disposition on its part to take in its notes became so apparent as to amount to a moral conviction that they would not be taken in, they would cease to have any value. It is in this way that their quantity may be said to control their value. It was the magnitude of the Revolutionary currency of the United States that forbade all thoughts of its payment. Its circulation was sought to be enforced by laws which were increased in number and severity, in ratio to its decline in price, — in other words, in ratio to the distrust entertained as to its value. When it was felt that it was worthless, neither the laws designed to secure its circulation, nor those which declared it to be legal tender in the payment of contracts, had any effect whatever; although the necessity for some medium of exchange increased in ratio to the disuse of that previously in circulation. The French Assignats went out of use from a conviction of their worthlessness, and in face of laws which made it a penal offence not to receive them; though great numbers were executed for such refusal, and the country left for the time almost wholly without a medium of exchange.

The only remedy for such a condition of things is repudiation, — not as a deliberate act, but as a matter of sheer necessity. It was far better to repudiate the French Assignats and the Revolutionary Currency of the United States, than to attempt to pay them. Such an attempt would only have prolonged the sufferings that had been endured. The wrong done was too monstrous ever to be repaired by human hands. There is no instance, so far, in which government currencies, that have been issued in any considerable amount, have been redeemed by full payment. Fortunately the most signal instance of recent times — the present currency of the United States — is not so excessive as to forbid the hope that it may avoid the fate which has so far overtaken all of its kind.

As paper money should be issued only as records of transactions, — as symbols of merchandise to serve in its distribution, — and as the test of its legitimacy or propriety is its return to the issuer in the payment of the bills in the discount of which it was issued, leaving his reserves intact, it follows by necessary sequence that not only every person possessing merchandise entering into consumption is competent to issue a convertible currency, but that every currency to be used by a community in the distribution of its merchandise should be issued within it, in order that the issuer may have the means of possessing himself of the standing and trustworthiness of the parties to the bills discounted, as well as of the profitableness or unprofitableness of their industries. Otherwise he would necessarily be constantly making losses by discounting fictitious or worthless bills. Local bills made in Texas might be very proper subjects for discount by Banks in that State, while they would be very improper subjects for discount by Banks situated in New York or Boston. The managers of the latter might have no personal knowledge of the character or responsibility of the parties to such bills, and might be wholly unable to obtain any satisfactory information in reference thereto. In such countries as Great Britain and the United States, local currencies are supplied by local institutions. Every community without a Bank, or banker, issuing currency, will be largely wanting in the instruments most essential to the promotion of its welfare. Were there no Banks in the State of Texas, for example, its currency, in the absence of United States notes, would of necessity consist chiefly in coin. As it had no Banks previous to the issue of such notes, its currency consisted in a great measure of coin. It prosecuted its industries, consequently, under great disadvantages compared with States possessed of symbolic currencies which discharged from use a large amount of coin, to be held as reserves against issues of paper exceeding many times the amount of coin which, in the absence of symbols, could have been maintained in circulation.

Paper currencies, so long as they are convertible, will never circulate in any considerable amount at a distance from the place of their issue. They cannot ordinarily get far distant therefrom, as they must, by the operations of trade, return to the Bank for redemption within three or four months

from their issue.   The notes of the Banks of the great centres
of trade in the Eastern States of the United States will be
readily taken in the most distant of the Western ; but they
will not circulate in them, as they will be immediately taken up
for remittances to the Eastern States, in favor of which there
is always a constant balance of indebtedness.   The notes of the
Banks of the Western States can never obtain circulation in
the Eastern.   They would be superfluous as currency in the
latter, and, as they would immediately go into the Eastern
Banks on deposit, they would speedily be returned to their
issuers for payment in coin.   Banks in all large cities make
daily settlements with each other through Clearing Houses,
the balances arising daily being discharged daily.   Country
Banks, not parties to Clearing Houses, are, no less than those
that are, compelled to take in daily a portion of their circulation, or such part of it as may be in excess of the wants of the
public for the distribution of merchandise.   All currencies, by
whomsoever issued, are subject to the same law of redemption
within the time ordinarily required for the distribution of
merchandise from producer to consumer.

Very different ideas, however, upon the subject of paper
money prevail.   It is assumed by all writers upon the subject
that, as a rule, currencies will remain indefinitely in circulation provided the credit of the issuer remain unshaken.   Paper
money is described by all as a " credit currency."   A currency
could never get into circulation unless it was supposed to represent capital, and to be payable on demand in coin ; but a currency with millions behind it is subject to the same necessity
of redemption as one that is not supported by a single dollar
(assuming, of course, that the latter circulates as currency
from the credit attached to it).   But for such credit it would
not go into circulation at all, or it would be immediately presented for redemption in coin.   This law of redemption has
been wholly overlooked by all writers upon monetary science.
It is the law of all convertible currencies that they must be redeemed within comparatively short periods.   If they represent
merchandise, they will be returned to the issuer by virtue of the
purchase and consumption of such merchandise.   Redemption
in such case is only a mutual offset of liabilities.   If not retired in this manner, it must be taken in by the Bank by the
payment of a corresponding amount of its reserves.

In that which has preceded, the question of money, in all its forms, has been treated as one coming within the range of the exact sciences, to be solved by purely scientific methods. As those here employed are entirely different from any previously used, the conclusions arrived at are wholly different. All previous attempts to solve this question have failed from the employment of the dialectical method in the investigation of questions which yield only to scientific analysis. Modern writers upon the subject of Political Economy, in which that of money has been included, are the legitimate descendants of the Schoolmen, with all their vain and frivolous distinctions and categories, delivered in a feeble and tumid rhetoric much better fitted to repel than attract investigation and inquiry by those not so tied to tradition and routine, so careless of truth, and so incapable of its investigation, as themselves. One of the imperative duties, in a work like the present, is to expose the false and vicious methods and theories which have so long been imposed upon the world, — an imposition which future times might well believe to have been impossible, but for similar illustrations of equally ignorant assumption on one side, and equally ignorant credulity on the other. The proper execution of such an attempt is well calculated to form one of the most interesting chapters in the history of society.

HISTORY OF MONETARY THEORIES.

The source of the monetary theories of ancient as well as modern times, as well as of the doctrine of the unlawfulness of usury which remained unchallenged till near the close of the eighteenth century, is Aristotle. His views upon both of these subjects will be sufficiently set forth in the following extracts from his works:[1]—

" There is, also, another kind of acquisition which men specially call pecuniary, and with great justice too ; and by this indeed it seems that there are no bounds to riches and wealth. Now many persons suppose, from their near relations to each other, that this is one and the same with the art just mentioned" (which he terms elsewhere natural acquisition, and in which he embraces what is captured in war, the products of the chase, of flocks and herds, and of the soil) ; "but it is not the same as that, though not very different ; for one of these is natural, the other is not, but rather arises from some art and skill. Now let us enter on our inquiry into the subject from the following point. The uses of every possession are two ; both indeed essential, but not in the same manner ; for the one is strictly proper to the thing, the other not ; as a shoe, for instance, may be either worn or exchanged for something else ; for both these are uses of the shoe ; for he who exchanges a shoe with some man who wants one, for money, or provisions, uses the shoe as a shoe, but not according to its proper use ; for shoes are not made to be exchanged. The same thing holds true of all other possessions ; for barter in general had its original beginning in Nature, from the fact that some men had a surplus, and others less than was necessary for them. And hence it is evident that the selling provisions for money is not naturally a part of pecuniary science ; for men were obliged to use barter as far as would supply their wants. Now it is plain that barter could have no place in the first community, that is to say in the household, but must have begun when the number of those who composed the community came to be enlarged ; for the former of these had all things the same and in common ; but those who came to be separated had in common many other things which both parties were obliged to exchange as their wants arose.". . . " This sort of barter, then,

---

[1] Aristotle's " Politics," Bohn's edition, Book i. Chap. ix.

is not contrary to Nature, nor yet is it any species of money-getting; but it is necessary in order to complete that independence which is natural. From this barter however arose the use of money, as might be expected; for as the needful means for importing what was wanted, or for exporting a surplus, was often at a great distance, *the use of money was of necessity devised.* For it is not every thing which is naturally useful, that is easy of carriage; and for this reason men *invented* among themselves, by way of exchange, something which they should mutually give and take, and which being really valuable in itself, might easily be passed from hand to hand for the purposes of daily life, as iron, or silver, or any thing else of the same nature. . . .

" Money, then, being *devised* from the *necessity* of mutual exchange, the second species of money-getting arose, namely, by buying and selling; and this was conducted probably at first in a simple manner, but afterwards it came to employ more skill and experience as to where and how the greatest profit might be made. For which reason the art of money-getting seems to be chiefly conversant about trade, and its end to be able to see where the greatest profit can be made; for it is the means of procuring abundance of wealth and possessions. For men oftentimes suppose wealth to consist in the quantity of money which any one possesses, as this is that medium with which trading and trafficking are concerned; others regard it as a mere trifle, as having no value by nature, but merely by arbitrary compact; so that, if those who use it should alter their sentiments, it would be worthless and unserviceable for any necessary purpose. *Thus oftentimes the man who abounds in money will want the necessary food; and it is absurd to say that wealth is a thing of such a kind that a man with plenty of it around him may perish with hunger,* like Midas [1] in the fable, who from his insatiable wish found every thing set before him turned into gold. For which reason, people look about for something else by way of riches and property, and rightly too; for the mere getting of money differs from natural wealth, and the

---

[1] It is remarkable, not that Aristotle should not have been able to appreciate the significance of a highly spiritual myth, but it is remarkable that he should have so misstated a fable which originated with his own race. Midas by no means wished that every thing set before him should be turned to gold; he wished that whatever he touched should be turned to gold. The table set before him was loaded with delicious viands, which were turned to gold in the attempt to convey them to his mouth. He was caught in his own trap. The moral intended to be drawn was, not that gold possessed no value, but that all inordinate desires defeat themselves; that avarice so deadens the higher faculties that the money gained by it is itself an instrument of punishment. It has already been demonstrated that gold and silver (money) are the most substantial of all kinds of wealth; that a person is rich in ratio to the amount of them that he possesses, as he can by their use command whatever other people possess, and can never come to want so long as there is food or clothing for the use of any one; while a person possessed of the greatest abundance of any other kind of property, such as food or clothing, may miserably perish from his inability to exchange that which he has for other articles necessary to sustain life.

latter is the true object of economy; while trade only procures money, not by all means, but by the exchange of it; and it seems to be chiefly employed about trading, for money is the element and the regulator of trade, nor are there any bounds to be set to the wealth which is thereby acquired. For just as there are no limits to the art of medicine with respect to health, and as all other arts with respect to their ends are infinite — (for those ends they desire to effect to the farthest possible extent) — but still the means used for those ends are limited, and their several ends are the limits of each; so too in the art of acquiring riches, its end has no limits, for its object is money and possessions; but economy has a boundary, though the former has not; for acquiring riches is not its real end. And for this reason it should seem that some boundary should be set to riches, though in practice we see the contrary of this taking place; for all those who get riches add to their money without end. The cause of this is the near connection of these two arts with each other, for they sometimes change employment with each other, as getting of money is their common pursuit. For they each employ the same thing, but not in the same manner; for the end of the one is something beyond itself, but the end of the other is merely to increase it; so that some persons are led to believe that this is the proper object of economy, and think that for this purpose they ought to continue to save or to hoard up money without end. . . . . Such persons make every art subservient to money-getting, as if this was the only end, and to this end every thing ought to contribute. We have now considered that art of money-getting which is not necessary, and have said what it is, and how we come to need it; and also that which is necessary, which is *different* from it; for that economy which is natural, and whose object is to provide food, is not infinite like this, but has its bounds. . . .

 " That which was doubted at the first is now clear, as to whether the art of getting money is the business of the head of a family or a State, or whether it is not, and yet must of necessity exist; for as the political science does not make men, but, receiving them from the hand of Nature, employs them to proper purposes; thus Nature, whether it be the earth, or sea, or any thing else, ought to supply them with provisions; and this it is the business of the master of the family to manage properly. For it is not the weaver's business to make yarn, but to use it, and to distinguish what is good and useful from what is bad and of no service; and in like manner some one may inquire why money-getting should be a part of economy, when the art of healing is not; since it is as requisite that the family should be in health as that they should eat, or have any thing else which is necessary. Now, as it is indeed in some sense the business of both the master of the family and the ruler of a State to see after the health of those under their care, but in another sense not, but the physician's; so, also, as to money, in some respects it is the business of the master of the family, in others not, *but of the servile art.* But, as we have already said, it is chiefly the part of Nature, for it is her part to supply her off-

spring with food; for nourishment is left for every thing born, by
that which gave it birth; and hence by the way, the natural riches
of all men arise from fruits and from animals.   But since these
riches may be applied, as we have said, to two purposes, the one to
make money of, the other for the service of the house; of these the
one is necessary and commendable, the other, which has to do with
traffic, is justly censured, for it has not its origin in Nature, but
amongst ourselves; for usury is most reasonably detested, as the
increase of our fortune arises from the money itself, and not by
employing it to the purpose to which it was intended.   For it was
devised for the sake of exchange, but usury multiplies it.   And,
hence, usury has received the name of ' τόχος ' or ' *produce*,' for
whatever is produced is itself like its parents; and usury is merely
money born of money : so that of all means of money-making this
is the most contrary to Nature."

Aristotle has been quoted at length, as a necessary condition of getting at his ideas upon the subject of money; as
the source of all theories or opinions which have prevailed in
reference to it from his time to our own; and to show the
methods pursued by him, by his legitimate successors the
Schoolmen of the Middle Ages, and by the Political Economists, the Schoolmen of modern times. His method of resolving
all questions by verbal distinctions, by dialectics, relieved him of
all necessity of investigation into, or analysis of their law.   Of
this, his treatment of money and of loans of it at usury affords
a striking illustration.   Money was an invention for the purpose of facilitating exchanges of property.   To use it for any
other purpose was against Nature; usury, — " money born of
money," — a crime ! It was the very falseness of his method
that gave him his prodigious ascendency. By means of it, he
was enabled within the period of a very few years to construct
what he assumed to be a universal science. His conclusions,
to which he gave all the authority of dogmas, were delivered
with an eloquence of language and a copiousness of illustration
which his successors could never hope to equal; still less, if
they had wished, to controvert. This could be done only by
the discovery of the law of that to which they related.   He
had an eminently active, but an eminently unscientific mind.
He epitomized his time and his race. When he wrote, the
world was in its infancy in every thing that characterizes scientific analysis. On a multitude of subjects it was in the highest degree impious to question the beliefs and traditions of the
past. Phenomenon still stood for law. Reflection and inquiry,

with the race as with the individual, come only with the maturity of age. He has been termed the father of the Inductive Method. He indeed said something as to the necessity of proceeding from particulars to generals, and of deducing from a comparison of facts their connection and law ; but it never occurred to him to question the testimony of the senses ; on the contrary, he made it the foundation of the vast super-structure he undertook to rear. His method was necessarily deductive, from his utter ignorance of, or inability to use, the inductive ; from the imperiousness and arrogance of his nature, and from the purpose he had in view, which was nothing less than to solve, in an age wholly incapable of any thing like an adequate investigation of natural law, every question coming within the range of human experience. He was the impressible child, full of animation and garrulity, not the mature man, silent and reflective from the consciousness of his own ignorance and impotence to interpret the mighty problems which confronted him on every side. Child as he was, his statements and illustrations were so grotesque and fanciful that it is to be wondered that he did not see their inconclusiveness and absurdity. Never disturbed by a doubt as to the soundness of his premises, he assumed to dispose by a single stroke, not only of problems for which, with all the lights of the present day, ages will hardly suffice, but those which wholly transcend human capacity. The manner in which he attempted to prove the world to be perfect is a capital illustration of his method and its results : " The bodies," he says, " of which the world is composed, are solids, and therefore have three dimensions. Now three is the most *perfect* number ; it is the first of numbers ; for of one we do not speak as a number ; of two we say both ; but three is the first number of which we say all ; moreover, it has a beginning, a middle, and an end ! " [1] By a similar method he undertook to prove the existence of a fifth element, or essence. " Simple elements," he tells us, " must have simple motions, and thus fire and air have their natural motions upward, and water and earth have their natural motions downward ; but besides these motions, there is motion in a circle, which is unnatural to these elements, but which is a more perfect motion than the other, because a circle is a per-

---

[1] Whewell's " Inductive Sciences," Am. ed. vol. i. p. 72.

fect line, and a straight line is not; and there must be something to which this motion is natural. From this it is evident that there is some essence or body different from those of the four elements, more divine than those, and superior to them. If things which move in a circle move contrary to Nature, it is marvellous, or rather absurd, that this, the unnatural motion, should alone be continuous and eternal; for unnatural motions decay speedily. And so, from all this, we must collect that besides the four elements which we have here and about us, there is another removed far off, and the more excellent in proportion as it is more distant from us." From this fifth essence the modern word *quintessence* is derived.[1]

The preceding illustrations will convey a sufficient idea of the method of Aristotle, and explain the barrenness of its results. The premises from which he reasoned were the untrained observations of phenomena, or the extravagant fictions of an ardent and fanciful mind. The conclusions to which he came were as grotesque and fanciful as the premises themselves. They were like attempts to solve mathematical problems by using numerals that accidentally presented themselves, and guessing at the results of their combination. If he could not discover the unsoundness of his premises and the inconclusiveness of his reasoning, still less could those whose only ambition was to implicitly adopt and unfold the doctrines of their great master. The more they commented, the more puerile and feeble, compared with his, their rhetoric and illustrations became. His mode of proof of the perfection of the earth possessed some charm and dignity as it fell from his lips. If it could have been accepted without discussion, no harm at the time could have come of it. The Greeks, incapable of scientific inquiry, would have been as well off with this as with any other explanation which was certain to be as far from the truth. The harm came from the discussions that followed. The freshness of the original propositions was wholly lost in the commentators; and as no truth, no goal, was ever arrived at, no end ever reached, proposition was piled upon proposition, and assumption upon assumption, till the faculty of reasoning, of perceiving the truth, was itself lost, and the race but little removed from a condition of mental idiocy. Absurd

---

[1] Whewell, vol. i. pp. 72, 73.

as were his teachings and pretensions, he is by no means yet fully dethroned. He still is an authority in our colleges, and a great many very important questions, which should be treated on a scientific basis, are still treated by his methods, — that of money being one of the most notable.

"It is highly instructive," says Whewell, in his History of the Inductive Sciences,[1] "to trace the principles of this undertaking (of Aristotle); for the course pursued was certainly one of the most natural and tempting that could be imagined. The essay was made by a nation unequalled in fine mental endowments, at the period of its greatest activity and vigor; and yet, it must be allowed (for, at least so far as physical science is concerned, none will contest this) to have been entirely unsuccessful. We cannot consider otherwise than as an utter failure, an endeavor to discover the cause of things, of which the most complete results are the Aristotelian Physical Treatises; and which, after reaching the point which these Treatises mark, left the human mind to remain stationary, at any rate, upon all such subjects for nearly two thousand years."[2]

It was not, however, till nearly fifteen hundred years after his decease, that Aristotle began to exercise a paramount and at the same time a most baleful influence over the human mind. He exerted little or none over his own nation; and, although

---

[1] Whewell, vol. i. p. 56.

[2] "Aristotle affords," says Bacon, "the most eminent instance of the first (sophistic philosophy); for he corrupted natural philosophy by logic: thus, he formed the world of categories, assigned to the human soul, the noblest of substances, a genus determined by words of secondary operation, treated of density and rarity (by which bodies occupy a greater or lesser space) by the frigid distinctions of action and power; asserted that there was a peculiar and proper motion in all bodies, and that, if they shared in any other motion, it was owing to an external moving cause, and imposed innumerable arbitrary distinctions upon the nature of things; being everywhere more anxious as to definitions in teaching and the accuracy of the wording of his propositions, than the internal truth of things. And this is best shown by a comparison of his philosophy with the others of the greatest repute among the Greeks. For the similar parts of Anaxagoras, the atoms of Leucippus and Democritus, the heaven and earth of Parmenides, the discord and concord of Empedocles, the resolution of bodies into the common nature of fire, and their condensation, according to Heraclitus, exhibit some sprinkling of natural philosophy, the nature of things, and experiment; whilst Aristotle's physics are mere logical terms, and he remodelled the same subject, in his metaphysics, under a more imposing title; and more as a realist than a nominalist. Nor is much stress to be laid on his frequent recourse to experiment in his books on animals, his problems, and other treatises; for he had already decided, without having properly consulted experience as the basis of his decisions and axioms, and, after having so decided, he drags experiment along, as a captive constrained to accommodate herself to his decisions; so that he is even more to be blamed than his modern followers (of the scholastic school) who have deserted her altogether. — *Novum Organum.* Book i. 63.

one of the greatest and wisest of her philosophers, that which he did exert only contributed to precipitate her fall. The practical and unimaginative Romans, who finally included Greece in the universal empire, regarded at first, with a like contempt, her literature and culture. At no time did these exert any considerable influence over the lives or fortunes of the conquerors; at least, none that served to arrest their decline and fall. That fall buried for ages all the culture of the past in its ruins. On the rise of the new nationalities, and on the revival of learning in the Middle Ages, it could not be otherwise than that scholars, whose own tongues were compounds of barbarous dialects, should become enraptured with a language the most perfect the world has yet seen; should without reserve accept Aristotle, one of the most accomplished writers of this language, as their master, and should regard his works as the great store-house of human wisdom.

"We may consider," continues Whewell, in his History of the Inductive Sciences, "the reign of mere disputation as fully established at the time of which we are now speaking" (the 12th and 13th centuries); "the only kind of philosophy henceforth studied was one in which no sound physical science had or could have place. The wavering abstractions, the indistinct generalizations, and loose classifications of common language which we have already noticed as the fountain of physics of the Greek Schools of philosophy, were also the only source from which the Schoolmen of the Middle Ages drew their views, or rather their arguments; and though these notional and verbal relations were invested with a most complex and pedantic technicality, they did not on this account become at all more precise as notions, or more likely to lead to a single real truth. Instead of acquiring distinct ideas, they multiplied abstract terms; instead of real generalizations, they had recourse to verbal distinctions. The whole course of their employments tended to make them not only ignorant of physical truth, but incapable of conceiving its nature.

"Having thus taken upon themselves the task of raising and discussing questions by means of abstract terms, verbal distinctions, and logical rules alone, there was no tendency in their activity to come to an end, as there was no progress. The same questions, the same answers, the same difficulties, the same solutions, the same verbal subtleties, — sought for, admired, cavilled at, abandoned, reproduced, and again admired, — might recur without limit. John of Salisbury observed of the Parisian teachers, that, after several years' absence, he found them not a step advanced, and still employed in urging and parrying the same arguments; and this, as Mr. Hallam remarks, 'was equally applicable to the period of centuries.' The same knots were tied and untied; the same clouds were formed

and dissipated. The poet's censure of the sons of Aristotle is just
as happily expressed : —

> " ' They stand
> Locked up together, hand in hand.
> Every one leads as he is led ;
> The same bare path they tread,
> And dance like Fairies a fantastic round,
> But neither change their motion nor their ground.[1] ' "

The ascendency of Aristotle upon the revival of learning
could not have become so paramount, but for the fact that he
was accepted as authority by the Church equally with the
Schools. The methods of the two were precisely the same.
Each assumed the truth of the premises upon which the systems of each were constructed. The Church had nothing to
fear from one who stood in the way of all inquiry by which
truth could be discovered, and, by rendering all progress impossible, gave for a time an historic truth to the famous boast
of " *Semper Eadem.*" Uniformity throughout the ages, whether
in science or in art, in religion or in dogma, is the uniformity of
death. In spite, however, of Church and of Aristotle, discoveries continued to be made, each one of which enlarged the
vision and means of those that followed. The spirit of freedom and inquiry came from the new races. They burst the
bonds, both physical and religious, in which the world had so
long been held. For such an effort, neither Greece nor Rome
had the aspiration nor the power. So firm, however, had become the grasp of the Church and the Schools upon the human
mind, that it was not till the beginning of the seventeenth century that Bacon, for the first time, displayed to the race, in
all their length and breadth, the methods by which truth is to
be discovered, — methods which cannot fail, so far as the faculties of man can go, to unfold all the laws of the universe.

The difference between the methods of Aristotle and Bacon
is, that to the Aristotelian, the sun *rises* and *sets ;* upon the evidence of his senses he immediately constructs a system which
assumes to explain all the phenomena of the heavens. To the
Baconian, the sun *appears* to rise and set ; but from this appearance he draws no conclusions whatever. His first essay is
to test the accuracy of the testimony of his senses. He finds
in the end that the phenomena entirely contradict the facts, —

---

[1] Whewell, vol. i. p. 234-5.

the law, the appearance ; that the earth moves about the sun, instead of the sun about the earth as a common centre. The system which he erects, consequently, differs wholly from that of the follower of Aristotle. Both, in one sense, have proceeded inductively, drawing their conclusions from premises which appear to each not to be controverted. Those of one are the testimony of his senses, or propositions framed by his own fancy; from these he immediately proceeds to conclusions. The other draws no conclusions from the testimony of his senses, from phenomena, nor from his fancies; but first proceeds to test their accuracy or truth. This done, his conclusions are demonstrations which irresistibly command assent.

The exact sciences — those which deal in space, quantity and number — were the first to emancipate themselves from the Aristotelian methods. When these are properly pursued the results are indisputable. Astrology, with all its monstrous fables, as unmeaning to those who proposed them as to the ignorant and unlearned, gave place to astronomy. Alchemy, with all its assumption of creative power, gave place to chemistry, which demonstrates beyond cavil that final causes lie beyond the reach of man. In these, investigation, whatever may be the progress made, at least proceeds by proper methods. In many of the moral sciences, however, — in those the truths of which are less demonstrable than those of astronomy and chemistry, — the Schoolmen still exert almost paramount authority. As Religion is largely a matter of race, there is probably no solution of the controversies growing out of it, but the law of the stronger. We can, however, already assume that the freer the articulation of the faculties in reference to it, the more effective and capable do man and the race become. The greater part of what we know of Medicine is that the schools are wider apart than ever: there is no concord, for the reason that there are no demonstrations that command assent. In this science the methods of the Schoolmen still hold sway. Negative progress, however, has been made. In the inability to propose remedies, Nature is in great measure allowed to do her own work, — a confession of ignorance and incompetency by which mankind has immeasurably gained.[1]

[1] Of what may be termed the Moral Sciences, that of Law seems to be the only one in which any considerable or satisfactory progress has yet been made.

Midway between these extremes are a vast number of subjects that relate to the economy of life, — law, government,
administration, production, distribution ; subjects which result
from the joint action of many and often apparently opposing
laws.   These become all the more difficult of solution as society
advances in civilization and wealth.   All, at the outset, so far
as they were treated, were necessarily treated after the manner of the Schoolmen.   The theories or opinions which related
to money, and to loans of money at usury, came directly
from Aristotle, and were accepted without examination or res-

The results or demonstrations in this rank among the highest achievements, — or,
rather, the ability to accept them is to be taken as the most decisive and satisfactory proof of the moral elevation of the race.   Other kindred sciences are
broken up into innumerable Schools, for the reason that, so far, there have in
these been no adequate demonstrations, no common points of agreement.   Schools
are another word for guesses at, or suggestions of probabilities.   There are no
Schools in Astronomy, for the reason that the truth or falsehood of all propositions in reference to it is a matter of proof.   There are, or should be, no Schools
in Chemistry.   If there are unsolved problems in this science, conclusion is to
be held in abeyance.   There are Schools in Medicine and Theology for the reason that the claims or propositions put forth by their teachers are inadequate or
partial, and are consequently untrue to the general sense of mankind.   From a
feeling of their inadequacy new hypotheses or explanations are put forth, to
give place, in time, to others perhaps equally unfounded and untenable.   There
are no Schools in Law, in its highest sense, for the reason that its conclusions
are based upon sentiments or convictions common to the race.   All have a similar sense of right and wrong, and when interest or passion is not involved,
every one wishes to see, in the laws, the embodiment of justice, not only for the
protection and welfare of others, which every one, ordinarily, desires to see promoted, but for his own, when his rights may be assailed.   As every legal proposition is open to criticism, every one that is not founded in justice, or in convenience, is sure to be eventually overthrown.   The Civil Law affords a splendid
illustration of the progress made in legal science long before others, now so prominent, may be said to have had an existence.   It is one of the greatest monu-
ments of human wisdom.   There never was a similar necessity or occasion.
The Roman Empire embraced the known world, with every variety of race and
nationality, and with ideas and institutions appropriate to each,   There was, so
far as administration was concerned, but one method by which all these incongruous elements could be fused into one homogeneous mass, — a Code to which
all were subject, and resting upon grounds and reasons appreciable by all, — upon
a sense of justice, and of fitness of things.   Although it was a maxim of the
Roman lawyers, " Quod principi placuit legis habet vigorem," yet the legislation of
the Emperors, if such it may be called, served as a rule, only to give the force of
law to the reasoning and conclusions of the wisest and purest jurists of the Empire.   In this way the Civil Law became, as far as possible, the expression of
pure reason when it dealt with principles, and of pure convenience when it dealt
with their application.   It is not probable that the world will ever see a similar
code, one so just in principle and so universal and beneficent in its operation,
for the reason that the world will never again see a universal Empire.

ervation. With him, money was invented for a specific purpose, and was entitled to no consideration, for the reason that
such purposes or objects were contrary to Nature. Those
that were according to Nature were war, the chase, the care of
herds, and the gathering of the fruits of the fields. Such
only were worthy of freemen who had a part in the administration of the government. With him, trade and the
mechanical arts were contrary to Nature, were servile; and, as
such, were worthy only of those who occupied an inferior
political or social condition, and of slaves. Money was held
in the same indifference or contempt as were those by whom it
was chiefly used. It was unworthy of notice or investigation;
it was base because those who used it, and the employments
in which it was used, were base. Such was the foundation upon which was reared a superstructure which has out-
lasted the ages.

The views of Aristotle on the subject of usury are a necessary
sequence of his views upon the subject of money. If money-
getting by trade, or by exchanges in which it was used, was contrary to Nature, loans of it at usury could be no less so. They
were only an aggravation of the original wrong. Contemp-
tible as such reasoning now appears, it controlled the judgment
of mankind for twenty-two hundred years! "This absurdity
of Aristotle," says Lecky,[1] "and the number of centuries during
which it was so incessantly asserted, without being, so far as we
know, once questioned, is a curious illustration of the longevity
of a sophism[2] when expressed in a terse form and sheltered by a
great name. It is enough to make one ashamed of his species
to think that Bentham, so late as 1787, was the first to bring
into notice the simple consideration that, if a farmer employs
borrowed money in buying bulls and cows, and if these produce calves to the value of ten times the interest, the money
borrowed can scarcely be said to be sterile, or the borrower
to be a loser!"

[1] History of Rationalism in Europe, vol. ii. page 251.
[2] The history of Medicine affords a still more striking instance of the "longevity of a sophism when sheltered by a great name." For more than 1,500
years, the system of Medicine established by the celebrated Galen, a Greek physician, held undisputed sway. By this system, to use the words of Sir William
Hamilton, "Four elementary fluids, their relations and changes, sufficed to explain the varieties of natural temperament and the cause of disease; while

After Aristotle, the first writer whose works on this subject possess any interest or value was the celebrated John
Locke. The silver currency of England (the only one then in
use) had become, in 1696, so reduced in value, from clipping
and wear, as to cause the greatest inconvenience in all the
operations of society. The coins in use, no matter how light,
could be still used in the payment of debts and of the taxes
due the government. The latter attempted for a long time to
correct the evil, by causing large quantities of silver to be
coined of the standard weight and fineness; but as the old
coins, with one-quarter or one-fifth less of pure metal, were

the genius, eloquence, and unbounded learning with which he illustrated this
theory mainly bestowed on it the ascendency, which, without essential alteration, it retained from the conclusion of the second to the beginning of the eighteenth century. . . . Nor was this doctrine merely an erroneous speculation; it
exerted the most decisive, the most pernicious influence on practice. The various diseased affections were denominated in accommodation to the theory. In
place of saying that a malady affected the liver, the peritonæum, or the organs
of circulation, its seat was assumed in the blood, the bile, or the lymph. The
morbific causes acted exclusively on the fluids; the food digested in the stomach,
and converted into chyle, determined the qualities of the blood; and poisons
operated through the corruption they thus effected in the vital humors. All
symptoms were interpreted in blind subservience to the hypothesis; and those
only attracted attention which the hypothesis seemed calculated to explain.
The color and consistence of the blood, mucus, feces, urine, and pus were carefully studied. On the other hand, the phenomena of the solids, if not wholly
overlooked, as mere accidents, were slumped together under some collective
name, and attached to the theory through a subsidiary hypothesis. By supposed changes in the humors, they explained the association and consecution of
symptoms. Under the terms *crudity, coction,* and *evacuation* were designated the
three principal periods of diseases, as dependent on an alteration of the *morbific
matter.* In the first, this matter in all its deleterious energy had not yet undergone
any change on the part of the organs; it was still *crude.* In the second, Nature
gradually assumed the ascendent; *coction* took place. In the third, the peccant
matter, now rendered mobile, was *evacuated* by urine, perspiration, dejection, &c.,
and equilibrium restored. When no critical discharge was apparent, the morbific matter, it was supposed, had, after a suitable elaboration, been assimilated
to the humors, and its deleterious character neutralized. Coction might be perfect or imperfect; and the transformation of one disease into another was
lightly solved by the transport or emigration of the noxious humor. It was
principally on the changes of the evacuated fluids that they founded their judgments respecting the nature, issue, and duration of diseases. The urine, in
particular, supplied them with indications to which they attached the greatest
importance. Examinations of the dead body confirmed them in these notions.
In the redness and tumefaction of inflamed parts, they beheld only a congestion
of blood; and in dropsies, merely the dissolution of that fluid; tubercles were
simply coagula of lymph; and other organic alterations, in general, naught but
obstructions from an increased viscosity of the humors. The plan of cure was
in unison with the rest of the hypothesis. Venesection was copiously employed

used as currency equally with the new, the latter were immediately taken up and melted down and exported at their value as bullion or merchandise ; so that no progress whatever was made in remedying an evil which, at the time Locke wrote, had become well nigh insupportable.

" The financiers of that age," says Macaulay, in his graphic picture of it, " seem to have expected that the new money, which was excellent, would soon displace the old money which was much impaired. Yet any man of plain understanding might have known that, when the State treats perfect coin and light coin as of equal value, the perfect coin will not drive the light coin out of circulation, but will itself be driven out. A clipped crown, on English ground, went as far in the payment of a tax or a debt as a milled crown. But the milled crown, as soon as it had been flung into the crucible or carried across the channel, became much more valuable than the clipped crown. It might therefore have been predicted, as confidently as any thing can be predicted which depends on the human will, that the inferior pieces would remain in the only market in which they could fetch the same price as the superior pieces ; and that the superior pieces would take some form or fly to some place, in which some advantage could be derived from their superiority.

" The politicians of that age, however, generally overlooked these very obvious considerations. They marvelled exceedingly that everybody should be so perverse as to use light money in preference to good money. In other words, they marvelled that nobody chose

to renew the blood, to attenuate its consistency, or to remove a part of the morbific matter with which it was impregnated; and cathartics, sudorifics, and diuretics were largely administered with a similar intent. In a word, as *plethora* or *cacochymia* were the two great sources of disease, their whole therapeutic was directed to change the quantity or quality of the fluids. Nor was this murderous treatment limited to the actual period of the disease. Seven or eight annual bleedings and as many purgations, — such was the common regimen the theory prescribed to assure continuance of health ; and the twofold depletion, still customary, at spring and fall among the peasantry of many European countries is a remnant of the once universal practice. In Spain, every village has even now its *Sangrador*, whose only art of surgery is blood-letting ; and he is rarely idle. The medical treatment of Louis XIII. may be quoted as a specimen of the humoral therapeutic. Within a single year, this theory inflicted on that unfortunate monarch above a hundred cathartics and more than forty bloodings. During the fifteen centuries of Humorism, how many millions of lives did medicine cost mankind ? " [1]

The permanence of such fallacies as the unlawfulness of interest, and the humoral theory in Medicine, will serve to lessen our astonishment at the continuance to the present time of monetary theories, equally absurd, which have never been challenged from the time they were delivered to the world by Aristotle.

[1] Sir William Hamilton's " Discussions on Philosophy and Literature," American edition, pp. 246-248.

to pay twelve ounces of silver when ten ounces would serve the turn. The horse at the Tower still paced his rounds. Fresh wagonloads of choice money still came forth from the mill; and still they vanished as fast as they appeared. Great masses were melted down; great masses exported; great masses hoarded: but scarcely one new piece was found in the till of a shop, or in the leathern bag which the farmer carried home from the cattle fair. In the receipts and payments of the Exchequer, the milled money did not exceed ten shillings in a hundred pounds. A writer of that age mentions the case of a merchant who, in the sum of thirty-five pounds, received only a single half-crown in milled silver. . . .

" The evils produced by this state of the currency were not such as have generally been thought worthy to occupy a prominent place in history. Yet it may well be doubted whether all the misery which had been inflicted on the English nation in a quarter of a century by bad kings, bad ministers, bad parliaments, and bad judges was equal to the misery caused in a single year by bad crowns and bad shillings. Those events which furnish the best themes for pathetic or indignant eloquence are not always those which most affect the happiness of the great body of the people. The misgovernment of Charles and James, gross as it had been, had not prevented the common business of life from going steadily and prosperously on. While the honor and independence of the State were sold to a foreign power, while chartered rights were invaded, while fundamental laws were violated, hundreds of thousands of quiet, honest, and industrious families labored and traded, ate their meals and lay down to rest, in comfort and security. Whether Whigs or Tories, Protestants or Jesuits were uppermost, the grazier drove his beasts to market: the grocer weighed out his currants: the draper measured out his broadcloth: the hum of buyers and sellers was as loud as ever in the towns: the harvest-home was celebrated as joyously as ever in the hamlets: the cream overflowed the pails of Cheshire: the apple-juice foamed in the presses of Herefordshire: the piles of crockery glowed in the furnaces of the Trent; and the barrows of coal rolled fast along the timber railway of the Tyne. But when the great instrument of exchange became thoroughly deranged, all trade, all industry, were smitten as with a palsy. . . .

" Since the Revolution, the state of the currency had been repeatedly discussed in Parliament. In 1689 a committee of the Commons had been appointed to investigate the subject, but had made no report. In 1690 another committee had reported that immense quantities of silver were carried out of the country by Jews, who, it was said, would do any thing for profit. Schemes were formed for encouraging the importation and discouraging the exportation of the precious metals. One foolish bill after another was brought in and dropped. At length, in the beginning of the year 1695, the question assumed so serious an aspect that the Houses applied themselves to it in earnest. The only practical result of their deliberations, however, was a new penal law, which, it was hoped, would prevent the clipping of the hammered coin and the melting and exporting of the milled coin. It was enacted that every person who informed against a clipper should be entitled to a reward of forty pounds, that every clipper who informed against two clippers should be entitled to a pardon, and that whoever should be found in possession of silver filings or parings should be burned in the cheek with a red-hot iron. Certain officers were employed to search for bullion. If bullion were found in a house or on board of a ship, the burden of proving that it had never been part of the money of the realm was thrown on the owner. If he failed in making out a satisfactory account of every ingot he was liable to severe penalties. This Act was, as might have been expected, altogether ineffective. During the following summer and autumn, the coin went on dwindling, and the cry of distress from every county in the realm became louder and more piercing.

"But, happily for England, there were among her rulers some who clearly perceived that it was not by halters and branding-irons that her decaying industry and commerce could be restored to health. The state of the currency had, during some time, occupied the serious attention of four eminent men closely connected by public and private ties. Two of them were politicians who had never, in the midst of official and parliamentary business, ceased to love and honor philosophy; and two were philosophers in whom habits of abstruse meditation had not impaired the homely good sense without which even genius is mischievous in politics. Never had there been an occasion which more urgently required both practical and speculative abilities; and never had the world seen the highest practical and the highest speculative abilities united in an alliance so close, so harmonious, and so honorable as that which bound Somers and Montague to Locke and Newton. . . .

"In whatever way the restoration of the coin might be effected, great sacrifices must be made, either by the whole community or by a part of the community. And to call for such sacrifices at a time when the nation was at war, and was already paying taxes such as, ten years before, no financier would have thought it possible to raise, was undoubtedly a course full of danger. Timorous politicians were for delay; but the deliberate conviction of the great Whig leaders was that something must be hazarded, or that every thing was lost. Montague, in particular, is said to have expressed in strong language his determination to kill or cure. If, indeed, there had been any hope that the evil would merely continue to be what it was, it might have been wise to defer till the return of peace an experiment which must severely try the strength of the body politic. But the evil was one which daily made progress, almost visible to the eye. There might have been a recoinage in 1694 with half the risk which must be run in 1696; and great as would be the risk in 1696, that risk would be doubled if the recoinage were postponed till 1698.

"Those politicians whose voice was for delay gave less trouble than another set of politicians who were for a general and immediate recoinage, but who insisted that the new shilling should be worth only ninepence or ninepence halfpenny. At the head of this party was William Lowndes, Secretary of the Treasury, a most respectable and industrious public servant, but much more versed in the details of his office than in the higher parts of political philosophy. He was not in the least aware that a piece of metal with the king's head on it was a commodity of which the price was governed by the same laws which govern the price of a piece of metal fashioned into a spoon or a buckle, and that it was no more in the power of Parliament to make the kingdom richer by calling a crown a pound than to make the kingdom larger by calling a furlong a mile. He seriously believed, incredible as it may seem, that if the ounce of silver were divided into seven shillings instead of five, foreign nations would sell us their wines and their silks for a smaller number of ounces. He had a considerable following, composed partly of dull men who really believed what he told them, and partly of shrewd men who were perfectly willing to be authorized by law to pay a hundred pounds with eighty. Had his arguments prevailed, the evils of a vast confiscation would have been added to the other evils which afflicted the nation : public credit, still in its tender and sickly infancy, would have been destroyed, and there would have been much risk of a general mutiny of the fleet and army. Happily, Lowndes was completely refuted by Locke in a paper drawn up for the use of Somers. Somers was delighted with this little treatise, and desired that it might be printed. It speedily became the text book of all the most enlightened politicians in the kingdom, and may still be read with pleasure and profit." [1]

The proposition of Lowndes was for a recoinage of the currency with one-fifth less metal than the standard of the old coins ; to raise, to use his own words, " the value of the silver in the coins to the foot of 6s. 3d. in every crown, because the price of standard silver in bullion is risen to 6s. 5d. an ounce." Bullion, when purchased and paid for in the debased coins, had risen in ratio to their depreciation ; in other words, five light coins were required to purchase a given weight of bullion which could have been purchased by four coins of full weight. Locke was called upon to prove, and did prove most conclusively, that equal weights of silver were equal in value to equal weights of equal fineness ; and, consequently, that nothing could be gained, at home or abroad, by altering the standard, as the coins, both at home and abroad, would pass only at their value measured by weight and fineness. It would seem that the conclusions to which Locke came might have been assumed as axioms, from which he might have commenced his argument. If so, the statement of the ques-

---

[1] Macaulay's " History of England," vol. iv.

tion contains its own answer. Locke was not content with this. He prepared a pamphlet of more than a hundred pages, in which he reënforced his argument by a wealth and conclusiveness of illustration which should have put the question for ever at rest. He did, indeed, carry the government with him, but by no means the conviction of mankind. Strange as it may seem, he is, as will be hereafter shown, the only writer except Law, upon the subject of currency, who has not assumed, much less attempted to prove that two and two make five. At the time that he wrote, the Bank of England had just gone into operation, and his attention was only called to the subject of metallic money. He appears to have been the only person that has ever had any thing like correct ideas as to its nature and functions, and there can be little doubt that, had he sufficiently pursued the inquiry, he would have unfolded its true laws. He not only stands alone in the position he undertook to demonstrate, but he committed another unpardonable offence with the Schoolmen in asserting, to use the words of Adam Smith, " that gold and silver are the most solid and substantial part of the movable capital of a nation ; " or, to quote the words of Locke himself, that " the only way to bring treasure into England is the well ordering of our trade ; and, further, that the only way to bring silver and gold to the Mint, for the increase of our stock of money and treasure which shall stay here, is the overbalance of our whole trade. All other ways to increase our money and riches are but projects that will fail us." [1]

The plan of relief finally adopted by the English government provided that the money of the kingdom should be recoined according to the old standard of weight and fineness; that all the pieces should be milled, and that the loss on the clipped pieces should be borne by the public. A time was fixed after which no clipped money should pass, except in payments to the government, and a later time after which it should not pass at all. To provide for the loss on the clipped coins, the Bank of England undertook, on the security of the window tax, to advance the government £1,200,000. This advance, however, afforded but a partial relief. Full relief

[1] Locke's Works, vol. v. p. 253.

could only be had when the new silver (the metal then
chiefly in circulation) came in in sufficient abundance to fill
up the vacuum made by calling in the old.

"Saturday, the second of May," (1696), continues Lord Macaulay,
"had been fixed as the last day on which the clipped crowns, half-
crowns, and shillings were to be received by tale in payment of
taxes.   The Exchequer was besieged from dawn till midnight by
an immense multitude.   It was necessary to call in the guards for
the purpose of keeping order.   On the following Monday began a
cruel agony of a few months, which was destined to be succeeded
by many years of almost unbroken prosperity.

"Most of the old silver had vanished.   The new silver had
scarcely made its appearance.   About £4,000,000, in ingots and
hammered coin, were lying in the vaults of the Exchequer; and
the milled money as yet came forth very slowly from the Mint.
Alarmists predicted that the wealthiest and most enlightened kingdom in Europe would be reduced to the state of those barbarous
societies in which a mat is bought with a hatchet, and a pair of moc-
casins with a piece of venison.   There were, indeed, some hammered
pieces which had escaped mutilation, and sixpences not clipped
within the innermost ring were still current.   This old money and
the new money together made up a scanty stock of silver, which,
with the help of gold, was to carry the nation through the summer.
The manufacturers generally continued, though with extreme difficulty, to pay their workmen in coin.   The upper classes seem to
have lived to a great extent on credit.   Even an opulent man seldom
had the means of discharging the weekly bills of his baker and
butcher.   A promissory note, however, subscribed by such a man,
was readily taken in the district where his means and character
were well known.   The notes of the wealthy money-changers of
Lombard Street circulated widely.   The paper of the Bank of
England did much service. . . .

"The directors soon found it impossible to procure silver to meet
every claim which was made on them in good faith.   They then be-
thought them of a new expedient.   They made a call of twenty per
cent on the proprietors, and thus raised a sum which enabled them
to give every applicant fifteen per cent in milled money on what
was due to him.   They returned him his note, after making a
minute upon it that part had been paid.   A few notes thus marked
are still preserved among the archives of the Bank, as memorials of
that terrible year.   The paper of the corporation continued to circulate; but the value fluctuated violently from day to day, and
indeed from hour to hour; for the public mind was in so excitable
a state that the most absurd lie which a stock-jobber could invent
sufficed to send the price up or down.   At one time the discount
was only six per cent, at another time twenty-four per cent.   A
ten-pound note, which had been taken in the morning as worth
more than nine pounds, was often worth less than eight pounds
before night. . . .

" Meanwhile, strenuous exertions were making to hasten the re-coinage. Since the Restoration, the Mint had, like every other public establishment in the kingdom, been a nest of idlers and jobbers. The important office of Warden, worth between six and seven hundred a year, had become a mere sinecure, and had been filled by a succession of fine gentlemen who were well known at the hazard-table at Whitehall, but who never condescended to come near the Tower. This office had just become vacant, and Montague had obtained it for Newton. The ability, the industry, and the strict uprightness of the great philosopher speedily produced a complete revolution throughout the department which was under his direction. He devoted himself to his task with an activity which left him no time to spare for those pursuits in which he had surpassed Archimedes and Galileo. Till the great work was completely done, he resisted firmly, and almost angrily, every attempt that was made by men of science, either here or on the Continent, to draw him away from his official duties. The old officers of the Mint had thought it a great feat to coin silver to the amount of fifteen thousand pounds a week. When Montague talked of thirty or forty thousand, these men of form and precedent pronounced the thing impracticable. But the energy of the young Chancellor of the Exchequer and of his friend the Warden accomplished far greater wonders. Soon nineteen mills were going at once in the Tower. As fast as men could be trained to the work in London, bands of them were sent off to other parts of the kingdom. Mints were established at Bristol, York, Exeter, Norwich, and Chester. This arrangement was in the highest degree popular. The machinery and the workmen were welcomed to the new stations with the ringing of bells and the firing of guns. The weekly issue increased to sixty thousand pounds, to eighty thousand, to a hundred thousand, and at length to a hundred and twenty thousand. Yet even this issue, though great, not only beyond precedent, but beyond hope, was scanty when compared with the demands of the nation. Nor did all the newly stamped silver pass into circulation ; for during the summer and autumn those politicians who were for raising the denomination of the coin were active and clamorous ; and it was generally expected that, as soon as Parliament should reassemble, the standard would be lowered. Of course, no person who thought it probable that he should, at a day not far distant, be able to pay a debt of a pound with three crown pieces instead of four, was willing to part with a crown piece till that day arrived. Most of the milled pieces were, therefore, hoarded. May, June, and July passed away without any perceptible increase in the quantity of good money. It was not till August that the keenest observer could discern the first faint signs of returning prosperity."

Immediately following Locke, came the celebrated John Law, who, about the year 1700, published a treatise entitled " Money and Trade Considered," the object of which was to show that articles of property, other than silver, — the money then chiefly in circulation, — might be made into money, or might be made the basis for the issue of a paper money in place of one of silver, to the great advantage of the public, and particularly of Scotland, his own country, then one of the poorest in Europe. Law possessed an acute intellect, which, when not influenced by the purposes he had in view, was capable of mastering almost any subject toward which it might be directed. " The value of silver as money," he says, " is its value in barter." This statement covered the whole ground. In his familiarity with financial affairs, in the clearness and vigor of his style, and in his knowledge of the principles of metallic money, he has no superior but Locke. He is, in fact, the one who, next to Locke, can be studied with most interest and profit. Had he done no more than to write his " Money and Trade Considered," he would now be regarded as an oracle of wisdom, instead of being, as he is, an object of universal obloquy and contempt. He was a remarkable instance of the union of an idealist and a man of affairs. There is every reason to believe that he was prompted by a sincere desire to promote the welfare of his species. That he left France in a state of utter destitution, although he might have laid aside millions after seeing his ruin to be inevitable, — a fact which he urged in vindication of his motives, however much his judgment might have been at fault, — is at least proof of the disinterestedness of his nature.

"It is reasonable to think," says Law, "silver was bartered as it was valued for its uses as a metal, and was given as money according to its value in barter. The additional use of money silver was applied to would add to its value, because as money it remedied the disadvantages and inconveniences of barter, and consequently, the demand for silver increasing, it received an additional value equal to the greatest demand its use as money occasioned.

"And this additional value is no more imaginary than the value silver had in barter as a metal; for such value was because it served such uses, and was greater or lesser according to the demand for silver as a metal proportioned to its quantity. The additional value silver received from being used as money was because of its qualities which fitted it for that use, and that value was according to the additional demand its use as money occasioned.

"If either of these values are imaginary, then all value is so; for no goods have any value but from the uses they are applied to, and according to the demand for them, in proportion to their quantity. . . .

"Money is not a pledge, as some call it; it is a value paid, or contracted to be paid, with which it is supposed the receiver may, as his occasions require, buy an equal quantity of the same goods he has sold, or other goods equal in value to them; and that money is the most secure value either to receive, to contract for, or to value goods by, which is least liable to change in its value. . . .

"Thus silver having a value and qualities fitting it for money, which other goods had not, was made money, and, for the greater use of the people, was coined." [1]

Law was entirely right in assuming that the value of silver was its value in barter. He was mistaken, however, in asserting that it derives a value from its use as money, unless by its use as money he meant its use as reserves. The value of the precious metals in barter is made up of their value in the arts and their value as reserves. A person possessing perishable property seeks to convert it into that which has a more permanent value. If he can find something that is imperishable and at the same time in universal demand, he will pay for it a price greater than its value in the arts; in other words, the value of gold and silver, as determined by their value in the arts, would be less than it is, were it not for the demand for them as reserves. It is not their use as a medium of exchange that constitutes their value: it is their value in the arts and their capacity to serve as reserves that give them their value in exchange. They are simply used as money from their value for other purposes. To say that they are valuable because they are used as money, is only saying that they are valuable in barter because they are used in barter.

Although silver was the money in use, and although its value as such was its value in barter, Law, to provide a way for his new money, proceeded to show that the former, though in use, was very poorly adapted to serve as money: —

"Silver money is more uncertain in its value than other goods, so less qualified to serve as money.

"Goods of the same kind and quality differ in value from any change in their quality, or in the demand for them. In either of these cases goods are said to be dearer, or cheaper, being more or less valuable, and equal to a greater or lesser quantity of other goods, or of money.

"Silver in bullion or money changes its value from any change in its quantity, or in the demand for it. In either of these cases goods are said to be dearer or cheaper; but 'tis silver or money is dearer

<hr>

[1] Money and Trade Considered, Chap. I.

or cheaper, being more or less valuable, and equal to a greater or lesser quantity of goods.

"Perishable goods, as corns, &c., increase or decrease in quantity as the demand for them increases or decreases; so their value continues equal or near the same.

"More durable goods, as metals, materials for shipping, &c., increase in quantity beyond the demand for them, so are less valuable." [1]

The preceding paragraphs contain assumptions which are exactly opposed to the fact. The value of silver is uniform from the uniformity of its production and of the demand for it. Should there be some excess in production for one or more years, such excess would be taken up at previous prices to be held as reserves (so long as silver is legalized as money). A large increase of production will be absorbed in this manner. Unlike other merchandise, the market for silver is the world. Until the markets of the world are glutted, it cannot fall materially in value from increase of production. Corn is an indispensable article of food; but corn-consuming countries are corn-producing countries. The greater part of the excess in one country must be consumed within the country producing it. It cannot, from its perishable nature, be held as reserves. As the amount of product depends upon the seasons, and as it may be twice as great in one year as it was in the one preceding, its market value will be somewhat in ratio to its quantity; in other words will fluctuate violently from year to year. Metals and materials for ship-building are produced very slowly, and, as they can be held without injury for long periods, their prices are much more uniform than those of most articles of food, which must presently be consumed or become valueless to their holder. Although at the outset some of Law's propositions in reference to money were eminently sound, he was compelled to sacrifice them so soon as he began to unfold his scheme. Those who came after him were incapable of appreciating him where he was right, but were certain to follow him wherever he was wrong. It was from him that Adam Smith got the doctrine which he asserted with so much emphasis, that corn was a better measure of value than coin. Like Adam Smith, all the Economists have borrowed greatly from Law, from whom, from the disgrace at-

[1] Money and Trade Considered, Chap. V.

tached to his name, they could copy without reference and with impunity. They constructed, in great measure, from the ruins he left behind, their grotesque and absurd edifices. Materials which he put together in a symmetrical manner were by them wholly misconceived and misapplied.

The substitute for silver money proposed by Law was a paper money based upon lands. To provide for its issue Parliament was, —

"1. To authorize the Commission to lend notes on land security, the debt not exceeding one-half or two-thirds of the value, and at the ordinary interest.

"2. To give out the full price of land, as it is valued, 20 years' purchase, more or less, according to what it would have given in silver money; the Commission entering into possession of such lands by wadset granted to the Commission or assignees, and redeemable betwixt, and the expiring of a term of years.

"3. To give the full price of land upon sale made of such lands, and disposed to the Commission or assignees irredeemably. . . .

"The paper money proposed will be equal in value to silver, for it will have a value of land-pledge equal to the same sum of silver money, that is given out for. If any losses should happen, one-fourth of the revenue (interest on the notes) issued of the commission will, in all appearance, be more than sufficient to make them good.

"This paper money will not fall in value as silver money has fallen, or may fall: goods or money fall in value if they increase in quantity, or if the demand lessens. But the Commission giving out what sums are demanded, and taking back what sums are offered to be returned, this paper money will keep its value, and there will always be as much money as there is occasion or employment for, and no more. . . .

"Land has a more certain value than other goods, for it does not increase in quantity, as all other goods may. The uses of goods may be discharged, or by custom be taken from them, and given to other goods: the use of bread may be taken from oats and wholly given to wheat; the use of money may be taken from silver and given to land; the use of plate, and the other uses of silver, as a metal, may be taken from silver and given to some other metal or some mixture that may be more fitted for these uses. In any of these cases these goods lose a part of their value, proportioned to the uses that are taken from them; but land cannot lose any of its uses. For as every thing is produced by land, so the land must keep its value, because it can be turned to produce the goods that are in use. If wheat is more used, and oats less, as the land can produce both, it will be turned to produce what is most used, because most valuable." [1] . . .

---

[1] Money and Trade Considered, Chap. VII.

What would be the object of borrowers in getting Law's land notes? Not land, for they could get that by direct purchase. Their object would be to obtain coin, or merchandise, the equivalent of coin, — capital that could be used in their industries. Unless they could obtain one or the other of these, they would not receive the notes, giving their own obligations therefor. They could not come into the possession of the lands by which the notes were secured, as these would be held by the Commission issuing the notes. The latter, consequently, would be simply forms of debt, and to be realized upon would have to be sold in open market, and, certainly, at a very great discount. As the borrower would have to give his own bills equal in amount to the notes received, he might be giving that which might be valuable for that which might be almost wholly worthless. Whether, therefore, the notes were well secured or not, they could never get into circulation. To get out of this dilemma, Law was obliged to assume, to use his own words, that, —

" Money is not the value for which goods are exchanged, but the value by which they are exchanged. The use of money is to buy goods ; and silver, while money, is of no other use." [1]

In developing his scheme, Law had, undoubtedly, all the time, a sort of consciousness that his land money would not be received in exchange for other articles. As he could not give up his scheme, his principles had to give way to his necessities, and he was forced to assert the exact opposite to that which he had affirmed, and the truth of which he had conclusively demonstrated. Money, consequently, "was not the value *for* which goods were exchanged, but the value *by* which they were exchanged." It was the yardstick by which goods were measured off, — a contrivance to assist in numeration, — a tally or counter to register the delivery of certain quantities or values of merchandise ; in other words, value was not a necessary attribute of money.

" Though silver were our product," says Law, " yet it is not so proper to be made money as land. Land is what produces every

---

[1] Money and Trade Considered, Chap. VII.

thing; silver is only the product. Land does not increase or decrease in quantity; silver or any other product may: so land is more certain in its value than silver or any other goods.

"Land is capable of improvement, and the demand for it may be greater; so it may be more valuable. Silver cannot be supposed to be applied to any other uses than it is now applied to, or that the demand will increase more than the quantity.

"Land cannot lose any of its uses, so will not be less valuable. Silver may lose the uses of money it is now applied to, and so be reduced to its value as a metal.

"It may likewise lose a part of its uses as a metal, these uses being supplied by other goods; so loses a part of its value as a metal; but nothing can supply the uses of land.

"Land may be conveyed by paper, and thereby has the other qualities necessary in money, in a greater degree than silver.

"Land has other qualities fitting it for the use of money that silver has not.

"Land applied to the use of money does not lose any other uses it is applied to; silver cannot serve the use of money and any of its other uses as a metal. . . .

"When a nation establishes a money, if the money they set up have a value equal to what it is made money for, and all the other qualities necessary in money, they ought to have no regard what value it will have in other countries. On the contrary, as every country endeavors by laws to preserve their money, if that people can contrive a money that will not be valued abroad, they will do what other countries have by laws endeavored in vain.

"No nation keeps to silver because it is used in other countries: it is because they can find nothing so safe and convenient. Trade betwixt nations is carried on by exchange of goods, and if one merchant sends out goods of a less value than he brings home, he has money furnished him abroad by another who brings home for a less value than he sent out. If there is no money due abroad, then the merchant who designed to import for a greater value than he exported is restricted, and can only import equal to his export; which is all the many laws to regulate trade have been endeavoring."[1]

From what has been shown in that part of this work which treats of the Laws of Money, it would be superfluous here to controvert Law's assumption that whatever possesses value can be made into money; or that real property is the best basis of money because the least liable to fluctuate in value. A mortgage on real property may possess a high value, and yet have no other attributes fitting it to serve as money. The assertion that a nation should have no regard, in its money, to its trade with others, was undoubtedly wholly false to Law

[1] Money and Trade Considered, Chap. VII.

in his sober moments. He saw that his paper money would never pass abroad. He was driven consequently to assert that it was not necessary that it ever should pass abroad; that the domestic trade of a nation was alone to be considered. He took the short cut of throwing his principles overboard without the least compunction, whenever they came into conflict with his purposes. He was a man of action, who never stopped to explain, but pushed right forward to the object he had in view. For him to doubt and inquire would be to give up the contest altogether. His life was a mission to promote, in the first place, the welfare of his own country, by supplying it with money — capital; and every consideration was subordinate to this grand idea.

Law found no one who would entertain his schemes for a Land Bank. He succeeded, however, in 1716, in establishing, in France, a Bank with a cash capital of 6,000,000 francs, which he appears to have conducted, so long as he was able to keep clear of government, in a safe and legitimate manner. The great want of France at the time was precisely the institution which Law succeeded in establishing. Her finances were in a most disorganized condition. The securities of government were hardly worth one-third their nominal value. Her metallic currency had been constantly tampered with, by reducing its value, in order to enable the government to pay its debts at one-half or one-third the value at which they were contracted. From the social disorder which prevailed, it was in the highest degree hazardous to forward coin from one province to another. Law undertook to make the notes he issued payable in coin at its value at the time they were issued, and as he promptly paid them on presentation, they soon began to be preferred to coin, which was liable at any moment to be debased in value by a royal edict. His notes soon attained circulation in the provinces, as they were received with coin in the payment of the revenues of government. His Bank had hardly been in operation a year before the most striking and beneficial consequences were everywhere apparent. Trade was greatly improved, the revenues of the government were increased, and were more promptly paid, and Law was hailed as the benefactor, if not the saviour, of the nation.

Having found, at last, an adequate theatre for the exercise of the great abilities which he undoubtedly possessed, Law seems to have forgotten his Land Bank schemes altogether. He was accustomed to affirm that every banker who issued notes without proper provision for their conversion into coin was deserving of death. He held, however, that his notes could be made the basis of industrial enterprises, in addition to being the instruments for the distribution of that which enterprise and industry had already produced. His Bank, therefore, became the guarantor for the success of all such undertakings. If these failed, its capital became responsible for the loss sustained. Acting upon this principle, he held that Banks should engage in all kinds of commercial and industrial pursuits; that they should, in fact, in imitation of the great monopolies which governments at the time were accustomed to grant, merge in themselves the whole commerce and industry of the nation. Here was his fundamental error, and here the rock on which he made final shipwreck. One of his great projects was the Mississippi scheme, the greatest " Bubble " the world ever saw, which at last involved Law, his Bank, and France herself, in a common ruin. An account of this, as well as of Law's operations, does not come within the object of this work.

From the publication of Law's " Money and Trade Considered," the subject of money attracted little attention till 1752, when Mr. Hume published his "Essays on Civil and Political Economy." The Bank of England went on its even way, discounting business paper at the rate of five per cent, a rate that was hardly changed for a generation. In Hume, Aristotle found a pupil worthy the master, with this difference: Aristotle was one of the most truthful of men, while with Hume truth was a matter of secondary importance. There is an earnestness in Aristotle which attracts our sympathy, if it does not command our assent. There is a want of earnestness in Hume that repels our sympathy, even if we cannot controvert his conclusions. Hume, like Aristotle, assumed all his premises without consideration or reflection, and disposed, by a single stroke of his pen, of questions, to solve which by any proper method a lifetime might hardly suffice.

" Money," says Hume (by which he means gold and silver), " having chiefly a fictitious value, the greater or less plenty of it is of no consequence.[1] . . . It is not, properly speaking, one of the subjects

[1] Hume's Works, Essay on Interest (Am. ed.), vol. iii. p. 325.

of commerce, but only the instrument which men have agreed upon
to facilitate the exchange of one commodity for another. It is
none of the wheels of trade : it is the oil which renders the motion
of the wheels more smooth and easy. If we consider any one
kingdom by itself, it is evident that the greater or less plenty of
money is of no consequence.[1] . . . It is only the public (government) which draws any advantage from the greater plenty of
money, and that only in its wars and negotiations with foreign
States.[2] . . . The greater the number of people, and their greater
industry are serviceable in all cases at home and abroad, in private
and in public. But the greater plenty of money is very limited in
its use, and may even sometimes be a loss to the nation in its commerce with foreigners.[3] . . . And, in general, we may observe that
the dearness of every thing, from plenty of money, is a disadvantage
which attends an established commerce, and sets bounds to it in
every country by enabling the poorer States to undersell the richer
in all foreign markets. This has made me to entertain a doubt concerning the benefit of Banks and paper credits.[4] . . . That provisions
and labor should become dear by an increase of trade and money, is
in many respects an inconvenience, but an inconvenience that is unavoidable, and the effect of that public wealth and prosperity which
are the end of all our wishes. It is compensated by the advantages which we reap from the possession of these precious metals,
and the weight which they give the nation in all foreign wars and
negotiations. But there appears to be no reason for increasing that
inconvenience by a counterfeit money which foreigners will not
accept of in any payment, and which any great disorder in the State
will reduce to nothing.[5] . . . And in this view it must be allowed
that no Bank could be more advantageous than such a one as
locked up all the money it received (as was the case with the Bank
of Amsterdam), and never augmented the circulating coin, as is
usual, by returning a part of its treasure into commerce. A public
Bank by this expedient might cut off much of the dealings of
private bankers and money-jobbers; and though the State bore the
charge of their salaries to directors and tellers of this Bank (for
according to the preceding supposition it would have no profit
from its dealings), the national advantage resulting from the lower
price of labor and the destruction of paper credit would be a
sufficient compensation.[6] . . .

" It was a shrewd observation of Anacharsis, the Scythian, who
had never seen money in his own country, that gold and silver
seemed to him of no use to the Greeks but to assist them in numeration and arithmetic. It is, indeed, evident that money is nothing
but the representation of labor and commodities, and serves
only as a method of rating or estimating them. . . . It can have
no effect, either good or bad, taking the nation within itself; any
more than it would make an alteration upon the merchant's books

[1] Essay on Money, vol. iii, p. 309.   [2] Ibid.
[3] Ibid. p. 310.   [4] Ibid. p. 311.
[5] Ibid.   [6] Ibid. p. 312.

if, instead of the Arabian method of notation, which requires few
characters, he should make use of the Roman, which requires a great
many. Nay, the greater quantity of money, like the Roman characters, is rather inconvenient, and requires greater trouble to keep and
transport it. But, notwithstanding this conclusion, which must be
allowed just, it is certain that since the discovery of the mines of
America industry has increased in all the countries of Europe,
except in the possessors of those mines, and this may justly be
ascribed, among other things, to the increase of gold and silver.
. . . This is not easily accounted for if we consider only the influence which a greater abundance of coin has in the kingdom
itself, by heightening the price of commodities, and obliging every
one to pay a greater number of these little yellow or white pieces
for every thing he has to purchase. And as to foreign trade it
appears that a plenty of money is rather disadvantageous by raising the price of every kind of labor." [1]

Hume followed Law where the latter was wrong, and rejected him wherever he was right. The value of money, he
tells us, is fictitious; its greater or less quantity, therefore, is
of no consequence; nothing is to be gained by increasing the
dimensions of a fiction; it is not valuable to a country in its
commerce, for it is not the subject of commerce, only the oil
which lubricates its wheels. Is not that a subject of commerce,
the possession of which is the great object of commerce, and in
which all the profits or balances arising in commerce are payable? According to Hume, its quantity becomes of importance
only in negotiations and wars with other countries. But if it
were a fiction in England when he wrote, why was it not a fiction in France, with which England was at war? Is it a law of
human nature that that which is a pure fiction in one country
should be solid reality in another? Is not that valuable which
every people seek to obtain by exchanging therefor whatever
they possess; and which will always, at its cost, command all
other kinds of property?

In all respects, except in wars and negotiations, the abundance of money, says Hume, may be, and often is, a disadvantage, as prices are raised thereby in ratio to its abundance.
In this way, poor countries having no money are enabled to
undersell the rich having a great deal of money, and drive them
out of their accustomed markets. The exact reverse of all this
is the truth. Prices are either low in ratio to the abundance of
money, or, what is the same thing, the amount which a people

[1] Essay on Money, pp. 313, 314.

are able to consume is in ratio to such abundance. Cocoa-
nuts are very cheap in the interior of Africa, and dates in the
interior of Arabia ; but the people of those countries may consume nothing but cocoa-nuts and dates.   They hâve no means
of purchasing other articles, because they have no means of
transporting that which they possess to markets where it would
have a high value.   Had they plenty of money, merchants
could afford to supply them at very low rates from the certainty of being paid.   With such people, therefore, the price
of all imported articles would be in inverse ratio to the amount
of their money.   So with a symbolic currency, — with paper
money.   This is the representative of capital.   If one be
abundant the other must be ; and, if abundant, prices must be
low, for prices are high or low in ratio to the abundance
or want of the articles to which they relate.   Whatever the
form of money or currency, therefore, the greater the abundance, the lower are prices.   If merchandise that is made
the basis of production be low, the price of the product must
be low.   Cheapness of production is always in ratio to the
abundance of means applicable thereto.   Rich nations can,
and always do, undersell the poorer, by force of natural
laws.   Does Spain undersell England, or Mexico the United
States, in the markets of the world ?   Paper credits — that is
currencies — issued by Banks are one of the most important
conditions of low prices, as they serve as the cheapest possible
means of distribution.

    There is some compensation, says Hume, for the inconven-
ience of too great an abundance of coin, that it can be used in
foreign wars, but Bank paper can never be used out of the
country in which it is issued.   No reason, therefore, can
be urged to palliate its issue.   But does not the cost of articles
used in foreign wars, other than coin, exceed tenfold that of the
coin required ?   If they can be had by means of paper money,
equally with coin, does not the former possess for the government the same value as coin ?   Hume would have all Banks like
the Bank of Amsterdam, or an improvement upon that Bank.
His Banks should collect every thing into their vaults, and let
nothing out !   But how, in such case, are exchanges to be
effected ?   There must be either coin or symbols, or all commerce must speedily come to a dead stand.   In such event, a
people, in the course of a few months, would be reduced to the
very brink of ruin.

With Hume, gold and silver derive their importance to a nation solely from their use in its wars and negotiations. Considered by itself, their abundance is of no consequence whatever. Suppose all people constituted one nation, would not gold and silver be held in the same esteem and possess the same value that they do with the vast number of nationalities and races which exist? Would they not appeal in the same way to the sense of beauty in man? Would they not have the same value in the arts? Would they not still be the most valuable of all kinds of property? and by virtue of such value serve as reserves in which all accumulations are to be held, whether in possession, or in loans at interest? When the first lump of gold was exchanged for some other article of property, did the person who received it consider that the profit of the exchange would depend upon the value of his gold in countries other than his own? Hume might just as well have affirmed that the only importance and value of iron was in dealing with other nations; that to a nation considered by itself it was of no consequence whatever.

Hume asserts the value of money to be imaginary, and at the same time that a great abundance of it is injurious by raising the price of commodities. But what constitutes the value of any article? The amount of demand that exists for it. There can be no other test or measure. We can form no idea of the value of any article but by comparing it with that of some other. If it have no exchangeable value, it has no value. It may have uses, without having values. The water that a person drinks from a river is useful in sustaining his life, but it has no value in the proper sense of the term. An imaginary value, therefore, is no value; so that the very foundation upon which Hume erected his argument has no existence whatever. Only that which possesses value can affect the value of other things. If money had no value, its greater or less abundance could exert no influence whatever on the value or price of other articles. A little thought and reflection would have shown all this, but this way was not Hume's way. Reflection and analysis are laborious and painful processes, to which he was by no means inclined. To truth he was wholly indifferent. His object was effect, provided that could be produced by very little labor and pains.

" Were all our money, for instance, recoined," says Hume, " and a penny's worth of silver taken from every shilling, the new shilling would probably purchase every thing that could have been bought with the old; the prices of every thing would be insensibly diminished ; foreign trade enlivened ; and domestic industry, by the circulation of a greater number of pounds and shillings, would receive some increase and encouragement.   In executing such a project, it would be better to make the new shilling pass for twenty-four half-pence, in order to preserve the illusion, and to make it be taken for the same.   And as the recoinage of our silver begins to be requisite by the continual wearing of our shillings and sixpences, it may be doubtful whether we ought to imitate the example in King William's reign, when the clipped money was raised to the old standard." [1]

Never did a person draw a more graphic picture of himself than did Hume in the preceding paragraph. He would debase money, and at the same time maintain its value. He would maintain its value, and at the same time derive an advantage from its debasement in diminishing prices. In the same sentence, the value of money was to be both maintained and reduced. From diminished prices at home, foreign trade was to be enlivened, and domestic trade receive some increase and encouragement from the greater number of pounds and shillings in circulation. But how could more pounds and shillings be in circulation, if the debased coins would purchase as much as those of full weight and value ? In executing the project it would be better, he says, to make the " new shilling pass for twenty-four half-pence, in order to preserve the illusion and make it be taken for the same ; " and he suggests that at the next coinage his project should be carried out, naïvely remarking, that it was doubtful whether King William's example in restoring the coinage should be followed. With Hume, from the perversity or credulity of human nature, a falsehood plausibly told, and well stuck to, would have all the potency of truth. Of this, his own works afford a memorable illustration. He contrived by artful fabrications to falsify the whole course of English history, and to make the world believe, almost for a century, that slavery, not freedom, was the birthright of Englishmen. Any one, by taking the pains, might easily have shown that his history must have been wholly untrustworthy, from the careless and flippant manner in which he wrote upon other subjects.

[1] Essay on Money, p. 816.

" The necessary effect is," he continues, "that, provided the money increase not in a nation, every thing must become much cheaper in times of industry and refinement, than in rude and uncultivated ages. It is the proportion between the circulating money and the commodities in the market which determines the prices. . . . But after money enters into all contracts and sales, and is everywhere the measure of exchange, the same national cash has a much greater task to perform : all commodities are in the market ; the sphere of circulation is enlarged ; it is the same case as if that individual sum were to serve a larger nation ; and, therefore, the proportion being here lessened on the side of the money, every thing must become cheaper and the prices gradually fall. "[1]

The degree of wealth of a people depends upon their means of distribution. The one must always be in ratio to the other. Their money must increase as their industries increase, by a law as inexorable as that of gravity. Hume's assumption, therefore, that wealth and industry may increase, the amount of money remaining unchanged, is to assume a half to equal the whole. His plan for benefiting the public by reducing prices, by reducing the amount of money, is equivalent to taking off one-half of the cars from a railroad, where the whole had only sufficed for its operations. Such a process would reduce greatly the price or value of merchandise to the producer. It would, at the same time, add very largely to the price paid by the consumer. Both would be equally injured by the restricted capacity of the instrument of distribution. The former would receive much less ; the latter would pay much more. So with money. With its decrease, production would decrease in far greater ratio. With such decrease, cost of production would increase. These are not assertions, but laws. By Hume's reasoning, money has only to be abolished altogether to have prices reach their minimum, or rather for merchandise to have no value at all.

" I scarcely know any method," he continues, " of sinking money below its level, but those institutions of Banks, Funds, and Paper Credit, which are so much practised in this kingdom. These render paper equivalent to money, circulate it throughout the whole State, make it supply the place of gold and silver, raise proportionably the price of labor and commodities, and by that means either banish a great part of those precious metals, or prevent their further increase. What can be more short-sighted than our reasonings on this head ? We fancy, because an individual would be much richer were

[1] Essay on Money, p. 320.

his stock of money doubled, that the same good effect would follow were the money of every one increased; not considering that this would raise as much the price of every commodity, and reduce every man in time to the same condition as before. It is only in our public negotiations and transactions with foreigners that a greater stock of money is advantageous; and as our paper is there absolutely insignificant, we feel, by its means, all the ill effects arising from a great abundance of money without reaping any of the advantages." [1]

"Suppose there are £12,000,000 of paper which circulate in this kingdom as money; . . . and suppose the real cash of the kingdom to be £18,000,000. Here is a state which is found by experience to be able to hold a stock of £30,000,000. I say, if it be able to hold it, it must of necessity have acquired it in gold and silver, had we not obstructed the entrance of these metals by this new invention of paper. Whence would it have acquired that sum? From all the kingdoms of the world. But why? Because if you remove these £12,000,000, money in this state is below its level compared with its neighbors, and we must immediately draw from all of them, till we be full and saturate, so to speak, and can hold no more. By our present politics we are as careful to stuff the nation with this fine commodity of bank bills, and cheque-notes, as if we were afraid of being overburdened with the precious metals." [2] . . .

"What a pity Lycurgus did not think of paper credit when he wanted to banish gold and silver from Sparta! It would have served his purpose better than the lumps of iron he made use of as money; and would have prevented more effectually all commerce with strangers." [3]

" These institutions of Banks and Paper Credits render paper the equivalent of money," says Hume. It is the capital such paper represents that makes it the equivalent of money. By representing capital, and serving in the place of coin as the means of its distribution, it reduces instead of " raising propor-

---

[1] Essay on Balance of Trade, p. 397.

[2] Ibid., vol. iii. p. 348. As Aristotle deduced the laws of money from the baseness of its uses, it is not improbable that Hume reasoned, or was biased, in a similar manner. He was a thorough Tory, holding the trading and mechanic classes in indifference, if not contempt, which, like that of Aristotle, may have attached itself to their methods and implements. It was natural that he should have a Tory's spite against the Bank of England, as it was founded by the King and Parliament that expelled the Stuarts, to vindicate and uphold whom was the great object of his life; and as the Bank was one of the greatest supporters of liberal principles and of constitutional government in England. With such sentiments, he was much more likely to utter a sneer, than to enter upon an inquiry which would show the Bank to be one of the most beneficent instruments in promoting the progress of the nation.

[3] Ibid. p. 349.

tionably the price of labor and commodities." His assumption consequently is exactly opposed to the fact. "We fancy," he says, "because an individual would be much richer were his stock of money doubled, that the same good effect would follow were the money of every one increased." But would not every one be richer by having his money doubled? If it were in coin, it could be used as capital, and its possessor's means of consumption be doubled. Its price at home would be regulated by its price the world over, so that an increase in its amount in any one country would by no means affect in like ratio, and permanently, the price of other commodities. Suppose the iron and breadstuffs in a community to be doubled, would it not be all the better off? If a symbolic currency be doubled, would it not be evidence that the means of consumption were doubled? What is wealth but an abundance of such means? With Hume, money was not capital at home while it was capital abroad. It is the highest form of capital at home, for the reason that it is the highest form of capital abroad.

With Hume, the evil of paper money is, that it displaces a corresponding amount of coin, — sinks it below its level, compared with other countries. How did he ascertain this? England, at the time he wrote, with £18,000,000 of coin and £12,000,000 of bank notes, might have had more than its share of coin. Its paper currency, by assisting in the exchanges, may have secured to it a larger amount of coin than it would have had without such currency. His assumption, therefore, that the notes in circulation replaced a corresponding amount of coin is wholly gratuitous. It is from this assumption, however, that Economists have drawn their celebrated dogma or axiom that the proper measure of issue of paper money is the amount of gold that would have been in circulation but for such issue ; overlooking the fact that paper money is not based upon coin so much as upon merchandise ; and that the amount of the coin of a nation is to be measured not by that which it possesses, but by that which it can command. England may not have so much coin within her borders as France has within hers ; but in England every coin that can be spared is loaned. Her money is in every quarter of the globe. Were her loans all called in, she would have an amount of coin far exceeding that which France could command. The latter country is the land of revolutions, and the greater part of the population prefer, for their better security, to keep their own cash, instead of intrusting it to Banks or bankers.

Hume was one of the earliest writers to refer to the subject of currency to be issued by Banks. An opportunity was thus opened to him, had he chosen, by unfolding its nature and laws, of performing a substantial service for mankind. He preferred to talk rather than to investigate, — to appear wise and learned rather than to be so. The Bank of England, when he wrote, had been in operation nearly sixty years, and the currency it then issued was precisely similar in kind to that issued at the present day. He had, therefore, every condition necessary to the scientific investigation of money in all its forms. The establishment of the Bank was an era not only in the history of money, but in that of the race. It was the first attempt, on any considerable scale, to symbolize merchandise, — to provide instruments of distribution other than coin. Nothing was better fitted to excite interest and investigation than the nature of such instruments. It seems marvellous that no adequate attempt at their analysis should ever have been made. This is very largely due to the influence exerted by Hume. As the reputation enjoyed by Aristotle forbade all investigation of the truth of his dogmas, and secured for them immunity through the ages, so Hume impressed himself so strongly upon the opinions of mankind as to be received, for nearly a century, as authority upon most of the subjects upon which he wrote, although his works were full of errors and falsifications. He is still constantly quoted, with approbation, upon the knotty points of monetary science; although, as far as any knowledge of the subject was concerned, a Kaffir might as well be quoted for an authoritative opinion upon the Code of Menu.

The anomalous character of the Bank of England has undoubtedly opposed a very serious obstacle to progress in monetary science. It was founded not so much to provide more convenient instruments of distribution and exchange, as to supply the necessities of government, of which it has, since its organization, been one of the most important departments. Its mixed or double functions, as an issuer of currency and as the fiscal agent of the government, have been well calculated to avert attention from its real nature, with which its relation to the latter had nothing to do. Its success is a striking illustration of the naturalness and necessity of its functions as an instrument of commerce. It was, fortunately, at the outset, restricted in its dealings to commercial bills, and was required to pay all claims upon it, on demand, in coin. It needed no book or instruction to teach an Englishman to demand gold and silver in payment of whatever might be due him, — to act like a man of sense, whatever may have been told him in books, — to teach the first managers of the Bank that the only way in which they could avoid paying out coin in taking in their notes was to issue them only in the discount of solvent bills, and that the only competent evidence of solvency was that bills were given for merchandise in demand for consumption. The liberties of Englishmen have not been got out of books, nor maintained by any fine-spun theories as to the value of freedom, but by a stolid determination on the part of each one to enjoy whatever he possessed in the manner that best suited him. To this the whole nation have clung with bull-dog tenacity, deaf to all threats or appeals of Church or State. It is almost the only right sacred in their eyes. The only way in which their government could exert power was by the possession of money; and the only way by which it could come into possession of money was through the voluntary gifts of the people. As each one used his own in his own way, the freest play was given to the peculiarities of each; and, out of such free play, whatever is great or good in the nation has sprung.

From Hume we have no writer of eminence on the subject of currency till we come to Adam Smith, who published his celebrated work on the " Wealth of Nations," in 1776, twenty-four years after the publication of Hume's " Civil and Political Essays." The latter were simply monographs upon various questions included in the general term of Political Economy. Smith undertook to treat the whole subject scientifically, and, including his work on the Moral Sentiments, to map out and classify all the motives which influence human action.

" In the ' Moral Sentiments,' " says Buckle, " Smith investigates the sympathetic part of human nature; in the ' Wealth of Nations,' he investigates the selfish part. And as all of us are sympathetic as

well as selfish ; in other words, as all of us look without as well as
within, and as this classification is a primary and exhaustive division of our motives to action ; it is evident, that if Adam Smith
had completely accomplished his vast design, he would at once have
raised the study of human nature to a science, leaving nothing for
subsequent inquirers except to ascertain the minor springs of affairs,
all of which would find their place in this general scheme, and be
deemed subordinate to it. In his attempt to perform this prodigious
task, and to traverse the enormous field which he saw lying before
him, he soon perceived that an *inductive* investigation was impossible, because it would require the labor of many lives even to assem-
ble the materials from which the generalization was to be made.
Moved by these reflections, and probably moved still more by the
intellectual habits which prevailed around him, he resolved on
adopting the deductive method instead of the inductive." [1]

It will thus be seen that Smith attempted an infinitely wider
task than Aristotle, and by precisely similar methods. The
latter had no conception whatever of those great questions
which now engross the attention of mankind. He had no idea
of social and moral progress as its highest condition and law.
For the ancients humanity had no claims. Aristotle was unable to raise himself above the low level of his age and race.
When his attention was turned to physical phenomena, the
great field open to him, he could, for the want of adequate
methods, make no progress whatever. If with so few questions, compared with those which pressed upon Smith, Aristotle made such an utter and disastrous failure, how was it to
be expected that the former, with no better methods, with a
far less acute intellect, and with infinitely more numerous and
difficult problems, could otherwise than share the fate of his
great master? The objects as well as the methods of the two
were almost precisely similar. Aristotle undertook to construct an universal science, and to pronounce authoritatively
upon every subject coming within the range of human observation, — subjects for the solution of a vast number of which, a
lifetime, with the best of training and helps, would have been
far too short. The still vaster undertaking of Smith left him
no alternative but to apply the Aristotelian method — that
of dialectics — to subjects which yield only to the most patient analysis, and in this way, by a stroke of his pen, to dispose of questions which have required years, if not cycles, to
solve. Like those of Aristotle, his teachings upon some of the

[1] History of Civilization in England, vol. ii. page 341, American edition.

most important subjects that concern the welfare of the race have been accepted without reserve, while the comments upon them by his followers have only served to perpetuate, and involve in still greater uncertainty and confusion, the errors and absurdities they contain.

It comes within the scope of this work to discuss only that part of Smith's " Wealth of Nations " that relates to the subject of money. Of the origin and nature of this he gives the following account : —

" When the division of labor has been thoroughly established, it is but a very small part of man's wants which the produce of his own labor can supply. He supplies the far greater part of them by exchanging that surplus part of the produce of his own labor, which is over and above his own consumption for such part of the produce of other men's labor as he has occasion for. Every man thus lives by exchanging, or becomes in some measure a merchant ; and society itself grows to be what is properly a commercial society. But, when the division of labor first began to take place, this power of exchanging must frequently have been very much clogged and embarrassed in its operations. One man, we shall suppose, has more of a certain commodity than he himself has occasion for, while another has less. The former, consequently, would be glad to dispose of, and the latter to purchase, a part of this superfluity. But, if this latter should chance to have nothing that the former stands in need of, no exchange can be made between them. The butcher has more meat in his shop than he himself can consume, and the brewer and the baker would each of them be willing to purchase a part of it ; but they have nothing to offer in exchange except the different productions of their respective trades, and the butcher is already provided with all the bread and beer which he has immediate occasion for. No exchange can, in this case, be made between them. He cannot be their merchant, nor they his customers ; and they are all of them thus mutually less serviceable to one another. In order to avoid the inconvenience of such situations, every prudent man, in every period of society, after the first establishment of the division of labor, must naturally have endeavored to manage his affairs in such a manner as to have at all times by him, besides the peculiar produce of his own industry, a certain quantity of some one commodity or other, such as he imagined few people would be likely to refuse in exchange for the produce of their industry.

" Many different commodities, it is probable, were successively both thought of and employed for this purpose of exchange. In the rude ages of society, cattle are said to have been the instrument of commerce, and though they must have been a most inconvenient one, yet, in old times, we find things were frequently valued according to the number of cattle which had been given in exchange for them. The arms of Diomede, says Homer, cost only nine oxen, but that of Glaucus cost an hundred oxen. Salt is said to be the common instrument of commerce and exchanges in Abyssinia; a species of shells in some parts of the coast of India; dried cod at Newfoundland; tobacco in Virginia; sugar in some of our West India colonies; hides, or dressed leather, in some other countries; and there is at this day a village in Scotland where it is not uncommon, I am told, for a workman to carry nails, instead of money, to the baker's shop or to the ale-house.

" In all countries, however, men seem at last to have determined, by irresistible reasons, to give preference to metals above every commodity. Metals can be not only kept with as little loss as any other commodity, scarce any thing being less perishable than they are, but they can likewise, without any loss, be divided into any number of parts, as by fusion those parts can easily be reunited again, — *a quality which no other equally durable commodities possess, and which, more than any other qualities, renders them fit to be the instruments of commerce and circulation.* . . .

" Different metals have been made use of by different nations for this purpose. Iron was the common instrument of commerce among the ancient Spartans; copper among the ancient Romans; gold and silver among all rich and commercial nations. . . .

" The use of the metals in their rude state was attended with two very considerable inconveniences: first, the trouble of weighing, and, secondly, that of assaying them. In the precious metals, where a small difference in the quantity makes a great difference in value, even the business of weighing with proper exactness requires at least very accurate weights and scales. . . . The operation of assaying is still more difficult and still more tedious. . . . To prevent such abuses and facilitate exchanges and thereby to encourage all sorts of industry and commerce, it has been found necessary, in all countries that have made any considerable advances toward improvement, to affix a public stamp upon certain quantities of such particular metals as were in those countries commonly made use of to purchase goods. Hence the origin of coined money, and of those public offices called Mints. . . .

" It is in this manner that money has become, in all civilized nations, the universal instrument of commerce, by the intervention of which goods of all kinds were bought and sold, or exchanged for one another. What are the rules which men naturally observe in exchanging them, either for money or for one another, I shall now proceed to examine. These rules determine what may be called the relative or exchangeable value of goods." [1]

From what has preceded, it will be seen that Smith fell into precisely the error of those who hold governments to have arisen, from a sense of their necessity, out of compacts formally proposed by the people, and entered into between the governments and the governed. Such writers imagine the people to

---

[1] Wealth of Nations, Book i. Chap. iv.

say: "We cannot get on any longer in this way. We must have a government to maintain order, protect property, and administer upon a great number of matters that concern the public welfare." So, says Smith, the butcher has more meat in his shop than he himself can consume, and of which the brewer and baker would each of them be willing to purchase a part, but they have nothing to offer in exchange except the different productions of their respective trades. The butcher, however, being already provided with all the bread and beer he has immediate occasion for, no exchange of commodities can take place between them. They, therefore, — the butcher, baker, and brewer of primitive times, — being at a dead-lock, put their heads together, and invented money, which each, and society as well, agreed to receive in exchange for whatever each had to sell.

In his illustrations, Smith, like the advocates of the "original compact," has inverted the whole order of Nature, — or of human development. Mankind never speculated upon governments, upon their necessity, or upon the modes of their organization and administration, until ages after governments, and powerful ones too, had existed. Smith committed the common error in assuming the conditions and operations which he saw about him to reflect those which took place while the race was in its infancy. If money, from any cause, had suddenly disappeared from his own country, he would, with others, have undertaken, from a sense of its necessity, to provide a new supply. What he and his associates would have done he supposed were the means by which money was first brought into use. But the early state or condition which he describes as leading to the use of money is purely mythical. Commerce, in the outset, resulted from no plan or method. It never occurred to any one to save or accumulate till he saw some object that took his fancy, and was told he could have it in exchange for some article which he could produce or acquire by his own labor. The motive had always to be first supplied. The most powerful incentive of all was the desire to possess the precious metals, which were undoubtedly among the first acquisitions of all races capable of civilization. Those articles which appeal most strongly to the sense of beauty in man, not those that discharge the primary wants of his nature, alone supply adequate motives to continued exertion — to those industries upon which civilization rests. Had man felt no other want than for food, he could have had no other existence than an animal one. Had the precious metals been found in any greater abundance at any time than they have been, their possession would not have required that persistent labor so necessary to his highest moral as well as material welfare. As they were indestructible, as well as in universal demand, their possessor, as far as they would go, became at once the master of the property and services of others who possessed them in a less degree. With their discovery, the power of acquisition, on any thing like a scale sufficient to constitute wealth or civilization, was for the first time secured to the race. Without them, a person in possession of herds, or of the productions of Nature, unlimited in number or quantity, might not be able to supply himself with a single article of which he might stand in need other than that which he possessed. As the precious metals in primitive times stood in precisely the same relations to the nature and wants of man that they do to-day, they served on their first discovery precisely as they do to-day, as money in trade. Discussion and agreement had nothing more to do with their adoption as money than they had with the adoption of eating as a means of sustaining life, or of clothing to protect from the cold. Nothing like an "instrument of commerce" was ever thought or conceived of. With the precious metals, all the conditions necessary for division of labor were supplied long before the necessity or importance of such division was felt, much less thought of. No mission or duty was ever assigned to the race till all the conditions for its fulfilment had been amply and generously supplied. To assume otherwise would be to impugn both Divine power and goodness. Man, in every stage of his progress, could always command the precious metals in abundance, provided he was possessed of a plenty of other articles in demand for consumption. The primitive butcher and baker were never in want of a circulating medium so long as there was a demand for their meat or bread. The existence of butchers and bakers implies division of labor and a highly advanced social condition, which would have been impossible but for the previous use of the precious metals as the universal solvents of transactions. They complained of the want of money, of a "circulating medium," only when the market was overstocked with their own particular goods.

Oxen, according to Smith, were money among the Greeks; tobacco among the Virginia colonists; dried cod in Newfoundland; and sugar in the West Indies. Such assertions are absurdities on their face. The use of all such articles in exchange, the one for the other, is simple barter, and can never be any thing else. An ox that is exchanged for a certain quantity of sheep is no more rendered money by such act of exchange than it is converted into the sheep. To call sheep or oxen, or tobacco money, is to say that oxen are sheep, or tobacco is gold and silver. They never were used as money, and they never can be used as money. Money is the universal equivalent, always accepted at its cost, for whatever a person has to sell. There can be no other definition of it. All other articles may or may not be accepted as such equivalents. A person who has an ox for sale will take nothing but money, unless he wishes to deal in simple barter, which is the exception, not the rule. He would gain nothing by exchanging it for a horse, or for sheep. He could barter his ox now with much less difficulty than in ancient times. He might not find it very difficult to dispose of its various parts, in such cities as New York and London, for such articles as he might wish to acquire. But had all parties possessed of merchandise no other modes of effecting their exchanges but those in kind, society would be speedily remitted to its original condition of barbarism. It may often happen that oxen, tobacco, codfish, and sugar may be largely received in exchange for what a person has to sell, to be held by him till they can be converted into money, just as they were produced to be converted into money. It makes no difference to their possessor whether they are acquired at first or second hand. The object is the same in either case. Their acceptance in barter does not make them money. A country shopkeeper may barter a portion of his stock for produce, which he transports to market, and there converts into money. But this process does not make either the goods money, or the produce money. He may "make money," as the phrase is, or he may be ruined by the fall of that for which he exchanges his goods. He can never tell the extent of his losses or profits till he has converted that which he has received into money.

The radical error, however, of Smith, with all his school, was the distinction which he made between money (gold and silver) and capital. "In all countries," he tells us, "men seem, at last, to have been determined, by irresistible reasons, to give preference for this employment to metals above every other commodity. Metals cannot only be kept with as little loss as any other commodity, but they can likewise, without loss, be divided into any number of parts ; as, by fusion, these parts can easily be reunited again, — *a quality which, more than any other quality, renders them fit to be the instruments of commerce and circulation.*" The intrinsic value of money (gold and silver), depending upon a preference which universally prevails for them, together with the regularity of their supply, — qualities by virtue of which they serve as money, — Smith wholly overlooked. With him their divisibility and capacity to be reunited, not their value, chiefly fitted them to serve as such. In this distinction between money and capital, Smith implicitly followed Aristotle and Hume ; and he has been implicitly followed by all subsequent writers in the assumption, that even the most worthless articles may serve as money, and be maintained at the par value of coin, provided they do not exceed in amount that necessary to effect the exchanges of the community using them.

From the distinction made between money and capital, it was natural that Smith should consider coinage as an essential quality of money. "It has been found necessary," he says, "in all countries that have made any considerable advance toward improvement, to affix a public stamp upon certain quantities of such particular metals as were in those countries commonly made use of to purchase goods." He was either ignorant of or overlooked the fact, that coinage was wholly unknown to the great nations of antiquity, — the Egyptians, Chaldeans, and Phœnicians. All history bears witness to the vastness of their commerce and wealth. Coinage is a very valuable contrivance ; but, in all great transactions at the present day, coins pass by weight, not by tale. In this way they pass at their actual, not at their denominational, value. The ancients were unquestionably experts in the refining of metals, and had all the means necessary for ascertaining their value by their weight.

As Smith made a wide distinction between money and capital, yet, as money was the standard by which all other articles were measured, he was necessarily driven to another distinction, equally absurd, — that of the real and nominal prices of commodities. Labor was the measure of their real value or price; money, of their nominal value. To use his own words : —

"But though labor be the real measure of the exchangeable value of all commodities, it is not that by which their value is commonly estimated. It is often difficult to ascertain the proportion between two different quantities of labor. The time spent in two different sorts of work will not always alone determine this proportion. The different degrees of hardship endured, and of ingenuity exercised, must likewise be taken into account. There may be more labor in an hour's hard work than in two hours' easy business ; or in an hour's application to a trade which it cost ten years' labor to learn, than in a month's industry at an ordinary and obvious employment. But it is not easy to find any accurate measure, either of hardness or ingenuity. In exchanging, indeed, the different productions of different sorts of labor for one another, some allowance is commonly made for both. It is adjusted, however, not by any accurate measure, but by the higgling and bargaining of the market ; according to that sort of rough equity, which, though not exact, is sufficient for carrying on the business of daily life. Every commodity, besides, is more frequently exchanged for, and thereby compared with, other commodities than with labor. It is more natural, therefore, to estimate its exchangeable value by the quantity of some other commodity than by that of the labor which it can purchase. The greater part of people, too, understand better what is meant by a quantity of a particular commodity than by a quantity of labor. The one is a plain, palpable object ; the other is an abstract notion, which, though it can be made sufficiently palpable, is not altogether so natural and obvious." [1]

The preceding paragraph refutes his own cardinal proposition, that labor is the proper measure of values. While assuming that labor is the measure of value, it is impossible, Smith tells us, that it should be a measure of value, for the reason that one hour's labor of one man may have a value equal to ten hours' labor of another man similarly employed ; and that, consequently, the true measure of value cannot be the conventional one, — that the true measure of value is an

[1] Wealth of Nations, Book i., Chap. v.

abstract notion, — that the conventional measure is a plain, palpable object. How can there be abstract measures of any thing? What is an abstract foot, yard, pound weight, dollar, or an abstract quantity of labor? All these are concrete, real things. Abstractions are not the subjects which men buy and sell. Why not accept the fact as proving what it does prove? That Smith in a single paragraph could assert a law, and at the same time show no such law to be possible, is evidence of such a want of the reasoning faculty as to throw a well-grounded distrust over all his conclusions, no matter the questions of which he may treat.

" When barter ceases, and money becomes the common instrument of commerce, every particular commodity is more frequently exchanged for money than for any other commodity. The butcher seldom carries his beef or mutton to the baker or brewer, in order to exchange them for bread or for beer ; but he carries them to the market, where he exchanges them for money, and afterwards exchanges that money for bread or for beer. The quantity of money he can get for them regulates, too, the quantity of bread or beer which he can afterwards purchase. It is more natural and obvious to him, therefore, to estimate their value by the quantity of money, — the commodity for which he exchanges them, — than by that of bread and beer, — the commodities for which he can exchange them only by the intervention of another commodity ; and rather to say that his butcher's meat is worth threepence or fourpence a pound, than that it is worth three or four pounds of bread or three or four quarts of small beer. Hence it comes to pass, that the exchangeable value of every commodity is more frequently estimated by the quantity of money than by the quantity either of labor or of any other commodity which may be had in exchange for it."[1]

" When barter ceases," says Smith, " money becomes the common instrument of commerce." Barter never ceases. There is an incomparably greater amount of barter in a civilized than in an uncivilized age, — when there are butchers and bakers than before. The exchange of money for bread or beer is just as much an act of barter as an exchange of bread for beer. As equal values are exchanged when money is used, that for which it is exchanged is just as much the instrument of commerce as the money. With Smith, however, money was not the subject, only the instrument, of commerce, like the yardstick or the railroad car, the value of which bears no

---

[1] Wealth of Nations, Book i., Chap. v.

relation to the value of the articles to be measured or transferred. To be the subject of commerce, it must, like all
other subjects, have a real equal to its nominal value. Figures
are the instruments, not the subjects, of commerce. So, with
Smith, money was the instrument, not the subject, of commerce. It had value; but it was not chiefly by means of that
value that it served as a medium of exchange.

From the discussion of the distinction between real and
nominal prices, Smith proceeds to show its importance in
practice.

"Gold and silver, like every other commodity, vary in value;
are sometimes cheaper and sometimes dearer, sometimes of easier
and sometimes of more difficult purchase. . . . But as a measure
of quantity, such as the natural foot, fathom, or handful, which is
continually varying in its own quantity, can never be an accurate
measure of the quantity of other things; so a commodity which is
itself constantly varying in its own value can never be an accurate measure of the value of other commodities. Equal quantities
of labor, at all times, may be said to be of equal value to the
laborer." . . .

"When a landed estate, therefore, is sold with a reservation of
perpetual rent, if it is intended that this rent should always be of
the same value, it is of importance to the family in whose favor it
is reserved that it should not consist in a particular sum of money.
. . . Rents which have been reserved in corn have preserved their
value much better than those which have been reserved in money,
even where the denomination of the coin has not been altered.
By the 18th of Elizabeth it was enacted, that a third of the rents
of all the college leases should be reserved in corn, to be paid
either in kind or according to the prices at the nearest public
market; the money arising from this corn rent, though originally
but one-third of the whole, is in the present time, according to
Blackstone, commonly near double what arises from the other two-
thirds. The old money-rents of colleges must, according to this
account, have sunk to almost a fourth part of their ancient value,
or are worth a little more than a fourth part of the coin which they
were formerly worth. But, since the reign of Philip and Mary, the
denomination of the English coin has undergone little or no alteration. This depreciation, therefore, in the value of money rents of
colleges has arisen altogether from the depreciation in the value of
silver (money). A rent, therefore, reserved in corn is liable only
to the variations in the quantity of labor which a certain quantity
of corn can purchase; but a rent reserved in any other commodity
is liable not only to the variations in the quantity of labor which
any particular quantity of corn can purchase, but to the variations
in the quantity of corn which can be purchased by any particular
quantity of that commodity.

" Though the real value of a corn rent, it is to be observed, however, varies much less from century to century than that of a money
rent, it varies much more from year to year. But the value of
silver, though it sometimes varies greatly from century to century,
seldom varies much from year to year ; but frequently continues the
same, or very nearly the same, for a half century or a century : the
ordinary or average money price of corn, therefore, may, during so
long a period, continue the same or very nearly the same, too, and
along with it the money price of labor; provided, at least, the
society continues in other respects in the same or nearly in the same
condition. In the mean time, the temporary and occasional price
of corn may frequently be double one year of what it had been the
year before, or fluctuate, for example, from twenty-five to fifty
shillings the quarter. But, when corn is at the latter price, not only
the real but the nominal value of the corn rent will be double of
what it is at the former, or will command double the quantity
either of labor or of the greater part of other commodities ; the
money price of labor, and along with it that of most other things,
continuing the same during all these fluctuations.

" Labor, therefore, it appears, evidently is the only universal as
well as the only accurate measure of value, or the only standard
by which we can compare the value of different commodities at all
times and places. We cannot estimate, it is allowed, the real value
of commodities from century to century by the quantities of silver
which can be given for them. We cannot estimate it from year to
year by the quantities of corn. By quantities of labor we can,
with the greatest accuracy, estimate it both from century to century
and from year to year. From century to century corn is a better
measure than silver, because from century to century equal quantities of corn will command the same quantity of labor more
nearly than equal quantities of silver. From year to year, on the
contrary, silver is a better measure than corn, because equal quantities of it will more nearly command the same quantity of
labor. . . .

" As it is the nominal or money price of goods, therefore, which
finally determines the prudence or imprudence of all purchases or
sales, and thereby regulates almost the whole business of common
life in which price is concerned, we cannot wonder it should have
been so much more attended to than the real price." [1]

Smith has already demonstrated it to be impossible that
labor should be the measure of value; yet he continually
repeats that it is the only true measure. As that cannot be
used, corn, he says, is a much better measure of value than
coin. This assertion, like the previous one, is contradicted by
the whole experience of society. If corn were a more accurate measure of value than coin, it would have been adopted

[1] Wealth of Nations, Book i., Chap. v.

as such. That it never has been adopted is proof that coin is the better measure. His assertion that the price of coin has fluctuated through long periods more than that of corn is not supported by a particle of evidence. No one has ever hesitated to enter into contracts payable in coin, no matter the time that was to elapse before they were to mature. No one would ever enter into contracts, the consideration or value of which was to be measured by corn, from an entire uncertainty as to its future value. This is decisive of the whole question. Coin is the better measure of values, because its value is more uniform. The illustration he uses, the leases of the college lands, proves the exact opposite of that which he assumed it to prove. With him, corn should be made a measure of value, from the greater uniformity of its value than that of coin. The leases should be made payable in corn, for the reason that it was certain to appreciate much more rapidly in value than coin, securing a corresponding advantage to the landlord. Here is another palpable contradiction almost in the same paragraph. In order to prove the depreciation in the value of silver, Smith should have shown it to have fallen in value in reference to other kinds of merchandise or property as well as food. It might require twice the weight of silver to purchase in his day a given quantity of corn that it did two centuries previous; but one-half or one-quarter of the weight of silver might purchase twice the quantity of iron, or of other articles entering into domestic economy, that it would in the sixteenth century. What does this prove? Not that the value of silver had changed; but that other articles had fallen in price, from their reduced cost of production. The increase of population in England may have increased the value of food, while such increase, from the better combination and direction of industries, may have greatly reduced the price of other articles. It is, therefore, just as proper to infer that the price of silver has appreciated from the fall in value of other articles than food, as that it has depreciated from the increase in the price of food. As the price of the greater part of articles entering into consumption is far lower than it was three hundred years ago, the evidence, if such reduction be evidence, is altogether on the side of an appreciation of the value of gold and silver. The rise or fall of commodities, however, proves nothing on either side. The value of coin depends upon its cost; that of all other articles, upon demand and cost. To prove the appreciation or depreciation of money, its price or value, which measures its cost, should be compared with the price of other articles whose cost has remained unchanged for long periods of years, or whose cost has changed no more than the cost of producing gold and silver; but all such comparisons amount to nothing, from the want of adequate data upon which they can be based. Whatever may be the fact, however, a little reflection should have shown Smith that no advantage could be gained from the application of his distinction between nominal and real price. If it were for the interest of lessors of lands to have their rents payable in corn, it would be equally against the interest of the lessees; and as it takes two to make a bargain, no lease would ever be made upon the terms suggested. Nothing can be more puerile than such illustrations and arguments. Of course, there is little use in replying to them, and they are referred to chiefly for the purpose of showing the total inadequacy of Smith's premises, and the absurdity of his conclusions from them.[1]

From the discussion of the distinction between real and nominal prices, Smith proceeds, in the second chapter of the second book of his " Wealth of Nations," to that of metallic and paper money; or, to use his own words, " money considered as a particular branch of the general stock of society, or the expense of maintaining the national capital."

" It has been shown in the first book " (that on division of labor), says Smith, " that the price of the greater part of commodities resolves itself into three parts : one of which pays the wages of the laborer; another, the profits of the stock; and a third, the rent of the land which had been employed in producing and bringing them to market. . . . The price of every commodity necessarily resolves itself into some one or other or all of these three parts. Every part of it which goes neither to rent or to wages being necessarily profit to somebody.

[1] Smith's assumption, which is awkwardly interpolated into his chapters on money, that corn is a better measure of value than coin, is wholly borrowed, and without acknowledgment, from Law, with this difference, that, while Law states the argument most fully in a single paragraph, Smith drags the reader through page after page of incoherent and inconclusive assertions, utterly foreign to his main argument, and winds up by proving the very opposite of the proposition with which he started.

" Since this is the case, it has been observed, with regard to every particular commodity taken separately, it must be so with regard to all the commodities which compose the whole annual produce of the land and labor of every country, taken complexly. The whole price or exchangeable value of that annual produce must resolve itself into the same three parts, and be parcelled out among the different inhabitants of the country, either as the wages of their labor, the profits of their stock, or the rent of their land.

" But though the whole value of the annual produce of the land and labor of every country is thus divided among, and constitutes a revenue to, its different inhabitants, . . . yet as in the rent of a private estate we distinguish between the gross and the neat rent, so we may likewise in the revenue of all the inhabitants of a great country. The gross rent of a private estate comprehends whatever is paid by the farmer ; the neat rent, what remains free to the landlord after deducting the expenses of management, of repairs, and all other necessary charges, or what, without hurting his estate, he can afford to place in his stock reserved for immediate consumption, or to spend upon his table, equipage, the ornaments of his house, his private enjoyments and amusements. His real wealth is in proportion, not to his gross, but to his neat, rent.

" The gross revenue of all the inhabitants of a great country comprehends the whole annual produce of their land and labor ; the neat revenue, what remains free to them after deducting the expense of maintaining, first, their fixed, and, secondly, their circulating, capital ; or what, without encroaching upon their capital, they can place in their stock reserved for immediate consumption, or spend upon their subsistence, conveniences, and amusement. Their real wealth, too, is in proportion, not to their gross, but to their neat, revenue.

" The whole expense of maintaining the fixed capital must evidently be excluded from the neat revenue of society. Neither the materials necessary for supporting their useful machines and instruments of trade, their profitable buildings, &c., nor the produce of the labor necessary for fashioning these materials into proper form, can ever make any part of it.

" The expense of maintaining the fixed capital of a great country may very properly be compared to that of repairs in a private estate : the expense of repairs may be frequently necessary for supporting the produce of the estate, and, consequently, both the gross and the neat rent of the landlord. When, by a more proper direction, however, it can be diminished without occasioning any diminution of produce, the gross rent remains at least the same as before, and the neat rent is necessarily augmented.

" But, though the whole expense of maintaining the fixed capital is thus necessarily excluded from the neat revenue of society, it is not the same case with that of maintaining the circulating capital. Of the four parts of which this latter capital is composed, — money, provisions, materials, and finished work, — the three last, it has already been observed, are regularly withdrawn from it, and placed either in the fixed capital of the society, or in their stock reserved for immediate consumption. Whatever portion of these consumable goods is not employed in maintaining the former, goes all to the latter, and makes a part of the neat revenue of the society. The maintenance of these three parts of the circulating capital, therefore, withdraws no portion of the annual produce from the neat revenue of the society, besides what is necessary for maintaining the fixed capital.

" The circulating capital of a society is in this respect different from that of an individual. That of an individual is wholly excluded from making any part of his neat revenue, which must consist altogether in his profits. But, though the circulating capital of every individual makes a part of that of the society to which he belongs, it is not upon that account totally excluded from making a part likewise of their neat revenue. Though the whole goods in a merchant's shop must by no means be placed in his own stock reserved for immediate consumption, they may in that of other people's, from whom a revenue derived from other funds may regularly replace their value to him, together with its profits, without occasioning any diminution either of his capital or of theirs.

" Money, therefore, is the only part of the circulating capital of a society of which the maintenance can occasion any diminution in their neat revenue.

" The fixed capital, and that part of the circulating capital which consists in money, so far as they affect the revenue of society, bear a very great resemblance to one another.

" As those machines and instruments of trade, &c., require a certain expense, first to erect them, and afterwards to support them, both of which expenses, though they make a part of the gross, are deductions from the neat, revenue of society : so the stock of money which circulates in any country must require a certain expense, first to collect it, and afterwards to support it ; both which expenses, though they make a part of the gross, are in the same manner deductions from the neat, revenue of the society. A certain quantity of very valuable materials, gold and silver, and of very curious labor, instead of augmenting the stock reserved for immediate consumption, — the subsistence, convenience, and amusement of individuals, — is employed in supporting that great but expensive instrument of commerce by means of which every individual in the society has his subsistence, conveniences, and amusements regularly distributed to him, in their proper proportions.

" As the machines and instruments of trade, &c., which compose the fixed capital either of an individual or of society, make no part of the gross or of the neat revenue of either, so money, by means of which the whole revenue of society is regularly distributed among its different members, makes itself no part of that revenue. The great wheel of circulation is altogether different from the goods which are circulated by means of it. The revenue of society consists altogether in those goods, and not in the wheel which circulates them. In computing either the gross or the neat revenue of any country, we must always, from their whole annual circulation of money and goods, deduct the whole value of the money, of which not a single farthing can ever make any part of either." [1]

The preceding extracts· are given at length, as the only mode of presenting Smith's notions upon the subject of money. Nothing can be more inappropriate than his method to scientific discussion. He has more than Aristotle's passion for elaborate classification, resting upon no better support than his own fancies. That which divides the circulating capital of society into money, material, provisions, and finished work, is wholly arbitrary and absurd. Money — gold and silver — is material in the same sense as is iron, wood, or wool. Like these, it is constantly going into the arts, — into tools and finished work. It is in one sense the highest kind of finished work, as it is always received by every one in exchange for what he may have to sell. The classification given by Smith, therefore, has no warrant whatever in the nature of things. The usual classification of property — that known to the law and to the books — into real and personal, is the only proper one, for the reason that it is the only one that rests upon a radical distinction in kind.

It is a capital defect in Smith, as well as in all the Economists, that he entirely overlooks interest as an element in price, and as a source of revenue. "The revenue of society," he tells us, "consists wholly of the three parts of the circulating capital, consisting of provisions, material, and finished work. The maintenance of these costs nothing; money — though a part of the circulating capital — is wholly to be deducted from the neat and gross revenue, of which not a farthing can ever make any part of either. The fixed capital and that part of the circulating capital which consists of money, have, so far as they affect the neat revenue of society, a very great resemblance the one to the other."

The expense of maintaining any kind of property is, in one very important particular, in direct ratio to its cost; and this is interest on its cost. Interest is always chargeable against every kind of property, for the reason that it could be realized on loans of the money paid for it. Interest, therefore, enters into the price of every article put upon the market. Take the case of a carpet: the importer of the wool used in its manu-

[1] Wealth of Nations, Book ii., Chap. ii.

facture charges interest on its cost from the time of its purchase, in Africa or Australia, till it is delivered to the manufacturer. If it be sold on time, interest in addition to cost is charged for such time. The interest the manufacturer pays is included in the price at which the finished goods are put upon the market. If sold on time, interest is charged on such sales. If the merchant pay cash, he includes interest on the price to his customers, as the only mode in which he can be reimbursed for the use of his capital. But for such payments, he might be receiving interest on loans of the money by which they were made. The price which the consumer pays is not only the cost, but interest on the same from the time of the purchase of the material till the finished product is taken for consumption; interest on the machinery and tools employed in its manufacture; on the cost of their maintenance, cost of warehousing, cost of distribution for consumption; and a profit to all parties engaged in the various processes described. It costs far less to maintain money than it does any other kind of capital. In such a country as the United States, for example, there is at the close of every harvest a year's stock of food on hand, the value of which may be estimated at $1,000,000,000. This food is to be carried by some one for an average of six months, for which service interest is charged to the consumers, amounting, say, to $30,000,000; the cost of warehousing this food may be estimated at $20,000,000; insurance, $10,000,000: making a total of $60,000,000, every dollar of which enters into the price. It costs very little to maintain $1,000,000,000 for six months. On the contrary, while that value of produce is to be carried without interest to the holder, an equal amount of money would produce him $30,000,000. Money can be used at all times; food must be held in very large quantities, in reserve, for future use. The maintenance of such reserves is a burden to which society must submit. Such comparisons or illustrations, however, are of very little importance; for the reason that every kind of property necessary to the operations of society is to be considered as equally expensive in its maintenance, equally valuable, and equally productive in its use. But for money, the exchanges of property could not be made; nor could it have any commercial value.

Money, therefore, as a medium of exchange, performs an indispensable function, and consequently is always a most important source of revenue. The revenue of society, in fact, is in ratio to the amount of property it possesses, whatever be its form, — whether fixed or floating, real or personal. It is not necessary even that capital — money — should be actively employed, in order that it may be regarded as productive. Every prudent person will always seek to have on hand an amount of it in excess of that necessary to his immediate wants, or uses, to meet unforeseen calls or emergencies. Such reserves will consist either of gold or silver, or of the notes and credits of Banks, which entitle their holder to gold and silver, or to whatever these will purchase. A merchant, whose profit is in the nature of a commission, is not expected to maintain on hand an amount of capital equal to the liabilities he assumes. Such liabilities may, and often do, exceed tenfold his means, apart from the merchandise in the purchase of which they were created. He is expected to discharge them by the sale of such merchandise. As he is, however, constantly liable to losses, he must maintain reserves in ratio to his liabilities; otherwise no one would trust him, as it would be seen that the first reverse might ruin him. With adequate reserves, however, the more favorable rates at which he would be able to purchase, and the greater degree of credit he would enjoy, would far more than compensate for the loss of interest on his reserves. Capital so held, therefore, though not immediately productive, may, in fact, be considered as the most productive and the most usefully employed of any that the merchant may hold. A very large amount of capital is always necessarily held in this manner. Every person has, or seeks to have, about him an amount of money, greater or less according to his means or ability, to meet future demands or opportunities; foregoing interest for the sake of having the immediate control of that which he may wish to use or spend. In some countries, from the want of social order or from the rapacity of governments, as a matter of safety and prudence interest may be foregone altogether. In all, very large amounts of capital must remain without drawing interest, involving a sacrifice for a greater good or convenience. It is a loss which society makes to secure a greater advantage or gain.

If Aristotle, Hume, Smith, and other Economists, in place of declaring money to have only a fictitious or conventional value, or its value and productions to be less than those of other kinds of property, had set themselves to work to explain the phenomenon of the universal demand for money at usury, the history of Political Economy would have been wholly different. Money was in as active demand when Aristotle wrote as to-day. The rate in Greece on such as was borrowed to be used in mercantile adventures averaged 30 per cent per annum, commerce being subject to much greater risks than at the present time. It was equally in demand, though loaned at less rates, at the time of Smith and Hume. Why should not such a demand have been accepted as evidence of value? The reason was the absurd dogma of Aristotle, which no writer till Bentham ever assumed to controvert.

As interest to be received on loans of capital is a prime factor in human affairs; as it is one of the most powerful motives to industry and exertion; as it is the great conservator of social order; as upon it rest institutions indispensable to the alleviation of human weakness and distress, and to the promotion of the moral, intellectual, and physical welfare of the race, without which it would relapse into a condition of comparative barbarism, — to wholly overlook it in a work the object of which is to treat of the laws upon which such welfare rests, marks such a want of the proper comprehension of the subject as to throw a well-grounded distrust over whatever conclusions its author may undertake to establish. No reliance can be placed upon those derived from premises from which the most important element is wholly excluded. It is like an attempt to solve complex geometrical propositions, taking no account of elemental truths. The conclusions arrived at would be mere hap-hazard guesses, which might never coincide with the law or fact. Such guesses were Smith's conclusions in his work on Political Economy. It cannot be otherwise with any work of the kind till the principles upon which the science treated of rests are adequately established. Those upon which the science of Political Economy rests, if there be such a science, are to be found, not in the intellectual, but in the moral part of man's nature. When proper moral conditions are secured, the highest possible material prosperity is the necessary result.

A distinction to which Smith is constantly returning is the difference between the wheel of circulation and the goods that are circulated by it. The one, he tells us, is wholly different from the other. Such distinction is entirely imaginary. If a person possessed of 1,000 barrels of flour sell it for $10,000 in gold, the flour may be said to move the gold. If a person possessed of such a sum in gold wish to purchase its equivalent in flour, the gold may be said to move the flour. The figure of the wheel is allowable only on the assumption that money, as such, is not capital; but an instrument of commerce, like a scale, a railroad car, or a steamboat. The wheels of the railroad car may very properly be said to be the wheels of commerce, because they are constantly moving merchandise the value and nature of which has no relation or resemblance to them ; but to call one kind of merchandise, and not the other for which it is exchanged, a wheel of commerce, is to use illustrations which have no correspondence in nature, but are simply inventions, which with the indolent or superficial take the place of fundamental principles or laws.

Smith, when treating of money, is always returning to his favorite distinction between money and capital, — between the real and nominal price of commodities.

"If," he says, " a guinea be the weekly pension of a particular person, he can, in the course of a week, purchase with it a certain quantity of subsistence, conveniences, and amusements. In proportion as this quantity is great or small, so are his real riches, his real weekly revenue. His weekly revenue is certainly not equal to the guinea and to what can be purchased with it : but only to one or other of these two equal values ; and to the latter more properly than to the former ; — to the guinea's worth, rather than to the guinea.

" If the pension of such a person was paid to him, not in gold, but in a weekly bill for a guinea, his revenue surely would not so properly consist in the piece of paper as in what he could get for it. A guinea may be considered as a bill for a certain amount of necessaries and conveniences, upon all the tradesmen in the neighborhood. The revenue of a person to whom it is paid does not so properly consist in the piece of gold as in what he can get for it, or in what he can exchange it for. If it could be exchanged for nothing, it would, like a bill upon a bankrupt, be of no more value than the most useless piece of paper.

" Though we frequently express a person's revenue by the metal pieces which are annually paid to him, it is because the amount of these pieces regulates the extent of his power of purchasing, or the value of the goods which he can annually afford to consume. We still consider his revenue as consisting in the power of pur-

chasing or consuming, and not in the pieces which convey it. . . .
His revenue, therefore, cannot consist of these metal pieces, of
which the amount is so much inferior to its value; but in the power
of purchasing, — in the goods which can successively be bought with
them as they circulate from hand to hand.

"Money, therefore, the great wheel of circulation, the great instrument of commerce, like all other instruments of trade, though
it makes a part and a very valuable part of the capital, makes no
part of the revenue of the society to which it belongs; and though
the metal pieces of which it is composed, in the course of their
annual circulation, distribute to every man the revenue which
properly belongs to him, they make themselves no part of that
revenue."[1] . . .

"It is not the guinea, but the guinea's worth," says Smith,
"that constitutes a person's income." Why not the guinea?
It is this that is paid him as his income; it is the value of this
which enables him to become possessed of articles necessary
for his comfort or support. Its value is the measure of his
ability to purchase such articles. What is gained by going
beyond the guinea, and making that which the guinea will purchase the measure of a person's income? He may not expend
his guineas; but may accumulate them for a lifetime, leaving
them for his heirs. Would he be all that time without any
income? Would his income be measured by what he might
purchase? If he hoarded his guineas, would not he have the
same income as if he expended them as fast as earned? Or he
might loan his guineas at interest, and in this way be receiving
a large income, never expending a penny of the principal.
"If gold could be exchanged for nothing," says Smith, "it
would be of no value." It is not a great stroke of genius to
tell us this. He might, without much danger, have affirmed
the same of every other kind of property. "But," says
Smith, "a person's income cannot be said to be equal both to
the money that is paid him, and the goods which such money
can purchase. It can equal only the one or the other of these,
and the latter more properly than the former." If it be a discovery to find out that one does not equal two, then Smith
should certainly have the honor of making it.

From the consideration of metallic, Smith proceeds to that
of paper, money:—

---

[1] Wealth of Nations, Book ii., Chap. ii.

"The machines and instruments of trade, which compose the fixed capital, have this further resemblance to that part of the circulating capital which consists in money : that as every saving in the expense of erecting and supporting those machines, which does not diminish the productive powers of labor, is an improvement of the neat revenue of the society, so every saving in the expense of collecting and supporting that part of the circulating capital which consists in money is an improvement of exactly the same kind.

" It is sufficiently obvious, and it has partly, too, been explained already, in what manner every saving in the expense of supporting the fixed capital is an improvement in the neat revenue of society. The whole capital of the undertaker of every work is necessarily divided between his fixed and his circulating capital. While his whole capital remains the same, the smaller the one part the greater must necessarily be the other. It is the circulating capital which furnishes the materials and wages of labor, and puts industry in motion. Every saving, therefore, in the expense of maintaining the fixed capital, which does not diminish the productive powers of labor, must increase the fund which puts industry in motion, and consequently the annual produce of the land and labor, — the real revenue of society. The substitution of paper in the room of gold and silver money, replaces a very expensive instrument of commerce with one much less costly, and sometimes equally convenient. Circulation comes to be carried on by a new wheel, which it costs less both to erect and maintain than the old one. But in what manner this operation is performed, and in what manner it tends to increase either the gross or the neat revenue of the society, is not altogether so obvious ; and may, therefore, require some further explication.

" There are several different sorts of paper money ; but the circulating notes of Banks and bankers are the species which is best known, and which seems best adapted for this purpose. When the people of any particular country have such confidence in the fortune, probity, and prudence of a particular banker as to believe that he is always ready to pay upon demand such of his promissory notes as are likely to be at any time presented to him, these notes come to have the same currency as gold and silver money, from the confidence that such money can at any time be had for them.

" A particular banker lends among his customers his own promissory notes, to the extent, we shall suppose, of a hundred thousand pounds. As those notes serve all the purposes of money, his debtors pay the same interest as if he had lent them so much money. This interest is the source of his gain. Though some of these notes are continually coming back upon him for payment, part of them circulate for months and years together ; though he has generally in circulation, therefore, notes to the extent of a hundred thousand pounds, twenty thousand pounds in gold and silver may frequently be sufficient provision for answering occasional demands. By this operation, therefore, twenty thousand pounds in gold and silver perform all the operations which a hundred thousand pounds would otherwise have performed. The same exchanges may be made; the same quantity of consumable goods may be circulated and distributed to their proper consumers, by the means of his promissory notes to the value of a hundred thousand pounds, as by an equal value of gold and silver money. Eighty thousand pounds of gold and silver, therefore, can in this manner be spared from the circulation of the country; and, if different operations of the same kind should at the same time be carried on by many different Banks and bankers, the whole circulation may thus be conducted with a fifth part only of the gold and silver which would otherwise have been requisite." [1]

" There are several kinds of paper money," says Smith; " but bank-notes seem to be the best to serve as money," and he therefore makes them the subject of his discussion. This paragraph describes exactly the nature of Smith's mind, and the method pursued by him. Bank-notes *seem* to him to be the best. Why did he not tell us which was the best? *Seem* has no place in scientific analysis. It belongs purely to the deductive method. Had Smith devoted himself to finding out what bank-notes were, instead of what they *seemed* to be, he might have rendered the world some service in the place of pouring forth such a mass of unmeaning verbiage in support of vain and frivolous distinctions, which had no existence but in his own imagination.

Smith's theory of the issue of paper money was this: a banker in good credit, and who has punctually met his payments, issues his notes for, say, £100,000. These he pays out, no matter for what objects. If the amount be not excessive, — that is, if it do not exceed the wants of the community for currency, — the notes will remain indefinitely in circulation. A few of them will be occasionally presented for payment, as their holders may happen to want coin. For such occasional calls, it will be prudent for the banker to keep on hand, say, £20,000 in coin. The measure of his profit will be the excess of interest on his notes over and above that on his reserves. By this substitution, £80,000 of coin are discharged from circulation, while the exchanges of the community will be effected equally well as with the corresponding amount of coin. In all this, he assumed that the operations referred to were all based upon credit, except the provision of £20,000 in coin; that the notes issued

---

[1] Wealth of Nations, Book ii., Chap. ii.

would serve as instruments of exchange, without any reference
to that which they represented. He overlooked the fact, that
all the notes issued in the discount of.bills return to the party
issuing them, for redemption or conversion, within periods of,
say, four months from their issue ; that, as they were issued in
the discount of bills, they must be returned on their payment.
That they were not demanded in coin, or, rather, that reserves
of £20,000 in coin were all that were found necessary for
the banker to hold, was due to the fact that he issued his notes
in the discount of business paper, and that the payment of such
paper returned to him his notes in the manner already described. If he discounted only such notes as were certain to
be paid, £10,000, or even £5,000, of coin reserves might be
adequate. The notes would return for redemption with the
same certainty and regularity, if they represented capital to
their full amount, as if they did not represent a penny.
Redemption within certain periods is the law of all convertible
currencies. There was in the case supposed no substitution of
credit for capital ; only that instruments other than coin were
used for the exchange or distribution of a corresponding
amount of capital. It by no means follows that there is any
less coin in a community for the use of symbols. There may
be a far greater amount from its increased wealth due to their
use, in all cases in which they can be used instead of coin.

To quote again : —

" Let us suppose, for example, that the whole circulating money
of some particular country amounted at a particular time to
£1,000,000, that sum then being sufficient for circulating the whole
annual produce of their land and labor. Let us suppose, too, that
sometime thereafter different Banks and bankers issued promissory
notes payable to the bearer, to the extent of £1,000,000, reserving
in their different coffers £200,000 for answering occasional demands.
There would remain, therefore, in circulation, £800,000 in gold and
silver, and £1,000,000 of bank-notes, or £1,800,000 of paper and
money together. But the annual produce of the land and labor of
the country had before required only £1,000,000 to circulate and
distribute it to its proper consumers, and that annual produce cannot be immediately augmented by the operations of banking.
£1,000,000, therefore, will be sufficient to circulate it after them.
The goods to be bought and sold being precisely the same as before,
the same quantity of money will be sufficient for buying and selling
them. The channel of circulation, if I may be allowed such an
expression, will remain precisely the same as before. £1,000,000

we have supposed sufficient to fill that channel. Whatever, therefore, is poured into it beyond that sum, cannot run in it, but must overflow : £1,800,000 are poured into it ; £800,000, therefore, must overflow, that sum being over and above what can be employed in the circulation of the country. But though this sum cannot be employed at home, it is too valuable to be allowed to lie idle. It will, therefore, be sent abroad, in order to seek that profitable employment which it cannot find at home. But the paper cannot go abroad, because at a distance from the Banks which issue it, and from the country in which payment of it can be exacted by law, it will not be received in common payments. Gold and silver, therefore, to the amount of £800,000 will be sent abroad, and the channel of home circulation will remain filled with £1,000,000 of paper instead of the £1,000,000 of those metals which filled it before. . . .

"When paper is substituted in the room of gold and silver money, the quantity of the materials, tools, and maintenance which the whole circulating capital can supply, may be increased by the whole value of gold and silver which used to be employed in circulating them. The whole value of the great wheel of circulation and distribution is added to the goods which are circulated and distributed by means of it." [1]

The effect of the issue of £800,000 (whatever its character) of currency upon a community accustomed to use £1,000,000 in coin would depend entirely upon that which the paper money represented. It is to be remarked, however, that no such certain or methodical issue or substitution of one kind or currency for another as that supposed by Smith is possible. The use of a symbolic currency is evidence of a high intellectual and moral condition. Such currency, valueless in itself, is taken, like a bill of exchange, upon the faith that it is what it is represented to be, — the evidence of capital, — and that it will secure to its holder such capital. We should no more expect to find in Spain or Turkey the currency of New England as it was, or Scotland, than we should expect to find in them the skill of the latter in the mechanic arts. A good currency, like elaborate mechanical contrivances, is a growth, not an improvisation. No people ever said to themselves, " We have put up with an expensive currency of coin long enough, we will now try the cheaper one of paper ; " any more than they said to themselves, " We have put up with poor mechanical contrivances long enough, we will henceforth use only such

[1] Wealth of Nations, Book ii., Chap. ii.

as are most perfectly adapted to their ends." Progress in distribution, so that it may be cheaply and expeditiously effected, is much more gradual than in production whereby quantity is increased and quality improved. Intellectual training will suffice for the latter; but for the former moral qualities must always be superadded. Symbolic currencies have come into use very gradually. They were never resorted to for the purpose of discharging from use a corresponding amount of coin; neither did their use necessarily discharge from employment a corresponding amount of coin; neither would they (provided they represented capital) increase the relative amount of money, as capital would necessarily exist in the same ratio. In such case, the channel of circulation (if the figure may be used) would never overflow, no matter the magnitude of the current. The banks would recede and contract with the current. Smith, however, assumed in his illustration the increase in paper money to be without a corresponding increase in capital; and that an equal amount of coin, discharged from employment as currency, would be immediately sent abroad as merchandise. But even if the £800,000 of paper money had been purely fictitious, — that is, if it had represented nothing but the promises of the issuers, — still the channel of circulation would no more have overflowed than if the new issue had represented a corresponding amount of capital. As the instruments of expenditure, in excess of capital, were increased, prices would rise in like ratio, so that relative to prices, the amount of money might not have increased a dollar. Till prices reached their maximum, there would be an active demand for all kinds of merchandise, foreign as well as domestic : and under the increased demand importations would be increased; to be paid for not by exports of merchandise, but of the coin reserves of the country. It would never occur to the holders of this coin that they must send it out of the country to find employment for it, or to get its worth. Such as they had to spend would be expended on objects lying immediately about them; and, if any portion went out of the country, it would be in payment of merchandise for which the ordinary exports of the country no longer sufficed. The expenditure would be made long before any one dreamed of exporting gold. In all these operations, there would be no plan or method, nor would it be supposed that any shipments of coin would be necessary. When an adverse movement of specie begins, people are always surprised, and wonder what can be the cause. As they are always sure to apply the proper remedy so soon as the movement appears to be a strong one, they would never, had they foreseen the consequences, have placed themselves in a position from which they immediately seek to escape. Coin, too, can be much better spared when it is the sole currency, than when a symbolic one is used in connection with it. In the latter case, a reduction of one dollar in coin may be equivalent to the reduction of five or ten dollars in the volume of symbols. Hence the extreme sensitiveness of such countries as England to the slightest foreign demand for specie. The illustration, therefore, that the moment a paper currency is used people methodically send abroad a corresponding amount of coin, is preposterous. The moment a symbolic currency is issued to the extent supposed by Smith, coin is carefully collected by the issuers of currency, as they can increase their issues in fivefold or greater ratio to the amount they hold. As soon as a symbolic currency begins to be issued, the motive to retain specie in the country becomes all the stronger in ratio to the amount of issue of such currency.

"When we compute," says Smith, "the quantity of industry which the circulating capital of any society can employ, we must always have regard to those parts of it only which consist in provisions, materials, and finished work; the other, which consists in money, and which serves only to circulate these three, must always be deducted. In order to put industry in motion, three things are requisite: materials to work upon, tools to work with, and the wages or recompense for the sake of which the work is done. Money is neither a material to work upon, nor a tool to work with; and, though the wages of the workmen are commonly paid to them in money, their real income consists, not in the money, but in the money's worth, — not in the metal pieces, but in what can be got for them.

"The quantity of industry which any capital can employ must evidently be equal to the number of workmen whom it can supply with materials, tools, and maintenance suitable to the workmen; but the quantity of industry which the whole capital can employ is certainly not equal both to the money which purchases, and to the materials, tools, and maintenance which are purchased with it: but only to one or other of these two values; and to the latter more properly than to the former."[1] "Money," he continues in

---

[1] Wealth of Nations, Book ii., Chap. ii.

a subsequent part of the work, "no doubt always makes a part of the national capital; but it has already been shown that it generally makes only a small part, and always the most unprofitable part of it." [1]

If money be capital, or the evidence of capital, then the amount of industry which any society can employ must be in ratio to its quantity. Money, in the form of coin, is capital, and as material, is constantly passing into the arts. It is capital, in being at all times exchangeable at its cost for all other articles of property. It is capital, in being always in demand at interest. It is one of the most valuable of tools or instruments, as without it no exchanges could be made, nor could other kinds of property have any exchangeable value. But for money, there could in fact, be no property worthy the name. If it be symbolic, it measures, so far, the quantity of merchandise in a country entering into consumption; and is the instrument, and the only one, by which the capital of a community in the form of merchandise can be loaned in any considerable amount. When loans by coin are made, the coin itself is loaned. When loans are made by means of symbolic currency, merchandise, or that which will purchase it, is loaned. Loans made by the issue of symbols are just as useful to the borrower as loans made in coin. What he wants is currency, — that which will reach some other article of merchandise. The quantity of industry, therefore, which any society can employ must be in direct ratio to the amount of its money, in whatever form. Smith's assumption, that, in estimating the quantity of labor that can be employed, money is to be entirely excluded from the calculation, is exactly opposed to the fact. That the quantity of industry which the capital of any society can employ is equal both to the money which purchases, and to the materials, tools, and maintenance which are purchased with it, is a suggestion too puerile and absurd for comment. To the assertion that money always forms the least productive part of the capital of society, it is sufficient to reply, that every kind of property necessary to its operations is to be considered equally valuable and equally productive.

[1] Wealth of Nations, Book iii., Chap. i.

Again : —

"What is the proportion which the circulating money of any country bears to the whole value of the annual produce circulated by means of it, it is, perhaps, impossible to determine. It has been computed by different authors at a fifth, at a tenth, at a twentieth, and at a thirtieth, part of that value. But how small soever the proportion which the circulating money may bear to the whole value of the annual produce, as but a part, and frequently but a small part, of that produce is ever destined for the maintenance of industry, it must always bear a very considerable proportion to that part. When, therefore, by the substitution of paper, the gold and silver necessary for circulation are reduced to perhaps a fifth part of the former quantity, if the value of only the greater part of the other four-fifths be added to the funds which are destined for the maintenance of industry, it must make a very considerable addition to the quantity of that industry, and consequently to the value of the annual produce of land and labor." [1]

The proportion which the money of the country bears, or should bear, to its capital or property in other forms, is a matter of very little speculative importance. So long as such money consists of the precious metals, the necessities of society or business will always tend to a proper adjustment of the relative amounts of the two. No theory, speculation, or method can change them. This is a matter which must be left to the operation of natural laws. If there be such an excess of coin in one country that its relative value in it is reduced, such excess will move off, by its own gravity, to places or countries where it is in less relative abundance. Paper money, on the other hand, is not capital. It is the evidence of capital ; and such evidences, provided they be of merchandise entering into consumption, serve all the functions of coin as currency. As the parties having the right to such merchandise, or its equivalent in coin, should always be possessed of the evidences of such right, it follows that paper money should equal in its nominal amount that of such merchandise,— in other words, that the symbol should always correspond to the substance ; that the money of commerce should equal the merchandise of commerce. There is a uniform tendency to such equalization in all countries making use of a symbolic currency. There is the same reason why all articles

---

[1] Wealth of Nations, Book ii., Chap. ii.

entering into consumption should be symbolized as that any one should be. In England, nearly the whole amount of the merchandise entering into consumption is symbolized. The money of that country approaches in its nominal value to that of her merchandise. Such a condition of things could by no means be possible but for the high moral qualities of her people, which lead a merchant or a banker in London to confide as implicitly in the undertakings of a merchant, banker, or manufacturer in Liverpool or Glasgow, as in those of his immediate neighbors. Domestic order is also a necessary condition to the use of such a currency. It is impossible, for the reasons stated, that it should be used to any considerable extent in Turkey or in Spain, or in the Southern, in the same degree as in the Northern United States of America.

Smith assumes that the only gain in the use of paper money is in the displacement of a corresponding amount of coin, and in its conversion into other uses than that of currency. It, however, by no means follows that the use of a symbolic currency diminishes the amount of metallic currency in a country. This is a matter which can never be accurately determined. It may be that the increase in production and trade, and consequently in wealth, and the necessity of providing reserves adequate for the maintenance of a very large amount of symbolic currency, may call for the use of a larger amount of coin than could have been maintained in circulation without the use of symbols. Be this as it may, the advantages of discharging a certain amount of coin from use, by means of paper money, are really insignificant compared with those which flow from its use. Without it, the commerce and wealth of such countries as Great Britain and the United States could not have reached one-fifth of their present prodigious proportions.

Again : —

" The whole paper money of every kind which can easily circulate in any country can never exceed the value of the gold and silver of which it supplies the place, or which (the commerce being supposed the same) would circulate there if there were no paper money. If twenty shilling notes, for example, are the lowest paper money current in Scotland, the whole of that currency that could easily circulate there cannot exceed the sum of gold and silver which would be necessary for transacting the annual exchanges of twenty shillings' value and upwards usually transacted in that country. Should the circulating paper at any time exceed that sum, as the excess could neither be sent abroad nor employed in the circulation of the country, it must return immediately upon the Banks to be exchanged for gold and silver. Many people would immediately perceive that they had more of this paper than was necessary for transacting their business at home; and, as they could not send it abroad, they would immediately demand payment for it at the Banks. When this superfluous paper was converted into gold and silver, they could easily find a use for it by sending it abroad; but they could find none while it remained in the shape of paper. There would immediately, therefore, be a run upon the Banks to the whole extent of this superfluous paper; and, if they showed any difficulty or backwardness in payment, to a much greater extent, the alarm which this would occasion necessarily increasing the run." [1]

In the preceding paragraph Smith asserts a principle which has since become a dogma with all succeeding Economists, that the amount of paper money that can be maintained in circulation can never exceed the amount of coin the place of which it supplies. A few remarks will show its utter absurdity. The currency of his own country, Scotland, when he wrote, equalled, he tells us, £2,000,000, of which gold and silver constituted only £500,000. If we add, to the £1,500,000 of notes in circulation, £500,000, as the deposits in the Banks, which are currency equally with the notes, the total circulation of the country equalled £2,500,000. The circulation of the Scotch Banks, including deposits, in 1873, was £82,000,000; the coin reserves equalled about £5,000,000; the coin actually in circulation equalled, probably, as much more: making a total currency of £92,000,000. The increase of currency in Scotland in the hundred years, consequently, has been £89,500,000. The amount of coin displaced by the issue of notes has been, according to Smith, £82,000,000.

It is absurd to suppose if there had been no increase of paper money in Scotland, that the amount of coin in circulation in it would have equalled £90,500,000 — a sum nearly equalling the estimated amount in circulation in the United Kingdom at the present time. The total amount of coin in England in 1776 was estimated at the time at about £20,000,000; the notes of the Bank of England in circulation equalled about £8,000,000; deposits about £5,000,000; the circulation

1 Wealth of Nations, Book ii., Chap. ii.

of, and deposits with, private Banks and bankers, £5,000,000 : the total being £38,000,000, of which £18,000,000 was made up of symbols. The currency in circulation in England at the present time, according to Palgrave, equals, probably, £100,000,000 of specie and £550,000,000 of various kinds of paper, making a total of £650,000,000 against £38,000,000 a hundred years ago. According to Smith, the paper money put in circulation within the century must have displaced £532,000,000 of coin — an assumption utterly incredible. With a specie currency only, there are limitations to production and distribution beyond which they cannot pass. A point would soon be reached in which, as in the speed of locomotive trains, the loss and inconvenience suffered would exceed all the profit to be derived from business operations. In widely extended communities, like those of the United States, gold and silver could never adequately fill the place of a symbolic currency ; and, if the latter should be disused, they would be forced to an enormous contraction of production and trade.

According to Smith, if an amount of paper money at any time exceed that of the metallic money displaced, the excess must return immediately to the Banks to be exchanged for coin. " Many people," he repeats, " would immediately perceive that they had more of this paper than was necessary for the transaction of their business at home ; and, as they could not send it abroad, they would immediately demand payment for it at the Banks. When the surplus paper was converted into gold and silver, they could easily find use for it by sending it abroad ; but they could find none while it remained in the shape of paper." How does paper money get into circulation ? From the confidence reposed in it. Those who receive it believe that it will secure to them, as currency, the same values of merchandise as an equal amount of currency of coin ; otherwise they would not have received it. So long as such confidence remains, — in other words, so long as, in the case supposed by Smith, it can be exchanged at Bank for coin, — it will be so exchanged only when the holders of the same wish to obtain coin for use in the arts, or in payments where coin only will be accepted, as in the case of tender in satisfaction of contracts. It never yet occurred to the holder of a note convertible on demand into coin, that he must go to the Bank and exchange it for coin before he could use it as currency. Of all Smith's fancies, this is one of the most untenable and absurd. Even if foreign merchandise were to be purchased, the notes, so long as they represented merchandise, would serve the holder precisely as well as coin. The holder of the merchandise to be purchased would receive them in payment equally with coin. He may pay for his importations, not in coin, but by bills drawn against a shipment of domestic merchandise. The drawer of such bill receives such notes in its sale equally with coin, as he can pay these out equally with coin in the payment of his debts or in the purchase of labor and material in the production of his industries. As a rule, specie is hardly more necessary in foreign than in domestic trade, — imports being paid for by exports. In countries that do not produce the precious metals, the two must, in the long run, nearly balance, the one the other. The amount of coin required in a healthy condition of trade, only equals that necessary for the discharge of balances, which may not equal one per cent of the merchandise moving between nations or between communities widely separated. Smith's assumption, therefore, that all excess of currency over and above that necessary to effect the exchanges of its holders must be returned to the Banks for coin, before it can be used as money or capital, is a pure fiction, having no counterpart whatever in any transaction in real life.

Again: —

"A banking company which issues more paper than can be employed in the circulation of the country, and of which the *excess* is continually returning upon them for payment, ought to increase the quantity of gold and silver which they keep at all times in their coffers, not only in proportion to this excessive increase of their circulation, but in much greater proportion ; their notes returning upon them much faster than in proportion to the excess of their quantity. Such a company, therefore, ought to increase the first article of their expense, not only in proportion to this forced increase of their business, but in much greater proportion. . . .

"The coffers of such a company, too, though they ought to be filled much fuller, must empty themselves much faster than if their business was confined within more reasonable bonds ; and must require not only a more violent, but a more constant and uninterrupted, exertion of expense in order to replenish them. The coin, too, which is continually drawn in such large quantities from their coffers cannot be employed in the circulation of the country. It comes in place of a paper which is over and above what can be employed in that circulation, and is, therefore, over and above what can be employed in it too. But, as that coin will not be allowed to lie idle, it must in one shape or another be sent abroad, in order to find that profitable employment which it cannot find at home; and this continual exportation of gold and silver, by enhancing the difficulty, must, necessarily, enhance still further the expense of the Bank in finding new gold and silver, in order to replenish their coffers which empty themselves so very rapidly. Such a company, therefore, must, in proportion to this forced increase of their business, increase the second article of their expense still more than the first." [1]

No Bank can issue "more paper than can be employed in the circulation of the country," provided such issues be made in the discount of bills representing merchandise. So far a perfect equilibrium is maintained between money and merchandise. But all the issues of paper money, not the excess alone, return regularly and within very short periods to the Bank for redemption, in the manner already described. As they were issued in the discount of bills, they must be returned in their payment. The whole process is automatic, so long as provision for their conversion is provided previous to their issue. If such be not made before their issue, it must be made subsequent to it, and ordinarily out of the reserves of the Bank. It is not a question of quantity, but of quality or kind. There can never be too much of a symbolic currency ; there can never be too little of such as is not properly symbolic. For the one, a Bank need keep on hand only a small percentage of coin in ratio to its issues, no matter how great these may be : for the other, it must keep on hand an amount equal to its issues, no matter how small these may be. With Smith, quantity was the only criterion of quality. He wholly overlooked the fact, that a currency not issued in excess has to be redeemed just as speedily, and to the same extent, as a currency issued in excess, or a currency that has nothing behind it. It is not the extent but the character of issues of paper money that calls for large reserves of coin. So long as they represent capital, — so long as they will secure to their holders the same value of other articles as coin, — there will be no object to exchange them for coin. But if the notes of a Bank be drawn in gold and silver, why may not the latter be as profitably employed at home as abroad ? Suppose the

[1] Wealth of Nations, Book ii. Chap. ii.

countries to which they were sent to be in the precise condition of that from which they were sent, they would then have to be sent off to some other. If all had their proper proportion of currency to property, such gold and silver as currency would find a resting-place nowhere ; they would be waifs which no one would touch. If, on the other hand, they were capital, they could as well be employed in one country as another : for no country can have too much capital, if it can have too much currency. But no country can have too much of that either, if it be capital, or its representative. In the illustration of his argument, Smith finds himself with too much money on hand — a larger quantity than that necessary to effect the exchanges, — and he packs it off without ceremony, as capital, to some other country. He should certainly have asked himself whether it might not be possible that such money might not be as unwelcome and out of place abroad as at home ; and whether it might not be immediately returned without breaking the wax. In such an event, which might be more than probable, his treatise could certainly not be considered complete till he had in some manner disposed of this refractory element in business affairs.

Smith is constantly talking of the expense of maintaining a currency which is in excess of the wants of a community, as if it cost nothing to maintain one that did not exceed its wants. It costs just as much, in ratio to its amount, to maintain a currency which equals only the wants of the people, as it does one that exceeds their wants. All currencies not legal tender have to be taken in within a comparatively short time from their issue. For this purpose, an adequate amount of capital must always be provided. If provided in merchandise previous to their issue, they convert themselves, in being returned to the Bank in payment of the bills in the discount of which they were issued. If such provision for their conversion be not made previous to their issue, they must be taken in by paying out therefor a corresponding amount of coin. A Bank, when it commences operations, must have its capital paid in either in coin, or the notes or cheques payable in coin of other Banks, or in good bills given for merchandise, and having a value in coin equal to their nominal amount. The substance must always equal the symbol. Such substance may be, and usually is, in the hands of the public. It does not, necessarily, ever come into the possession of the Bank. It must, however, be provided just as much in the one case as the other.

Again : —

"What a Bank can with propriety advance to a merchant or undertaker of any kind, is not either the whole capital with which he trades, or even any considerable portion of that capital, but that part of it only which he would otherwise be obliged to keep by him unemployed, and in ready money for answering occasional demands. If the paper money which the Bank advances, never exceeds this value, it can never exceed the value of the gold and silver which would necessarily circulate in the country, if there were no paper money ; it can never exceed the quantity which the circulation of the country can easily absorb and employ." [1]

A Bank, as a rule, should advance nothing to merchants. If they conduct their business properly, they have no need of banking accommodations. They have abundant capital in the merchandise intrusted to them. They are purchasers on time for distribution. It is their bills given to manufacturers, or producers, that are discounted. Such discounts are made to supply the cost of such merchandise to manufacturers or producers, for the purpose of enabling them to prosecute their industries during the periods for which the credits are given, and until the merchants return to them the proceeds of their sales. It is only when merchants have made purchases of merchandise which they cannot sell within the time within which their bills are to mature, that they call upon the Banks to supplement the credits first given to the manufacturers. No well-conducted Bank will take paper manufactured by merchants, for the reason that by doing so it is making loans upon merchandise which is shown to be unsalable. No loans should ever be made to an undertaker or contractor. Undertakers and contractors cannot make business paper. It is their object to get the possession of merchandise for their own use, not to sell it. As Smith would not allow Banks to issue a greater amount of currency than that necessary to be held by merchants to meet occasional demands, it is plain that he had no idea of the nature or value of a symbolic currency. It has already been shown that such currency,

---

[1] Wealth of Nations, Book ii. Chap. ii.

to be fully adequate to its objects, should equal in amount the total value of the merchandise entering presently into consumption. Paper money does not supersede metallic money: it only supplements it. To say, therefore, that it should never exceed in amount the coin previously in circulation, is to say that a railroad constructed along an old highway should never transport a greater amount of merchandise than had been transported over it. The railroad may still leave the old highway well employed, while reducing the cost of transportation five or ten fold. It does not supersede, it supplements, the old highway ; and, by supplementing it, adds almost infinitely to production and wealth.

" Whatever currency a Bank issues over and above what a community can absorb, is," says Smith, " constantly returning to it for redemption." A country will absorb all the currency it can get. If the present amount of United States notes should be quintupled, the country would absorb them, just as it has absorbed those at present in circulation, which, as far as the exchanges were concerned, were wholly superfluous. Prices rose in ratio to the amount issued, so that, so soon as the effect of the inflation had expended itself, money was in no greater relative abundance than before. So with the issues of a Bank. If they represented consumable merchandise, the country would absorb all that could be issued ; money, in the mean time, remaining in the same relative abundance. As whatever was issued by Banks would be speedily returned to them for redemption, and would have to be retired by the payment of coin, provided they did not represent merchandise, the country could not " absorb " such notes a second time, for the very good reason that they could not be reissued. When a currency is irredeemable, the country will absorb all it can get, so long as any credit whatever is attached to it. It can absorb whatever represents capital, for the reason that an equilibrium is in such case maintained between prices and the amount of currency issued.

" When it was observed that, within moderate periods of time, the repayments of a particular customer were upon most occasions fully equal to the advances which a Bank had made him, it might be assumed that the paper money which had been advanced to him had not at any time exceeded the quantity of gold and silver which he would otherwise have been obliged to keep by him for answering occasional demands ; and that, consequently, the paper money which had been circulated by his means had not at any time exceeded the quantity of gold and silver which would have circulated in the country had there been no paper money. The frequency, regularity, and amount of his repayments, would sufficiently demonstrate that the amount of the advances made had at no time exceeded that part of his capital which he would otherwise have been obliged to keep by him unemployed, and in ready money for answering occasional demands. . . .

" The advances of the Bank paper, by exceeding the quantity of gold and silver, which, had there been no such advances, he would have been obliged to keep by him for answering occasional demands, might soon come to exceed the whole quantity of gold and silver which would have circulated in the country had there been no paper money, and, consequently, to exceed the quantity which the circulation of the country could easily absorb and employ ; and the excess of this paper money would immediately have returned upon the Bank to be exchanged for gold and silver." [1]

As prices would rise in ratio to the amount of paper money issued, an increase of currency over that which had been in use would, in the outset, tend to make merchants more prompt in their payments, from a corresponding increase of demand for merchandise. Promptness in payment would, for a time, be rather an evidence of an excess of currency than otherwise. An inflation, or an excessive issue, of paper, might go on for years, even when the currency could be converted on demand into coin, provided all the Banks and bankers were affected by similar sentiments, and moved in the same direction. The greater part of the notes and credits issued would be retired by mutual offset in the manner already described; so that only a small amount of coin might, for a long time, be drawn. In this way, the amount of paper in circulation might very largely exceed the amount that could eventually be sustained. In time, however, some event or another would disclose the weakness of the financial situation, of which the wisest and most experienced in the community might, up to the very time of the catastrophe, be almost wholly unconscious. Then would come the scramble, — the *sauve qui peut*, — which, in a few months, might reduce the currency far below the point at which it stood when the inflation commenced. Even in such a case, the Banks might not be

[1] Wealth of Nations, Book ii. Chap. ii.

compelled to suspend specie payment ; but they might lose a very considerable portion of their reserves, and might require years to recover the ground lost. Unfortunately, the history of Banks is one of constant alternation between excessive issues and excessive contractions. The first lesson is yet to be learned by their managers, that all loans, except those made upon business paper, always inflict an injury upon the public, and usually recoil with greater or less force upon those making them.

"It is not by augmenting the capital of the country," says Smith, " but by rendering a greater part of that capital active and productive than would otherwise be so, that the most judicious operations of banking can increase the industry of the country. That part of his capital which a dealer is obliged to keep by him unemployed, and in ready money for answering occasional demands, is so much dead stock, which, so long as it remains in this situation, produces nothing to himself or to his country. . . . The gold and silver money which circulates in any country, and by means of which the produce of its lands and labor is annually distributed to the proper consumers, is in the same manner as the ready money of a dealer a dead stock. It is a very valuable part of the capital of the country which produces nothing to the country. The judicious operations of banking, by substituting paper in the room of the greater part of this gold and silver, enables the country to convert a great part of this dead stock into active and productive stock, — into stock which produces something to the country. The gold and silver money which circulates in any country may very properly be compared to a highway, which, while it circulates and carries to market all the grass and corn of the country, produces itself not a single pile of either. The judicious operations of banking, by providing (if I may be allowed so violent a metaphor) a sort of wagon-way through the air, enable the country to convert, as it were, a great part of its highways into good pastures and cornfields, and thereby to increase, very considerably, the annual produce of its land and labor. . . .

"The increase of paper money, it has been said, by augmenting the quantity, and consequently diminishing the value, of the whole currency, necessarily augments the money price of commodities; but as the quantity of gold and silver which is taken from the currency is always equal to the quantity of paper which is added to it, paper money does not necessarily increase the quantity of the whole currency."[1]

Smith's assertions, that all reserves and all money are so much dead capital, and that it is only by the use of paper

[1] Wealth of Nations, Book ii. Chap. ii.

money that gold and silver, being discharged from use as currency and exported, can produce any thing to a country holding them, have been sufficiently refuted. " These are," he tells us, " like highways, which, while they circulate and carry to market all the grass and corn of a country, produce not a pile of either." He forgot that it was the highway that gave the grass and corn whatever marketable value they possessed; and, that, consequently, the highway was as productive as were the soils upon which they were grown. His " violent metaphor," that a judicious process of banking was like a wagon way through the air, enabling the country, as it were, to convert the greater part of highways into good pastures and corn-fields, and thereby increase the annual produce of its land and labor, is a false one: for the reason that as there may be no less gold in a country possessing a symbolic currency, so there are no fewer, but more, ordinary highways for every railway that is constructed; showing that the improvement does not supersede, but supplements, the old method.

Among the subjects which Smith discussed, as having an intimate relation to that of money, was " Balance of Trade," of which he treats in the chapter in the " Wealth of Nations," entitled " The Principles of the Commercial or Mercantile System." As there has been no subject upon which the Economists have been better agreed, nor one more thoroughly misunderstood, it may be well to set out briefly the ideas and conditions upon which this system was founded; and to show, that while the methods resorted to were calculated to defeat the end sought, a favorable, or, rather, a not unfavorable, " Balance of Trade " is that which is always uppermost in the minds of individuals as well as nations; and every community, at least every one using a symbolic currency, must constantly look to it that the " Balance of Trade " is not adverse, and must be able to prevent the withdrawal of an excessive amount of coin, and to recall such as may have been lost from an unfavorable state of its industries and trade.

It is well known to every student of history, that the assumed science of Political Economy is a modern one. Such part of it as relates to symbolic currencies dates from the foundation of the Bank of England, — an event, or institution, which has changed the whole face of modern society. Although somewhat addicted to commerce, the Greeks never appear to have speculated upon subjects coming within the range of the economic sciences. Their industries were chiefly conducted by, and their incomes derived from, the labor of slaves ; and it was hardly to be expected that subjects or callings which were held by the wisest and best of their race in disesteem, or as contrary to nature, should be thought worthy to be erected into the dignity of a science. The Romans, never a commercial or manufacturing people, sustained themselves very largely by war during the period of their conquests ; and after the world was subjected to their arms, by requisitions upon the provinces. For ages the race was under one vast military *régime*, which left no room for, or effectually stifled all discussion upon subjects which now chiefly engross the attention of mankind.

The Northern races which overthrew the Empire, and erected the new nationalities upon its ruins, were radically unlike all that preceded them. The spirit of independence, which pervaded them all, rendered it impossible that the arms of one state or nation should become paramount, so as to draw from others its means of support. Wealth, consequently, if gained at all, had finally to be gained by industry and trade, in what, compared with Southern Europe, was a country forbidding in its aspect, and possessed of a cold and inhospitable climate. Unlike the Romans, all the Northern nations were addicted to adventure and to nautical life. They had a passion for wealth and luxury which industry and commerce could alone supply. The new civilizations, consequently, rested upon foundations wholly different from the old. With the old, almost the only idea of a city was as a means of attack or defence; with the new, the city had hardly any other purpose than as a mart of trade. Those founded by them frequently rose to great wealth and power ; and combining with each other, like the Hanse Towns, were in time able not only to protect their commerce and industries, but to oppose an effectual resistance to the utmost power that could be brought against them. As freedom is the necessary condition of commerce, these cities became the asylums and champions of the liberties of mankind. But for them, these could not have survived the assaults

alike of the clerical and secular powers. But for the commercial
spirit common to all the Northern nations, it is impossible to
see how the race could ever have emancipated itself from the
influence and traditions of the past, and from the ignorance
and moral degradation which preceded and followed the fall
of the Empire.

A radical distinction between the old and the new civilizations was the difference in the esteem in which the useful arts
were held. In the reign of Athelstan, in the early part of the
tenth century, a merchant who made three foreign voyages in
his own ship was ennobled. Plato banished tradesmen and
mechanics from his imaginary Republic. He pronounced
the trade of a shop-keeper to be a degradation to a freeman,
and wished it to be punished as a crime. Augustus Cæsar
condemned a senator to death, who had debased his rank by
taking part in a manufacture. Cato the Elder, on being
asked what he thought of lending money at usury, replied,
" What do you think of the crime of murder? " Aristotle
everywhere speaks in the most contemptuous terms of artisans
and tradesmen, who, he says, are not to be classed as citizens,
but *things* useful to the state. To use his own language : —

" In the best governed States, where the citizens are really of
intrinsic, and not of negative goodness, none of them should be
permitted to exercise any low mechanical employment or traffic, as
being ignoble and destructive to virtue. Neither should they who
are destined for office be husbandmen ; for leisure is necessary in
order to improve in virtue, and to perform the duty which they owe
to the State.

" Every work is to be esteemed mean, and every art and every
discipline as well, which renders the body, the mind, or the understanding of freemen unfit for the habit and practice of virtue ; for
which reason, all those arts which tend to form the body are called
mean, and all those employments which are exercised for gain, for
they take off from the leisure of the mind, and render it sordid.
There are, also, some liberal arts which are not improper for freemen to apply to in a certain degree ; but all sedulous endeavor to
acquire a perfect skill in them is exposed to the faults I have just
mentioned, for there is a great deal of difference in the reason for
which any one does or learns any thing: for it is not illiberal to
engage in it for the sake of one's self, or one's friend, or in the
cause of virtue ; while, at the same time, to do it for the sake of another may seem to be acting the part of a servant and slave." [1]

With such teachers as Plato and Aristotle, so wanting in
all sense of the rights of humanity, and so ignorant of all the

[1] Aristotle's Politics, Book vii. Chap. ix.

methods and conditions of human progress and of scientific inquiry; the highest virtues of whose civilizations are the worst vices of the new; whose propositions were fancies, and whose conclusions fables, — was it strange that, when they came to be authorities in the Church as well as in the Schools, a night of intense darkness settled over Europe, — a darkness which could never have been dispelled, but for the new races in whom a sense of duty, and the worth of man apart from his relations to the State, were most potent springs of action, and but for whom the picture presented by Western Asia might have been that presented to-day by those portions of Europe still occupied by what are termed the Latin Races?

The existence of independent commercial communities in constant intercourse, having similar objects and pursuits, and acting and reacting upon each other, laid the foundation, not only of the laws of nations, but of those economic and political systems which so strikingly distinguish modern from ancient society. Their passion for luxury and wealth could only be gratified by the possession of the precious metals, of which their own countries furnished but a scanty supply. These are the only materials out of which races unskilled in the mechanic arts can easily create articles of beauty and ornament, and which can be transported to the most distant points at small cost compared with their value. From the want of highways into the interior, the most important productions of Northern and Western Europe had a commercial value only along the navigable water-lines. Their wealth, therefore, necessarily came to be largely measured by the amount of gold and silver they possessed; and, in accordance with the spirit of the age, in which, from the teachings of the Church — which had assumed nothing less than entire authority in affairs, human as well as divine — the protective sentiment or idea was carried into, and sought to be enforced in every walk and department of life. It was regarded as a proper function of government to re-enforce by legal enactments individual enterprises in bringing the precious metals into, and retaining them within the country. The error consisted, not in an undue importance attached to the precious metals, and the desirableness of their possession, but in the methods by which it was sought to secure them. The nations had not then, if they have yet, learned that production must be in ratio to the freedom enjoyed by their people, — intellectual, political, and religious ; and that, as all balances in trade are always payable in coin, the people producing the greatest amount of merchandise will always have, relatively, the greatest amount of the precious metals ; and that, consequently, the wisest policy is to leave their articulations perfectly free. The amount of the precious metals of a nation is not to be measured by that which it actually has in hand, but by the quantity of them to which it has the right of possession. A capitalist may not have a dollar in hand who has millions loaned and payable in coin, at call. At the time when what is called the Mercantile System was in full vigor, usury was forbidden by law as well as by the teachings of religion. Had it been allowed, the political and religious disturbances which almost universally prevailed would have rendered it wholly unsafe for one people to have intrusted large amounts of capital to the safekeeping of another, and, perhaps, far distant one. At that time, usury, which now plays such a transcendent part in human affairs, was practised only by Jews and Lombards, and was often, itself, a fruitful cause of social disturbance.[1]

---

[1] The subject of usury is well fitted to form one of the most interesting chapters in the history of mankind. Upon none has there been a wider difference of opinion; of none has the importance been so little appreciated and understood ; none has been a more fruitful source of political and social disquiet; and none has presented to legislators more difficult problems for solution.

The earliest historical reference to the subject is to be found in the Mosaic law : " If thou lend money to any of my people that is poor by thee, thou shalt not be to him as an usurer, neither shalt thou lay upon him usury."— Exodus xxii. 25. "Thou shalt not lend upon usury to thy brother ; usury of money, usury of victuals, usury of any thing that is lent upon usury : unto a stranger thou mayest lend upon usury ; but unto thy brother thou shalt not lend upon usury, that the Lord thy God may bless thee." — Deuteronomy xxiii. 19, 20. These extracts recognize the abstract lawfulness of usury. Aristotle forbade it as against nature, that is, against the dignity of citizenship. As the Greeks, however, were inclined to nautical adventure and to commerce, the use of money in their operations was indispensable ; and, as the teachings of their philosophers carried very little moral obligation, usury was an almost universal practice among them, nor do there seem to have been any legal enactments against it. From the frequency of civil and political commotions, the rates charged were necessarily high. With the Romans, usury was practised from the foundation of the city. By the Twelve Tables, which probably did little more than embody the customary law, the rate for the use of money was fixed at twelve per cent. The penalty imposed for exacting a greater rate was the forfeiture of three times the amount usuriously taken. Such rate, for a new people, was not excessive, and would undoubtedly have given no sufficient ground of complaint but

The principles of the Mercantile System, as set out by
Smith, were as follows :—

" Two principles being established, — that wealth consisted in
gold and silver; and that these metals were brought into a country

for the terrible penalties which followed the non-payment of the debt. " The
cruelty," says Gibbon, "of the Twelve Tables against insolvent debtors still
remains to be told. After judicial proof or confession of debt, thirty days of
grace were allowed before a Roman was delivered into the power of his fellow-
citizen. In this private prison, twelve ounces of rice was his daily food; he
might be bound with a chain of fifteen pounds' weight, and his misery was
thrice exposed in the market-place to solicit the compassion of his friends and
countrymen. At the expiration of sixty days, the debt was discharged by the
loss of liberty or life; the insolvent debtor was either put to death or sold into
foreign slavery beyond the Tiber: but, if several creditors were alike obstinate
and unrelenting, they might legally dismember his body, and satiate their revenge by this horrid partition."—Decline and Fall of the Roman Empire,
Chap. xliv.
Although the severity of the Roman law in reference to usury became in
time greatly mitigated, usury under the Empire as well as under the Republic
was a standing grievance, and was one of the most difficult problems that
engaged the attention of the government. In the year 407, U. C., the rate was
lowered to five per cent. In the year 412, U. C., the taking of interest at any
rate was forbidden. This, like all similar laws, wherever enacted, was almost
wholly inoperative. Usury continued to be practised, the rates charged being
regulated according to the nature and risk of the transaction. Under the dic-
tatorship of Sulla, the rate was fixed at three per cent. Julius Cæsar attempted
to control it by police regulations. All such attempts, which were utterly futile,
only served to show the difficult nature of the subject with which they dealt.
They only aggravated the evils which they sought to cure. In the reign of the
Emperor Tiberius, the city was threatened with insurrection by those oppressed
by the exorbitant rates which continued to be charged. "Usury," says
Gibbon, " the intolerable grievance of Rome, was discouraged by the Twelve
Tables, and abolished by the clamors of the people. It was revived by their
wants and idleness; tolerated by the discretion of the prætors; and finally determined by the Code of Justinian. By that code, persons of illustrious rank
were confined to the moderate rate of four per cent; six was pronounced to be
the ordinary and legal standard of interest; eight was allowed for the convenience of manufacturers and merchants; twelve was granted to nautical
insurance, which the wiser ancients had not attempted to define. But, except
in this perilous adventure, the practice of exorbitant usury was severely restrained. The most simple interest was condemned by the clergy of the East
and West; but the sense of mutual benefit, which had triumphed over the
laws of the Republic, has resisted with equal firmness the decrees of the Church,
and even the prejudices of mankind."— Decline and Fall of the Roman Empire,
Chap. xliv.
Usury, among the ancients, does not appear to have been regarded as morally
wrong. With the Hebrews, it might be practised with the Gentiles. With
the Greek, it was against nature, — that is, was unworthy of a free citizen. It
might be practised by slaves, or by persons occupying an inferior political position, from whom the duties of the citizen were not required. With him, virtue

which had no mines, only by the 'balance of trade,' or by exporting to a greater value than it imported, — it necessarily became the
great object of Political Economy [1] to diminish as much as possible

was the synonyme of the modern word "honor." Neither term raised or involved
moral distinctions. Usury was detested by the Romans, chiefly from the cruelties
to which debtors were exposed. It was, perhaps, from such a sentiment that
Cato made his famous reply, when asked what he thought of the practice of usury.
No sooner, however, had the Empire been converted to Christianity than its
sinfulness came to be an established dogma. As the Hebrews were considered
as constituting one family, between the members of which usury was not to be
tolerated, so the early Christians regarded themselves in the same light, and
applied to themselves the same rule; and the Church, so soon as it acquired
sufficient power to speak authoritatively, declared it to be a crime punishable
by the severest penalties. Upon the revival of learning, the teachings of Aristotle came in to reënforce most powerfully the Mosaic injunction; and, as for
ages the Church was the paramount power, its teachings were accepted with
blind and unreasoning submission.

It may seem remarkable that a principle or practice from which the Church,
or the religious organizations at the present day, derive so vast an advantage,
and upon which are acknowledged to rest the moral as well as the material
welfare of society, should at the outset have encountered from them such bitter
hostility. The wonder ceases when the condition of the race at the time of its
conversion to Christianity, and the nature of the religious instinct, is considered.
It was inevitable that the early Christians should regard themselves as one
family, and apply to their condition the Mosaic rule. With such sentiments,
the teachings of Aristotle would be eagerly accepted. The unlawfulness of
usury having become a dogma, it was established for all time: for a dogma that
is proper for one age must be proper for all ages. It was *res judicata*. To
again raise the question, would have been to impugn the authority of the
Church, — a presumption upon no account to be tolerated. While the Church denounced usury as a deadly sin, and thundered its anathemas against all offenders,
for the discovery of whose crimes torture might be used, to whom the rites of
religion were refused in their lifetime, and who were condemned to eternal
punishment after death, the natural instinct of man still asserted itself. None
but Churchmen or Schoolmen felt it to be a sin to receive compensation for the
loan of that from which by its use they might derive an income; nor could a
borrower see any reason why he should not pay a part of the advantage which
a loan secured to him. If other articles of property, which might be returned,
were chargeable for their use, it was naturally asked why a charge might not be

---

[1] Smith has the folly to assume that Political Economy existed as a science as
early as the fifteenth or sixteenth centuries! There was no more notion of it
at the time he supposed, than there was of the laws of gravity. No higher or
broader sentiment was involved in the efforts of a nation, three hundred years
ago, to bring in and retain the precious metals within it, than that now felt by a
miser to get and hoard all he can. Both act in obedience to a common instinct
to accumulate the greatest possible amount of the highest form of property.
The whole system about which Smith makes so much ado, and the idea that
mediæval legislation in reference to the precious metals proceeded from, or represented any thing like, a deliberate study or investigation of the laws of money,
or of Political Economy, are sheer absurdities.

10

the importations of foreign goods for home consumption, and to increase, as much as possible, the exportation of the produce of domestic industry. Its two great engines, therefore, for enriching

made for the use of money? It was replied, that when a horse, for example, was borrowed and returned, the use of the horse was an advantage distinct from the horse; and for such an advantage a charge might properly be made. But, when money was borrowed and used, the thing itself was consumed. It was no longer in the hands of the borrower, nor had it any value distinct from its use. When, therefore, the borrower returned a sum equal to the loan, he had done all that was required of him. To make him pay for the use of the money borrowed, was to make him pay for that which, as far as he was concerned, did not exist; that is, to make him pay something which he did not receive, or to make him pay twice for the same thing. Such arguments, however conclusive with the Churchmen, were not so readily appreciated by the people. The authority of the former, however, was sufficient to confine the loaning of money to the Jews; to whom, as beyond the pale of the Church, its reasoning did not apply. In this way this class was vested, as it were, with the monopoly of money-lending, and became the money-changers and bankers of the world. Nothing can be more striking than their continuance and success in a calling which subjected them not only to the denunciations of the Church, and to the contempt and hatred of all Christians, but to the rapacity and lawlessness of the feudal tyrants of the countries in which they sojourned. They were outside the protection of the law; and it was a virtue, rather than a crime, to rob and persecute them. Yet they still continued to acquire and hold the greater part of the money of the world. About the close of the eleventh century, however, upon the revival of commerce in the free cities of Italy, their inhabitants became so far emancipated from the teachings and rules of the Church that usury was not only tolerated, but held to be an honorable calling. Its practice was one of the causes of the marvellous progress of those cities. Florence became what London is at the present time,—the monetary centre of the world. Their commercial spirit spread itself over the rest of Europe; and Italian bankers, known as the Lombards, soon became the rivals of the Jews, and were seated in every great mart of trade. It was from them that Lombard Street, in which they were chiefly collected in London, took its name. As they were Christians, and consequently tolerated, they soon eclipsed the Jews in their peculiar calling. The Church, however, did not change its attitude, nor was there any considerable amelioration in England of the laws against usury until 1546, in which its lawfulness was especially recognized by an act of Parliament. It was not till the Reformation, which emancipated the mind from the dogmas of the Church, that the subject of usury came to be treated in a manner which could lead to its proper solution. It could then be discussed upon its own merits. A large number of the leading reformers proclaimed its lawfulness; although to establish the rate to be charged was still considered to be, as it is to-day in many countries, a proper function of government. Even in the State of New York, the taking of more than seven per cent is punished by very severe penalties.

No proposition seems better established at the present time than that the charge for the use of money should, like that for all other kinds of property, be regulated by the demand; that the price of a horse, in the form of money, should be just as valuable to the holder as the horse. That so simple a truth should require ages to gain admittance into the mind or conviction of mankind must be almost wholly due to its teachers, and, in modern times, to Churchmen and Schoolmen. These classes have been the most formidable obstacles to the progress of society.

the country were restraints upon importation, and the encouragement of exportation.

" 1st. The restraints upon importation of such foreign goods for home consumption as could be produced at home, from whatever country they could be imported.

" 2d. Restraints upon the importation of goods of almost all kinds, from those particular countries with which the balance of trade was supposed to be disadvantageous.

" Exportations were encouraged, sometimes by drawbacks, sometimes by bounties, sometimes by advantageous treaties of commerce, and sometimes by the establishment of colonies in distant countries. . . .

" The two sorts of restraints upon importations above mentioned, together with these four encouragements to exportation, constitute the six principal means by which the commercial system proposes to increase the quantity of gold and silver in any country, by turning the 'balance of trade' in its favor."[1]

Smith has properly stated the theory upon which the so-called Mercantile System was based, — that the precious metals can be brought into a country not producing them, only by exporting a greater value of merchandise than is imported, — the balance being payable in coin. Hence the attempts by legislation to increase such balance. He opposed it on two grounds : first, the inadequacy of the object ; secondly, the inadequacy of the means to the object. The means were absurd, for the reason that the ends were equally so ; for why should the least valuable articles of commerce be the great object of commerce ?

" That wealth," to give his own words, " consists in money, or in gold and silver, is a popular notion which naturally arises from the double function of money, as the instrument of commerce and as

Man has risen in the scale just in ratio as their power and influence have declined. As there is no motive so strong as that which leads to the acquisition of property, so no motive or incitement, on the whole, can be more beneficent in its results. Capital is always a great moral agency in society. Some one always stands ready to take every dollar that is produced, in the hope that by uniting it with his own labor he can greatly benefit his condition, and still return a fair compensation for its use. But for such capital, he might be compelled to remain in indolence, a prey to all its evils. As he acquires strength, he accumulates for the purpose of lending to others. Every dollar he gains becomes a co-worker with him. His labor not only raises him above want, but is the condition of his highest moral training, and, by the capital it acquires, is the foundation of those institutions which in the highest degree alleviate the sufferings, and promote the advancement and welfare, of the race.

[1] Wealth of Nations, Book ii. Chap. i.

the measure of value. In consequence of its being the instrument of commerce, when we have money we can more readily obtain whatever else we have occasion for than by means of any other commodity. The great affair, we always find, is to get money. When that is obtained, there is no difficulty in making any subsequent purchase. In consequence of its being the measure of value, we estimate that of all other commodities by the quantity of money which they will exchange for. We say of a rich man, that he is worth a great deal, and of a poor man, that he is worth very little, money. A frugal man, or a man eager to be rich, is said to love money ; and a careless, a generous, or a profuse man is said to be indifferent about it. To grow rich is to get money; and wealth and money, in short, are in common language considered as in every respect synonymous.

" A rich country, in the same manner as a rich man, is supposed to be a country abounding in money; and to heap up gold and silver in any country is supposed to be the readiest way to enrich it. For some time after the discovery of America, the first inquiry of the Spaniards, when they arrived upon any unknown coast, used to be, if there was any gold or silver to be found in the neighborhood. By the information which they received, they judged whether it was worth while to make a settlement there, or if the country was worth the conquering. Plano Carpino, a monk, sent ambassador from the King of France to one of the sons of the famous Genghis Khan, says that the Tartars used frequently to ask him if there was plenty of sheep and oxen in the kingdom of France. Their inquiry had the same object with that of the Spaniards. They wanted to know if the country was rich enough to be worth the conquering. Among the Tartars, as among all other nations of shepherds, who are generally ignorant of the use of money, cattle are the instruments of commerce and the measures of value. Wealth, therefore, according to them, consisted in cattle, as, according to the Spaniards, it consisted in gold and silver. Of the two, the Tartar notion, perhaps, was the nearest to the truth. . . .

" It is not because wealth consists more essentially in money than in goods, that the merchant finds it generally more easy to buy goods with money than money with goods ; but because money is the known and established instrument of commerce, for which every thing is given in exchange, but which is not always with equal readiness to be got in exchange for every thing. The greater part of goods, besides, are more perishable than money, and he may frequently sustain a much greater loss by keeping them. When his goods are upon hand, too, he is more liable to such demands for money as he may not be able to answer, than when he has got their price in his coffers. Over and above all this, his profit arises more directly from selling than from buying ; and he is, upon all these accounts, generally much more anxious to exchange his goods for money than his money for goods. But though a particular merchant, with abundance of goods in his warehouse, may sometimes be ruined by not being able to sell them in time, a nation or country is not liable to the same accident. The whole capital of a merchant frequently consists in perishable goods destined for purchasing money. But it is but a very small part of the annual produce of the land and labor of a country which can ever be destined for purchasing gold and silver from their neighbors. The far greater part is circulated and consumed among themselves; and, even of the surplus which is sent abroad, the greater part is generally destined for the purchase of other foreign goods. Though gold and silver, therefore, could not be had in exchange for the goods destined to purchase them, the nation might not be ruined. It might, indeed, suffer some loss and inconvenience, and be forced upon some of those expedients which are necessary for supplying the place of money. The annual produce of its land and labor, however, would be the same, or very nearly the same, as usual; because the same, or very nearly the same, consumable capital would be employed in maintaining it. And though goods do not always draw money as readily as money draws goods, in the long run they draw it more necessarily than even it draws them. Goods can serve many other purposes besides purchasing money; but money can serve no other purpose besides purchasing goods. Money, therefore, necessarily runs after goods; but goods do not always or necessarily run after money. The man who buys does not always mean to sell again, but frequently to use or to consume; whereas, he who sells always means to buy again. The one may frequently have done the whole, but the other can never have done more than the one-half of his business. It is not for its own sake that men desire money, but for the sake of what they can purchase with it."[1]

The distinction that Smith made between money as an instrument of commerce, and as a measure of value, is wholly fanciful. Money is an instrument of commerce for the reason that it is a measure of value; and a measure of value for the reason that it is an instrument of commerce. The instrument and the measure are always identical. They can never be separated. A person sells a barrel of flour for ten dollars in gold, for the reason that the gold has the same value with the flour. Equivalents are exchanged. Five dollars in gold would not be accepted for the flour, for the very good reason that they are not worth as much. The instrument and the measure pass from buyer to seller at the same moment and by the same act, and *vice versa ;* for the flour is the instrument of commerce which measures the value of the gold, just as much as the gold is the instrument of commerce which measures the value of the flour. The measure is never separated from the value, as in the case of the yardstick, which never passes with the goods it measures. Smith's double function of money, there-

[1] Wealth of Nations, Book iii. Chap. i.

fore, which he took without credit from Law, is a pure fiction, — a fiction, unfortunately, which has done a vast amount
of mischief; for it is one which has been accepted as a fundamental principle in monetary science from his day to our own,
and is the great cause of the confusion and error which still
prevail.

As a person is rich in proportion to the amount of coin — the
highest form of property — which he holds, so a person is rich
in proportion to the number of oxen and horses he owns.
Money is not every thing, no more than oxen and horses. The
Spaniards were right, as their only object was wealth, in making gold and silver in South America and Mexico their chief
object, in place of the other products of these countries. They
grew rich much faster by wringing these articles out of the
natives, than they could by any other mode. The amount of
gold and silver they collected was something the like of which
was never seen. They enriched themselves beyond measure.
There is, however, another side to this picture. The adventurers
were a set of robbers and cut-throats, and in the end shared
the fate of robbers and cut-throats. Like all of their class,
they were speedily rid of their ill-gotten gains ; and both Spain
and her colonies have ever since been paying the penalties of
their follies and crimes in impoverishment, a prey to intestine
feuds, without ambition, without capacity or hope, — a by-word
and reproach among the nations. The Tartars inquired, and
very properly, of an ambassador sent by the King of France,
whether there were many sheep or oxen in that country, as a
means of informing themselves of the degree of its wealth,
their wealth consisting chiefly in their herds. This does not
prove them to be a higher form of capital ; only that, from their
want of exchangeable commodities, it was the only kind of
capital they could acquire in any considerable amount. These
could not be sent to Peru and Mexico in exchange for gold.
In the same sense, an Esquimaux would ask a West Indian
whether there were many seals and walruses in his country.
By such inquiries by a people ignorant of, or possessing little
gold and silver, Smith would infer that these articles did not
constitute wealth. Indeed, he seems to think such inquiries
to be conclusive ; as he intimates that the Tartars' test of
wealth — sheep and oxen — was a better one than that of the
Spaniards — gold and silver.

"It is not," says Smith, "because wealth consists more exclusively in money than in goods that the merchant finds it generally more easy to buy goods with money than to buy money with goods, but because money is the known and established instrument of commerce, for which every thing is readily given in exchange, but which is not always with equal readiness to be got in exchange for every thing." Why did money become an established instrument of commerce for which every thing is readily given in exchange? Does not such universal experience establish a law, and could not Smith have been much better employed in investigating the phenomena, for the purpose of deducing the law, than in wearying the reader with page after page of loose and vague assumptions, not one of which will bear the test even of ordinary scrutiny? In the discussion of money, he failed to solve a single proposition. He is like a traveller who, lost in a wood or fog, always speedily comes round to the point at which he started. No progress is made, — only constant iteration of the same circle; so that any account he might give of his wanderings would be but the repetition of the same experiences and the description of the same scenes. So Smith's argument upon the nature and origin of money; upon the real and nominal price of commodities; upon metallic and paper money, and upon the mercantile system, is but a repetition that money is an invention from the sense of its necessity; that in its use it is wholly unproductive; that only such an amount of it can remain in circulation as is necessary to effect the exchanges of society; that an issue of paper money always displaces from circulation an equal amount of coin; and that the only mode by which the latter can be made productive is to send it to other countries. He uses, throughout, arguments precisely similar to sustain propositions wholly different in kind.

Another fiction is his assertion that a profit more frequently arises from selling than from buying; and that the merchant, consequently, is much more anxious to sell his goods for money than his money for goods. The old adage, that goods well bought are half sold, is exactly opposed to this assumption. It is utter folly, however, to assume any thing of the kind. The profit or loss of a transaction cannot be told till after the goods that have been purchased are sold. It hinges as much upon one act as upon the other. To attempt to decide in which act is the greater profit is on a par with an attempt to determine which of two equal quantities is the larger.

Not content with asserting that goods can be more readily obtained for money than money for goods, Smith proceeds immediately to prove the converse of this proposition. " Though goods," he says, " do not always draw money so readily as money draws goods, in the long run they draw it more readily than it draws them. Goods can serve many other purposes beside purchasing money ; but money can serve no other purpose beside the purchase of goods. Money, therefore, necessarily runs after goods ; but goods do not always, or necessarily, run after money. The man who buys does not always mean to sell again ; whereas he who sells always means to buy again. It is not for its own sake that men desire money ; but for the sake of what they can purchase with it." As in all transactions for the sale of merchandise equivalents are exchanged, or are assumed to be exchanged, and as each party equally assents thereto, it is difficult to see that the running which he describes is more on one side than the other. The illustration is simply an attempt to prove that of two equally strong motives, or inclinations, one is stronger than the other ; or that the tide flows inland with more strength than it flows outward. His assertion, that goods can serve many other purposes than the purpose of money, while money can serve no other purpose than the purchase of goods, shows that he had not the least comprehension of the matter upon which he wrote. The exchange of money for goods, or goods for money, is simply an exchange of one kind of merchandise for another. To assert that one of the subjects of exchange can have no use but to serve as the instrument of exchange, is equivalent to asserting that it has no value in itself, or that it is, like a yardstick, the mere instrument of exchange. It is the old story which Smith is always repeating under all possible forms, that money is not merchandise, and that value is no necessary attribute of it. The exact opposite to his assertion is the truth. Money — gold and silver — serves vastly wider uses than any other kind of merchandise. Food can have no other purpose than to be eaten ; cloth, no other than for making garments. The precious metals, on the other hand, enter into almost every department of social economy. It is the variety of their uses which renders their value more uniform than that of any other

articles. They are the only articles which can serve as reserves. It is these, with other qualities which they possess,
that fit them to serve as money. No other articles of property
have such a wide range of use. Smith and the Economists have
adopted exactly the opposite theory, — that the precious metals,
of all articles, had the narrowest range of use; that their possession was to be avoided, was to be discouraged rather than
encouraged, and that the only way to turn them to account
was to send them abroad in exchange for what was useful.
In reply to his assertion, that it is not for its own sake that men
desire money, it may be replied that it is for its own sake that
they do desire it; as by means of its intrinsic value they can
always obtain that of which they stand in need. It frequently
happens when money is acquired its possessor has no notion of
the objects for which he may expend it; or he may intend never
to expend it, but to invest it for the income it will yield.
A man labors for money just as diligently when he has a hundred times more than he knows how to spend, as he does when
he is pinched with hunger.

Money, Smith tells us, is the least valuable part of the capital
of a community. In the same breath, almost, he tells us that
the great thing is to get money. That got, every thing else
follows. If money be the master of every thing else, and if
it secure by direct exchange whatever its possessor may wish
to purchase, how is it that it is the least valuable and least
productive part of a person's capital? What constitutes value
but demand and uses?

"Although," says Smith, "gold and silver could not be
had" [to serve as money] "in exchange for goods destined
to purchase them, the nation would not be ruined. It might,
indeed, suffer some loss and inconveniency, and be forced
upon some of those expedients which are necessary for supplying the place of money. The annual produce of its land
and labor, however, would be the same, or very nearly the
same, as usual; because the same, or very nearly the same,
consumable capital would be employed in maintaining it."
What expedients would he use? Not legal tender surely?
That he never contemplated. He could not have a symbolic
currency without reserves of coin. The nation, consequently,
would be without any currency whatever. Its industries, notwithstanding, were to go on as before. Some inconvenience,

but no considerable loss, would result. It has been shown that life without money is the life of the savage. To give it up is, at the same moment, to give up our cvilization. Smith would have all our present conditions maintained, throwing away the very foundation upon which they rest. Such were his ignorance and incapacity that he could hardly venture upon an assertion that did not involve him in the grossest contradictions and absurdities.

The reason why the dogmas of Aristotle and Smith have had such universal acceptance is the absence of all attempt at proof in their support. They are pure assumptions. Had it been attempted to establish them by any process of reasoning, the utter inadequacy of the evidence would have been fatal to the attempt. To offer a reason is always a dangerous expedient. If one would command assent, his words must be those of an oracle. He must transcend the vulgar processes of reason and induction, of proof. The public do not want to be told how a thing is true, but that it is true. A mere charlatan, consequently, will often for a time find wider acceptance than a man of the most solid qualities. An affirmation without a reason may be above the reach of reason. How is it to be demonstrated that Aristotle's fifth element or essence does not exist? — how that all diseases do not operate through the fluids rather than through the solids? All that is wanting, often, to the perpetuation of a theory or error, no matter how gross, is its mere statement. The moment assent is secured, it may defy for ages all assault; for the reason that the methods likely to be brought to its attack have no adaptation to their object.

The doctrines of the Economists in reference to " Balance of Trade " are the necessary sequence of those held by them in reference to money. What could be more absurd than to make that the object of commerce which was the least valuable subject of commerce, or which was not even a subject of commerce? The premises admitted, the conclusions were inevitable. With them, the suggestion of the importance of a favorable balance of trade was the red rag to the bull: it was enough to throw them into paroxysms of rage and fury. The welfare of a nation was to be measured by the amount of the precious metals it could get rid of. In parting with them, it parted with that which was comparatively valueless for that which might be highly valuable. Better to part with them for silks and wines than to keep them; as some use and satisfaction, at least, could be got out of the former, while little or nothing could be got out of the latter. If, on the other hand, gold and silver be the highest, instead of the lowest, form of capital, then the greater the amount accumulated the richer the nation becomes. As they are capital, a favorable balance payable in them is that for which every individual and nation has always been and is constantly striving. The amount of such balances measures the degree of their acquisition or wealth. It is not necessary that the balances arising should be immediately paid over, or paid over at all, in coin. If the immediate payment of such balances be forborne, the party in whose favor they are found is compensated by receiving interest on the amount. Such interest or income makes a part of his wealth. Even Huskisson, one of the most intelligent of Englishmen, and hardly to be named in connection with the Economists, fell into their common error. In his essay in vindication of the Report of the Bullion Committee, of which he was a distinguished member, he uses the following language: —

"Two very erroneous opinions on this subject are most generally received in the theory of the mercantile world: —

"1st. That, whenever the exchange is against any country, the natural and general course of balancing the account is by a payment in bullion.

"2dly. That the balance of these payments in favor of any country is finally to be measured by what is called the *balance of trade*, or the excess of exports above imports. . . . Such is affirmed to be the present situation of this country, and the true explanation of the very depressed state of our foreign exchanges.

"The first of these positions is so little conformable to truth, and to the real course of business between nations, that there is, perhaps, no one article of general consumption and demand which forms the foundation of so few operations of trade between the different countries of Europe as bullion; and that the operations which do take place originate almost entirely in the fresh supplies which are yearly poured in from the mines of the New World, and are chiefly confined to the distribution of those supplies through the different parts of Europe. If this supply were to cease altogether, the dealings in gold and silver, as objects of foreign trade, would be very few, and those of short duration." [1]

[1] Huskisson on the Depreciation of the Currency, pp. 48–50.

Huskisson could not have written so carelessly, but for the acceptance of dogmas the truth of which it never occurred to him to examine. He had been told that gold and silver were not the subjects — only the instruments — of commerce; that the only way in which a nation could avail itself of their value was to export them. No man knew better than he "that," to repeat him, "whenever the exchange is against any country, the natural and obvious course of balancing the account is by payment in bullion." No man more often asserted, in general terms, such fact or law. It was the great theme and conclusion of the Bullion Report: yet, when he sat down to write upon it, he fell into the grossest of errors, simply for the reason that, from the want of a little reflection, he adopted the language and nomenclature in common use; and, in doing so, he asserted what he must have known to be exactly contrary to the fact. From the phenomena — from the sale of every thing for coin — it might well be inferred that the possession of gold and silver was the only object of commerce, instead of being, as he tells us, "the one article of general consumption and demand which forms the foundation of the fewest operations of trade between the different countries of Europe;" and that, "were it not for the supply constantly coming in from the New World, dealings in bullion would in great measure cease." Was there ever an instance of a man of such real ability and originality so completely mastered by Bacon's "idol of the theatre"?[1]

There can be no doubt that the welfare of each nation is best promoted by the distribution of the precious metals the world over in proper equilibrium. Such equilibrium tends to a harmonious condition of production and trade; and, as all civilized nations form one great commercial community, the

[1] There are idols which have crept into men's minds from the various dogmas of peculiar systems of philosophy, and also from the perverted rules of demonstration; and these we denominate idols of the theatre. For we regard all the systems of philosophy hitherto received or imagined as so many plays brought out and performed, creating fictitious and theatrical worlds. Nor do we speak only of the present systems, or of the philosophy and sects of the ancients; since numerous other plays of a similar nature can be still composed and made to agree with each other, the causes of the most opposite errors being generally the same. Nor, again, do we allude merely to general systems, but also to many elements and axioms of sciences, which have become inveterate by tradition, implicit credence, and neglect. — Novum Organum, Book i. 44.

welfare of all is measured by that of each. Money, as such, is an instrument in production and distribution, and should be supplied in proper measure to all. If a balance result in favor of any one nation to be paid in coin, — if that balance, or the greater part of it, can be employed more profitably by the community from which it is due than by the one to which it is due, — it is for the interest of both that such balance should remain within the indebted community; the proper compensation to be paid for its use, till a balance arises against the community which is for the present the creditor. The one indebted can frequently pay interest with much less inconvenience than it could immediately pay the principal sum. Forbearance of present payment, as a rule, can always be had by payment of interest at some rate. In this way, if, from accidental causes, such as the failure of crops, any community be unable to meet its accruing obligations by exports of merchandise, it is not compelled to draw too largely upon its reserves of coin. It is of the utmost importance to communities making use of symbolic currencies that such reserves should not suddenly be drawn from them; for the reason that, if they be drawn, such currency must be reduced in far greater ratio. The currency of Great Britain, as already shown, equals, say £550,000,000. The reserves held by the Banks and bankers issuing it do not exceed, probably, seven per cent of its amount, or, say, £35,000,000. As the percentage of reserves to liabilities must be maintained, it follows that if £10,000,000 of such reserves be permanently drawn, the currency must be reduced by nearly £175,000,000. Of course, new reserves would be provided with all possible speed; but not before a large contraction had been made, and great loss and suffering caused. "The state of the trade" in that country is watched with the utmost care and anxiety by the only power competent to deal with the subject, — the Bank of England. Should it appear that any considerable portion of its reserves, in which are included those of the whole country, are likely to be drawn, it would meet the emergency by an immediate advance in the rate of interest, and in this way reduce the volume of the currency by rendering it unprofitable for the public to borrow. What, therefore, the government could by no means do, the Bank, an *imperium in imperio*, is fully competent to do. The former might prohibit the export of coin; but it could add no proper sanctions to its decrees,

and a law without a sanction is no law. If it were for the
advantage of a party holding coin to export it, the government
could not prevent its export. But the Bank can always enforce its legislation by an appropriate sanction. From such
legislation there is no appeal. From the penalty imposed
there can be no escape. The Board of Directors of the Bank
meets weekly to consider the situation, and legislate as it may
require. It may not directly attempt to import gold, assuming the action of natural law will bring in a quantity sufficient
for its needs. It does undertake, and most vigilantly, that
such quantity as is necessary for the proper maintenance of
its industry and trade shall not suddenly be taken from it.
The efficiency of its action, unsupported by a single legal
enactment, in matters where governments wielding the
power of life and death are wholly impotent, is a striking
proof of the wisdom of that policy by which individuals, as
well as nations, commit themselves to the guidance of natural
laws in reference to production and trade, in preference to
those of human contrivance. It is also a triumphant vindication of the soundness of the doctrine of the " Balance of Trade ; "
and proves that the founders of the Mercantile System — if
such system were ever deliberately founded, which is by no
means probable — were wrong, not in assuming gold and silver
to be the highest and most desirable form of property, but only
in the means by which they sought to acquire their possession.

It is assumed by the admirers of Smith that he proved the
policy of Free-Trade to be preferable to that of Protection.
As an abstract proposition, it may be preferable, as peace may
be preferable to war. But such questions are to be decided by
concrete — if the word may be used — rather than by abstract
reasoning. It may be that war will be accepted by a people
as far preferable to peace. They may admit all the objections
that can be urged against it, yet obey sentiments or principles
which transcend argument or reason. They may engage in it
to avoid something worse than all the calamities it can impose.
To such a people there may be things more to be dreaded than
annihilation. So the abstract argument in favor of Free-Trade
carries no sense or conviction to the Australian or Canadian.
When it is addressed to him, he replies : " That may be a very
good doctrine for you in England, but a very poor one for me

in Australia. You are so strong there that you will declare
war upon me the moment you see that I am about to engage
in any industry which threatens to deprive you of your markets ; and will certainly overthrow me, unless the community
in which I live will, in self-defence, combine to keep you at a
distance. Protection, with us, is but another word for self-
defence. It is the only means by which we can secure a material, economic, and, perhaps, political independence. What
you call Protection is with us self-sacrifice. It is a sacrifice
which individuals as well as communities must make, as a
necessary condition of wealth and prosperity. A man just
entering upon life with nothing but his hands, cannot indulge
in the same habits, expenditures, and methods of business as
one possessed of wealth, experience, and the confidence of the
public, — all of them acquired by long years of patient sacrifice and industry. The new rival must go through a similar
experience and training, before he can engage in enterprises on
a similar scale, or indulge himself in similar habits and expenditures." The truth, therefore, of the doctrine of Free-Trade,
as a rule of universal application, can never be demonstrated
by proof or argument. It results from a condition, not from
a law. What is evidence to one party or community is no
evidence to another. A Free-Trader is such from interest, not
from benevolence or principle. So with the doctrine of Protection. In England, Free-Trade is accepted as an elemental
truth. In her colonies, Protection is accepted with equal confidence. The same man, with the same reason, is a Free-
Trader in one country and a Protectionist in another. In
England, a manufacturer believes that, from the low price of
labor and material, from the high mechanical skill and great
abundance of capital at his command, and from his unrivalled
means of distribution, he can supply goods at a lower price
or cost than they can be produced in any other country in the
world. He feels, therefore, that his success is assured, provided
his fabrics, when they reach the consumer, shall be charged
with no other burden than cost, and that the material he works
up shall reach him charged with no other burden. He believes,
consequently, that Free-Trade should be the policy of mankind. The same person placed in the colonies would very
well know that he could not compete with manufacturers in
England, — of textiles, for example. He would feel, however,

that the raw material of his new home should be worked up, in part at least, upon or near the spot where it was grown. He would understand that to undertake its manufacture, exposed to the competition which he would be sure to encounter from the mother country, would be fatal to him, unless he were protected by some law or impost duty which would give him the home, or a part of the home, market. He would gladly make any personal sacrifice, if this would avail. As it would not, he appeals to the community in which he lives to unite with him in making it, by paying him higher rates for what he may produce than they would be compelled to pay for the imported article. He is supported by the colonists, from a conviction that his success will promote their advantage by increasing the prices of their products, by adding to their numbers and their means of consumption. They might, to be sure, believe that when manufactures became well established among them the impost duties might be removed, — their imposition being only a temporary expedient. The same men, therefore, are Free-Traders in one country and Protectionists in another. To say that either doctrine is absolutely true is to beg the question altogether. There is the same reason for affirming each to be true under certain conditions. To prove the superiority of Free-Trade, the home manufacturer must show that it is for the interest of the colonists to allow him to work up their raw material, and send back the finished product. The Australian or the Canadian replies that his country can never come to any thing so long as its products are restricted to wool or wheat. The conviction and reason on one side are as strong as they are in the other. The Protectionist, struggling for something better, and prepared to make great sacrifices to secure it, is certainly more fitted to enlist sympathy than the Free-Trader, who stands ready to crush out every rival by means of the experience, training, and capital he has acquired. The age of Protection, therefore, is the heroic one, — the age of self-sacrifice, of achievement : that of Free-Trade, of realization, of enjoyment, — in other words, of selfishness. The one bears the same relation to the other that the ardor, generosity, and sympathy of youth bear to the cold, calculating selfishness of wealth and age.

It may be urged, that, all things being equal, freedom of trade would promote the highest condition of the race. But all things can never be equal. One nation or community will, in some particulars, either from situation, natural resources, a greater abundance of capital, or a better trained industry, always excel others; so that the same disparity of conditions witnessed to-day is likely to prevail for all future time, dividing the world, as it is now, into two great camps, each using the same arguments with those now urged. While neither of the two doctrines—Free-Trade or Protection—can be shown to be of universal application, or reconciled the one with the other, the latter is the more liable of the two to abuse; as it is, compared with Free-Trade, a positive and active principle, and as it is supported by far the greater number of communities or nations. It is often made the pretext for the creation, by government, of odious and oppressive monopolies. When excessive, it is liable to give a most unhealthy impulse to the industries of those adopting it, and become most vexatious by raising prices of many articles far beyond the reach of the working or laboring classes. As a rule, individuals are wiser as to the industries they may pursue, and the methods by which these may be conducted, than governments. The latter, consequently, should be very careful in interposing in such matters. The tendency of the age is in striking contrast with the protective spirit, which, hardly a generation ago, prevailed among every people in matters of education, religion, and opinion, as well as in those which related to production and trade. The sentiment which inspired such interference was dictated, not so much by a desire to promote the welfare of the people, as to merge all power in the hands of government. Protection in matters of trade, therefore, is now regarded with suspicion as an instrument of oppression and as a relic of barbarism. This tendency favors the free articulation of every individual in what concerns his own welfare. It increases in strength with the progress of mankind in intelligence and morals. The condition of the great mass of humanity is almost infinitely superior to what it was, even a few generations ago, when art, religion, government, education, personal freedom, were monopolies, — the result of an exclusively protective spirit. As Free-Trade is certain to have the support of those who have made the greatest progress, it is constantly gaining strength at the expense of Protection, in having for its advocates those who from their wealth and intelligence give direction to the ideas and sentiments of mankind. The reason why no progress is made in determining the relative value of the two systems, is because the question, as treated, is an insoluble one. Argument leaves the question precisely in the condition in which it is taken up; and is no more likely to dispose of it than are the deliberations of peace societies to put an end to war. No argument can convert a nation to the doctrines of Free-Trade whose condition does not, without argument, beget such sentiments; or to the opposite doctrine, one who does not feel in its condition the necessity of Protection.

For merchants and manufacturers Smith had a contempt as great as ever that felt by Plato or Aristotle. They were the authors of all the illiberal doctrines in reference to commerce, and of all the restrictions imposed upon it. From these the nobility and gentry learned what little they knew. This contempt may have not a little to do with his ideas as to the insignificance of money.

"The sneaking arts of underling tradesmen," he says, "are thus erected into political maxims for the conduct of a great empire; for it is the most underling tradesmen only who make it a rule to employ chiefly their own customers. A great trader purchases his goods always where they are cheapest and best, without regard to any little interest of this kind.

"By such maxims as these, however, nations have been taught that their interest consisted in beggaring all their neighbors. Each nation has been made to look with an invidious eye upon the prosperity of all the nations with which it trades, and to consider their gain as its own loss. Commerce, which ought naturally to be, among nations as among individuals, a bond of union and friendship, has become the most fertile source of discord and animosity. The capricious ambition of kings and ministers has not, during the present and the preceding century, been more fatal to the repose of Europe than the impertinent jealousy of merchants and manufacturers. The violence and injustice of the rulers of mankind is an ancient evil, for which, I am afraid, the nature of human affairs can scarce admit of a remedy. But the mean rapacity, the monopolizing spirit, of merchants and manufacturers, — who neither are nor ought to be the rulers of mankind, — though it cannot perhaps be corrected, may very easily be prevented from disturbing the tranquillity of anybody but themselves."[1]

The impotent spite which dictated this incoherent passage borders very nearly upon untruth. It was the underling, the

[1] Wealth of Nations, Book iv. Chap. iii.

shopkeeper, — the impersonation, with Smith as with Aristotle, of baseness and selfishness, — who directed and controlled the policy of nations, who taught them that their
advantage was best promoted by beggaring all their neighbors.
How did these underlings get at the ears of kings and cour-
tiers, and instil into their minds such pernicious doctrines?
In the very same breath, he tells us that merchants and manufacturers neither are nor ought to be the rulers of mankind.
Whether its rulers or not, they are the class which, throughout
the ages, has nurtured and sustained the spirit of freedom,
without which there could have been neither material progress
nor moral life. Without these classes, a despotism must have
prevailed so universal and inexorable that the race itself must
have become extinct or savage. A nation is rich, intelligent,
and free in ratio as it collects within and appropriates to itself,
not only the products, but the ideas and methods, of all other
lands. The story of foreign countries, of their inhabitants,
their institutions, their wealth, — of their physical aspects, so
inviting or so terrible, — excites the imagination, and gives an
impulse to enterprise and adventure that faces every danger,
and triumphs over every obstacle. It is the school which
trains the individual to deeds of heroic daring and faith, and
which develops and perfects the highest faculties of his nature.
The story of the Argonautic Expedition, whether fabulous or
true, exerted a most powerful influence over the pursuits, the
ideas, and the imagination of the Greeks, and was one of
the means which helped to raise that people to its high place
among the nations. With the Northmen, a love of nautical
adventure was both the outgrowth and support of that spirit
of freedom which so distinguishes them from all other races,
and modern from ancient society. By means of it, the moral,
as the intellectual qualities of the race have alike been nurtured and strengthened. To come down to modern times,
who in England first welcomed that great reformation in religion which gave to the nation a new consciousness and a new
life? The commercial and industrial classes. Who met and
overthrew the Great Armada, and saved their country from a
foreign yoke? The merchants of England, with ships fitted
out and manned at their own cost. Who preserved her liberties in the great crisis in which those of all other nations were
overthrown, and when the Stuarts sought to model her consti-

tution after the despotism of France? The tradesmen and tradesmen's clerks, — the train-bands of London. Who contributed most to expel that odious dynasty, and restore to their country her liberties; who have made England another England; and who, if the enemies of progress are to be believed, have subverted her constitution by restoring to it its original spirit? The merchants of London, the same who founded the Bank of England, which so earnestly and efficiently sustained the government in preventing the return to power of that detested family. Who, within the memory of the living, carried through those great reforms which gave to the people cheap food, and removed those social and political distinctions which had so long been a disgrace to the nation? Its merchants and manufacturers, so well known as the Manchester School. The tendency of agricultural pursuits, from the iteration of seasons and employments, is to so limit the range and deaden the faculties that, were there no other pursuits, the race, if it had ever risen by other helps, would become a mere machine, would lose all aspiration and capacity for progress, and relapse into brutal stolidity. The merchant, on the other hand, creates his conditions. With him, nothing is fixed: every thing is changing. He adds to and enlarges his ideas by constant contact with all lands and races. His ventures are stimulated by the possibility of gains far beyond those usually falling to the lot of the tiller of the soil. His profession demands the constant exercise of the highest qualities; the combination and execution of great plans; a knowledge of the character, wants, and means of those with whom he has to deal, and of the condition of trade and the money markets throughout the world. His field is the world. He soon learns, instinctively as it were, if he be fitted to become a great merchant, that his success must be in ratio to his probity. It is for these reasons that the merchant is necessarily the highest type of a man of affairs. There is no morality like mercantile morality; for nowhere else is morality so indispensable to success, or exercised on so grand a scale. We do not admire the force that draws a pin to the earth; but we stand in awe of that which directs the motions of the planets, and holds them within their appropriate spheres.

"That it was the spirit of monopoly," says Smith, "which originally both invented and propagated this doctrine, cannot be doubted ; and they who first taught it were by no means such fools as they who believed it. In every country, it always is and must be the interest of the great body of the people to buy whatever they want of those who sell it cheapest. The proposition is so very manifest that it seems ridiculous to take any pains to prove it ; nor could it ever have been called in question, had not the interested sophistry of merchants and manufacturers confounded the common sense of mankind. Their interest is, in this respect, directly opposite to that of the great body of the people." [1]

" Such as they were, however, those arguments [in favor of the protective system] convinced the people to whom they were addressed. They were addressed by merchants to parliaments and to the councils of princes, to nobles and to country gentlemen, by those who were supposed to understand trade, to those who were conscious to themselves that they knew nothing about the matter. That foreign trade enriched the country, experience demonstrated to the nobles and country gentlemen, as well as to the merchants ; but how, or in what manner, none of them well knew. The merchants knew perfectly in what manner it enriched themselves : it was their business to know it. But to know in what manner it enriched the country was no part of their business. The subject never came into their consideration. But, when they had occasion to apply to their country for some change in the laws relating to foreign trade, it then became necessary to say something about the beneficial effects of foreign trade, and the manner in which those effects were obstructed by the laws as they then stood. To the judges who were to decide the business, it appeared a most satisfactory account of the matter when they were told that foreign trade brought money into the country, but that the laws in question hindered it from bringing so much as it otherwise would do. These arguments, therefore, produced the wished-for effect." [2]

No sooner had Smith come to the discussion of a class of men whom he despised, than his doctrines of Free-Trade were thrown to the winds. Mankind, he says in effect, are divided into two classes, knaves and fools ; merchants forming the first. " Their interest," he tells us, " is directly opposed to that of the great body of the people." How ? It is certainly for the interest of the great body of the people to buy whatever they want of those who sell the cheapest. Such a sentiment, so plain, he tells us could not have been called in question but for the sophistry of merchants and manufacturers, who tell the people that they should not buy where they can buy cheapest, but where they must buy dearest. But why should not merchants buy where they can buy cheapest ? The lower

[1] Wealth of Nations, Book iv. Chap. iii.
[2] Wealth of Nations, Book iv. Chap. i.

the rate the greater their profit.   Would they not be likely to
seek the best markets ; and, if they appealed to government,
would it not be to open up those where the cheapest goods
were to be found ?   Would not their interests and those of the
people lie in the same direction ?   He says they knew perfectly
well how to enrich themselves, but cared nothing whether or
not they enriched the public.   How could they enrich themselves without enriching the public ?   Is not public wealth
made up of individual wealth ? Supposing them to be the selfish
and unscrupulous creatures he assumed, would they not, for
their own interest, adopt precisely the same policy as those
who were benevolent and upright, — buy in the cheapest and
sell in the dearest market, — even if they were in conspiracy
against mankind, and found no difficulty in imposing upon the
feeble and derelict minds of noblemen and princes, — the rulers
of the nation, — so as to bend the law to their base purposes?
But if merchants are not to be trusted, if they are certain to
combine against the welfare of their fellows, and are only kept
to their duties by the strong arm of the law, what becomes of
the doctrine of Free-Trade, which is based upon the assumption that the merchant, when left to himself, is certain to act
in reference to the welfare of others in acting in reference to
his own.   According to Smith, the very agents who are to
carry it out are certain to prove false to it.   If they are not
to be trusted, who are ?   They were as honest and straight-
forward in his day as they are now, or as they are ever likely
to be.   He had, however, no faith in them, and vented his spleen
and hatred, as the only mode by which they could be made to
pay some penalty for their rascalities and oppressions.   He
certainly spent a lifetime to very little purpose in erecting a
system impossible for the want of proper instruments of
execution.

It is by the " sneaking arts of underling tradesmen " that
England is what she is.   As the gains of the merchant must
be in ratio to the means of those with whom he deals, it must
be for his interest, and consequently his object, to do all he can
to enrich instead of beggaring them.   At the time that Smith
wrote, commerce was almost the only pacific influence at work
in Europe.   It was the bond of friendship, so far as any such
bond existed.   It was the ruling classes — the landholders,
with the dynastic pretensions and ambitions of princes — that

converted Europe into one vast military camp. His whole
tirade is entirely misdirected. There was commercial ignorance enough, no doubt. Compared with the present, his was
a barbarous age; but the progress which has since been made
has not been the work of kings or princes, or of owners of the
soil, but of the wider scope and influence of principles or
causes then at work, though sadly hampered and thwarted by
that ambition, ignorance, and selfishness which have gradually
yielded to a higher and better law. Smith saw no hope of a
better state of things, because he wholly ignored the moral
elements — the sense of duty — as chief factors in civilization.
The foundations upon which he erected the superstructure of
his " Wealth of Nations " are the selfish instincts of the race.
With such premises, it was inevitable that he should make a
disastrous failure. He is the legitimate founder of the school
which assumes to treat man by the same methods that it would
a lump of earth, or the laws of gravity or motion, — which
assumes that as gravity or attraction is in ratio to quantity, so
man's nature is affected in the same way; so much attraction,
so much compliance, — with whom, as with Buckle, civilization
is the necessary product or evolution of given quantities of
moisture and heat!

"Country gentlemen and farmers," Smith continues, " are, to
their great honor, of all people the least subject to the wretched
spirit of monopoly. . . . They have no secrets, such as those of the
greater part of manufacturers; but are generally rather fond of
communicating to their neighbors, and of extending, as far as
possible, any new practice which they have found to be advantageous. . . . Country gentlemen and farmers, dispersed in different
parts of the country, cannot so easily combine as merchants and
manufacturers, who being collected into towns, and accustomed to
that exclusive corporation spirit which prevails in them, naturally
endeavor to obtain against all their countrymen the same exclusive
privilege which they generally possess against the inhabitants of
their respective towns. They accordingly seem to have been the
original inventors of these restraints upon the importation of foreign goods, which secure to them the monopoly of the home market. It was, probably, in imitation of them, and to put themselves
upon a level with those who, they found, were disposed to oppress
them, that the country gentlemen and farmers of Great Britain
so far forgot the generosity which is natural to their station, as to
demand the exclusive privilege of supplying their countrymen with
corn and butcher's meat. They did not, perhaps, take time to consider how much less their interest could be affected by freedom of
trade, than that of the people whose advantage they followed." [1]

[1] Wealth of Nations, Book iv. Chap. ii.

Country gentlemen and farmers are undoubtedly a very worthy class, and much to be envied. If one possess a better variety of turnips or pigs or horses than his neighbor, he will be very likely to share his good fortunes with him. But that they are by nature opposed to the wretched spirit of monopoly, and fell from their gracious state through the instructions of merchants, who plied them with arguments and reasons which they could not understand, much less refute, and made good their instructions by imposing prohibitory duties upon corn and butcher's meat, — could never have occurred to the imagination of any one but Smith; for it is difficult to conceive any other person so ignorant, not only of history but of human nature, who could, where he was not interested, assert that which is exactly opposed to the fact. The market of the merchant is the world; and to assume that he would deliberately adopt a policy destructive to his own welfare, is to assert that the motive of self-interest — the very motive which Smith assumes to be the ruling principle of all action — has no place in the human mind. He might not have intended to state an untruth: the difficulty with him was that he lacked the power of distinguishing between the true and the false.

By nature, Smith was wholly unfitted to conduct a scientific discussion of any kind. He was a dreamer, not a reasoner. He evolved, to use a cant phrase, his systems from his own consciousness. He knew nothing of affairs, and could learn nothing from others. In his antipathy to merchants, or in a freak of passion, he lost sight of his principles altogether. " He was," says Dugald Stewart, in his memoir, " certainly not fitted for the general commerce of the world or the active business of life. The comprehensive speculations with which he had been occupied from his youth, and the variety of materials which his own invention continually supplied to his thoughts, rendered him habitually inattentive to familiar objects and to common occurrences, and he frequently exhibited instances of absence which have scarcely been surpassed by the fancy of La Bruyère. Even in company he was apt to be engrossed with his studies, and appeared at times, by the motion of his lips, as well as by his looks and gestures, to be in the fervor of composition. . . . He was peculiarly ill-qualified to take care of his own estate, for the proper management of which he was indebted to the attention and care of kind-hearted relations." It is not strange that a person so wholly wanting in practical sense should be equally wanting in the perception of principles, in method, and in originality. He borrowed his ideas of money very largely from Law; following him, like Hume, where he was wrong, and rejecting him where he was right. In urging the advantages of freedom of trade, he was fully anticipated by Hume, "whose political discourses," says Stewart, "were of greater use to him than any other works which had appeared prior to his lectures." Had neither of them lived, the whole question of Free-Trade and Protection would have been precisely where it is to-day. As already shown, the opinions held upon this subject do not result from argument or statement, but from the conditions in which individuals or communities find themselves placed. Whoever feels that he can undersell every one else, welcomes competition, — is a Free-Trader; he who is conscious that he cannot, fears competition, — is a Protectionist. There can be no doubt that liberal sentiments are gaining ground in trade, as in all other questions; but in Free-Trade and Protection, in the sense in which these words are ordinarily used, there will always remain the positive and negative poles.

When the ignorance of Smith upon the subject upon which he wrote, his want of scientific method, the groundlessness of his assumptions and conclusions, especially in reference to money, are considered, the influence he has exerted over succeeding generations is well fitted to excite astonishment. It is to be remembered, however, that mankind always demand some positive and authoritative statement of belief or faith, and of the nature and significance of the problems or phenomena by which they are surrounded, — and necessarily accept that which appears most reasonable, although it may have no foundation whatever. Of this the Ptolemaic system of astronomy is a striking example. Nothing could be more true to sense, or untrue to the fact. There was nothing to violate the ordinary sense of mankind in the teachings of Aristotle. If he could not see their unreasonableness, much less could those who followed, none of whom, for ages, possessed any thing like his intellectual acuteness. Galen's system of medicine gained possession of the public mind, and became a despotism which lasted more than fifteen hundred years, only for the reason that it was stated more authoritatively, and with greater show of learning, than any other. By it he assumed to meet every possible condition of body as well as mind ; to be as universal in medicine as Aristotle assumed to be in the far broader field, — the world. The truth or falsehood of what either proposed had nothing to do with its acceptance. In the moral as well as the material world, that which appears most reasonable to what may be termed the natural sense of mankind is untrue. As the instincts are never to be implicitly trusted, but are always to be referred and subjected to a sense of duty, no matter with what struggle or at what cost, so, in the material world, phenomena are always to be referred to a law which may wholly contradict the conclusion of the senses. That which is dearest to the human heart, as well as to untutored observation, is always to be put under the foot of duty and reason. Nothing is to be taken on trust ; every thing is to be referred to an inexorable law, — in other words, self-sacrifice, self-denial, is the condition of all scientific as well as of moral progress. Of all this the Greeks and Romans had no conception. To them the very foundation of the sciences was wholly wanting.

The systems of Aristotle and Galen, by absorbing the attention and satisfying the reason of mankind, effectually blocked the way to all progress in the discovery of truth. With them, in their respective departments, the age of invention, of originality, came to an end. That which followed was one of imitation, of comment, of refinement in error, by means of which the race itself became reduced to a condition ot mental imbecility. In the same way Smith, for a hundred years, has been the great obstacle to all progress in the subjects upon which he wrote. As his teachings upon money were almost universally accepted, all that subsequent writers have done has been to develop and push his doctrines to their extremest terms. In them was wholly lost whatever of freshness or strength their master possessed. The crowning mistake of all, however, was in assuming that what they erected with so much labor and pains deserved even the name of a science. They have wholly mistaken the foundations upon which that of Political Economy is to be erected. If such a science be possible, it must be based upon the moral, rather that the intellectual nature of man. With adequate moral, the highest material conditions follow as a necessary result. Smith failed in his attempt, as all must fail who ignore the moral or the sentimental side of man's nature. This is but another name for the ideal which far transcends all human effort. Hence the insupportable weariness of his works. It is in the unattainable that lies the great charm of life, the great incentive to exertion. The goal reached, the wished-for one is still in the distance, and is still for ever to remain so. Smith and his school placed all good within the reach of human effort. They gave nothing, in assuming to give all.

The first writer following Smith upon the subject of money, deserving attention, was Dugald Stewart, Professor of Moral Philosophy in the University of Edinburgh, who delivered, in the early part of the present century, an elaborate course of lectures upon the subject of Political Economy. Stewart was an ardent admirer of Smith, and assumed to reduce to precise and logical terms what his great master only more generally outlined. With Smith, he held " that division of labor, wherever it existed to any considerable extent, presupposed the establishment of some common medium of exchange. Without this previous arrangement, it would be impossible for an individual to devote himself exclusively to a particular species of employment. . . . In process of time, among all civilized nations, gold, silver, and copper have supplanted all other commodities, as the great instruments of commerce." Smith, however, held that the value of these metals depended largely upon their beauty, utility in the arts, and scarcity ; that such qualities, among others still more important, fitted them to serve as money. To this, however, Stewart strongly demurred.

" I certainly agree with Mr. Smith," he says, " excepting where he states that the intrinsic value of gold and silver was the quality which fitted them for their employment as coin. It appears to me that this intrinsic value, which I shall allow to gold and silver to its fullest extent, ought to be regarded in the theory of money as merely accidental circumstances, from which it is proper to abstract with all possible care, as tending only to embarrass our conceptions; for the same reason that, in studying the theory of mechanics, we abstract from the effect of friction, the rigidity of the ropes, and the weight of materials of which the machines are composed. . . . When gold is converted into coin, its possessor never thinks of any thing but its exchangeable value, or supposes a coffer of guineas to be more valuable because they are capable of being transferred into a service of plate for his own use. . . . Why, then, should we suppose that, if the intrinsic value of gold and silver were completely annihilated, they might not still perform, as well as now, all the functions of money, supposing them to retain all those recommendations (durability, divisibility, &c.) formerly stated, which give them so decided a superiority over every thing else which could be employed for the same purpose. Supposing the supply of the precious metals at present afforded by the mines to fail entirely the world over, there can be little doubt that all the plate now in existence would be gradually converted into money, and gold and silver would soon cease to be employed in the ornamental arts. In this case, a few years would obliterate entirely all trace of the intrinsic value of these metals, while their value would be understood to arise from those characteristical qualities (divisibility, durability, &c.) which recommend them as media of exchange. I see no reason why gold and silver should not have maintained their value as money, if they had been applicable to no other purposes than to serve as money. I am, therefore, disposed to think, with Bishop Berkeley, whether the true idea of money, as such, be not altogether that of a ticket or counter. . . . It is general consent alone which distinguishes them, when employed as money, from any thing else which circulates in a country ; from the paper money, for instance, which circulates in Scotland and England. Were this island insulated from the rest of the world, the former, as a medium of exchange, would possess no advantage over the latter, excepting in so far as it diminished the opportunities of fraud ; nor would it make the slightest difference on the national wealth whether the circulating medium consisted of gold or paper, or whether the materials were abundant or scanty." And he continues, "this observation is to me a self-evident proposition.

"In a country which had no communication with others, it is obvious and indisputable that the precious metals, when formed into money, would be useful only as a medium of exchange and scale of valuation. On this supposition, the observation of Anacharsis the Scythian, quoted by Mr. Hume in one of his political discourses, seems to be perfectly just, that gold and silver appeared to be of no use to the Greeks but to assist them in enumeration and arithmetic. . . . The only utility which is essential to gold and silver as media of exchange is their peculiar adaptation (divisibility, durability, &c.) to this purpose. And, though I would not take it upon me to say that their uses in the arts detract from their value in this respect, yet these are so far from being essential to their quality as money that they are, in some respects, disadvantageous, by rendering the theory of money more complicated than it otherwise would have been."[1]

The groundlessness of Stewart's assumption, in common with Smith, that money was an invention, — an arrangement entered into from a sense of its necessity, — has already been

[1] Lectures on Political Economy, Part i. Book ii.

sufficiently shown. The conclusion, however, to which Stewart came, that value is not a necessary attribute of money; and, if not necessary, it is no attribute of it, was the logical sequence of the premises laid down by the former. Smith would by no means have admitted that money might be wholly without value, — only that value was not its most essential attribute; that the qualities which chiefly fitted gold and silver to serve as money were their divisibility, fusibility, durability, and the like. As they must be taken from commerce at their value as merchandise, the substitution of a less expensive article therefor was so much clear gain. An inexpensive wheel of commerce took the place of an expensive one. Assuming, for the moment, Smith's premises to be correct, his next step should have been to show how far the value of money was intrinsic, and how far it was factitious; how inexpensive might be the medium employed, — in other words, how far its nominal might exceed its real value: for it is evident that, if media of exchange pass at their real value, one must be as expensive as another. When reduced to such terms, the untenableness and absurdity of Smith's propositions will at once be seen. There is no middle ground: the real value of money must equal its nominal value, or, in case of symbols, the values of what they represent must equal their nominal value in coin, or value is no attribute of money whatever. The latter conclusion is an irresistible one, from the premises which Smith laid down, and Stewart has the merit of first giving a logical and precise form to that which came from his great master as a very indistinct and ill-defined proposition.

"We never think," says Stewart, "when we receive the precious metals as money, of their value in the arts." But were they not first taken, and chiefly, for their value in the arts? and if we do not now consciously go through the same mental process that was gone through when they were first taken, is it not that such consciousness is concealed from us by habit, not that it does not exist? We are constantly practising, without apparent reflection or thought, processes which, in the outset, cost us infinite attention, labor, and painstaking to acquire. That we at last come to practise these unconsciously, is no proof that the mind is not engaged in one case as in the other. Stewart, however, wholly misstated the fact that gold and silver are taken without any consciousness of

their value in the arts.   As a rule, we do not raise the inquiry ;
we assume from experience that coins are what they purport to
be: but let it be noised abroad that debased coins of a particular denomination are in circulation, then every one of the
kind, good or bad, will be subjected to the closest scrutiny,
and, if taken at all, will only be taken at its value in the
arts, measured by the amount of pure metal it contains.

"If all the mines," says Stewart, " should become exhausted,
then all the gold and silver in the arts would be converted into
coin ; and all remembrance of their value in the arts would
inevitably fade away.   As there would be no idea of their
value, they would have no value."   Suppose a physician, in
erecting a system of hygiene, should make provision for the
total disappearance of oxygen from the air.   The only proper
answer would be, that oxygen will not disappear.   It is in the
air by Divine ordination.   If the physician persist, the only
proper course for him is to attack and upset the Divine order.
It is just as absurd to deduce a law in reference to money by
assuming that gold and silver may cease to be produced.
There is no more probability that they will not be produced
than that oxygen will cease to be an element of the air.   When
gold and silver disappear, civilization will disappear with them.
The one is reared upon the other.   That Stewart could use
such illustrations shows how incompetent he was for all such
investigations.   He was the Schoolman over again, in assuming
to solve by dialectics what will yield only to scientific analysis.   But, even if the mines should fail, all the gold and silver
in existence would by no means go into money.   It is not
probable that for a long time the relative proportions of that
held as money and that going into the arts would be materially changed.   As it gradually disappeared from loss and attrition, commerce and trade, and with these, civilization and
wealth, would gradually die out.   As these disappeared, gold
and silver would gradually flow back into the arts, and almost
wholly in time ; for, as there would be no trade, money would
not be wanted.   It is a fact of universal observation, that gold
and silver possessed by the savage races are not used as money,
but almost wholly in the arts.   They cover themselves, if they
can, with them, and have little other sense of their value
or use.

"If England were insulated from the rest of the world,"

says Stewart, "then, for that country, gold and silver, as a
medium of exchange, would possess no value over the most
worthless of substances." This absurdity is repeated by every
subsequent writer upon the subject of money. Suppose England to be the world, what then? Would all sense of beauty,
of utility or value be lost to its people? Suppose, as Stewart
assumes, England isolated, a Yorkshire grazier should take with
him to London a lot of beeves; and upon their sale should be
offered a leather medal, with curious hieroglyphics stamped
upon it, in payment. The seller at first might consider
the offer as a good joke; but, on finding the purchaser in
earnest, he would believe himself to be dealing with a
madman, and would take good care to get his beeves into
his possession again, and to rid himself of such a dangerous
customer. To be logical, Stewart must assume that, were
England isolated from all the world, its people would have
a sense of neither use nor beauty; in other words, that
they would be lower in the scale than any race or tribe ever
yet discovered. If the precious metals have no intrinsic value,
then the Scythian was correct in assuming money to be useful
only for the purpose of assisting in numeration and arithmetic.
It is for this reason that Stewart held their value to be disadvantageous, in complicating thereby the theory of money. If
value be not an attribute of money, he was quite right in
eliminating from it all idea of such quality. Figures convey
to us only ideas of numbers. If they conveyed other ideas,
they might, from the distraction that would be caused, render
it impossible to use them for the purpose of making any calculation whatever.

Again:—

"It must not therefore be imagined," says Stewart, "when I lay
so great a stress on the properties of the precious metals (divisibility, durability, and the like), abstracting from their intrinsical
value, in studying the theory of money, that I would mean to
insinuate any apology for these arbitrary operations in coinage
which have been so often practised by different princes. If gold
and silver possessed no intrinsic value, such operations might be
no less iniquitous than they always have been; for their iniquity
arises not from the useful purposes to which the precious metals are
subservient in the arts, but from the universality of their employment as media of exchange; and, indeed, one of my chief reasons

for dwelling so long upon the present subjects was to prevent so very important a truth as that which relates to the good faith that ought to be maintained with regard to the coinage, from being placed on what I conceive to be an unsound foundation ; and," he continues, quoting approvingly from Law, " money is not the value for which goods are exchanged, but the value by which they are exchanged." [1]

Now, if value be wholly abstracted from money, what harm can come of the arbitrary operations of princes in coinage ? They never change the denominations of the coin they debase. If the sole use of money, as asserted by Stewart, be to assist in numeration and arithmetic, then the different denominations of coin have only the force of numerals ; and a piece of leather upon which is imprinted the word " dollar " is in its proper essence the same thing as a piece of gold upon which the same word is impressed. Hume was more logical and consistent. Agreeing with Stewart that the only value of money, as such, was to assist in numeration and arithmetic, he took the ground that the currency should be debased, as the means of eliminating value from it ; naïvely remarking, that such debasement should be effected in such a sly way that the people should not discover the swindle. Of the two, Hume is to be preferred. The admission that the debasement was a swindle had the merit, at least, of putting the people on their guard. It suggested reasons for inquiry and investigation ; while Stewart, assuming similar grounds to Hume as to the nature of money, while expressing horror at the legitimate consequences of his doctrines, leaves the reader without even a thread to lead him out of the labyrinth in which he is involved.

Again : —

" From the functions of the precious metals as media of exchange," says Stewart, " they gradually and naturally came to form the common scale of valuation. For this end, indeed, they are naturally adapted, from the mathematical exactness with which metals, in consequence of their divisibility and fusibility, are fitted to express every conceivable variation of value, — a quality, indeed, of so much importance in their use as money that it probably contributed more than any thing else to establish their employment among commercial nations. The existence, too, of such a standard would necessarily render the ideas of relative value much more

[1] Lectures on Political Economy, Part. i. Book ii.

precise and definite than they otherwise would have been, by leading men to an arithmetical statement of relations which, in the
infancy of commerce, would have been estimated in a very gross
and inaccurate manner." [1]

In the preceding paragraph, in place of "standard of value,"
Stewart has "scale of valuations." He certainly has the advantage of Smith and the Economists in the accuracy of his definitions. It would be a contradiction in terms to call that a
standard of value which had no value. A thing may be a
scale, without being a standard. A yardstick is a scale for
measuring distance or extension, but not the standard of distance or extension.

If all value is to be abstracted from money, then of what
advantage are the qualities of divisibility and fusibility, in
the materials composing it? Why not have the denominations
which are fitted to express "every conceivable variation of
value" all of the same size and fineness? A bank-note for a
thousand dollars has precisely the same size and quality of
material as a note for one dollar. The only difference is in
their inscriptions. There could be no possible advantage in
making the size of the notes correspond with their nominal
values: in making, say, the surface of a dollar note equal to
one square inch, and the surface of a thousand dollar note
equal to a thousand square inches. According to Stewart's
theory, the qualities which fit gold and silver for money —
divisibility and fusibility — are of the least importance; for
pieces of similar size may be made by their inscriptions to
express "every conceivable variation of value." The existence
of a scale of valuation like that proposed by him would, he
says, render the ideas of value much more precise and definite
than they otherwise would have been. But how can ideas of
relative value be made more precise by comparing them with
a scale from which all value is abstracted? How can nothing
be made to be the measure of the value of something? A
definite idea is conveyed in the statement that a gold dollar
measures the value of a bushel of corn; but what idea can be
formed of the value of the corn from a statement that its value
is that expressed upon a worthless piece of leather or paper?

[1] Lectures on Political Economy, Part i. Book ii.

Stewart was among the earliest writers to suggest that the quantity of money required by a community was in ratio to the rapidity of its circulation. This suggestion, which naturally resulted from the assumption that money is not capital, but a scale of valuation, or an aid in enumeration and arithmetic, has become an axiom among all modern Economists. Stewart undertakes to prove his assumption in the following manner : —

" In Mr. Pinto's ' Treatise on Circulation and Credit,' it has been shown, with much ingenuity, how a quick circulation makes money go far in exchanges. And the following anecdote is mentioned by this very well informed writer as an illustration : ' During the siege of Tournay, in 1745, and for some time before, all communication being cut off, it was a matter of some difficulty to pay the garrison, for want of money. It was thought advisable to borrow from the *cantines* [sutlers] the sum of 7,000 florins. It was all that they had. At the end of the week, the 7,000 florins had come back to the *cantines*, when the same sum was borrowed again. This was repeated for seven weeks, until the surrender ; so that the same 7,000 florins did the work of 49,000 florins. It was, therefore, with very good reason that Bishop Berkeley long ago proposed the following query : Whether less money swiftly circulating be not in fact equivalent to more money slowly circulating ? ' " [1]

Suppose the sutlers had had the whole 49,000 florins, and that these had been borrowed at once, Stewart's illustration would have had no meaning or significance whatever. What was this transaction? The garrison was in arrears of pay. No money could be obtained but of the sutlers, and they had but a small amount compared with what was wanted. They had, however, a plenty of camp supplies. The money they had was borrowed, and paid out to the soldiers. Such as received any went immediately to the sutlers, and supplied their wants as far as the money received would go. It was then reloaned, again paid out to the soldiers, and again paid out for supplies. It required seven different transactions to accomplish that which, had a sufficient amount of money been in hand, would have been accomplished by one. It was precisely like a process in mechanics, where the time required for lifting a given weight depends wholly upon the degree of power applied. The same amount is expended whether the

---

[1] Lectures on Political Economy, Part i. Book ii.

weight be lifted in one minute or in one hour. The less the degree of power the greater the time. The result of these transactions was, that in the course of seven weeks the garrison had been paid 49,000 florins, the sutlers had sold supplies to the amount of 49,000 florins, and the commandant or government owed them 49,000 florins: so that in the end the latter had converted their supplies into money, and had in hand 7,000 florins, and a debt against the government or commandant for 49,000 florins. From all this Stewart deduces a law, — that the amount of currency required is in ratio to its activity. Suppose the garrison had required a certain amount of forage lying twenty miles off; and that, having but one· horse, ten days were required for its transportation. With ten horses, the same work might have been done in a single day. Would Stewart from this fact have attempted to prove that one horse could do the work of ten? We wonder he did not fortify his argument by the following syllogism: "ten horses can do so much work in one day; one horse can do the same work in ten days; therefore one horse can do the work of ten horses." It is really astonishing how great men, or those who have the reputation of being such, can repeat such puerile and unmeaning nonsense, and flatter themselves that they have proved some grand principle thereby.

"From these observations, it seems evident," says Stewart, "that the quantity of money and notes in circulation must bear but a small proportion to the value of the goods to be bought and sold, and that this proportion must vary according to the quickness with which the money circulates or shifts from one hand to another. According to Mr. Pinto, there is not in the whole world half the silver coin which would pay all the expenses of Paris for a single year, if the same piece were never to change its possessor but once." [1]

If the proportion of money to the goods to be bought and sold be small, then the amount of goods bought and sold will be small. Stewart has only shown that, with a small amount of money, seven weeks were required to effect exchanges which might, with an adequate amount, have been made in one. There is no more escape from this law of proportion between money and transactions than there is from the law of gravity. The one is as deeply grounded in the nature of

[1] Lectures on Political Economy, Book i. Part ii.

things as the other. Whether there were or were not a sufficient amount of silver in the world to pay the expenses of
Paris for a single year has nothing more to do with the question of the activity of money, and the quantity dependent
upon such activity, than if there had been silver enough in
the world to pay the expenses of Paris for a thousand years.

"In order to illustrate this subject a little farther," says Stewart,
"I shall suppose that a laboring man gains ten shillings a week,
which he receives always on Saturday. This man may be said, on
a medium, to be possessed of five shillings; and a hundred men in
this situation may be said to be in possession of £25. This is all
they have used, though they have each of them spent ten shillings
a week.

"I make a second supposition, — that each of these men lives on
credit; that his ten shillings are spent by the time they are earned;
and that every man pays his debt when he receives his weekly
wages. In this case, the money may never have been a single hour
in their hands; and it is a chance of a hundred to one if they are
masters of twenty shillings amongst them; and yet each of them,
as before, spends ten shillings a week.

"I have only another supposition to make : that each of these hundred laborers will live at the same rate as formerly; that they ask
no credit; and that they are paid their wages once a year. They
will thus receive at once £26, which, having no other use for their
money, they will gradually spend on their families, in the course of
a year, at the rate of ten shillings a week. It is evident that these
men will, *at a medium*, be possessed of £13 apiece, and that their
whole money will be equal to £1,300; though their wage and consumption are the same as those of a hundred men who could not
produce twenty shillings among them.

"The obvious inferences from these suppositions are: *firstly*,
that £25 with a quick circulation will go as far as £1,300 with
a slow circulation; *secondly*, that, even where the circulation is
equally quick, £1 with credit will purchase as much as £25 without
credit; and, *thirdly*, that, as both the *circulation and quantity of
money* may vary in consequence of a variety of causes, both natural and moral, it is extremely improbable that the money in circulation should always bear a fixed and invariable proportion to the
value of all the commodities used in commerce."[1]

If money be capital, or the representative of capital, and if
when it is exchanged it is exchanged for other kinds of capital,
then there can be no greater activity in money than in other
kinds of capital; and there can be no relation whatever between its activity and quantity. There would be just as much

[1] Lectures on Political Economy, Part i. Book ii.

sense in saying that the quantity of wheat necessary for the consumption of a community was in ratio to the rapidity of its movement: that is, if the rapidity of its motion be made twice as great, one-half the ordinary quantity will suffice. Or, to give another illustration. It not unfrequently happens that a pair of steelyards for weighing large quantities will serve for half-a-dozen families. It is borrowed, or passes from one to the other as they have occasion to use it. If all can use it, then the rapidity or diligence with which it is used marks its value. If such pair of scales cost a hundred dollars, and if it will suffice for the wants of the six families, it saves the purchase of five other pair, although each family may frequently use it. This is precisely Stewart's idea as to money, and this is the meaning of his " rapidity of circulation." He overlooked the fact, that, when money was used as the measure of value or the scale of valuation, the thing, the scale itself, passed from the party using it to the party whose goods had been purchased and measured by it. The scale no longer remains with the six families; but may pass into the next neighborhood, or into England or France or China, if the goods of those countries were purchased by its use.

With Stewart and the modern Economists, money is an entity, possessed of volition and will, flying about the country eager to do some good deed; an active and lively piece doing twice the work of a dull, phlegmatic one. But money cannot move unless something else moves, no matter how eager it may be for work. Its eagerness must find its complement in some other kind of property; so that if volition, will, and activity be predicated of one, volition, will, and activity must be predicated of the other. Money has no attribute of activity different from that possessed by all other kinds of merchandise. The use of one involves the use of the other; the employment of one involves the employment of the other. In the illustration given by Stewart, just as much money was required when the laborers used that received by them in the payment of debts contracted during the week just closed, and had possession of it for only an hour or so, as when they used it in payment of merchandise purchased during the one ensuing. Equal provision of money had to be made in either case. It mattered little in whose hands the money might be, for a few days, whether in those of the laborer or shopkeeper. In the case where the laborers were paid at the end of the year, and held on hand, during the succeeding one, one-half, on an average, of their wages, they simply allowed their employers the use, without interest, of the whole amount of their wages for the year. If they held them on hand till they were expended, they deprived themselves of interest upon the amount so held. If 100 men should hold unemployed, for six months, £1,300, society would be deprived of the use of a corresponding amount of capital, in the same way as it would if an equal amount of money, previously in circulation, were to be hoarded. But to infer from such operations that the amount of money required by a community is to be measured by the degree of its activity, is an absurdity that can only be matched by Aristotle, by the Schoolmen, or by modern Economists, who are more wild and extravagant, if possible, than either.

One of the great evils resulting from the reputation of such a man as Dugald Stewart is, that every word that he uttered, which was recorded by himself or by others, is carefully gathered up and put into his " works." In the case of Stewart, these are swelled to eleven ponderous volumes, full of propositions of the correctness of not one of which the reader can have the least assurance. Had his " literary executor," instead of carefully raking up, burned three quarters of all he left, he would have rid the world of a vast mass of rubbish, and the painstaking student of a great deal of the most irksome toil. It may be set down as a maxim, that a person who assumes to write authoritatively upon every subject will write well upon none. Life is not long enough for one man to know every thing, or to construct an universal science.

Simultaneously, almost, with the publication of Stewart's Lectures on " Political Economy " came the report of the famous Bullion Committee, which has occupied so wide a space in the discussion of financial and monetary subjects. It is well known that the Bank of England, in obedience to an " Order in Council," suspended payment in February, 1797. The suspension was caused by the extraordinary demands made upon it by the government in the wars growing out of the French Revolution. The financial position of England had been previously somewhat weakened by enormous exportations of bullion in the purchase of bread-stuffs, in consequence of disastrous harvests, particularly that of 1795. Wheat, which in January of that year was worth 55s. the quarter, reached, in August, 108s. the quarter. Enormous importations were the consequence. At the same time, government was in the market for a large loan, the proceeds of which were in a great measure to be expended abroad. Similar loans had been made in 1793.and 1794: that for 1793 being £701,475; that for 1794 being £2,601,053; and that of 1795 being £6,253,151: making a total, in three years, of £9,555,679, to be used chiefly in military operations. The means for meeting these loans were supplied through the Bank, as the great financial institution of the kingdom.

In order to convey an adequate idea of the nature and functions of the Bank, and of the influence it exerted as an instrument of commerce and as an arm of the government, it is necessary to give a brief sketch of its organization and history. The Act by which it was established was entitled, " An Act for granting to their Majesties several duties upon tonnage of ships and vessels, and upon beer, ale, and other liquors; and for securing certain recompenses and advantages in said act mentioned, to such persons as should voluntarily advance the sum of £1,500,000 toward carrying on the war with France." After a variety of provisions relating to the duties to be imposed, the Act went on to declare that the subscribers to a loan of £1,200,000 might be formed into a corporation to be styled " The Government and Company of the Bank of England." The whole sum was subscribed within ten days after the opening of the books. The charter was thereupon issued (July 27, 1694), and the Bank went immediately into operation. For the sum of £300,000, which was to form no part of the capital of the Bank, the subscribers were to receive annuities for one, two, and three lives. Upon the loan to the government, which formed the capital of the Bank, the latter was to receive interest at the rate of eight per cent, with an additional annual allowance of £4000 for management; making the whole income from this source £100,000 annually. The Bank was authorized to issue its notes as money, to an amount equalling its capital. It was to deal in bills of exchange, and in gold and silver bullion; but was restricted from

trading in any "goods, wares, and merchandise whatsoever."
It was to make no loans to government but by permission of
Parliament. Its charter was to extend for twelve years, or
till twelve months' notice to be given after August 1, 1705.

It will thus be seen that the entire capital of the Bank was
loaned to the government. Provision for the redemption of
its notes, consequently, had to be made by that for which they
were issued, and by the deposits, which, upon its organization,
it received in very considerable amounts. In 1697, its charter
was extended till twelve months' notice after August 1, 1710.
In 1708, it was again extended till twelve months' notice
after August 1, 1732; the Bank advancing to government
£2,175,027 17s. 10d., its capital being increased by a like
amount. By the provision of this Act, authority was given to
the Bank to issue its notes for any amount whatever. The
Act of 1708 further provided: "That, during the continuance of
the corporation, it shall not be lawful for any body, politic or
corporate whatsoever, created or to be created, or for any
other persons whatsoever, united or to be united in covenants or
partnership, exceeding the number of six persons, in that part
of Great Britain called England, to borrow, owe, or take up
any sum or sums of money on their bills or notes, payable on
demand, or at less time than six months from the borrowing
thereof."

It will thus be seen, that the Act of 1708 gave to the Bank the
power of unlimited, and, within certain restrictions, exclusive
issue of notes. By virtue thereof, it became the "manager
and regulator of the currency;" standing in the relation to
paper that the government did to metallic money. As the
former was bound to coin whatever metal was brought to it,
it became, by necessary inference, obligatory on the part of the
latter to supply its notes upon all applications that came within
the rules prescribed for making its loans. The Act of 1708,
therefore, was that upon which the Bank, as it subsequently
existed, was based. It gave to the monetary system of England its peculiar character, and was the chief cause of the
ignorance which has prevailed in that country in reference to
the laws or principles of currency. As for nearly one hundred years after this Act was passed the Bank enjoyed almost
uninterrupted prosperity, and as during that period very little
disturbance occurred in commercial or financial circles, it came

to be assumed that the Act, in reference to its objects, expressed the sum of human wisdom. No occasion arose for inquiry and investigation till the phenomena to which it gave rise were erected into maxims or rules, which from that to the present time have held unquestioned sway over the opinions and judgment, not only of the people of England, but of the world. In 1713, the charter of the Bank was again extended till twelve months' notice after August 1, 1742. In 1716, it advanced to government £2,000,000 ; and, in 1721, £4,000,000. Of these sums, £275,027 17s. 10d. were repaid to the Bank ; so that its share capital stood upon their payment in 1738 at £9,100,000. In 1742, its charter was extended till twelve months' notice after August 1, 1764 ; the Bank advancing to the government £2,586,800, increasing its capital to £11,686,800. In 1764, the charter was extended till twelve months' notice after August 1, 1786 ; in 1781, till twelve months' notice after August 1, 1812 ; in 1800, till twelve months' notice after August 1, 1833. In 1816, the Bank was authorized to increase its capital from £11,686,800 to £14,553,000, being an addition of twenty-five per cent to its stock ; the increase being paid by, and representing, a portion of its accumulated or *net* earnings, which on the 29th February, 1816, equalled £8,639,000.

The Act of 1816 provided for the payment by the government of one quarter of the advances made by the former, reducing the debt of the government to it, to £11,015,100. Although the Bank, for almost the whole of the first century of its existence, was forbidden by its charter to make any advances to government, it acted from the outset as its fiscal agent in collecting and disbursing its revenues, and in paying the interest upon the public debt.

Although the government in establishing the Bank had no higher or broader purpose than temporary relief from a present emergency, it was no sooner set in motion than its operations, whatever may have been thought of its conduct in aftertimes, were immediately followed by the most beneficent results. Its notes served for the collection and disbursement of the revenues ; while such as were not required for these purposes were fully employed in the distribution of merchandise. It laid, in fact, the foundation of that manufacturing, commercial, and political supremacy which enabled England to wield a paramount influence over the destinies of mankind. While the paper issued by a Bank, that it may return without effort on its part, should always symbolize merchandise, it is perfectly competent for a government, without a dollar in its vaults, to issue a currency which shall, by its power of levying and collecting taxes, return to it automatically, after having performed all the functions that could have been performed by coin in a similar use. If its revenues equal, say, £30,000,000 annually, and it issue during the year £10,000,000 of its notes receivable in the payment of taxes, these would (the taxes being certain to be paid) be maintained very nearly or quite at the par of coin, from the uses they served. If they would pay taxes equally with coin, they would be preferred by taxpayers to coin. The debts due from the people to the government — and taxes that are levied may be called such — are a consideration which may give its notes a high value. Such debts take the place of merchandise, which must form the basis and security of loans made by Banks. A considerable portion of the issues of the Bank were from the outset constantly employed by the public in manner described, and returned to the former as its fiscal agent. Such as were not taken in in this manner were sufficiently provided for by the commercial paper discounted; the deposits in the form of coin providing adequate reserves. The issues of the Bank, compared with their present magnitude, were for a long time on a small scale. Its notes in circulation, from 1694 to 1716, averaged only about £800,000 annually. From 1716 to 1770, the annual average did not much exceed £4,000,000; and from 1770 to the suspension of payments in 1797, only about £8,500,000 annually.

Although the Bank, as the issuer and manager of the currency, stood out in bold relief, and was for a long time the paramount financial power, it was at no period the only one. As early as 1650, the merchants of London were accustomed, for greater security, to deposit their surplus cash with the goldsmiths. The holders of such deposits as were likely to remain for some time undrawn loaned them, and thus realized a considerable revenue. It was in this way that banking became a trade, and deposits were solicited in the same manner that customers are solicited by merchants at the present time.

The receipts given for deposits would naturally circulate as currency. In time, checks were drawn against them ; so that, before the establishment of the Bank of England, the greater part of the surplus cash of the merchants was regularly deposited, and was loaned, drawn upon, and disbursed, precisely as are deposits with London bankers at the present day. The establishment of the Bank was violently opposed by the goldsmiths, — the bankers of that time, — and undoubtedly made a serious inroad upon their operations. As, however, every great institution like the Bank must regulate its affairs by strict and inexorable rules, the mass of borrowers would prefer to deal with private bankers, although paying a greater rate of interest, from the better accommodations they could secure ; so that, during the whole period of its existence, large amounts of loans were made, and paper discounted, by private bankers, whose issues, in form and kind, were precisely similar to those made by the Bank. After the relations of the latter to the government became changed, so that it could rely upon it as its chief customer, the Bank naturally withdrew from the field of discount, leaving it in the hands of private parties ; although during the period of Restriction, when it was under no obligation to take in its notes in coin, it discounted business paper very largely. It ceased to be, relatively, the great instrument of commerce it once was ; and was content to loan its deposits on the highest form of security at very low rates, certain from their amount of being constantly in the receipt of very large revenues.

While the Bank has had the competition of private bankers during the whole period of its existence, — a competition so effective as to drive it in great measure out of the discount market of the metropolis, — it has for the last hundred years had that of country Banks, which at one time rivalled it in the amount of their note circulation, and, perhaps, far exceeded it in the extent of their operations. By common law, any person might become a banker, — might issue notes and receive deposits ; or, to quote the language of Lord Liverpool in a speech delivered in Parliament in 1826, when the subject of authorizing joint-stock Banks was under consideration : "small tradesmen — a cheesemonger, a butcher, or a shoemaker, may open a Bank. The exclusive privileges of the Bank of England do not touch such cases ; but an association of persons with sufficient fortune to carry on a banking business with security was not permitted." [1]   Lord Liverpool seems to have been the first to recognize the glaring absurdity and disastrous consequences of allowing the issue of notes to serve as money, at the same time restricting the number of those who unite for their issue to six persons or less.   If any other party than the Bank were allowed to issue notes, the most careful provision should have been made that " small tradesmen, — cheese-mongers, butchers, and shoemakers," — not, perhaps, masters of a shilling, should not exercise a function which the greatest authorities on monetary science declare to be a prerogative of government, and which, certainly should not be exercised by any but those of undoubted substance.   No other evidence is needed of the utter ignorance and folly which has uniformly characterized the legislation of Parliament upon the subject of money, than that an Act like that of 1708 should have remained untouched till 1826.   It was then only so modified as to allow banking associations of more than six members to be formed in England, for the issue of notes, at places sixty-five miles distant from London.

Only a small number of country Banks were in existence prior to the war of American Independence.   They increased very rapidly after the conclusion of peace.   It was at that period that those great improvements were made in the mechanic arts which so enormously increased the productive industry of the nation, and which enabled it to bring to a triumphant conclusion the gigantic struggle with France.   The creation of country Banks was, in a great measure, due to the progress made in manufactures and commerce.   They were the natural result of the increased wealth, and increased necessity for a symbolic currency.   There were, according to Thornton, 353 country Banks in operation in 1797, 366 in 1799, and 386 in 1801.   No account of these institutions was required by government ; and there was no means of ascertaining the amount of their note circulation till 1804, when a stamp duty was imposed.   It was admitted, however, that the amount of duties paid was by no means an accurate measure of the amount of notes issued.   It was not until 1808 that country Banks were required to take out licenses.   The

---

[1] Knight's History of England, vol. viii. p. 200.

number of licenses issued in 1809 was 702; showing an increase, in a period of five years, of 316 Banks. In 1814, the number of licenses taken out was 940. No statements were ever furnished of the amount of capital invested, of deposits received, nor, till 1833, of the amount of notes issued; the amount of the latter till that time being only a matter of inference from the number of stamps sold.[1]

Although the amount of issues of London bankers and of country Banks was in great measure a matter of conjecture, it is certain that for nearly a hundred years past by far the greater portion of the exchanges were effected by them. In 1795, the average amount of commercial bills under discount at the Bank equalled only £2,996,000. The average amount under discount in the whole country must have been tenfold greater. In 1796, the bills under discount averaged £3,505,000. The amount gradually increased after the suspension, reaching as high as £20,070,000, in 1810. The Bank began to withdraw from this kind of business so soon as it was seen that preparations must be made to resume.[2]

As the notes and credits issued by the bankers and country Banks exerted, in ratio to their amount, precisely the same influence over the operations of production and trade as those of the Bank of England, and as we are in great measure ig-

---

[1] Statement showing the number of licenses issued to country Banks, and the number of commissions of bankruptcy issued against them, from 1809 to 1832, inclusive.

Years.	No. of licenses granted.	No. of Commissions of Bankruptcy issued.	Years.	No. of licenses granted.	No. of Commissions of Bankruptcy issued.
1809	702	4	1821	781	10
1810	782	20	1822	776	9
1811	779	4	1823	779	9
1812	825	17	1824	788	10
1813	922	8	1825	797	87
1814	940	27	1826	809	48
1815	916	25	1827	665	8
1816	831	37	1828	672	3
1817	752	3	1829	677	3
1818	765	3	1830	671	14
1819	787	13	1831	641	
1820	769	4	1832	686	

[2] Statement showing the average note circulation of the Bank of England and of the country banks; deposits in the Bank of England; the amount of

norant of the amount of the formêr, compared with those of the latter, it is impossible to say how much of the aberration or disturbance occurring from time to time in commercial affairs was due to the one, and how much to the other. It was possible that the greatest degree of disturbance may have arisen almost wholly from the action of bankers and country

commercial bills under discount by the bank; the amount of private deposits held by the bank; and the amount of loans by the bank upon public and private securities from 1814 to 1832 inclusive.

(000s omitted; thus, £1,000 = £1,000,000.)

Years.	Note circulation of the Bank of England.	Note Circulation of the country Banks.	Aggregate Note Circulation of the Bank and of country Banks.	Deposits in the Bank of England.	Commercial Bills under Discount by the Bank.	Amount of Private Deposits in the Bank.	Amount of Loans upon Public Securities.	Amount of Loan upon Private Securities.
1814	£24,801	£22,700	£47,501	£13,602	£13,285	£2,874	£29,316	£15,865
1815	27,281	19,011	46,272	12,199	14,957	1,690	25,858	18,852
1816	27,013	15,096	42,109	12,122	11,416	1,333	22,761	17,575
1817	27,397	15,894	43,291	9,954	8,980	1,672	26,328	7,123
1818	27,775	20,507	48,282	7,962	4,325	1,640	27,085	4,552
1819	25,227	15,701	40,928	6,358	6,515	1,790	24,887	7,710
1820	23,509	10,576	34,085	4,256	3,883	1,325	20,444	4,571
1821	22,971	8,256	31,227	5,720	2,676	1,326	15,881	3,853
1822	18,172	8,416	26,588	5,544	3,866	1,873	13,073	8,558
1823	18,176	9,920	28,096	7,504	8,123	2,321	12,750	5,142
1824	19,927	12,831	32,758	9,876	2,369	2,389	14,495	5,367
1825	26,069	14,980	41,049	8,299	4,941	2,607	18,431	6,597
1826	23,515	8,656	32,171	7,067	4,908	3,322	19,143	9,857
1827	22,318	9,985	32,303	8,426	1,240	3,031	18,494	4,117
1828	21,668	10,121	31,789	9,699	1,167	5,701	20,501	8,492
1829	19,708	8,130	27,838	9,294	2,250	5,217	19,904	5,118
1830	20,757	7,841	28,598	11,181	919	5,562	20,475	8,909
1831	19,019	7,914	26,933	10,141	1,533	5,202	18,992	5,564
1832	18,185	8,221	26,306	9,607		. . .	19,665	5,992

Statement showing the amount of commercial bills under discount at the Bank from 1795 to 1813, inclusive.

Years.	Amounts.	Years.	Amounts.	Years.	Amounts.
1795	£2,996,000	1802	£7,528,000	1808	£12,951,000
1796	3,505,000	1803	10,747,000	1809	15,175,000
1797	5,350,000	1804	9,982,000	1810	20,070,000
1798	4,490,000	1805	11,365,000	1811	14,355,000
1799	5,403,000	1806	12,380,000	1812	14,291,000
1800	6,401,000	1807	13,484,000	1813	12,330,000
1801	7,905,000				

Banks, for which the Bank of England was in no way to be censured; or its action may have produced great commercial convulsions, for which bankers and country Banks were by no means chiefly responsible. The action of both, however, is always to be taken into account, in every attempted explanation of a great rise in prices, of great speculative movements, and of great financial revulsions, and in applying the proper remedy. Whichever be at fault, the cause will always be found in a nut-shell: in an issue of money, — of notes and credits, which act powerfully upon prices, for the reason that they do not represent merchandise, but debt. Englishmen have been taught, that only such paper is deserving the name of money as displaces a corresponding amount of coin; and that the only paper that effects such displacement is bank-notes. The moment there is a disturbance, or any great movement in financial affairs, they instantly begin, for a proper explanation or remedy, to pore over the tables of the amount of issue of Bank of England notes. They might as well infer the wealth of the nation from the petty sums hoarded in its vaults, or measure the volume and effect of an Amazon or a Niagara by the contracted and noiseless flow of their Thames. As the action of the private Banks and bankers does not enter into their calculation, they cannot get rid of the conviction that the quantities with which they are dealing make up only a small part of those necessary to a proper equation, — to a proper understanding of the situation. In the uncertainty as to the future, all monetary and commercial operations are brought to a dead stand, to resume their wonted movement only when time shall have fully revealed the extent of their conjectures and fears.

By the terms of its charter the Bank was forbidden to make loans to the government without the sanction of Parliament, for fear that it might at some time become involved in the precise condition in which it found itself in 1795 and for a long time thereafter. It had, however, from a very early period, been in the habit of making advances on such Treasury bills of exchange as were made payable at it. These advances, or "discounts," as they may be more properly termed, were usually for small sums only. Such transactions were made subjects of complaint on the part of the Bank, if the sums so advanced reached at any one time £50,000. During the American War of Independence, however, such advances rose as high as £150,000. As grave doubts had always existed as to the legality of such transactions, the Bank determined to apply for an Act of Indemnity for the past, and for permission to make such advances in the future to a limited amount. Mr. Pitt, then at the head of the government, brought in a bill for this purpose, with an understanding, as it was claimed, on the part of the Bank, that such advances for the future were not to exceed £50,000, or £100,000 at most, at any one time. Mr. Bosanquet, the President of the Bank, intrusted on its part with the matter, being about to go out of office, left it mainly in charge of Mr. Pitt; who, probably foreseeing the advantage to be gained thereby, pushed through the bill, leaving out the limitation clause altogether. By its passage, he had now the Bank, and with it the whole monetary power of the kingdom, under his control, as there was no limit to the price at which he could sell the securities of the government. There was hardly any, consequently, to the means at his command. He armed all Europe against his great enemy, and waged, while he lived, by no means 'an unequal contest. If worsted on land, England remained mistress of the seas; making good, in the end, the prediction of Cicero in reference to the struggle between Pompey and Cæsar: " *Qui mari potitur, eum rerum potiri.*" The magnitude of his combinations, and the vast power he was enabled to wield through the Bank, are still the wonder and admiration of the world. The Bank Directors, however, were by no means the willing victims and slaves of their imperious master. In addition to the drain upon the country for military subsidies, large amounts of bullion were sent abroad for other purposes: the amount of exports in 1793 being £2,715,232; in 1794, £8,335,592; and in 1795, £11,040,236: the total for the three years equalling £22,091,060. In addition to the exports of bullion, the amount of Treasury bills made payable or negotiated at Bank increased enormously. The demands of merchants and manufacturers were equally pressing with those of the government. So clamorous were the calls for accommodation, that the Directors, in the latter part of 1794, represented to Mr. Pitt the condition of affairs, and the dangers which threatened. Early in 1795 they adopted a resolution, that, in view of a loan of £6,000,000 to be raised for foreign, and one of £18,000,000 for home purposes, the Chancellor of the Exchequer be requested to make his financial arrangements for the year without aid from the Bank ; and that they would make no advances upon Treasury bills, exceeding, at any one time, the sum of £500,000.

Although Mr. Pitt promised a ready compliance with the requests of the Directors, he acted only in reference to his own necessities ; and notwithstanding their remonstrance, he wrung from the Bank, in August, 1795, the sum of £2,000,000. In the mean time, the Bank, in face of the loans it was called upon to make, as well as others that were proposed, and which it might have to aid in making, largely increased its issues of notes, although at the same time there was a constant and heavy outflow of specie. Its notes, which in August, 1794, stood at £10,000,000, reached £14,000,000 in February, 1795, the increase being made chiefly in payment of bills drawn upon the Treasury in behalf of foreign governments. The point was already reached at which it could consult its own safety only at the cost of declaring government bankrupt.

As the outflow of specie continued to increase in force, its Directors, in October, 1795, again made a formal representation to the government of their apprehensions growing out of the condition of affairs, and the absolute necessity of a reduction in the amount of their advances. They called its attention to the fact that the representations made at the commencement of the year as to the dangers likely to arise from foreign loans were being fully realized, and that numerous payments were yet to be provided for. They showed the market price of gold to have risen to a considerable premium ; and, with the extraordinary call for it which had caused the rise, they declared they could make no further advances. The rumors that new loans were contemplated were at first denied by Mr. Pitt. At subsequent interviews, however, he stated to the Directors that a new loan of £2,000,000 to the Austrian government would be of great aid to the common cause of which he was the master-spirit, the object of which was to humble the power and ambition of France. He stated, at the same time, that if such a loan would hazard the welfare or stability of the Bank, all thought of it should be abandoned.

As the Bank had in great measure exhausted its means by its loans to the government, which were, necessarily, very largely drawn in coin, it had no other alternative than to reduce its accommodations to the public. Its Directors accord ingly announced, that such advances as they could make 'ly by day, should be divided proportionably among the appli- cants. This determination caused great alarm and distress in commercial circles. In spite, however, of all expedients, mat- ters continued to go from bad to worse; the Bank, in the mean time, remonstrating in the strongest, and Mr. Pitt always replying in the most compliant terms. On the 14th of February, 1796, the Directors formally represented to Mr. Pitt, " That it is the opinion of this Court [of Directors,] founded on its experi- ence of the effect of the late Imperial loan, that if any further loan or advance of money to the Emperor [of Germany], or other foreign state, should, in the present state of affairs, take place, it would in all probability prove fatal to the Bank of England. The Court of Directors, therefore, do most earnestly depre- cate the adoption of any such measure; and they solemnly protest against any responsibility for the calamitous conse- quences that may follow therefrom." Mr. Pitt replied in his usual strain, that no further loan should be made without communicating with them; that he saw no reason for their apprehension; and that their representations must have been made in a moment of needless alarm.

As the stringent measures adopted by the Bank, for the pur- pose of contracting its issues, produced great distress among all classes, various propositions were made for relief; and among them, that a Committee of twenty-five members be appointed by Parliament, authorized to issue notes payable six months after date, bearing interest at the rate of $1\frac{1}{4}$ pence daily per £100, upon receiving their value in gold and silver, Bank of England notes, or bills of exchange having not more than three months to run. Such a suggestion was made, probably, in consequence of an issue of Exchequer bills for the purpose of arresting the commercial and financial panic of 1793. All such propositions, however, came to nothing. In the mean time, Mr. Pitt applied, in July, 1796, for a loan of £800,000 on Treas- ury bills (the Bank being already in advance on account of such bills to the amount of over £1,200,000); and for a similar sum in August. The Directors agreed to advance the first sum, but refused to advance the second. Mr. Pitt replied, that without the second the first would be of no use to him, and they were driven most reluctantly to make both loans. They again addressed an earnest remonstrance to the government, a:'" ʰeclared that they yielded to its demands only from fear of the consequences that would follow a refusal. " They consented," they said, " to this measure, in a firm reliance that the repeated promises, so frequently made to them, that the advances on the Treasury bills should be completely done away, may be actually fulfilled at the next meeting of Parliament, and the necessary arrangements taken to prevent the same from ever happening again ; as they conceive it to be an unconstitutional mode of raising money, what they are not warranted by their charter to consent to, and an advance always extremely inconvenient to themselves." The immediate response to this remonstrance, so pertinent and reasonable, was a fresh demand upon the Bank for £2,750,000, on the security of the malt and land taxes ; which was granted upon condition that the advances on the Treasury bills, then amounting to £1,513,345, were to be paid out of it. Mr. Pitt pocketed the new loan, without paying off any advances that had been made on the Treasury bills. The Directors again demanded payment ; as the advances on such bills had increased to £1,554,635, and would, in a few days, be increased to £1,854,635. Mr. Pitt was full of excuses for non-payment, made abundant promises for the future ; but hinted at the same time, that a large amount of bills, estimated at £700,000, had come in from San Domingo. He further hinted, at the same time, that he should presently want £200,000 for Ireland. All that the Directors could do was to repeat their remonstrances, and picture the ruin which now stared them in the face. Pitt, in fact, knew no law but that imposed upon him by the situation in which he was placed. With vast military operations, of which he was the centre, he would have been in the greatest straits for money with tenfold the advances that were made. It was a struggle which of the two mighty geniuses that were brought into collision should become master of the destinies of the world. In all this Pitt simply impersonated the spirit of the nation, then roused to a pitch of fervor and determination which perhaps occurs but once in a nation's history. It was a struggle for every thing the preservation of which gave value to life. It was a struggle which absorbed the will of the nation, and in which the Bank Directors, though foreseeing certain ruin in their path, stood ready to sacrifice themselves upon what they believed to be the altar of their country's good. The attitude of England to the French republic was in every respect selfish and unjustifiable; but when the liberties of France were surrendered to a remorseless and unprincipled despot, the only course for England was to fight the battle to the bitter end. Her crowning triumph would have been wholly impossible but for the aid furnished by the Bank. By means of it, she availed herself of the whole financial power of the nation; and was enabled to carry on for twenty years a struggle in which, without the Bank, she must have been ignominiously driven from the field.

The action of the Bank in restricting its issues, to which it rigidly adhered in endeavoring to save itself from what appeared to be nothing less than certain destruction, precipitated the crisis which was impending, and which could not then probably have been avoided. In a period of eighteen months, it reduced its circulation from £14,017,510 to £8,640,250, — a reduction of nearly one-half. A wide-spread panic was the natural result of the unexampled distress which was caused, and by which all classes were alike affected, and greatly increased the run for coin. The Directors, now fully comprehending the situation, sent, on the 21st of February, 1797, a deputation to Mr. Pitt to ask him how much longer he thought the Bank should continue to pay specie, and when he should think it advisable for him to interfere. Mr. Pitt replied that, as a preliminary step, the affairs of the Bank should be examined by a secret committee; to which request the Directors promptly assented. The specie on hand on that day was reduced to £1,272,000. It was evident that it could go on no longer; and, on the 25th of February, a meeting of the Cabinet was held, and an "Order in Council" issued, directing the Bank to suspend all payments in specie until the sense of Parliament should be known. Accompanying this order was a statement of the Directors, that the affairs of the Bank were in a prosperous condition, and that it was possessed of ample means for the ultimate payment of all its liabilities. Its specie was reduced, on the day of the suspension, to £1,086,000. With the announcement of the suspension, the panic instantly subsided. The relief was immediate and complete. The merchants and bankers of London, immediately upon the announcement, held a meeting, at which they resolved, " That, being highly sensible how necessary the preservation of public credit is at this time, we do most readily declare, that we will not refuse to receive bank-notes in payment of any sum of money to be paid us; and we will use our utmost endeavors to make all our payments in the same manner." This resolution was subsequently signed by nearly four thousand individuals and firms. The Bank immediately began to expand its issues; increasing them within one week by the sum of nearly £2,000,000. Confidence being fully restored, a return flow of specie into it immediately set in; for the run upon it, for some time previous to the suspension, was not caused by the foreign demand, but by hoarding in consequence of the distrust which had prevailed. The foreign exchanges had for some time previous to the suspension been in favor of the country, and continued in its favor for a considerable period thereafter. An Act of Parliament was speedily passed, " for continuing for a limited time the restriction contained in the Minute of Council for the 25th of February, 1797, on payment of cash by the Bank." By this Act the Bank Directors were indemnified for having complied with the Order in Council. They were forbidden to pay cash, except in sums under 20s.; but, if any person lodged specie with them, he might be repaid in kind to the extent of three-fourths of the sum deposited, provided such sum were not less than £500. Payments, in the notes of the Bank were to be deemed as payments in specie, if accepted as such. The notes were also to be received in payment of taxes; and no debtor was to be held to special bail, unless the affidavit stated that payment in bank-notes had not been offered. The Act was continued in force till June 24th of the same year. The Bank was also at the same time authorized to issue notes under £5. Within six months after the suspension, it held £4,089,620 in specie and bullion against £1,086,000 held by it on the day of the suspension. On the 28th of February, 1798, one year after the suspension, the amount of specie held equalled £5,828,940. The amount of notes outstanding on the day of the suspension was £8,640,250. The amount on the 31st of August, 1797, was £11,114,130; on the 28th of February, 1798, £13,095,320; and on the 28th of February, 1799, two years after suspension, £12,959,800. These changes were a decisive proof of the healthy condition of production and trade, and the ease with which they adjusted themselves on a sound basis the moment apprehension and uncertainty as to the future were removed. Nothing could have been more admirable than the conduct of the Bank. Relieved of the necessity of paying specie, it increased in one year its coin reserves in ninefold greater ratio than its liabilities in the form of notes. It had seldom or never been in a stronger position than it was during the two years after its suspension ; and early in 1799, it signified its ability, and, with the consent of government, its willingness, to resume payment. But the latter, influenced by other considerations than those which relate to commercial and mercantile affairs, replied that it was inexpedient to resume in the present state of the country. With the suspension of specie payments came the abundant harvests of 1797 and 1798. Wheat fell to 41s. the quarter in January, 1799. The seasons of 1799 and 1800 were unpropitious, and the price of wheat rose in May of the first year to 61s. the quarter ; and, at the end of the year, to 94s. 2d. the quarter. In June, 1800, it rose to 134s. the quarter ; and, in March, 1801, to 156s. the quarter. The market price of gold, however, remained at the mint price, £3 17s. 6d., till June, 1800, when the price of foreign gold suddenly rose to 4s. 6d. the ounce. Early in 1801, the value of domestic coins had risen 1s. per ounce ; and foreign exchange, payable in bank-notes, particularly in Hamburg, was depressed 14 per cent below par. The cost of remitting gold from London to Hamburg at the time did not exceed 7 per cent. The difference between the rate of exchange and the cost of remitting specie could only result from depreciation of the currency.

The restriction of specie payments had been continued by various acts, the last of which was to expire within six months after a definitive treaty of peace (with France) was signed. This was concluded at Amiens, on the 27th of March, 1802. Although the Bank at that time signified its readiness to resume, the restriction was continued till March 1st, 1803. The price of gold, which averaged £4 5d. the ounce for 1801, and £4 4s. the ounce for 1802, fell in 1803 to £4 the ounce, and continued at that figure till 1809, when it rose to £4 10s. the ounce, or to a premium of 13½ per cent ; the restriction having been, of course, continued for this period. The sudden rise in 1809 caused great alarm ; and, early in 1810, a Committee was moved in the House of Commons by Mr. Francis Horner, " to inquire into the cause of the high price of gold bullion, and to take into consideration the state of the circulating medium and of the exchanges between Great Britain and foreign parts." [1] The Committee consisted of twenty-one members, among whom were those most distinguished in the kingdom for their experience and knowledge in monetary and commercial affairs.   Among these, in addition to the chairman, were Alexander Baring, Henry Thornton, William Huskisson, and Spencer Perceval, then Chancellor of the Exchequer.   The Committee, in the course of their inquiries, examined thirty persons, most of them eminent merchants and bankers and thoroughly familiar with all the operations of business and trade.   They submitted their Report on the 8th of June, 1810 ; but this was not considered in Parliament till the

[1] Statement showing the average market price, in bank-notes, of bullion, and the average value and average percentage of depreciation of the notes of the Bank of England, in each year from 1797 to 1821 inclusive.

Years.	Average value of gold in bank-notes.			Average percentage of the value of bank-notes.			Average depreciation per cent.		
	£	s.	d.	£	s.	d.	£	d.	s.
1797	3	17	10½	100	0	0		Nil.	
1798	3	17	10½	100	0	0		Nil.	
1799	3	17	10½	100	0	0		Nil.	
1800	3	17	10½	100	0	0		Nil.	
1801	4	5	0	91	12	4	8	7	8
1802	4	4	0	92	14	2	7	5	10
1803	4	0	0	97	6	10	2	13	2
1804	4	0	0	97	6	10	2	13	2
1805	4	0	0	97	6	10	2	13	2
1806	4	0	0	97	6	10	2	13	2
1807	4	0	0	97	6	10	2	13	2
1808	4	0	0	97	6	10	2	13	2
1809	4	5	0	91	12	4	8	7	8
1810	4	10	0	86	10	6	13	9	6
1811	4	4	6	92	3	2	7	16	10
1812	4	15	6	79	5	3	20	14	9
1813	5	1	0	77	2	0	22	18	0
1814	5	4	0	74	17	6	25	2	6
1815	4	13	6	83	5	9	16	14	3
1816	4	13	6	83	5	9	16	14	3
1817	4	0	0	97	6	10	2	13	2
1818	4	0	0	97	6	10	2	13	2
1819	4	1	6	95	11	0	4	9	0
1820	3	19	11	97	8	0	2	12	0
1821	3	17	10½	100	0	0		Nil.	

The highest point to which gold rose was £5 10s. the ounce, on the 6th of August, 1813. The premium equalled 29 per cent.

following year. It reported that the price of gold bullion, which by the regulations of His Majesty's mint was £3 17s. 10½d. per ounce of standard fineness, was during the years 1806, 1807, and 1808, as high as £4 in the market. Toward the close of the year 1808, it began to advance very rapidly, and continued very high during the year 1809; the market price of standard gold in bank-notes fluctuating from £4 9s. to £4 12s. the ounce; the market price at £4 10s. the ounce being about 15½ per cent above the mint price. The Committee then proceeded to inquire as to the cause or reasons for such advance; and ascribed it, in the conclusion of their Report, to an excessive issue of notes by the Bank. The Bank, on the other hand, contended that, from the manner in which it conducted its business, — that is, as it only discounted paper based upon and representing actual mercantile transactions, and payable within short and fixed periods, — the currency could not be in excess. It was contended, also, by the public more than by the Bank, that the price of gold had risen in consequence of the excessive demand for it upon the Continent; that the value of its notes was not depreciated. The Committee, however, assumed that its notes were depreciated; and that the only check upon over-issues was a liability for the redemption of its notes upon demand; or that its issues should be made in reference to the state of foreign exchange; and that, specie payments being forbidden, the Bank was bound to conduct its operations in reference to the latter test or standard.

"It is important," said the Committee, "to observe, that when the Bank was bound to answer its notes in specie on demand, the state of foreign exchanges and the price of gold did most materially influence its conduct in the issue of its notes, though it was not the practice of the Directors systematically to watch either the one or the other. So long as gold was demandable on their paper, they were speedily apprised of a depression of the exchange, and a rise in the price of gold, by a run upon them for that article. If at any time they incautiously exceeded the proper limit for their advances and issues, the paper was quickly brought back to them by those who were tempted to profit by the market price of gold or by the rate of exchange. In this manner, the evil soon cured itself. The Directors of the Bank, having their apprehensions excited by the reduction of their stock of gold, and being able to replace their loss only by restricted purchases of bullion at a very losing price, naturally contracted their issues of paper; and thus gave to the remaining paper, as well as to the coin for which it was interchangeable, an increased value; while the clandestine exportation either of coin or the gold produced from it combined in improving the state of the exchange, and in producing a corresponding diminution of the difference between the market price and mint price of gold, or of paper convertible into gold.

"It was a necessary consequence of the suspension of cash payments," continued the Committee, "to exempt the Bank from that drain of gold which was sure to result from an unfavorable exchange and a high price of bullion; and the Directors, released from all fear of such drain, and no longer feeling any inconvenience from such a state of things, had not been prompted to restore the exchanges and the price of gold to their proper level, by a reduction of their advances and issues. The Directors in former times did not, perhaps, perceive and acknowledge the principle more distinctly than those of the present day; but they felt the inconvenience and obeyed its impulse, which practically established a check and limitation to the issue of paper. In the present times, the inconvenience is not felt; and the check, accordingly, is no longer in force.

"Your Committee beg leave to report it to the House, as their most clear opinion, that, so long as the suspension of cash payments is permitted to subsist, the price of gold bullion, and the general course of exchange with foreign countries, taken for any considerable period of time, form the best general criterion from which any inference can be drawn as to the sufficiency or excess of paper currency in circulation; and that the Bank of England cannot safely regulate the amount of its issues without having reference to the criterion presented by these two circumstances. And, upon a review of all the facts and reasonings which have already been stated, your Committee are of the further opinion, that, although the commercial state of the country and the political state of the Continent may have had some influence upon the high price of gold bullion, and the unfavorable course of exchanges with foreign countries, this price and this depreciation are also to be ascribed to the want of a permanent check, and a sufficient limitation of the paper currency in this country.

"In connection with the general subject of this part of their Report, the policy of the Bank of England respecting the amount of their circulation, your Committee have now," said the Report, "to call the attention of the House to another topic, which was brought under their notice in the course of their inquiry, and which, in their judgment, demands the most serious consideration. The Bank Directors, as well as some of the merchants who have been examined, showed a great anxiety to state to your Committee a doctrine of the truth of which they professed themselves to be most thoroughly convinced: that there can be no possible excess in the issue of Bank of England paper, so long as the advances in which it is issued are made upon the principles which at present guide the conduct of the Directors; that is, so long as the discount of mercantile bills is confined to paper of undoubted solidity, arising out of real commercial transactions, and payable at short and fixed periods. That the discounts should be made only upon bills growing out of real commercial transactions falling due in a fixed and short period, are sound and well established principles. But that while the Bank is restrained from paying in specie, there need be no other limit to the issues of their paper than what is fixed by such rules of discount, and that during the suspension of cash payments, the discount of good bills falling due at short periods cannot lead to any excess in the amount of Bank paper in circulation, appears to your Committee a doctrine wholly erroneous in principle, and pregnant with dangerous consequences in practice."

" If at any time," say the Committee, " they " (the directors) " incautiously exceeded the proper limit for their advances and issues, the paper was quickly brought back to them by those who attempted to profit by the market price of gold, or by the rate of exchange." But all the issues of the Bank are speedily brought back to it in the payment of its bills, or for coin, if these be not paid, only after they have performed their function as currency. The method by which, according to the Committee, they were brought back was a pure fiction. They assumed, with Adam Smith, that the moment there was an excess of paper, such excess would instantly cause a rise in the exchanges, and would immediately be taken back to the Bank for coin by its holders, in order to profit by such advance. But an excess of currency acts upon exchanges, not directly, but through its consequences or effects. If an amount be issued for which there is no constituent, there will be an increased consumption of foreign goods, to pay for which coin must be exported. The consumers of such goods pay the importer in Bank of England notes, which are drawn by him in coin. A long period, however, may elapse between importation and payment, as the purchases may be made on very long time, or may be carried for a long time on bankers' credits. The effect of an over-issue, therefore, is remote and consequential, seldom direct. Nothing whatever would be gained by buying up the notes of the Bank, for the sake of obtaining coin for the purpose of profiting by the rise of exchange, for the reason that the notes would cost their purchaser their value in coin. The only parties who would profit by a rise in exchange would be importers who had accumulated notes when the exchanges were at par, and who could put up the price of their goods with the rise in the price of the former. The Committee simply repeated Smith in saying, that " the whole paper money which can easily be circulated in a country can never exceed the value of the gold and silver of which it supplies the place. Should the circulating paper at any time exceed that sum, as the excess could neither be sent abroad, nor employed in the circulation of the country, it must return immediately upon the Banks, to be exchanged for gold and silver. Many people would immediately perceive that they had more of this paper than was necessary for transacting their business at home; and, as they could not send it abroad, they would immediately demand payment for it at the Banks. When this superfluous paper was converted into gold and silver, they could easily find a use for it by sending it abroad; but they could find none while it remained in the shape of paper." [1] Such was precisely the idea of the Committee. The assumption and process, however, were purely imaginary. All the issues of the Bank, so long as confidence is felt in them, return to it with equal regularity and in equal volume, whether they represent capital, or whether they are purely fictitious. If loans are properly made, its issues are returned [2] by its customers; if not, they must be taken in out of its reserves. The result alone can determine the character of the issue, and such result may be postponed for a long time; for an excess of issue, by inflating prices, will, for a time, cause payments to be made more promptly in consequence. Years may elapse before the period of liquidation comes round. The question, therefore, is not one of quantity, but of quality. The issues of

[1] See ante, p. 129.

[2] A calculation made by the Bank in 1818, to ascertain the number of days that bank-notes of each denomination remained in circulation, showed the following results:—

Notes of £1 and £2, 147 days		Notes of £40, 38 days.	
„ 5	148 „	„ 50	72 „
„ 10	137 „	„ 100	49 „
„ 15	60 „	„ 200	18 „
„ 20	121 „	„ 300	14 „
„ 25	43 „	„ 500	14 „
„ 30	55 „	„ 1,000	13 „

The average time the notes remained in circulation, assuming that equal amounts of the different denominations were issued, equalled about twenty-eight days. The one, two, and three pound notes remained in circulation about four and a half months. The time in which the notes of £300 and upwards, by means of which the greater portion of the exchanges must have been effected, remained in circulation, equalled thirteen and one half days. — Gilbart on Banking, p. 43.

the Bank, if properly made, can never be in excess.   If improperly made, every note will be in excess.   The Committee
simply reiterated, in effect, the dogma of Smith, that money
was an instrument, — a wheel of commerce, — the value of
which depended upon the relation its quantity bore to the
quantity or value of goods to be exchanged; and that inherent
value was no necessary attribute of it.

  So long as the Bank was liable, say the Committee, to discharge its notes in coin on presentation, it conducted its affairs
in view of such a liability.   Relieved from this obligation, it
should have conducted them in reference to the price of gold
and the condition of the exchanges.   To act in reference to such
standard or rule would be to resume; for it could make its
notes equal in value to coin, only by paying coin when demanded.   This it was forbidden to do.   It could not do this so
long as it remained in the power of government; and there was
no hope that the latter would relax its grasp till peace was
finally established.   The proposition of the Committee, therefore, was an absurdity upon its face.   No contraction of the currency in the condition of affairs would have increased the
amount of gold in the Bank.   It could not expect its bills to be
paid in any other currency than its own notes ; and, if it had not
reissued them, the country would speedily have been without
any currency whatever.   The nation would have succumbed
in the tremendous struggle in which it was engaged, while
society would speedily have been remitted to a condition of
barter.   In the emergency, the Bank adopted the only possible
course open to it: it continued to pursue that which had enabled it to maintain specie payments for more than a hundred
years consecutively, previous to the Restriction Act.   By a rigid
adherence to it, it restored its position, after suspension, with
marvellous celerity.   So rapidly did it recover itself, that in
1800 it was perfectly able to resume payment, and would have
resumed could the consent of government have been obtained.
It is very probable that the Directors did not realize the great
importance of such a step, or they might have brought the
government to their views.   The rule they followed during
suspension, of discounting paper representing merchandise and
having a short time to run, was the only possible one for them
to follow.   It not only saved the nation from ruin, but promoted

its welfare in the highest degree. While acting in such manner, they did not see that suspension removed the real check to an undue expansion of the currency. In this they were not wiser than their time. So long as a Bank pays specie, every mistake it makes, every improper discount, has finally to be made good by paying out a corresponding amount of coin. As this is drawn, its ability to make further loans is lessened in the same degree. After suspension, in case its notes are not retired by the payment of its bills, its ability to make loans in the future is not reduced, for the reason that, by creation of new notes which cost nothing, it can replenish its reserves, consisting of notes, to any amount. It is like a ship at sea that has lost its compass, and all means of determining its position. It must sail, if it sail at all, by the best lights it has; and, although its general direction may be plain enough, it may in time find itself far out of its proper course; so that, when it makes land, it may be wrecked, or may have to refit, and so reach its destined harbor with great loss and damage. It was only when the Bank came into port, as it were, — when it undertook to resume by converting its assets into coin, — that the degree of its departure and the losses it sustained could be ascertained. It was not shipwrecked, although it suffered great loss. With the lights it had, it pursued the course best fitted to promote the welfare of the nation as well as its own. The error of the Committee consisted not only in denying the correctness of the rule followed by the Bank, which was the only practicable one, but in imposing one impossible to be followed. It never occurred to them to inquire whether the evils complained of might not have arisen from other modes by which the Bank made its loans. At that time it had loans upon governments, Exchequer bills, to the amount of fully £17,000,000; the amount of loans upon bills at the time equalling about £20,000,000. Such inquiry, if made, might have shown that the condition of affairs might be almost wholly referrible to the action of the Bank in its relation to the government. The sudden recovery of the former, after the passage of the Restriction Act, — a recovery wholly due to a rigid adherence to the principles upon which a convertible currency must rest, — attracted no attention whatever. It would be supposed that so remarkable a phenomenon would have received the most careful investigation. That neither such recovery, nor the relation of the Bank to the government, were made subjects for consideration by the Committee, shows how narrow were their vision and scope. It is not improbable, however, that both Directors and Committee assumed that no inflation or harm could come of loans made upon public securities; that the value of such must be a sufficient guarantee of the propriety and value of all issues made upon them. Nothing can be more natural than such inference, as the share capital of the Bank had, from the outset, been wholly invested in public securities; and as the Bank, so organized, had continued to pay specie for more than one hundred years consecutively. With Englishmen, a precedent — an ounce of the past — outweighs a ton of the future; so that, with them, the old disappears only by being absorbed or overlaid by the almost imperceptible growth of the new. Such trait may be referred to in their praise, and may be the reason why their progress, though so slow, has been so uniform and sure, and, through the ages, so immense.[1]

[1] Economists have never been able to master the reason of the sudden recovery of the Bank after the Restriction Act, due wholly to the prudent conduct of the Directors in making their loans. For them, it only re-enforced the old dogma, that the value of the currency depends upon quantity alone. The rise of the notes of the Bank to par after the suspension is now accepted as fully proving such assumption. The explanation given by Tooke is a curious illustration of the treatment by the Economists of this as well as of similar subjects: —

"It becomes a curious matter of speculation to inquire, how, with motives so strong to constant and progressive excess, and under the guidance of maxims and principles so unsound and of such apparently mischievous tendency as those professed by the Governor and some of the Directors of the Bank, in 1810, such moderation and (with some exceptions which will be noticed hereafter) such regularity of issue should, under chances and changes in politics and trade unprecedented in violence and extent, have been preserved, as that a spontaneous readjustment between the value of gold and the paper should have taken place, as it did, without any reduction of their circulation.

"The explanation of the difficulty seems to be this: the rule by which the Bank Directors professed to be, and were in the main, guided, — viz., the demand of good mercantile bills, not exceeding sixty-one days' date, at the rate of five per cent per annum, — did, with the necessary policy of government in periodically reducing the floating debt within certain limits by funding, operate as a principle of limitation upon the total issues of the Bank. And the reason of the rule having so operated is to be found in the fact, that the market rate of interest for bills of the description which were alone discountable at the Bank did not materially, or for any length of time together, exceed the rate of five per cent per annum. But the Bank Directors seem to have been unaware of the precise mode of operation by which their rule had the effect of a principle of limitation against great or permanent excess in their circulation." — Tooke's History of Prices, Vol. i. p. 158.

The rule of the Bank in discounting bills having sixty-one days to run, at the

" By far the most important of these consequences," continues the Report, " is, that while the convertibility into specie no longer exists as a check to an overissue of paper, the Bank Directors have not perceived that the removal of that check rendered it possible that such an excess might be issued by the discount of perfectly good bills. So far from perceiving this, your Committee have shown that they maintain the contrary doctrine with the utmost confidence, however it may be qualified occasionally by some of their expressions. That this doctrine is a very fallacious one, your Committee cannot entertain a doubt. The fallacy upon which it is founded lies in not distinguishing between an advance of capital to merchants and an addition of supply of currency to the general mass of circulating medium. If the supply of capital only is considered, as made to those who are ready to employ it in judicious and productive undertakings, it is evident there need be no other limit to the total amount of advances than what the means of the lender, and his prudence in the selection of borrowers, may impose. But in the present situation of the Bank, intrusted as it is with the function of supplying the public with that paper currency which forms the basis of our circulation, and at the same time not subjected to the liability of converting the paper into specie, every advance which it makes of capital to the merchants in the shape of discount, becomes an addition also to the mass of circulating medium. In the first instance, when the advance is made by notes paid in discount of a bill, it is undoubtedly so much capital, so much power of making purchases, placed in the hands of the merchant who receives the notes ; and, if those hands are safe, the operation is so far, and in this its first step, useful and productive to the public. But as soon as the portion of circulating medium in which the advance was thus made performs, in the hands of him to whom it was advanced, this its first operation as capital, as soon as the notes are exchanged by him for some other article which is capital, they fall into the channel of circulation as so much circulating medium, and form an addition to the mass of currency. The necessary effect of every such addition to the mass is to diminish the relative value of any given portion of that mass, in exchange for commodities. If the addition were made by notes convertible into specie, this diminution of the relative value of any given portion of the whole mass would speedily bring back upon the Bank which issued the notes, as much as was excessive. But if by law they are not so convertible, of course this excess will not be brought back ; but will remain in the channel of circulation, until paid in again to the Bank itself in discharge of the bills which were originally

rate of five per cent, did, according to Tooke, " operate as a principle of limitation upon the total issues of the Bank." And why ? Because " the market rate of interest for bills of the description which were alone discountable at the Bank did not materially, or for any length of time together, exceed the rate of five cent per annum ! " Such is the argument and conclusion of one of the great lights among the modern Economists, whose works are probably more referred to, and quoted with more approbation, than those of almost any one of his school.

discounted. During the whole time they remain out, they perform all the functions of circulating medium ; and, before they come to be paid in discharge of those bills, they have already been followed by a new issue of notes in a similar operation of discounting. Each successive advance repeats the same process. If the whole sum of discount continue outstanding at a given amount, there will remain permanently out in circulation a corresponding amount of paper ; and, if the amount of discounts is progressively increasing, the amount of paper which remains out in circulation over and above what is otherwise wanted for the occasions of the public will progressively increase also, and the money prices of commodities will progressively rise. This progress may be as indefinite as the range of speculation and adventure in a great commercial country."

As the Bank, in making its loans, pays out its notes instead of capital, these, if they represent capital, will as a rule be discharged only by its consumption. That they are outstanding, is evidence that the merchandise they represent is not consumed. They have, therefore, until taken in by the Bank, the same value, by virtue of representing the same merchandise, no matter into whose hands they may fall. It is their possession which entitles their holder to the merchandise they represent. That they change their character before their retirement — being capital in the hands of the party to whom they were first issued, and currency, representing no capital, in the hands of all subsequent holders — is an assumption which is exactly opposed to the fact. They are never discharged of their value till they come back to the party issuing them. Whatever are issued, equally fall into the channel of circulation, and alike return to the Bank for retirement; so that, unless they were reissued, there would presently be no currency outstanding. Just in ratio that the bills of a Bank are paid are its liabilities taken in. They will be paid in equally after as before suspension by the Bank. If, at a particular moment, currency, which was capital in the hands of one person ceased to be capital in the hands of another, without any change in its form, or in that which it represented, certainly the Committee should have shown, or have attempted to show, the process by which, and the time at which the change in value was effected. A moment's reflection would have shown that no such change could have taken place ; but such is not the way with the Economists. Not one of them ever broke through the crust of words and assumptions by means of which the real principles of currency have been concealed from sight. How the fictions they uttered could have been accepted as sober truths by Horner, Thornton, and Huskisson exceeds belief. It is infinitely more incredible than that those of the Alchemists should have been accepted in a credulous and un-scientific age. The transmutation of lead, tin, and quicksilver into gold was a proposition ten times more credible than the transmutation of a bank-note from something into nothing. That such fables could really have been accepted as funda-mental truths by the wisest, most discreet, and most earnest of our race, is mortifying evidence of our weakness, and shows how little confidence we are entitled to place even in our strongest convictions.

" We must not omit," continues the Committee, " to state one very important principle : that mere numerical return of the amount of bank-notes out in circulation cannot be considered as at all decid-ing the question whether such paper is or is not excessive. It is necessary to have recourse to other tests. The same amount of paper may, at one time, be less than enough, and, at another time, more. The quantity of currency required will vary in some degree with the extent of trade ; and the increase of our trade, which has taken place since the suspension, must have occasioned some increase in the quantity of our currency. But the quantity of currency has no fixed proportion to the quantity of commodities ; and any inferences proceeding upon such a supposition would be entirely erroneous. The effective currency of a country depends upon the quickness of circulation, and the number of exchanges performed in a given time, as well as upon its numerical amount ; and all the circumstances which have a tendency to quicken or to retard the rate of circulation render the same amount of cur-rency more or less adequate to the wants of trade. A much smaller amount is required in a high state of public credit than when alarms make individuals call in their advances and provide against accidents by hoarding, and in a period of commercial security and private confidence, than when mutual distrust discourages pecuni-ary arrangements for any distant time. But, above all, the same amount of currency will be more or less adequate, in proportion to the skill which the great money-dealers possess in managing and economizing the use of the circulating medium. Your Committee are of opinion, that the improvements which have taken place of late years in this country, and particularly in the district of Lon-don, with regard to the use and economy of money among bankers, and in the mode of adjusting commercial payments, must have had a much greater effect than has hitherto been ascribed to them, in rendering the same sum adequate to a much greater amount of trade and payments than formerly. Some of those improvements will be found detailed in the evidence. They consist principally in the increascd use of banker's drafts in the common payments of London; the contrivance of bringing all such drafts daily to a common receptacle, where they are balanced against each other; and the intermediate agency of bill-brokers. And several other changes in the practice of London bankers are to the same effect, of rendering it unnecessary for them to keep so large a deposit of money as formerly. Within the London district, it would certainly appear that a smaller sum of money is required than formerly, to perform the same number of exchanges and amount of payments, if the rate of prices had remained the same. It is material also to observe, that both the policy of the Bank of England itself, and the competition of the country Bank paper, have tended to compress the paper of the Bank of England more and more within London and the adjacent districts. All these circumstances must have co-operated to render a smaller augmentation of Bank of England paper necessary to supply the demands of our increased trade, than might otherwise have been required; and show how impossible it is, from the numerical amount alone of that paper, to pronounce whether it is excessive or not. A more sure criterion must be resorted to; and such a criterion, your Committee have already shown, is only to be found in the state of the exchanges and the price of gold bullion.

" Upon a review of all the facts and reasonings which have been submitted to the consideration of your Committee in the course of their inquiry, they have formed an opinion, which they submit to the House: That there is, at present, an excess in the paper circulation of this country, of which the most unequivocal symptom is the very high price of bullion, and, next to that, the low state of the Continental exchanges; that this excess is to be ascribed to the want of a sufficient check and control in the issues of the paper from the Bank of England, and, originally, to the suspension of cash payments, which removed the natural and true control. For, upon a general view of the subject, your Committee are of opinion, that no safe, certain, and constantly adequate provision against an excess of paper currency, either occasional or permanent, can be found, except in the convertibility of all such paper into specie."

If money be capital, it must obey the laws of capital. For the movement of the latter, two parties must consent, each governed by considerations having reference to his interests alone. Suppose one hundred hogsheads of sugar to be sold and paid for three times during the same day: no one would say that the activity of its movement had any necessary relation to its value, or that a less quantity was required by reason of such activity. Precisely the same law holds as to money. That it changes hands several times in a day does not increase or diminish its value; nor is a greater or less quantity required in consequence. If money be active, merchandise must be active. The relation of one to the other, both in quantity and activity, must be uniform. When symbolic money is used, the title to that which it represents is transferred with the transfer of the instrument. It is only upon the supposition that money is not capital, nor the representative of capital, that the assumptions of the Committee can be sustained. If not capital, it is a scale of valuation, — an instrument of commerce like a set of weights. If a community consisting of a hundred families possess only one scale or set, the whole must use it. The degree of its activity or use, in such case, measures its value. In its use, however, it is not parted with as the equivalent in value of that which it measures. So soon as it is used by one family it is passed to another, to come round again in time to the one first using it. But money, by its use, for ever passes from the hands of the party using it. He cannot hand it over to his neighbor, to perform the same service that it did for him. When properly analyzed, therefore, no more meaning can be attached to the statement, that " the effective currency of a country depends upon the quickness of circulation and the number of exchanges performed in a given time, as well as upon its numerical amount," than to a statement, that one barrel of flour, by the rapidity of its circulation, may serve the purposes of three barrels. The quantity of money must always be in ratio to the exchanges that are made. When a symbolic currency is used, the tendency of all merchandise entering into consumption is to express itself in it.

The Committee asserted that a much smaller amount of money — coin and bank-notes — sufficed for the wants of the public than formerly, from the greater economy of their use ; checks upon Banks and bankers having taken their place. What is the difference between checks on Banks and bankers and their notes? Nothing, whatever, but form. Neither are, in themselves, capital. Both equally represent capital. Both serve as instruments for the exchange of capital. Both equally entitle their holder to coin, and both are equally entitled to be called money. To say that fewer notes are required from the economy of their use, is the same as to say that a nation economizes in sailing vessels by the employment of steam ships. The latter tend to supersede the former, from the greater convenience of their use. To assign to the two kinds of ships functions wholly unlike, in the transportation of merchandise, is to make distinctions where no differences whatever exist. So checks drawn upon Banks and bankers tend, for the same reason, to supersede the notes issued by them. To erect a system of finance upon a radical difference between the two kinds of currency is the very climax of folly.

The Report of the Bullion Committee was accompanied by a series of resolutions embodying the conclusions to which it finally came, and declaring that cash payments ought to be resumed by the Bank within the period of two years. Mr. Vansittart, in behalf of the government, moved a series of opposing resolutions, in which he declared that the cause of the difference in the market price of bank-notes and gold was, not that the value of notes had depreciated, but that the value of gold had risen. In his speech on the occasion, he declared that a standard such as that supposed by the Committee, consisting of a fixed and invariable weight of the precious metals, had never existed in England; that the legal coin of the country never possessed a value estimated by a fixed quantity of gold and silver bullion; that the notes of the Bank never had any other than a current value, founded on the public confidence in it; that a diminution in the value of the currency might have had the effect of improving the exchange, but could not by any possibility depress it. Mr. Horner's resolutions were defeated in the House of Commons by a very large majority; that requiring the Bank to resume within two years being rejected by a vote of 180 to 45. Upon the defeat of Mr. Horner's resolutions, those of Mr. Vansittart were taken up, and passed by a vote almost equally decisive. Nothing, of course, could be more absurd than the statements embodied in the latter resolutions. A person who should offer similar ones at the present day would be treated as a lunatic. The action of the House had no reference whatever to the merits of either. The great majority of its members were the pliant tools of the government, which had no idea of depriving itself of the means of carrying forward the vast military operations in which it was engaged.

In order to give a proper sanction to the action of the House upon Mr. Vansittart's resolution, Lord Stanhope brought in a Bill which made it a misdemeanor to make any difference in

payment between guineas and bank-notes. This was passed
by a large majority in both Houses. The act proved, as might
have been expected, wholly inoperative ; guineas continuing to
sell at a high premium compared with notes. The Courts of
law, to their credit, declared it to be no crime to sell guineas
at a premium, and set aside the conviction of a party who had
made such sales. Lord Stanhope's bill, however, remained on
the Statute Book during the whole period of the Restriction Act.

There can be no doubt that the high price of coin and exchange was due to an excess of Bank of England notes. To
restore their equilibrium, their amount, say the Committee, must
be reduced. But no reduction in amount of paper improperly
issued will bring up its value, except so far as such reduction
indicates the means of the issuer. No amount of reduction
of legal-tender notes will have the effect to bring their value
to par, even if there be not a dollar of other kind of paper
money in circulation. So far as the Bank of England notes
resembled legal-tender notes, no amount of reduction would
have brought them to par. Their price would equal their real
value. The question of all others, therefore, — the manner
in which the notes should be issued, in order to render
them at all times the equivalent of coin, — the Committee
wholly overlooked. What their Report did prove or establish
has been a riddle compared with which that of the Sphinx
was of the easiest solution. That it established no truth,
that it did not advance monetary science a single step, is
proved by the fact, that, instead of reconciling, it only served
to increase the confusion, and exasperate the differences which
already prevailed. It divided England into two great camps, —
Bullionists and Anti-Bullionists, — separated by hardly any
other than verbal distinctions ; each waging a fierce and incessant
war of words, in which the discussion of principles had no
place whatever. The more consistent party were the Anti-
Bullionists, who altogether ignored value as an attribute of
money. On the other hand, the Bullionists held that value
might or might not be an attribute of it. They held the test
of the propriety of its issue to be its convertibility into coin ;
at the same time holding that it would have a value equal to
that of coin, and consequently would be exchangeable at all

times for it, although no provision were made for its conversion, provided its amount did not exceed that required by a community for its exchanges. The only effect of the Report, therefore, was to establish on a still firmer basis that absurdest of all errors in monetary science, that value is no necessary attribute of money. It was claimed by the Bullionists that the Report proved the superiority of a metallic over a paper currency. It proved nothing of the kind, for the reason that nothing of the kind can be proved. The Committee might just as well have attempted to prove the superiority of iron over wood in the arts. Each is superior in its way. Paper money, properly issued, is, from its greater convenience, superior to gold in exchanges of property. It is far more convenient to use a thousand dollar bank-note than it is a thousand dollars in gold or silver. On the other hand, a metallic is superior to a paper currency, if it be necessary to send money to other countries, or if the object be to hold it as reserves, or to pay balances resulting after symbols are exhausted. The report, undoubtedly, contained much useful information as to the state of exchanges and the financial condition of the country at the time, and proved the depreciation in value of the bank-notes. It settled, however, not a single principle; while the sanction given to the errors which it contained, by the great names of those by whom it was prepared, has been one of the most formidable obstacles to the progress of monetary science.

The opinions of contemporaneous writers confirm in a striking manner the conclusions in the preceding paragraph as to the meaning and effect of the Bullion Report. In 1802, pending the Restriction Act, Mr. Henry Thornton, afterwards a member of the Bullion Committee, and an acknowledged authority in financial affairs, published "An Inquiry into the Nature and Effect of the Public Credit of Great Britain," in which he draws the following comparison between the nature of real and fictitious bills : —

" They agree, inasmuch as each is a discountable article ; each has also been created for the purpose of being discounted ; and each is, perhaps, discounted in fact. Each, therefore, serves equally to supply means of speculation to the merchant. So far, moreover, as bills and notes constitute what is called the circulating medium, or paper currency, of the country (a topic which shall not be here anticipated), and prevent the use of guineas, the fictitious and the real bills are upon an equality ; and, if the price of commodities be raised in proportion to the quantity of paper currency, the one contributes to that rise exactly in the same manner as the other. . . .

"In order to justify the supposition that a real bill (as it is called) represents actual property, there ought to be some power in the bill-holder to prevent the property which the bill represents from being turned to other purposes than that of paying the bill in question. No such power exists : neither the man who holds the real bill, nor the man who discounts it, has any property in the specific goods for which it was given ; he as much trusts to the general ability to pay of the giver of the bill as the holder of any fictitious bill does. The fictitious bill may, in many cases, be a bill given by a person having a large and known capital, a part of which the fictitious bill may be said, in that case, to represent. The supposition that real bills represent property, and that fictitious bills do not, seems, therefore, to be one by which more than justice is done to one of these species of bills, and something less than justice to the other. . . .

"A fictitious bill, or bill of accommodation, is evidently, in substance, the same as any common promissory note ; and even better, in this respect, that there is but one security to the promissory note, whereas in the case of the bill of accommodation there are two." [1]

If Thornton had taken the pains to inquire into the effects produced by the use of a currency based upon fictitious bills, in comparison with one based upon bills representing merchandise, he would readily have discovered the wide difference between the two. He saw no necessity for this, for the reason that he held, with the Economists, that paper money was an "instrument of commerce" of which value was no necessary attribute. That which has preceded, however, shows the absurdity of his assumption, that fictitious bills as well as those representing transactions in merchandise are equally " discountable articles." [2]

---

[1] Inquiry into the Nature and Effect of the Public Credit of Great Britain, Chap. ii.

[2] It is hardly necessary to notice, at any length, Lord King's pamphlet, "Thoughts on the Restriction of Specie Payments by the Bank of England," published in 1803. Lord King, as is well known, acquired no little celebrity by refusing to receive the notes of the Bank from his tenants, except at their value in coin. This act, which was considered as in the highest degree disloyal, involved him at the time in great odium. His pamphlet opens with the following statement of the laws of money, taken from Adam Smith : —

"The use of a paper currency in any particular country, so far as it displaces coin which would otherwise be employed, diminishes the demand for gold and silver for the purpose of coinage, and has precisely the same effect in reducing their general value as an actual increase of their quantity to the same amount. On the supposition, therefore, of the whole quantity of gold and silver remain-

A far more important illustration, however, of the meaning conveyed or intended to be conveyed by the Bullion Report, is to be found in an elaborate essay in its vindication by Mr. William Huskisson, a member of the Committee, and published almost simultaneously with the report. His essay opens with the following definition of the nature and laws of money : —

" The various definitions of the word ' money,' and the different acceptations in which the word is used in the ordinary transactions of life, have contributed to produce much of the doubt and uncertainty which prevail at this moment respecting the state of our currency.

" Money, in the popular sense, is frequently considered as having no other value than one purely arbitrary and conventional. It is sometimes defined to be the representative of all other commodities, and sometimes the common measure of them. These definitions are both incomplete as applied to money ; because they are equally applicable to every description of currency, whether consisting of the precious metals, of paper, or of any other article.

" It is of the essence of money to possess intrinsic value.

" The quality of representing commodities does not necessarily imply intrinsic value ; because that quality may be given either by confidence or by authority. The quality of being a common measure does not necessarily imply intrinsic value, any more than the possession of a foot-rule entitles us to the power of acquiring whatever it enables us to measure. Money, or a given quantity of gold or silver, is not only the common measure and common representative of all other commodities, but also the common and universal equivalent.

" Paper currency has, obviously, no intrinsic value.

" A promissory note, under whatever form, or from whatever source it may issue, represents value. It does so, in as much as it is an undertaking to pay, in money, the sum for which it is issued.

" The money, or coin of a country, is so much of its capital. Paper currency is no part of the capital of a country : it is so much circulating credit.

" Whoever buys, gives, whoever sells, receives, such a quantity of pure gold or silver as is equivalent to the article bought or sold ; or, if he gives or receives paper instead of money, he gives or receives that which is valuable only as it stipulates the

ing the same, they must in a certain degree be rendered cheap by every increase of paper currency. It must, however, be evident that the advantages which do result from the use of a paper currency depend upon its exactly supplying the place of the coin it represents. This quality can be only possessed by a currency which is immediately convertible into specie at the option of the holder." (pp. 2–5.)

This preface was followed by a temperate argument against the Restriction Act, wholly inconclusive, from the writer's ignorance of the laws upon which a convertible currency must rest. His protest, notwithstanding, had a value in helping to keep up a spirit of opposition to the Restriction Act, which finally ended in its repeal.

payment of a given quantity of gold or silver. So long as this engagement is punctually fulfilled, paper will, of course, pass current with the coin with which it is thus constantly interchangeable. Both money, therefore, and paper promissory of money, are common measures and representatives of the value of all commodities. But money alone is the universal equivalent; paper currency is the representative of that money.

"Of paper currency, however, there are two sorts: the one resting upon confidence, the other upon authority. Paper resting upon confidence is what I have described as circulating credit, and consists in engagements for the payment, upon demand, of any specific sums of money; which engagements, from a general trust in the issuers of such paper, they are enabled to substitute for money in the transactions of the community. Paper resting upon authority is what, in common language, is called paper money; and consists of engagements issued or circulated under the sanction, and by the immediate intervention, of the public power of the State."[1]

The quality of representing commodities cannot be given either by confidence or authority. That a person believes that a note which he takes represents commodities does not make it the representative of them, any more than the belief of the Alchemists made the baser metals in combination the representatives of gold, into which they so long sought to convert them. If confidence would create values, the silliest dunce would be the Crœsus of the race. "Why not authority?" it is asked. "Government can declare that a foot-rule shall have the capacity of measuring extension. Why may it not declare that a bank-note shall have the capacity of measuring value? Intrinsic value is no more necessary in one case than in the other." But would the owners of estates accept in their sale the instruments by which their areas were measured? They might receive the surveyor's chains at their value as "scrap-iron," but in no other way. When men buy and sell, they exchange, or intend to exchange, articles possessing equal values. It is astonishing that Huskisson could have allowed himself to be taken captive by the theories or statements which he found in the books; which, upon the slightest examination, would have vanished in empty air. With all his acuteness, he did not get an inch beyond Smith's " instrument of commerce," — his "wheel" the value of which bore no relation whatever to the value of the articles moved by it.

---

[1] Question Concerning the Depreciation of our Currency, pp. 1–3.

"If the circulation," continues Huskisson, " of any country were performed exclusively by gold, for instance, and the supply of that metal in any such country were, from any imaginable cause, doubled, whilst the quantity of gold and the demand for it should continue the same in all other markets of the world, the value of gold in such country would be diminished. This diminution in the value of gold would appear in the proportionate rise of all commodities; but gold, being so much cheaper in the country in which its quantity had been increased, it would be bought by other countries, and exported from that country till its value was restored again to a level in the different parts of the world.

"If the circulation of a country were supplied partly by gold and partly by paper, and the amount of that circulation were doubled by an augmentation of that paper, the effect upon prices at home would be the same as in the former case ; but gold not becoming, by this augmentation of currency, more abundant in such country than in other parts of the world, as a commodity its relative value to other commodities would remain unaltered. As a commodity also, its price would rise in the same proportion as that of other commodities ; although, in the state of coin of which the denomination is fixed by law, it could only pass current according to that denomination.

"When paper is thus augmented in any country, the exportation of the gold coin, therefore, will take place ; not because gold, as a commodity, is become more abundant and less valuable with reference to other commodities in such country, but from the circumstance of its value as currency remaining the same, while its price in that currency is increased in common with the prices of all other commodities. So far as such exportation takes place, the diminution which it effects in the total amount of the currency has a tendency to support the value of the remainder, just as much, and for the same reason, as if, in the case of the circulation consisting wholly of gold, first an augmentation, and then an exportation to the same amount, had taken place, according to the first supposition.

"An excess of paper has, in the first instance, the same effect upon prices as an excess of the precious metals, to the same amount, would have, in any particular country. But it does not admit of the same relief : it cannot right itself by exportation.

"The currency of a country, then, is depreciated, —

"1. If its standard coin contain less of gold or silver than it is certified to contain. In that case, the paper, as representing the coin, is also depreciated, and precisely in the same degree as the coin.

"2. If the standard coin being of full weight, and the paper which represents that standard coin, and is, or purports to be, exchangeable for it, is not exchangeable, at the same time, for so large a quantity of gold or silver as is contained in the coin which it represents. In that case, the coin, though undiminished in value, must, as part of the currency, partake of the depreciation of the whole.

"Consequently, if the coin be itself, as coin, depreciated, the paper which circulates with it cannot be otherwise than depreciated to the same degree. But if the coin be undepreciated as coin, and there be, notwithstanding, a depreciation of the general currency, the cause of that depreciation can only be in the paper; and that cause can be no other than the excess in which that paper is issued."[1]

In the case supposed, where the currency was supplied partly by gold and partly by paper, and the two were of equal value, the latter must have been symbolic. If such a currency be doubled, the whole increase being, as Huskisson assumes, of the kind previously in circulation, there would be no inflation. Prices would, in reference to money, remain unchanged. So long as gold and paper possessed the same value, an increase, or, rather, an inflation, of the currency, would not inflate or increase the price of gold bullion, — gold as merchandise, — while it might increase the value of all other kinds of merchandise, for the very good reason that gold cannot rise in value in reference to itself; that is, a sovereign after the inflation would purchase the same amount of bullion as before. Huskisson took precisely the ground of Lowndes, who would " raise the value of silver in the coins to the foot of 6s. 3d. in every crown, because the price of standard silver in bullion had risen to 6s. 5d. the ounce." This was the very proposition that Locke was at such pains to refute, — that the value of silver cannot rise in reference to silver. Huskisson's assertion was only the old impossibility over again.

So long as coin would purchase no more than an equal nominal amount of paper, gold would have no more tendency to go abroad than before such increase. Indeed, its tendency would be inward to provide adequate reserves for the increase of paper. If the currency were inflated, that is, if it did not to its full extent represent merchandise other than gold, it might still remain at par with gold, provided the parties who issued it possessed sufficient reserves. If adequate provision, either in merchandise or coin, were not made for its redemption, it would become depreciated: it would not be exchangeable for an equal quantity of gold, nor would it command an equal amount of merchandise with gold, no matter whether it rested upon confidence or authority. The value of gold would not be influenced in any degree by the amount or value of the paper outstanding. That of the former would still depend

[1] Question Concerning the Depreciation of our Currency, pp. 26–29.

upon cost: that of the latter, upon cost and demand. If the latter rested upon confidence, its depreciation would tend to bring gold into the country; for it would be disused so soon as a currency that was not depreciated could be got to fill its place. Currency resting upon confidence that is depreciated always speedily goes out of circulation. If it rested upon authority, which was really the fact with regard to the Bank of England currency during the suspension, and was issued in very large amounts, it would, in great measure, drive the coin previously in circulation out of the country. But this fact would not tend, in any degree, to raise the value of the currency "resting on authority." Its value in exchange would be its estimated value. The exportation of coin would tend to reduce the value of such currency, instead of raising it, by rendering it all the more difficult to resume, from the impoverishment of the people, which would be measured by the amount of gold — capital — that had been drawn from them. Huskisson's assumptions, therefore, in whatever light viewed, are exactly opposed to the fact. It is wholly beyond the power of government to create the values upon which a currency must rest, except in the manner already described. If it be competent for it to make its notes legal tender, then they may, for a time, have a value for those who can use them exceeding their intrinsic value. But such accidental value would be lost so soon as the contracts existing at the time of their issue were discharged.

As money resting upon confidence or authority was with Huskisson equally a measure of value with gold, the decline in the value of the former, from whatever cause, carried down, and equally, the price of the latter; for the reason that one competent measure of value must be equal in potency or effect to any other competent measure. This is the way he reasoned in an essay the whole scope and object of which was to prove the exact opposite, — that the paper money of the country, though declared to have a value equal to that of an equal nominal amount of gold, did not possess such value; that the values of the two, though equally supported by authority, had no necessary relation the one to the other; and that their wide divergence was well calculated to excite the most profound alarm. He could not go into the market to make any purchase, without having thrust into his hand two scales of prices, —

one in paper, the other in gold ; yet, in the face of all this, he was so tied to tradition as to assert that money resting upon authority — the assignats of France and the Revolutionary Currency of the United States — was as competent a measure of values as gold and silver.

Immediately following Huskisson, but of much greater reputation and influence upon the subject of money, and whose writings reflected far more vividly the ideas of the Bullion Committee, was the celebrated David Ricardo, the author of several works upon money and kindred subjects, who has always been one of the great authorities in Political Economy. He was actively engaged in business as a banker during almost the whole period of the restriction. In 1809, he published a " Treatise on the Price of Bullion ; " in 1816, " Proposals for an Economical and Secure Currency ; " and, in 1817, his great work entitled " The Principles of Political Economy and Taxation," esteemed by the Economists to be the most important treatise on that science, with the single exception of Smith's " Wealth of Nations." As he was a member of Parliament, and took a leading part in the debates on the Restriction Act, his writings are of especial value as illustrating the opinions prevailing at the time. He is the central figure among the later school of Economists, as Smith is among the old. The latter lived almost wholly in an ideal world. The former was as wanting in ideas as the latter in knowledge of affairs. Accepting without reservation the theory of Smith, that value was not a necessary attribute of money, Ricardo was driven to explain the principle on which it circulated. He made short work of it, by declaring that money became such by virtue of the insignia of government; that its value was in ratio to its quantity, — that the most worthless pieces of paper, or the most debased coin, might be raised to the highest pitch of value simply by limiting their amount. In the same way, as will be hereafter seen, when called upon to reconcile Smith's doctrines of Free-Trade with the apparent necessity for Protection, he invented a dogma, which, so far as the doctrine of rent is concerned, is now universally accepted, — that prices are regulated by the least and not by the most favored of producers ; that the least favored is certain of a profit, although far below that of the most favored ; and, consequently, that the value or price of merchandise depends upon cost alone.

"The quantity of money," he says, "that can be employed in any country must depend upon its value. . . . A circulation can never be so abundant as to overflow; for, by diminishing its value, you will in the same proportion increase its quantity, and, by increasing its value, diminish its quantity. . . .

" While the State coins money, and charges no seigniorage, money will be of the same value as any other piece of the same metal of equal weight and fineness ; but, if the State charges a seigniorage for coinage, the coined piece of money will generally exceed the value of the uncoined piece of metal by the whole seigniorage charged, because it will require a greater quantity of labor, or, which is the same thing, the value of the produce of a greater quantity of labor, to procure it.

" While the State alone coins, there can be no limit to this charge of seigniorage ; for, by limiting the quantity of coin, it can be raised to any conceivable value.

" It is on this principle that paper money circulates : the whole charge for paper money may be considered as seigniorage. Though it has no intrinsic value, yet, by limiting its quantity, its value in exchange is as great as an equal denomination of coin or of bullion in that coin. On the same principle, too, namely, by a limitation of the quantity, a debased coin would circulate at the value it should bear if it were of the legal weight and fineness, not at the value of the quantity of metal which it actually contained. . . .

" After the establishment of Banks, the State has not the sole power of coining or issuing money. The currency may as effectually be increased by paper as by coin : so that if a State were to debase its money, and diminish its quantity, it could not support its value ; because the Banks would have an equal power of adding to the whole quantity of circulation.

" On these principles, it will be seen that it is not necessary that paper money should be payable in specie to secure its value : it is only necessary that its quantity should be regulated according to the value of the metal which is declared to be its standard. If the standard were gold of a given weight and fineness, paper might be increased with every fall in the value of gold, or, which is the same thing in its effects, with every rise in the price of goods . . .

" Dr. Smith appears to have forgotten his own principle in his argument on colony currency. Instead of ascribing the depreci- ation of that paper to its too great abundance, he asks whether, allowing the colony security to be perfectly good, a hundred pounds payable fifteen years hence would be equally valuable with a hundred pounds to be paid immediately. I answer, Yes, if it be not too abundant.

" Experience, however, shows that neither a State nor a Bank ever have had the unrestricted power of issuing paper money, without abusing that power. In all States, therefore, the issue of paper money ought to be under some check and control ; and none seems so proper for that purpose as that of subjecting the issuers of paper money to the obligation of paying their notes, either in gold coin or bullion.

" A currency is in its most perfect state when it consists wholly of paper money, but of paper money of an equal value with the gold which it professes to represent. The use of paper instead of gold substitutes the cheapest in place of the most expensive medium, and enables the country, without loss to any individual, to exchange all the gold which it before used for this purpose, for raw materials, utensils, and food, by the use of which both its wealth and its enjoyments are increased." [1]

Suppose government to charge nine sovereigns for coining one, — that is, that for metal equal in weight to ten, it should return, to the party bringing it to the mint, only one, the insignia affixed to the coin declaring that it should have a value in exchanges equal to ten times the amount of the metal it contained, — could such declaration make the exchangeable value of the coin equal to its nominal value? Ricardo replies, " Yes, for the public must have money — must have yardsticks and scales — or their operations must cease." But if government should offer to return in coin only one-tenth of the metal received, no one would take bullion or dust to it. The metal would be privately assayed, and would pass by weight. A person possessing bullion might wish to sell it for use in the arts, or for the purchase of foreign commodities; for which it would be received at its full value. If government should persist in returning only one-tenth of the metal in the form of coin, its action might cause no little inconvenience; but great commercial communities existed long before coinage was invented. The inconvenience resulting from the want of coinage, relative to the magnitude of the transactions taking place, would be much less now than before the invention or use of symbolic money; for the reserves necessary for the conversion of such currency may be in the form of bullion, nearly as well as in that of coin. They are now largely held in bullion. Government can create debts which have a value equal to that which is to be eventually paid, less the charge for interest for forbearance of present payment; but it can no more create values by its insignia without an obligation, than the Alchemist could create gold out of curious and fanciful combinations of the baser metals.

Paper money with Ricardo having necessarily no intrinsic value, and his assumption having become a dogma with the modern school, the only question really involved in the discus-

[1] Principles of Political Economy and Taxation, Chapter xxv.

sion which followed has been that of quantity. As governments were the proper parties to coin metals, they were, by necessary inference, the proper parties to issue paper. Experience, however, proved that they were not to be trusted where the temptation was so great. Their necessities, real or fancied, would always be pushing them beyond the proper limit. Paper money, therefore, was to be issued by private parties or bankers, who were always to be under the check of its conversion into coin. If, for example, a currency of £50,000,000, consisting of £30,000,000 of paper and £20,000,000 of coin, sufficed for the wants of a community in their exchanges, and an addition to it of £10,000,000 of paper, no matter how issued, were made, — the currency would be in excess; and that portion of it consisting of gold, being the only part of it that was exportable, would seek other markets in which the currency was in less relative abundance. If the addition of £10,000,000 in the case assumed were convertible into coin, it would be drawn, in order to supply the export demand. This demand would continue till equilibrium was restored; that is, till the amount of currency was reduced to that required by the community in their transactions, — to the original sum of £50,000,000. Provided the parties issuing the excess were able to take in their notes on demand, all aberrations in the volume of the currency would correct themselves. Convertibility of paper at all times into coin, consequently, was the only certain test of the propriety of its issue.

But convertibility of issue may have no relation whatever to propriety of issue. A person may be able to pay a bill he has uttered; but by doing so he may strip himself of every dollar he possesses. The question, therefore, far in advance of convertibility, and which is the only one important to be considered, is the manner in, or cost at which, convertibility is sought to be secured. The notes of the Bank of England have been uninterruptedly convertible for the last fifty-five years; yet the fear that they might not be convertible has, during that whole period, kept the public mind in constant agitation, and has often culminated in panics which carried ruin and dismay throughout the land. The spectre has yet lost none of its terror or power to harm. How to create a currency which shall at all times be convertible without drawing capital from its issuers, and without creating disturbance in monetary and financial circles, is a problem no nearer solution than it was a hundred years ago. The principles on which all commercial currencies must be based, as set out in the first part of this work, have only to be referred to, to place the whole subject in a light to command universal assent. Where bills are discounted, obligations are mutually created; and, so long as such bills represent merchandise entering into consumption, their payment is certain to return to the Bank its obligations, without the withdrawal of any considerable portion of its means. So long as such rule is followed, so long as a currency is issued only in the discount of bills representing merchandise, there can be no inflation; nor is there any danger that the Bank issuing it will be called upon for any considerable amount of coin. No ordinary alarm can take the notes so issued out of the channels of circulation, so that they will be presented for payment in coin. But so soon as the Bank ceases to discount bills, and puts its means, whatever they may be, into governments — into consols, it alone undertakes to take in its own currency; and it may be laid down as an axiom in monetary science, that unless provision be made for the retirement of a currency without any act of the issuer, it is certain to involve both himself and the public in great embarrassment and loss, and the former, perhaps, in absolute ruin. The only proper mode of issuing a currency is that which shall provide for its retirement automatically, by the operation of the laws of trade, — by the debtors of the Bank, instead of the Bank itself. That such mode of issue has never yet been made the subject of discussion by the Economists, is a sufficient explanation of the utter want of progress in monetary science.

It has already been sufficiently shown, that in all exchanges, equivalents, or what are assumed to be equivalents, are exchanged; that when one of the subjects of exchange is a promise or undertaking of government, its price is its real or estimated value; and that the insignia of government, unless they carry with them some obligation, are of no value. A government currency, which may at first have a value in coin nearly equal to its nominal value, may become wholly valueless; but its price at any given time is to be accepted as its value. In other words, money will no more be taken but at its value than any other kind of merchandise or property. This may, like that of all other kinds, be overestimated; the market price of any article, however, at any one time, must always be considered to measure its value. Ricardo, however, with the Economists, held value to be no attribute of money; but that it was an instrument of commerce precisely in the same manner that scales or balances are instruments of commerce, the value of both depending upon their quantity. If only one set of scales were allowed to be used, if the weight of all merchandise entering into commerce were to be ascertained by it, it might to its possessor have an almost fabulous value, as all would have to use it upon his own terms. If Ricardo be correct, then provided there be but one shilling in the world, and that a debased one, its value might be equal to all the money in it at the present time. If he be correct, then the debasement of a currency, provided its nominal amount be not increased, is the wisest possible policy both for princes and people.

"In a national point of view," continues Ricardo, "it is of no importance whether the issuers of this well-regulated paper money be the government or a Bank; it will on the whole be equally productive of'riches, whether it be issued by one or by the other : but it is not so with respect to the interest of individuals. In a country where the market rate of interest is 7 per cent, and where the State requires for a particular expense £70,000 per annum, it is a question of importance to the individuals of that country, whether they must be taxed to pay this £70,000 per aunum, or whether they could raise it without taxes. Suppose that a million of money should be required to fit out an expedition. If the State issued a million of paper, and displaced a million of coin, the expedition would be fitted out without any charge to the people; but if a Bank issued a million of paper, and lent it to government at 7 per cent, thereby displacing a million of coin, the country would be charged with a continual tax of £70,000 per annum. The people would pay the tax, the Bank would receive it, and the society would in either case be as wealthy as before : the expedition would have been really fitted out by the improvement of our system; by rendering capital, of the value of a million, productive in the form of commodities, instead of letting it remain unproductive in the form of coin. But the advantage would always be in favor of the issuers of paper; and, as the State represents the people, the people would have saved the tax, if they, and not the Bank, had issued this million. . . .

"It has already been observed, that if there were perfect security that the power of issuing paper money would not be abused, it could be of no importance, with respect to the riches of the country collectively, by whom it was issued; and I have now shown that the public would have a direct interest that the issuers should be the State, and not a company of merchants and bankers.

The danger, however, is, that this power would be more likely to be abused, if in the hands of government, than in the hands of a banking company. A company would, it is said, be more under the control of law; and, although it might be their interest to extend their issues beyond the bounds of discretion, they would be limited and checked by the power which individuals would have of calling for bullion or specie. It is argued, that the same check would not be long respected, if government had the privilege of issuing money; that they would be too apt to consider present convenience rather than future security, and might, therefore, on the alleged grounds of expediency, be too much inclined to remove the checks by which the amount of their issues was controlled.

"Under an arbitrary government, this objection would have great force; but in a free country, with an enlightened legislature, the power of issuing paper money, under the requisite checks of convertibility at the will of the holder, might be safely lodged in the hands of commissioners appointed for that special purpose, and they might be made totally independent of the control of ministers." [1]

As money, with Ricardo, possessed no value, it was immaterial who issued it, — government or the Bank. It would in either case be equally productive of riches. Why? Because government would pay nothing for its use, thereby saving the people an equal amount in taxes, while Banks would receive an interest on that which cost them nothing. It made, however, a great difference to the public who issued it; for the reason that its issue by government saved them an equal sum. The saving effected by such a currency, Ricardo illustrates by the fitting out of an expedition, the whole cost of which was borne by an issue of government notes. The notes would necessarily be legal tender; for the reason that, if they bore no interest, the people would not willingly receive them on any other terms. If they bore interest, nothing would be saved to the public. If they were made legal tender, the effect would be to drive out of the country a corresponding amount of specie. The nation, consequently, would be so much the poorer. It could only pay its notes by bringing back the coin it had parted with. If it repudiated them, it could not resume its industries on their wonted scale till the amount lost had been brought back. Ricardo assumed that a nation might waste a large portion of its capital in bootless military operations, and still have the whole of it in hand. He made nothing of over-

[1] Principles of Political Economy and Taxation, Chap. xxv.

ruling natural laws, in order to give consistency to his theories
or schemes.

Suppose the government of the United States to undertake
the issue of a currency by a commission having its office in
the City of New York, as the commercial centre of the country,
upon what principle or rule would it act? How would the
right of a person to receive this currency be ascertained? If
it were issued in the discount of bills, how could the sufficiency
of their makers be determined? By evidence, of course, — by
proof of their solvency. It might require a day to collect and
weigh the evidence presented in any one case, so that the
commission might be able to make only a few hundred loans
each year; no more than could be made by any one of the
twenty-two hundred Banks in the country. How would such
a commission, having no capital, take in its notes when presented for payment? Large losses would inevitably be incurred. How would these be made good? If any doubt
were thrown upon the ability of the commission to redeem its
notes when presented, no one would receive them, or, if in circulation, they would speedily be returned for payment in coin.
The moment the plan of a single office of issue is examined,
its absurdity is so palpable as to transcend all argument.
Government might with the same propriety undertake to
supply its people with food and clothing as with money.
Money is the equivalent of food and clothing.

"In another part of this work" says Ricardo, "I have endeavored to show that the real value of a commodity is regulated,
not by the accidental advantages which may be enjoyed by some
of its producers, but by the real difficulties encountered by that
producer who is least favored. It is so with respect to the interest
for money: it is not regulated by the rate at which the Bank will
lend, whether it be 5, 4, or 3 per cent, but by the rate of profits
which can be made by the employment of capital, and which is
totally independent of the quantity or of the value of money.
Whether a Bank lost one million, ten millions, or a hundred millions, they would not permanently alter the market rate of interest:
they would alter only the value of the money which they thus
issued. In one case, ten or twenty times more money might be
required to carry on the same business than what might be required
in the other. The applications to the Bank for money, then, depend
on the comparison between the rate of profits that may be made by
the employment of it, and the rate at which they are willing to
lend it. If they charge less than the market rate of interest, there
is no amount of money which they might not lend. If they charge

more than that rate, only spendthrifts and prodigals would be found to borrow of them. We accordingly find, that, when the market rate of interest exceeds the rate of 5 per cent, at which the Bank uniformly lends, the discount office is besieged with applicants for money; and, on the contrary, when the market rate is even temporarily under 5 per cent, the clerks of that office have no employment.

"The reason, then, why for the last twenty years the Bank is said to have given so much aid to commerce by assisting the merchants with money, is because they have, during that whole period, lent money below the market rate of interest; — below the rate at which the merchants could have borrowed elsewhere; but I confess, that to me this seems rather an objection to their establishment than an argument in favor of it.

"What should we say of an establishment which should regularly supply half the clothiers with their wool under the market price? Of what benefit would it be to the community? It would not extend our trade, because the wool would equally have been bought if they had charged the market price for it. It would not lower the price of cloth to the consumer; because the price, as I have said before, would be regulated by the cost of its production to those who were the least favored. Its sole effect, then, would be to swell the profits of a part of the clothiers beyond the general and common rate of profits. The establishment would be deprived of its fair profits, and another part of the community would be in the same degree benefited. Now this is precisely the effect of our banking establishments. A rate of interest is fixed by the law below that at which it can be borrowed in the market; and at this rate the Bank is required to lend, or not to lend at all. From the nature of their establishment, they have large funds which they can only deal with in this way; and a part of the traders of the country are unfairly, and for the country unprofitably, benefited, by being enabled to supply themselves with an instrument of trade at a less charge than those who must be influenced only by market price."[1]

It was upon the theory that the least favored, not the most favored, control prices, that Ricardo built his doctrine of rent, now universally accepted by the Economists. According to this, the cost at which a farmer can afford to sell a bushel of corn produced among the hills of New Hampshire regulates the price which one producing it upon the bottom lands of Illinois can obtain for it; or the cost at which cloth can be produced by the spinning-wheel and hand-loom regulates the price which can be obtained for that produced by the most approved machinery. The difference of cost of production between the two methods is profit to the most favored. This assumption was preceded by another, for which Ricardo has been

[1] Principles of Political Economy and Taxation. Chap. xxv.

greatly praised, — that price is regulated by cost alone. The one is a proper sequence of the other. His doctrine, if true, is a most comforting one to all classes. By it the least favored are secured from loss, while the most favored are certain of enormous profits. None can be losers, all will be gainers, and mankind will at once enter upon a financial millennium. Poverty will be banished from the earth. Unfortunately, the very reverse of this picture is too often the rule. The most favored often find themselves in the greatest straits ; and, if they can sustain themselves, may have to work for years without any profit whatever. What, in such case, becomes of the least favored? They are, as it were, swept out of existence. Ricardo's assumption, consequently, is exactly opposed to the universal experience of mankind. The Bank, in the case supposed, was enabled to loan below the market rate from being the most favored of lenders. It was intrusted with the custody of immense sums, upon which it paid no interest. The public were gainers in ratio to the lowness of the rates charged, as the capital loaned became the basis of production or distribution, the price of the product being in ratio to the price of capital. That the Bank favored one class more than another was unquestionably a pure fiction. The rates at which it loaned depended, as they will always depend, upon the goodness of the security offered. Those who offered the best fared the best. There was in all this no injustice, but the greatest justice. Reward followed desert. If, in the case supposed, an institution supplied one-half the clothiers with wool under the market price, what would be lost on one hand would be gained on the other, as the price of the product would be in ratio to the cost of the material. The illustration, however, goes for nothing ; for there never was and never will be a case in which the arbitrary distinctions he supposed were made.

The following extract will show the manner in which Ricardo proposed to establish an Economical and Secure Currency : —

" A well-regulated paper currency is so great an improvement in commerce, that I should greatly regret if prejudice should induce us to return to a system of less utility. The introduction of the precious metals for the purposes of money may, with truth, be considered as one of the most important steps towards the improvement of commerce and the arts of civilized life; but it is no less true, that, with the advancement of knowledge and science, we discover that it would be another improvement to banish them again from the employment to which, during a less enlightened age, they had been so advantageously applied.

"If the Bank should be again called upon to pay their notes in specie, the effect would be to lessen greatly the profits of the Bank, without a corresponding gain to any other part of the community. If those who use one and two, and even five, pound notes should have their option of using guineas, there would be little doubt which they would prefer; and thus, to indulge a mere caprice, a most expensive medium would be substituted for one of little value.

" Besides the loss to the Bank, which must be considered as a loss to the community, general wealth being made up of individual riches, the State would be subjected to the useless expense of coinage; and, on every fall of the exchange, guineas would be melted and exported.

" To secure the public against any other variations in the value of the currency than those to which the standard itself is subject, and, at the same time, to carry on the circulation with a medium the least expensive, is to attain the most perfect state to which a currency can be brought; and we should possess all these advantages by subjecting the Bank to the delivery of uncoined gold or silver at the mint standard and price, in exchange for their notes, instead of the delivery of guineas; by which means paper would never fall below the value of bullion without being followed by a reduction of its quantity. To prevent the rise of paper above the value of bullion, the Bank should be also obliged to give their paper in exchange for standard gold at the price of £3 17s. per ounce. Not to give too much trouble to the Bank, the quantity of gold to be demanded in exchange for paper at the mint price of £3 17s. 10½d., or the quantity to be sold at the Bank at £3 17s., should never be less than twenty ounces. In other words, the Bank should be obliged to purchase any quantity of gold that was offered them, not less than twenty ounces, at £3 17s. per ounce, and to sell any quantity that might be demanded at £3 17s. 10d. While they have the power of regulating the quantity of their paper, there is no possible inconvenience that could result to them from such a regulation.

" The most perfect liberty should be given, at the same time, to export or import every description of bullion. These transactions in bullion would be very few in number, if the Bank regulated their loans and issues of paper by the criterion which I have so often mentioned, namely, the price of standard bullion, without attending to the absolute quantity of paper in circulation." [1]

Ricardo would maintain the value of paper money by having it represent gold, but would prevent a resort to gold by throw-

[1] Proposals for an Economical and Secure Currency, Section iv.

ing inconveniences in the way of its use. He assumed, of course, that only a small amount of gold would be required to meet occasional calls; for nothing would be gained, provided the amount of gold to be held in reserve equalled the amount of notes issued. But, if it were optional with the public whether or not they would receive the notes of the Bank, they would not receive them, if they could get nothing for them but bullion. They would not subject themselves to the expense, delay, and annoyance of having the bullion that might be paid them coined. Ricardo proceeded upon the assumption, that what the public wanted was currency, — a medium of exchange, — not capital. If perfect freedom were allowed, the people, Ricardo says, from mere caprice, would indulge in a most expensive medium, in place of one of little or no value. Such caprice must not be submitted to. It must be corrected by the inconvenience of indulging it. This inconvenience must exceed the convenience of the use of coin over bullion. If no one would go after it, the Bank or mint would be under no necessity to maintain on hand any considerable quantity, while there would be no occasion to coin even such quantity. In this way, says Ricardo, a perfect currency would be realized; costing nothing in itself, yet always at the standard of coin! He would invite the whole world to a Barmecide feast, crowned with every thing but that necessary to gratify the appetite. One such feast would be enough for those invited to it; for, it is to be feared, that, had Ricardo received the treatment properly due to the giver of such an entertainment, his barren nature would hardly have imitated the generous and hospitable spirit of the inventor.

Whoever follows the Economists must make up his mind to be surprised by no folly or absurdity which he may meet: he is in the land of delusions and dreams. The moment one crosses the line between the world of affairs, and the world of theories which relate to money and subjects kindred to it, his whole nature seems changed. He has drunk of the cup of Circe till he is deprived alike of sense and reason. Ricardo possessed in an eminent degree the gift of money-making, and undoubtedly ranked high as a man of affairs. He, however, no sooner took up his pen than he seemed instantly discharged of all reasoning faculty. In the same sentence, he could affirm propositions exactly opposed the one to the other, without the least perception of their incongruity. Never was there a more striking instance of confident assumption on the one hand, and fatuity on the other. To add to the strangeness of the picture, he occupies the front rank among the Economists as an original and profound thinker, — one who exploded many of the radical errors, who placed on firm foundations some of the most important truths of Political Economy, and to whom it is more indebted than to any writer but Adam Smith. His name is never mentioned but with expressions of profound respect. From his example, it would seem that no mind is capable of discussing the subject of money, and of preserving, at the same time, its balance and integrity. The charm or influence which so subverts the sense of mankind is a problem in psychology well worthy the most careful investigation. Its solution might help the race to attack and overthrow delusions upon other subjects, equally deep-rooted and far more mischievous; for, in the matter of money, the most groundless and absurd theories are often found intimately associated with the greatest practical talent for its accumulation and administration. Life nowhere else presents an example of such complete disassociation between the practical and speculative sides of our nature.

As the recommendations contained in the Report of the Bullion Committee were rejected, the condition of the Bank and its relations to the government and the public remained unchanged. The price of gold, however, gradually rose; and, after numerous fluctuations, reached its highest point, £5 10s. the ounce, in August, 1813. Upon the abdication of Napoleon, in 1814, it fell off to £4 6s. On his return from Elba, in 1815, it rose to £5 7s. Upon his final overthrow, its price rapidly declined; and in October, 1816, it was as low as £3 18s. 6d. the ounce. On the 17th of April, 1817, the Bank gave notice of its readiness to pay off its £1 and £2 notes dated prior to January 1, 1816; and, on the 18th of September of the same year, of its readiness to pay off all its notes dated prior to January 1, 1817. This action was voluntary on the part of the Bank, as the restriction, which was to expire at the end of six months after a definitive treaty of peace, was extended, in 1815, to July 5, 1816; again extended to July 5, 1818; and again, to July 5, 1819. On the 28th of

February, 1817, the Bank had in its vaults £9,680,000 in coin
and bullion; on the 31st of August, of the same year,
£11,688,000; and on the 28th of February, 1818, £10,055,000.
Its liabilities on its notes and deposits, on the 28th of February, 1817, equalled £38,223,000.   It was at that time,
apparently, in position to attempt resumption.   But, although
peace had for some time been established, order had by no
means been restored in commercial circles; and as the Bank
possessed no available capital of its own, except its accumulated
profits, amounting only to a few millions, it had really no control over the coin that had accumulated in its vaults.   This
was speedily drawn out in the adjustment of the enormous
debts growing out of the recent gigantic struggle, and in consequence of the commercial embarrassments and disasters
which necessarily accompanied the attempt to resume.   On the
27th of February, 1819, the coin at the Bank was reduced to
£4,184,000; and as it was seen that if it continued to pay
its means would speedily become exhausted, Parliament
early in 1819, again interposed, forbidding any further cash
payments.   At the same time, it took the whole subject vigorously in hand, and with little delay passed an act, of which
the following are the most important provisions: —

"1. The Restriction Act was continued, absolutely, from the 5th
of July, 1819, to February 1, 1820.

"2. Between February 1 and October 1, 1820, the Bank was
required to pay its notes in gold bullion, of standard fineness, at
the rate of £4 1s. per ounce; but not to be liable to a demand for a
less quantity than sixty ounces at one time.

"3. Between October 1, 1820, and May 1, 1821, the Bank was
required to pay its notes in gold bullion upon the same plan, at
the rate of £3 19s. 6d. per ounce.

"4. Between May 1, 1821, and May 1, 1823, the Bank was to
pay in gold bullion upon the same plan, at the rate of £3 17s. 10½d.
per ounce, which was the mint price of gold.

"5. From May 1, 1823, the Bank was to pay its notes in the
gold coin of the realm.

"6. But between February 1 and October 1, 1820, the Bank
might make payments at a less rate than £4 1s., and not less
than £3 19s. 6d. per ounce; and between October 1, 1820, and
May 1, 1821, the Bank might pay at any rate less than £3 19s. 6d.,
and not less than £3 17s. 10½d., on giving three days' notice in the
Gazette.   Such payments to be made in ingots or bars of gold, of
the weight of sixty ounces.   The Bank was also permitted to pay
in gold coin on or after May 1, 1822.

"7. All the laws which restrained the exportation of gold and silver coin were repealed, and the coin was allowed to be exported or melted without incurring any penalty."

It will thus be seen that the law providing for resumption was based upon Ricardo's proposition for a Secure and Economical Currency; according to which, if 'called upon, the Bank might pay in bullion, the object being to protect it from demands for small sums. The Bank, however, did not avail itself of this privilege; while it anticipated the time fixed by Parliament, by resuming payment in coin on the first of May, 1821.

Simultaneously with the passage of the act providing for resumption, was that of another forbidding the Bank to make loans to government without permission of Parliament. The value of such provision, however, was wholly negatived by a clause allowing the Bank to continue the purchase of Exchequer bills.

The signal failure which followed the attempts at resumption, in 1817–18, taught the Bank a lesson which was well heeded in making its preparations for resumption in pursuance of the Act of 1819. No sooner was that Act passed than it immediately began to contract its issues, and continued to do so till the close of 1822. On the 31st of August, 1821, its note circulation equalled £20,295,000; its deposits, £5,818,000, and its specie, £11,233,000: against £25,252,000 of notes, £6,304,000 of deposits, and £3,595,000 of specie, on the 31st of August, 1819; and against £29,543,000 of notes, £9,084,000 of deposits, and £11,688,000 of specie, on the 31st of August, 1817. The reduction of liabilities from the time the Bank attempted to resume in 1817, to 1821, when it did resume, equalled £12,514,000. The circulation was still further reduced in 1822; averaging, for that year, £18,165,000. Its deposits for that year averaged £5,544,000; its total liabilities, only £23,704,000, — a smaller sum than for any year since 1802. Its average liabilities for 1814 equalled £40,246,000; the reduction from that year to 1822 equalling £16,502,000. From 1822 to 1824, the Bank did not materially increase its note circulation; that for the former year averaging £18,811,000, and, for the latter, £19,934,000. Its deposits, growing out of the operations of government, however, increased from £5,544,000, in 1822, to £9,888,000, in 1824. It maintained a very large average of specie until 1824; holding, on the 31st of August of that year, £11,787,000. In the latter part of 1824, however, a heavy demand set in, which continued uninterruptedly through 1825, reducing the amount in the Bank on the 28th of December of that year to £1,027,000, against £14,142,000 held by it on the 20th of December, 1823; the reduction in two years equalling £13,115,000. The year 1825 appeared to open most auspiciously. Even the King's speech dismissing the Parliament on the 6th of July of that year congratulated the country upon its " general and increasing prosperity." The more sagacious, however, by no means concurred in such an opinion. There was vast activity, based, as events proved, upon no substantial foundation. Never since the South Sea scheme had there been a spirit of speculation so excessive and universal as that which prevailed in the latter part of 1824 and through- out 1825. It was natural that the people, released from the apprehension with which resumption of specie payments was so long viewed, and from the restraints which such apprehension necessarily imposed, should lose control of themselves, and rush wildly into all sorts of visionary and extravagant schemes. This could not have been possible but for the country Banks, which issued their notes in a most profuse and reckless manner, fancying that they were possessed of the same impunity as during restriction. The conduct of the Bank, as far as its issues of notes were concerned, does not appear to have been at all censurable. The average amount of these in circulation in 1825 equalled only £20,076,000, against £22,000,000 in 1821, the year of the resumption, and against £18,065,000 in 1822. The increase was certainly no greater than might have been expected from that of the business of the country in the three years. The action of the Bank, however, did materi- ally assist to increase the inflation, in connection with that of the government, which, in 1824, undertook to reduce £80,000,000 of four per cents to three and one-half per cents. The dissentients, of whom there were a large number, the Bank undertook to pay off. This threw a great amount of money into circulation. It also induced great numbers to sell their governments, for the purpose of realizing higher rates of interest. The public mind, therefore, was well prepared for the reception of any plausible scheme that promised great returns upon very small investments; and it was abundantly supplied. In less than two years, ending with 1825, six hundred and twenty-four speculative companies were formed and put upon the market, whose share capital equalled £372,173,000.[1] At the same time, foreign loans were negotiated to the amount of £52,994,000, upon a considerable portion of which little or nothing was ever paid.[2]

[1] These companies were classified as follows : —

		Capital.
74	Mining Companies	£38,370,000
29	Gas Companies	12,077,000
20	Insurance Companies	85,820,000
29	Investment Companies	52,600,000
54	Canal and Railroad Companies	44,051,000
67	Steam Companies	8,555,500
11	Trading Companies	10,450,000
26	Building Companies	13,781,000
24	Provision Companies	8,360,000
292	Miscellaneous Companies	148,108,600
	Total	£372,173,100

The amount actually advanced on account of these companies equalled £17,605,625. It is needless to say, that nearly this whole sum was lost, and, with it, a vastly larger sum, in the extravagance and folly which always accompany an intense speculative movement.

[2] The following is a list of foreign loans concluded in England at the period under discussion, the rate per cent, and the rate at which they were put upon the public : —

		Rate of Interest per cent.	Price at which put upon the market per cent.
Austrian	£2,500,000	5	82
Brazilian	8,200,000	5	75
„	2,000,000	5	85
Buenos Ayres	1,000,000	6	85
Chilian	1,000,000	6	70
Columbian	2,000,000	6	84
„	4,750,000	6	88¼
Danish	5,500,000	3	75
Greek	800,000	5	59
„	1,000,000	5	56½
Guatemala	1,428,571	6	73
Gaudalajara	600,000	5	60
Mexican	8,200,000	5	58
„	8,200,000	6	89¼
Neapolitan	2,500,000	5	92¼
Prussian	5,000,000	5	72
„	8,500,000	5	84¼
Portuguese	1,500,000	5	87
Peruvian	450,000	6	88
„	750,000	6	82
„	616,000	6	78
Russian	8,500,000	5	82
Spanish	1,500,000	5	56
„	1,500,000	5	80¼
Total	£52,994,571		

But speculation was by no means confined to fictitious or fraudulent enterprises and companies, nor to worthless foreign loans. It invaded every walk of life and every department of industry and trade. In the general delirium, the relation between values and price was wholly lost sight of. For a brief period, the people rioted in their imagined wealth; coming to consciousness only when their actual means were well-nigh dissipated, to see no trace of their magnificent bubbles but the ruins left behind.

The Bank, for a considerable time after the drain set in, endeavored to protect itself by refusing to make loans. Such refusal only added to the alarm which prevailed, and to the run upon it. Seeing nothing but certain destruction in such a course, the Bank suddenly changed its policy, and determined, as far as its means would go, to meet all calls that could properly be made upon it. The mint was driven to its utmost capacity; turning out daily 150,000 guineas. Notes could not be so readily provided. The Bank luckily, however, found a large package of £1 and £2 notes which had been taken in, but by some accident had not been cancelled. Before these were wholly paid out, the panic subsided. " During its continuance," said Mr. Harmon, Governor of the Bank at the time, in his evidence before a Committee of the House of Commons, " we lent by every possible means, and in modes that we never had adopted before. We took in stock as security; we purchased Exchequer bills; we made advances on Exchequer bills; we not only discounted outright, but we made advances on deposits of bills of exchange to an immense amount, — in short, by every possible means consistent with the safety of the Bank; and we were not, upon some occasions, over-nice. Seeing the dreadful state in which the public were, we rendered every assistance in our power. . . . As far as my judgment goes, the discovery of the package of £1 notes saved the credit of the country."

The events of 1826 were well calculated to arrest the attention of government. No sooner had the panic subsided than Lord Liverpool addressed a communication to the Bank, remarkable for being one of the few papers in the literature of finance in which there is any recognition of the principles upon which a symbolic currency must rest.

" However much," said Lord Liverpool, "the recent distress may have been aggravated, in the judgment of some, by incidental circumstances and particular measures, there can be no doubt that the principal source of it is to be found in the rash spirit of speculation, which has pervaded the country for some time, supported, fostered, and encouraged by the country Banks.

" The remedy, therefore, for this evil in future must be found in an improvement in the circulation of the country paper; and the first measure which has suggested itself to most of those who have considered the subject, is a recurrence to gold circulation throughout the country, as well as in the metropolis and its neighborhood, by a repeal of the Act which permits country Banks to issue £1 and £2 notes, until the year 1833; and by the immediate enactment of a prohibition of any such issues at the expiration of two or three years from the present period. . . .

" But though a recurrence to gold circulation in the country, for the reasons already stated, might be productive of some good, it could by no means go to the root of the evil.

" We have abundant proof of the truth of this position in the events which took place in the spring of 1793, when a convulsion occurred in the money transactions and circulation of the country more extensive than that which we have recently experienced. At that period, nearly a hundred country Banks were obliged to stop payment, and Parliament was induced to grant an issue of Exchequer bills to relieve the distress; yet in the year 1793 there were no £1 or £2 notes in circulation in England, either by country Banks or by the Bank of England.

" We have a further proof of the truth of what has been advanced, in the experience of Scotland, which has escaped all the convulsions which have occurred in the money market of England for the last thirty-five years; though Scotland, during the whole of that time, has had a circulation of £1 notes, and the small pecuniary transactions of that part of the United Kingdom have been carried on exclusively by means of such notes.

" The issue of small notes, though it be an aggravation, cannot, therefore, be the sole, or even the main, cause of the evil in England.

" We have, to a considerable degree, the proof of this position in the very establishment of so many country Banks.

" Within the memory of many living, and even of some of those now engaged in public affairs, there were no country Banks except in a few of the great commercial towns.

" The money transactions of the country were carried on by supplies of coin and bank-notes from London.

" The extent of the business of the country, and the improvements made from time to time in the mode of conducting our increased commercial transactions, founded on pecuniary credit, rendered such a system no longer adequate; and country Banks must have arisen — as, in fact, they did arise — from the increased wealth and new wants of the country.

" The matter of regret is, not that country Banks have been

suffered to exist, but that they have been suffered to exist so long
without control or limitation, or without the adoption of provisions
calculated to counteract the evils resulting from their improvidence
or excess.

" It would be vain to suppose that we could now, by any act of
the Legislature extinguish the existing country Banks, even if it
were desirable: but it may be within our power, gradually at
least, to establish a sound system of banking throughout the
country ; and, if such a system could be formed, there can be little
doubt that it would ultimately extinguish and absorb all that is
objectionable and dangerous in the present banking establishments.

" There appear to be two modes of attaining this object : —

" 1st. That the Bank of England should establish branches of
its own body in different parts of the country.

" 2dly. That the Bank of England should give up its exclusive
privileges as to the number of partners engaged in banking except
within a certain distance of the metropolis.

" It has always appeared to me, that it would have been very
desirable that the Bank should have tried the first of these plans, —
that of establishing branch Banks upon a limited scale.

" But I am not insensible to the difficulties which would have
attended such an experiment ; and I am quite satisfied that it would
be impossible for the Bank, under present circumstances, to carry
into execution such a system to the extent necessary for providing
for the wants of the country.

" There remains, therefore, only the other plan, — the surrender
by the Bank of their exclusive privileges as to the number of
partners within a certain distance from the metropolis.

" The effect of such a measure would be the gradual establishment of extensive and respectable Banks in different parts of the
country ; some, perhaps, with charters from the Crown, and some
without.

" Here we have again the advantage of the experience of Scotland.

" In England, there are said to be between eight and nine hundred country Banks ; and it is no exaggeration to suppose that a
great proportion of them have not been conducted with a due attention to those precautions which are necessary for the safety of
all banking establishments, even where their property is more ample.
When such Banks stop, their creditors may ultimately be paid the
whole of their demands ; but the delay and shock to credit may, in
the mean time, involve them in the same difficulty, and is always
attended with the greatest injury and suffering in the districts where
such stoppages occur. If this be the case where the solidity of the
Bank is unquestionable, what must it be, as too often happens, when
they rest on no solid foundation ?

" In Scotland there are not more than thirty Banks, and these
Banks have stood firm amidst all the convulsions in the money
market in England, and amidst all the distresses to which the manufacturing and agricultural interests in Scotland, as well as in
England, have occasionally been subject.

" Banks of this description must necessarily be conducted upon the general, understood, and approved principles of banking.

" Individuals are, from the nature of the institutions, precluded from speculating in the manner in which persons engaged in country, and even in London Banks speculate in England.

" The failures which have occurred in England, unaccompanied as they have been by the same occurrences in Scotland, tend to prove that there must have been an unsolid and delusive system of banking in one part of Great Britain, and a solid and substantial one in the other.

" It would be entirely at variance with my deliberate opinion, not to do full justice to the Bank of England as the great centre of circulation and commercial credit.

" I believe that much of the prosperity of the country for the last century is to be ascribed to the general wisdom, justice, and fairness of all its dealings; and I further think, that, during a great part of that time, it may have been in itself and by itself fully equal to all the important duties and operations confided to it : but the progress of the country during the last thirty or forty years in every branch of industry — in agriculture, manufactures, commerce, and navigation — has been so rapid and extensive as to make it no reflection upon the Bank of England to say that the instrument, which by itself was fully adequate to former transactions, is no longer sufficient, without new aids, to meet the demands of the present times.

" If the concerns of the country could be carried on without any other Bank than the Bank of England, there might be some reason for not interfering with their exclusive privileges ; but the effect of the law at present is to permit every description of banking except that which is solid and secure." [1]

The Bank, conscious of its impotence, contented itself with a feeble protest.   An Act was presently passed allowing the formation of banking companies to be composed of any number of partners or members.   It also authorized the Bank to establish branches in various parts of England.   Its object was to increase the value and stability of the country circulation.   It had been claimed, some time previous to its passage, that joint-stock Banks consisting of more than six persons might be organized under existing laws, although not possessing the power of issuing notes.   The right to form them was now declared to exist in all parts of England, with right to issue notes except within sixty-five miles of London.   If Banks, other than the Bank of England, were allowed this privilege, there was every reason, argued Lord Liverpool, why they should be so organized as to give the highest value to their

[1] Correspondence between the Government and the Bank of England, 1826.

issues. Although the continued issue of £1 and £2 notes
was revoked, Lord Liverpool by no means referred the panic
chiefly to their use. The Scotch Banks, he said, issued £1
and £2 notes; indeed, exchanges in that part of the country
were largely effected by the use of such; yet during the panic
of 1826 not a single Scotch Bank failed, nor were the business
operations of that country materially affected by the panic of
that year. Scotland almost wholly escaped the disasters that
befell England. The Scotch system was shown, in its results
at least, to be an admirable one. It seems incredible, considering the magnitude and importance of the subject, and in view
of the terrible losses on one, and the uniform prosperity on
the other side of an imaginary boundary between sections
composing a political, geographical, and commercial unit, only
with different monetary systems, that neither Parliament nor
its Committees, writers upon the subject of money, — nor, in
fact, the English people, — should have taken the least pains to
trace out the cause of the wonderful difference between the
two. An examination of the Scotch system, in a proper
spirit, would have readily solved all the laws on which a symbolic currency rests. It was certainly the duty of those who
assumed to unfold the principles of money, to give the reasons
of the widely different phenomena presented by the two systems. Instead of doing this, they shrugged their shoulders
when the Scotch system was referred to, with an — " Ah! Scotland is a very different country from England;" while one of
the most distinguished among the Economists, in reply to an
assertion of the excellence of the Scotch system, replied:
" Yes; but a lion's tail is a very different affair from his
maw."

The Bank, upon its recovery from the effects of the panic of
1826, held a pretty even course till 1832, when it was subjected to a heavy drain of specie, to check which no extraordinary means were resorted to. In that year, as was the wont
of the House of Commons upon similar occasions, a Committee were appointed to consider the subject of the extension
of the charter of the Bank, which was to expire in 1834. It
took an enormous amount of evidence; the number of questions put to the persons examined being nearly six thousand. The substance of its report is embraced in the following
paragraph: —

" The principal points to which the Committee directed their attention were : —

" 1st. Whether the paper circulation of the metropolis should be confined, as at present, to the issues of one Bank, and that a commercial company ; or, whether a competition of different Banks of issue, each consisting of an unlimited number of partners, should be permitted.

" 2dly. If it should be deemed expedient that the paper circulation of the metropolis should be confined, as at present, to the issues of one Bank, how far the whole of the exclusive privileges possessed by the Bank of England are neceessary to effect this object.

" 3dly. What checks can be provided to secure for the public a proper management of Banks of issue ; and, especially, whether it would be expedient and safe to compel them periodically to publish their accounts ?

" With respect to the circulation of paper in the country, the Committee have examined, first, into the effect produced by the establishment of branch Banks of the Bank of England ; and, secondly, into the expediency of encouraging the establishment of joint-stock Banks of issue in the country.

" On all these, and on some collateral points, more or less information will be found in the ' Minutes of Evidence ; ' but on no one of them is it so complete as to justify the Committee in giving a decided opinion." [1]

The Committee showed wisdom in their Report. An attempt to draw a conclusion from the evidence would be to draw order out of chaos ; or to establish propositions from statements which, taken in the mass, disproved every thing sought to be proved. The whole affair resembled a *mêlée* in which all the combatants are concealed from view by the clouds of dust they raise. The evidence given was a re-statement of the dogmas of Adam Smith, furbished up and amplified by the Economists of the later school. It is important only from its bearing upon future legislation, and particularly as leading the way to the Act of 1844. That of the more important witnesses is sufficiently shown in the following extracts, copied from the " Digest of the Evidence on the Bank Charter taken before the Committee of 1832."

Mr. Jones Loyd (now Lord Overstone) : —

" The establishment of joint-stock Banks in London, by increasing the demand for bullion, it is to be presumed would have

[1] Report of the Committee of the House of Commons upon the Bank of England Charter, 1832.

the effect of raising the market price of gold. A greater amount of gold would be required to manage the same amount of paper circulations, upon the system of multiplied issues, than at present; but any advantage produced by the existence of a greater quantity of gold would be at the sacrifice of the benefit intended to be produced by the paper currency, viz; the transference of capital from the unproductive state of bullion to a productive state. Joint-stock Banks are deficient in every requisite except extended responsibility. Acting through agents, and not by principals, they cannot decide upon special cases with so nice a reference to circumstances as the private banker; nor can they exercise that promptitude and hourly watchfulness, nor preserve that secrecy, which is so essential in banking operations." — Digest, pp. 62, 63.

Mr. Ward, one of the Directors of the Bank : —

" The immediate profit of the Bank requires the smallest possible amount of treasure, and the public interest likewise requires it; for otherwise the currency would be too much depressed. . . . The Bank, in 1822, violated its principles by keeping an excess of gold; but the altered law compelled it. It is the prerogative of the crown to decide what the gold currency shall be, and the Bank does its duty by making its paper issues represent the gold coin as nearly as possible."—Digest, pp 26–28.

Mr. Norman, one of the Directors of the Bank : —

" There can be no depreciation (from over-issue), unless every article rises in price. . . . Paper money is depreciated by excess, just as metallic coin is depreciated by a deduction from its weight. . . . Notes should not be issued without securities. If the customers of any Bank are satisfied with its solidity, the public at large has very little more to do with it. The objection is *in toto* to the establishment of joint-stock company Banks in London, or increased competition among the issuers of paper money. . . . Exchequer bills, mortgages, and even bonds, might be taken to a certain amount. . . . Landed security might be taken, and the responsibility should be limited or unlimited, as that of other mercantile concerns might. The Bank of England, for instance, has its capital lent to government, — the dead weight and Exchequer bills. All these might be made securities for its issues. The Legislature ought to guard, as far as possible, against the insolvency of Banks of issue : their deposits are voluntary transactions on the part of the public. Perhaps, compelling country bankers to give security might induce them to issue Bank of England notes instead of their own. Ninety-nine monopolies out of one hundred are mischievous; but the monopoly of the Bank of England is an exception. The supply of paper money is precisely the case in which monopoly is not a disadvantage. The government might determine to issue £20,000,000 of paper, payable in gold, or secured on bullion to the amount, and then the banking trade of

London might be thrown open; but, even then, in times of difficulty, some advantage is derived from one great establishment of undoubted solidity and untarnished credit. Issues of gold are unavoidable: the Bank has no control. Issues of government securities are not so absolutely necessary: but this concerns the Bank, not the public; for the note issued is money, and the Bank must provide for the demand on it. In 1825, the issues might have been made a hundred times over without producing excitement."—Digest, 39, 42, 43.

Mr. Tooke: —

"There exists no more reason for two or more Banks than for two or more mints. . . . If the cash of the Bank of England were completely drained, and the government issued paper on their own responsibility, the confidence of persons would be increased. All paper money should be issued by the government, on the same ground that coin is. . . . The issuing of paper notes by bankers is a source of profit, which coin is not. The State, therefore, is entitled to a very large portion of the profits arising from the circulation. . . . The establishment of joint-stock companies would be in opposition to the principle of having one Bank of issue for the whole country. . . . The amount of issues of the Bank of England does not influence prices, without a consideration of the circumstances at the time. . . . Neither paper nor credit is capital, but investments. All paper (such as the Bank of England's £20,000,000), that bears interest may be called investments in productive securities. The issue of paper money through discount (of bills) or accommodation is objectionable, for the demand in that way prevails most generally at the time when it is most essential to contract the circulation. Therefore, there is often an excess of issue through the medium of private credit, which would not occur if paper were substituted for gold. . . . An increase of paper is most commonly the consequence of a tendency, from other causes, to a rise of prices. In every original instance, the rise or fall of prices has preceded, and therefore could not be the effect of an enlargement and contraction of the Bank circulation. . . . There cannot be an excessive issue of convertible paper as relates to the Bank itself; but there may be as regards the public."—Digest, p. 78, 80, 81, 90.

Mr. Grote: —

"I would have the Bank of England compelled to pay over all the profits of their circulation to the public, saving so much as might be a fair remuneration for the trouble and risk of administering the details of it. This should be accounted for directly to government, and not be made a set-off in any bargain made as to the management of the national debt. In point of principle, the country bankers might also be called upon to give up their profits on the circulation; but, seeing that the number of parties everywhere out of the metropolis had acquired a certain established interest in the circulation, it would be throwing them out of their business to deal similarly with them. Had they all charters expiring, like the Bank, they might be ruled afresh. It is in consideration of the circulation of London being capable of yielding a profit, and of that circulation being at the disposal of Parliament, witness holds that terms may be exacted from the body to be endowed with its administration.

" More than one joint-stock Bank of issue in the metropolis would be mischievous. If you have only one such Bank, you get a circulation, considered as a whole, which would be impossible were it distributed among six or eight or ten Banks. No one among these competing Banks would be either able or willing to measure its separate issues in reference to the total amount of circulating medium required. Each might unseasonably maintain or extend its issues ; taking the chance of being able to supplant the notes of other Banks. In the provinces, evils of the same nature would arise. Many stock Banks in a district would present less security against over-issue than a single Bank. Under a single Bank, that contraction of the currency which is incident to a fall in prices would be earlier foreseen, and more gradually brought about, than by a number of competing Banks ; because their rivalry would induce each to delay the moment of beginning the contraction until its necessity became both urgent and notorious. Then the thing having been too long deferred, would be carried into effect with rigorous violence.

" Witness does not see that a metallic currency would give any protection against fluctuations in the price of commodities, in the rate of exchanges, and in the rates of commercial discounts. These would partly depend on the state of the harvest, and the circumstances of dividends being paid in at fixed periods. Fluctuations would occur in a currency referrible to any definite standard whatever ; and, doubtless, our present standard is less liable than any other to variations." —Digest, pp. 97–99.

Mr. Glyn : —

" The exclusive privileges of the Bank of England are decidedly advantageous to the London bankers, because the existence of more than one Bank of issue would expose the commercial world to fluctuations, and cause such bankers, in particular, great inconvenience in the details of their business. It would compel them to keep, probably, three or four times the amount of gold in hand now necessary. The establishment of competition among the Banks of issue would affect the circulating medium, exposing it to certain increase and reduction. The natural inclination of all banking companies seeking profit for their proprietors must be to extend their issues. The sense of danger attending over-issues would be a very doubtful check ; for, under competition, though a return of paper might be apprehended, every company would speculate on its coming back more upon its competitors than upon itself. The scramble for profits would prevent that due regulation of issues essential to a safe circulation. Joint-stock Banks have been established in the country; but are not, in general opinion, fitted for London and its trade. The competition of four or five joint-stock Banks in London would compel private houses to answer drafts in their own notes, if demanded. To keep cash by them to make payments in gold, whenever the paper of another company was demanded, would be exceedingly inconvenient." — Digest, p. 54.

Mr. Gurney : —

"A mixed circulation is the best state of currency. Such a circulating medium as we now have has the most wholesome effect in controlling these variations (in prices). It is not assumed, in the nature of a paper circulation, that with rising prices there would be enlarged issues, and with falling prices, a contraction; having a tendency in each case to increase the prevailing disposition, so as to lead to greater fluctuations than a metallic currency would ; for, in this country, paper money is mainly concerned, and that fluctuates wholly and solely with the state of prices and transactions in the district (where it is issued). The amount cannot be increased beyond what is called for. It cannot be governed by any act of the banker.

"No country banking establishment can issue more than there is a demand for. . . . What has been said of the impossibility of an over-issue by country bankers does not apply to the Bank of England. To a considerable degree, the Bank circulation is founded on government securities, which the witness thinks is the best foundation." — Digest, pp. 70–74.

Such are the most material portions of the evidence given before the Committee by men of the very highest repute in their respective callings ; men of great wealth, largely acquired by their own exertions, and wielding a wide social and political influence. Mr. Ward and Mr. Norman were Directors of the Bank, while no persons enjoyed a greater reputation in monetary circles than Mr. Glyn, Mr. Loyd, Mr. Gurney and Mr. Grote. Yet their statements and conclusions were as groundless as, and far less valuable than, the speculations of the Alchemists as to the proper combination of the baser metals necessary to produce gold. The Alchemists did make some discoveries of great value, and laid the foundation of a science which, working by exact methods, always advances the inquirer on his way. The evidence or speculations of the witnesses before the Committee, who were favorable to the Bank, did not disclose a single principle, did not lead to a single discovery, in reference to the laws of money. On the contrary, they overlaid the whole subject with such a mass of verbiage, of false assumptions, of vain and frivolous distinctions, that, like the Report of the Bullion Committee, their conclusions have been formidable obstacles to the progress of monetary science.

Mr. Loyd, now Lord Overstone, held joint-stock Banks to be "deficient in every requisite but extended responsibility." In this he was sustained by every witness an abstract of whose testimony has been given. Experience has shown the exact opposite to be the fact. All were opposed to "plurality of issue." A greater amount of gold, said Lord Overstone, would be required from a greater number of issuers. A far less amount is required relative to that of the currency issued, for the reason, that, the greater the number of issuers, the greater the degree of scrutiny in making loans. Parties seeking to make them must go to those to whom they are well known : to go elsewhere would be a sufficient cause for distrust. "Plurality of issue," therefore, is a necessary condition of a sound currency. Where there are a great number of issuers, as in London and New York, there will always be settlements, by which each will be compelled to make good his issues day by day. The weaker must daily come up to the standard set by the stronger, in order to insure confidence in their issues. There can be no "competition" of issue, in the sense in which this word is ordinarily used, for the reason that capital must stand behind every issue, and must always speedily discharge it. Competition of issue, if there can be such, is competition in the employment of capital. To this there can be no objection. Upon the same principle that Lord Overstone objected to "plurality of issue," would he object to plurality in drawers of bills. The right to issue notes as well as to draw bills is based upon the possession of something to issue, or draw against. If perfect freedom were allowed, then every one, according to him, would begin drawing, and the world would soon be flooded with bills, — some good, some worthless ; and great losses would be the result. He forgot that it takes two to give utterance to a bill, as well as to the notes of a Bank. When a person receives such notes as the equivalent of what he has to sell, he will take good care that that which he receives shall equal in value that with which he parts. Self-interest, therefore, is all the check needed upon plurality of issue. A person has only to be imposed upon once or twice, to refuse the issues of all parties that are not entitled to confidence. A few lessons of the kind will do no one any harm. The public are just as competent to take care of themselves in the matter of bank-notes as in bills of exchange, or in the purchase of property of any kind. It is in this very matter of issue of paper money that the greatest scope and freedom should be allowed, not only for the purpose of placing it upon the most stable foundations, but for the purpose of supplying, in the place of coin, adequate instruments of distribution. It is natural for an Englishman to repeat to himself, "One Government, one Bank." That would be all very well, were government possessed of all the capital of the country, — if it had the same right to the administration of such capital as it has in the enactment and administration of the laws. But having no capital other than that drawn from the public by taxation, for immediate expenditure, it has no more to do with the issue of paper money than it has with the quantity of food to be raised, or of yards of cloth to be woven. According to Mr. Ward, the public interest requires the Bank to hold the smallest possible amount of treasure; otherwise the currency would be too much depressed. Properly managed, the amount of circulation would be in five or tenfold greater ratio than the amount of treasure held by the Bank. Loans should never be made for the purpose of getting rid of the gold held by it, on the assumption that its accumulation in the Bank is the withdrawal of a corresponding amount from the channels of circulation. Its accumulation in it may simply mean its transfer from one country, place of deposit, or hoard, to another. The accident that brought it into the Bank may speedily carry it from it. In such case, if loaned, it must be collected from the public, — a process which may cause no small disturbance and loss. If the stock of gold in the Bank be permanently increased, say £5,000,000, its loans might be increased by £25,000,000 or £50,000,000, the gold serving as reserves, provided an adequate amount of good bills were offered. That they were not offered would be evidence of a want of merchandise to be symbolized. Mr. Norman would have no notes issued that did not rest upon securities other than commercial bills, — upon Exchequer bills, government stock, bonds, lands, &c. He objected *in toto* to the existence of joint-stock Banks in London, or to increased competition among issuers of paper money. But every person possessed of merchandise is just as competent to issue paper money as the Bank of England ; and far more so, as the Bank is now conducted, as his issues would be based upon that which would return them to him without any act on his part ; while the Bank might have to take in no small part of its own, by paying out a corresponding amount of its reserves, which it hardly ever does without loss to itself as well as the public. According to Mr. Tooke, there exists no more reason for two Banks than for two mints. All paper money should be issued, as coin is, by government — by the exclusive privilege of the State. But the only function of government in coinage is assaying and affixing upon the piece assayed the quantity of pure metal it contains. How can it assay paper? Its insignia does not give value in one case ; how can it in the other? It creates no obligation when it coins gold ; and, if it does not when it issues paper, the only effect of its insignia upon it is to render worthless what otherwise might have had value. The value of gold is measured by its cost ; that of paper, by that which it represents. If government possess capital, — merchandise, — it may issue symbols against it, to serve in its distribution. So far it may secure to itself the profit resulting from its use, — that is, interest on a sum equal to its amount. It may, if it will, turn banker, and issue notes, holding a proper amount of reserves. If it would be successful in such rôle, it must issue no paper that does not represent merchandise. But even such a wild and visionary theorist as Tooke would hardly venture to impose upon government such a function. If not, then he must leave the issue of paper money to those who have capital to lend. " An increase of paper money," says Tooke, " is the consequence of a tendency from other causes to a rise in prices." Tooke, as will be hereafter seen, was the great apostle of the doctrine, that an excess of paper money follows, instead of preceding, a rise in prices. Mr. Grote, like Mr. Tooke, " would have the Bank pay over to the public the profits of its circulation ; retaining such portion of them as would be a fair remuneration for the trouble of administering it. A metallic currency would give no protection against fluctuation of commodities." How could any considerable fluctuation occur with a currency exclusively metallic, and so long as equivalents are exchanged?

Fluctuations occur when merchandise is purchased on credit in some form, and when the credit is not the equivalent of that purchased by it.   In such case, credits, as well as capital, are competitors in the market, and prices rise in ratio to their quantity, or to the demand.   When the credits mature, and payment is not made, then the prices of merchandise which has been purchased and held on speculation fall, from being thrown upon the market.   So long as paper money is the representative of merchandise in demand for consumption, the effect of its issue upon the whole market is to reduce, instead of to increase, prices, by discharging a corresponding amount — or a certain amount — of capital from use as money. "Fluctuations would occur," says Mr. Grote, "in a currency referrible to any definite standard whatever; and, doubtless, our standard is less liable than any other to variations."   This single paragraph epitomizes whatever of speculation and theory there is in England upon the subject of money: "Fluctuations are inevitable in all systems; but ours is the best." Mr. Glyn opposed plurality of issues on the ground that the natural inclination of all Banks is to seek profit for their proprietors by extending their issues; forgetting that the only check to such inclination is to place all issues in a position in which they cannot indulge in any thing of the kind without being immediately called to account.   Mr. Gurney held that "no country banking establishments can issue more notes than there is a demand for."   There will always be a demand for whatever issues are made, so long as they will be the equivalent of capital to the holders.   There is no more limit to the demand for paper money, so long as it will exchange for any thing, than there is for capital.   Mr. Gurney, like the other witnesses favorable to the Bank, held that paper money should be based upon governments in preference to bills; that is, that the principles upon which the operations of the Bank were conducted were wise and proper.

Those who were examined as representatives of joint-stock Banks — Mr. Stuckey, Mr. Wilkins, Mr. Dyer, Mr. J. B. Smith, and Mr. Burt — ventured mildly to suggest, that Free-Trade might prove as advantageous in banking as in commercial and manufacturing industries; and that in ratio as such freedom was secured at the expense of the exclusive privileges of the Bank of England would the value and stability of the country circulation of all kinds be increased. Such representations — coming from feeble and struggling institutions, as they were at the time — had no more influence over the public mind than would propositions at the present day for the abolition of the House of Lords and the distribution of the royal revenues — even the crown itself — among the people. Englishmen bow reverently before quantity and force. These, under their system, — which allows great freedom to individual action, and secures to it its proper reward, — are the certain product of time. The joint-stock Banks, which existed in the outset by sufferance as it were, biding their time, have now grown into such colossal proportions as to challenge the reverence which the Bank of England once wholly engrossed; and their managers, who for a long time stood, hat in hand, in presence of its Directors, now do not scruple to hustle them off the walk whenever the crowd is too dense for ease of movement. The very privileges and monopoly of the Bank have now come to involve great burdens and great responsibilities. As "manager of the currency," it has to supply reserves for that of the whole kingdom; amounting, including deposits as well as notes, to some £550,000,000. The least disturbance in the money market, or in commerce and trade, or the slightest foreign complication, are warnings to the Bank. How to strengthen its position and increase its reserves has for years been the paramount question in the monetary and commercial circles of England. At present its only means of defence is in its power of exacting exorbitant rates on its loans. This is a very feeble one against an excited crowd ready to sacrifice whatever they possess for the maintenance of their credit. In olden times, the Directors of the Bank might set its operations upon a given key, and go to sleep for a half century. The rates now charged appear and disappear with the celerity of the figures in Punch and Judy. The wider the discussion of the problem, the more difficult appears its solution. Fortunately, in such a country as England, where every valuable achievement or step that is gained serves as vantage-ground for something beyond, all such questions solve themselves. From the foundation of the Bank in 1694 to 1797, there was very little fluctuation in commercial or monetary affairs, for the reason that it was an instrument of commerce, not of the government. Its

loans were made upon such securities only as were fitted
to return to it, in their payment, its own liabilities. It was
for more than one hundred years restricted by its charter from
dealing in any thing but " bills of exchange and gold and silver
bullion." The result was uniformity in the volume of the currency, and in the operations of production and trade.[1] From
1797 to the present time, it has been little more than an arm of
the government. The result has been constant and excessive
fluctuations in such operations. Although nominally the manager of the currency, it has never attempted to manage any
but its own. Such as it has issued, being at all times largely
based upon governments, has necessarily been a great disturbing element in financial affairs. This evil, so deeply grounded,
could only be reformed by a currency properly issued, and
sufficient in amount for the exchanges of the country. Such
a currency has now been created through the action of parties
and institutions other than the Bank, and in such volume that
the disturbing influence of the latter is no longer paramount.
It is taken up and absorbed into the greater magnitude of
that with which it moves. In this way, by a new growth, the
English system of finance is passing from a condition of
excessive fluctuation, due to its inherent defects, to one of comparative uniformity both as to quantity and value. The joint-

---

[1] Although, for a long time previous to the repeal, in 1793, of the provision
in the charter of the Bank forbidding it to make loans to government, the
obligations of the latter were largely made use of by its customers as the basis of
loans, or as collateral to them, borrowers, undoubtedly, frequently preferred
to make loans upon " public securities " rather than upon bills; holding the
latter to meet their loans on " securities," when they fell due. Loans made at
Bank by private parties are not for the purpose of supplying to them the
means of consumption, but for use in their various industries or callings.
None but the thrifty classes could get access to it: there is, therefore, no reason
to suppose that the greater part of the loans made by the Banks previous to
1793 were not properly made, although only a portion, and sometimes the
smaller portion, of them seemed to be made upon bills. This assumption is fully
supported by the experience of the Bank through more than a century, during
which the fluctuations in its issues, as well as in production and trade, were very
slight. A government is a very different kind of borrower from an individual;
as its loans are made, not for the purpose of supplying symbols for the distribution of merchandise, but for its profitless consumption. Loans to individuals tend to keep the volume of currency uniform, as they serve as the basis of
reproducing merchandise (which will also, in its turn, be symbolized), equal to,
and, perhaps, greater in amount than, that which has been consumed. Loans to
the government tend to disturb such uniformity; for the reason, that that which
is borrowed is not repeated in kind, but is unproductively expended.

stock Banks and private Banks and bankers are now the issuers and managers of the currency, while the Bank contents itself with the more humble, but still honorable, office of the safe-keeping of the reserves of those, by whom, as issuers of the currency, it is now in great measure supplanted.

While the evidence given before the Committee, already quoted, sufficiently illustrates the ideas prevailing at the time upon the subject of money, and upon the questions considered by it, the following summary of the evidence given before it by Mr. J. Horsley Palmer, then Governor of the Bank, and Mr. Ward and Mr. Norman, Directors, will illustrate the system of management which prevailed from the panic of 1826 to 1837, — and, in fact, to 1844, when the great change in its organization took place : —

" The principal functions which it is the ordinary duty of the Bank to perform, consist in its furnishing the public with paper money, convertible on demand into coin and bullion, and in affording a place of safe deposit for the money of the government, as well as for that of individuals who may prefer it to a private Bank.

" It is not deemed desirable that, in ordinary times, the Bank of England should systematically regulate the amount of its issues, through commercial discounts in London. There are, usually, in the possession of the bankers of London, and other individuals, large deposits waiting for employment, with which it would not become the Bank to interfere. But upon occasions when there is a scarcity of money, or when a season of commercial alarm occurs, it is then the duty of the Bank to step forward to the aid of public and private credit, by discounting commercial bills. The Bank, for this purpose, occasionally fix, by official notice, a public rate of interest, at which they are willing to receive approved bills of a given description. Being the only body issuing money *ad libitum*, within the sphere of the circulation of such bills, the Bank define the maximum rate of interest, by such notice, during its continuance. The consequence is, that all persons having money to employ must necessarily offer to lend it under that rate, unless, by the pressure of the moment, the market rate of interest advance to that fixed by the Bank.

" But in ordinary times, when there is no such scarcity of money, or when no commercial discredit exists, if the Bank were to found their issue principally upon commercial bills, they would be under the necessity of entering into competition with all other parties in the purchase of bills of exchange, at the market rate of interest. Such competition would be justly deemed objectionable. All banking business is better done by private bankers than by public bodies. More facilities are afforded in the way of credit by the

former, than can be offered under the existing regulations by the
Bank Directors, who give no credit to any one, and exact an adherence to forms which are not required by private bankers.

" No inflexible rule, indeed, exists that the Bank shall not, even
in ordinary times, afford accommodation to the commercial classes.
But the Bank do not, in general, found their issue upon commercial discounts. According to their present principles of management, they extend their assistance in that way only when any
serious exigency arises. Being required to provide a requisite supply
of money for the average circulation of the sphere in which they
act, it is also their duty to uphold public and private credit when
called upon ; and, when so appealed to, it is then that the resources
of a great body like the Bank of England may be rendered available to the commercial stability of the country.

" In the latter part of the year 1825, when the great panic
occurred, the discounts of the Bank rose to about fifteen millions.
The interest was raised from four to five per cent, with a view to
limit the issue ; but it did not produce the desired effect. On other
occasions, it might be more successful ; and it seems much better,
when possible, to diminish the issue upon bills, by raising the rate
of interest, than by caprice, by rejecting a portion of the paper that
is offered. . . .

" Since the resumption of cash payments, which can hardly be
said to have been completely under the control of the Bank until
after the events of 1825, and the entire suppression of the £1 and
£2 notes in the country, the rule of that establishment has been to
preserve in its coffers an amount of bullion equal to one-third of the
whole of its liabilities. Thus, if we assume the circulation to be
£21,000,000, and the deposits to be £6,000,000, the Bank would
then, according to its principles of management, retain £9,000,000
in bullion in a period of full currency. The currency is said to be
full when the exchanges are at par, or, rather, when they are on
the point of becoming unfavorable, prior to the commencement of a
demand for bullion. In that state of things, the circulation of the
Bank is supposed to be neither more nor less than is necessary for
the transactions of the country. The moment the exchanges become unfavorable, the fact is discovered by a demand for gold at
the Bank ; and, as notes must then be given by the parties who
wish to procure it, the consequence is, that the circulation becomes
pro tanto diminished, and the gold obtained in lieu of the notes
goes abroad. When the demand ceases, and the exchanges take a
favorable turn, then the Bank is in a progressive state towards re-
assuming its proportion of bullion. In May, 1832, the resignation
of Lord Grey's ministry having produced great agitation throughout the country, there was a drain for gold upon the Bank, arising
entirely out of political distrust. Before that drain began, the
bullion in the Bank amounted to about £6,500,000. The total absorption of gold which took place at that period, including the sums paid
on account of dividends, was near £2,000,000. Nevertheless, after
the drain had ceased, the bullion in the Bank had accumulated to
£5,500,000, in consequence of there having been a natural influx

of gold during that interval; and that, too, at a very high rate of exchange.

"But when the drain upon the Bank for gold arises from the unfavorable state of the foreign exchanges, and bullion is wanted for exportation, then the Bank would wait, under ordinary circumstances, until the exchanges should take a turn the other way, before it would replenish its coffers. If, however, an extraordinary demand arose, and continued to go on increasing, the Directors, in order to provide for the safety of the Bank, would have recourse to operations for the contraction of the circulation. Thus, for instance, if they foresaw a bad harvest, or any other circumstance likely to turn the exchanges against the country, they would, even if the exchanges were at the moment favorable, anticipate their becoming unfavorable, and make their preparations accordingly. They would, in such a case, proceed to shorten the amount of the currency in this way. The Bank is possessed of a certain number of securities, always coming into it. A considerable amount of these arises from the annuities, the dead weight, and other assets of that description. These moneys they would not reissue. If they had silver at their disposal, they would, perhaps, as a further measure, send it to Paris, and draw against it; and, finally, if the extraordinary necessity of the case required it, they would sell all their Exchequer bills, and reduce the amount of their other securities. They would not thus forcibly contract their issues in anticipation of uncertain events, or of events not likely to be of any magnitude. Their object in taking such precautions would be to prevent sudden jerks in the currency, and to provide against the extraordinary demand they saw coming, before it was actually at their door. If they did not thus anticipate the period of the exchanges becoming unfavorable, they would have to buy gold at a very high price, and to furnish those who demanded it in exchange for notes at a low price; the Bank losing the difference upon the transaction. . . .

"But, when matters assume this momentous character, the conduct of the Bank becomes a question of State policy: and it is but justice to that institution to remember, that when it was within a few hours of losing all its gold, in consequence of the panic of 1825, instead of separating itself from the interests of the country, it was deliberately identified with them; and the resolution was taken, that the interests of the Bank and the nation should fall or stand together. It should never be forgotten, that all the principles of management upon which the Bank ordinarily acts were flung to the winds upon that occasion; and that their discounts and advances upon all kinds of securities were swelled to upwards of fifteen millions, at an hour when their bullion was reduced below one.

"If, therefore, an emergency should arise, in which, referring to their general rules, the Directors might deem it prudent to contract their circulation, they would probably recollect that no state of commercial alarm has ever yet affected the character of the Bank; but that, on the contrary, the credit of that establishment has risen above the common credit of other bodies of individuals, at such periods, higher than at any other time. There is little doubt that, under such circumstances, the Governor would communicate with his Majesty's ministers, and consult with them as to what would be the most expedient course for the Bank to adopt, with a view to the general welfare of the kingdom. There is no resolution recorded on the point, whether the Directors shall wait until the demand for gold actually arises, before they contract the currency, or whether they shall anticipate the period of such demand. But there is not one person in the Directors who does not consider it a sacred duty to do always the very best that can be done, in order to preserve the principle of the currency.

" During the last two years, the Directors of the Bank have spontaneously taken no measures for the purpose of contracting the circulation. Whatever diminution has occurred, has been effected almost entirely by the return of notes for gold. Their policy is to keep in view the foreign exchanges and the state of the bullion market ; and to be prepared for the increase of their issue when favorable, as well as for a diminution of it when they are unfavorable, seeing that such increase and diminution would take place if there were no notes in existence. With the exception of the special circumstances above alluded to, the principle of the Bank is, when the currency is full, and the exchanges consequently at par, to invest and retain in securities bearing interest the proportion already mentioned of the deposits, and the value already received from the notes in circulation, the remainder to be held in coin and bullion ; the circulation of the whole currency of the country, so far as the same may depend upon the Bank, being subsequently regulated by the action of the foreign exchanges. Whatever power the Bank may have in reference to the currency, they are very desirous not to exercise it, but to leave individuals to use the right which they possess of returning bank-notes for bullion. The exchanges are in due season corrected, when left wholly in the hands of the community. If the Bank be adequately supplied with bullion, as they usually are, when the exchanges are full they experience no inconvenience by waiting to have the exchanges corrected by the operations of the public." [1]

Such is a picture of the management of the Bank from the time that it fairly surmounted the effects of the Act of Restriction to 1844, and in reality from that to the present time.[2] The Bank, in possession of great sums from depositors, used them in the purchase of securities, wholly regardless of the consequences. Loans of deposits made in the purchase of governments do not necessarily cause an inflation. None, certainly, would be caused, if depositors, instead of putting their money into the Bank, had invested it in the

---

[1] Quinn's Trade of Banking in England, pp. 4–6, 85–96.

[2] The following statement will show the character of the loans of the Bank,

same manner as the Bank.   The same amount would be in circulation after as before.   It would only have changed hands.   Sales and purchases made by individuals produce little disturbance, for the reason that they do not usually act in mass, — in one direction.   It is not when the Bank purchases governments, but when it seeks to sell them, that the mischievous character of the transaction shows itself.   When it wishes to sell, it cannot.   To go into the market with its securities in seasons of great pressure, or in a panic, would only serve to increase the run upon it.   Should it attempt this, it would only be an additional competitor for money which it would have to pay out again as soon as received.   It might be utterly powerless, from inability to convert its means.   In such a crisis, the public do not want securities, but money, — that which will instantly discharge their liabilities.   If, on the other hand, its loans were made wholly in the discount of bills, no panic, or run upon it, could arise, that could not be speedily checked by a refusal to make further discounts.   There can be no considerable inflation, so long as the currency is symbolic, for the reason that the public, in such case, deal in actual values, — in equivalents, whose real, or representative, equals their nominal value.   A panic arises only when it is seen or feared that, in the exchanges that have taken or are taking place, equivalents are not exchanged, — that the currency does not entitle its holder to a corresponding amount of capital.   If such fear or suspicion become a conviction, there

___

and of its assets, other than its share capital, as they were on the 29th of February, 1832.

Exchequer bills	£6,884,940
Advances on account of the purchase of the annuity of £585,740 for 44 years	10,897,880
Stock purchased	764,600
City bonds	500,000
Loans on mortgages	1,452,100
London Dock Company	227,500
Advanced on security and various articles	570,690
Bills discounted	2,951,970
Coin and bullion	5,293,150
Total	£29,492,880

Of its advances on various accounts, only one tenth was in commercial bills. Its liabilities of the same date were: notes, £18,051,710 ; deposits, £8,937,160 : total of £26,988,870.   Its rest, or accumulated earnings, equalled £2,687,760.

is a contest of speed to see who shall secure to himself whatever reserves the issuer of the currency may hold. If this be issued in large amount, the panic may become excessive and general, involving issuers whose currency was purely symbolic, as well as those whose currency was wholly fictitious. As a rule, no issuer of currency, no matter how legitimate, will be able to liquidate all his liabilities upon the instant. As the parties to whom the issues upon bills have been made are the very ones who undertake to return them, they will, so long as they are solvent, seldom or never seek to draw coin for what they may hold, when they must speedily return it to the Bank in payment of their bills. The danger arises when there are no reciprocal obligations between the issuer and holder of currency. If the Bank were to make an issue in the purchase of government stock, for example, against a large amount of gold which it might happen to hold, it might have to provide all the means for taking it in; and it would be almost certain to have, not the support, but the opposition, of the public, who would not only refuse to purchase its securities, by the sale of which it must replenish its means, but present all the notes they held for payment in coin. What adds to the peril is, that the Bank must, as a " manager of the currency," issue to all parties who come within its rules in the matter of security, — rules that were established, very likely, when the demand for money was far below the supply. The public, in such case, not the Bank, are the judges of the amount of money required. Its only means of defence is in its power to raise the rate of interest to a point that shall render it unprofitable for them to borrow, — a most impotent defence, as the catastrophies of 1847, 1857, and 1866, abundantly prove.

The state of the exchanges is a wholly inadequate test whereby to regulate the issues of the Bank, for the reason that the causes which are to render them unfavorable may be in most active operation at the very time they are in the highest degree favorable — when every thing wears the appearance of the greatest prosperity. The currency may be, and often is, excessive in amount — more than full — long before the exchanges become unfavorable. Such, indeed, is usually the case. To take them as a rule for the regulation of the currency has the same and no higher wisdom than to lock the door after the horse is stolen. Gold is not exported, as Smith and the Economists assume, the moment an excess of paper is issued; but only when the paper has been expended in the purchase of that which can be paid for only in gold. The final payment in gold, with the facilities which now exist for renewing and extending banker's credits, may be put off for years; so that the state of exchanges may not, for years, sufficiently indicate the financial condition of a country. A rule or test, to be worth any thing, must be that which shall prevent the possibility of an adverse exchange, which shall put it out of the power of a people to consume more than they possess or produce. This can only be done by restricting the currency to the amount of merchandise fitted for consumption; the instruments, to the means of expenditure. This done, exchanges could never be long unfavorable, and never excessively so. In the ratio that such rule is not followed, — in the ratio that the currency is not symbolic, — will the exchanges be unfavorable; the degree of aberration in one case measuring very accurately that in the other.

The agreeable picture drawn by Mr. Palmer and his associates of their happy lot as managers of the Bank, having nothing to do but to allow the oscillations in the amount of its circulation and coin to regulate themselves with a certainty and uniformity far transcending human skill, was soon to give place to a very different one. The oscillation which carried gold into the Bank in 1832 and 1833 began, in 1834, to carry it in an opposite direction. The amount held by it on the 31st of August, 1833, was £10,870,000. This was reduced, on the 31st of August, 1834, to £7,303,000; on the 31st of August, 1835, to £6,255,000; and on the 21st of February, 1837, to £4,077,000, — the last-named sum equalling only one-seventh of its liabilities, instead of one-third, according to the rule claimed to have been laid down for the management of the Bank. The reduction in the amount of specie in the three and a half years equalled £6,793,000. In the same period its note circulation was reduced from £19,925,000 to £18,165,000; its deposits from £11,927,000 to £10,040,000: the total reduction being only £3,647,000, — a sum equalling only about half of the reduction in the amount of its coin. The balance of the coin lost, that is, £3,146,000, must have been paid out in new loans; these being increased from £23,245,000, in 1833, to £27,297,000, in 1837. The action of the Bank, therefore, in increasing its loans while its specie was being withdrawn, was enough to defeat the operation of the rule laid down for its guidance, assuming its competency when no increase of loans was made. As there was no evidence that a return flow of specie was likely to set in, and as great alarm and disturbance in monetary circles were the natural consequences, Mr. Palmer felt called upon to explain the reason why the rule was no longer observed, or refused to work. This he attempted to do in an elaborate essay published in the early part of 1837.

"The system" (prescribed for the conduct of the Bank), he said, "appeared to work satisfactorily, and without any forced action on part of the Bank in contracting its circulation. It was tried upon the change of government in France in July, 1830, when credit throughout that kingdom was shaken to its foundation. At that period, the Bank of England was possessed of about twelve millions of bullion. Immediately upon the events referred to taking place, the currency of England exhibited an excess compared with that of France and other parts of Europe. The consequence of that derangement between the currencies of this and other countries was a continued diminution of the bullion held by the Bank from July, 1830, to February or March, 1832, when the increased value of money in England, and the gradual restoration of credit upon the Continent, gave a favorable turn to the foreign exchanges; which continued in our favor till the autumn of 1833, at which time the bullion in deposit at the Bank amounted to nearly eleven millions. At this period, an exportation of the precious metals again commenced, from causes that will hereafter be explained, as well as the reason why that system, which appeared to adjust itself so satisfactorily from 1830 to 1832, failed from 1833 to 1836: for, although during the former period the bullion of the Bank was diminished from twelve to five millions, yet in the progress of this reduction, as there was no excitement, and no undue credit given by the Banks in the interior of the country, the interest of money gradually rose from $2\frac{1}{2}$ to 4 per cent per annum for first-rate commercial paper; and then, without discredit or distrust of any kind, the bullion returned into the coffers of the Bank, and money nearly resumed its former value, the rate of interest having gradually fallen from 4 to $2\frac{3}{4}$ per cent in July, 1833. . . .

"But, before preceding farther, it is necessary to allude to the rise and progress of joint-stock Banks in England, Wales, and Ireland. Scotland having, fortunately for that part of the empire, kept itself free from the mania for the extension of these companies, it is unnecessary particularly to allude to the proceedings of its Banks.

"Immediately subsequent to the panic of 1825, which affected almost every banking establishment in London as well as the country, the government of that day was unfortunately induced to call upon the Bank of England to relinquish, beyond sixty-five miles from London, its exclusive privileges as to the number of partners authorized by law to be associated for the formation of Banks, in order to enable ministers to frame regulations authorizing the establishment of joint-stock Banks throughout all parts of the country beyond the limit above specified; thereby virtually declaring that the existing private Banks were unworthy of credit. The term ' unfortunately ' is used ; for, perhaps, there never was a measure more uncalled for by the wants of the community. The existing system was intimately connected with the prosperity of the country, and was good in all parts, except the power of issuing paper money *ad libitum*. The change in question laid the foundation of a new system, to be brought into the field by competition in the issue of paper money, — the most prejudicial means that could be devised. A reluctant concession was obtained from the Bank; and, in order to place the whole subject before the public, the correspondence which then took place between the government and Banks is annexed to the present statement. Very little progress was made in the formation of those projected institutions prior to the year 1830, when a further application was made by government to the Bank for concessions intended to have formed part of the conditions at that time for the renewal of the charter. The opinion of the Bank remained unchanged as to the danger to be apprehended from the extension of the system of joint-stock Banks, and this opinion was pressed upon the government at that period. . . .

— " Having thus briefly stated the proceedings which have occurred in the establishment of joint-stock Banks prior· to the renewal of the charter of the Bank of England, it may, perhaps, be proper to state the periods of increase of those of issue from the year 1826. They are as follows, taken from returns furnished by the Stamp Office : —

IN ENGLAND AND WALES.

1826 were established	. . . .	3
1827 ,, ,,	. . . .	4
1828 ,, ,,	. . . .	nil
1829 ,, ,,	. . . .	7
1830 ,, ,,	. . . .	1
1831 ,, ,,	. . . .	8
1832 ,, ,,	. . . .	7
1833 ,, ,,	. . . .	10
1834 ,, ,,	. . . .	11
1835 ,, ,,	. . . .	9
1836, from 1st January to 26th November	. . . .	42
Total	. . . .	102

IN IRELAND.

There were formed prior to 1834	. . . .	3
In 1835	. . . .	2
In 1836	. . . .	8
Total	. . . .	13

" Until the year 1833, the action of the Banks, as already stated, appears to have been perfectly regular. From that point, the increase in the number of joint-stock Banks in England and Wales, to the 26th November last has been seventy-two, and in Ireland ten ; making an aggregate of eighty-two, exclusive of their innumerable branches, formed in almost every town in the two kingdoms, which are, in fact, equivalent to so many additional Banks.

" It next remains to be shown what was the amount of paper money in circulation in England and Wales and Ireland, other than that issued by the Banks of England and Ireland. The average in England and Wales, on the 29th of March, 1834, was £10,200,000; and in June, 1836, £12,200,000. In Ireland, the average in June, 1834, was £1,300,000 ; and in June, 1836, £2,300,000. It thus appears that there was a total increase in this portion of the paper money of the two kingdoms, in 1836 over 1834, of no less than £3,000,000, or more than 25 per cent.

" Having thus stated the action of the different bodies through which the extension and contraction of the paper money of England and Ireland have been effected from the year 1833 to the present time, it may be now expedient to show the causes which appear to have occasioned the reduction of the circulation of the Bank of England. It is the more important to submit these causes to the notice of the public, as they seem in no degree to have arisen from over-trading, or from any undue speculative advance in commercial prices. Occurrences of that nature tend to produce an unfavorable foreign exchange ; an evil only to be remedied by that contraction of the circulation which eventually restores prices and currency to a level with those existing in foreign countries. If, therefore, upon reference being made to the state of the foreign exchanges during the period to which the inquiry relates, it be found that no material derangement existed, our attention is naturally directed to the consideration of the other causes that have occasioned the demand upon our metallic currency. In order to establish the position that the commercial exchanges were not against England, it may be right to refer to the increase or decrease of gold at the Bank, from which alone any correct inferences are to be drawn as to the state of our currency in comparison with that of foreign countries.

" The first period may be taken from October, 1833, to April, 1835, during almost the whole of which time there was a continued purchase of gold by the Bank at £3 17s. 9d. per ounce. The exchange on Paris never fell below 25.35 for short paper, and the premium upon gold remained in Paris at about 9 per mille : thus showing that, during that period, there was no demand upon the Bank for bar gold, and no profit upon the export of that metal or the gold coin of the realm.

" The second period was from April, 1835, to April, 1836 ; during the whole of which time the foreign exchanges were considerably higher than during the preceding eighteen months, and, consequently, the influx of gold correspondingly increased at the Bank.

" The third and last period is that from April to December of the past year, during the whole of which time the foreign exchange on Paris was seldom under 25.35. The premium upon gold, however, was for a short time as high as 13 or 14 per mille, which occasioned a loss of about £100,000 of the Bank's stock of gold bullion, — an amount too trifling to establish the fact of an unfavorable commercial rate of exchange.

" With this statement of the actual bearing of the foreign exchanges upon the gold currency of the country, it may, perhaps, excite some surprise as to the mode in which the large reduction in the bullion held by the Bank was effected, and which, in its consequences, from that body having been governed by the principle laid down in the evidence of 1832, ought to have had the same effect upon the general currency of the empire, as if the reduction had been occasioned by any cause other than that from which it is believed to have arisen. . . .

" According to the principles laid down in the evidence referred to, the rate of interest ought to have been advanced by the Bank, in order to throw back that excess upon the market. It is admitted, however, that we have not been placed in ordinary circumstances since the discredit which occurred in Ireland. In consequence of that event, there was, in the first instance, an undue return of Bank of England notes for coin ; and secondly, it is believed, that, in this country, from apprehension of consequences, a much larger amount of bank-notes has been, and still is, retained in reserve by bankers generally, than they are ordinarily in the habit of holding. At any rate, it is evident that the additional issue by the Bank has not caused any foreign demand for gold ; and, unless that be exhibited, the Bank ought not, under circumstances of an unnatural pressure, strictly to enforce the principle laid down. . . .

" We must keep in mind that England is the centre of the whole commerce of Europe and America, if not the world ; and any hasty or unnecessary step taken will not only affect the credit and prices of this country, but, to a certain degree, those of all parts of the Continent, from whence we are to obtain that bullion which we have lost. . . .

" Allusion has already been made to the effect upon the currency from a deranged state of commercial prices between this and foreign countries. It must be evident to every one reflecting upon the subject, that similar effects may be produced by employing capital in speculative loans to foreign powers, or investing it abroad at a higher rate of interest than the securities of this country may afford. This, it is obvious, may occasion large and sudden foreign payments, without any reference to the exchanges. And it is to payments of that character that we may attribute the loss of bullion which took place from October, 1833, to April, 1835 ; and to which the public attention should be directed, that remedies may be devised for mitigating the evil which must otherwise attend similar transactions hereafter. . . .

" Adverting to the excess of the country issues, and looking to the race running with increased violence in Ireland as well as in England, the Bank was fully justified in attempting to arrest the evil which might attend a continuance of the export of bullion from the redundancy of money, by making an advance in the rate of interest in London and at the branch Banks. In fact, the only question about which there can be any real difficulty is, whether she ought not to have taken this step somewhat earlier. To have acted, however, in anticipation of events likely to occur, would have been in direct violation of that principle upon which the Bank professed to be guided, and which Parliament had tacitly sanctioned. It would, moreover, have established a precedent, and imposed future responsibilities upon the directors, which it is questionable whether they should ever incur, either upon their own account or that of the public. The Bank acted precisely as any board of commissioners empowered solely to issue notes for bullion would have done, and can in no way be chargeable with the consequences. . . .

"The demand for bullion continuing, the Bank further advanced the rate of interest in August to £5 per cent per annum, which forced additional securities upon many of those country Banks that adhered to a lower rate. Their surplus funds in London being soon absorbed, they all eventually adopted the rate of interest established in London. There was, however, an effect created by this act on the part of the Bank far more powerful than the actual advance in the value of money. It was a moral apprehension, in all prudent minds, that there was mischief abroad; and those who had been promoting and applauding the action of the joint-stock Banks began to doubt the solidity of the system. The feeling so created was probably further extended by the publication of the evidence already alluded to. The consequence of this altered state of confidence was first shown in Ireland, where the competition had assumed a more violent character than in England. A run upon all the joint-stock Banks in that part of the empire ensued, which terminated in the stoppage of the Agricultural. The direct effect of that discredit upon the Irish Banks was an immediate drain upon the Bank of England and its branches of nearly one million of sovereigns, obtained by the return of notes to that amount. None of these Banks having been previously provided with coin, or the direct means of obtaining it, the only mode of getting possession of it was by forced sales of securities in London. A moment's reflection will show the derangement in the London circulation, necessarily consequent on such proceedings, as well as the difficulty under which the Bank is placed by the total amount of coin or bank-notes on the part of issuing Banks to uphold the credit of their circulation. It may be assumed as a fact, that profit is their only object, and that not a single issuing Bank in England, Ireland, or even Scotland, has ever been provided with bank-notes or coin adequate to meet a demand upon their respective liabilities. Their assets, beyond the ordinary wants of their customers are all vested in securities bearing interest; trusting to the realization of those securities in bank-notes in case of need, which, thus abstracted from the public market, either inflicts a most inconvenient pressure upon London, or, in order to prevent

that pressure, the Bank is required to reissue the amount of notes
so cancelled, without reference to the amount of bullion in its possession. . . .

" Under the system which now exists, embracing a total amount
of bank-paper circulation in Great Britain and Ireland of about
forty-five millions, the half of which may be assumed to be unpro-
tected by an adequate reserve of either Bank of England notes or
coin, it certainly is impossible to insure the convertibility of paper
even for foreign payments. Nothing can guard against the effects
of mismanagement, and consequent excess, by such a numerous mass
of issuing bodies as overspread the empire. If, however, the
amount of paper money be limited, and it be issued by one body,
with an adequate reserve of bullion, expanding and contracting as
the currency may fluctuate in value with reference to foreign countries, there could be no difficulty in preserving it against depreciation
for all purposes of foreign payment. If paper money ever become
discredited by any internal political convulsion, it can then only be
upheld by the power of government; and in such times it becomes
the duty of the ministers of the Crown to undertake the responsibility of upholding public credit. For relief against commercial
discredit, the issuing body should be so formed as to be able to
afford protection.

" With reference to the past action of the Bank, there is no reason
to doubt that the value of the currency would have been maintained
without occasioning any severe pressure upon the money market,
had the countervailing issues by other parties not occurred : still,
if there exist any well-founded reasons for supposing that the principle explained in the evidence of 1832, and acted upon by the
Bank, is not sound, or that the proportion of one-third of bullion
with reference to the liabilities of the Bank at the period of a full
currency be not sufficient, — it merely remains for Parliament to
express an opinion upon either of these points, and there can be
no question but that the Bank will immediately regulate its course
accordingly. The principle referred to was never intended to apply
under any extraordinary events that might arise. In such times,
it would become the duty of the Bank to reduce their securities
without delay, and thus to increase the relative proportion of bullion
to their liabilities, prior to the commencement of a foreign demand,
which, in such altered state of circumstances, might be expected
to occur.

" Having thus endeavored to show the rise and progress of the
contraction in the circulation of the Bank of England, which has
terminated in the pressure upon the money market, it remains to
be considered, what are the consequences likely hereafter to ensue
from a continuance of the present system. . . .

" The consideration of the joint-stock system had been, for some
time prior to the year 1825, forced upon public attention by the
many failures which had taken place, subsequently to 1810, in private banking-establishments, amounting to more than one hundred
and fifty; and, as about eighty private banks suspended their payments in 1825, the government thought themselves then called

upon, without further delay, to endeavor to change the system altogether, — a sound system of banking being an object of the highest importance to the whole community. The view taken by government was strengthened by observing the little comparative derangement sustained by Scotland under the joint-stock Banks, by which the monetary concerns of that part of the kingdom have been almost exclusively conducted. Looking to that country as an example, it was perhaps natural to conclude that what afforded evidence of advantage in one part of the kingdom would be equally good for all the rest. There is no intention to criticise the Scottish system of banking; but, were it narrowly examined, it might not appear so perfect in all its parts as its many warm advocates are inclined to believe. Suffice it to say, that it has produced great benefit to Scotland, which is a sufficient reason for leaving it untouched so long as it commands public confidence. . . . The two systems were different in origin and principle. That of England had been formed upon the Bank of England, and private establishments precluded by Parliament from embracing more than six partners, while the system of joint-stock Banks had ever been the main support of the circulation of Scotland. Both systems existed with equal advantage in the several districts where established. A change in either could only be accomplished by competition, endangering the credit and currency of the country. . . . So dangerous does this system appear, as it now stands, that it becomes questionable whether the Bank of England and the bodies in question can permanently exist together." [1]

Such was the attempted explanation of the abandonment or failure of the rule requiring the Bank, on a full currency, to maintain reserves in coin equalling one-third of its liabilities. In adopting it, it merely followed the dogma of the Bullion Committee, that the condition of the currency was indicated by that of foreign exchange. If the latter were at par, the currency was necessarily in a healthy and normal condition. The Bullion Committee did not attempt to prescribe the requisite amount of coin to be held, when the exchanges were at par, and the currency consequently full. The managers of the Bank adopted the " one-third rule " for no other reason than that, for some time after it recovered from the effects of the panic of 1826, it held specie equalling about one-third its liabilities ; the former averaging, from 1827 to 1830, inclusive, about £10,000,000 ; the latter, about £30,000,000. As the proportion was purely accidental, the rule was equally accidental. The exchanges being at par, the currency was full, and in a

---

[1] Causes and Consequences of the Pressure in the Money Market.

healthy and normal condition. An adverse exchange caused contraction, which was still to disturb only temporarily the relation between liabilities and reserves, as the rate of interest would be raised to such a pitch that the coin lost would flow back into the country, and into the Bank, from being more valuable there than elsewhere. This doctrine was implicitly adopted by the Bank, and appeared to work satisfactorily in the drain which began in 1830, and continued until 1832, although the proportion of one-third between reserves and liabilities was by no means maintained. The drain continued so long as it was profitable to export gold, or so long as the country had no means of discharging its liabilities but by export. It turned, when it became profitable to import it, or when England became the creditor instead of the debtor nation. During these automatic movements, as they may be called, every thing worked pretty smoothly. In the mean time, the Bank conducted its operations as if the currency had been full, and had the satisfaction of seeing its gold brought back to it in full volume, without raising a finger on its part. The correctness of the dogma of the Bullion Committee seemed to be established beyond cavil. From 1833 to 1837, however, the exchanges remaining at par, the Bank was subjected to a steady drain for coin, which took from it, in a period of three and a half years, nearly £7,000,000. The rule no longer worked; or, rather, the Bank no longer followed the rule. It no longer applied, for the reason that the demand for coin was domestic, not foreign. This demand, to use the language of Mr. Palmer, "seems in no degree to have arisen from overtrading, or any undue speculative advance in commercial prices: occurrences of that nature tend to produce an unfavorable foreign exchange, — an evil only to be remedied by that contraction of the circulation which eventually restores prices and currency to a level with those existing in foreign countries." With conditions not contemplated by the Bullion Committee, the Bank was no longer to be governed by the rules it had laid down. It must meet a domestic demand both for currency and coin; otherwise there would be a domestic convulsion or disturbance most fatal in its effects. "It is evident," said Mr. Palmer, "that the additional issue by the Bank has not caused any foreign demand for gold; and, unless that be exhibited, the Bank ought not, under circumstances of unnatural pressure, strictly to enforce the principle laid down. We must keep in mind that England is the centre of the whole commerce of Europe and America, if not of the world ; and any hasty or unnecessary step taken will not only affect the credit and prices of this country, but, to a certain degree, those of all parts of the Continent from whence we are to obtain that bullion which we have lost. . . . And, in order to prevent that pressure, the Bank is required to reissue the amount of notes so cancelled " (taken in), " without reference to the amount of bullion in its possession." While no longer recognizing the old rule under the new condition of things, Mr. Palmer seems measurably to have lost confidence in its value in reference to the exchanges. " It remains for Parliament," he says, " to express an opinion upon either of those points " (that is, whether the rule should hold in reference to the currency when exchanges are even, or whether it should be abandoned when they are even, but when the demand for coin is a domestic one) ; " and there can be no question but that the Bank will immediately regulate its course accordingly. . . . If, however, the amount of paper money be limited, and it be issued by one body with an adequate reserve of bullion, expanding and contracting as the currency may fluctuate in value with reference to foreign exchanges, there could be no difficulty in preserving it against depreciation for all purposes of foreign payment. If paper money ever become discredited by any internal convulsion, it can then be only upheld by the power of the government ; and in such cases it becomes the duty of the ministers of the Crown to undertake the responsibility of upholding the public credit. For relief against commercial discredit, the issuing body should be so formed as to be able to afford protection."

With such incoherency and incompetency on the part of its managers, no wonder that the Bank constantly found itself involved in the greatest straits, and commerce and trade in great uncertainty, embarrassment and loss. The reserves held by the Bank are, at all times, to have reference as much to a domestic as to a foreign demand, — to its own condition as to that of the public. They are held to make good losses, however arising. That coin is drawn from it in considerable quantities, and continuously, is evidence that large losses have been made. It is the same, so far as the volume of the currency is concerned, whether they have been made by the Bank or by its depositors. If the Bank make a loss of a million of sovereigns, it must reduce its issues in far greater ratio. If its depositors make a similar loss, and draw in consequence a corresponding amount of coin, it must reduce its issues in the same ratio as if the loss were its own. The capital on which it bases the greater part of its operations, belongs to the public; but, whether belonging to the public or itself, its loans must always be in ratio to its reserves. As already shown, the drain upon it for specie does not begin till the goods, the payment of which is to cause the foreign or domestic demand for coin, have been purchased for consumption, and probably in great part consumed. But for the instruments issued by the Bank, such purchases for consumption would never have been made. The Bank, when it makes its loans, has no means of knowing the purposes for which their proceeds may be applied. Their use in the purchase of imported merchandise may be upon a full currency; when, in fact, specie is flowing into its vaults. At that very moment it may be pursuing a course which imperils its condition. To make two sets of rules in reference to its reserves — one having reference to a foreign, and one to a domestic, demand — is to make distinctions where no differences whatever exist. To assume the Bank to be in a perfectly safe condition when it is not being called upon for specie, is an absurdity which any tyro in finance should be able to detect. The step or act, which is to involve it in future embarrassment or loss, is always taken in a period of apparent prosperity, — in a period of full currency, and when it is not on its guard.

No such rule, however, as that formally set forth by Mr. Palmer ever did exist; nor could it exist, considering the manner in which the Bank is organized and conducts its operations. It can make no rule which shall control the operations of its depositors. They will draw the coin which belongs to them as it suits their necessities. It might as well make a rule that the exports of the United Kingdom shall not exceed a certain tonnage and value. In a panic, its gold as well as its rules are scattered to the winds. No more meaning was attached to the phrase "full currency" than to "rapidity of circulation." A paper currency can be said to be full, only

when all articles entering into consumption are symbolized.
" Full currency " was borrowed from the Bullion Committee.
It meant with them the equilibrium of the currency. If it
were more than full, if it were redundant, then the rates of
exchange rose, to be brought down again only by a reduction
of the excess, — by export of coin, which was the only part of
the currency that could be exported.· The reason that gold
goes forward is not because the proper equilibrium in the circulating medium common to all commercial countries has been disturbed, but for the reason that, from an excess of instruments
of expenditure, the country in which such excess exists has
created debts which can be discharged only by an exportation
of coin, in default of the ordinary subjects of commerce.

The holding, by the Bank, of an amount of gold unusually
large, is always proof that the currency is, or, rather, that production and trade are or have been, in an unhealthy condition; that liquidations to a large extent have taken place;
and that the business public, in their distrust, or want of opportunities, have deposited in Bank the balances due them,
which have been liquidated in gold, for safe-keeping and to
wait a favorable turn of affairs. A large amount of gold in
its vaults, therefore, indicates the exact opposite of what it is
supposed to indicate. With the Bank of England it is always
a prelude to, or always follows, great speculative movements.
It is the rule with it to issue notes against the coin it holds.
If the amount be large, the issues act correspondingly upon
prices and upon expenditure. As a necessary consequence,
gold is drawn from the Bank to meet such expenditure, and
in the adjustment of balances that necessarily arise. This
done, the gold returns to it again, to be made the basis of
loans to be drawn from, and again to be returned in manner
described. As the viciousness of the system is not seen, the
same inflations and contractions periodically occur, alike disastrous to itself as to the public, until their regular recurrence
has come to be regarded as a necessary law or condition of
all' currencies.

There can be no doubt that the condition of the country in
1836 and 1837 seemed to call for extraordinary exertions on
the part of the Bank; nor that, in making them, it was guided

by the most laudable intentions. In November of the former year, the Northern and Central Bank, which had thirty-nine branches, and whose central office was at Manchester, finding itself in trouble, applied to the Bank of England for help to the extent of £500,000. This, after some hesitation, was granted, from fear of the consequences that might follow the failure of such an extensive concern. It was soon found that the sum first applied for was by no means sufficient, and further aid had to be granted, till the whole amount reached £1,370,000. This application was quickly followed by one from a leading London house, which was granted upon the guarantee of other houses. Applications for aid to other concerns, both in London and in the provinces, followed; which were granted for the same reason as the preceding. To meet the demands for such aid as was regarded indispensable to avert a general crash, the Bank advanced, in a short time, fully £6,000,000. The final repayment of these advances, and the great relief they seemed to afford, might be considered as a precedent to be followed in similar emergencies. It must, however, so long as the Bank is conducted as at present, be regarded as a very questionable one. The Bank makes its loans by issuing its own obligations, payable presently, for those of its borrowers or of other parties, payable at a future day. The safety of the transactions on its part is in having its obligations circulate as money, until those upon which they were based become payable. In ratio as they are returned, previous to the maturity of the securities for which they were issued, the Bank must pay out a corresponding amount of its own means. It should never attempt to loan its capital, or to make loans that are likely to impair its amount. This is always to be held in reserve to meet such portions of its liabilities as are not seasonably returned to it by its securities. As its issues, however, so far as their credit is maintained, serve to it as capital, it is under the greatest temptation, in an active demand for money, to make an excessive use of them. In case of a temporary pressure, were its loans properly made, it might act with a good degree of liberality, by increasing them to a considerable amount; as in such case there would be a reasonable probability that all its issues, however made, would be seasonably returned. But as itself is its chief customer, — that is, as it makes its loans chiefly in the purchase of governments, not, perhaps, to mature within the time that its notes will find their way back to it, — it is, when subjected to a drain of specie, in the dilemma of being liable to have the issues it may be called upon to make immediately presented for payment in coin, or notes, or to aggravate the alarm and run upon it by refusal to make any. In such a state of things, to discount the best paper may be as fatal, in its immediate consequences, as to discount the most worthless. It can neither act nor refuse to act with safety. It is impossible for it to liquidate all its obligations upon the moment, and this is what a panic calls upon it to do. As it is, it is wholly incompetent to manage or allay it. Its real and only safety, as well as that of the public, is in rendering panics, or any considerable aberration in production and trade, impossible, by making no issues that will not be taken care of by the borrowers, — by discounting no paper and taking no securities that have not a constituent in merchandise.

The advances that were made in 1836–37 seemed to have accomplished their object; but, after all, they only perhaps postponed, while they aggravated, the crisis which was already inevitable. In 1839, after a partial recovery from 1837, the Bank was again subjected to a drain far more excessive than that of the former year; a drain which indicated a most unsound condition of affairs, — which had, perhaps, been only skimmed over, instead of being healed. It was finally driven to make large loans at the Banks of France and Hamburg, to save it from what seemed to be impending bankruptcy.

Mr. Palmer was very probably correct in ascribing the drain upon the Bank, or a considerable part of it, to the rapid formation and increased operations of the joint-stock Banks. It was inevitable, in the outset, that their action, for the want of adequate experience and training, should have been somewhat eccentric, and should have led to excessive expenditures, not only in consumption, but in enterprises of various kinds. As the notes of the Bank were then legal tender, they constituted the reserves of all other issuers. It had thus to stand in the gap, and make good, from reserves held to meet its own liabilities, the mistakes and losses of every petty issuer in the kingdom. For all this, it was by no means prepared. The losses sustained by the joint-stock and other Banks, and from over-production and over-trading, proportionably reduced its means, as well as those of the public.   Its condition for a long period after 1837 was one of great comparative weakness, for which all the issuers of currency, including itself, were responsible.   From the passage, in 1826, of the Act authorizing the formation of joint-stock Banks, and especially from 1833, previous to which no considerable number of these were in operation, a great revolution has been going on in the monetary system of the kingdom.   Instead of holding reserves applicable only to its own operations, it has now, from the fact that its notes are legal tender, to hold them for those exceeding in amount ten times its own ; and if its managers do not yet comprehend the principles upon which a symbolic currency must rest, they make good the lack by an excess of caution, which now holds out the signal of alarm at the least freshening of the breeze and the slightest turn of the vane.

Mr. Palmer had no sooner laid down his pen than he was instantly assailed on all sides, with no little vehemence, by a crowd of writers, the most distinguished of whom was Mr. Loyd, — Lord Overstone ; whose reply chiefly deserves consideration from the fact, that it prepared the way for the Act of 1844, of which he was the originator and virtually the author.

" The principle upon which the Bank professes to be guided in the regulation of the currency," said Lord Overstone, " is this : to meet its outstanding liabilities, consisting of circulation and deposits, it holds at its disposal securities and specie ; and its principle of action is, to keep the amount of its securities fixed, and to leave any variation in the amount of circulation and deposits to be balanced by a corresponding variation in the amount of specie. This principle was set forth by the Bank Directors in their evidence before the Parliamentary Committee, previous to the last renewal of the charter, and was recommended principally upon the ground, that the effect of it would be to render the Bank a passive agent, and that all variations in the amount of specie would thus become the result, not of any direct action on the part of the Bank, but solely on that of the public.   If they demanded specie, it could be obtained only by paying in notes or diminishing deposits ; and if, on the other hand, the specie was increased, there must at the same time be a corresponding increase in the amount of circulation or deposits.   Under this view of its probable action, the principle above stated met with a degree of acquiescence which a more close examination of the subject will hardly warrant.

" The Bank, it must be observed, acts in two capacities : as a manager of the circulation, and as a body performing the ordinary functions of a banking concern.   The duties of these two characters, though very often united in the same party, are in themselves perfectly distinct.   In the principle laid down by the Bank for its own guidance, the separate and distinct natures of these two characters has not been sufficiently attended to.   The rules applicable to its conduct as manager of the currency are mixed with the rules applicable to its conduct as a simple banker, and the rule or principle under discussion is the result of this mixture.   As a manager of the currency, it is undoubtedly a sound rule by which to guide itself, that against the amount of notes out it should hold at its disposal securities and specie ; that the amount of securities shall be invariable ; and that, consequently, all fluctuations in the amount of notes out shall be met by a corresponding fluctuation in the amount of specie on deposit; and thus the public, and not the Bank, will be made the regulators of the amount of the circulation ; and that amount will, by this principle, be made to fluctuate precisely as it would have fluctuated had the currency been purely metallic.

" For the regulation of the conduct of the Bank as a manager of the currency, this rule is perfectly unobjectionable, and rests, indeed, upon the soundest principles.

" But when the same rule is further applied to the regulation of its conduct as a banking concern, it is necessarily found to be wholly impracticable.   It is in the nature of banking business that the amount of its deposits should vary with a variety of circumstances ; and, as its amount of deposit varies, the amount of that in which those deposits are invested (viz., the securities) must vary also.   It is, therefore, quite absurd to talk of the Bank, in its character of a banking concern, keeping the amount of its securities invariable. . . .

" The rule is, ' that, the securities being kept equal, any diminution in the amount of specie may be met by a corresponding decrease in the aggregate amount of circulation and deposits.' The possible consequence is, that a large diminution of specie may take place, and be met, not by a corresponding decrease of circulation, but solely by a decrease of deposits.   Thus, a heavy drain upon the treasury of the Bank might take place under this rule, without any contraction of the currency by which that drain is to be checked or the Bank to be protected.

" To those who are practically conversant with banking business, or who have reflected upon the nature of it, it can hardly be necessary to point out the simple considerations, that banking deposits are necessarily variable in their amount and duration; and that, with such variation, the amount of the securities held by the Bank will fluctuate.   It is, therefore, unreasonable to talk of the invariable amount of a banker's securities ; and this observation is equally applicable to banking business when conducted by the Bank of England as when it is conducted by any other body. On the other hand, I apprehend there will be no difference of opinion, amongst those who have reflected upon the principles of paper currency, as to the soundness of the rule, — that the amount of the paper issued shall be represented by an amount of securities which never varies, and an amount of specie which is left to fluctuate with the fluctuations of the amount of notes out.

"If these rules be correct, it follows, that the rule now adopted by the Bank is incorrect, and cannot be safely relied upon in the management of the currency. The rule ought to be, that the variations in the amount of circulation shall correspond to the variations in the amount of bullion ; and the adherence of the Bank to this rule ought to be obvious on the face of its published accounts. By this means, and by this means only, can we obtain ' a paper circulation varying in amount exactly as the circulation would have varied had it been metallic ; ' and, in addition to the establishment of this only sound principle of currency, shall we obtain a simple and intelligent account, requiring no further explanation, nor the production of any information not at the command of the public, to enable them to come to a correct understanding of it.

"Was the management of the currency intrusted to a body established exclusively for that purpose, this is the rule by which such body must govern its operations. It is only by an adherence to such a principle that a paper currency can be made to vary in amount precisely as the circulation would have varied had it been exclusively metallic. The importance of a rigid adherence to this rule cannot be over-estimated ; and, if it be incompatible, as is alleged by some, with the mixed functions of the Bank of England, it seems to become a very serious question, whether it is not better to separate altogether the business of banking from that of regulating the currency, rather than suffer so essential a rule to be in any degree compromised. It is not, however, very easy to perceive any insuperable difficulty in rendering the currency department of the Bank of England totally distinct and separate from the management of its other business ; so that the one should not interfere with or affect the other more than they would do where they were under the control of different bodies. In proportion as these two functions are kept distinct, will each be rendered more effectual for its proper purpose. The two branches of the business of the Bank, thus divided, will proceed with equal efficiency, and without mutual interruption. Like those animals described by naturalists, whose pecular property it is, that, when cut into two parts, they move off in opposite directions, each half full of life and energy ; thus, if the two natures of the Bank of England were completely dissociated, each would proceed to the discharge of its respective functions with more simplicity and efficiency, unencumbered by the conflicting tendencies and opposite action of its former companion. . . .

"We impose upon the Bank of England the duty of regulating the value of the currency, and providing for the payment of the whole of it in specie, without giving to that body the exclusive power of issuing the paper money, or investing it with any direct control over the conduct of rival issuers. We look to the Bank for a strict regulation of the amount of its issues according to the state of the exchanges and the drain for bullion, while, at the same time, we very inconsistently look to it, also, as responsible for the maintenance of public credit in a period of pressure.

" We thus unite in the same body functions which, it can be easily shown, are in many cases conflicting, and therefore incompatible ; viz., those of ordinary banking business, and of regulating the amount of a paper currency.   And, lastly, to perform those very delicate duties, in every step of which the personal interests of the mercantile, trading, and money classes must be immediately affected, we select, not a body of individuals, qualified (by their total separation from all such interests) to exercise a dispassionate and disinterested judgment, but, on the contrary, men the most largely engaged in mercantile and moneyed operations, and, therefore, more than any other exposed in their private interests to the immediate effects of any action upon the currency.

" Again, with respect to joint-stock Banks, we create by law large and powerful establishments, to which is given the right to issue paper money without any absolute restriction ; and even that knowledge of the action of the Bank which is essential to enable them to take a just view of the condition of the currency, and of their corresponding duty, is afforded them only through such imperfect and delusive accounts as those published by the Bank are represented by the Bank Directors themselves to be. . . .

" A Bank of issue is intrusted with the creation of the circulating medium.

" A Bank of deposit and discount is concerned only with the use, distribution, or application of that circulating medium.

" The sole duty of the former is to take efficient means for the issuing its paper money upon good security, and regulating the amount of it by one fixed rule.

" The principal object and business of the latter is to obtain the command of as large a proportion as possible of the existing circulating medium, and to distribute it in such manner as shall combine security for repayment with the highest rate of profit.

" That those two functions are perfectly separate and distinct, and that there is no connection between them which renders it necessary that they should be administered by the same parties, is very clear.   A very short explanation will be sufficient to show that they are, in many respects, conflicting duties.

" The history of what we are in the habit of calling the ' state of the trade ' is an instructive lesson.   We find it a subject to various conditions which are periodically returning; it revolves apparently in an established cycle.   First, we find it in a state of quiescence; next, improvement, growing confidence, prosperity, excitement, over-trading, convulsion, pressure, stagnation, distress ; ending again in quiescence.

" Now during the progress of trade through this circular course, what is the necessary situation, and the inevitable conduct of the banker ?   The connection between him and his customers is necessarily very close and intimate : they must sympathize with each others' views and feelings, and act, to a considerable degree, in concert. When confidence is increasing, the spirit of enterprise beginning to expand itself ; when hope in all its forms is coming into active operation ; when prices are rising, profits increasing, and every merchant and tradesman, with a view of benefiting by these circumstances, is desirous of extending his operations, — the banker is looked to by his customers to act in concert with them ; to facilitate their operations, and to distribute amongst them all the aid which the extent of his resources enables him to command. It would be difficult to show that it is not his duty, properly understood, to obey this call, and to assist the expanding energies of trade. At all events, it would be practically impossible for him to act otherwise : he must conform to the tendency of circumstances about him ; he must breathe the atmosphere of opinion which surrounds him, and suffer himself to be moved onward by the stream of events in which he is placed. For the practical truth of this view, we may safely appeal to the experience of all those who are concerned with business of this nature. A banker cannot contract, by operations in a period when the whole trading and mercantile world are acting under one common impetus of expansion. If, under these circumstances, the banker, in addition to what may be properly called his ordinary and legitimate resources, is also intrusted with the power of issuing paper money *ad libitum*, is it not inevitable that he should abuse that power ? Can we expect, under such circumstances, while all his other resources are strained to the utmost for the accommodation of his customers, he will still keep a firm and unyielding restraint over the amount of his issues ? Will he, under such temptations, in no respect confound or compromise his respective duties as a banker of issue and a banker of deposit and discount ? Or must we not rather conclude, whether we look to the principles of human conduct or draw our conclusions from the lessons of experience, that he will certainly blend together his deposits and circulation on the one side, and his gold and securities on the other ; and thus produce an account which shall throw a plausible appearance over the abusive use which he is making of his power as an issuing banker? Look to the published accounts of the Bank, and to their avowed rule of conduct, — ' *Habes confitentem reum.*' The effect, of course, of such an application by the banker of his power of issue will be to give a further stimulus to the existing tendencies of the trading world, and ultimately to aggravate the convulsion to which they must lead. . . .

" With this view, it seems important to direct the attention of the public to the following points : —

" 1. The propriety of securing and strengthening, and, if possible, of extending the monopoly, as regards the currency, of the central issuer, with a view of rendering the indirect control which she can exercise over subordinate issuers more powerful and effectual.

" 2. The propriety of making some gradual approach toward the separation of the banking functions from those of the management of the currency, with the view of rendering the body that undertakes the latter duty free from all conflicting interests and motives, and at the same time making her responsibilities distinct and complete, and the nature of her proceedings simple and easily understood.

"3. The propriety, in the mean time, of a distinct separation in the accounts of the Bank of the management of currency from every other branch of business; of subjecting the superintendence of this department to a 'separate committee of currency,' and of associating with this committee a representative of the government whose presence should be always requisite to constitute this committee efficient for business. . . . The presence of a member of the government in all the deliberations of this committee would prevent the Bank in any tendency to abuse her power over the currency, for the promotion of her banking purposes, and the Bank would exercise a similar restraint over the government." [1]

An examination of Lord Overstone's reply to Mr. Palmer, and of the doctrines or propositions set forth in the same, will more appropriately follow the extracts which will be given from his evidence before the Parliamentary Committee of 1840.

The crisis past, a return flow of specie set in. On the 31st of August, 1837, the Bank held £6,548,000 of specie, against £4,077,000 on the 28th of February of that year. On the 28th of February, 1838, it held £10,471,000 of coin; its liabilities at that time amounting to £29,800,000. On the 31st of August, 1838, its specie was reduced to £9,540,000; its liabilities, to £28,410,000. On the 28th of February, 1839, its specie was reduced to £6,773,000, and its liabilities to £25,837,000. On the 31st of August of that year its specie stood at £2,420,000; its liabilities, at £24,471,000. As it appeared to be drifting toward bankruptcy, it was driven to the mortifying necessity of making large loans in Paris and Hamburg. In July, 1839, Messrs. Baring Brothers & Company made an arrangement with twelve of the leading bankers of Paris, by which that house was to draw for £2,000,000; the Bank of France undertaking to see that the acceptances were paid. A similar arrangement was made with the Bank of Hamburg for £900,000. With every bill drawn, the Bank put up with trustees, securities as collateral for its payment. These loans served not only to increase largely the means of the Bank, but to allay, in a great measure, the alarm which had prevailed. A return flow of specie soon set in, increasing the amount in the Bank on the 28th of February, 1840, to £4,311,000; its

[1] Reflections Suggested by a Perusal of the Pamphlet of Mr. J. Horsley Palmer.

liabilities at that time standing at £23,060,000. The recovery of the Bank, however, was much more gradual than from previous panics. The amount of gold held by it for 1840, averaging the amounts for February and August, equalled only £4,305,000 ; and for 1841, only £4,528,000 ; against liabilities for £23,282,000 for the former and £23,575,000 for the latter year. In 1842 it increased its coin to £7,924,000 ; and on the 28th of February, 1843, to £11,016,000, its liabilities at that time standing as high as £31,738,000.

It is impossible, in a work of the character of the present, to enter into a full discussion of the alleged causes of the violent fluctuations in the currency, and in production and trade, during the period referred to. The real cause was an excess of paper money ; or, to state the case more accurately, of paper money that did not symbolize merchandise, — paper that did not seasonably return to its issuers their own liabilities. As already stated, and perhaps more than once, there can be no considerable inflation or contraction where the currency is merchandise or the representative of merchandise. There may, in such case, be much waste ; but, where equivalents are always present in exchanges, neither consumption nor credit can, to any considerable extent, anticipate future accumulations. Large operations are made upon credit, only when the seller can convert the paper he receives into money. He sells in order to avail himself of the proceeds. If he cannot get his bills discounted, he has, as a rule, no motive to sell. He is much stronger with his merchandise in hand, than with the paper taken for it, but which he cannot convert. He will sell on credit, only when he knows or believes a Bank stands ready to discount the paper. Its issues are to him the equivalent of coin for whatever object he may have in view. By means of Banks, therefore, a very large proportion of the merchandise of a community — whether or not fitted for consumption — can be turned into paper money having, for the time, all the potency of coin. Accommodation notes, to a very large amount, may in the same way be turned into money, — the equivalent, to the holders, of coin. If a portion of the bills, and not a very considerable one, which have been discounted be not paid by their makers, the Banks must take in their notes and credits, by paying out a corresponding amount from their reserves. So soon as this is done, the currency becomes contracted in far greater ratio. Alarm is created lest the Banks themselves should not be able to meet the calls upon them, and a wild rush is made for whatever they hold. The alarm quieted, all attempt to account for the fluctuations and the disasters that have been suffered. Bad crops are the argument of one ; excessive importations, of another ; foreign loans, of a third ; — the Bank laying the blame upon the joint-stock and country Banks and bankers, and the latter upon the former. But all such explanations amount to nothing. A bad crop may happen, involving large importations ; but, if the currency be capital or the representative of capital, then its amount measures the ability of the country to purchase. So with foreign loans : if the currency be capital, their purchase may involve those who take them in loss, but can involve no others ; nor can it anticipate the future earnings of themselves or the country.

The disasters of 1839 were well calculated to provoke the attention of government ; and, as was its wont on such occasions, the House of Commons, on the 10th of March, 1840, appointed a special Committee, consisting of twenty-six members, to " consider the subject of Banks of issue." Upon this Committee was Mr. Thomas F. Baring (then Chancellor of the Exchequer), Mr. Hume, Sir Charles Wood, Sir Robert Peel, Mr. Grote, with many others almost equally distinguished in financial and political circles. . The Committee passed in review before them a great number of merchants and bankers. It is only important to refer to this evidence as leading to the Act of 1844, and only to that portion of it given by Lord Overstone ; which, with the extracts already given from his essay published in 1837, is all that is needed by way of introduction to that Act. The great question discussed by the Committee was the difference or resemblance between the liabilities of a Bank in the form of deposits and its notes in circulation. Lord Overstone's evidence was accepted as conclusive of a radical difference between the two. The Act of 1844 is simply an embodiment of his views. These are sufficiently shown in his answers to the questions put to him by the Committee.

Question 2661. " In your definition of the word ' circulation ' do you include deposits ? " — " No, I do not."

Question 2663. " Why do you not include deposits in your

definition of circulation?"—"To answer that question I believe I must be allowed to revert to first principles. The precious metals are distributed to the different countries of the world
by the operation of particular laws, which have been investigated,
and are now well recognized. The laws allot to each country
a certain portion of the precious metals, which, whilst other
things remain unchanged, remains itself unchanged. The precious
metals, converted into coin, constitute the money of each country.
That coin circulates somewhat in kind; but in highly-advanced
countries it is represented, to a certain extent, by paper notes
promising to pay the coin to bearer on demand,— these notes
being of such a nature, in principle, that the increase of them supplants coin to an equal amount. Where these notes are in use,
the metallic coin, together with these notes, constitutes the money
or currency of that country. Now, this money is marked by certain distinguishing characteristics: first of all, that its amount is
determined by the laws which apportion the precious metals to the
different countries of the world; secondly, that it is in every
country the common measure of the value of all other commodities,
— the standard by reference to which the value of every other
commodity is ascertained, and every contract fulfilled; and, thirdly,
it becomes the common medium of exchange for the adjustment of
all transactions, equally at all times, between all persons, and in all
places. It has, further, the quality of discharging those functions in endless succession. Now, I conceive, that neither deposits nor bills of exchange in any way whatever possess those
qualities. In the first place, the amount of them is not determined
by the laws which determine the amount of the precious metals in
each country; in the second place, they will in no respect serve as
a common measure of value, or a standard by reference to which
we can measure the relative values of all other things; and, in the
next place, they do not possess that power of universal exchange-
ability which belongs to the money of the country. If the Committee will allow me to refer to it, there is a passage in the Report of
the French Chamber, which has recently been appointed to inquire
into a subject very similar to that which this Committee is now
investigating, which seems to put the point of the universal ex-
changeability of money in a very striking way:—

"'If we reflect upon the innumerable commercial transactions
which daily take place, from those which furnish the most inconsiderable results to those which express the boldest speculations
of international commerce, we may readily perceive that they could
not be accomplished without the assistance of an intermediate value,
which can successively be brought into comparison with all others,
and serve among them as a standard and a medium of exchange.'"

Question 2667. "What are the elements which constitute
money in the sense in which you use the expression 'quantity
of money'? What is the exact meaning you attach to the
words 'quantity of money, — quantity of metallic currency'?"—
"When I use the words 'quantity of money,' I mean the quantity
of metallic coin, and of paper notes promising to pay the coin on
demand, which are in circulation in the country."

Question 2668. "Paper notes payable by coin?" — "Yes."

Question 2669. "By whomsoever issued?" — "Yes."

Question 2670. "By country Banks as well as other Banks?" — "Yes."

Question 3101. "Are not the Bank of England notes, deposited by you in the Bank of England, as much at your disposal as if they were in your own banking-house?" — "No."

Question 3102. "What is the difference?" — "In the one case I am sure I can have them when I like, and in the other case I have only a general belief that I can have them when I like."

Question 3106. "Are you aware that, in the official return of the Bank of England, the notes deposited by you appear as deposits?" — "Yes."

Question 3107. "Are you aware that the notes that are kept in your own banking-house appear, in that official return, as circulation?" — "Yes."

Question 3108. "Does the circumstance of a certain amount of bank-notes belonging to you being returned by the Bank of England, as deposits, alter their nature or change their value?" — "It does."

Question 3109. "Why?" — "Deposit business is a mode of economizing the use of the circulation. By means of resorting to that process, a greater amount of obligations or of transactions can be adjusted with a smaller amount of circulating medium than could otherwise take place. The amount of deposits which the Bank of England, or any other Bank, holds, is worked by that concern with a certain reserve of bank-notes, which reserve is measured in its extent by what that concern considers to be the average quantity of demand that will be made upon it. By that means, that reserve is enabled to perform an amount of business, which, without the process of banking deposit business, it would have required an amount of circulation equal to the whole deposits to have performed. By that means, undoubtedly, an economic use of the circulation is effected; but an economic use of the circulation is not itself circulation. When you put the question, Are not the bank-notes in my till, and the bank-notes deposited by me in the hands of the Bank of England, equally at my disposal? it is undoubtedly true that they are; but it is true only with respect to the bank-notes which I have in the Bank of England, upon the supposition that all other persons similarly circumstanced with myself do not act simultaneously. The Bank of England, or any other banker, can clearly pay his deposits only to the extent of the banking reserve in his till. The banking reserve in his till is the money with which that business is worked, and constitutes the amount of circulation. It is to mistake the amount of business done for the instrument with which it is done, — to call deposits circulation. Deposits are the business worked; the reserve in the banking-till is the instrument with which they are worked; and the business by which your instrument is worked is the circulation or money of the country."

Question 3121. "What difference, then, is there between the bank-note you hold in your hand, and the money you deposit in the Bank?"—"The difference is this: in one case, the debt has assumed that form which makes it the representative of metallic coin for all purposes; in the other case, it has not assumed a form which gives it those properties."

Question 3182. "Are there any circumstances you can suppose which would prevent a deposit in the Bank of England, belonging to you, as a banker, being applied to discharge, if you think proper to give an order on the Bank, any debt to the amount you may have in deposit?"—"Yes, there are."

Question 3184. "Is there any thing, then, to prevent your going to the Bank, and receiving bank-notes or sovereigns for that amount, and then paying the notes or sovereigns over to that person who you suppose may refuse the check?"—"No."

Question 3185. "Then, have not the deposits in that case all the characteristics of money which the notes have?"—"No, they have not."

Question 3186. "Have they not discharged the debt that you owed?"—"No: the notes have, but not the deposit."

Question 3187. "Did you not obtain notes to the amount of the deposit you had in the Bank?"—"I obtained a discharge of my credit in bank-notes."

Question 3190. "Did you not obtain the notes by means of the credit?"—"I did."

Question 3196. "Is it your opinion that the Bank of England should increase or diminish its circulation, according to the increase or decrease of the influx of bullion, without regard to the amount of deposits?"—"Certainly."

Question 3222. "Have you not stated that, when the Bank wishes to increase the quantity of currency, they will purchase securities?"—"I certainly think that to purchase securities, and issue money against that purchase, is the mode by which the Bank should increase the circulation."

Question 3226. "Is it not your opinion that the Bank should sell securities, to effect that decrease of currency?"—"No: I think that the proper course is for the Bank to cancel their notes as they are paid in for gold."

The preceding extracts from the arguments of Mr. Palmer and Lord Overstone fully present the method of the management of the Bank from its recovery from the panic of 1826 down to the famous Act of 1844; while those from that of the latter, and from his evidence before the Committee of 1840, fully set forth the grounds for that Act. It turned wholly on the distinction in kind between notes, and deposits growing out of such notes. The former, whether issued by the Bank or by country Banks, were money; the latter, not. "The Bank," said Lord Overstone, "acts in two capacities,—as a manager of the circulation, and as a body performing the ordinary functions of a banking concern. The duties of these two characters, though very often united in the same party, are in themselves perfectly distinct." The rule by which, at the time, the Bank claimed to be managed, was to hold a certain quantity of securities, invariable in amount, and allow the circulation over and above such amount to fluctuate as gold was drawn from, or was returned to the Bank. This rule, he said, was perfectly correct when applied to the Bank as issuer and manager of the circulation, for the reason that the latter was uniform, or very nearly uniform in amount; but was wholly inapplicable to the Bank doing a general banking business, as, from their nature, its deposits, which were to be paid in coin equally with notes, fluctuated constantly and excessively in amount. The withdrawal of such deposits in specie might wholly exhaust its resources, leaving its notes — the circulation — entirely unprovided for. The remedy was the division of the Bank into two distinct Departments; one of Issue, the other of Banking. The rule then professed to be followed would be perfectly correct as applied to the circulation. "All fluctuations in its amount," said Lord Overstone, "would then be met by a corresponding fluctuation in the amount of specie on deposit: thus the public, not the Bank, would be made the regulators of the amount of the circulation; and that amount, by this principle, would be made to fluctuate precisely as it would have done had it been purely metallic. . . . By this means, and by this means only, can we obtain a paper circulation varying in amount exactly as it would have had it been metallic." To repeat his summary : —

" A Bank of Issue is entrusted with the creation of the circulating medium.

" A Bank of Deposit and Discount is concerned *only* with the use, distribution, or application of that circulating medium.

" The sole duty of the former is to take efficient means for issuing its paper upon good security, and regulating the amount of it by one fixed rule.

" The principal object and business of the latter is to obtain the command of as large a proportion as possible of the existing circulating medium, and to distribute it in such a manner as shall combine security for repayment with the highest rate of profit."

The two functions of issue and banking, being wholly distinct and antagonistic, should never be exercised by the same institution or party, for the reason, that, if it possessed the power, it could never resist, in periods of great monetary stringency, the importunities of its customers for an excessive issue of notes, as means of re-enforcing its banking resources. The latter were to arise wholly from notes; their distribution and use, in a manner to combine security with the highest rate of profit, being the sole function of a Banking Establishment or Department. The complete separation of issue and banking was the condition upon which a circulation, always the equivalent in quantity and value of coin, and consequent exemption from commercial and financial disasters, could alone be secured. To accomplish such results, all future legislation in reference to the Bank should be directed : —

" 1. To the strengthening, and, if possible, the extending, the monopoly, as regards currency, of the *central* issuer, with a view of rendering the indirect control which it can exercise over subordinate issuers more powerful and effectual.

" 2. The propriety of making some gradual approach toward the separation of the banking functions from the management of the currency. . . .

" 3. Of subjecting the superintendence of the issue department to a separate Committee of currency, and of associating with this Committee a representative of the government, whose presence should always be requisite to constitute this Committee efficient for business. . . . The presence of a member of the government in all the deliberations of this Committee would prevent the Bank in any tendency to abuse its power over the currency, for the promotion of her banking purposes, and the Bank would exercise a similar restraint over the government."

Here we have foreshadowed, seven years before its final adoption, all the material provisions of the Act of 1844. It was simply an attempt to secure a legislative sanction for the dogma of Adam Smith, "that the whole amount of paper money of every kind that can easily circulate in any country can never exceed the value of the gold and silver of which it supplies the place, or which would circulate if there were no paper money;" [1] and to limit its amount to that of the coin which otherwise would have been in circulation. The nature of a symbolic currency wholly escaped Lord Overstone. It could not be otherwise so long as he held to the dogma that money was not necessarily capital, only the wheel of commerce, the

---

[1] See *ante*, p. 127.

value of which bore no relation to that which it moved. But, if some repetition may be allowed, the very object of all paper currencies is not to supplant a corresponding amount of coin, but to supplement it. A far greater amount of the latter may be in circulation after than before the use of paper money, and by reason of such use. The rapid increase in production and trade in such countries as Great Britain and the United States has arisen almost wholly from improved methods of distribution, among the most valuable of which is a symbolic currency. A reduction in the amount of the latter, from whatever cause, would be followed by a proportional reduction in the amount of the former, which, to a very large extent, is the creation of the latter. Paper and coin, instead of being antagonistic, or supplanting the one the other, are, so far as currency is concerned, the components or conditions of a perfect means of distribution. Paper symbolizing merchandise is the more convenient agent for its distribution than coin. The latter is more appropriate for the discharge of balances, and to serve as reserves, which must be maintained in ratio to the magnitude of the transactions that are taking place. As the value of metallic money in no way depends upon the form it takes, — pieces of the same weight being equivalents the one of the other, — so the value of paper money in no way depends upon the form it takes. Notes and checks are the equivalents of each other. Neither are in themselves capital; both are equally the representatives of capital; both are equally payable on demand; they are convertible into each other at the will of the holder; they act equally upon prices and the rates of exchange. The assertion, therefore, that "deposits are business worked, and the notes the instruments by which they are worked," has no more meaning than an assertion " that the bullion in the Bank is the business worked, its coin is the instrument by which it is worked." There is the same identity in principle in one case as in the other.[1]

Lord Overstone held that the sole function of the Banking Department was to deal in the notes of that of Issue. It might

---

[1] Banks of deposit, which do not issue notes in their ordinary form, are constantly issuing "certificates of deposit," which are undertakings, on their part, to pay a corresponding amount of coin, which is all that notes undertake to do. So far they are, in a technical sense, Banks of issue.

deal wholly in such notes, and yet have deposits to the amount
of millions, and not a note remaining in its till, having loaned
them as fast as received.   Is there any difference between
deposits arising in this manner, and for the discharge of which
the Bank has no other means than its securities, and deposits
arising from the discount bills, their proceeds being placed to
the credit of the borrowers?   If not, then the function of the
Banking Department is a much more comprehensive one than
Lord Overstone would allow.   But restricting it to dealing
solely with the notes of the Issue Department, why should it
not be allowed to repay obligations incurred by receiving notes
on deposit, by notes of its own creation, if the depositors prefer
to receive in this manner what may be due them?   The
nature of its indebtedness would not be changed thereby.
This would merely take a different form.   In either case, it
would be payable on demand, in coin.   Neither the Bank, its
creditors, nor the public could be any worse off in one case
than in the other.   Why not, then, let the parties to the transactions solve them in any way they choose?   Whatever the
manner, the currency would not be potentially increased.

Bank-notes, not deposits, according to Lord Overstone, constituted money, circulation, for the reason that " their amount
is determined by the laws which apportion the precious metals
to the different countries of the world, and by the fact, that, in
every country, they are the common measure of the value of all
other commodities, — the standard by reference to which the
value of every other commodity is ascertained, and every contract fulfilled, — the common medium of exchange for the adjustment of all transactions equally, at all times, between all
persons, and in all places; and they have the further quality
of discharging these functions in endless succession.   Now, I
conceive that neither deposits nor bills of exchange in any way
whatever possess these attributes."   Deposits, certainly, do not
possess such attributes; although it might be supposed that
those in the Bank of England arising out of, and the equivalent of, its notes, might at least possess qualities as exalted as
the notes issued by "small tradesmen, cheese-mongers, shoemakers, and butchers," so graphically described by Lord Liverpool in 1826, who had the same right of issue in 1840, and
whose notes, according to Lord Overstone, possessed everywhere, and in endless succession, all the potency of coin.

It is to be feared that Lord Overstone possesses no exemption from the danger common to all who undertake to give reasons. With him, the notes of the Bank differed wholly from deposits, even when the latter arose out of the former, for the reason that (as in his answer to question 3109) " the amount which the Bank of England, or any other Bank, holds, is worked by that concern with a certain reserve of bank-notes, which reserve is measured in its extent by what that concern considers to be the average quantity of demand that will be made upon it. By that means, that reserve is entitled to perform an amount of business which, without the process of banking deposit business, it would have required an amount of circulation equal to the whole deposits to have performed." That the notes of the Bank, but for the deposits, would have to be increased by the amount of the latter, can hardly be held to prove, beyond cavil, a radical difference between the two. The inference from the statement, on the other hand, would seem to favor their perfect identity in principle. Lord Overstone himself appears to have entertained some misgivings: for in the same paragraph he proceeds to say, that " deposits are business worked ; the reserve in the banking till is the instrument by which they are worked ; and the business by which your instrument is worked is the currency of the country "! The conclusion to which he finally comes, that both forms of paper are equally circulation, — money, — is very satisfactory, whatever may be thought of the process by which it was reached, and however unintelligible it may be to those not familiar with Aristotle, Adam Smith, and the Schoolmen. As it was, " his wit was too courtly " for the simple natures of the Committee ; " and they rested." It must, however, be remembered that question 3109 was the 457th that had been asked him consecutively. By that time he had them in a state of mind as wild and incoherent as his own.

The next extension of the charter of the Bank was the occasion of giving a legal sanction to Lord Overstone's schemes. On the 14th of May, 1844, Sir Robert Peel, then at the head of the government, moved a resolution that it was expedient to continue, for a limited time, the privileges enjoyed by the Bank of England, subject to such conditions as Parliament might think fit to impose : —

"I must state, at the outset," he said, in introducing the measure, "that in using the word 'money,' I mean to designate by that word the coin of the realm, and promissory notes payable to bearer on demand. In using the words 'paper currency,' I mean only such promissory notes. I do not include in these terms bills of exchange, or drafts on bankers, or other forms of paper credit. There is a natural distinction, in my opinion, between the character of promissory notes payable to bearer on demand, and other forms of paper credit, and between the effects which they respectively produce upon the price of commodities, and upon the exchanges. The one answers all the purposes of money, passes from hand to hand without indorsement, without examination, if there be no suspicion of forgery; and it is, in fact, what its designations imply it to be, — currency, or circulating medium. . . . I think experience shows that the paper currency, that is, the promissory notes payable to bearer on demand, stands in a certain relation to the gold coin and the foreign exchange, in which other forms of paper credit do not stand. There are striking examples of this adduced in the Report of the Bullion Committee of 1810, in the case both of the Bank of England and of the Irish and Scotch Banks. In the case of the Bank of England, shortly after its establishment there was a material depreciation of paper, in consequence of its excessive issue. The notes of the Bank of England were at a discount of 17 per cent. After trying various expedients, it was at length determined to reduce the amount of bank-notes outstanding. The consequence was an immediate increase in the value of those which remained in circulation, the restoration of them to par, and a corresponding improvement in the foreign exchanges. In the case of Ireland, in 1804, the exchange with England was extremely unfavorable. A Committee was appointed to consider the causes. It was denied by most of the witnesses from Ireland that they were at all connected with excessive issues of Irish notes. . . . In the spring of 1804, the exchange of Ireland with England was so unfavorable that it required £118 10s. of the notes of the Bank of Ireland to purchase £100 of the notes of the Bank of England. Between the years 1804 and 1806, the notes of the Bank of Ireland were reduced from £3,000,000 to £2,410,000; and the effect of this, taken in conjunction with an increase of the English circulation, was to restore the relative value of Irish paper, and the exchange with England to par. In the same manner, an unfavorable state of the exchange between England and Scotland has been more than once corrected by a contraction of the paper circulation of Scotland. In all these cases, the action has been on that part of the paper credit of the country which has consisted of promissory notes payable to bearer on demand. There has been no interference with other forms of paper credit; nor was it contended then, as it is now contended by some, that promissory notes are identical in their nature with bills of exchange, and with checks on bankers, and with deposits, and that they cannot be dealt with on any separate principle."

To justify the proposed measure, Sir Robert had to go farther than Lord Overstone, and assert, not only the distinction in kind between notes and deposits, but that notes were the great cause of the commercial and financial disasters that were constantly occurring, and were to be subjected to a rigid restraint; while the influence exerted by deposits was so wholly innocuous as to require no legislative interposition whatever. If, however, according to Lord Overstone, the notes of Banks by their inherent qualities supplanted an equal amount of coin, — if " they were standards of value in all transactions, between all parties, and at all times, and in endless succession," — what need of legislation in reference to them that coin did not require ? Sir Robert's refinement of Lord Overstone's distinction is as absurd as the distinction itself. He might, with equal propriety, have based his measure upon the influence that the color of the notes of the Bank exerted upon the rates of exchange: those printed upon paper of a certain tinge of green having a tendency to put up the rates of exchange, while those that had a certain tinge of blue tended to put them down. His illustrations, when examined, will be seen to have no better foundation than his assumptions. In 1697, the notes of the Bank were at a discount; for the reason that, during the recoinage of 1696, it issued them in considerable amounts in exchange for debased coin then in circulation. This coin went out of use, so that all contracts entered into previous thereto had to be made good in coin of standard value. The Bank further embarrassed itself by making large loans to government, in order to aid it through the period of the recoinage. It also suffered discredit in being unable to get standard coin in sufficient abundance to meet its wants, from the inability of the mint to turn it out. A variety of causes, therefore, operated to depreciate its notes; among them, the want of adequate means. To provide such, it was compelled to make two calls of 20 per cent. each upon its stockholders. With their proceeds it was enabled to take in its notes at par. No reduction in their amount would have increased the price of those outstanding, unless it had been attended by an increase in value. With Sir Robert Peel the question was one of quantity, not of quality. He assumed, with the Bullion Committee, that all that was necessary to raise the value of depreciated notes to par was to reduce their amount. The depreciation of the notes of the Irish and Scotch Banks could only be remedied by increasing their value. They had, undoubtedly, too many notes out; but no amount of reduction would have brought up their price, unless attended with an increase of their value. In all the examples referred to, the value of notes and deposits in Bank was always the same, as they were always convertible the one into the other. The Banks could not bring up the price of one without bringing up the price of the other. Both were in excess, and both had to be reduced as a means of bringing up the value of either one remaining outstanding. Sir Robert's illustrations, therefore, are nothing to the purpose; or, if they prove any thing, they prove the exact opposite of that sought to be proved.

Sir Robert Peel enforced his argument as to the necessity of government taking the currency under its control, so far as related to competition or freedom of issue, from the experience of banking in the United States : —

" It appears to me," he said, " that the conclusions of reason against unlimited competition of issue are amply confirmed by the admissions of the advocates for it. Are the lessons of experience at variance with the conclusions we are entitled to draw from reason and from evidence? What has been the result of unlimited competition in the United States? In the United States, the paper circulation was supplied not by private bankers, but by joint-stock Banks established on principles apparently the most satisfactory. There was every precaution taken against insolvency; unlimited responsibility of partners; excellent regulations for the publication and audit of accounts; immediate convertibility into gold. If the principles of unlimited competition, controlled by such checks, be safe, why has it utterly failed in the United States? How can it be shown that the experiment was not fairly made in that country?"

In the debate which followed, he was sustained by Sir Charles Wood, now Lord Halifax; who, in reference to American Banks, said : —

" We are not without experience as to the value even of convertibility as a safeguard for the preservation of the standard. . . . In America, the convertibility of bank-notes is a fundamental article of the Constitution; provisions more stringent than in this country are enacted to enforce it in practice; every precaution is taken to render the Banks safe and sound. They are all joint-stock Banks, with limited liability, and restrictions on issues, paid up capital, and whatever other precaution can be devised for this purpose. What has been the result?"

Mr. Goulburn, then Chancellor of the Exchequer, who took part in the debate, spoke as follows: —

" Was there not, then, in the United States a paper that was perfectly convertible? Was there not, then, a precise regulation that every note should be payable on demand in coin? Still, in consequence of competition, there was an excess of issues; and this, though there was a perfect publicity as to accounts, a rigid inspection by the government, and a rigorous control; and yet from the competition of issues they reduced the country to that state, that, as the honorable gentleman himself had said, they overlooked morality, and suspended cash payments. There was no want, then, of a convertibility of paper enforced by law; but the competition of issues defied all law, and made every man in the community anxious to increase the circulation, in order that he might be able to promote his own wild speculations."

Schoolboys in England who should repeat such stuff as this should be sent to the bottom of their forms. That men at the head of a great empire should fabricate or utter it exceeds belief. At that time the United States, as a nation, had no more relation to the Banks within it than it had to the Bank of England. It was held, at the time, to be unconstitutional for the nation to establish Banks, or, indeed, any corporate company whatever. The extension of the charter of the United States Bank, which expired in 1836, was refused on this very ground. In the twenty-nine States, of which the nation was composed, there were as many systems. The operation of these might be said to prove almost every thing except the assertions made in reference to them, or to the assumed one of the United States. The States of Arkansas, Florida, and Mississippi had systems peculiar to themselves, which consisted of borrowing large sums of money for the ostensible purpose of founding Banks, squandering it, and winding up by repudiating payment. Their systems were a full proof of the barbarous and dishonest character of their people. They had neither capacity to manage Banks, nor, in Mississippi at least, the integrity to admit even a legal liability for the money borrowed, which they seized and made way with as lavishly and absurdly as if they had been tribes of savages. Sir Robert Peel and his associates should have known something about the systems of these States, as the money to found them had been in great part borrowed in London, and the whole city was then ringing with denunciations of the defaults that had

been made.   The Banks nominally set on foot in these States
were, according to Sir Robert, among those for the publication
and audit of whose accounts, and for the payment of whose
notes in coin, such wonderful provisions had been made, —
provisions, unfortunately, rendered wholly inoperative by the
competition of the issuers.   In some of the Western States
there were what were very appropriately termed " wild-cat "
systems, — no wilder, however, than that which only a short
time ago prevailed in every part of England.   The object of
such Banks in the United States, and, indeed, everywhere
else, was, in the first place, to impose their notes upon the public, and then to provide for their redemption as could best be
done.   If there were no downright dishonesty in these systems, they were entirely without any stable foundation, and in
the United States they all disappeared like a growth of mush-
rooms.   Fortunately, very little money was borrowed to set
them up.   The principal sufferers were the note-holders. Other
States, like that of New York, had, in fact, two systems: one
in the cities, founded on adequate means and well conducted ;
the other in districts far removed from the sea-board, in which
the wild-cat element largely prevailed.   This element, however, in this State as through the country, steadily tended to
disappear with the increase of wealth ; for this always brings
with it the lessons proper for its management, to those by whom
it is acquired, whether it be a Bank, or some industrial enterprise, in which it may be invested.   The systems of Pennsylvania, and of the States lying to the South, repeated in their
double character that of New York ; some parts of them very
good, some very vicious.   Legislation could do little in those
States, nor can it anywhere, unless seconded by integrity and
business training.   That which is to render a system perfect
far transcends legislative skill or power.   The best system, if
perfect freedom be allowed, grows naturally out of, and is
thoroughly adapted to the wants of production and trade, like
all other contrivances having similar objects.   Such a system,
resting wholly upon the voluntary consent of its members,
and as perfect as is possible in all its important features,
had existed in the New England States for twenty years previous to the Act of 1844.   It continued in operation down
to the establishment of the national system of 1861, which,
being purely a creation of law, is vicious in every part, and

which, until repealed or modified in every important particular, will be found to be an insuperable barrier to the restoration of the currency of the country. From the New England
system, English statesmen and financiers might have learned
whatever could be known of the principles of a paper currency,
and of their application. All they had to do to secure the best
possible system for themselves was to copy the example set
them, which was equally adapted to their country as it was to
the New England States. The latter formed a geographical
and commercial unit, with Boston for its centre. As that city
was the creditor of them all, the issues of all their Banks naturally tended toward it. All that was wanting, under such
conditions, to a perfect currency, was for every Bank to make
good all its issues in coin, at the point at which the greater
part of them were used, and to which, by a law of gravitation
as it were, whatever was issued tended constantly to flow, as
the most convenient point at which to hold it, while it was
awaiting employment. To this end, all the Banks of these
States, numbering at one time five hundred, entered into an
agreement to make daily redemptions of their notes and credits,
in coin or its equivalent, at the Suffolk Bank, Boston, from
which Bank the system, if such it may be called, took its name.
A homogeneous currency was thus created everywhere within
such territory, the equivalent of coin, and everywhere accepted
by the Banks and by the public as such. Whatever was the
equivalent of coin in Boston was equally so in every part of
the territory dependent upon it. By being so in Boston, the
notes of every Bank belonging to the system were the equivalent of coin in every part of the United States, less the rate of
exchange or cost of remitting coin, wherever such notes circulated, to that city. As a rule, they were, throughout the whole
country, preferred to coin, from the greater ease and safety of
their remittance; and for the reason that they were the equivalent of coin in New York, whenever the exchange between
that city and Boston was in favor of the former. While the
issues of these Banks were thus everywhere the equivalent of
coin, the system from its perfection required the least possible
amount of coin, as the daily redemptions of the issuers rendered
it impossible that any considerable excess of currency should
at any time get into circulation, or that any considerable balances should arise in production and trade. It has already

been shown that were all the interests of a community or nation maintained in perfect equilibrium, its exchanges might be effected almost wholly by the use of symbols. Such a condition of equilibrium, as perfect as is possible in any country, was, probably, obtained in the New England States under the system described. Only a small amount of specie had to be maintained at the central point; while such country Banks as had sufficient credit in Boston, or an abundance of good bills which could be readily sold in the market, had to keep on hand only such amount as was required by way of change. As the contracts or bills upon which the currency was issued ran off on an average every ninety days, the currency was retired within the same periods. So perfect was this system, that it is not probable that at any period there was a necessity for the suspension of the Banks composing it, arising out of their own condition. In 1837, 1847, and 1857, they followed the suspension of the Banks of other parts of the country, only for self-protection. They were, in all instances, the last to suspend and the first to resume. With the adoption of this system for the whole country, with New York as the central point, the issuing of the currency might, without the least danger or apprehension, be thrown open without regulation or restraint. The public, for their own safety and convenience, would impose limitations upon issue and provisions for redemption far more stringent and adequate than can ever be provided by law. The currency so issued would reflect, and be entirely adapted to, the wants of the country; and would be regulated as to its quantity by the same laws by which the quantity of a metallic currency, or of bills of exchange, is regulated. For Englishmen to draw their reasons against competition of issue, and in favor of a single issuer, from the assumed system of the United States, is as absurd and inadequate as for a traveller to describe London from observations made among the mud huts of Ireland, or the New England States from those made among the tribes of savages of the Pacific coast.

The Act of 1844, among other things, provided: —

1. That on and after August 31, 1844, the issue of notes by the Bank should be wholly distinct from its general banking business, and managed by a Committee of Directors, under the name of "The Issue Department of the Bank of England."

2. That there should be transferred to the Issue Department securities to the value of £14,000,000 (since increased to £15,000,000); of which the debt owed by the government to the Bank, amounting to £11,015,100, was to form a part; and also such gold coin and gold and silver bullion as the Bank at that time possessed, not needed to conduct the operations of the Banking Department. In exchange therefor, the Issue Department was to deliver over to the Banking Department an amount of notes equalling in nominal value the securities held by the former, that is, £14,000,000, and the bullion so transferred to it. No increase was to be made to the securities in the Issue Department. Their amount, however, might be decreased to any extent, and again increased, but not beyond the limit prescribed. The amount of securities and coin and bullion transferred to the Issue Department at the time equalled £28,351,295; that is, £14,000,000 of securities, £12,656,200 of gold coin and bullion, and £1,695,095 of silver bullion. The notes delivered at the time to the Banking Department equalled £8,175,025; the balance, that is, £20,176,070, being at the time in the hands of the public. The amount of gold and silver coin retained by the Banking Department equalled £857,765; making the total capital with which it began business £9,032,790. The only mode by which this department, as well as the public, could draw coin from the Issue Department was a presentation of notes, which were cancelled as they were taken in. The coin and bullion drawn, in theory, entered into circulation in ratio to the amount of notes withdrawn. The Department of Issue was required, upon an increase of its coin or bullion, to issue to the Banking Department a corresponding amount of coin. By these contrivances the circulation was, in theory at least, to be always uniform in amount; such amount to depend not upon the action of the Bank, but upon that of the public.

3. The amount of silver bullion in the Issue Department was never to exceed one-fourth part of the gold coin and bullion held by it.

4. The Issue Department was required to purchase, in exchange for its notes, all standard gold bullion, at the rate of £3 17s. 9d. the ounce.

5. If any banker issuing notes on the 6th of May, 1844, should cease such issue, the Bank might, by the permission of

government, increase its issues upon securities equal to two-thirds the amount so lapsed.

6. After the passage of the Act, no person, other than a banker who was lawfully issuing his own notes on the 6th of May, 1844, should issue bank-notes in any part of the kingdom.

7. Any banker who should cease to issue his own notes, from any cause whatever, after the passage of the Act, was not to resume their issue.

8. All existing Banks of issue were required to certify forthwith the places, name, and firm, at, and under which they issued notes during the twelve weeks which preceded the 27th of April, 1844, and the average amount of such issue ; and no Bank or banker was, for the future, to be allowed to exceed the amount of such average ; if, however, any two or more Banks of issue had become united within the said twelve weeks, the issues of the united Bank might equal the aggregate of those composing it. If two or more Banks became united after the passage of the Act, each of less than six partners, the new Bank might issue notes equalling the amount of the separate issues ; but if the partners in the new or consolidated Bank exceeded six members, then its right of issue was to cease.

Such, in its more important features, was the Act of 1844. Its effect was, in the place of one, to create two Banks of issue. The first was to hold, or was assumed to hold, at all times, means (securities and coin) equal in value to its liabilities, and sufficient for their immediate conversion into coin. The credit or value of these, consisting wholly of notes, was further sustained by their being made legal tender everywhere but at the Bank ; and also by being receivable in payment of the revenues, which exceeded the notes by three times the amount ordinarily in circulation ; so that, should the means provided for their redemption wholly fail, their value, from the uses to which they could be applied, could never fall much, if any, below their par in coin. In case of a panic, their holders owing debts due, either presently or in the future, including the revenues and taxes of all kinds, would have no motive to convert them into coin, for the reason that it would be of no greater value to them than notes, wherever the latter could be used. With the provision described, a few millions in coin would be all that would ever be required for the Issue Department to hold to meet all demands likely to be made upon it. Experience has shown that such arguments or inferences would have been entirely correct. No panic that has occurred since the Act went into effect has ever caused a considerable reduction in the amount of notes in the hands of the public. A large part of the coin held by the Issue Department always has been, and always will be, wholly superfluous to its objects. The holders of its notes are the very parties who do not want the coin for them, and would not draw it if they could; at least, so long as they were assured that they would discharge their own liabilities.

The provision made for the conversion of the liabilities of the other Bank — that is, of the Banking Department, which is equally with the former a Bank of issue, and whose issues and liabilities are, equally with notes, payable on demand in coin — is a small amount of coin, and the notes of the Issue Department which it may happen to hold. The Banking Department, of course, always holds securities exceeding its liabilities; but these are not coin, nor are they immediately convertible into coin. Its issues have no other support than that described. They are not legal tender, nor are they receivable in the payment of the revenues. It would naturally be supposed, that, if something like the present system were to be established — that is, if the Bank were to be divided, as at present, into two departments, — the amount of coin that would be transferred to that of issue would be only so much as would be required to meet the demands liable to be made upon it: the balance, whatever it might be, which would always be the greater portion of what the Bank might hold, would be allotted to the Banking Department, as the one chiefly concerned in production and trade, and upon which rest the whole commercial and financial interests of the kingdom. This is an obvious mode of reasoning; but reason had no more to do with the matter of the present organization of the Bank than it has with the shape or color of an amulet which is to serve as a fetish to shield one from harm.

The passage of the Act of 1844 exerted no apparent influence at the time; for, so long as there was no considerable

demand for money, it was immaterial in which till of the Bank
its notes lay, or what proportion of them was in the hands of
the public. So long as the condition of production and trade
existing at the time of the reorganization remained unchanged,
the Act was a dead letter. At that very time, however, causes
were at work that were soon to put it to the test. The mania
for the construction of railways, which culminated in 1847,
had already gained no little strength. Up to the 17th of
November, 1845, the amount already expended upon the completed railways in the United Kingdom equalled £70,680,877 ;
that expended, or to be expended, upon those in process of
construction, £67,317,325. The amount which the companies
chartered up to January 1, 1849, were entitled to raise upon
share capital and debentures, equalled £320,000,000, as
follows :—

Years.	Acts.		Years.	Acts.	
1801 to 1840	299	£69,000,000	1846	270	£120,000,000
1841 to 1844	113	18,000,000	1847	184	35,000,000
1845	120	59,000,000	1848	83	19,000,000

The total amount called up in 1847 by the railway schemes
put upon the London market, including foreign railways,
equalled the enormous sum of £47,000,000, or more than
£800,000 weekly. During the same year, the greatest fluctuation in the amount of bank-notes in circulation equalled only
about £1,500,000. The monetary transactions having reference to railways were carried on almost wholly by means of
checks drawn against deposits ; the notes of the Bank, as well
as country Banks, being hardly a makeweight in the general
mass. The enormous amount expended on account of these
works, in 1846 and 1847, would have produced a financial
crisis, even had the crops for those years been favorable. They
proved very unfavorable. The Irish potato crop, which began
to fail in 1845, was almost wholly cut off in 1846 and 1847.
Large importations of food had to be made, requiring the
exportation of considerable amounts of gold, but not sufficient
to seriously affect the money market, or the ability of the
Bank, as the great monetary institution of the kingdom, to
lend. It was the immense investments in railways, many of
which proved unproductive, and the consequent stimulus given
to all branches of production and trade, and which affected
every class and every interest in the kingdom, that caused, by

a necessary recoil, the panic of 1847. It would have occurred, only perhaps a little later, even if the crops had not been unfavorable ; and with almost equal severity, had not the Bank of England aided it to the extent of a single penny. The Bank undoubtedly contributed something, but by no means in the ratio that its capital bore to that of the other Banks and bankers of the kingdom. Its means, during the whole period under discussion, were in great measure employed in the methods and according to the precedents of the past ; so that only a comparatively small fraction of them found its way into railways, or into other speculative schemes, which, for a time, so engrossed the attention and absorbed the means of the nation.

The enormous amount of deposits of the Bank in 1846 was full proof of the magnitude of the financial operations of that year. Their excessive reduction showed the severity of the contraction which followed. Their amount, at the reorganization of the Bank, on the 7th of September, 1844, equalled £12,274,000 ; their average for 1845 equalled £17,300,000 ; for 1846, £21,500,000. For the first three quarters of that year, their average equalled £23,100,000. The average amount held in 1847 equalled £14,750,000. The amount of notes in circulation on the 7th of September, 1844, equalled £20,176,270. In 1845, the average was £21,000,000 ; in 1846, £20,300,000 ; and in 1847, £20,000,000. The drain upon the Bank, chiefly by its depositors, began in the latter part of 1846 ; reducing the amount of deposits in February, 1847, to £14,600,000. The drain, which had to be met by the notes in the Banking Department, reduced these, on the 1st of January, 1847, to £6,500,000, and on the 3d of July, 1847, to £5,015,000. From that time it steadily continued till the 23d of October, 1847, when the notes in the Banking Department were reduced to £1,540,000 ; its deposits at that time standing at £13,500,000 ; its specie, at £7,860,000 ; and its notes in circulation, at £20,860,000. It was evident that the Bank could not go on much longer ; and, on the 23d of October, a deputation of London bankers waited upon the government to represent the position of affairs, and the consequences that must result from the inability of the Bank to make further loans. On Monday following, October 27th, Lord John Russell, then Chancellor of the Exchequer, addressed a communication to the Directors,

informing them, that, should they deem it necessary to exceed
in their issues the limit prescribed by the Act of 1844, the
government, upon the assembling of Parliament, would apply
to it for an Act of Indemnity. The communication suggested
that such advances as might be made by notes issued in excess
of the provisions of the Act, should be at a rate of interest not
less than 8 per cent. The communication was no sooner made
public than confidence was instantly restored. The notes
which had been hoarded were at once brought into use, and
discounts were everywhere attainable. So instant and complete was the relief, that the Bank was not compelled to avail
itself of the authority to increase its circulation.[1]

The crisis past, Parliament was speedily called together;
for, although the Act of 1844 was not violated, the authority
to do so had been given, and must be condoned. Upon its
assembling, the Chancellor of the Exchequer moved for the
Committee usually appointed in such cases "to inquire into
the causes of the recent commercial distress, and how far it
had been affected by the Act of 1844." In the course of his
remarks, after describing the progress of the panic, which he
largely ascribed to the failure of the Bank in not taking earlier
measures for its arrest, he said: —

"The Bank of England were pressed directly for assistance from
all parts of the country, and indirectly through the London bankers,
who were called upon to support their country correspondents.
The country Banks required a large amount of notes, to render

---

[1] When the Bank, in 1847, was compelled to invoke the aid of government,
it had £7,860,000 of coin in its vaults. Of this sum, only £440,000 were in the
Banking Department. That department had at the same time only £1,540,000
in notes, making a total of £1,980,000 wherewith to carry forward the operations of an empire. This is the only available sum it had for the discharge of
£13,500,000 of deposits, and to provide the means for the loans it was called upon
to make. When the panic was at its height, over £7,000,000 coin were unavailable in its vaults. The average amount of the note circulation for 1847 equalled
£20,000,000. The amount in circulation, October 25th, 1847, when an increase of
its notes was authorized, equalled £20,860,000, — a sum considerably larger than
the average for the year. The panic had no tendency to reduce the amount of
the circulation. It resulted, so far as the Bank was concerned, not in any want
of confidence in it, or in the solvency of its notes, only from fear that a sufficient
amount of these could not be had. The moment such fear was allayed, the
demand for them instantly ceased. If it were proper to quiet this alarm by enlarging the authority of the Bank, why not invest it permanently with such
power, instead of compelling it to throw itself upon the government whenever a
crisis arises?

them secure against possible demands, not so much for payment of their notes as of their deposits.   Houses in London were applying constantly to the Bank for aid.   Two bill-brokers had stopped, and the operations of two others were nearly paralyzed.   The whole demand for discount was thrown upon the hands of the Bank of England.   Notwithstanding this, as I before said, the Bank never refused a bill which it would have discounted at another time ; but still the large mass of bills which, under ordinary circumstances, are discounted by bill-brokers, could not be negotiated.   During that period, we were daily — I may say hourly — in possession of the state of the Bank.   The Governor and Deputy-Governor at last said they could no longer continue their advances to support the various people who applied to them ; that they could save themselves, — that is, they could comply with the law ; but that they could not do so without pressing more stringently on the commercial world.   At this crisis, a feeling as to the necessity of the interposition of government appeared to be generally entertained ; and those conversant with commercial affairs, and least likely to decide in favor of the course we ultimately adopted, unanimously expressed an opinion that, if some measure were not taken by the government to arrest the evil, the most disastrous consequences must inevitably ensue.   Evidence was laid before the government which proved, not only the existence of severe pressure from the causes I have stated, but also that it was aggravated in a very great degree by the hoarding, on the part of many persons, of gold and bank-notes, to a very large extent ; in consequence of which an amount of circulation which, under ordinary circumstances, would have been adequate, became insufficient for the wants of the community.   It was difficult to establish this beforehand, but the best proof of the fact is in what occurred after we interfered.   As soon as the letter of the 12th October appeared, and the panic ceased, thousands and tens of thousands of pounds were taken from the hoards, — some from boxes deposited with bankers, although the parties would not leave the notes in their banker's hands.   Large parcels of notes were returned to the Bank of England cut into halves, as they had been sent down into the country ; and so small was the real demand for an additional quantity of notes, that the whole amount taken from the Bank, when the unlimited power of issue was given, was under £400,000.   The restoration of confidence released notes from their hoards ; and no more was wanted, for this trifling quantity of additional notes is hardly worth notice. . . . Parties of every description made application for assistance to us, with the observation, ' We do not want notes ; but give us confidence.'   They said ' We have notes enough ; but we have not confidence to use them.   Say you will stand by us, and we shall have all that we want ; do every thing, in short, that will give us confidence.   If you think that we can get bank-notes, we shall not want them.   Charge any rate of interest you please ; ask what you like.' " — (Mr. Spooner, " No, no ! ") — " I beg pardon of the honorable gentleman ; but I may be permitted to know what was actually said to me.   I say, that what I have stated was the tenor of the applications made to me.   Parties said to me, 'Let us have notes, charge 10 to 12 per cent for them ; we don't care what the rate of interest is. We don't mean, indeed, to take the notes ; because we shall not want them. Only tell us that we can get them, and this will at once restore confidence.' We have been asked what was the change of circumstances which induced us to act on Saturday, when we declined acting a day or two before. I reply, that the accounts which we received on Thursday, Friday, and Saturday, were of a totally different description from those which had been previously brought us. It was on Saturday, and not before, that this conviction was forced upon us ; and it was not till then that we felt it necessary to sanction a violation of the law."

Sir Robert Peel followed, in a more apologetic strain. As the responsible author of the Act of 1844, he was not a little chagrined at the result. It was unfair, he said, that he should be singled out as the great object of attack. The Act was not his own, but of Parliament. It had been alleged that it had been passed without due consideration ; but the subject was one upon which Committees had sat for five years, and during their investigations had asked more than 14,000 questions, and received more than 14,000 answers. As nothing practical had come of them all, the government determined to pass some measure upon its own responsibility. If the one adopted were inadequate to its objects, he was ready to accept any provision necessary to render it so.

" There has," said Sir Robert, " been some misrepresentation respecting the object of this Act. I do not deny that one of the objects contemplated by the Act was the prevention of the convulsions that had heretofore occurred in consequence of the neglect by the Bank of England to take early precautions against the withdrawal of its treasure. I did hope that, although there was no imperative obligation on the Bank of England to take these precautions, that the experience of 1825, 1836, and 1837, would have induced that establishment to conform to principles which the Directors of the Bank acknowledged to be just, and which they had more than once professed to adopt for their own regulation. Sir, I am bound to say that in that hope, that in that object of the bill, I have been disappointed. I am bound to admit, seeing the extent of commercial depression which has prevailed, and the number of houses which have been swept away, — some of which, however, I think, were insolvent long before the bill came into operation, and others of which became insolvent in consequence of the failure of those who were connected with them and were imprudent in their speculations, — I am bound to admit, that that purpose of the bill of 1844, which sought to impress, if not a legal, at least a moral obligation on the Bank, to prevent the necessity for measures of extreme stringency by timely precautions, has not been fulfilled. Sir, I must contend, that it was in the power of the Bank, if not to prevent all the evils that have arisen, at least greatly to diminish their force. If the Bank had possessed the resolution to meet the coming danger by a contraction of its issues, by raising the rate of discount, by refusing much of the accommodation which they granted between the years 1844 and 1846; if they had been firm and determined in the adoption of these precautions, — the necessity for extrinsic interference might have been prevented; it might not then have been necessary for the government to authorize a violation of the Act of 1844. . . . The bill of 1844 had a triple object. Its first object was that in which I admit it has failed; namely, to prevent, by early and gradual, severe and sudden contraction, and the panic and confusion inseparable from it. But the bill had, at least, two other objects, of at least equal importance : the one to maintain and guarantee the convertibility of the paper currency into gold; the other to prevent the difficulties which arise at all times from undue speculation being aggravated by the abuse of paper credit in the form of promissory notes. In these two objects, my belief is that the bill has completely succeeded; my belief is, that you have had a guarantee for the maintenance of the principle of convertibility, such as you never had before; my belief also is, that, whatever difficulties you are now suffering, from a combination of various causes, those difficulties would have been greatly aggravated if you had not wisely taken the precaution of checking the unlimited issues of the notes of the Bank of England, of joint-stock Banks, and private Banks."

Whenever there is an eccentric movement or disturbance in the money market, the Bank always comes in for censure. It is always made the universal scape-goat. After such crises as those of 1847, 1857, and 1866, the censure is unmeasured. " The Bank should not have reissued its notes; " "it should long ago have refused to make any further loans; " "it should have contracted the circulation by the sale of its securities." The Bank can do nothing, nor does it attempt to do any thing, of the kind. It is the regular issuer and manager of the currency, and must issue it to every one who comes within rules established, not in periods of panics, but when the supply of money may have exceeded the demand. The public, not itself, is the judge of the amount of circulation required. It met all applications in 1847, 1857, and 1866; it can adopt no other rule. It says, to the government, in effect: " As we are to supply the circulation, we shall do so as long as we have a note in our till; you have provided the mode in which it is to be issued. When our notes are exhausted, you are to make

further provision, or assume responsibility for the consequences." Such is the construction which has always been
put upon the Act, both by the government and by the Bank;
and this is the only logical one. If the currency is to be provided by legislation, such legislation must in some form be
adequate to its objects. The mint must turn into coin all the
bullion offered to it. The Bank in the same way must turn
into notes all the securities of the proper kind offered to it.
There is no more discretion in one case than in the other. The
operations of society are not to be blocked by any such folly
as that of 1844. When these are imperilled, the Act is but a
straw in the current of a Niagara. Its suspension, which is a
matter of necessity, is universally acquiesced in. No act, however, can be more revolutionary than for a government to
arrest the operation of a law, and still continue it in full force
on the statute-book. Such is the respect for order in England
that such precedents are little to be feared. For the most commercial and one of the most .intelligent people in the world,
however, to make a public confession of their inability to deal
with such a matter as the Bank, but by declaring it, when a
crisis arises, to be absolved from the observance of its organic
rule or law, implies an ignorance or an impotence certainly not
very flattering to their national pride.

Sir Robert Peel frankly admitted the Act of 1844 to be no
safeguard against commercial or monetary disturbance. So
far it was an entire failure. It was, however, he claimed, successful in guaranteeing the convertibility of the notes of the
Bank into coin, and in preventing an aggravation of the panic
by their excessive issue. As it was not the coin in the Bank
which maintained its notes at par, — such coin at one time
equalling only about one-third their amount, — but the other
provisions in their favor which have already been described,
Sir Robert was reduced to one advantage only as resulting
from the Act. As, however, deposits exert precisely the same
influence as notes, in causing lavish expenditures and inflation
of prices, which must always end in a panic greater or less in
severity, it is not easy to see that any thing was gained by
restricting the issue of notes, when deposits, which can always
be created in unlimited amounts by Banks and bankers and
their customers, were certain to take their place. He might

with equal propriety have congratulated the good fortune of a man, who, having become thoroughly intoxicated by the excessive use of brandy, of which he had a profuse supply, could not supplement his brandy by an excessive use of whiskey. Sir Robert's two advantages, therefore, have only to be very briefly analyzed to vanish in empty air.

The crisis of 1847 was no sooner past than the inevitable Committee or Committees — for in this case each House raised its own — was appointed "to consider the subject of the recent commercial distress." These Committees added some 10,000 more questions and answers to the 14,000 which had been put and received by previous ones, — all, or nearly all, upon the nature of paper money, and the constitution and conduct of the Bank. Lord Overstone, as usual, was the conspicuous figure.

Question 5126 (of the House Committee). "When the Act of 1844 was brought in, I think (said the Chairman) there was an impression, upon the minds of some parties at least, that the operation of the Act would tend to mitigate those convulsions when they came on, even supposing it was impossible that that Act, or any Act, could prevent them; there was an impression that they would be of a less sudden character than they were before; was that your expectation?" — "My expectation was, that the Act would mitigate that portion of commercial pressure, which was justly attributable to the mismanagement of the circulation; and the only point upon which any difficulty could exist was in determining what portion of the pressure of the different crises had really arisen from the mismanagement of the circulation, and what portion had arisen entirely from the ordinary excess of mercantile enterprise. I think the Act has completely realized all that was reasonably expected of it, and has verified every principle upon which it was established. I think that the pressure of 1847 would have been considerably more severe, postponed probably to rather a later period, but, when it came, much more severe, if there had been, in the early part of 1847, a power of mismanaging the circulation of the country; the Act of 1844, by preventing that power, brought on the pressure earlier, and by that means rendered the pressure much less severe than it would have been at a later period, and with the bullion reduced to a much lower amount."

Question 5127. "Will you allow me to call your attention to that part of the question which relates to the suddenness of the difficulties? I think there was an impression at the time of the passing of the Act, that, the withdrawing of the circulation being gradual, the pressure would be extended over a longer time, and that it would not be sudden, and the pinch would not be so great when it came. Do you think the Act has been effective in that respect, or that the circumstances under the Act have been such as you expected in regard to that?"—"The course of events under the Act has not been at all different from what I should have expected; it was anticipated that the Act would produce this effect, viz., that it would cause a gradual contraction of the circulation, and that, under ordinary circumstances, a certain portion of that contraction of the circulation would fall upon the notes in the hands of the public; at the same time, it was perfectly true that the contraction of the circulation might assume one of two forms,—either a contraction in the numerical amount of the notes in the hands of the public, or, in lieu of that, a contraction in the efficiency of the existing amount of notes; in which form the contraction, on any given occasion, will take place, will depend in some degree on accidental circumstances; it seems to me that two accidents occurred in the year 1847: the mismanagement of the banking business of the Bank in the spring of 1847, and the extraordinary extent of commercial failures in the autumn of 1847; had these two accidents not occurred, I apprehend that the course of things in 1847 would have been precisely identical with that which is intimated in the question; viz., that we should have had a considerable export of bullion, and a considerable contraction in the numerical amount of the notes in the hands of the public, followed by a high rate of interest, and that, probably, continuing for several months. That high rate of interest so continuing would have corrected the exchanges, and have gradually brought back the gold; that would, probably, have been the course of things under the pressure of 1847, barring the two accidents already alluded to."

This answer reminds one of Leech's illustration of the Irishman's boat: "And shure if yer honors sit parfectly still, and don't cough or snaze, she'll carry you all illigant." The passengers did cough and sneeze, and the crazy craft went to the bottom.

Committees of Parliament to consider grave questions, as they arise, have come to be institutions with Englishmen. Those appointed previous to and in 1848, to consider the subjects of currency and the Bank, were years in session, and asked and received some twenty-five thousand questions and answers; not one of which, it may safely be assumed, was asked or answered with any appreciation whatever of the laws or principles of paper money, except such answers as were made, in 1810, by the Directors of the Bank, in their examination before the Bullion Committee.[1] It could not be otherwise.

[1] The answers to the Bullion Committee of the Directors of the Bank, which maintained its loans to be properly made so long as it discounted bills having sixty days to run, and representing real transactions in merchandise, were at the

With that single exception, all the questions and answers assumed the correctness of the dogmas of Adam Smith, each one of which was wholly without adequate foundation.   With such premise it was inevitable that, the greater the number of questions asked and answered, the more involved in confusion and error the subject became.   Their almost infinite number, when half a dozen, properly put and answered, would have made the whole matter palpable to the meanest understanding, is of itself full proof of the utter ignorance and chaos of opinion which prevailed.   When truth is discovered, opinions are in accord.   When it is not, individuality asserts itself, and there are as many theories and explanations as there are parties to give them.

Englishmen assume themselves to be the especial champions of freedom of trade.   This is based upon the idea that individuals know better than governments the methods and conditions necessary to their own welfare, and that individual welfare makes up that of society.   If one in that country embark in any industrial enterprise, government does not prefer its advice as to its nature and management.   If a ship be to be built, it does not insist upon the model.   If a bill of exchange be offered for sale, it does not interpose in order that the purchaser may get an equivalent for his money.   In all such matters it adopts, to the fullest extent, the *laissez faire* policy.   But, when a person wishes to exchange his own obligation for the notes of the Bank, it then steps in to provide the conditions upon which the exchange shall be made.   Why should not the same freedom be allowed in one case as in the other?   Why should not the holder of a bill and the Bank enter into any agreement for the exchange of their obligations in whatever form they please?   It is not a question of morals, but of affairs.   Why should not the Bank determine the proper limit of issue of notes, as the public does the amount of commercial bills proper to be drawn?   The answer is, that the issue of paper money is really a function of the government, which, when usurped by

ime, and have ever since been, received with derisive jeers. Mr. Bagehot, in aying "that their answers made nonsense classical;" and that "very few persons could have managed to commit so many blunders in so few words," expresses the general contempt felt for the answers, as well as for their authors. — ,ombard Street, pp. 175, 176.

individuals, is to be tolerated only from necessity, not encouraged. But a note of the Bank does not differ in its nature from, nor has it inherently any higher dignity than, a note or a bill given for a sheep or a cow. The right to issue notes to serve as money was a right at common law previous to the Act of 1844. Are not the Bank and the public competent to decide what is for the advantage of each? If the holder of a bill wish it converted into money, why not allow this to be done in whatever manner suits his convenience or that of the issuer? A currency, to be adequate to its objects, should symbolize all merchandise entering into consumption. If the right to issue notes be unrestricted, the nation, it is urged, will be flooded with them, and the most terrible disasters will be the result. But if notes be not allowed, the money created in other forms will equal the notes which, but for the restriction, would have been issued, and produce precisely the same consequences. But would a perfect freedom in the issue of either form of money be likely to produce the disasters predicted? For every issue of notes or credits it makes, the Bank undertakes to pay out, and, if it make an improper issue, must pay out, an equal amount of coin. It will, therefore, be under no more inducement to spread its notes broadcast than coin, or its liabilities in other forms in the creation of which it is wholly unrestricted. How, then, is an excessive issue of notes to be got into circulation? The Bank will not knowingly fool away its capital. Every borrower, also, undertakes to pay coin, or its equivalent, for the notes and credits issued to him; so that he will take good care to receive no notes that are not of equal value to that which he contracts to pay. Both Bank and borrower are constantly on their guard; neither will incur a liability without receiving an equivalent; and, so long as equivalents are exchanged, no harm can come therefrom, but great good, as the welfare of society depends upon the freedom with which its exchanges are made. The theory, therefore, upon which the Act of 1844 proceeds, is that mankind, that the holders of capital, are not to be trusted with its management; that they are imbeciles, not to be freed from the leading-strings of government. Such is the monstrous conclusion to which the Act necessarily leads.

Among the witnesses examined before the Committee o

1848 were the Governor and Deputy-Governor of the Bank. These were, at last, the loudest in praise of the virtues of the Act of 1844; the object of which, they said, repeating the words of Lord Overstone, "was to place the circulation of the country exactly in the position that it would have been had it been purely metallic." They declared "that, with regard both to the contraction and expansion of the currency, they would both have taken place under the Act precisely in the same mode, and to the same degree had the currency been purely metallic." They had learned their lesson well. They had had enough of parliamentary and financial Petruchios; and were only too happy to purchase quiet, and exemption from further interference, by declaring the same object to be white or black, according to the caprice of their imperious masters. They even volunteered to reproach themselves for their conduct in not arresting the course of the panic, by raising the rate of interest in the spring of 1847. They claimed, however, that the action of the government in setting aside the Act of 1844 was not solicited, and that it was not necessary to the solvency of the Bank, although it was of great use in quieting the panic; which would, probably, have occurred had the Act never been passed. Its severity was greatly mitigated by the action of the government. The great merit claimed by them for the Act was, that when the pressure did come, it left the Bank in the possession of £8,000,000 of coin and bullion, which those who were entitled to draw it did not want, and which those to whom the Bank was indebted to a much greater amount did want, and could not reach. If one-half this sum could have been transferred from the branch in which it was lying wholly useless to the one which was rapidly becoming exhausted of its means, the panic might have been averted without the action of the government, and long before its interference. The timely transfer of such a sum would have saved the nation ten times its amount. The generalship of the Act is that of a commander who fights the battle with only one-half the forces he has in hand, and suffers in consequence, disastrous defeat, although complete victory would have been assured had he brought the other half into the field. There was all the time an abundance of money; but for fear that the issues of the future might be greatly restricted, every one holding a note or a guinea hoarded it against a wet day. The consequence was that business men, who had been quietly occupied with their affairs, suddenly woke up to the conviction that the ordinary instruments of exchange might, in a short time, be wholly refused them. It was as if the air necessary to sustain life were to be so reduced in amount as to suffice for only one-tenth the number accustomed to breathe it. Hence the frantic struggle which followed: it was a struggle for dear life. As soon as it was seen that there was to be enough for all, apprehension instantly subsided: affairs at once relapsed into their accustomed routine. Is it wise, every ten years, to put the nation into such an extremity by allowing an institution, upon whose operations the affairs of a world, as it were, turn, to create enormous liabilities, at the same time denying to it all means for their payment?

The Governor and Deputy-Governor, in the conclusion of their evidence, prayed that government would make no alteration in the Act, save perhaps to allow a larger issue of notes upon silver bullion.

The Act of 1844 has been dwelt upon at length, for the reason that it afforded a suitable opportunity for illustrating the principles laid down in the first part of this work, and the opinions prevailing in England, as well as in this country, upon the subject of money; for opinions on this only echo those on the other side of the water. From the vast mass of works on the subject, it is possible only to present the arguments and views of the leading authorities. The literature of money and banking, probably, exceeds in extent that upon any other subject whatever. It is all the same in kind; so that when the theories of a representative writer are presented, those of all others are matters of easy inference. The science of money, as laid down in the books, bears the same relation to the subject itself that Alchemy did to chemistry. Having once demonstrated that gold cannot be produced by any mixture of the baser metals, it is useless to spend time in proving that it cannot after the method of Geber or of Raymond Lulli. To refute each one of the Alchemists who claimed such power, a life-time would not suffice. So a refutation of Adam Smith may be properly accepted as a refutation of all his followers. So with the Bank. Lord Overstone, the real author of the Act of 1844, was to it what Adam Smith was to

Political Economy: the greater includes the less. All the writers upon the Bank since Lord Overstone's Essays, in 1837, have simply repeated one far greater, in statement at least, than themselves. The lesser lights, therefore, need not be dwelt upon. To do this would swell into a dozen volumes what is intended to be embraced in one. The curious may, if they will, enter the boundless field; from which they will be likely to return, if ever, far less wise than when they started upon their perilous and weary way. What the public require is an outline which shall be measurably brief, and still shall present all that is really necessary to be known.[1]

A prominent figure before the Committees of Parliament, upon the subject of money and the Bank, as well as a great authority with modern Economists, was Mr. Thomas Tooke, who dedicated a life-time to the work of proving that a rise in prices always precedes, and causes an increase of money, in whatever form; in other words, that a rise of water in rivers always precedes and is the cause of rainfall. The following are among the questions put to him by the House Committee of 1840. The *Italics* are his own: —

Question 3292, by *Mr. Hume.* "Will you state what part of the currency or circulating medium affects prices, under the definitions which you have now given?" — "No one part of them affects the prices of commodities more than any of the other parts."
Question 3293, by *Mr. Grote.* "Do you mean, not more in degree, or not in any different way?" — "Not more in degree."
Question 3295, by *Mr. Hume.* "Do you mean, that every transaction of purchase or sale, by any of the means which you have mentioned as included in the circulating medium, equally affects prices?" — "Yes, and that was my reason for caring so little about making a distinction among them. I doubt whether they operate upon prices at all."
Question 3296, by *Mr. Grote.* "You mean, that none of those items which you have enumerated under the general term 'circulating medium' have, in your opinion, any effect upon prices?" — "Yes. I mean that they are not operative causes of prices."
Question 3297, by *Mr. Hume.* "What is it, then, which does

---

[1] The crises, similar to those of 1847, which the Bank went through in 1857 and 1866, are not referred to here, for the reason that an examination of them would add nothing to our knowledge of the laws of money. That of 1847 has been dwelt upon chiefly for the purpose of illustrating the principles laid down in the first part of this work. Any further illustration of them, by reference to the operations of the Bank, would be in great measure superfluous.

affect prices?" — "*The cost of production limiting the supply on
the one hand, and the pecuniary means of the consumer limiting
the demand on the other.*"

Question 3298. "Will not the variations in the quantity of the
circulating medium affect prices?" — "No."

Question 3299. "Will it not, if abundant, be more at the disposal
of individuals for purchasers than when it is scarce?" — "It will
be more easily disposable; but it will not be necessarily so disposed
of. *I believe that the amount of the circulating medium is the effect,
and not the cause, of variations in prices.*"

Question 3301, by *Mr. Warburton.* "Supposing the quantity of
the precious metals in the world to remain constant, and that in
any country you go on increasing the quantity of the notes payable
on demand, will the prices of commodities estimated in those notes
undergo a variation proportionate to the increase of the notes?" —
"*Not if the notes are payable in gold, on demand,* unless in the
degree in which it may be supposed that the value of gold is
affected in the commercial world by an extensive substitution of
paper for gold: I consider that those points were distinctly understood as the only conditions by which the money prices of commodities were likely to be affected, independently of the circumstances
affecting the articles themselves."

Question 3303. "Suppose, as before, the quantity of precious
metals in the world to remain constant, and that the number of
deposits in banker's hands available to the purchase and sale of
commodities is doubled, trebled, and so on, will the prices of commodities vary in proportion to that increase of deposits in banker's
hands?" — "*Not in the slightest degree.*" [1]

The following extracts from Mr. James Wilson's "Essay on
Capital, Currency, and Banking," are quoted by Mr. Tooke
approvingly, as fully expressing his own views: —

"The assumption before us involves two questions: first, expansion and contraction of the currency at pleasure; and, second, as
the consequence, a corresponding action on prices. Many authors,
in treating of the latter as a consequence, and even combating its
truth, have labored under great difficulties, by proceeding upon the
admission of the former; but, if the former be admitted, we confess we cannot understand how the latter can be denied as the
legitimate consequence. If, in the language of Mr. Horner, there be
any means by which 'the quantity of circulating medium (being
convertible paper and coin) can be permanently augmented, without
a corresponding augmentation of internal trade, a rise will unavoid-
ably take place in the price of exchangeable commodities.' Such
means, as we have already seen, do exist in the case of an inconvertible currency; but the rise in price in consequence is only
nominal in that case, being immediately compensated to other

[1] History of Prices, vol. iv. p. 461 *et seq.*

countries by a fall in the exchange. But with a convertible currency, *if such means exist at all*, the rise in price would not be nominal, but real; as it would be expressed either in coin, or notes convertible into coin, and, therefore, would not, as in the other case, be compensated by any fall in the exchange. But this fact shows at once the impossibility of the '*augmentation*' alluded to in the premises, when the currency is *convertible*. A currency ' augmented without any corresponding augmentation of the internal trade,' implies a quantity of notes retained in circulation, at the will of the issuers, which the public do not require. Now, the public do not receive notes from a banker without paying interest for their use; and, however low that may be, they will take no more than they absolutely require; nor do they retain notes in their possession beyond what the convenience of trade requires; and, therefore, if issued in excess of that quantity, and if convertible, a portion would be instantly returned upon the issuers. Nor can we conceive any means whatever by which the circulation could be so augmented; and we have deeply to regret that, although such a power on the part of Banks has been taken for granted by most of the writers during the last twelve years, no one has yet attempted to explain by what process it could be accomplished; and we are compelled to think that impressions which gained ground many years since as applicable to an inconvertible currency have been inadvertently associated also with a convertible currency.

" The impossibility of increasing the quantity of paper in circulation (when convertible), except as the effect of a corresponding increase of an internal trade, or of any depreciation in its value taking place, will be more evident when it is considered by what process an inconvertible currency becomes depreciated. On all hands it is admitted, that, as long as inconvertible paper is not issued in excess, as long as coin continues freely to circulate with it, the paper will not become depreciated; but as soon as the paper is issued in excess, and the coin is pressed out of circulation, it becomes depreciated, and the prices of commodities rise in consequence; though it is only a nominal rise, which would be better expressed by depreciation of the circulation. Now, how does this depreciation and rise of price take place? During the early issue of the French assignats, no depreciation or rise in price of commodities took place until the coin was pressed out of circulation; because, as the paper was issued, the tendency to a redundant currency was constantly corrected by the withdrawal of silver, which, being a commodity having a general value in the markets of the world, could be exported or taken for the general uses of the cambist or the silversmith. But as soon as silver was exhausted from the circulation, the issue of assignats still continuing, and the same quantity of internal exchanges only remaining, the currency became redundant; there being no means of absorption except in the existing quantities of commodities.[1]

" Money " (says Tooke, on a preceding page) "has two functions: the one, that of serving as an instrument of exchange; the other,

---

[1] History of Prices, vol. iv. pp. 194–196.

that of being the subject of contracts for future payment. It is in the latter capacity that the fixity of a standard is the most essential. As a mere instrument or medium of exchange,' at the same time and in the same place, invariableness of value, though desirable, is not of so much importance; the immediate purpose of money in this capacity being to serve as a point, or rather a scale, of comparison more convenient than actual barter between any two commodities or sets of commodities. It is in the latter capacity, that is to say, as the subject of engagements or obligations for future payment, that, in every view of justice and policy, the specific thing promised, in quantity and quality, should be paid at the expiration of the term." [1]

The sum of all this is, that convertible paper money cannot affect prices under any conditions. So far Tooke simply follows Adam Smith, that "the amount of paper money of every kind that can circulate in a nation can only equal the amount of coin which would otherwise have been in circulation. All excess of issue would immediately return upon the Bank for coin. As its holders can make no use of such excess, they will immediately convert it into a form in which, by its exportation, they can use it." Such was Tooke's argument. If there could be no excess, then a convertible paper money could not affect prices. Neither could a government inconvertible paper currency affect prices, so long as it was not in excess of the wants of those using it in their exchanges. It became depreciated only for the reason that it was in excess of a currency of coin. Value was no necessary attribute of it. It might be a convenient attribute: that is, if a person parted with merchandise, to be paid for in six months, it would be well that that in which he was to be paid should have a uniform value; but where the transaction was to be immediately closed, that is, where a person sold a barrel of flour for the purpose of purchasing with the proceeds a hat or a coat, the value of the medium to such person, says Tooke, would be unimportant. But would it be unimportant to the seller of the coat or hat? He might wish to hold the proceeds in reserve for future use; or suppose he wished immediately to purchase something, must he not be prepared to offer that which could be held in reserve for any length of time, its value remaining unchanged. Whatever is to serve as money, in the last resort, must always possess uniformity of value, not only for months and years, but for ages.

[1] History of Prices, vol. iv. pp. 145-146.

The fallacy of Tooke's distinction ought to be palpable to the dullest apprehension. Yet he drags the reader through six volumes, one of them containing nearly a thousand pages, — the greater portion of them all devoted to the task of proving this, and propositions, if possible still more absurd. So with prices: these with him depend upon cost, and the ability, not the will, of the public to consume. The public are able to consume a thousand things they will not. At one time they will not purchase a particular style of goods, which is all the rage at another, although it would be twice as valuable, as far as its wear is concerned, as that which they will purchase. Had Tooke understood the laws and effects of paper money, he would have seen that it is possible for prices to fall enormously, even when it is greatly inflated. The effect of an inflation is to advance prices, from an increase of the instruments of expenditure, and from its tendency to excite speculation, which may be carried to such a pitch as to seize and attempt to hold all the food, for example, upon the market. In such case, it not unfrequently happens that the public can be supplied from other sources, or that, from the excessive rates charged by holders, consumption will be so much reduced that those who attempted to control prices find themselves unable to carry their purchases, and are forced to throw them upon the market; in consequence of which, prices may for a time be far below what they would have been under a metallic currency. Such fluctuations, which are constantly occurring, or were occurring during the suspension of the Bank, — a period from which he drew the greater part of his illustrations, — have been assumed by Mr. Tooke to prove prices to be wholly independent of the quantity of the circulating medium. He might as well have attempted to prove that indulgence in liquor had no tendency to elevate one, from the exhaustion or syncope resulting from its excessive use. So, under an inflation of the currency, prices may fall in much greater ratio than the inflation, from the decreased cost of production, or from the falling off, from any cause, of the demand. None of these causes or influences were properly considered by him. He sought to erect a science from an observation of certain phenomena, without sufficient reference to their cause or law. It is as useless, however, to attempt to reason with him as it was with the philosopher in the tale of " Rasselas." It was, probably, from

an examination or an attempted examination of his works, that
Mr. Gladstone declared the study of money to be a fruitful
cause of insanity.

An authority far greater than Tooke, and whose works may,
indeed, be said to epitomize all that is known or held at the
present time upon this subject, is Mr. J. R. McCulloch, late
Professor of Political Economy in the University of London,
author of the "Cyclopædia of Commerce," of a "Statistical
Account of the British Empire," of the "Principles of Political Economy," and of numerous other works on kindred subjects. He also edited the works of his great master, Adam
Smith, to which he added elaborate notes of his own; the
works of Lord Overstone, of David Ricardo, and of other
lesser lights of the modern school. No one in his particular
province ever covered so broad a field; no one was ever so
familiar with the Economists; and no one ever so completely
epitomized their speculations and views. He was, among
them, eminently *omnium hominum facile princeps.* Fully
accepting the doctrines of Smith, and the wide distinction
which he made between the qualities of the precious metals
which fit them for money and those which determine their
value in exchange, he proceeds to consider the laws by which
their value is determined when their movement is perfectly free;
and those by which they are affected when artificial restraint
is imposed upon it: —

"It appears that when gold and silver are produced under a system of free competition, their value depends, like that of all other
commodities, on the cost of their production. While they form the
currency of the commercial world, the price of commodities, or
their value estimated in money, will consequently vary not only
according to the variation in the cost, demand, and supply of commodities, but also according to the variations in the cost of the gold
and silver with which they are compared. . . .

"We now come to the second branch of our inquiry, or that
which has for its object to discover the laws which regulate the
value of gold and silver, when the power to supply them is placed
under a restraint. It is obvious, supposing competition were not
allowed to operate in the production of the precious metals, that
their value would no longer depend on the principles previously
laid down. Whenever the supply of money is limited, its value
varies in inverse ratio to its quantity as compared with the quantity
of commodities brought to market, or with the business it has to
perform. If, on one hand, double the usual supply of commodities

were brought to market with a limited currency, their money price
would be reduced a half; and if, on the other hand, only half the
usual supply of commodities were brought to market, their price
would be doubled; and this, whether the cost of their production
was increased or diminished. Sovereigns, shillings, livres, dollars, &c., would then really constitute mere tickets or counters, to
be used in computing the value of property, and in transferring it
from one individual to another. And, as small tickets or counters
would serve for that purpose quite as well as large ones, it is unquestionably true that a debased currency may, by first reducing,
and then limiting its quantity, be made to circulate at the value it
would bear were the power to supply it unrestricted, and were it of
the legal weight and fineness; and, by still further limiting its quantity, it may be made to pass at any higher value. It appears, therefore, that whatever be the matter of which money is made, and
however destitute of intrinsic value, it is yet possible, by sufficiently limiting its quantity, to raise its value to any conceivable
extent. . . . Assume the currency of Great Britain to consist of
fifty or sixty millions of sovereigns; suppose now that government
withdraws them, and supplies their place with fifty or sixty millions
of half sovereigns, and that the issue of additional coins and of
paper money is effectually prevented; in this case it is plain,
should the same quantity of commodities be brought to market,
there would be the same number of coins to exchange against them.
There would not, therefore, unless the supply of commodities
varied, be any change in their price. The hat that had previously
sold for a gold coin would still sell for one. It ·is true that the
coin for which it now sells is only half the intrinsic value of the
one previously in circulation; but this deficiency has been fully
compensated by the artificial value given to it by the monopoly.
The country has a certain number of exchanges to perform; and it
is quite obvious, that, were the currency which is to perform them
sufficiently limited, a shilling or a sixpence might be made to do
the business, or to pass at the value of a sovereign.

"These are principles of the greatest importance to a right
understanding of the real nature of money. In inquiring into the
circumstances on which its value depends, we must always ascertain, in the first place, whether it be free or monopolized. Down
to a recent period, it was universally maintained that the value of
money depended entirely on the relation between its amount and
the demand. But this is true only of a gold and silver currency
when its quantity is limited; and of a currency formed of materials
having little intrinsic worth, when its quantity is limited, and it is not
convertible, at the pleasure of the holder, into some more valuable
commodity. It is obvious, indeed, without any reasoning on the
subject, that the value of a currency consisting of inconvertible
paper, or of any other very cheap material, must depend on the
proportion which its amount bears to the commodities brought to
market, or to the demand; and wherever a currency of this kind,
or a limited gold currency, is in circulation, the common opinion
that the price of commodities depends wholly on the proportion

between them and the supply of money is quite correct. But it is altogether different with a freely supplied currency consisting of gold and silver, or of any article possessed of considerable value. The fluctuations in the supply and demand of such currency have no permanent influence over its value. This is determined by the cost of its production. If a sovereign commonly exchange for a couple of bushels of wheat or a hat, it is because its production has cost as much as either of these commodities ; while, if with a limited and inconvertible paper money, the latter is exchanged for a one pound note, it is because such is the proportion which, as a part of the mass of commodities offered for sale, they bear to the supply of paper or money in the market. This proportion would, it is evident, be not only immediately, but permanently, affected by an increase or diminution of the supply of paper or of commodities ; but the relations which commodities bear to a freely supplied metallic currency cannot be changed, except by a change in the cost of producing the commodities. Such are the circumstances which determine the value of money, both when the power to supply it is not subjected to any species of control, and when it is controlled and limited. In the former case, its value depends, like that of most other things, on the cost of its production ; while, in the latter case, its value is totally unaffected by that circumstance, and depends on the extent to which it has been issued compared with the demand." [1]

Mr. McCulloch might as well have assumed a particular county of England to be fenced off by a wall so high that only a small amount of vital air could get into it ; and that, in such case, the right to breathe would sell at an enormous price ; and have inferred, therefrom, that, should the amount of money be limited, its price would rise in like ratio. One illustration is as pertinent, or rather as impertinent, as the other. Whoever gets gold, gets it to spend. There may be quarrels between those who dig and those who rule as to who shall enjoy the product ; but, whatever the result, it would immediately go into circulation. Such will be the law so long as mankind must be fed and clothed, or will waste its means in pageants and wars. In his " Political Economy " and other works his great theme always was the impossibility that government should control the movement of the precious metals, and consequently, the utter folly of attempting to do so. They obey a law far higher than that of human provision. His illustrations, however, are in keeping with those of the school to which he belonged, which is always assuming impossible instances as a

[1] Notes to Smith's Wealth of Nations, pp. 482, 483.

means of setting forth its conclusions and beliefs. It is the way of children, not the method of men of full stature. Neither the production nor possession of the precious metals can be monopolized. Their value everywhere, under all conditions (allowing for the influence of accidental circumstances), is measured by their cost. Every one can, at all times, possess himself of them to any extent, on the condition only of paying their price. No rule or law is more universally recognized than this ; yet, from conditions declared by Mr. McCulloch himself to be utterly impossible, he, with the Economists, deduces an inexorable law, — and attempts to prove that, if a sixpence could be cut into a sufficient number of pieces, it would suffice for the exchanges of the world, — not from its intrinsic value, for Mr. McCulloch assumes that this would not be affected by the restraint to be imposed upon it ; — and that, consequently, the most worthless thing serving as money might, by a similar restraint or limitation upon its quantity, be raised to the highest possible pitch of value.

All this is but the repetition of the argument of Lowndes at the period of recoinage in 1696 ; which Locke, at the request of the government, was at such pains to refute. Such repetition is all the more wonderful for the reason, that the experience of 1696 conveyed a lesson as conclusive as Locke's demonstration. All the conditions assumed by Mr. McCulloch and the Economists for raising debased money to any conceivable pitch of value, then met, from causes which far transcended human power. The proof, if ever to be made, was to be made then. For a time, the amount of coin in circulation, or currency of all kinds, equalled hardly a tithe of that required for the exchanges of the country. These, for a considerable period, had to be made by means of credit or barter. Yet the necessity which then existed for a " circulating medium " did not exert the slightest influence in raising the value of the debased coins. The value of each was measured by the cost of the metal that each contained. Had their value risen greatly above their cost, supplies would immediately have flowed in from other countries. If tickets or counters were all that were wanted, these could easily have been provided, as McCulloch suggests, by cutting the pieces in circulation into a sufficient number of parts. It was capital, not counters, that was wanted, and relief came only when that was supplied.

But even admitting that, by reducing the amount of metal in coins, their value might be maintained from the necessity of their use, there was still an important link wanting to connect his premise with his conclusion. Gold gets into circulation by means of its value. It circulates at its value. If its amount were permanently decreased, its value would increase. This is palpable enough; but how is that which is valueless in itself to get into the category of values? It is easy to see that the value of a handful of sand circulating as money would increase as its quantity was decreased. But how was it, in the first place, to get into circulation? From the necessity, says McCulloch, of some medium of exchange, and from the agreement of mankind that sand should be such medium. After what has preceded, it is useless to reply to such assumptions as these. They are the dreams or vagaries of persons bereft of all sense in reference to the subjects to which they relate, and who, unfortunately, are wholly impervious to reason.

Again: —

"In the first part of this note we endeavored to show, in the first place, that, when the power to supply money is not restricted, its value depends, like that of most other commodities, entirely on the cost of its production; and that, in the second place, or when the power to supply money is monopolized, its value does not depend on the cost of its production; but on the quantity in circulation compared with the demand. . . .

"It may be worth while, perhaps, to observe that neither the existence nor the want of confidence in the solvency of the issuers exercises the smallest influence over the value of paper money, properly so called. Notes not legal tender, and payable on demand, or at some stipulated period, are not paper money, though they serve the same purposes during the time they continue to circulate. The value of such notes is wholly derived from the confidence placed in the ability of the issuers to retire them when presented for payment, or when they become due. Whenever, therefore, this confidence ceases, their circulation necessarily ceases also. But no such circumstances affect *paper money;* meaning by paper money, paper made legal tender, and not legally convertible into gold, or any thing else, at the pleasure of the holders, or at any given period. No part, whatever, of the value of paper money is derived from such confidence. It circulates because it is made legal tender, and because the use of a circulating medium is indispensable; and its value, supposing the demand to be constant, is, in all cases, precisely as the quantity in circulation. . . .

"It would not be difficult for the issuers of inconvertible paper, were they so disposed, to preserve its value on a par with that of gold or silver. Suppose, for example, that there are no gold coins in circulation in Great Britain, and that our currency consists *wholly* of inconvertible paper issued by government, or by a board acting under its orders; under these circumstances, it is quite plain that no gold would be imported, either to be used as money or to be kept as reserves in the coffers of the bankers. But the demand for it in the arts would, notwithstanding, cause it to be imported in large quantities; and it might still be made a standard by which to regulate the issues of paper. Thus, when the holders of $£3\frac{143}{160}$ ($£3$ 17s. $10\frac{1}{2}d$.) of paper could readily exchange it for one ounce of gold bullion of 22 carats fine, it would be a proof that it was exactly of the same value as gold, and that, consequently, its quantity should neither be increased nor diminished. But if more or fewer than $£3\frac{143}{160}$ in paper were required to buy an ounce of bullion, it would show, in the one case, that the value of paper had fallen too low, and that its quantity should be lessened; and, in the other, that its value had risen too high, and that its quantity should be increased. By acting in this way, or, which is substantially the same thing, by attending to the exchanges, and lessening the supply of currency when they begin to fall, and increasing it when they begin to rise, the value of paper money might be kept very nearly on a level with the value of the metallic money that would circulate in its stead were it withdrawn. This conduct is that, in fact, of every prudent banker obliged to pay his notes on demand. He does not defer narrowing his issues until a heavy drain for bullion has set upon his coffers, but sets about their contraction the moment he observes the price of bullion rising, and the exchanges falling; enlarging them under the opposite circumstances. The obligation to pay in bullion compels attention to be paid to principles that might otherwise be contemned; but that is all, and hence it follows, that, if sufficient security could be obtained that the power to issue inconvertible paper would not be abused, and that its amount would be enlarged and diminished so as to preserve its value on a par with gold, the latter might be entirely dispensed with for all pecuniary purposes, except as a standard, though it might still be expedient to use a subsidiary silver and copper currency, as at present, for small payments."[1]

It is very true, that, if $£3\frac{143}{160}$ of paper would exchange for one ounce of gold, twenty-two carats fine, the value of one would equal that of the other. But was not Mr. McCulloch a little hasty in assuming an inconvertible government note of the nominal value of an ounce of gold, to be of equal value, and exchangeable therefor? It is to be remembered, that it was not necessary that any provision should be made for its payment, or even that it should ever become due. It

---

[1] Notes to Smith's Wealth of Nations, pp. 489–491.

circulated, not from any value it possessed, but from the necessity for its use as a ticket or counter of exchange. Neither was it necessary that it should be made legal tender. Suppose government to set up a board for the issue of inconvertible notes. How are these to be issued? Would any thing be paid to the board on their issue? If not, then there would be likely to be no little scramble for them ; as they would be worth a struggle, so long as they would sell in the market at one-half per cent of their nominal value. If any thing were to be paid, how much? If fifty per cent of their nominal value, then those who received them would sell them at a trifling advance for the profit to be made. They would only, however, command their value; for no one would pay more when he could get them himself by application to the board. They would sell, therefore, only at their worth or cost. How was any excess issued to be taken in? By paying out, of course, a corresponding amount of coin. The board, then, must start with some provision therefor. Such provision, in order to secure that degree of confidence necessary to cause them to circulate as currency, must, in some form, equal their whole value. They would be subject to the same laws as all other kinds of currency. Who is to supply such provision? Those, of course, who receive the notes. Those who derive no advantage therefrom are not to stand in the gap. If those to whom the notes were paid could only get their value or cost in exchange, their nominal would be made to express their real value, if only as a matter of convenience. If the process be traced, it will be seen that notes can get into circulation as money, only in the manner in which they do get into circulation, and that the inconvertible ones of Mr. McCulloch (for the notes supposed by him were not to be legal tender) could not get into circulation at all. It is certainly useless to repeat his folly by replying to assertions which the briefest examination shows to be wholly gratuitous and false.

Again : —

" But, notwithstanding the economy of money, and the saving of risk and trouble resulting from the use of bills of exchange and Banks of deposit, there is still a very heavy expense attendant upon the employment of the precious metals as currency. The impossibility of employing bills of exchange in the settlement of the great majority of transactions renders the employment of a large quantity of money indispensable ; while the State loses the whole value of the bullion or capital that is locked up in the coffers of the deposit Banks. Should, therefore, means be devised for fabricating that portion of the currency required for the settlement of such transactions as cannot be adjusted by bills of exchange, of some material having little real value, the cost of its maintenance would be proportionally diminished ; and the bullion in the coffers of the deposit Banks would be disengaged for other purposes. Of the materials suggested for this purpose, paper has been by far the most generally resorted to, and is in every respect the most eligible. By using paper instead of gold, we substitute the cheapest in room of the most expensive currency ; and enable the society, without loss to any individual, to send abroad all the coins rendered superfluous by the use of paper, getting in return from the foreigner an equivalent in raw materials or manufactured goods." [1]

McCulloch objects to the use of coin as money, from its excessive cost. It is to be supplemented, in consequence, by paper. Still, to render this paper convertible into coin or its equivalent, considerable sums of the latter have to be maintained. Such a system, he says, is very imperfect. To render it perfect, the reserves of coin now held should be supplied by some material costing nothing. The whole amount of the precious metals in the country might then be sent out of it, in exchange for useful merchandise or machinery. The monetary millennium would then dawn on the world. But what does every one seek in exchanging that which he possesses? To better his condition ; to get something which will be more valuable to him than that with which he parts ; in order to have that which,. when he wishes to use it, will bring to him the greatest possible amount of values in other forms. Gold and silver, therefore, are always demanded in exchange, for the reason that they are values in their highest forms. The whole effort of mankind is to convert its industries and products into such values, or into that which shall produce them ; and which, till its possession be demanded, is drawing interest in kind for the benefit of the party entitled to it. The whole effort of nature is in the same direction, — to convert lesser into greater values. McCulloch and the Economists would invert all this order, by converting whatever a person has to sell, not into the most valuable, but into the least valuable form. Could they have their way, six months would suffice for them to

---

[1] Notes to Smith's Wealth of Nations, pp. 487, 488.

point out the "last man;" for they are pests which seem likely to survive to witness the final doom.

McCulloch fully sustained the policy of Sir Robert Peel in the Act of 1844, on the ground that the whole currency should vary in amount and value exactly as a metallic currency would do were the paper currency withdrawn and coin substituted in its place. In order to a perfect currency, he would, in another place, have it consist of a material wholly costless in itself, the value of which was to be derived wholly from its use in the exchanges. He re-enforced his argument in favor of restriction upon the issues of paper by the following reference to the system of the United States: —

"If the reason of the thing, and the revulsion and bankruptcy it has repeatedly occasioned in England, had not been sufficient to convince the Parliament and the public of the propriety of restricting the issue of notes, the example of America would have supplied the deficiency. There are Banks of issue in all considerable towns throughout the Union; and the different State legislatures have exhausted their skill in devising schemes for the regulation of these Banks, by ordering that certain portions of their capital shall be paid up before they begin business, and that the amount of their issues and engagements of all sorts shall be governed by the amount of this paid-up capital. And, not satisfied with laying down rules for the guidance of the Banks, they make the Directors swear their observance, order returns of their affairs to be made public, and sometimes appoint inspectors to see that the regulations are complied with. The result of all this cumbrous quackery is precisely such as every man of sense would anticipate. The banking system of America is the bane of the country; it is, in fact, as bad as can well be imagined, and has been the means of alternately diffusing a spirit of improvident and wild speculation throughout the Union, and then of plunging it into all but universal bankruptcy. The rules devised for the regulation of the Banks are good for nothing, unless it be to delude or deceive. They restrain none but the opulent, honest, and conscientious bankers, who do not require to be placed under any sort of surveillance; and afford every one else an opportunity, by misleading the inspectors and making false and exaggerated statements of their affairs, to get their condition represented as most prosperous, when, perhaps, it is very much the reverse." [1]

In reference to the system of the United States, Mr. McCulloch only repeated, parrot-like, the lesson taught him, with no more understanding of the subject than of the configuration

[1] Notes to Smith's Wealth of Nations, p. 502.

of the opposite side of the moon. Nothing can be more disgraceful in a man like him, — Professor of Political Economy in the university of a city which, commercially, is the very eye of the world, and standing at the very apex of his school, — than the ignorance and assurance he displayed. Among the numerous systems in them, if the Banks erected by the several States are to be called systems, there were many bad enough, as there was at the time any amount of rottenness in the English system, or in the Banks of which it may said to be composed. Human nature is the same on both sides of the water. There are plenty of adventurers in both countries, who will, if they can, impose their issues upon the public to serve as money; who will either make no provision at all for their redemption, or only such as they can make after the issues are made. In the large towns of both countries, the systems were good; that is, those who issued notes were compelled to make adequate provision for their redemption, previous to their issue, as the necessary condition of getting them into circulation. Mr. McCulloch might just as well have said that the Americans were too dishonest to construct good roads or warehouses, as to create good Banks and properly administer them. There is always more of adventure, and a far feebler sense of the importance of what is called commercial integrity, among a pioneer than among a trading people; but, under similar circumstances, similar results are produced the world over; and, in the end, the best methods will always be made use of, or will always be sought. To assume otherwise is to adopt a conclusion far worse than the baldest pessimism, — that society itself is incapable of continued existence.

In passing in review before us the arguments and conclusions upon the subject of money of Hume, Smith, Stewart and McCulloch, — all Scotchmen, and among the most distinguished of their race, — nothing can excite greater wonder than the incapacity of all to conduct an argument upon it through even a single paragraph, without involving themselves in the grossest mistakes and contradictions; and that, too, upon a subject coming almost wholly within the range of the exact sciences. To what is this apparent feebleness of intellect — this inability to make even ordinary distinctions, and this passion for finding them where no differences exist, due? No

other explanation can be given than the uniformity in religion
and dogma which so long prevailed in their country.   The
reasoning faculty of her people was, as it were, lost, for want
of proper objects for its exercise, or from its improper exercise.   When emancipation, or whatever it may be termed,
came, the habit of assuming, instead of proving, had become
too strong even for such men as Hume and Smith, who
were certainly no churchmen.   When they began to inquire in reference to matters other than those which related
to religious dogma, they used precisely the same methods as
were used by those remaining within the pale.   It was far
easier to assume than to investigate ; but very unsafe when
the subjects for investigation were the phenomena of the
physical world, the operations of society, or the laws of matter.   When Smith asserted that " the amount of paper
money which can circulate in any country can never exceed
the amount of coin which would have circulated in its place ; "
that " money has two distinct and separate functions, — one
as an instrument of commerce, the other as a measure of
value ; " that " the great wheel of circulation " (metallic
money) " is altogether different from the goods which are circulated by it ; " that " it forms no part of the revenue of an
individual or nation ; " and that, " of all kinds of capital,
money is the least valuable," — it never occurred to him that
these statements were not proofs.   He assumed them as axioms
with which to construct his more complex propositions.   He
might just as well have entered upon solutions in geom-
etry by assuming an acute angle to always equal a right
angle.   As his premises were wholly false, his conclusions
could not be less so.   His followers, bowing abjectly in so
great a presence, accepted without the least reservation or
qualification the assumptions upon money of their master.
Unfortunately, he was as lacking in intuition as in method.
He had not a touch of that inspiration by means of which
great truths first find their expression, to become, in time, the
property of the race.   He could never forget himself, or get
away from himself.   He could not even stop to analyze the system of his own country, which, when he wrote, had been in operation nearly a hundred years ; an examination of which would
have completely disproved every proposition made by him in reference to money.   What he did not propose or attempt, it would

have been in the highest degree irreverent for his followers to do. It was natural that an ignorant or excited people in a great extremity, and conscious of their impotence, should take refuge in theories and conclusions laid down by authority, as it were, in the books, without the least comprehension of their validity or effect. It is in this way that speculation, grounded on no principle or law, gets its power to harm. The Act of 1844, with all its consequent disasters, was the natural and direct result of Smith's propositions upon money, incessantly reiterated by the Economists from his time to our own. The Scotch people, however, have been far wiser than Scotch thinkers or metaphysicians. With the absurdest theories in their books, they have the best system of banking now existing, and one of the best that has ever existed. With them theory and practice have been as wide apart as the poles. In this respect, they closely resemble the Puritan emigrants to this country. Were one to examine the literature and legislation of the latter, he would suppose religious metaphysics to be their only occupation in life. Their theme, from morning till night, appeared to be the truth of their peculiar views; and their chief labor, to sustain them from Bible texts. Yet there was another side to this picture, if possible far more striking. Their discussions in theology took very little time or thought necessary for the discharge of the graver duties of life. In all their affairs they displayed an energy, persistency, and soundness of judgment which made them one of the greatest marvels of material prosperity and success the world has yet seen. The wrongs and mistakes they did commit came, like those of the Scotch, from the speculative side of their nature. A traveller who visited them in the earlier part of the eighteenth century, after describing their formal manners, their uncouth scriptural language, their constant and rigid observance of religious forms, by no means agreeable to him, winds up the strange picture with the statement of a fact which still more excited his wonder, and defied explanation, — "but great numbers among them are damnably rich!" Indeed, a strong religious sentiment seems to exert a powerful influence favorable to the accumulation of wealth, for the reason that a people subject to it are the more persistent in their industries, and the more economical in their expenditures.

If we must go to McCulloch to learn the opinions and theories held by the Economists, particularly those which relate to the subject of money, we must go to Mr. Stuart Mill to learn what is now taught in reference to it. His work on Political Economy is the great text-book on both sides of the water. It is made a part of the course in nearly all the institutions in which this science is, or is assumed to be taught. If his own works are not directly used, it is only for the reason that it has become a habit with almost all teachers or professors of Political Economy in this country, to get up works of their own; based, however, almost wholly upon the teachings of this, the great light in modern Economy.

" Money," says Mill, " when its use has grown habitual, is the medium through which the incomes of the different members of the community are distributed to them, and the measure by which they estimate their possessions. As it is always by means of money that people provide for their different necessities, there grows up in their minds a powerful association, leading them to regard money as wealth in a more peculiar sense than any other article; and even those who pass their lives in the production of the most useful objects acquire the habit of regarding those objects as chiefly important by their capacity of being exchanged for money. A person who parts with money to obtain commodities, unless he intends to sell them, appears to the imagination to be making a worse bargain than a person who parts with commodities to get money; the one seems to be spending his means, the other adding to them: illusions which, though now in some measure dispelled, were long powerful enough to overmaster the mind of every politician, both speculative and practical, in Europe.

" It must be evident, however, that the mere introduction of a particular mode of exchanging things for one another, by first exchanging a thing for money, and then exchanging the money for something else, makes no difference in the essential character of transactions. It is not with money that things are really purchased. Nobody's income (except that of the gold or silver miner) is derived from the precious metals. The pounds or shillings which a person receives weekly or yearly are not what constitute his income: they are a sort of tickets or orders which he can present for payment at any shop he pleases, and which entitle him to receive a certain value of any commodity that he makes choice of. The farmer pays his laborers and his landlord in these tickets, as the most convenient plan for himself and them: but their real income is their share of his corn, cattle, and hay, and it makes no essential difference whether he distributes it to them direct, or sells it for them and gives them the price; but as they would have to sell it for money if he did not, and as he is a seller at any rate, it best suits the purposes of all that he should sell their share along with his own, and leave the laborers more leisure for work, and the landlord for being idle.[1] The capitalists, except those who are producers of the precious metals, derive no part of their income from those metals, since they only get them by buying them with their own produce; while all other persons have their incomes paid to them by the capitalists, or by those who have received payment from the capitalists; and, as the capitalists have nothing from the first except their produce, it is that and nothing else which supplies all incomes furnished by them. There cannot, in short, be intrinsically a more insignificant thing in the economy of society than money, except in the character of a contrivance for sparing time and labor. It is a machine for doing, quickly and commodiously, what would be done, though less quickly and commodiously, without it; and, like many other kinds of machinery, it only exerts a distinct and independent influence of its own when it gets out of order.[2]

Mankind, from habit, says Mill, came to regard money as being peculiarly wealth; and that objects are useful and valuable in ratio to their capacity of being exchanged for it. But is not such capacity a proper test of value? Have articles that will not exchange for money any value? Is not the uniform experience of mankind, from the time that exchanges first began to be made, of more force than Mill's assertion to the contrary? Are not gold and silver something beyond mere tickets or orders invented "for doing quickly and commodiously what would be done, but less quickly and commodiously, without them?" Are they not the most, instead of being the least, significant things in the economy of society? As capital, they can always be loaned at interest. They are the universal equivalent, — that into which every one seeks to convert whatever he acquires not necessary to his immediate wants. They are the only articles fitted to constitute the reserves of society, as they are imperishable, and preserve their value, uniform, from age to age. They are the only articles which can be sent to every part of the world with the certainty of always being accepted at their cost. If the precious metals alone, of all articles of merchandise or property, possess such attributes, then Mill's description of their nature and function is inadequate and puerile to the last degree.

---

[1] Nothing more strikingly illustrates Mill's incapacity for scientific inquiry, the puerility of his mind, and the infirmity of his temper, than his assertion that one reason for the conversion by the farmer of his products into money was to give his landlord "more leisure for being idle." He could not discuss a purely scientific subject without intruding spiteful and irrelevant personalities and flings.

[2] Political Economy, vol. ii. pp. 7–9.

"When," says Mill, "one person lends to another, as well as when he pays wages or rent to another, what he transfers is not the mere money, but a right to a certain value of the produce of the country, to be selected at pleasure; the lender having first bought this right by giving for it a portion of his capital. What he really lends is so much capital; the money is the mere instrument of transfer. But the capital usually passes from the lender to the receiver, through the means either of money or of an order to receive money; and, at any rate, it is in money that the capital is computed and estimated. Hence, borrowing capital is universally called borrowing money; the loan market is called the money market; those who have their capital disposable for investment on loan are called the moneyed class; and the equivalent given for the use of capital, or in other words, interest, is not only the interest of money, but, by a grosser perversion of terms, the value of money. This misapplication of language, assisted by some fallacious appearances which we shall notice and clear up hereafter, has created a general notion among persons in business, that the value of money, meaning the rate of interest, has an intimate connection with the value of money in its proper sense, — the value or purchasing power of the circulating medium. We shall come to this subject before long; at present, it is enough to show that by value I shall always mean exchange value; and by money, the medium of exchange, not the capital which is passed from hand to hand through that medium. . . .

"As the whole of the goods in the market compose the demand for money, so the whole of the money constitutes the demand for goods. The money and the goods are seeking each other, for the purpose of being exchanged. They are reciprocally supply and demand to one another. It is indifferent whether, in characterizing the phenomena, we speak of the demand and the supply of goods, or the supply and demand of money: they are equivalent expressions. . . .

"Supposing the money in the hands of individuals to be increased, their wants and inclinations collectively, in respect to consumption, remaining exactly the same, the increase of demand would reach all things equally, and there would be a universal rise of prices. We might suppose, with Hume, that some morning every person in the nation should wake and find a gold coin in his pocket; this example, however, would involve an alteration of the proportion in the demand for different commodities; the luxuries of the poor would, in the first instance, be raised in price, in a much greater degree than other things. Let us rather suppose, therefore, that to every pound or shilling or penny in the possession of any one, another pound, shilling, or penny were suddenly added. There would be an increased money demand; and, consequently, an increased money value, or price, for things of all sorts. This increased value would do no good to any one; would make no difference, except that of having to reckon pounds, shillings, and pence in higher numbers. It would be an increase of values only as estimated in money, — a thing only wanted to buy other things with; and would not enable any one to buy more of them than before. Prices would have risen in a certain ratio, and the value of money would have fallen in the same ratio. . . .

" The very same effect would be produced on prices, if we suppose the goods diminished, instead of the money increased; and the contrary effect, if the goods were increased or the money diminished. If there were less money in the hands of the community, and the same amount of goods to be sold, less money altogether would be given for them, and they would be sold at lower prices; lower, too, in the precise ratio in which the money was diminished. So that the value of money, other things being the same, varies inversely as its quantity; every increase of quantity lowering the value, and every diminution raising it in a ratio exactly equivalent.[1]

If the money (gold and silver) of every person in a community were suddenly doubled, without any act of his own, would not every one be better off? No, says Mill: you have, in such case, two tickets, indeed, instead of one; but they will bring you only the articles or values that one would before. But suppose a person holding 10,000 sovereigns has added to them another 10,000. Having no occasion for the use of the latter amount for the purchase of food or clothing, or for expenses of any kind, he might, with great advantage, supplement his domestic utensils of iron by those of gold and silver. He might erect structures, or cover his roof, with a substance wholly indestructible by the elements. When the vast number of uses to which they could be applied, which now have to be supplied by materials so perishable as to impose, in their cost and repair, the greatest of burdens upon society, is considered, it would seem to have been an oversight in nature that that which is fitted to serve the highest uses should not have been produced in greater abundance. But the designs and scope of Providence embrace other matters than domestic utensils, fair structures, and impervious roofs. A solvent of all transactions had to be provided as the prime condition of human progress, and of high value in ratio to its quantity, to be easily borne about by those who were to use it. Gold and silver, therefore, could not be supplied in the same profusion as iron, without losing the greater part of the attributes which constitute their value as agencies in the progress and welfare of mankind. If they were to become as abundant as iron, all the operations of society

[1] Political Economy, vol. ii. pp. 9-12.

would have to pause till the place they now supply was made good by articles having similar attributes or functions in the new order of things.   In the world constructed by the Economists, gold is almost wholly dethroned, without any other provision in its place.   A world of their own creation would be the best commentary upon their absurd and incoherent theories.

" When a person lends," says Mill, in effect, " as well as when he pays money or wages to another, that which he lends is not the money, but capital.   The money is the mere instrument of transfer.   But as capital usually passes from lender to receiver through the means of money, it is in money that the amount of capital is computed and estimated.   Hence, the borrowing of capital is universally, but very improperly, called the borrowing of money.   The language is just as much misapplied as it would be to call the transaction by· which a person borrowed a load of potatoes for consumption, and a cart for the purpose of bringing them home, the borrowing of a cart: it is not the cart that is borrowed, but the potatoes.   So when a man borrows a sovereign: the sovereign is not the capital borrowed, but the means by which it is borrowed."   With Mill, as with Smith, it is not money (gold and silver) which constitutes a man's capital or his income, but that which gold and silver buys.   The absurdity of all such distinctions has been already sufficiently demonstrated.

" If we assume," continues Mill, " the quantity of goods on sale, and the number of times these goods are resold, to be fixed quantities, the value of money will depend upon its quantity, together with the average number of times that each piece changes hands in the process.   The whole of the goods sold (counting each resale of the same goods as so much added to the goods) have been exchanged for the whole of the money, multiplied by the number of purchases made in the average by each piece.   Consequently, the amount of goods and of transactions being the same, the value of money is inversely as its quantity, multiplied by what is called the rapidity of circulation.   And the quantity of money in circulation is equal to the money value of all the goods sold, divided by the number which expresses the rapidity of circulation." [1]

After referring to the increased amount of money (bank-notes) wanted for extraordinary payments at certain periods of the year, he goes on to say : —

[1] Political Economy, vol. ii. p. 16.

"If extra currency were not forthcoming to make these extra payments, one of three things must happen : Either the payments must be made without money, by a resort to some of those contrivances by which its use is dispensed with ; or, there must be an increase in the *rapidity of circulation*, the same sum of money being made to perform more payments; or if neither of these things took place, money to make the extra payments must be withdrawn from the market for commodities, and prices, consequently must fall. An increase of the circulating medium, conformable in extent and duration to the temporary stress of business, does not raise prices, but merely prevents this fall.

"The sequel of our investigation will point out many other explanations and qualifications with which the proposition must be received, that the value of the circulating medium depends on the demand and supply, and is in the inverse ratio of the quantity." [1]

The value of money, says Mill, is in inverse ratio to its quantity multiplied by the rapidity of its circulation. He might as well have framed a similar formula in reference to the value of a loaf of bread : — " a loaf sufficient for the breakfast of one man, moving at the rate of one foot per second, will be sufficient for the breakfast of ten men, and of equal value to ten loaves, by moving at the rate of ten feet per second." In the application of his doctrine, the choice of position might be considered of some consequence. So, "if more money be required to move the crops, one of three things must happen : either the payments must be made without money ; or there must be an increase in the rapidity of the circulation, the same amount of money being made to do double duty ; or money must be withdrawn from the market for other commodities." The better way would seem to be to make money do double duty. " A nimble sixpence is better than a slow shilling " may be quoted in proof. An objection to the forced activity, or, indeed, to any activity of money, is the attrition which is estimated to reduce its value at the rate of one per cent annually. If made to do double duty, its wear would equal two per cent. A piece would then last only fifty years. But if one could be made to do the duty of two, the relative gain would still be enormous. It would have been well for Mr. Mill to have detailed the process by which increased " rapidity of circulation " is to be secured. As by its use the ownership of money is always parted with, and as the propriety of its use depends

[1] Political Economy, vol. ii. p. 21.

upon the equivalent received, the holder might well object to part with it to help forward the operations of his impecunious and less fortunate neighbors. Where their wants were the greatest they would have the least to offer for it. The greater the demand, the greater the distrust, and the more tenaciously would it be held by its churlish and selfish owners. As the need of money is the imperative one the world over, and as it should be relieved once for all, Economists should set themselves to work, either to provide a sufficient quantity, or to show how, by " rapidity of circulation," an infinitesimal quantity, as it were, may do the work of a mass as big as the moon. If money could be made to revolve with sufficient rapidity, every one now having but one dollar in his pocket, in a given period, might have ten. But such a result would after all, according to Mill, be a very bootless one ; for if every one had ten dollars in his pocket where he now has but one, the prices of every thing else would rise in like ratio ; so that he would be no better off with ten than with one. The great problem, therefore, which the Economists should lose no time in solving is to secure a rapidity of the circulation ten times greater than its present rate, prices of all kinds remaining the same. This done, the financial and material millennium would for the first time dawn upon the race, and the Economists, for once, would have turned their labors to some account.

But may there not be some fallacy in Mr. Mill's assumption that money has, or may have, an activity greater than that of other kinds of merchandise ? Suppose a person in his purchases not to part with his money; that as a yardstick, as a measure of extension, is always retained by its owner, whether he be purchaser or seller, so money serves as the measure of values without being parted with. In such case, a person whose expenditures were $100 a week would require only that amount of money, or only one-seventh of it, provided an equal amount of purchases was made daily. It is plain, in such case, that there would be no more activity of money than merchandise, — no more than of the yardstick. The same would be the case if he used the money but once : he can use it only once. But the person who receives it from him can use it only once : it is then *functus officio* to him. So far as each is concerned, there is the same activity in the merchandise as in the money paid for it, and the converse. Equivalents are exchanged. Their activity in the exchange, if such attribute can be predicated of either, is precisely the same. As the purchases a person makes equal the money he is possessed of, and the converse, so the purchases made by society equal the money it is possessed of. The money of society, therefore, and the merchandise fitted for or entering into consumption, necessarily equal the one the other. There must, therefore, be the same activity of its merchandise as of its money. It is true that the merchandise has been consumed while the money has not; but the merchandise has been productively consumed, to reappear in the same or other forms. When it reappears, it is then ready for exchange for the very money its antecedent was exchanged for, the place of which it has taken. If it do not reappear, the money has nothing to do, and will be exported as an article for which there is no domestic use. It is demonstrable, therefore, that the merchandise of society at any one time entering into consumption equals the money of society; and that the one possesses precisely the same degree of activity as the other. No assumption has been more dwelt upon by the Economists than the superior activity of money to merchandise, while there is none so utterly absurd.

" It is not, however," continues Mill, " with ultimate or average, but with immediate and temporary, prices that we are now concerned. These, as we have seen, may deviate very widely from the standard or cost of production. Among other causes of fluctuation, one we have found to be the quantity of money in circulation. Other things being the same, an increase of the money in circulation raises prices; a diminution lowers them. If more money is thrown into circulation than the quantity which can circulate at a value conformable to its cost of production, the value of money, so long as the excess lasts, will remain below the standard or cost of production, and general prices will be sustained above the natural rate.

" But we have now found that there are other things, such as bank-notes, bills of exchange, and checks, which circulate as money, and perform all the functions of it; and the question arises, Do these various substitutes operate on prices in the same manner as money itself? Does an increase in the quantity of transferable paper tend to raise prices in the same manner and degree as an increase in the quantity of money? . . . .

" I apprehend that bank-notes, bills, or checks, as such, do not act on prices at all. What does act on prices is credit, in whatever shape given; and whether it gives rise to any transferable instruments capable of passing into circulation, or not.

" I proceed to explain and substantiate this opinion.

" Money acts upon prices in no other way than by being tendered in exchange for commodities. The demand which influences the prices of commodities consists of the money offered for them. But the money offered is not the same thing with the money possessed. It is sometimes less, sometimes much more. In the long run, indeed, the money which people lay out will be neither more nor less than the money which they have to lay out; but this is far from being the case at any given time. Sometimes they keep money by them for fear of an emergency, or in expectation of a more advantageous opportunity for expending it. In that case, the money is said not to be in circulation; in plainer language, it is not offered, nor about to be offered, for commodities. Money not in circulation has no effect on prices. The converse, however, is a much commoner case; people make purchases with money not in their possession. An article, for instance, which is paid for by a check on a banker, is bought with money which not only is not in the payer's possession, but generally not even in the banker's, having been lent by him (all but the usual reserve) to other persons. We just now made the imaginary supposition that all persons dealt with a Bank, and all with the same Bank, payments being universally made by checks. In this ideal case, there could be no money anywhere except in the hands of the banker; who might then safely part with all of it, by selling it as bullion, or lending it, to be sent out of the country in exchange for goods or foreign securities. But though there would then be no money in possession, or ultimately, perhaps, even in existence, money would be offered, and commodities bought with it, just as at present. People would continue to reckon their incomes and their capitals in money, and to make their usual purchases with orders for the receipt of a thing which would have literally ceased to exist. There would be in all this nothing to complain of, so long as the money in disappearing left behind it an equivalent value in other things, applicable when required to the reimbursement of those to whom the money orignally belonged.

" In the case, however, of payment by checks, the purchases are at any rate made, though not with money in the buyer's possession, yet with money to which he has a right. But he may make purchases with money which he only expects to have, or even only pretends to expect. He may obtain goods in return for his acceptances payable at a future time, or in his note of hand, or on a simple book credit, that is, a mere promise to pay. All these purchases have exactly the same effect on price, as if they were made with ready money. The amount of purchasing power which a person can exercise is composed of all the money in his possession or due to him, and of all his credit. For exercising the whole of this power, he finds a sufficient motive only under peculiar circumstances; but he always possesses it, and the portion of it which he at any time does exercise is the measure of the effect which he produces on price.

" Suppose that, in the expectation that some commodity will

rise in price, he determines not only to invest in it all his ready
money, but to take up on credit, from the producers or importers,
as much of it as their opinion of his resources will enable him to
obtain. Every one must see that by thus acting he produces a
greater effect on price than if he limited his purchases to the
money he has actually in hand. He creates a demand for the
article to the full amount of his money and credit taken together,
and raises the price proportionally to both. And this effect is
produced, although none of the written instruments called substitutes for currency may be called into existence, though the transaction may give rise to no bill of exchange, nor to the issue of a
single bank-note. The buyer, instead of taking a mere book credit,
might have given a bill for the amount, or might have paid for the
goods with bank-notes borrowed for that purpose from a banker ;
thus making the purchase not on his own credit with the seller,
but on the banker's credit with the seller, and his own with the
banker. Had he done so, he would have produced as great an
effect on price as by a simple purchase to the same amount on a book
credit, but no greater effect. The credit itself, not the form and
mode in which it is given, is the operating cause." [1]

Two things, or influences, according to Mill, act upon
prices, — money (coin) and credit, — each in ratio to its quantity or amount. Bills, notes of Banks, checks, and the like, do
not act upon them. It is undoubtedly possible that all the
sugar in the market might be bought on a credit to mature in
six months. The contract might not even be reduced to writing.
The purchaser might then put up the price. So far, credit
may be said to act upon prices. But the same result might
have been produced without any credit whatever. The
holders of the sugar, which they purchased and paid for, might
put up its price, by refusing to sell except at an advance ; or a
purchaser might secure the whole for an advance, by paying
cash or bank-notes for it. The same result would be produced without credit as with. Credit, consequently, may or
may not be the cause of the rise. If it were unaccompanied
by any contract or bill, then the rise in price would be confined to the specific article operated in. But suppose the
purchase, for speculative purposes, to be made by a three-
months' bill, and that this be discounted, the holder of the
sugar purchased in the mean time refusing to sell it, the
credit in such case would affect the price of every article
upon the market. The sugar would have been converted
into money, or into that which had all the potency of money,

[1] Political Economy, vol. ii. pp. 50–53.

equal in amount to its whole value, to act upon the price of articles other than that which it represented. The sugar would not be on sale, but would at the same time be a purchasing power to the whole extent of its value. It is impossible, however, that any considerable number of sales in large amounts should be made by book account, for the reason that holders of merchandise will as a rule, not sell, unless they can either get money, or that which by means of Banks can be turned into money. If they can get no other acknowledgment than book accounts, they will prefer to hold, unless they are disposed to sell on speculation. It is to be remembered, that they are usually owing for what they hold ; and they must sell for that which will pay their debts, — for that which can be turned into money. Ordinarily, a bill given for merchandise is equivalent to money. The object of Banks is to turn the representatives of *bona fide* transactions into money, for the purpose of enabling production to anticipate the sale and collection of the proceeds of the merchandise already put upon the market. It is the only way in which consumption can be anticipated ; in which the producer, the moment he parts with his merchandise, is in the same condition as he would be after his products were sold and their proceeds paid over to him. Where merchandise is sold on book account, its consumption and payment cannot be anticipated by the seller. A book account is not a proper subject for discount. He can get his money only when the credit falls due. The assertion of Mill, therefore, that purchases made by bills can exert no more influence over prices than purchases made by book account is directly opposed to the fact. It is the notes of and checks upon Banks which chiefly, with money, do act upon prices. But to go a step further : credits by book account can only act upon the merchandise that is in actual existence, and can affect only that to which they relate ; but by means of Banks moonshine itself — accommodation bills — may be turned into money. Now it is impossible that such a result could have been produced without the process and instruments described. It is demonstrable, therefore, that whatever may be the effect of credit upon prices, the most direct and potent of all are negotiable instruments, which may or may not represent capital, but which exert as money precisely the functions of a currency of coin.

From a convertible, Mill proceeds to the discussion of an inconvertible, currency.

"After experience had shown that pieces of paper of no intrinsic value, by merely bearing upon them the written profession of being equivalent to a certain number of francs, dollars, or pounds, could be made to circulate as such, and to produce all the benefit to the issuers which could have been produced by the coins they purported to represent, governments began to think that it would be a happy device if they could appropriate to themselves this benefit, free from the condition to which individuals issuing such paper substitutes for money were subject, — of giving, when required, for the sign, the thing signified. They determined to try whether they could not emancipate themselves from this unpleasant obligation, and make a piece of paper issued by them pass for a pound, by merely calling it a pound, and consenting to receive it in payment of the taxes. And such is the influence of all established governments, that they have generally succeeded in attaining this object. I believe I might say they have always succeeded for a time ; and the power has only been lost to them after they had compromised it by the most flagrant abuse.

"In the case supposed, the functions of money are performed by a thing which derives its power of performing them solely from convention. But convention is quite sufficient to confer the power ; since nothing more is needful to make a person accept any thing as money, and even at any arbitrary value, than the persuasion that it will be taken from him on the same terms by others. The only question is : What determines the value of such a currency ? since it cannot be, as in the case of gold and silver (or paper exchangeable for them at will), the cost of production.

"We have seen, however, that even in the case of a metallic currency, the immediate agency in determining its value is its quantity. If the quantity, instead of depending on the ordinary mercantile motives of profit and loss, could be arbitrarily fixed by authority, the value would depend on the fiat of that authority, not on cost of production. The quantity of a paper currency not convertible into the metals at the option of the holder can be arbitrarily fixed, especially if the issuer is the sovereign power of the State. The value, therefore, of such a currency is entirely arbitrary.

"Suppose that, in a country of which the currency is wholly metallic, a paper currency is suddenly issued to the amount of half the metallic circulation ; not by a banking establishment, or in the form of loans, but by the government, in payment of salaries and purchase of commodities. The currency being suddenly increased by one-half, all prices will rise, and, among the rest, the prices of all things made of gold and silver ; an ounce of manufactured gold will become more valuable than an ounce of gold coin by more than the customary difference which compensates for the value of the workmanship ; and it will be profitable to melt the coin for the purpose of being manufactured, until as much has been taken from the currency by the subtraction of gold as has been added to it by the issue of the paper. Then prices will relapse to what they were at first, and there will be nothing changed, except that a paper currency has been substituted for half of the metallic currency which existed before. Suppose, now, a second emission of paper : the same series of effects will be renewed ; and so on, until the whole of the metallic money has disappeared : that is, if paper be issued of as low denomination as the lowest coin ; if not, as much will remain as convenience requires for the smaller payments. The addition made to the quantity of gold and silver disposable for ornamental purposes will somewhat reduce, for a time, the value of the article : and as long as this is the case, even though paper has been issued to the original amount of the metallic circulation, as much coin will remain in circulation along with it as will keep the value of the currency down to the reduced value of the metallic material ; but, the value having fallen below the cost of production, a stoppage or diminution of the supply from the mines will enable the surplus to be carried off by the ordinary agents of destruction, after which, the metals and the currency will recover their natural value. We are here supposing, as we have supposed throughout, that the country has mines of its own, and no commercial intercourse with other countries ; for, in a country having foreign trade, the coin which is rendered superfluous by an issue of paper is carried off by a much prompter method. Up to this, the effects of a paper currency are substantially the same, whether it is convertible into specie or not. . . .

" In order that the value of the currency may be secure from being altered by design, and may be as little as possible liable to fluctuation from accident, the articles least liable of all known commodities to vary in their value — the precious metals — have been made in all civilized countries the standard of value for the circulating medium ; and no paper currency ought to exist of which the value cannot be made to conform to theirs. Nor has this fundamental maxim ever been entirely lost sight of, even by the governments which have most abused the power of creating inconvertible paper. If they have not (as they generally have) professed an intention of paying in specie at some indefinite future time, they have at least, by giving to their paper issues the names of their coins, made a virtual, though generally a false, profession of intending to keep them at a value corresponding to that of the coins. This is not impracticable even with an inconvertible paper. There is not, indeed, the self-acting check which convertibility brings with it ; but there is a clear and unequivocal indication by which to judge whether the currency (inconvertible) is depreciated, and to what extent. That indication is the price of the precious metals. When holders of paper cannot demand coin to be converted into bullion, and when there is none left in circulation, bullion rises and falls in price like other things ; and if it is above the mint price, — if an ounce of gold, which would be coined into the equivalent of £3 17s. 10d., is sold for £4 or £5 in paper, — the value of the currency is sunk just that much below what the value of a metallic currency would be. If, therefore, the issue of inconvertible paper were subjected to strict rules, — one rule being that, whenever bullion rose above the mint price, the issues should be contracted until the market price of bullion and the mint price were again in accordance, — such a currency would not be subject to any of the evils usually deemed inherent in an inconvertible paper.

"But, also, such a system of currency would have no advantages sufficient to recommend it to adoption. An inconvertible currency regulated by the price of bullion would conform exactly, in all its variations, to a convertible one; and the only advantage gained would be that of exemption from the necessity of keeping any reserve of the precious metals; which is not a very important consideration, especially as a government, so long as its good faith is not suspected, needs not keep so large a reserve as private issuers, being not so liable to great and sudden demands, since there never can be any real doubt of its solvency. Against this small advantage is to be set, in the first place, the possibility of fraudulent tampering with the price of bullion, for the sake of acting on the currency, in the manner of the fictitious sales of corn, to influence the averages, so much and so justly complained of while the corn laws were in force. But a still stronger consideration is the importance of adhering to a simple principle, intelligible to the most untaught capacity. Everybody can understand convertibility; every one sees that what can be at any moment exchanged for five pounds is worth five pounds. Regulation by the price of bullion is a more complex idea, and does not recommend itself through the same familiar associations. There would be nothing like the same confidence, by the public generally, in an inconvertible currency so regulated as in a convertible one; and the most instructed person might reasonably doubt whether such a rule would be as likely to be inflexibly adhered to. The grounds of the rule not being so well understood by the public, opinion would probably not enforce it with as much rigidity, and, in any circumstances of difficulty, would be likely to turn against it; while to the government itself a suspension of convertibility would appear a much stronger and more extreme measure than a relaxation of what might possibly be considered a somewhat artificial rule. There is, therefore, a great preponderance of reasons in favor of a convertible in preference to even the best-regulated inconvertible currency. The temptation to overissue in certain financial emergencies is so strong, that nothing is admissible which can tend, in however slight a degree, to weaken the barriers that restrain it."[1]

"After experience had shown," says Mill, in effect, "that the inhabitants of a particular country could get on just as well, could be just as comfortable and strong without food and clothing as with, governments began to think it would be a happy device to appropriate to themselves the benefit of being thus relieved from providing for these two great wants; and

[1] Political Economy, vol. ii. pp. 76–78.

they determined to try whether they could not emancipate
the people from these unpleasant obligations, by substituting
words or declarations or hieroglyphs in place of coats and
beef; and such is the strength of combination or union, that
they pretty nearly succeeded in obtaining their object. Indeed,
they fully succeeded for a time, only to lose their power by
the flagrant conduct of those who went so far as to starve and
freeze themselves to death. Convention was competent to
decide, and did decide, the matter; but mankind were so
perverse that they would not contain themselves within any
reasonable bounds. A grand principle, therefore, which might
have revolutionized society, had, notwithstanding all the benefits which might have flowed from it, to be abandoned."

Mill might have used either illustration with equal perti-
nence and force. The value and use of gold and silver as
money was no more a matter of convention than the value and
use of food and clothing. Money is just as necessary to
society, as at present constituted, as is food and clothing. No
experience has ever shown that " pieces of paper of no intrinsic
value, by merely bearing upon them written professions of
being equivalent to a certain number of francs, dollars, or
pounds, could be made to circulate as such, and produce all
the benefits to the issuers which could have been produced by
the coins which they purported to represent." Experience
never will show such a result, unless, perchance, in a world
peopled wholly by Economists. That fictions — mere pieces of
paper professing to be the equivalent of coin, but representing
nothing and carrying with them no obligation whatever for
their payment, — cannot have the value of coin, has been made
a matter of demonstration over and over again. A currency
such as Mill assumes could not even get into circulation. If
made legal tender, which he did not contemplate, then an
attribute of value would be given to it other than that of a
plain note, which was to be his currency ; but even the price
of legal-tender notes would soon come to be measured by their
value. Men deal or intend to deal in values, — in substantial
things, not in shams. If they were unable to make the
distinction, as Mr. Mill assumes, the race itself would soon
cease to exist.

Mill's method for detecting, and determining the degree of
the depreciation of an inconvertible currency, is this : " When
the holders of paper cannot convert it on demand into bullion,

and when there is no coin in circulation by means of which bullion can be demanded, paper having driven it wholly out of circulation, then bullion rises and falls in price like other things ; and, if its value be above the mint price of gold, — if an ounce of gold, which is the equivalent of £3 17s. 10d., be sold for £4 or £5 in paper, — the value of the currency is sunk just that much below what the value of a metallic currency would be. In such case, the paper must be proportionally taken in. So when all the coin is driven out of circulation, and £3 17s. 10d. of irredeemable paper will purchase an ounce and a quarter of bullion, the paper is deficient in amount, and its value, consequently, excessive. The remedy is a proportional increase. By observing such rules, the currency would not be subject to any of the evils usually deemed inherent in an inconvertible paper." His statement, when reduced to its proper terms, is this : " When something exceeds nothing, either in quantity or value, the nothing is to be divided by two, the product being equal to the quantity of the something : when nothing exceeds something in quantity or value, it must be multiplied by two, the product being of the same value as the something." These propositions, which embody in a concise and accurate form Mill's more elaborate statement, may well take their place beside that which assumes "the value of money to be in inverse ratio to its quantity multiplied by the rapidity of its circulation."

" Although," says Mill, in effect, " the value of an inconvertible currency, so long as it does not exceed the wants of a community in its exchanges, might, by the rules laid down, be made to conform exactly to the value of gold, it is hardly worth while to issue it, as the only advantage gained would be an exemption from the necessity of maintaining reserves of the precious metals, — a matter of very little importance. So long as the good faith of the government issuing it was not suspected, it would have to keep on hand only a very small amount of reserve, even when it undertook to issue a convertible currency. A million or two of coin or bullion would be all that would be required against an issue of twenty millions of notes. What is the interest on such a paltry sum, set off against a possibility of tampering with the value of bullion?" But the motive for tampering with bullion would be when it was held as reserves, precisely as coin has been oftentimes tampered with for the purpose of enabling governments to pay their debts at one-half the value at which they were contracted. There would be no motive to tamper when there was no bullion to be paid. In this case, Mill seems, without being aware of it, to have altogether inverted his argument. But a still stronger consideration, he says, is the importance of a rule which the most untaught capacity can readily understand. When an issuer says, " I will pay ten dollars, on demand, in gold," the note will be readily accepted so long as the maker is in good credit ; for the holder knows that all he has to do is to demand and receive the gold for it, if he have occasion to use it, or if he suspect any thing wrong. An " untaught capacity " could hardly be made to understand the process by which a note he might hold could be made to have a value equal to that of gold, when not a particle of gold could be had for it. So far Mill was right. The regulation of the value of an inconvertible currency, so as to render it the equivalent of gold, is a very complex process. It is not illustrated in the " ordinary operations of society." Even some well-taught people might well doubt whether the rule would produce the assumed result, or whether it would be rigidly adhered to. Public opinion might not sufficiently support it. The government itself might recommend its relaxation ; for, as the object of such currency was to supply the lack of gold, government would not be very likely, after its issue, to take measures to give it the value of gold, when the same measures would have rendered its issue unnecessary. This is one of those cases in which it is not wise to attempt to enforce a rule or principle wholly correct, and of great value in itself, simply from the perversity or weakness of human nature.

" The same effects," says Mill, " which would arise from the discovery of a treasure accompany the process by which bank-notes, or any of the other substitutes for money, take the place of the precious metals. Suppose England possessed a currency wholly metallic, of twenty millions sterling, and that suddenly twenty millions of bank-notes were sent into circulation. If these were issued by bankers, they would be employed in loans, or in the purchase of securities, and would therefore create a sudden fall in the rate of interest, which would probably send a great part of the twenty millions of gold out of the country as capital, to seek a higher rate of interest elsewhere, before there had been time for any action on prices. . . .

" Effects of another kind, however, will have been produced.

Twenty millions, which formerly existed in the unproductive form of metallic money, have been converted into what is or is capable of becoming productive capital. This gain is at first made by England at the expense of other countries, who have taken her superfluity of this costly and unproductive article off her hands, giving for it an equivalent value in other commodities; by degrees, the loss is made up to those countries by diminished influx from the mines; and, finally, the world has gained a virtual addition of twenty millions to its productive resources. . . .

" The value saved to the community by thus dispensing with metallic money is a clear gain to those who provide the substitute. They have the use of twenty millions of circulating medium which have cost them only the expense of an engraver's plate. If they employ this accession to their fortunes as productive capital, the produce of the country is increased, and the community benefited as much as by any other capital of an equal amount. Whether it is so employed or not, depends, in some degree, upon the mode of issuing it. If issued by the government, and employed in paying off debt, it would probably become productive capital. The government, however, may prefer employing this extraordinary resource in its ordinary expenses, may squander it uselessly, or make it a mere temporary substitute for taxation to an equivalent amount; in which last case, the amount is saved by the tax-payers at large, who either add it to their capital or spend it as income."[1]

It seems that the assumption of Mill and the Economists, that the issue by a country — England, for example — of £20,000,000 of currency, thereby enabling her to export a corresponding amount of specie in exchange for productive capital, increasing her wealth in an equal degree, might well be objected to from its apparent injustice. A principle applicable to one should be applicable to all other nations. That one is to be benefited without desert, and another injured without wrong, is not sound in morals, if it be so in Political Economy. What is to become of the unfortunate race of Midases reduced to the necessity, not only of eating and drinking, but of wearing gold? Their wrongs and sufferings are certainly fitted to excite sincere commiseration. Why should ———, a country known only to the Economists, be, whether it will or no, the dumping ground for the gold of all the rest of creation? A science that is not true for such countries as England, France, or the United States, cannot be true for any other. Each should be compelled to keep its proper proportion of its own incumbrances or impediments, and should not be allowed to

[1] Political Economy, vol. ii. pp. 174–177.

palm them off as tickets or counters, at their nominal value, for the good things of others. How such wrong and injustice are to be prevented is not clear to ordinary understandings. It ought to be to the Economists, who make no ado of creating something out of nothing. One mode suggests itself: " As the value of money is inversely as its quantity multiplied by the rapidity of its circulation," its value might be reduced by reducing such rapidity ; that is, if one ounce of gold moving at the rate — an excessive one, perhaps — of ten feet per second, be worth ten ounces moving at the rate of only one foot per second, then if to the quantity ordinarily in circulation in England, and moving only at the rate of, say, five feet per second, an equal amount were added, and the movement of the whole be limited to two and a half feet per second, her money, though doubled in quantity, would be no more abundant, relatively, than before ; and none could be spared to be sent abroad. There would be nothing to complain of in all this. England might have the misfortune to gather in too much of this unproductive superfluity ; but she should have looked out for it. She might, in the same way, have improvidently accumulated too much cloth and too much iron. Political Economy is not to allow her to throw the loss upon unoffending, but less powerful, neighbors, who had steered clear of a similar folly. Mill admits that " this gain is first made by England at the expense of other countries, who have taken her superfluity of this costly and unproductive article off her hands, giving for it an equivalent value in other commodities ; " but claims that " by degrees, however, the loss is made up to those countries by diminished influx from the mines, and, finally, the world has gained a virtual addition of £20,000,000 to its productive resources " ! But the " other countries," having already their quota of the precious metals, have now a superfluity equal to the whole amount thrown upon them. If England be so much the richer, they are so much the poorer ; while the aggregate wealth of all, the world over, is not, for the present, increased a single penny. We say for the present ; for if, by the above process, the mines could be closed, then the labor of those who had been unproductively employed might be turned to some useful account. In time, too, by the loss and attrition of the coin in circulation, the superfluity England had luckily got rid of might be partly required in her channels of circulation. Twenty or thirty, or, perhaps, fifty years, might be required to bring about such a result. In the mean time, the interest account running against this " unproductive superfluity " might equal twice or thrice its amount. Nothing, therefore, could be gained to the world at large, while great injustice might be done to some of the nations that compose it. This should not be allowed. It is submitted that the Economists should reconsider Mill's statement in this particular, to see if it cannot be placed upon broader and more equitable foundations.

So much for Mill's assumption that the wealth of England might be increased by the substitution of worthless paper to serve as currency in the place of coin, and an advantage secured in ratio thereto. But if the gold, demonetized as it were, could be made available for export, is it certain that it would be exchanged for an equal value of commodities to be made the basis of reproduction? The first effect of the issue of paper, even if it were legal tender, would not be to send abroad, immediately, a corresponding amount of gold. The rates of exchange might be such that it could not be exported without a loss. It would only be exported to discharge balances· arising in foreign trade, to be created in consequence of the excessive issues of paper. As the effect of such issues would be to advance prices, an amount of the gold would still be required as currency, in addition to the paper, and in ratio to such advance. From increased consumption, increased importations would be made, and gold would be finally exported in ratio thereto. The movement, however, would always be gradual, and would· be the direct, not the indirect, effect of the increase of the currency. Whatever was exported would be for articles ordinarily entering into consumption, which exceed tenfold such as are imported to serve as the basis of production. It might be that very little would be brought into the country which it could not do as well without as with. Useful articles, that is, those which can be made the basis of production, are not usually the kind imported under the stimulus of an issue of worthless paper. All such improvident measures are always followed by others equally or still more improvident. It is to be remembered that all such issues are made only as the last alternative; that they are always tainted by the necessity of resorting to them. They inevitably first fall into the hands of the creatures of the government, who have no adequate personal interest in the result. Sellers of merchandise would, therefore, as a matter of precaution, always demand a much larger price in paper than in coin, and would always be in a position to exact their own terms. As it costs no more to engrave the word "two" than "one," there would be no lack of money so long as it had any exchangeable value whatever. The recklessness of government would soon beget a corresponding recklessness and extravagance on the part of the people. Thrift does not go hand in hand with such proceedings as these. The product of such industrial operations as were still carried on would be at an enormously high cost ; so that, when the reverse came, — as it would come sooner or later, either from an excessive decline in the value of the paper money or from its retirement, — the most as well as the least deserving would be involved in a common ruin. If the currency were ever redeemed, then the gold driven out of the country by its issue would have to be brought back. If finally repudiated, the gold must still be brought back to provide a new, or the basis for a new, currency ; so that, in either alternative, nothing but loss could be the result.

Again : —

"When metallic money has been entirely superseded and expelled from circulation by the substitution of an equal amount of bank-notes, any attempt to keep a still further quantity of paper in circulation must, if the notes are convertible, be a complete failure. The new issue would again set in motion the same train of consequences by which the gold coin had already been expelled. The metals would, as before, be required for exportation, and would be for that purpose demanded from the Banks, to the full extent of the superfluous notes, which thus could not possibly be retained in circulation. If, indeed, the notes were inconvertible, there would be no such obstacle to the increase of their quantity. An inconvertible paper acts in the same way as a convertible, while there remains any coin for it to supersede ; the difference begins to manifest itself when all the coin is driven from circulation (except what may be retained for the convenience of small change), and the issue still goes on increasing. When the paper begins to exceed in quantity the metallic currency which it superseded, prices, of course, rise ; things which were worth £5 in metallic money become worth £6 in inconvertible paper, or more, as the case may be. But this rise of price will not, as in the cases before examined, stimulate import and discourage export. The imports and exports are determined by the metallic prices of things, not by the paper prices; and it is only when the paper is exchangeable at pleasure for the metals that paper prices and metallic prices must correspond." [1]

" When metallic money," says Mr. Mill, " has been entirely superseded and expelled from circulation by the substitution of an equal amount of bank-notes, any attempt to keep a still further quantity of paper in circulation, must, if the notes are convertible, be a complete failure." No further issue of convertible paper can be made, for the reason that nothing remains into which it can be converted. An inconvertible currency, he says, produces precisely the effects of a convertible one, so long as there is any coin in circulation to be supplanted or displaced by either. The difference between the two only begins to manifest itself when there is no more coin to be superseded. The issue of convertible currency must then cease, while that of an inconvertible one may still continue. This statement is additional proof of Mr. Mill's complete misconception of the nature of paper money. Although all convertible currencies are nominally payable in coin, they are seldom discharged in it. The provision made for their convertibility is not coin, but merchandise. They must all be taken in by their issuers within periods, say, of ninety days. Assuming the currency of all kinds afloat in Great Britain to be £450,000,000, the amount daily taken in, assuming the period of its circulation to be ninety days, is £5,000,000 ; or assuming (which is nearer the mark) that its circuit is performed in sixty days, the amount daily taken in, or converted, equals £7,500,000. The whole amount of coin or bank-notes actually interposing would not exceed £25,000 in the one case, or £37,500 in the other. All the rest is taken in by mutual offset of the instruments of which it is composed. The condition of the circulation of such a currency is not the displacement of a corresponding amount of coin. No matter what its amount, not a penny less of coin may be in circulation. It supplements the use of coin. If it cause any amount of the latter to be drawn from circulation, it is only that it may be collected into hoards as reserves, to discharge such currency as is not discharged by merchandise. The effect of such a currency is to reduce instead of advancing prices, tak-

[1] Political Economy, vol. ii. pp. 178, 179.

ing the whole range of articles upon the market. Now, an inconvertible currency, provided it be legal tender, — for no other could ever get into circulation, — drives metallic money out of circulation, for the reason that it renders it in great measure superfluous in domestic exchanges. It supplants instead of supplementing coin; causes a rise in prices, in being an instrument in excess of the means of expenditure, or by being depreciated in value below that of coin. Mill asserts, that as inconvertible currency cannot be exported, it cannot stimulate import or discourage export, for the reason that " imports and exports are determined by the metallic prices of things, not by the paper prices." But as by means of an excessive issue of paper its holders can command any amount of coin, and whether the coin be expelled or not, can bring into the country an excessive amount of merchandise, the additional amounts of paper exert an influence over importations precisely as would corresponding additions of gold. It is the paper price, rather than the gold price, of values that determines the amount of imports and exports. If the paper price of a shawl be a thousand dollars, and the gold price five hundred, and if the paper at the time the order is given can be converted into gold at sixty per cent of its nominal value, the merchant will take the risk of importing it, from the apparent profit of the transaction, although, before it is received, the paper may have fallen to forty per cent of its nominal value, involving a large loss instead of a profit. Every transaction made with an inconvertible currency would always involve the risk of a loss; but there would always be plenty to assume the risk of its use. Mr. Mill's assertion, therefore, that it is the gold, not the paper, price by which exports and imports are determined, is exactly opposed to the fact.

From the following quotations from the chapter on the " Regulation of the Currency," it will be seen that Mill fully agreed with Tooke, that a convertible currency could not be issued in excess. They are simply a reiteration of his assumption, that neither bank-notes nor checks exert any influence over prices or the rates of exchange : —

" Before touching upon the practical provisions of Sir Robert Peel's Act of 1844, I shall briefly state the nature and examine the grounds of the theory on which it is founded.

"It is believed by many that Banks of issue universally, or the Bank of England in particular, have a power of throwing their notes into circulation, and thereby raising prices arbitrarily; that this power is only limited by the degree of moderation with which they think fit to exercise it; that, when they increase their issues beyond the usual amount, the rise of prices thus produced generates a spirit of speculation in commodities, which carries prices still higher, and ultimately causes a reaction and recoil, amounting in extreme cases to a commercial crisis; and that every such crisis which has occurred in this country within mercantile memory has been either originally produced by this cause, or greatly aggravated by it. To this extreme length the currency theory has not been carried by the eminent Political Economists who have given to a more moderate form of the same theory the sanction of their names. But I have not overstated the extravagance of the popular version, which is a remarkable instance to what lengths a favorite theory will hurry, not the closet students whose competency in such questions is often treated with so much contempt, but men of the world and of business, who pique themselves on the practical knowledge which they have, at least, had ample opportunities of acquiring. Not only has this fixed idea of the currency as the prime agent in the fluctuations of price made them shut their eyes to the multitude of circumstances which, by influencing the expectation of supply, are the true causes of almost all speculations and of almost all fluctuations of price; but, in order to bring about the chronological agreement required by their theory between the variations of Bank issue and those of prices, they have played such fantastic tricks with facts and dates as would be thought incredible, if an eminent practical authority had not taken the trouble of meeting them, on the ground of mere history, with an elaborate and systematic exposure. I refer, as all conversant with the subject must be aware, to Mr. Tooke's 'History of Prices.' The results of Mr. Tooke's investigations were thus stated by himself on his examination before the Commons Committee on the Bank charter question, in 1832, and the evidences of it stand recorded in his book. 'In point of fact and historically, as far as my researches have gone, in every signal instance of a rise or fall in prices, the rise or fall has preceded, and therefore could not be the effect of, an enlargement or contraction of the Bank circulation.'

"The extravagance of the currency theorists, in attributing almost every rise or fall of prices to an enlargement or contraction of the issues of bank-notes, has raised up, by reaction, a theory the extreme opposite of the former, of which, in scientific discussion, the most prominent representatives are Mr. Tooke and Mr. Fullarton. This counter theory denies to bank-notes, so long as their convertibility is maintained, any power whatever of raising prices, and to Banks any power of increasing their circulation, except as a consequence of, and in proportion to, an increase of the business to be done. This last statement is supported by the unanimous assurances of all the country bankers who have been examined before successive Parliamentary Committees on the subject. They all bear testimony, that (in the words of Mr. Fullarton) 'the amount of their issues is èxclusively regulated by the extent of local dealings and expenditures in their respective districts, fluctuating with the fluctuations of production and price ; and that they neither can increase their issues beyond the limits which the range of such dealings and expenditures prescribes, without the certainty of having their notes immediately returned to them, nor diminish them, but at an almost equal certainty of the vacancy being filled up from some other source.' From these premises, it is argued by Mr. Tooke and Mr. Fullarton, that Bank issues, since they cannot be increased in amount, unless there be an increased demand, cannot possibly raise prices, cannot encourage speculation, nor occasion a commercial crisis ; and that the attempt to guard against that evil by an artificial management of the issue of notes is of no effect for the intended purpose, and liable to produce other consequences extremely calamitous.

"As much of this doctrine as rests upon testimony, and not upon inference, appears to me incontrovertible, I give complete credence to the assertion of the country bankers, very clearly and correctly condensed into a small compass in the sentence just quoted from Mr. Fullarton. I am convinced that they cannot possibly increase their issue of notes in any other circumstances than those which are there stated. I believe, also, that the theory grounded by Mr. Fullarton upon this fact contains a large portion of truth, and is far nearer to being the expression of the whole truth than any form whatever of the currency theory."[1]

After what has preceded, the following quotations require no comment. They relate to the question of "plurality of issue " : —

"There remain two questions respecting a bank-note currency, which have also been a subject of considerable discussion of late years : whether the privilege of providing it should be confined to a single establishment, such as the Bank of England, or a plurality of issuers should be allowed ; and, in the latter case, whether any peculiar precautions are requisite or advisable to protect the holders of notes against losses occasioned by the insolvency of the issuers.

"The course of the preceding speculations has led us to attach so much less of peculiar importance to bank-notes, as compared with other forms of credit, than accords with the notions generally current, that questions respecting the regulation of so very small a part of the general mass of credit cannot appear to us of such momentous import as they are sometimes considered. Bank-notes, however, have so far a real peculiarity, that they are the only form of credit sufficiently convenient for all the purposes of circulation, to be able entirely to supersede the use of metallic money for internal

[1] Political Economy, vol. ii. pp. 195–197.

purposes. Although the extension of the use of checks has a tendency more and more to diminish the number of bank-notes, as it would that of the sovereigns or other coins which would take their place if they were abolished, there is sure, for a long time to come, to be a considerable supply of them, wherever the necessary degree of commercial confidence exists and their free use is permitted. The exclusive privilege, therefore, of issuing them, if reserved to the government or to some one body, is a source of great pecuniary gain. That this gain should be obtained for the nation at large is both practicable and desirable; and, if the management of a bank-note currency ought to be so completely mechanical, so entirely a thing of fixed rule, as it is made by the Act of 1844, there seems no reason why this mechanism should be worked for the profit of any private issuer rather than for the public treasury. If, however, a plan be preferred which leaves the variations in the amount of issues in any degree whatever to the discretion of the issuers, it is not desirable that to the ever-growing attributions of the government so delicate a function should be superadded; and that the attention of the heads of the State should be diverted from larger objects by their being besieged with the applications, and made a mark for all the attacks, which are never spared to those deemed responsible for any acts, however minute, connected with the regulation of the currency. It would be better that Treasury notes, exchangeable for gold on demand, should be issued to a fixed amount, not exceeding the minimum of a bank-note currency; the remainder of the notes which may be required being left to be supplied either by one or by a number of private banking establishments. Or an establishment like the Bank of England might supply the whole country, on condition of lending fifteen or twenty millions of its notes to the government, without interest; which would give the same pecuniary advantage to the State as if it issued that number of its own notes." [1]

The preceding extracts present adequately the views of Mr. Mill and his method upon the subject of money. To quote and comment further would be to go over again the ground already many times retraced. It is doubtful whether modern literature presents a more striking example of unwarranted assumption on one side, and impotent conclusion on the other. He has all the vices of the Scotch school, without their excuse. The emancipation, however partial, of the English intellect preceded by a considerable period that of the Scotch. It was, however, inevitable that the English as well as Scotch Economists should make disastrous failure, from a total misconception of the principles upon which the science of Political Economy, if there be such, must rest, and of the

[1] Political Economy, vol, ii. pp. 220, 221.

methods by which every science is to be pursued. If it be the object of Political Economy to unfold the laws by which nations or communities are enriched, its first and obvious step would be a study of the most striking examples of the kind which history affords. A signal one is that of the Hebrew race. Their great Law-giver enjoined morality as the highest condition of material welfare. " Obey the law, and you shall have gold and silver and cattle and possessions as you do obey it." The result in their case established the value of morality as an essential condition of wealth; for this race has throughout history been alike conspicuous for its morality and wealth. But morality may be wholly wanting in that necessary for its own preservation. The lawfulness, and consequent morality, of slavery was recognized by all ancient codes, although it tended to the destruction of all virtue and all material welfare. Hence the need of a rule or principle by which morals themselves may be enlightened and guided, and conduct subjected to a sense of duty, — to a law higher than that of human enactment. Such a principle or sense abolishes slavery, and so becomes a far more potent force than morality itself. Without it, all the obligations that morality can impose can never maintain society at its proper level and bent. This proposition, then, being established, the next question arises, Where is the most perfect expression of this principle to be found? History points to the teachings of Christ. We must weigh and estimate all teachings by their results. If Christianity, as a principle, appear to have exerted a more powerful influence over the race than any other statement or revelation of the kind; if it attack more effectually than any other the wrongs and vices which afflict society, and if by its observance the greatest degree of material prosperity be secured, — then the record of its teachings should become, as it were, the primer of the Political Economist. The conclusion seems to be irresistible. Christianity is not a dogma nor a system : these are conditions imposed upon and foreign to it. It is secular at the same time that it is religious. It forbids an act like the expulsion of the Moors from Spain, and the revocation of the Edict of Nantes, as wrongs done as much to the material as to the moral welfare of the authors of those monstrous crimes. As ethnic religions have no proper sense of the infinite immorality and improvidence of such acts, the necessity for a higher rule for their guidance and control is at once apparent. Moral and material prosperity must always go hand in hand ; but as the idea or intent must always precede the act, and as every act must be followed by its appropriate sequence or reward, the first thing always to be considered is the germ, the motive, that led to it. Political Economy, therefore, as a science, if it be such, must include in its range every motive and principle that can influence human action, as well as every method or law of human progress or acquisition. That " the meek shall inherit the earth " was not stated as a matter of senti-ment, — as compensation for losses, sufferings endured, — but as illustrating the power resulting from proper spiritual conditions, — conditions through which the best gifts of Providence, material as well as moral, come to the race. It may yet be seen that the injunction to give the coat where the cloak is taken expresses a principle most perfectly calculated for the protection of property, although its higher meaning may not yet have penetrated this " muddy vesture of decay." The Economists have not even comprehended the grounds upon which the science, if there be such, must rest. They begin by erecting their petty postulates, which partake of their own weakness ; and from these proceed to deduce the law of human life and progress, and even the nature of the Supreme Being himself. As the postulates of each necessarily express the peculiarities of each, the result is universal chaos of opinion and statement, without any possible means or stand-point for reconciliation. Mr. Mill, the great apostle of the modern school, expressed its condition when he declared that Adam Smith, the great apostle of the old, " is in many respects obsolete ; in all, imperfect." Principles, certainly, cannot be-come obsolete ; and, if Smith have become so, it is only because he was wanting in them. Each one has his own system ; and if he borrow any thing from another, it is always with a quali-fication to show his own superiority. They have all moved so long in their little spheres, without once seeking wisdom from a source higher than their own, that the race has become effete, not a few of them being only a little removed from a condition of mental imbecility.

An illustration, perhaps still more striking and pertinent than that afforded by the Hebrews, of the dependence of material prosperity upon morals, or upon a principle far higher than morals, is that afforded by the Seven United Provinces. Their territory was made up of marshy and sandy wastes, exposed to constant overflow from the great rivers which traversed them, and the still more terrible invasion of the sea. Before the beginning of our era, Julius Cæsar describes its inhabitants, the Batavians, as addicted to a seafaring life, and as relying upon their fisheries for the greater part of their subsistence. Their country itself, before it could be made to contribute in any considerable degree to their support, had first to be reclaimed by mounds and dykes, only to be reared at vast expense and labor. The territory was almost wholly wanting in forests, so that all the material for their ships, even, had to be brought from other lands. After the reclamation of their country, their food had always, in great measure, to be imported. The sea was both their element and their resource. This swarmed with fish, particularly herring ; the mode of curing and preserving which was fortunately discovered by an inhabitant named Beukels or Beukelzoon, about the middle of the fourteenth century. At that time, the eating of butcher's meat during two days each week, and forty days before Easter, was forbidden by a dogma of the church. As its place had to be supplied by some other kind of animal food, this prohibition opened a market, at highly remunerative rates, for all the fish that could be taken. From the time of the discovery of Beukels, therefore, the Hollanders had open before them the richest mine as it were, the greatest opportunity that ever presented itself to an adventurous, painstaking people. Their position, their nautical skill, together with their art of preserving fish, gave them, for centuries, the monopoly of supplying the Christian world. The result equalled the opportunity. They became the richest and most commercial people in the world. Their wealth was soon turned to political account by the power possessed by the Hanseatic League, of which several of their cities were important members. In 1477, Philip of Burgundy wrote to the Pope that, " Holland and Zealand are rich islands inhabited by a brave and warlike people, who have never been conquered by their neighbors, and who prosecute their commerce in every sea." " These people," said Sir Walter Raleigh, " are never without 700,000 quarters of corn, none of it the growth of the country; and a dearth of only one year in any other part of Europe enriches Holland for seven years. In the course of a year and a half, during a scarcity in England, there were carried away, from the ports of Southampton, Bristol, and Exeter alone, nearly £200,000; and, if London and the rest of England be included, there must have been £2,000,000 more." The celebrated John de Witt estimated that every fifth person in Holland, at the middle of the seventeenth century, derived his subsistence from the herring fishery; which employed, at that time, 3,000 vessels in the bays and inlets of their own coast, 800 in the seas around the Orkney and Shetland Islands, and 1,600 upon the coast of England. Including the vessels employed in the carriage of salt to be used in preserving the fish, and those employed in its distribution to consumers, the whole number of ships to which their fisheries gave employment equalled 6,400, manned by 112,000 seamen. The whole number of persons employed in the fisheries and dependent upon them for support, including those employed in building, rigging and fitting out ships, with provisions, nets, casks, salt, &c., numbered 450,000. " At that time," says De Witt, " Holland could boast of 10,000 sail of shipping, and 168,000 seamen;" "although," he adds, " the country itself affords them neither materials, victual, nor merchandise." In 1690, Sir William Petty estimated the shipping of Europe at about 2,000,000 tons: namely, England, 500,000; France, 100,000; Hamburg, Sweden, Denmark, and Dantzic, 250,000; Spain, Portugal, and Italy, 250,000; and Holland (the Seven United Provinces), 900,000, or nearly one-half of the whole. " Holland," said Sir William Temple, " did not grow rich by any native commodities, but by the force of industry; by the improvement and manufacture of all foreign growths; by being the general magazine of Europe, and furnishing all parts with whatever the market wants or invites; and by their seamen being, as they have been properly called, the common carriers of the world." Each city was distinguished by some special trade it carried on, or country with which it dealt. Middleburgh was chiefly concerned in the wine trade; Flushing, in that of the West Indies; Swaardam, in ship-building; Sluys, in the herring fishery; and Amsterdam, in the East India, Spanish, and Mediterranean trades. The prosperity of all, however, was based upon the fisheries: it became a common saying with them, that the foundation of their chief city, Amsterdam, was laid on herring bones.

It is unnecessary to remark that, during all this period, Holland was eminently a free State. The supreme government was vested in the " Assembly of the States," which met whenever occasion required; and without whose consent no taxes could be imposed, nor wars entered upon, nor treaties nor alliances concluded. That country was almost the only part of Western Europe never subdued by the Roman empire, and never affected by its corruptions and superstitions; or the still grosser ones of the empire which succeeded. She opposed as dauntless a front to the second as to the first, and contributed, in her long and desperate struggle with Spain, more than any other people to break that power; for in that struggle Spain was but an instrument in the hands of a will higher than her own. In that struggle, a people not two millions in number, proved more than a match for the greatest monarchy in Europe, and reduced it from the highest to the lowest rank among the nations. With the progress of other countries, however, — particularly that of England, — it was inevitable that Holland should lose the monopoly she once enjoyed, and should decline relatively in the scale. The wars in which she was exposed imposed upon her a large debt, which weighed upon her industries, and all the more so as she was compelled to divide with others the monopoly which she had so long enjoyed. After the peace of Aix-la-Chapelle, in 1748, the attention of the nation was directed to the decline of its shipping, and of its foreign commerce; and a circular was addressed to the leading merchants of the republic, by the Stadtholder, William IV., desiring answers to the following questions: —

" 1. What is the actual state of trade? And, if the same should be found to be diminished and fallen to decay, then, —

" 2. To inquire by what methods the same may be supported and advanced, or, if possible, restored to its former lustre, repute, and dignity?"

To these inquiries, numerous answers were received, which, by the direction of the Stadtholder, were embodied in a report or memoir, in which the former prosperity of the country was referred to three causes: 1. Physical or natural; 2. Moral; 3. Adventitious or external. Their operation and result were set out in detail as follows: —

" I. The natural and physical causes are the advantages of the situation of the country, — on the sea, and at the mouth of considerable rivers ; its situation between the northern and southern parts, which, by being in a manner the centre of all Europe, made the Republic become the general market where the merchants on both sides used to bring their superfluous commodities, in order to barter and exchange the same for other goods they wanted.

" Nor have the barrenness of the country, and the necessities of the natives arising from that cause, less contributed to set them upon exerting all their application, industry, and utmost stretch of genius, to fetch from foreign countries what they stand in need of in their own, and to support themselves by trade.

" The abundance of fish in the neighboring seas put them in a condition not only to supply their own occasions, but with the overplus to carry on a trade with foreigners, and out of the produce of the fishery to find an equivalent for what they wanted through the sterility and narrow boundaries and extent of their own country.

" II. Among the moral and political causes are to be placed the unalterable maxim and fundamental law relating to the free exercise of different religions ; and always to consider this toleration and connivance as the most effectual means to draw foreigners from adjacent countries to settle and reside here, and so become instrumental to the peopling of these provinces.

" The constant policy of the Republic to make this country a perpetual safe and secure asylum for all persecuted and oppressed strangers ; no alliance, no treaty, no regard for, or solicitation of any potentate whatever, has at any time been able to weaken or destroy this law, or make the State recede from protecting those who have fled to it for their own security and self-preservation.

" Throughout the whole course of the persecutions and oppressions that have occurred in other countries, the steady adherence of the Republic to this fundamental law has been the cause that many people have not only fled hither for refuge, with their whole stock in ready cash and their most valuable effects, but have also settled, and established many trades, fabrics, manufactories, arts, and sciences in this country, notwithstanding the first materials for the said fabrics and manufactories were wholly wanting in it, and not to be procured but at great expense from foreign parts.

" The constitution of our form of government, and the liberty thus accruing to the citizen, are further reasons to which the growth of trade and its establishment in the Republic may fairly be ascribed ; and all her policy and laws are put upon such an equitable footing that neither life, estates, nor dignities depend on the caprice or arbitrary power of any single individual ; nor is there any room for any person, who by care, frugality, and diligence has once acquired an affluent fortune or estate, to fear a deprivation of them by any act of violence, oppression, or injustice.

" The administration of justice in the country has, in like manner, always been clear and impartial, and without distinction of superior or inferior rank, — whether the parties have been rich or poor, or were this a foreigner and that a native; and it were greatly to be wished we could at this day boast of such impartial quickness and despatch in all our legal processes, seeing how great an influence it has on trade.

" To sum up all: amongst the moral and political causes of the former flourishing state of trade may be likewise placed the wisdom and prudence of the administration; the intrepid firmness of the councils; the faithfulness with which treaties and engagements were wont to be fulfilled and ratified; and, particularly, the care and caution practised to preserve tranquillity and peace, and to decline, instead of entering on a scene of war, merely to gratify the ambitious views of gaining fruitless or imaginary conquests.

" By these moral and political maxims was the glory and reputation of the Republic so far spread, and foreigners animated to place so great a confidence in the steady determinations of a State so wisely and prudently conducted, that a concourse of them stocked this country with an augmentation of inhabitants and useful hands, whereby its trade and opulence were from time to time increased.

" III. Amongst the adventitious and external causes of the rise and flourishing state of our trade may be reckoned : —

" That at the time when the best and wisest maxims were adopted in the Republic as the means of making trade flourish, they were neglected in almost all other countries; and any one reading the history of those times may easily discover that the persecutions on account of religion throughout Spain, Brabant, Flanders, and many other States and kingdoms, have powerfully promoted the establishment of commerce in the Republic.

" To this happy result, and the settling of manufacturers in our country, the long continuance of the civil wars in France, which were afterwards carried on in Germany, England, and divers other parts, have also very much contributed.

" It must be added, in the last place, that, during our most burdensome and heavy wars with Spain and Portugal (however ruinous that period was for commerce otherwise), these powers had both neglected their navy, whilst the navy of the Republic, by a conduct directly the reverse, was at the same time formidable, and in a capacity not only to protect the trade of its own subjects, but to annoy and crush that of their enemies in all quarters."

The preceding extracts contain more wisdom, and present more accurately the laws that govern the acquisition and preservation of wealth, than all the books on Political Economy ever written. They contain, in fact, all that is necessary to be known to reach the highest pitch of material greatness. Patient industry, religious toleration, the acknowledgment and sense of a law higher than any of man's provision, and exact justice and good faith in dealing with others, are certain to receive the highest benediction and reward that Providence can bestow. Among a people by whom such virtues were cultivated, the Political Economist would have been as superfluous and as much out of place as a fortune-teller.

The strange contrast to this picture is to be equally heeded, if the true method of human progress would be fully learned. It was the want of that which raised Holland to the highest pitch of prosperity that reduced Spain to the lowest abyss of impotence and decay. The latter should have learned to correct and abate dogma by reference to the material result.` The religious must be summoned to plead at the bar of the secular, as the secular at the bar of the religious. They must mutually correct the vices and excesses of each other. A nation or people who cannot do this is far gone in the downward road, to fall an easy victim to the higher powers that surround it, which are as remorseless and inexorable as the laws of nature itself.[1]

After leaving Mill, we come to a vast swarm of writers, all of whom repeat him with a greater or less degree of extravagance, with the exception, perhaps, of Mr. H. D. Macleod, who has erected a vast system, measured by the number of pages devoted to it, the fundamental principle of which is that gold and silver serve as money by reason of being representative of debt; that paper serves as such by reason of being the representative of transferable debt; and that whatever represents transferable debt is currency, — paper money. The italics and capitals are his own.

"In this sentence," says Macleod (referring to Law's commentary upon Chamberlain's plan for a bank based upon real estate), "is concentrated the whole essence of that eternal delusion, so specious and plausible, and so fatal, which we designate as LAW-ISM. It is, indeed, nothing but the stupendous fallacy that *money represents commodities, and that paper currency may be based upon commodities.* This delusion is deeply prevalent in the public mind at the present day, and probably there are few persons, except those who have studied the true philosophical principles of Political Economy, whose views are not deeply tainted with this infection. No man who does not thoroughly understand the great

---

[1] Charles V. being, in 1550, in Biervliet, where Beukels was buried, visited his grave, and ordered a magnificent monument to be erected to the memory of one to whom his country owed so much. What would have been his emotions could the veil of the future have been lifted so as to disclose the real significance and effect of Beukels' discovery in the disaster and ruin brought upon his house?

fundamental doctrine established by Turgot and others, *that money does not represent commodities*, can ever have sound ideas on this subject. MONEY DOES NOT REPRESENT COMMODITIES AT ALL, BUT ONLY DEBT ; OR SERVICES DUE, WHICH HAVE NOT YET RECEIVED THEIR EQUIVALENT IN COMMODITIES. Now, the views of Law are much more extensively prevalent than is generally supposed. All who think that there is any necessary connection between the quantity of money in a country and the quantity of commodities in it are influenced by them. Take the case of a private individual. Is there any necessary relation between the quantity of money he retains and the quantity of commodities he purchases ? The quantity of money he has is just the quantity of debt of services due to him, — which he has *not yet* parted with for something else. It is the quantity of power for purchasing commodities he has over and above what he has already expended. And the quantity of money a nation possesses is simply the quantity of accumulated industry it possesses over and above all commodities ; but they have no relation to each other. Now, money does not represent commodities ; but it represents that portion of a man's industry which is reserved for future use. Whatever a man earns is the fruit of his industry, money included ; and none of the separate items *represent* any thing else, though it may be *exchanged* for other things. Now, the value of money depends upon its relations to what it represents, namely, debt, and not to commodities. If money or currency increases faster than debt or services due, it immediately causes a diminution of its value. If debt increases faster than money or currency, then the value of money is raised. The infallible consequence, therefore, of an increase of currency, without a corresponding increase of debt, is to change the existing proportion between debt and currency, and to cause a depreciation of the latter commensurate to the changed proportion. The necessary and inevitable consequence, then, of issuing vast quantities of paper currency on the assumed value of property, is simply to cause a total subversion of the foundation of all value and of all property, and to plunge every creditor into irretrievable ruin. . . .

"We must, therefore, be careful to be just to Law. He was no advocate of an unlimited inconvertible paper currency. Quite the reverse. But, seeing that a convertible paper currency could only be based upon bullion to a certain limited extent, preserving its equality in value with bullion, his idea was to base a paper currency upon some other article of value ; and he thought that it might preserve its equality in value to silver on an independent basis. His idea was, that it was only necessary to have it represent some article of value. But this attempt was contrary to the nature of things. His paper currency, though avowedly based upon things of value, had exactly the same practical effects as if it had been based upon silver. It became redundant, and swamped every thing. And the reason is plain : it was a violation of the fundamental principle we have obtained — ' *Where there is no debt, there can be no currency.*' And the fresh quantities of currency issued on such a principle only represent the previously existing amount of debt, and then suffer a necessary diminution in value.[1] . . .

" The foregoing considerations also show the complete fallacy of the theory we have been discussing, — of issuing notes upon 'good bills.' In a banker's sense, a 'good bill' means simply a bill which is duly paid by the proper party at maturity. It is not of the smallest consequence to him whether the transaction out of which the bill originated is a profit or a loss to the person who incurred the obligation, as long as he is paid. But if the expression 'good bill' be taken in a more extended and philosophical sense to denote a bill upon which it is safe to issue currency, it is a very different matter indeed; for then a 'good bill' can only mean one generated by a successful operation.

" It is not a little remarkable that Adam Smith adopts both the theories of paper currency which have imposed so extensively on the banking and mercantile world, and that within a very few pages of each other: the one theory, that which the Bank Directors and merchants adopted in 1810; the other, which is the great currency fallacy of the present day. The two theories are utterly irreconcilable and inconsistent with each other: the one necessarily leads to the most excessive overissues and depreciation of the paper currency ; the other, if carried out in all its integrity, would be utterly destructive to the business of banking.

" What, then, is the only true foundation of a paper currency? Every consideration of sound reasoning and science proves that the only true foundation of a paper currency is that substance which is the legal or the universally accepted representative of DEBT, *i.e.*, of services due, whatever that substance may be. Now, among all civilized nations, gold or silver bullion is the acknowledged representative of debt. Consequently, gold or silver bullion is the only true basis of a paper currency. Among all civilized nations, the *weight of bullion is the acknowledged measure of value ;* and, consequently, bullion is the only true basis of the 'promises to pay.' * Many unthinking persons declaim against the absurdity of founding a paper currency upon the *commodity* of gold bullion, rather than any other commodity, such as wheat, or silk, or sugar. But it is not as a *commodity* that bullion is the basis of a paper currency, but as the substance which is the accepted representative of *debt*. It would be perfectly possible to make a yard of broadcloth, or a Dutch cheese, representative of debt and the measure of value. Then broadcloth or Dutch cheeses would be the only true basis of a paper currency; and to issue paper upon the basis of bullion would, in such a case, be as improper as to issue paper upon the basis of broadcloth or Dutch cheeses, under existing circumstances. But all nations are agreed that bullion is better fitted by nature for such purpose than broadcloth or Dutch cheeses ; and, consequently, as it seems to be the substance pointed out by Nature herself for representing debt, it is the substance which forms the only true basis of a paper currency.

[1] Macleod on Banking, vol. ii. pp. 172–174.

"Bullion, then, as the symbol of debt, is not only the sole proper basis of a paper currency, but is the only true regulator of its amount. As all paper currency is a 'promise to pay' gold or silver bullion at some definite time, it is quite evident that the 'promises to pay' floating in a nation must bear some proportion in quantity to the actual quantity of the bullion. It is quite impossible to fix any definite proportion; because that depends upon a multitude of peculiar circumstances. Experience is the only guide on the subject. Specie and credit, or money and promises to pay money, then, form the only true circulating medium or currency; and they are its limits.[1] . . .

"But, while we contend that Lord Overstone's criterion of a currency is fatal to his own view, we are quite willing to accept it. For what is it that exists in all places, in all times, and among almost all persons? DEBT, or SERVICES DUE. And what is it that is universally required to measure, record, and transfer them? *Some material.* But we see that all currencies are more or less local: none are universal. The idea, or the want alone, is universal. The notes of a country banker, only circulating in his own neighborhood, are like a country *patois:* each district has its own. A national currency rises to the dignity of a language. But even that is only local, on a larger scale. The ideas only expressed in the language are universal. We are, therefore, strengthened in our conviction, that the only true idea of a currency is that it is the *Representative of Transferable Debt,* and that *whatever represents Transferable Debt* is *Currency.*"[2]

It will be time enough to reply to such flippant and incoherent nonsense, swollen into two spacious volumes, when Dr. Schliemann shall have dug up at Troas or Mycenæ Dutch cheeses perfectly fresh and sweet, and bearing upon their surfaces the dimples in the exact form and shape in which they were impressed by the tiny fingers of the pretty Dutch milkmaids three thousand years ago. Till then the habit or prejudice of mankind in assuming gold, as money, to be capital instead of debt, will be considered as resulting not from accident, but from law.

"We must now consider," he says, "the effect of an inconvertible paper currency on the foreign exchanges and the market price of bullion. So long as paper is convertible, that is, the holder of it has the power to demand payment in gold for it at sight, it is very clear that it cannot circulate at a discount; because, if it fell to a discount, every person who held it would immediately go and demand gold for it. But if, while it enjoys considerable

[1] Macleod on Banking, vol. ii. pp. 191, 192.
[2] Macleod on Banking, vol. i. p. 209.

circulation, the power of convertibility is suddenly taken away, then it becomes, in all respects, equivalent to a new standard, just as much as gold or silver; and its value will be affected by the same principles as these two, viz., by the sole question of the quantity of it in circulation compared to the operations it represents.

" Now if, for the public convenience, it be deemed advisable to issue an inconvertible paper currency, the only way of maintaining its currency at par is by limiting its quantity. We do not mean by this, limiting its quantity to an absolute fixed amount; but by devising some means whereby *a greater quantity of it shall not be issued than if it were convertible into gold.* If more than this be issued, it will be followed by the same result as attends an excessive issue of silver: it will fall to a discount, which in this case is *depreciation;* and the necessary consequences of a depreciated currency will follow, viz., the market price (or paper price) of bullion will rise above the mint price, and the foreign exchanges will fall.

" Now, if such a state of things happens, the proper remedy is to *diminish* the quantity of the paper in circulation until the market price of bullion is reduced to the level of the mint price. If the direct power of demanding five sovereigns be taken away from the holder of a £5 note, still, if he can purchase bullion with it in the market to the amount of five sovereigns, it is an infallible proof that the note is current at par; and the limitation need not proceed beyond that.

" Whenever the currency of a country becomes redundant, that is to say, that prices rise so much higher in one country than in its neighbors that the value of money sensibly diminishes, the natural corrective for such a thing is to take a certain portion of it out of circulation; so that, by diminishing the quantity of it, its value may be raised. When people find that the same quantity of gold will not purchase an equal amount of commodities in this country as they will in another, their own natural instincts will lead them to purchase commodities abroad, where they are cheap, and bring them for sale here where they are dear. The natural instincts of trade will, therefore, produce an equilibrium in value in the currency of neighboring countries.

" Now, when the currency of a country consists partly of paper and partly of gold and silver, it is quite clear that only the metallic portion of it can be exported in payment of foreign commodities. The paper portion of it which has no value abroad must remain at home. If the issues of the paper be continued so as to prevent the currency from recovering its value, the process of the exportation of the metallic portion will go on until it is entirely exhausted. If this be the case, the only method of restoring the currency to its former value is by diminishing the quantity of the paper until the drain is stopped by the enhancement of the value of the whole quantity." [1]

[1] Macleod on Banking, vol. i. pp. 257–260.

This is only the old story over again, that value is not necessary to the circulation of a government or inconvertible currency ; that, no matter how worthless it may be, it will circulate at the value of coin, if it do not exceed the amount of convertible paper which would have circulated in its place, or if its quantity do not exceed the wants of the community in its exchanges. It is useless to repeat the demonstration that all currencies circulate at their real or assumed values.

The late Mr. James W.. Gilbart was a striking instance of a voluminous writer upon money, without any proper comprehension of its nature and laws. He was the author of an elaborate work upon " The Principles and Practice of Banking," and of half a dozen others upon that and kindred subjects. He was, for a long time, manager of the London and Westminster Bank, which he conducted with no little ability and success. As a Political Economist, he belonged to the school of Tooke and Mill, in holding that the convertible notes of no other Bank than that of the Bank of England could influence prices or the rates of exchange. His reasons are sufficiently set forth by the following extracts from the evidence given by him before the House Committee of 1840–41 upon " Banks of issue."

" What reference is made in the issue of paper to the quantity of gold in the country, and to the ultimate ability of the parties to discharge their paper engagements in gold ? — The bankers in issuing their notes do not make any reference to the quantity of gold in the country ; but they make reference to their ability to discharge these notes when returned to them for payment.

" What is the nature of the reference which they make ? — By keeping securities available for the purpose of being sold, in order to discharge those notes whenever presented to them for payment.

" Suppose there was one Bank which had the charge of the paper circulation of the country, and had the means, therefore, by constant reference to the state of the exchanges, of determining the amount of the paper circulation, do not you think that there would be a greater security against a sudden demand for gold, and an inability to pay that gold, than there is when there are a great many issuers, none of whom, according to your own statement, pay the slightest regard to the state of the exchanges ? — No ; I think not.

" What, then, supplies the check ? — The check upon the private bankers is, that their circulation cannot be issued to excess ; whereas, if you had a Bank which should issue notes for so much gold, then every time there was a favorable course of exchange there would be a large issue of notes, which notes would necessarily reduce the rate of interest, lead to speculation, and turn the exchanges again by causing investments to be made in foreign countries. Now, as issues are at present conducted, bankers are under several checks which would not apply to such a Bank, — for instance, the check of the interchange with each other of their different notes once or twice a week, and the check of having their notes payable on demand; whereas, the notes of such a Bank as you suppose would not be diminished except when gold was wanted to be sent abroad. Another check is the practice of giving interest upon deposits, by which all the surplus circulation is called in and lodged with the Banks. Now, such a Bank as you have supposed would not be under the control of those checks, and it would be under the necessity of increasing the circulation whenever the exchange became favorable; and we know by experience that the most sure way of making the exchanges unfavorable is a previous excessive issue; that previous excessive issue would necessarily arise, on the principle you have supposed, every time the exchange was favorable.

"You think that there is some cause in operation which applies equally to all issuers of paper, and prevents any undue issue of paper, and dispenses with the necessity of any reference on the part of each issuer to the state of the exchanges? — That is the case with all country issuers of paper. With regard to the Bank of England, who have the power of issuing their notes in exchange against bullion, in the purchase of Exchequer bills and government stock, it is quite clear that notes put into operation in that way, being thrown in a mass upon the previously existing state of trade, will have the effect of raising prices and reducing interest, and turn the exchanges; but if notes are issued merely to pay for transactions that have previously taken place, and are drawn out by the operations of trade, those notes will have no such effect. . . .

" Then, you do think that the expansion of the circulation of the Bank of England may cause unfavorable exchanges? — Yes.

" Why should not the expansion of the circulation on the part of the country issuers produce the same effect? — Because the country circulation is under checks, whereas the Bank of England circulation is not: the country circulation can be issued only in consequence of transactions which have taken place, and to the extent only required by the wants of the district; whereas it is obvious that the Bank of England has the power of increasing the circulation by the purchase of Exchequer bills or stock, or by purchasing bullion, and throwing a mass of notes on the market when the state of trade does not require it.

" *Chairman.* Have you any further observations to make to the Committee? — When the first question was asked of me, at the commencement of my examination, I stated that I appeared before the Committee as the representative of the joint-stock Banks, and that, therefore, in expressing any opinions consistently with the resolutions which they had passed, I wished to be considered as speaking the sentiments of the joint-stock Banks; but, should the

Committee ask me any question not connected with the circumstances of country issues, that I wish to be considered as speaking my own individual opinions.   The points upon which I wish to be considered as speaking the sentiments of the joint-stock Banks are as follows : I speak the opinions of the joint-stock Banks in saying that their circulation cannot be made to fluctuate in exact conformity with the circulation of the Bank of England, or with the stock of gold in the Bank of England ; that the country issue is drawn out by the demands of trade, and is subject to checks to which the circulation of the Bank of England is not liable ; that the country bankers have not the power of issuing their notes to excess ; that they cannot contract their circulation, or expand it, as they please ; and, also, that the country circulation does not influence the prices of commodities, and that it cannot be regulated by the principles of the foreign exchanges." [1]

The issues of private Banks and bankers, says Mr. Gilbart, can never be in excess, for two reasons : 1st, from their constant retirement " by the interchange by the Banks with each other of their different notes and checks, once or twice a week ; " and, 2d, for the reason that, by allowing interest on deposits, " all the surplus circulation is called in, and lodged with the Banks."   Suppose all the Banks to largely increase their issues, the exchange of £10,000,000 per week would be no more of a check than the exchange of £5,000,000.   One quantity could be exchanged as well as another.   An inflation may take place to a very large extent where exchanges are daily made, and where the Banks are on a specie basis, provided the issuers are all actuated by similar sentiments and move in a similar direction.   This is the way inflations do take place, and continue till some link in the chain snaps, to disclose the weakness of all.   Suppose all excess of currency to be called in by reason of an allowance of interest by the Banks, how is such interest to be paid ?   Of course, by reloaning the " excess " so deposited, as fast as received.   The " excess " would be in circulation as much after as before it was taken in, only in a different form.   Both of his checks, therefore, are only creations of his own imagination.

The issues of country Banks, says Mr. Gilbart, cannot affect prices like those of the Bank of England, for the reason that they are issued merely to pay for transactions that have pre-

---

[1] Principles and Practice of Banking, pp. 477–481.

viously taken place, or are drawn out by the operations of trade; while, "with regard to the Bank of England, which has the power of issuing its notes in exchange against bullion, in the purchase of Exchequer bills and government stock, it is quite clear that notes put into operation in that way, being thrown in a mass upon the previously existing state of trade, will have the effect of raising prices and reducing interest, and turn the exchanges," — an effect which the issues of country Banks will not produce. Now a £1,000 bank-note of a country Bank, or a check for a like amount drawn against deposits in it, will exert precisely the same effect upon prices, and upon the rates of interest and exchange, as a £1,000 note or check upon the Bank of England. The one is thrown in mass upon the previously existing state of trade as much as the other. The Bank throws its notes into the market for the purchase of Exchequer bills and securities; the country Bank, in the purchase of similar securities, or to help forward some enterprise or speculative scheme. The impulse or motive that gave birth to each is precisely the same. Once in the market, they perform precisely the same functions, and are subject to precisely the same laws. They are equally promises to pay coin on demand; and must be equally discharged within similar periods, by the payment of coin or its equivalent. Mr. Gilbart assumed that the Bank of England notes, when issued against bullion and used in the purchase of securities, would remain in circulation till the gold, by the turning of the rates of exchange, is wanted for export; and, by remaining in circulation, would affect prices in a manner which the notes of private Banks and bankers could not, for the reason that the latter were called into existence only by commercial operations taking place, or which were to take place, and must be speedily retired. But years may elapse after the loans for getting rid of the bullion in the Bank were made, before the exchanges would turn sufficiently to cause an export of gold. In the mean time, the notes so issued would have been taken in and reissued, or others issued in their place, a dozen times; and in every case, by the payment of gold or its equivalent. When the notes of the Bank, or of any private Bank or banker, get into circulation, they produce an effect in ratio to their quantity or amount; and as the issues of the private Banks and bankers in England, including joint-stock Banks, exceed tenfold those of the Bank of England, their effect must be in like ratio, — that is, ten times greater than that exerted by those of the Bank. It is certain that the former do exert a much greater influence over prices and the rates of exchange, in ratio to their amount, than the latter; for the reason that they have a much more intimate connection than those of the Bank with the foreign commerce of the country, and are usually made upon securities, as a class, inferior to those which the rules of the Bank allow it to take. Mr. Gilbart's assumption, therefore, that the notes of the Bank exert an influence over prices and rates of exchange greater than those exerted by the notes of country Banks, is as wanting in meaning as was Lord Overstone's distinction between the effect produced by the notes of the Bank and checks drawn upon it.

To questions put to him by the Committee of 1840–41 as to what course he would advise the Bank to pursue in the event of a war, he replied as follows : —

Question 1064. " Your answer assumes that the exchanges are never likely to be adverse during the period of a war, or that the drain of gold is not likely to be considerable ; how do you reconcile that with the circumstances attending the last war, or with the war in 1797, when the Bank was reduced to a state of exhaustion of its treasure ? " — " I do not know that any answer assumes that ; but, however, as a political question, rather than a banking one, I confess that, if I were the Prime Minister, I would immediately, on the commencement of a war, issue an order in council for the Bank to stop payment."

Question 1065. " Then, you are of opinion that a suspension of payment is necessarily the consequence of a war ? " — " ' Necessarily ' is a strong term ; but I should think it the best measure to adopt, and I should decidedly adopt it."

Question 1144, *Sir Thomas Fremantle.* " Do you mean to say that the Bank would be able to do so in a time of war ? " — " In a time of war I should stop payment at once. It would be better to stop before the gold was gone than afterwards."

Question 1145, *Mr. Warburton.* " You would recommend that as a desirable thing in itself ? " — " Yes, as an expedient thing."

Question 1148, *Sir Robert Peel.* " You would advise, under certain circumstances, a Bank-restriction as a immediate measure ? " — " If you had a war, a Bank-restriction I should immediately recommend."

Question 1149. . . . " When you issued your measure of restriction, what is the corresponding security that you would take to prevent that excess of issue which you have admitted to be an evil ? " — " In advocating immediate restriction, I am not speaking as a banker, but a politician. I should certainly enact the restriction of cash notes, to prevent the enemy withdrawing the gold from this country."

Mr. Gilbart, in the event of a war, would suspend specie payments, — would demonetize gold and silver, as a means of retaining them in the country. He would cut off the handle of your axe, and render it useless, so as to prevent an enemy from striking off your head. But how was the enemy to get hold of the handle? By paying the price both for that and the axe. If he paid the price, he might thereby put in the hands of the owner that wherewith to defend himself far better than with the axe. In a war, men do not pelt each other with paper bullets and guineas, but with what those purchase; so that a nation cannot, perhaps, do a better thing than increase its means of defence by parting with its gold. The better way is to leave the handle in, and let the enemy take it at his peril. But if the gold of a country at war be demonetized, the enemy or some other nation will be sure to get it, not in exchange for powder and ball, but for wines and silks, — for that which, instead of arming and furnishing it for the fight, would inevitably tend to its emasculation, to the destruction of all patriotism and manhood. The effect of a war is always to turn the exchanges of a country engaged in it in its favor, for the reason that every one orders home the proceeds of his exports in coin, in order to have in hand that upon which he can certainly rely, should the event prove unfavorable, should domestic order be disturbed, or the wonted industries of the country fail. The exchanges were instantly turned in favor of the United States upon the outbreak of the war of the Rebellion, and gold continued to flow into the country in immense volume until the suspension of specie payments. The exports of coin and bullion from the United States in 1860, the year preceding the Rebellion, equalled $66,546,289; the imports, $8,550,135. The imports for 1861, the first year of the war, during which the country remained on a specie basis, equalled $46,359,601; the exports, $23,800,810. Specie payments were suspended near the close of 1861, through the perverse action of the Secretary of the Treasury. The first issue of legal-tender notes was authorized Feb. 25, 1862. The imports of specie for that year equalled $16,415,012; the exports, $36,886,956. The exports for 1863 equalled $100,321,731;

the imports, $13,115,612. These facts show the effect of demonetizing the currency of a country. The exports for 1863, 1864, and 1865, equalled $220,932,000 ; the imports, $32,504,000. For the years last named, legal-tender notes were worth hardly fifty per cent of their par value. The retaining of gold in the country was a matter wholly within its power. If legal-tender notes had not been issued, the United States would have laid all the world under tribute. The first impulse of a people when they find themselves about to be plunged into a war is to forego every article that does not rank among the necessities of life. Their silver and gold are the first things they place beyond the reach of harm. Foreigners cannot get them, unless they pay more than they are worth. This they will not do, for the reason that they can get them of nations at peace, for their worth. The position of the United States, so far as its currency was concerned, was impregnable, but for its voluntary demonetization. Both England and the United States are striking examples of the effect of Mr. Gilbart's method. Both lost their gold as soon as it could be taken away from them by lavish and wasteful expenditure. By reason of an inconvertible currency, England probably doubled her national debt. It might not have been one-tenth its present amount ; for if her gold had not been demonetized, she might have escaped or avoided wars which, with all the success achieved, brought unnumbered woes upon her people. The civil war in the United States would have been ended in half the time, and at half the cost, but for demonetizing their coin. But for this, the nation, when it came out of the conflict, would have been in position to have at once started upon a new career of prosperity, the vast incubus of slavery having been shaken off. Twelve years have elapsed since order was restored, and it is still confronted with a problem far more difficult of solution than that of the subjection of the Slave States.

The following extract will show the modes by which, according to Mr. Gilbart, banking capital may be raised : —

"Now, it is obvious that these two kinds of banking are adapted to produce precisely the same effects. In each case, a banking capital is created, and each capital is employed in precisely the same way ; namely, in the discounting of bills. To the parties who have their bills discounted, it matters not from what source the capital is raised : the advantage is the same to them, and the effects upon trade and commerce will be the same. Let us suppose that in each case the banking capital created is £50,000. Now, the Bank of circulation will have increased the amount of money in the country by £50,000. The Bank of deposit will not have increased at all the amount of money in the country ; but it will have put into motion £50,000 that would otherwise have been idle. Here, then, is a proof that to give increased rapidity to the circulation of money has precisely the same effect as to increase the amount. Here, too, is a proof of the ignorance of banking on the part of those writers who consider that the Banks which issue notes are the sole cause of high prices, over-trading, and speculation ; whereas, it is obvious that if those effects are to be attributed to banking at all, they may as fairly be ascribed to Banks of deposit as to Banks of circulation." [1]

The difference in the two cases is, that in one the £50,000 of capital provided for the Bank is capital in a form proper to be loaned ; in the other, no capital whatever is created or provided. To say that notes, without the least provision for their redemption, are the equivalent of deposits, which may be wholly in the form of coin or of notes representing coin, is to say that fiction equals reality, and shadow substance. The difference in effect in the operations of the Bank would equal the difference in fact. The issue of the £50,000, without any thing to support it, would in all probability involve all parties to it in embarrassment and loss, while the loaning of the capital made up of deposits might prove most advantageous to all parties to the loan. The distinction, however, between the effect of issues based upon capital, and such as are purely fictitious, has been too fully shown to require comment here. Mr. Gilbart, undoubtedly, possessed a capacity of intuitively measuring the person who wanted to borrow his money ; but he was wholly out of his sphere when he undertook to write upon its laws.

Among the more recent publications is the " Manual of Political Economy," by Mr. Henry Fawcett, Professor of this science in the University of Cambridge, England. The following is his account of the nature and function of paper money : —

[1] Principles and Practice of Banking, p. 88.

" A moment's consideration will show that a bank-note, whether issued by a State establishment or by a private firm, is simply a convenient form for bringing into practical use the credit which may be possessed by the Bank. . . . A banker, therefore, whose credit is good can circulate a great number of his notes in his own neighborhood; his notes being willingly accepted by those to whom he is known. . . . It is manifestly to his advantage to issue notes; for, suppose £60,000 of these notes are kept in circulation, it is ascertained by experience that an amount of legal tender equivalent in value to one-third of the notes issued will be sufficient, if kept as a reserve, to meet all the notes which are presented for payment. A banker, therefore, whose notes circulate to the extent of £60,000, has £40,000 at his free disposal to invest in some profitable investment. . . .

" It may be asked, What would be the effect upon prices if the bank-note circulation were suddenly increased? This suggests one of the most disputed of the currency questions. As previously stated, the bank-note circulation of England is placed under various restrictions, the nature of which will be presently detailed. The purpose we have in view, at this stage of our inquiry, is to investigate the effect which would be produced on prices if the bank-note circulation were largely increased by a removal of all restrictions which now limit its amount. We conceive that the effect which would be produced entirely depends upon circumstances. Let it be supposed that there is no change in the population, or in the commercial condition of the country. If, under these circumstances, an increased issue of notes were added to the money circulation of the country, prices would manifestly rise; because there would be now more money in circulation to carry on the same amount of buying and selling which was previously conducted by a smaller amount of money. If, however, the additional notes which are issued simply cause a corresponding amount of bullion to be withdrawn from circulation, it is manifest that no effect is produced on prices. The only result is, that the trade of the country is carried on more economically; because these notes, which are simply pieces of paper of no intrinsic value, perform with equal efficiency all the purposes which were previously fulfilled by the gold, now supposed to be dispensed with. Consequently the economy of this substitution is evident. Gold is a valuable commodity, requiring much labor and capital to obtain it. We therefore have the following principles to guide us in an inquiry into the effects of a bank-note circulation : —

" 1. If bank-notes simply occupy, in the monetary circulation of the country, the place of a corresponding value of bullion, these notes produce no effect on prices.

" 2. If it can be shown, that, either by the repeal of the Bank Charter Act or by any other cause, the bank-note circulation of the country can be increased without withdrawing from circulation a corresponding amount of coin, it is manifest that the aggregate money circulating in a country will be augmented, and general prices will, as a consequence, undoubtedly rise. . . .

"In discussing the laws of price, the principle was established, that general prices depend upon the quantity of money in circulation compared with the wealth which is bought and sold with money, and also upon the frequency with which this wealth is bought and sold before it is consumed. If more wealth is produced, and an increased quantity of wealth is also bought and sold for money, general prices must decline, unless a large quantity of money is brought into circulation. Suppose, for instance, that the production of every kind of wealth is doubled in this country, that every one doubles his purchase of commodities, and, at the same time, there is no increase in the amount of money in circulation: upon this hypothesis, each individual, although he is supposed to purchase twice as much of every commodity as he did before, will only possess the same amount of money with which to effect these purchases. He will, therefore, be only able to give the same amount of money for double the quantity of each commodity he purchases; but this is tantamount to saying that general prices have declined one half. In fact, if there should be an increased production of wealth, if there should be more buying and selling, or if any other circumstance should occur the effect of which is to require the circulation of a larger amount of money, the value of money must rise; or, in other words, general prices must decline, unless an increased supply of money is forthcoming, so that a larger amount may be brought into circulation. When buying and selling are effected by bills of exchange, the necessity for money is as completely dispensed with as if the transaction was carried on by barter: these trading transactions, therefore, in which bills of exchange are employed may be almost indefinitely extended, without rendering it necessary to bring an increased amount of money into circulation.

"A consideration of some of the consequences which would ensue if bills of exchange did not exist will perhaps more plainly indicate the influence which they exert upon prices. Suppose that all the commodities which are now bought and sold by means of bills of exchange were paid for by money, a largely increased amount of money would be required to be brought into circulation. If this additional supply were not forthcoming, money would rise in value; or, in other words, general prices would decline. Hence bills of exchange, in many classes of transactions, are a convenient and complete substitute for money. Consequently, if it were not for bills of exchange, one of two things must happen: either the money in circulation must be increased, or the money already in circulation must become more valuable, since a greater amount of money will be required to carry on the trade and commerce of the country. But to say that money becomes more valuable is equivalent to stating that general prices decline.

"It therefore appears that we cannot, by a simple negative or affirmative, answer the question, whether an increased issue of bills of exchange affects prices. All that can be said is this: if the buying and selling now carried on by bills of exchange were effected by money, then one of two things must occur, — either more money must be brought into circulation, or general prices must decline. The influence, however, which is exerted upon prices by bills of exchange is not due to any thing peculiar in the nature or form of a bill of exchange : it is not the bill which produces the influence, but the influence is produced by the credit which is given. The bill is not this credit; but is simply a testimony or record of its existence. The truth of this assertion is illustrated by the fact, that buying and selling may be carried on by book credits, instead of by bills of exchange. . . . In this case (the illustration given), although the buying and selling are nominally made for money, yet the resort to book credits enables money to be as completely dispensed with as if bills of exchange had been used. It is therefore credit, and not the particular form which credit may assume, that enables money to be dispensed with, and consequently produces an influence on prices."[1]

Experience when appealed to in the case of the issue of the £60,000 of notes, as assumed in the first of the preceding paragraphs, would have shown that all issued would return to the banker for redemption regularly, and within periods of from sixty to ninety days from their issue, to be discharged by an equal amount of coin, or the equivalent of coin. How were these to be met? If the banker discounted bills representing merchandise, his notes would be returned to him by their makers in their payment. If he discounted those that would not be paid, then the notes issued would have to be presently taken in by him, by paying out a corresponding amount of his reserve. The debts created by their issue are to be discharged by their use, or by that of coin. Every note issued, therefore, must have a provision of an equal amount of capital for its discharge, and must be discharged by such provision. Its value depends upon its capacity of being discharged, of being retired from circulation. If it could never be discharged, it could have no value. Such is the law of all convertible currencies. Notes get into circulation upon the credit of the issuer ; but it is always upon the assumption that means, their equivalent in value, are first provided for their redemption. Without such confidence, no one would take them. The basis of their circulation is not credit, but capital. Credit is but another word for confidence that such capital exists, and can always be had when wanted. It may as well be in the hands of the public or of the merchant, and on its way to the con-

---

[1] Manual of Political Economy, pp. 427-433.

sumer, as in the hands of the issuer. If it be in the hands of the public or the merchant, then £3,000 is all that the issuer need hold against an issue of £60,000, as the return of the notes would be insured by the capital for the distribution of which they were the instruments. The reserve is not held to meet such notes as occasionally return, such as are assumed to be issued in excess; for the reason that all will return within their appointed periods. Mr. Fawcett wholly misconceived the law or nature of paper money. A similar answer may be given to his statement that notes can be substituted, as currency, for a corresponding amount of gold; the saving to the country being in the amount of the substitution, "because notes, which are simply pieces of paper of no intrinsic value, perform with equal efficiency all the purposes which were previously fulfilled by the gold which is now supposed to be dispensed with." Notes which are constantly being retired from circulation cannot take the place of gold which remains, as currency, unchanged and permanently in circulation. Whether convertible or not, they cannot perform, with equal efficiency, all the purposes which are fulfilled by gold. Their value is representative, not intrinsic; that of gold is intrinsic, not representative. Notes become valueless if their constituent become valueless; the value of gold depends upon nothing but itself. Gold is legal tender in the discharge of contracts; paper, such as that of which Mr. Fawcett was speaking, is not. Gold can be used in the arts; notes cannot. Gold can discharge indebtedness to foreign countries; notes cannot. Gold can discharge balances arising in the domestic trade of a country; notes cannot. Gold can be held as reserves by the issuers of paper money, and by society, and for all time; notes cannot in either case, as they are necessarily speedily retired by the use, or disappearance from any cause, of their constituent. Notes are accepted within the country in which they are issued, by reason of their representative character. They can perform only one function of gold, — that of effecting domestic exchanges. Mr. Fawcett should have been logician enough to have seen that the less cannot include the greater. Paper discharges gold from use in one particular; but can no more be substituted for it in all the functions which the latter has to perform in the economy of society than a mere promise can be substituted for the performance, or sugar for iron.

As the substitution is impossible, the advantage resulting therefrom is impossible. Great advantages result from the use of paper money, and in ratio to its use, in the same way that great advantages result from the use of ships and railroads. In ratio to its use, will the gold of a country, or the power to command and consume it, be increased. But paper can no more be substituted for gold than can ships and railroads.

Mr. Fawcett's theory of the effect upon prices of credit in the form of paper money is singularly unphilosophic and inadequate. With him, the whole thing is a mere piece of mechanism: so much money, so much price; and the reverse. His conclusions are based upon assumptions wholly impossible in themselves. " If," he says, " the amount of money be reduced one-half, that of merchandise remaining the same, prices will fall one-half; if it be increased, prices will rise in like ratio. So, if the production of all kinds of wealth in a country be doubled, and every one doubles his purchase of commodities, the amount of money in it remaining the same, prices will fall one-half." But production and consumption cannot be doubled, the amount of money remaining the same; both must, as a rule, proceed in ratio to the amount of money in circulation. Paper money is the symbol of merchandise: the one must be in ratio to the other, as the necessary condition of production and consumption. He might as well have assumed the commerce of a country to be doubled for the reason that the ships employed carried twice as much as they have the ability to carry. His statements and illustrations are nothing less than contradictions in terms. Credit in the form of money has an effect entirely different from that due to its quantity. " If," says Fawcett, in effect, " one would lift two pounds of merchandise with a one pound weight, he must double, or reduce one-half, the length of one arm of the scale." The true object of paper money is to raise the two pounds of merchandise without the employment of any weight whatever. So far as this can be done, can the cost of the operations of weighing be saved, and prices reduced in like ratio; and so far can the coin of a country be employed in the discharge of functions peculiar to itself, and which neither symbols nor paper money of any kind can discharge. Such a relation of currency to prices wholly escaped him. He

assumed an increase of currency to be followed by an increase
of prices. The whole question turns upon the nature of
the currency. If it be neither capital nor the representative of
capital (merchandise) ; if it be that kind of currency which can
be substituted for gold, like legal tender, then he was quite
right ; for an increase of such currency always tends to advance prices in being in excess of the means of consumption.
If it be capital or the representative of capital, then he was
wholly wrong ; for prices must be in ratio to the amount of
merchandise fitted for consumption, or in ratio to the perfection
of the instruments for its distribution.

The same remarks apply with equal force to bills as currency
as to bank-notes. Bills are, equally with bank-notes, the representatives of values, — of merchandise ; and would have no
value but for their capacity of being discharged by it. As
they must always speedily disappear if they possess any value,
they can no more be substituted for coin than can notes. Mr.
Fawcett predicates the same results of them as of bank-notes,
and assumes that their use may discharge that of gold altogether. An increase in their amount puts up prices ; a decrease in it puts them down. Suppose, he says, " that all the
commodities which are now bought and sold by means of bills
of exchange were paid for by money, a largely increased
amount of money would be required to be brought into circulation." But if bills of exchange, that is, symbolic money,
were not used, " all the commodities now bought and sold "
would not be bought and sold, — probably not one-quarter the
present amount. They would not exist. They are bought and
sold, that is, they do exist, by reason of the use of symbolic
money. With a return to a metallic currency, the amount of
commodities would not only be greatly reduced, but the cost
to consumers would be greatly increased.

Such is the confusion which prevails as to the nature and effect upon prices, of credits in the forms in which they are chiefly
used, that it may be well, at the risk of some repetition, to re-
state the whole subject. The lending of his name by a party
possessed of means in real estate or securities, to another of integrity and enterprise, is one of the usual illustrations of the
beneficent results that may flow from the use of credits. The
capitalist, as he is termed, will make a profit in the form of

interest upon the amount of the credit he extends. The borrower gets that upon which he can profitably exercise his industry and skill. But such credit, as a rule, is valueless until it is turned by a Bank into money. This done, the borrower contracts to pay the amount of the loan in money, within a comparatively brief period. This is to be provided out of the proceeds of the enterprise or industry in which he may engage. If he cannot turn this to account within the time within which the loan of the Bank is to be repaid, then the credit will prove to him a source of loss far greater than its amount. It was the means of anticipating — of putting into the form of money — that which perhaps existed only in idea, or which, if well based, might require years for its proper development. If the borrower cannot pay, then the capitalist, at the last moment, will be called upon. He may not be able to take in his credit immediately, although possessed of large means ; and, consequently, becomes involved and discredited by the operation. If he cannot seasonably pay, the Bank must take in its notes, by paying out a corresponding amount of coin. Its ability to discount, and with it the amount of the currency, will be reduced in like degree. The currency, which was inflated by the amount of the discount above the ordinary range, is now reduced as far below it ; and prices fall in like, or in still greater, ratio. All credits, therefore, of the kind described produce, as a rule, two effects : a rise, from an issue of instruments in excess of the means of consumption ; and then a fall, far greater and of longer continuance than the rise, from a reduction of the currency as far below as it had exceeded its ordinary range, and from the improvident expenditure of capital equal to the amount of the credit given. Such credits, therefore, should never be made the basis of industrial enterprises. Another form of credit, the process of which has already been fully detailed, is that by which bills given in the purchase of merchandise, for its distribution, are converted by Banks into paper money, by means of which producers can anticipate the sale of their products and collection of the proceeds. By this process they are enabled to continue their industries on their wonted scale. The effect is greatly to reduce prices to the consumer, while usually increasing the profits of the producer. A third form — that out of which bills which form the basis of paper money chiefly arise — is the intrusting to the merchant such possession of that in which he deals as is necessary for the discharge of his particular function. Such credit may be given by bill, or by book account. By its means, merchandise reaches the consumer with no other burden resting upon it than cost, and the necessary charge and compensation for the labor employed in its distribution. When it reaches the consumer, and is paid for, the proceeds return through the same channel through which it was distributed, discharging the obligations incurred in the several stages; to be finally paid over to the producer, or to the Bank, assuming the merchandise to have been sold upon credit and a bill given therefor, and turned into notes. The credit last described exerts a most powerful influence in the reduction of prices. In one sense, it includes the previous one, as it lays the foundation for bankers' credits, to be given in the discount of bills. The two last are the only ones that act to any considerable extent upon prices; and their effect in the end is always to produce a fall when the prices which the consumer pays, as well as those which the producer realizes, are taken into account. Were the effect of credits, in their proper sense, to raise instead of reducing prices, they would be the greatest of evils, instead of being, as they are, most valuable contrivances in the economy of society.

The only effect of the Act of 1844 would be to allow perfect freedom in the form of the currency issued. There might be an increased use of notes, and fewer checks; but this is not probable.

"Inconvertible notes," says Fawcett, "will be as freely accepted as coin, if people have confidence that an inconvertible currency is only a temporary expedient, and that the government will take scrupulous care never to permit the issue of inconvertible notes to exceed an amount which can with certainty be ultimately redeemed.

"It is, therefore, possible to conceive that exceptional circumstances may occur, during which an inconvertible currency may be issued, if kept within proper limits, without disturbing the finances of the country. For instance, there can be little doubt that the American civil war created a demand for a greater amount of money to be circulated in that country. More money was in fact required; because the raising of a large army, and supporting it in the field, would render it necessary to make many more payments in money. If the issue of an inconvertible currency in America had gone no further than to satisfy this demand for a greater sum of money to be brought into circulation, no one's confidence in the financial credit of the government would have been shaken, and the inconvertible currency would have exerted no effect on prices. But the American government far outstepped their legitimate limits."[1]

People accept an inconvertible currency of government notes, as it will discharge their own debts existing at the time, by virtue of its being legal tender, and from a belief that it will speedily be redeemed by an equivalent in some form.   If government be competent to issue it, it would have a high value for a time, even if it were believed that it would not be paid.   While there are grave objections to such a currency, says Mr. Fawcett, it is possible that if its issue were confined within reasonable limits, it might be issued without disturbing the finances of a country.   If, for example, the United States, in the late civil war, had issued notes only in ratio to their increased necessity for money, the issue could have exerted no influence over prices.   The yearly average expenditures of that country previous to the war equalled, say, $45,000,000. They went up during the war to $750,000,000 annually, for three years.   The demand for money, measured by the price of the notes issued, exceeded sixteen-fold the amount of previous expenditure.   To that extent, said Mr. Fawcett, government notes might be issued, and the currency increased in like ratio, without exerting any influence upon prices; for the reason that the money issued would only be in ratio to the increased necessity for its use.   But how could the expenditures of a government be increased sixteen-fold, or even eight-fold, without any increase of capital, or fund to draw upon, and prices remain at their old figures?   It is the same as to say that a demand multiplied by one per cent equals a demand multiplied by eight or sixteen per cent.   If gold could have been supplied wherewith to meet all expenditures growing out of the war, prices would still have increased enormously, from the excess of demand over supply.   Gold was not, or could not be, had.   Legal-tender could ; and prices rose in ratio to its use, and to the necessities of the government.   At one time, $281 of paper would purchase only $100 of coin.   Prices rose, there-

---

[1] Manual of Political Economy, p. 443.

fore, in ratio to the demand; in other words, in ratio to the inflation of the currency. If Mr. Fawcett had paused long enough to ask himself weather or not a sovereign to be received six months hence had the same value to the person who was to receive it as a sovereign in hand; or whether a government note having one year to run, without interest, equalled in value its note having the same time to run, bearing interest, — the answer, properly made, would have unlocked to him all the mysteries of money. Instead of this, he contented himself with a mild restatement of all the old dogmas, every one of which he accepted without reservation, and every one of which is exactly opposed to the principles upon which money is based. It must, however, be said in his favor, that his style is in agreeable contrast to the incoherent extravagance of Macleod and the fantastic nonsense of Bonamy Price.

Mr. W. Stanley Jevons, Professor of Political Economy in the University of London, in a recently published work, entitled "Money and the Mechanism of Exchange," gives the following account of the nature of paper money, and the manner in which it gets into use: —

"Metallic money, as we have seen, immensely facilitates, and, so to speak, lubricates the operation of exchange. But nations employing gold and silver money have usually discovered, in the course of time, that tokens of small metallic value, or even pieces of leather and paper of nominal value, might be passed from hand to hand as signs of the ownership of coins. That which replaces gold or silver or copper money is at first of a purely representative character. But, when a community has become thoroughly habituated to the circulation of a currency of this character, it is often found possible to remove the basis of valuable metal which it is supposed to represent, and yet to maintain the valueless bits of leather or paper in circulation as before. Thus arises the abnormal phenomenon known as an *inconvertible paper money*. . . .

"Although we now distinguish money according as it is metallic or paper money, because paper has in recent times been universally adopted as the material for representative money, yet it is well to remember that various other substances have been used for the purpose. We may pass, in fact, by gradual steps, from the perfect standard coins, whose nominal value is coincident with their metallic value, to worthless bits of paper, which are yet allowed to stand for thousands, or even millions, of pounds sterling. . . .[1]

"Persons who have long been accustomed to pay away certain pieces of paper without loss will continue to regard them as good

[1] Money and the Mechanism of Exchange, pp. 191–194.

currency, until some rude shock is given to their confidence. This may go so far that a dirty bit of paper, containing a promise to pay a sovereign, will be actually preferred to the beautiful gold coin which it promises. The currency of Scotland is a standing proof of this assertion; and the same may be said of Norway, where, until 1874, no gold at all was in circulation, and notes for one, five, or ten dollars formed the principal part of the currency.

" There is one all-important point in which representative differs from metallic money: it will not circulate beyond the boundaries of the district or country where it is legally current or habitually employed. No doubt, Bank of England notes are frequently carried abroad by travellers, and are in most places readily exchanged for the money of the locality; but they never circulate, and are treated as bills upon London, forming a convenient mode of remittance. They do not satisfy a debt from this to another country; but rather create it, an English bank-note in the hands of a Paris banker representing a claim which he has upon the Bank of England. The only money which can really be exported in payment of debts due to foreign merchants is standard metallic money. Hence paper money has exactly the same capacity for driving out standard money that light or depreciated coins possess.

" In the case of inconvertible notes, this has always been most obvious. As the quantity of such notes issued progressively increases, as almost always happens, coin must be exported; otherwise the currency would be excessive. But when most of the coin is gone, need begins to be felt for making foreign payments, and then the value of the paper falls below that of the coin which it is supposed to correspond to." [1]

As all convertible currencies, as already shown, are regularly retired within periods of, say ninety days from their issue, worthless bits of leather and paper can only " stand for thousands and millions sterling " for such a length of time. If they get into circulation, confidence must therefore be very frequently shocked. It does happen that large amounts of paper money get into circulation, having no more value than worthless bits of leather or paper; but they get into circulation for the reason that it is always believed that a metallic basis of value underlies them. If they have no such basis, those who take them are deceived. Mr. Jevons fortifies his statement by reference to the notes of Scotch Banks; but confidence was never shocked in reference to these, for the reason that it was always known that they rested on a basis of metals, or upon that which would produce metals. He assumed that worthless bits of paper — the basis of metal being wholly removed —

---

[1] Money and the Mechanism of Exchange, pp. 214, 215.

circulated by the same law as that which controls the circulation of coin, or that which was convertible on demand into coin. Paper money, he continues, has exactly the same capacity for driving out standard money that light or depreciated coins possess. What kind of paper money? Convertible paper money exerts no such tendency: on the contrary, its tendency is to bring metallic money into the country to form the basis of its issue. The two are equal in value, and move harmoniously side by side. Debased coin drives out standard coin, only for the reason that it has the same competency in the payment of debts; and, of two equally competent instruments, the less costly will be preferred. The example of England, in 1694, is strikingly in point. The coin was debased, but not demonetized; and those who had occasion to pay debts would use that which would cost the least. So soon as the debased coin was demonetized, it passed at its real — not at its denominational — value. Mr. Jevons holds that all kinds of paper money displace corresponding amounts of coin; or, to speak more to the point, he held to the traditions which he found in the books.

Again: —

" We may now proceed with advantage to consider the various methods in which the issue of paper money may be conducted. This question is, perhaps, the most vexed and debatable one in the whole sphere of Political Economy; but, by carefully adhering to the analysis of facts, we may, perhaps, get a view of the subject free from the great perplexities in which it is commonly involved. The elementary principles of the subject are not of a complex character; and, if we hold tenaciously to those principles, we may, perhaps, be saved from that dangerous kind of intellectual vertigo which often attacks writers on the currency.

" The State may either take the issue of representative money into its own hands, as it takes the coining of money; or it may allow private individuals, or semi-public companies and corporations, to undertake the work under more or less strict legislative control. We will afterwards briefly consider the relative advantages of government and private issues; but, in either case, we may lay down the following series of methods, according to which the amount of issue may be regulated, and the performance of the promises guaranteed."[1]

What would the money of a State represent? A beggared treasury and a parcel of ignorant and listless officials. No

[1] Money and the Mechanism of Exchange, pp. 217, 218.

State money issued as currency ever represented any thing else. Whoever issues it, however, or currency in any form, has nothing to fear, so long as they observe " fourteen series of methods " laid down and fully exploited by Mr. Jevons. We spare the reader their exploitation, in order not to inflict upon him the money-writer's malady. They should, however, be none the less studied. They should be placarded before the desk of every young man ambitious to rise and shine in the financial world. The heads or titles of Mr. Jevons's " fourteen series of methods " are as follows : —

1. The Simple Deposit Method.
2. The Partial Deposit Method.
3. The Minimum Reserve Method.
4. The Proportional Reserve Method.
5. The Maximum Issue Method.
6. The Elastic Limit Method.
7. The Documentary Reserve Method.
8. The Real Property Reserve Method.
9. The Foreign Exchanges Method.
10. The Free Issue Method.
11. The Gold Par Method.
12. The Revenue Payments Method.
13. The Deferred Convertibility Method.
14. The Paper Money Method.[1]

The following is Mr. Jevons's mode of maintaining the value of inconvertible paper money at the par value of gold : —

" Assuming an inconvertible paper currency to be issued, and to be entirely in the hands of government, many of the evils of such a system might be avoided, if the issue were limited or reduced the moment that the price of gold in paper rose above par. As long as the notes, and the gold coin which they pretend to represent, circulate on a footing of equality, they are as good as if convertible." [2]

Admitted. But suppose that a person holding sovereigns will not exchange them for equal amounts of inconvertible paper, what then ? We know of no other advice than that given

---

[1] Several of the above methods have much to commend them to the people of the United States ; especially the " Maximum Issue Method," the " Elastic Limit Method," the " Free Issue Method," and the " Deferred Convertibility Method." The last two, it is probable, would be the most popular. The others, however, would be received with more or less favor. It is to be regretted that space does not allow their further presentation here.

[2] Money and the Mechanism of Exchange, p. 231.

by Dogberry to the watch : " If he will not 'exchange,' let him go, and thank God you are rid of a knave " !

Again : —

" We now come to the undisguised *paper money* issued by government, and ordered to be received as legal tender. Such inconvertible paper notes have in all instances been put in circulation as convertible ones, or in the place of such ; and they are always expressed in terms of money. The French mandats of one hundred francs, for instance, bear the ambiguous phrase, " Bon pour cent francs." The wretched scraps of paper which circulate in Buenos Ayres are marked " Un Peso Moneda Corriente," reminding one of the time when the peso was a heavy standard coin. After the promise of payment in coin is found to be illusory, the notes still circulate, partly from habit, partly because the people must have some currency, and have no coin to use for the purpose, or, if they have, carefully hoard it for profit or future use. There is plenty of evidence to prove that an inconvertible paper money, if carefully limited in quantity, can retain its full value. Such was the case with the Bank of England notes for several years after the suspension of specie payments in 1797 ; and such is the case with the present notes of the Bank of France." [1]

After what has preceded, the above paragraph does not call for comment.

" When prices are at a certain level," says Mr. Jevons, " and trade in a quiescent state, a single banker is, no doubt, unable to put into circulation more than a certain quantity of bank-notes. He cannot produce a greater effect upon the whole currency than a single purchaser can, by his sales or purchases, produce upon the market for corn or cotton. But a number of bankers, all trying to issue additional notes, resemble a number of merchants offering to sell corn for future delivery ; and the value of gold will be affected, as the price of corn certainly is. We are too much accustomed to look upon the value of gold as a fixed datum line in commerce ; but, in reality, it is a very variable thing. . . . Every one who promises to pay gold on a future day, thereby increases the anticipated supply of gold ; and there is no limit to the amount of gold which can thus be thrown upon the market. Every one who draws a bill or issues a note, unconsciously acts as a " bear " upon the gold market. Every thing goes well, and apparent prosperity falls upon the whole community, so long as these promises to pay gold can be redeemed, or replaced by new promises. But the rise of prices thus produced turns the foreign exchanges against the country, and creates a balance of indebtedness which must be paid in gold. The basis of the whole fabric slips away, and produces that sudden collapse known as a commercial crisis." [2]

[1] Money and the Mechanism of Exchange, pp. 234, 235.
[2] Money and the Mechanism of Exchange, pp. 314–316.

We are afraid that gold cannot be thrown in any amount upon the market, simply by the issue of promises to pay it at a future day; and, also, that Mr. Jevons's illustrations borrowed from the stock market will hardly stand a critical examination. A "bear" sale is one in which the seller contracts to make future delivery of something, — not money, — receiving its present price in money. When a banker issues his notes, promising to pay a certain amount of coin, he takes the obligations of those who receive them to repay at a future day an equal, and, in fact, a greater, amount of coin as compensation for standing in the gap for the time that his borrowers' obligations have to run. As he may be called upon to pay all his liabilities immediately in coin, he must make provision of coin in ratio to the amount of his notes. In other words, he "bulls" the gold market just in ratio to the extent of his operations.

"What is true of credit generally," says Mr. Jevons, "is still more true of the special form of credit involved in Bank promissory notes. These purport to be payable in gold coin on demand, so that they are taken by every one as equivalent to the coin. Even bills of exchange can be paid in notes; and, as regards internal trade, no difficulty would be felt in maintaining credit so long as promises to pay gold circulate instead of gold. But foreigners will not hold such promises on the same footing; and, if the exchanges are against us, the metallic, not the paper, part of the currency will go abroad. It is at this moment that bankers will find no difficulty in expanding their issues; because many persons have claims to meet in gold, and the notes are regarded as gold. The notes will thus conveniently fill up the void occasioned by the exportation of specie; prices will be kept up; prosperity will continue; the balance of foreign trade will be still against us; and the game of replacing gold by promises will go on to an unlimited extent, until it becomes actually impossible to find more gold to make necessary payments abroad. . . .

"According to the view which I adopt, the issue of notes is more analogous to the royal function of coinage than to the ordinary commercial operation of drawing bills. We ought to talk of *coining notes*, as John Law did; for, though the design is impressed on paper instead of metal, the function of the note is exactly the same as that of a representative token. As to the right to issue promises, it no more exists than the right to establish private mints. For our present purposes, that alone is right which the legislature declares to be expedient to the community at large. As almost every one has long agreed to place the coinage of money in the hands of the executive government, so I believe that the issue of paper representative money should continue to be practically in the hands of the government, or its agents, acting under the strictest legislative control. M. Wolowski, in his admirable works on banking, has maintained that the issue of notes is a function distinct from the ordinary operations of a banker ; and Mr. Gladstone has allowed that the distinction is a wholesome and vital one. Bankers enjoy the utmost degree of freedom in this country at present in every other point ; so that it is wholly a confusion of ideas to speak of the unrestricted emission of paper representative money as a question of free banking." [1]

The preceding paragraphs may serve as illustrations of the History of Monetary Theories.

A striking illustration of the present condition of the science of Political Economy is furnished by Mr. Jevons in his Introductory Lecture at the opening of the session of 1876–77, at the University of London, to be found in the "Fortnightly Review" for November, 1876. The hundredth anniversary of the publication of the "Wealth of Nations" was celebrated by a dinner given in London by the "Political Economy Club," which was founded in 1821 by Ricardo, Malthus, Tooke, James Mill, Grote, and others. Mr. John Stuart Mill was afterwards among its most prominent members. At the dinner, Mr. Gladstone occupied the chair ; Mr. Lowe, and M. Léon Say, the French Minister of Finance, holding the seats next in honor. Mr. Jevons, in giving an account of this dinner, in the address referred to, says : —

" I was much struck with the desponding tone in which Mr. Lowe spoke of the future of the science I have the honor to teach in this college. He seems to think that the work of the science is to a great extent finished. He said : —
" ' I do not feel myself very sanguine that there is a very large field — at least, according to the present state of mental and commercial knowledge — for Political Economy beyond what I have mentioned ; but I think that very much depends upon the degree in which other sciences are developed. Should other sciences relating to mankind, which it is the barbarous jargon of the day to call "Sociology," take a spring and get forward in any degree towards the certainty attained by Political Economy, I do not doubt that their development would help in the development of this science ; but, at present, so far as my own humble opinion goes, I am not very sanguine as to any very large or any very startling development of Political Economy. I observe that the triumphs which have been gained have been rather in demolishing that which has been found to be bad and erroneous, than in establishing new truth ;

[1] Money and the Mechanism of Exchange, pp. 316–318.

and imagine that, before we can attain new results, we must be furnished from without with new truths to which our principles may be applied. The controversies which we now have in Political Economy, although they offer a capital exercise for the logical faculties, are not of the same thrilling importance as those of earlier days : the great work has been done.'

" I am far from denying that there is much to support, or at any rate to suggest, this view of the matter. Some of the greatest reforms which Economists can point out the need of, have been accomplished, and there certainly is no single work to be done comparable to the establishment of free-trade. But this does not prevent the existence of an indefinitely great sphere of useful work which Economists could accomplish, if their science were adequate to its duties. To a certain extent, again, I agree with Mr. Lowe, that there is much in the present position of our science to cause despondency. A very general impression to this effect seems to exist. Some of the newspapers hinted, in reference to the centenary dinner, that the Political Economists had better be celebrating the obsequies of their science than its jubilee. The *Pall Mall Gazette*, especially, thought that Mr. Lowe's task was to explain the decline, not the consummation, of economical science. Perhaps with many people the wish was the father of the thought. I am aware that Political Economists have always been regarded as cold-blooded beings, devoid of the ordinary feelings of humanity, — little better, in fact, than vivisectionists. I believe that the general public would be happier in their minds for a little' time, if Political Economy could be shown up as imposture, like the greater part of what is called ' Spiritualism.'

" It must be allowed, too, that there have been for some years back premonitory symptoms of disruption of the old orthodox school of Economists. Respect for the names of Ricardo and Mill seems no longer able to preserve unanimity. J. S. Mill himself, in the later years of his life, gave up one of the doctrines on which he had placed much importance in his works. One Economist after another — Thornton, Cairnes, Leslie, Macleod, Longe, Hearn, Musgrave — have protested against some one or other of the articles of the old Ricardian creed.

" At the same time foreign Economists, such as De Laveleye, Courcelle-Seneuil, Cournot, Walras, and others, have taken a course almost entirely independent of the predominant English school. So far has this discontent gone, that Mr. Bagehot has been induced to re-examine the fundamental postulates of economy from their very foundation, in his most acute papers published in the ' Fortnightly Review.' He remarks (p. 216, Feb. 1, 1876) : —

" ' Notwithstanding these triumphs, the position of our Political Economy is not altogether satisfactory. It lies rather dead in the public mind. Not only it does not excite the same interest as formerly, but there is not exactly the same confidence in it. Younger men either do not study it, or do not feel that it comes home to them, and that it matches with their most living ideas. . . . They ask, often hardly knowing it, will this " science," as it claims to be, harmonize with what we now know to be sciences, or bear to be tried as we now try sciences? And they are not sure of the answer.'

"In short, it comes to this : that, one hundred years after the first publication of the 'Wealth of Nations,' we find the state of the science to be almost chaotic. There is certainly less agreement now about what Political Economy is than there was thirty or fifty years ago. Under these circumstances, I will now draw your attention for a short time to the apparently rival sects which seem likely to arise from the break-up of the old Ricardian school.

"In the first place, it is impossible to ignore the fact, that there has been gradually rising into prominence a school of writers who take a very radical view of the reforms required in our science. They call in question the validity even of the deductive method on which Smith mainly relied. They hold that the science must be entirely recast in method and materials, and that it must take the form of an historical or archæological science. At the centenary dinner, this view of the matter was boldly stated by one of the most distinguished of European Economists, namely, M. de Laveleye. His own words, translated into English, will best explain his opinions : —

"' It is principally at this point that there has recently arisen a division in the ranks of Economists. Some, the old school, whom for want of 'a better name I will call the " Orthodox School," believe that every thing regulates itself by the effect of natural laws. The other school, which its adversaries have named the " Socialists of the Chair," the " Katheder Socialisten," but which we ought rather to call the " Historical School," or, as the Germans say, the " Realist School " — this school holds that distribution is governed in part, doubtless, by free contract ; but also, and still more, by civil and political institutions, by religious beliefs, by moral sentiments, by custom and historical tradition. You see that there opens itself here an immense field of studies ; comprehending the relations of Political Economy with morals, justice, right, religion, history, and connecting it to the *ensemble* of social science. That, in my humble opinion, is the actual mission of Political Economy. This is the path pursued by nearly all German Economists, several of whom have a European reputation, — such as Rau, Roscher, Knies, Nasse, Schäffle, Schmoller ; in Italy, by a group of writers already well known, Minghetti, Luzzati, Forti ; in France, by Wolowski, Lavergne, Passy, Courcelle-Seneuil, Leroy-Beaulieu ; and in England by authors whom it is unnecessary to name or estimate here, because you know them better than I.' "

Such is the sad picture of the condition of this great science. "At the end of one hundred years from the first publication of the 'Wealth of Nations,' we find," says Mr. Jevons, " the state of the science to be almost chaotic. There is certainly less agreement now about what Political Economy is than there was thirty or fifty years ago. Rival sects seem likely to arise from the break-up of the old Ricardian " (Adam Smith) " school. . . . It must be allowed that there have been for some years back premonitory symptoms of disruption of the old orthodox school of Economists. Respect for the names of Mill and Ricardo seems no longer able to preserve unanimity. J. S. Mill himself, in the later years of his life, gave up one of the doctrines on which he placed much importance in his works." (Would that his life had been longer preserved!) " One Economist after another — Thornton, Cairnes, Musgrave, and others — have protested against some one or other of the articles of the old Ricardian creed." These extracts are not more significant of the breaking up of the old school than is the disgust universally felt for it. "I am aware," says Jevons, " that Political Economists have always been regarded as cold-blooded beings, devoid of the ordinary feelings of humanity. I believe that the general public would be happier in their minds for a little while if Political Economy could be shown up as an imposture, like the greater part of what is called 'Spirit-ualism.' " " Happier " is a word far too weak to express the satisfaction which society would feel if those who have pestered it for a hundred years with their frivolous distinctions and inane talk, against which no seclusion, no bolts or bars, are proof, and who weigh like a nightmare upon the race, were never, as a class, to be heard of again. How great, therefore, must be the satisfaction of all to find that the centenary dinner, given in honor of the great apostle of the English system, became the melancholy occasion of its last obsequies! One does not know at which to be most struck, — the sadness which weighed upon the Economists, or the still sadder irreverence of the greater part of those who surrounded the table, in whose thoughts Adam Smith had no more place than the "lost tribes." With the statesmen who did the chief part of the talking, Political Economy, as a science, was held to be pretty thoroughly *functus officio*. Mr. Lowe's melancholy refrain has already been given. Mr. Newmarch insisted upon a larger "negative development" of this science, by which the functions of the government were to be greatly abridged: —

" On one of the points," he said, " mentioned by Mr. Lowe, with respect to Political Economy in its relation to the future, I am sanguine enough to think that there will be what may be called a large 'negative development' of Political Economy, tending to produce an important and beneficial effect; and that is such a development of Political Economy as will reduce the functions of government within a smaller and smaller compass. The full development of the principles of Adam Smith has been in no small danger for some time past; and one of the great dangers which now hangs over this country is that the wholesome spontaneous operation of human interests and human desires seems to be in course of rapid supersession by the erection of one government department after another, by the setting up of one set of inspectors after another, and by the whole time of Parliament being taken up in attempting to do for the nation those very things which, if the teachings of the man whose name we are celebrating to-day is to bear any fruit at all, the nation can do much better for itself."

Mr. Forster, on the other hand, a member of the government, and who had had some experience of the weakness of our race, would still further invoke legislative action in social economy : —

" I am strongly of the contrary opinion," he said, "that we cannot undertake the *laissez-faire* principle in the present condition of our politics, or of parties in Parliament, or in the general condition of the country. I gather from Mr. Newmarch's remarks that he is an advocate of the old *laissez-faire* principle. Well, if we were all Mr. Newmarches, if we had nothing to deal with in the country but men like ourselves, we might do this. But we have to deal with weak people; we have to deal with people who have themselves to deal with strong people, who are borne down, who are tempted, who are unfortunate in their circumstances of life, and who will say to us, and say to us with great truth, 'What is your use as a Parliament, if you cannot help us in our weakness, and against those who are too strong for us?'"

Mr. Forster opened a pretty wide field, and disclosed the full antagonism which prevails in the English schools. On the subject of the interposition of government, its members are as wide apart as the poles. A person experienced in affairs soon learns that the motives or principles which guide him are no criterion of those by which others, and in fact the masses, may be swayed; and he may well feel, whether wisely or no, that the innocent weak would have good ground for complaint, unless protected from the criminal or grasping strong. The " Wealth of Nations " is hardly the work to be appealed to as arbiter in questions such as these.

Mr. Jevons was also much struck with the contracted view

which seemed to be entertained by Mr. Gladstone as to the amount of work remaining to be accomplished by the Economists, and quoted him to the following effect : —

" ' I am bound to say that this society has still got its work before it. . . . I do not mean to say that there is a great deal remaining to be done here in the way of direct legislation, yet there is something. It appears to me at least that, perhaps, the question of the currency is one in which we are still, I think, in a backward condition ; our legislation having been confined in the main to averting great evils, rather than to establishing a system which, besides being sound, would be complete and logical. With that exception, perhaps, not much remains in the province of direct legislation.' "

The following extracts from Mr. Jevons' address will show the extremities, both in thought and style, to which the English school is reduced : —

" Passing now to a second aspect, Political Economy will naturally be divided according as it is abstract or concrete. The theory of the science consists of those general laws which are so simple in nature and so deeply grounded in the constitution of man and the inner world, that they remain the same throughout all those ages which are within our consideration. But, though the laws are the same, they may receive widely different applications in the concrete. The primary laws of motion are the same, whether they be applied to solids, liquids, or gases, though the phenomena obeying these laws are apparently so different. Just as there is a general science of mechanics, so we must have a general science or theory of economy. Here, again, there is a difference of opinion. There are those who think that dealing as the science does with quantities, economy must necessarily be a mathematic science if it is any thing at all. There are those, on the other hand, who, like the late Professor Cairnes, contest, and some who even ridicule, the notion of representing truths relating to human affairs in mathematical symbols. It may be safely asserted, however, that if English Economists persist in rejecting the mathematical view of their science, they will fall behind their European contemporaries. How many English students, or even professors, I should like to know, have sought out the papers of the late Dr. Whewell, printed in the *Cambridge Philosophical Transactions*, in which he gives his view as to the mode of applying mathematics to our science ? What English publisher, I may ask again, would for a moment entertain the idea of reprinting a series of mathematical works on Political Economy ? Yet this is what is being done in Italy by Professor Gerolamo Boccardo, the very learned and distinguished editor of the ' Nuova Enciclopedia Italiana.' Professor Boccardo has also prefixed to the series a remarkable treatise of his own on the application of the quantitative method to economic and social science in general. This series, which forms the third portion of the well-known ' Bibliotheca Economista,' will be completed with an Italian translation of the works of Professor Léon Walras, now Rector of the Academy of Lausanné, who has in recent years independently established the fact, that the laws of supply and demand, and all the phenomena of value, may be investigated algebraically and illustrated geometrically. From inquiries of this sort the curious conclusion emerges, that equilibrium of exchange of goods resembles in mathematical conditions the equilibrium of. weights upon a lever of the first order. In the latter case, one weight multiplied by its arm must exactly equal the other weight multiplied by its arm. So, in an act of exchange, the commodity given multiplied by its degree of utility must equal the quantity of commodity received multiplied by its degree of utility. The theory of economy proves to be, in fact, the mechanics of utility and self-interest."

In spite of the authority of Professor Léon Walras, now Rector of the Academy of Lausanne, supported by that of Mr. Jevons, we must be permitted to entertain grave doubts whether " the laws of supply and demand, and all the phenomena of value, may be investigated algebraically, and illustrated geometrically." Neither does it " emerge " to us, that, admitting the fact that " a commodity given multiplied by its degree of utility must equal the quantity of commodity received multiplied by its degree of utility," all the laws of value are settled thereby; or that " the theory of Economy is thereby proved to be the mechanics of utility and self-interest."

To continue : —

" So much for the theory of Economy, which will naturally be one science, remaining the same throughout its applications, though it may be broken up into several parts; the theories of utility, of exchange, of labor, of interest, &c., partly corresponding to the old division of the science into the laws of consumption, exchange, distribution, production, and so forth. Concrete Political Economy, however, can hardly be called one science, but already consists of many extensive branches of inquiry. Currency, banking, the relations of labor and capital, those of landlord and tenant, pauperism, taxation, and finance, are some of the principal portions of applied Political Economy, all involving the same ultimate laws, manifested in most different circumstances. In a subject of such appalling extent and complexity as currency, for instance, we depend upon the laws of supply and demand, of consumption and production of commodities as applied to the precious metals or other materials of money. In the science of banking and the money market, we have a very difficult application of the same laws to capital in general. This separation of the concrete branches of the science is, however, sufficiently obvious and recognized, and I need not dwell further upon it. The general conclusion, then, to which I come is, that Political Economy must for the future be looked upon as an aggregate of sciences. A hundred years ago, it was very wise of Adam Smith to attempt no subdivision, but to expound his mathematical theory (for I hold that his reasoning was really mathematical in nature) in conjunction with concrete applications and historical illustrations. He produced a work so varied in interest, so beautiful in style, and so full of instruction, that it attracted many readers, and convinced those whom it attracted. But Economists are no more bound to go on imitating Adam Smith in the accidental features of his work than metaphysicians are bound to write in the form of Platonic dialogues, or poets in the style of the Shakespearean drama. With the progress of industry, how many hundreds, or even thousands, of trades have sprung up since Smith wrote! With the progress of knowledge, how many sciences have been created, and subdivided again and again! The science of electricity has been almost entirely discovered since 1776; yet now it has its abstract mathematical theories, its concrete applications, and its many branches; treating of frictional or static electricity, dynamic electricity or galvanism, electro-chemistry, electro-magnetism, magnetism, terrestrial magnetism, atmospheric electricity, and so forth. Within the same century, chemistry, if not born, has grown, and is now so vast a body of facts and laws that professors are appointed to teach different parts of it. Yet the Political Economist is expected to teach all parts of his equally extensive and growing science, and is lucky if he escape having to profess also the mental, metaphysical, and moral sciences generally."

In striking contrast, however, to the above, and to what was said by Englishmen at the dinner referred to, was the brief account given by M. de Laveleye, of the new Continental or "Realist School;" which holds "production and distribution to be governed in part by free contract, but also, and still more, by civil and political institutions, by religious beliefs, by moral sentiments, by customs and traditions, — that morals, justice, right, religion, history, altogether go to make up the *tout ensemble* of social or political science." After naming those esteemed worthy to be enrolled in the new school, having for its basis the whole nature of man, and whose method is investigation, not assumption, he, with matchless politeness and irony, left it to the Englishmen present to add their own illustrious names to the list. Echo was silent; and will remain silent till Adam Smith, with his deductive method and the school founded upon it, all ignorant of any higher force in human development than the selfish instincts of the race, are thrown into the common receptacle of the incongruous and useless rubbish of the past.

There is, however, a lower depth than even Mr. Jevons sounded, and that was touched by Mr. Bonamy Price, Professor of Political Economy in the University of Oxford, as will be seen by the following extracts from lectures delivered by him in that institution, and embodied in a work entitled the " Principles of Currency."

" Political Economy, in respect of the range of its subject-matter," says Mr. Price, " has no superior, if indeed it has an equal, among the sciences. It treats of wealth, of its production and of its distribution, and the larger part of human life is spent in the exercise of these two functions. Political Economy is often spoken of as a modern science ; but it has existed in all ages, and amongst all civilized nations. Men at all times have occupied themselves with the creation of wealth according to certain rules and ideas ; for no laborious employment can be extensively carried on without the existence of some notions as to the right way of working, and the most fitting methods for attaining the end desired. It is a mistake, though a very common one, to suppose that practical men, as they are called, are destitute of theory. The exact reverse of this statement is true. Practical men swarm with theories ; none more so. They abound in views, in ideas, in rules, which they endow with the pompous authority of experience ; and when new principles are proposed, none so quick as practical men to overwhelm the innovator with an array of the wisdom which is to be found in prevalent practice. I know of no place which is so entirely under the dominion of loudly corrected theories as the city. In some departments of Political Economy, the doctrines of merchants and bankers have subdued the whole land, and almost put a stop to all independent thought which should presume to contradict the established theories of men of business. Adam Smith's illustrious work is almost wholly devoted to the demolition of the huge superstructure of doctrine which traders had reared up on their practice. The difference which separates the man of science from the man of practice does not consist in the presence of general views and ideas on one side, and their absence on the other. Both have views and ideas. The distinction lies in the method by which these views have been reached ; in the breadth and completeness of the investigation pursued ; in the rigorous questioning of facts, and the careful digestion of the instruction they contain ; in the co-ordination and the logical cohesion of the truths established.

" No science has suffered so severely at the hands of practical and empirical men as Political Economy. They have at all times propounded and acted on doctrines of the most elaborate kind. The more directly engaged in business was the speaker, the more complicated, the more artificial, the more mysterious, have been the rules he laid down for the attainment of wealth. ˙Monopolies were proclaimed to be the infallible means for creating good and trustworthy quality in manufacture. . . . Then, again, when the discovery of the New World enlarged geography with colonies of a novel kind, the practical man speedily stepped forward with his theory, and taught the statesman that the secret of the new and boundless wealth engendered by colonies lay in the exclusive appropriation of their trade by the mother country. His teaching was adópted by every civilized country, and became the recognized policy of all Europe. Great wars were waged in the name of the practical man's ideas: his views were supreme over all colonial relations. . . . The practical man's ascendency thus rose ever higher and higher, till it reached its culminating point in the famed mercantile theory, — the crowning embodiment of the wisdom which practical prudence and experience had inspired. The precious metals were held up as the one supreme object of industrial ambition. . . .

" I am constrained to acknowledge that Political Economy finds itself, even at this time of day, in a most unsatisfactory position. Two causes, it seems to me, have mainly brought about this result. The first and most influential is the singularly undefined character of the boundary line which encloses the subject-matter of Political Economy. The example set by the illustrious expounder of Political Economy has not been faithfully observed by his successors. In the 'Wealth of Nations,' the frontier line which separates Political Economy from cognate sciences is rarely transgressed. Adam Smith seldom runs away from his true subject, or mixes it up with foreign elements. His followers have too often written in a less philosophical spirit. Political Economy is infested with an incessant tendency to commingle with general politics. The confusion was natural: for wealth and finance form a large part of the business which occupies every government; and a philosophy which augmented the riches of a people, stimulated their industry, poured expanding streams into the national exchequer, and spread contentment with prosperity over the country, could not fail to look exceedingly like the science of good government. And so it is, in a sense; but still only within the limits of its appropriate province. But to identify Political Economy with statesmanship, with the science of government, — to suppose that a great Political Economist is *ex vi termini* a great statesman, — is as absurd as to identify the science of jurisprudence, or the building of ironclads, with politics, or to imagine that a great general is infallibly a scientific statesman. This confusion has shown itself in other branches of knowledge which are largely made use of by governments; but nowhere has it prevailed so widely or worked so much mischief as in Political Economy. Its name is unfortunate, and only too well calculated to precipitate its writers into this delusion. They never seem quite able to escape the impression that Political Economy is a branch of politics. . . . It may be very important; it may furnish more occupation to the statesman than any other province of human life; it may have to be consulted more frequently, and its suggestions may be very closely connected with the happiness of the whole people, — nevertheless, it is the knowledge of a single department only. They may be overridden, modified, or rejected at the dictation of a yet more universal science, by the order of a still wider and higher knowledge. The function of the Economist is solely to report, on matters within his cognizance, to the statesman; but it is the statesman, and the statesman alone, whose prerogative it is to judge of their application. . . .

"So much for the first of the two great difficulties which weigh on the pursuit of Political Economy, — the one, namely, which is derived from its own nature, and the subject-matter which it explores. I now come to the second, — the one which assails it from without, and which, as far as I am aware, Political Economy alone, of all the sciences, is compelled to endure. It never seems to make a final and permanent lodgement of any of its truths in the public mind. They float on a tide which often carries the vessel backward as fast as it progresses forward. The tendency to backslide seems to be incessant and irresistible, — not from any fault of its own, or from want of ability and demonstrating power in its teachers, but from the strength of the adverse forces which every one of its conclusions is ceaselessly obliged to encounter. A centrifugal force is ever acting on some large section of society, — sometimes, even, on a whole population, — which makes it forget all that it has learned, and draws it back into the darkness of ignorance. In other sciences, a truth once won is won for ever. No one challenges the principle, or acts in defiance of its law: no one slides back into the belief that the sun revolves round the earth; no one contradicts the truths once established by the chemist or hydraulist. The reason of this difference of fortune does not consist in the certainty attached to the subject-matter of the one, and the inherent uncertainty of the other. Some of the positions reached by Political Economy attain the quality of demonstration; and yet they are denied or ignored as readily as if they were the hypothesis of an empiric. They are not argued against and refuted; no second trial is summoned to retest their value: they are simply passed over; and then the error which they were supposed to have dispelled resumes its possession of the public mind, just as if it were the infallible suggestion of instinct. It seems like lost labor to waste instruction on those who listen and are convinced, and then, under some indescribable impulse, rebel against the light. And what is this impulse? How is a phenomenon apparently so discreditable to the human understanding to be explained? How comes Political Economy to have been born under so unlucky a star as to be doomed to teach and persuade, only to be repudiated? The explanation is to be found in the ceaseless action of selfishness, in the never-dying force of class and personal interests, in the steady and constant effort to promote private gains at the cost of the whole community. The foremost lessons of Political Econ-

omy are directed against narrow visions of private advantage; and
they strive to show how the welfare of each man is most effectually
achieved by securing the welfare of all. But it seems otherwise
to the natural mind. The immediate gain lies before it, can be
seen and handled; and the law which demands its sacrifice, in order
to arrive at a wider and more prolific result, appears to contradict
the senses, and to bring ruin and not benefit in its train. . . .

"And, now, what is the moral to be drawn from these ever-recur-
ring sins against light and knowledge? That Political Economy is in possession of no truth? that the experience of life,
and the surer intelligence of the whole people, refute the illusions with which a few subtle thinkers bewilder themselves in
the closet? that practice is wiser than theory? Nothing of the
kind. Such practice contains no refutation of theory; it puts forward no argument; it makes no appeals to reason; it pretends to no
better thought-out opinions. We can trace here only the action of
disturbing influences, — the power of selfishness in combination
with the most limited narrowness of vision. The moral to be drawn
is the importance of thoroughly imbuing the mind with accurate
principles, before prejudice has had time to build itself up, whilst
the mind is impressible by reason, and truths firmly implanted retain
their hold for life. The moment you see nations and legislatures
carried away by the strength of the tide into narrow empiricism,
determine resolutely to be a good Political Economist. . . . Here,
then, is the mercantile theory. Let us now take up the newspapers
of to-day. Read the city articles of every one of them. Look at
the cast of thought, at the style of literature, at the principles proceeded upon, at the whole spirit of the language. What is thought
most deserving of record? The sums of gold taken to the Bank of
England, or taken away from it; the amount of bullion; the vessels laden with gold on their passage to England from California
and Australia; the state of the exchanges. The beloved phrase of
the mercantile theory, 'favorable exchanges,' is dwelt upon with
satisfaction; unfavorable exchanges, and the departure of gold to
foreign countries, are bemoaned with anxiety as a loss; prognosti-
cations are made of a languishing or flourishing trade, according to
the influx or reflux of bullion; and weekly returns are proclaimed
of ingots buried out of sight in the cellars of the Bank. The
doctrine that gold is wealth — the doctrine which Mr. Mill paints
as an absurdity so palpable that the present age regards it as incredible, as a crude fancy of childhood — breathes in every line of
the city articles of all our daily newspapers. . . . What is this, I
ask, but the mercantile theory, pure and fresh, as you heard Mr.
Mill describe it? What is it but the resurrection of the Practical
Man, — the reassertion of himself, of his experience, his appeal to
outward form, to what may be touched and handled? The world
fondly imagined that he was vanquished and gone; that Adam
Smith had finally disposed of him; that boys and students had
learned to pity him, and to pride themselves on having been born
after the great Scotch genius : never was there a greater mistake.
It takes many Adam Smiths in Political Economy to kill off for

ever genuine mercantile superstitions. The great authority, the man of millions, who is supposed to understand the theory of business precisely because he has made millions, revives in every age. *Uno avulso, non deficit alter, aureus.* The mercantile theory may be consigned by philosophers to the limbo of nursery toys; but it lives on all the same, is master of the mind of the city, is supreme over city articles, and regulates the barometer of commercial weather, and, above all, is held to know the great secret of trade, and to be able to show men the way to get rich. . . .

" The mercantile theory lives, and one of two inferences from this fact must be accepted. Either it is the true theory of trade, and Adam Smith is not the great benefactor of mankind which he is supposed to have been; or else, in the department of science which has for its object the wealth of the community, error possesses a vitality which is more than a match for the keenest logic and the strongest common sense.

" The mercantile theory has given birth to a child to which the whole literature of the world affords no parallel, — the doctrine of currency as exhibited in the nineteenth century. I fear, almost, to utter its name; and yet it will form the subject of the following lectures. The very sound of the word 'currency' makes every man turn his back or shut his ears. His immediate instinct is to fly from a subject with which he associates every kind of jargon and unendurable phraseology. Yet it was the very repulsiveness of currency which induced me first to embark upon its study. It seemed to me a marvellous phenomenon, well worth investigation, that there should be at this period of the world's history an article of the most universal use in daily life which seemed to defy explanation in plain and intelligible language. Other subjects of the most recondite abstruseness had been mastered. Hieroglyphics had been read, mysterious inscriptions cleared up, the profoundest depths of physics sounded, and the most subtle problems in mathematics conquered. Few, indeed, might be the hearers that these successful investigators could attract; but those hearers listened with delight, and could feel that they had made an acquisition of real knowledge. What, then, was this so-called science, from which all men seemed to turn away in disgust, — even those whose lives were spent in handling the objects of which it treats? How was so astonishing an event to be explained? What causes had rendered currency the reproach of our age? What was there in sovereigns and bank-notes so inscrutable as to baffle the sharpest intellect, and to be incapable of clear and simple exposition? The cause of this strange spectacle presently became evident. The philosophic spirit had been absent; the right method of investigation had been, I will not say neglected, but absolutely despised; the method of Bacon, to which modern science owes its strength, — patient and accurate analysis, — had been scorned, as if fit only for physical subjects, but too mechanical for such subtle substances as the instrument of finance. *A priori* assumptions prevail on every side, in the discussion of currency. Every one starts with some arbitrary hypothesis. Can we wonder, after that, to find universal confusion and obscurity? Currency has been the jumble that it is, authority contradicts authority, no first principles are recognized as the common basis from which reasoning may take its origin, and, when some practical measure has been discussed, the cry of salvation for commerce is met by the counter shriek of ruin, — simply because no one will condescend to analyze facts, and to explore their meaning. The world has chosen to refer to great bankers and merchants, — to men who have conducted vast businesses, and have realized gigantic fortunes. These men, the world said, have spent their lives in dealing with money. Must they not know the nature of money and its laws? Must we not take our theory at their hands? And so mankind did take the theory of money from commercial authority, and the result has been currency in the state in which we now find it.[1]

" We have learned what coin is ; we have become acquainted with a metallic currency and its nature : but what are checks and bills, which make up the banking trade? Many would say they are papers which represent money; but I cannot accept the word 'represent' in currency, for I can never understand its meaning. It has no definite meaning for me ; nor, as far as I can perceive, for any one else. Anyhow, checks and bills are not money. They may, in their respective spheres, do the same work as money ; but in this place, where we are speaking of a purely metallic currency, they are not money. What are they, then? Orders to pay money, which can be legally enforced; title-deeds to money which lead directly to the obtaining of money. They are all warrants or evidences of debt. . . . A check on a banker implies a debt due by the banker as its basis : a bill is an admission of the acceptor that he owes money, and an undertaking to pay it on a particular day. Here, then, we have the things a banker deals in, — the resources of which he disposes. Bankers deal in debts, and a Bank is an institution for the transfer of debt. Bankers deal in orders to pay money in discharge of debts. . . . So far a banker's business is identical with that of a clerk sent around by a great shop to collect its bills. . . . So much for a banker's receipts : he does not obtain them in money ; they come to him as checks and bills. These are his resources. . . . The all-important question is, how these checks and bills are born into the world, what is it that makes a banker have few or many of them at different times. People are ever saying that Banks have much or little money ; that money is abundant or scarce. This is very erroneous and very misleading language. Money, cash, sovereigns, and bank-notes vary very little indeed. . . . The language should be, — bills and checks, or, if an abstract word is preferred, deposits are scarce or abundant : many checks have arrived at the Bank to-day : it will lend freely, and charge a low rate for its loans.' How, then, do these checks and bills come into existence ? Omitting accommodation bills, which are foreign to this discussion, they denote goods bought and paid for, either by a transfer of debt or by a promise to pay later. Every man who

[1] Principles of Currency, Inaugural Lecture.

gives a check has previously sold something, and charged his banker to get the payment for him. . . . If the customer buys more than he sells, if he makes losses in business, or lives beyond his income, the balance now falls the other way. The banker's power to lend to others, his resources, his means, depend entirely on his customer buying less than he sold. The banker finds that more checks are drawn upon him than are sent to him to collect payment for, his means are reduced; he is less able to lend: he makes difficulties about loans; the rate of discount rises, and the city, which has never investigated the matter, screams in astonishment or indignation. Money, coin and bank-notes have no part in this matter, except as small change. All the buying and selling, all the borrowing and lending, takes place by exchanging debts: actual payment is so rare as not to be worth considering. 'Give me your oil-cake,' says the farmer, 'and I will tell my banker to pay you.' Does he make an actual payment? No: the cake-merchant gives the check to his own banker, and forthwith proceeds to buy linseed, and tells the Russian in turn, 'I will tell my banker to pay you.' And so it goes on in every trade.[1]

"The check has furnished us with a very natural introduction to the discussion of paper money. . . . The bill and the check in time generated the bank-note. . . . And now let us watch the process by which the bank-notes issue forth into circulation. It is full of instruction on the fundamental points of a paper currency. We all know how an ordinary check makes its appearance in the world: goods are bought, a check is signed for the cash, and so it commences its short-lived existence. The birth of the bank-note takes place in a different manner. It is signed and made ready at the Bank; but how does it come forth? Through payments, few though they be, which the Bank makes in cash. It is the office of the banker to lend; and he lends the more freely in proportion as his borrowers carry away the loans in notes. I am speaking of the first establishment of its notes in public circulation at its origin. Observe the fact well: it is the root of most of the strange delusions afloat in the world about paper currency. It indissolubly associates in the commercial mind the issue of notes with perpetual ability to lend. 'The banker,' cries the world, 'most of all, the Bank of England, in the hour of panic, can issue notes which will do the work of money, and he can lend all the more to traders accordingly.' And then this fact is insisted on, that, by issuing notes the banker acquires additional means for lending. This fact is perfectly true; but there is an enormous fallacy lurking beneath it. . . .

"And now we reach the most important question of all — in what numbers will these bank-notes circulate? It is the crucial question wherewith to test the soundness of every theory of currency. It is a question which every merchant, every banker, every chamber of commerce, every member of Parliament who speaks on currency, ought to push home to his mind, and not be content till he has attained to a clear, precise, and intelligible answer. It is the

---

[1] Principles of Currency, Lec. iii.: "What is a Bank?"

centre of every theory of currency, whether metallic or of paper. Every doctrine which is mistaken on this central principle is worthless as an interpreter of the science of currency. Mr. Tooke discerned the true answer: Mr. Mill, with some little wavering, and a few others, have seen the light; but the general literature on money matters throughout the world profoundly ignores the fact. The answer is the same with that which has already been given to the parallel question respecting sovereigns. So many bank-notes as the public wants and can use will circulate, and no more. . . . This is the truth of truths in currency. . . . An expanded or inflated circulation of bank-notes is an absurdity, nothing better than pure nonsense. It would be just as sensible to speak of an expanded or inflated circulation of hats." [1]

It is hardly necessary to comment upon all this. Indeed, an apology is due for encumbering this work by copying so largely. It may do some good, however, to show the incoherent buffoonery taught in the name of Political Economy in one of the first universities in Christendom. Where are her purists, that they tolerate within her sacred precincts a fustian rhetoric to be matched only by that of Pistol? which proclaims " merchants and bankers to have subdued the whole land, and to have almost put a stop to independent thought; that the more directly one is engaged in business, the more complicated, the more artificial, the more mysterious, are the rules laid down by him for the attainment of wealth." The present unsatisfactory position of the science is charged to " the ceaseless action of selfishness, the never-dying force of class and personal interests, to promote private gain at the cost of the whole community. Here," he continues, " is the Mercantile Theory. Read the city articles of every one of the newspapers. Look at the cast of thought, at the style of literature, at the principles proceeded upon, at the whole spirit of the language. What is thought most worthy or deserving of record? The vast sums of gold taken to the Bank of England, or taken away from it; the state of the exchanges, and the weekly returns of ingots buried out of sight in the cellars of the Bank. The doctrine that gold is wealth — the doctrine which Mr. Mill paints as an absurdity so palpable that the present age regards it as incredible, as a crude fancy of childhood — breathes in every line of the city articles of all our daily newspapers. What is this, I ask, but the Mer-

[1] Principles of Currency, Lec. iv.: "Paper Currency."

cantile Theory, pure and fresh, as you heard Mr. Mill describe it ? What is it but the resurrection of the Practical Man, — the reassertion of himself, of his experience, his appeal to outward form, to what may be touched and handled. The world fondly imagined he was vanquished and gone; that Adam Smith had finally disposed of him; that boys and students had learned to pity him, and pride themselves on having been born after the great Scotch genius: never was there a greater mistake. The Mercantile Theory lives, and one of two inferences from this fact must be accepted : either it is the true theory of trade, and Adam Smith is not the great benefactor of mankind which he is supposed to have been; or else in the department of science which has for its object the wealth of the community, error possesses a vitality which is more than a match for the keenest logic and the strongest common sense."

A reader of the Economists cannot fail to be struck with the hostility, not to say hatred, which all of them display toward merchants. Adam Smith, when he called them " sneaking underlings," struck the key-note for all his followers. What is the reason of this hatred, with a sharper tooth even than that of the *odium theologicum?* — the practice of treating gold as wealth, and the highest form of wealth, in the very face of the teachings of the Economists that it is not wealth; or that it is the lowest form of wealth. It was a reflection not to be tolerated. Smith did his best to sustain his theory by sneers and flings at those who grew rich by its violation. He declared them to be a mean and selfish race, the abettors of the worst forms of monopoly, and the disturbers of the peace of the world. Price, in his grotesque way, attempts to paint them in still blacker colors. He admits that if the merchant, if the universal instinct of the race, is to be trusted, the teachings of Adam Smith, so far as they relate to money, are shams; that one of the two must go to the wall. The only refuge of the Economists is in crying that the science has been overborne by the selfishness of men of affairs. They cannot deny that these grow rich by pursuing methods precisely the opposite to those which they lay down. The man of millions vaunts his methods; and, in reply to criticism upon them, shakes his money-bags. The Economists fiercely reply that truth is sacrificed to mammon; but if it be the office of

Political Economy to teach the method of wealth, why has not the man of millions the true method; and what need of going beyond his rules? As for the selfishness of the race, we fear that Political Economists have no prescription for its cure.[1]

In a history of monetary theories, it will be necessary to refer only very briefly to American writers, as they simply echo, without one spark of originality or independence, but with an extravagance perhaps characteristic of the nation, what they have found in the books written on the other side

---

[1] It is hardly necessary to take into account Continental writers upon the subject of money. None of them have treated, to any considerable extent, of symbolic currencies. When these are referred to, Adam Smith seems to have been implicitly followed. The most distinguished of them is Jean-Baptiste Say, whose first work, entitled "A Treatise on Political Economy," &c., was published in 1803. It was for a long time a text-book in the schools of this country. He held with Smith and English Economists, that the value of money depended, or might depend, upon the necessity that existed for a medium of exchange. "The intense demand for money," he says, "has sometimes been sufficient to make paper employed as money equal in value to gold of the same denomination; of which the money of Great Britain is a present example. It must not be imagined that the paper money of that country derives its value from the promise of payment in specie which it purports to convey. That promise has been held out ever since the suspension of cash payment by the Bank in 1797, without any attempt at performance, which many people consider impossible. . . . Yet the paper, though depreciated, is invested with value far exceeding that of its flimsy material. Whence, then, is that value derived? From the urgent want, in a very advanced stage of society and industry, of some agent or medium of exchange.[1] . . . Paper money is thus left in the exclusive possession of the business of circulation; and the absolute necessity of some agent of transfer in every civilized community will then operate to maintain its value. So urgent is this necessity that the paper money of England, consisting of the notes of the Bank, has been kept at par with specie simply by the limitation of the issue to the demands of circulation."[2] In other words, so intense at times has been the demand for food, that people have been forced to eat their knives and forks to appease hunger and support life! Chevalier hardly touches upon the subject of paper-money. He confines himself almost exclusively to metallic money,—its sources of supply, distribution, &c. His treatise upon the probable fall of gold, which was translated by Mr. Cobden, seems to be very inadequate, in not sufficiently taking into account, not only the increased amounts necessary to be held for the support of symbolic currencies, but also the vastly increased power of consumption due to the increased wealth of the leading European nations and the United States. Wolowski, whose work is of more recent date, appears to have been wholly ignorant of the nature and object of paper money, as he quotes approvingly Mr. Amasa Walker's *dictum*, that paper should symbolize nothing but gold.

[1] Say's Political Economy, Book i. Chap. xxi.
[2] Ibid., Chap. xxii.

of the water. Among the most conspicuous of them is Mr. Francis Bowen, lately Professor of Political Economy in Harvard University, who, pending his professorship, published a voluminous work facetiously entitled "American Political Economy," which was long used as a text-book in that institution. It is a feeble and garrulous restatement of Adam Smith, Stewart, Ricardo, Tooke, McCulloch, and Mill, to whose absurdities and errors an emphasis is given by no means to be found in the originals.

"I say, then, that money is merely a contrivance for diminishing the friction of exchange; and, though safe and convenient, it is also a very costly contrivance for this end. . . . It is a portion of the wealth of the country, it is true; but it is a portion of our unproductive wealth, not our capital. We are the poorer by the loss of profit or interest on all of it which we are obliged to keep on hand. Money (paradoxical as the assertion may seem) yields neither profit nor interest. It is only the goods or commodities that are transferred by means of money which yield profit; and this profit or interest, as we have seen, depends on the mutations or changes of form that they undergo. The very reason which Locke adduces for the high estimate put upon money in comparison with other objects of wealth, — namely, its durability, or the fact that it cannot be consumed, — is the cause why it is not productive. The specie which a merchant or a banker holds in store, to provide against daily calls or sudden emergencies, is the only unproductive portion of his capital: he is subject to a loss of interest on the whole amount thus retained. It has been already proved that it is only through the constant transformation of capital, through its repeated consumption and reproduction, that it is made to yield a profit. And even as an article of unproductive wealth, it may be said of money that it gratifies no taste, and in its capacity as money, apart from its character as a portion of wealth, it yields no enjoyment. The coin which a man keeps in his pocket does not, like his shoes or his hat, contribute to his comfort: it is a convenience to him only as it supplies immediate means for making small purchases or satisfying small demands." [1]

We have already sufficiently dealt with all such statements as these. It is enough to reply here, that coin has a great many functions beside "diminishing the friction of exchange." It cannot be called unproductive so long as it can be loaned at interest, and is absolutely indispensable in the process of distribution, without which there can be no capital worthy the name. It would be just as proper to say that a wagon or

---

[1] American Political Economy, pp. 281, 282.

railroad car was unproductive, for the reason that it did not produce the merchandise transported by it.

"In every exchange," he continues, "the two values which are exchanged are supposed to be equal. Every exchange is a barter of a quantity of merchandise for a certain sum of money which is its equivalent. But it does not follow that there must be in the community as much money as there is merchandise; for, as the money is not consumed by effecting this exchange, it is ready immediately to effect another purchase. The same piece of money may be exchanged successively for any number of articles of merchandise of the same value; or, in other words, any sum of money can purchase successively a quantity of merchandise worth an infinitely larger sum.

"The circulation of money and of merchandise bears some relation to the *momentum* spoken of in physical science, which is composed of the velocity multiplied by the mass; the *momenta* are equal, though the velocity should be increased tenfold, provided that the mass is but one tenth part as great. So, also, the *momentum* of wealth is its value multiplied by the rapidity of its circulation. As money circulates far more rapidly than merchandise, it is evident that (the number of exchanges on both sides being equal) there must necessarily be less value in the money than in the merchandise, and as much less as the circulation of the money is more rapid than that of the merchandise. If the value of the merchandise which changes hands in a country in the course of a year amounts to a thousand millions, and the circulation of the money is ten times as quick as that of the merchandise, a hundred millions of money will effect all the exchanges. Let the quickness of the money circulation be doubled, and fifty millions will suffice.

"Mr. J. S. Mill has stated this point very clearly: 'If we assume the quantity of goods in sale, and the number of times those goods are resold, to be fixed quantities, the value of money will depend upon its quantity, together with the average number of times that each piece changes hands in the process. The whole of the goods sold (counting each resale of the same goods as so much added to the goods) have been exchanged for the whole of the money, multiplied by the number of purchases made on the average by each piece. Consequently, the amount of goods and of transactions being the same, the value of money is inversely as its quantity multiplied by what is called the rapidity of circulation. And the quantity of money in circulation is equal to the money value of all the goods sold (including all the resales as additional goods) divided by the number which expresses the rapidity of circulation.'

"Stating the matter algebraically, we have

$$g\,s = m\,r\,;$$

where $g =$ quantity of goods on sale;

    $s =$ number of times the goods are resold;

    $m =$ quantity of money in circulation;

    $r =$ number of purchases effected by each piece of money.

"Of course, any three of these quantities being given, the fourth can be deduced from them. Thus,—

$$m = \frac{g\,s}{r};$$

which is the principle just enunciated. It is also evident, that the value of money will be inversely as its quantity; for, if we suppose the quantity of money to be doubled, we still have

$$g\,s = 2\,m\,r;$$

whence,

$$2\,m = \frac{g\,s}{r};$$

that is, $2\,m$ is worth only the same value which was formerly represented by m."[1]

The value of money, says Mr. Bowen, is in ratio to its momentum; that is, "to its quantity multiplied by what is called the rapidity of circulation." The degree of one measures that of the other. "If the value of the merchandise which changes hands in a country in the course of a year amounts to $1,000,000,000, and the circulation of money is ten times as quick as that of the merchandise, $100,000,000 will effect all the exchanges. Let the quickness of money be doubled, and $50,000,000 will suffice." So, also, he says, "the momentum of wealth is its value multiplied by the rapidity of its circulation." Momentum and effective value are identical terms. All kinds of merchandise, wealth being a generic term, obey the same law. Whatever value can be predicated of one kind, due to the rapidity of its circulation, can be of all other kinds. Assuming the correctness of his proposition, the great problem for society is to determine the degree of momentum that can be secured for its merchandise, as its wealth will be increased in like ratio. As Mr. Bowen has applied his illustration to only one kind of merchandise, money, we will extend it to others: thus, —

$$g\,s = m\,r.$$

The algebraical formula is the same in its characters; but for the present purpose g stands for goose instead of goods. Now, "the value of the goose is inversely as its quantity multiplied by the rapidity of its circulation." Assuming the formula given to express the ordinary rapidity of circulation, or, what is equivalent, the momentum, and consequently, value of

[1] American Political Economy, pp. 306–308.

the goose; then, if its momentum, or value, be doubled, the
formula has only to be altered; thus: —

$$g\,s = 2\,m\,r,$$

or

$$m\,r = \frac{g\,s}{2}$$

The goose has now a value twice greater than it had before.

Of course, any three of these quantities being given, the
fourth can be deduced from them; thus: —

$$m = \frac{g\,s}{r},$$

which is the principle just enunciated. As the value of the
goose will be inversely as its quantity, if this quantity be
reduced one-half (the demand the same), we still have

$$\frac{g\,s}{2} = m\,r,$$

whence,

$$2\,m = \frac{g\,s}{r};$$

that is, $2\,m$ will have only the value that was formerly possessed by m. If the crop of geese should be short, and it
should be desirable to increase their momentum, or effective
value, say tenfold, all that would have to be done would be to
increase their rapidity of circulation to be expressed by the following change in Mr. Bowen's formula; thus: —

$$\frac{g\,s}{10} = m\,r,$$

or

$$10\,m\,r = g\,s.$$

When the last degree of momentum was secured, a wing or a
leg of the goose would have a value equal to that of the whole
bird. Society will be the gainer in an equal degree, by being
able to devote to other purposes the land formerly dedicated to
goose-culture. Admitting the conclusiveness of his demonstration, it must be applicable to all kinds of merchandise; for,
as has already been shown, money, after it has been spent, is as
functus officio to its late owner as is the goose to its owner after
it is eaten. If it be objected that the money is still in existence, and the goose is not, it may be replied: that the goose
has indeed been eaten, but productively, to appear in new
geese, or in other kinds of merchandise; so that whoever uses

the money the second time is still confronted by a new
goose or its equivalent. If the goose or its equivalent do not
reappear, then the money does not. Each responds, and with
equal alacrity, to the call of the other.

"It is possible," he continues, "to displace a portion, or even the
larger part, of the specie currency, and make paper currency, or
some other substitute, take its place; and the specie thus displaced will either go abroad or be melted up. But the total amount
of the currency will remain just as before: the value of the paper
and the precious metals, taken together, will be just what the specie alone would be if paper were not used.[1]

"We thus gain a more correct idea of the comparatively limited
functions of money; which common persons are led grossly to
exaggerate, merely because, at any one time and place, it is a common measure of value, a universal denomination of account.

"All wealth, all commodities, are estimated in dollars, francs,
pounds sterling, and the like; and it is by the aid of such estimates that all exchanges are made. Thus, the idea of money aids
us, when the reality is seldom employed. As pounds sterling were
a universal denomination of account for a long period during
which there was no such thing as a pound sterling in existence, so
the idea or abstract conception of numerical values expressed in
coin would be a convenient, even an essential, implement or contrivance in mercantile transactions, though all exchanges should be
made by direct barter of one commodity for another. Without
such a contrivance, the merchant could not keep his books of
record intelligibly, or preserve his accounts with individuals in his
large and complicated business. Money is even now only a hypothetical or abstract medium of exchange in all the larger transactions of commerce. I almost anticipate the time, in the progress of
invention and the discovery of new expedients and facilities in
commerce, when it will become so universally; when, at any rate,
so costly and useless a realization of the idea as gold and silver coin
will be entirely done away. Only practical difficulties, or what
may be called difficulties of detail, even now obstruct this desirable
consummation.[2]"

Mr. Bowen is certainly mistaken. Society has not as yet
advanced so far in the substitution of ideas for things as he
supposes. Money is still, as many find to their cost, far more
than a mere scale of valuation. The holders of property,
when they sell it, still persist in demanding something more
than "hypothetical or abstract media of exchange." They
may be very uncivilized and selfish to demand a *quid pro quo*

[1] American Political Economy, p. 311.
[2] Ibid., p. 334.

in all transactions, and the laws which uphold them very barbarous; but these laws, nevertheless, have maintained their
force since laws existed. The longing of the Economists for a
world in which ideas stand for things carries them too far.
Mr. Bowen, before he vacated the chair of Political Economy,
should have reconciled this conflict between the ideal and
actual. He would then have ranked among the great benefac-
tors of his race. But if wishing were having, if the good
things of life could be had without desert, no one would do
any thing deserving of them; so that, after all, it may be well
to let money remain the expensive thing it is.

"We are now prepared to explain the great difference between
convertible bank currency and inconvertible bills, or paper money,
properly so called, — that the latter is liable to issue in excess, and
consequent depreciation, while the former is not. . . . Those who
fear an excessive issue of convertible bank-bills might as well apprehend that Lake Erie would overflow its banks, and flood all the
surrounding country, because it is constantly receiving the surplus
waters of the three upper lakes and of innumerable tributary
streams. They forget that the average level of the lake depends,
not upon the quantity of water flowing into the lake, but upon the
quantity that flows out of it over Niagara Falls; and that no cause
could affect the level, except by raising or lowering the bar at the
opening of Niagara River, which regulates the rate of the efflux.[1]

"It follows from this whole review of the subject of paper money,
which I have intentionally based, as far as possible, upon historical
facts rather than abstract reasoning, that the depreciation of it is
attributable solely to excess in its issue. If this excess could be
prevented, that is, if the amount of paper currency could be kept
precisely equal to what the amount of metallic currency would be
in case there were no paper in circulation, then there would be no
depreciation of the paper; nay, the paper might even command a
premium over the coin, if the aggregate value of it were made less
than what the coin would amount to, and if it were also possible to
prevent the importation of specie. Money acquires the power of
exercising its functions, not from any intrinsic quality that it possesses, but solely from convention. To adopt Mr. Stuart Mill's
language, 'Convention is quite sufficient to confer the power;
since nothing more is needful to make a person accept any thing
as money, and even at any arbitrary value, than the persuasion
that it will be taken from him on the same terms by others.' The
value of paper money, not depending at all upon its cost of production, is regulated solely by its quantity. A certain determinable sum of money is needed in every nation to effect its current
exchanges, and to maintain prices at an equilibrium with the aver-

_____
[1] American Political Economy, pp. 382–384.

age prices of commodities throughout the commercial world. Coin being banished, if the issue of paper money is less than this sum, the paper will be at a premium; if greater, it will be at a discount." [1]

In the preceding paragraph, Mr. Bowen only repeats what the English Economists have labored a century to prove. If they have been answered, he has been; if not, he cannot be.

Were Mr. Bowen the only one to be affected by his opinions, they would be of very little consequence; but they become of the greatest importance when taught to young men about to enter the world of affairs, especially when they relate to a subject which concerns, more deeply almost than any other, the welfare of society. What would be thought of a professorship in a university that should still seek to establish the wonderful properties of the philosopher's stone? The attempt would not be a whit more absurd than his teachings upon the subject of money. The thing chiefly to be regretted is, that there does not seem to be any way in which to rid the universities and the world of such nonsense. So far as money is concerned, all are Alchemists, all are believers in the philosopher's stone, all are intent upon its realization. The first step in the way of reform should be to abolish the "professorship of Political Economy," not only in this, but in all institutions in which it is now pretended to be taught; and either abandon instruction in it altogether, or put its duties in commission. In the latter case, whatever was taught would at least have the merit of being as broad as the course of instruction would allow.[2]

[1] American Political Economy, pp. 388, 889.

[2] The following propositions, taken from the last catalogue of Harvard University, make up a part of the course upon which its students are called to exercise their wits : —

"Compare the generally received principle, that paper money tends to expel coin from circulation, with the following:

"All commodities tend to move toward those places at which they are the most utilized. Notes and checks increase the utility of the precious metals; and therefore it is that money tends to flow toward those places at which notes and checks are most in use, passing in America from the Southern and Western States toward the Northern and Eastern, and from America toward England."

Some kinds of paper money tend to expel coin from circulation, and some to increase the amount in circulation. If any question were to be asked, it should have been the manner in which the two differ. How do notes and checks increase the utility of the precious metals? In the same way that they increase the utility of a barrel of pork. Whether they do increase its utility, and, if so,

Another American writer upon the subject of money is Mr. William G. Sumner, Professor of Political Economy in Yale College, who has recently published a work entitled " History of American Currency." The only part of it calling for notice is that which discusses the report of the Bullion Committee, which, Mr. Sumner claims, solved the whole subject of money : —

" The question involved " (referring to the report), " was, therefore, this : Is an adverse balance of trade the explanation of an outflow of gold? or : Is a favorable balance of trade the force to which we must look to bring an influx of gold ? There is no question in finance which now demands our study so imperatively as this one. The false notions of the balance of trade infest almost every discussion of our present circumstances which one reads or hears. It is assumed that the movement of the precious metals from country to country is caused by the balance of trade one way or the other ; and, as the movement of the metals is a phenomenon of the first importance in any question of resumption, the reasoning which starts with this doctrine is all fallacious. The balance of trade was exploded by Quesnay and his followers a century ago, and was gibbeted in the Bullion Report, but it stalks the money market and the national treasury to-day, an uneasy ghost, which it seems impossible to lay.

" It is a vexatious task, and one which always makes a scientific man feel ridiculous, to set vigorously to work to demolish

in what way, would be a proposition upon which the youths might exercise their wits to some profit. It is not true that money tends to flow from the Southern and Western to the Eastern States, and from them to England, in greater quantity than in opposite directions. If money (commodities) united to flow to those places at which it is the most utilized, it is from the cities and the richer part of the country to the poorer, — from the Northern and Eastern to the Southern and Western States. Ten per cent is not an extravagant rate to be paid on loans of money either in Kansas or Texas, from the profitable manner in which it can be used in them. It consequently flows toward them from its greater utility there than elsewhere. There are ten dollars to-day in Kansas where there was one ten years ago; and this money came almost wholly from the Eastern States, in which the ratio of its increase within the period named has not been one-twentieth of that in Kansas. That money did tend to flow from the Southern and Western States toward the Northern and Eastern, and from these toward England, would, if true, be a very comforting proposition for the latter countries. Even the professor who propounded it seems to entertain doubts whether it ever reaches them. He alleges a tendency, without daring to affirm a result. This tendency, it is to be feared, is, after all, only a piece of sickly sentimentalism, not having force enough to surmount the Alleghanies in one case, or pass the Grand Banks in the other.

Here is another puzzle put by the professor of Political Economy in that institution to the Harvard wits : " Mention the three classes into which commodities are divided in relation to their value. In which class do you place gold and silver ? "

an old error which no well-informed man any longer holds ; but in our present situation, and under our political system, popular errors are of the utmost importance, and no pains should be spared in patiently exposing them. The fallacy here is in the word ' balance.' If it means *equilibrium*, it may be used correctly to denote the equality of exports and imports ; but then it regulates itself, and no power can control it. If it means *remainder*, and suggests analogies of book-keeping, it is a mere myth to which no fact corresponds, and is to be entirely rejected. . . .

" The report of this committee is perhaps the most important doctrine in financial literature. Its doctrines have been tested both ways, — by disbelief and by belief, by experiment of their opposites and by experiment of themselves. They are no longer disputable. They are not matter of opinion or theory, but of demonstration. They are ratified or established as the basis of finance. They may be denied, as the roundness of the earth was denied five years ago, and as Newton's theory of the solar system was denied until within twenty-five years; but they have passed the stage where the scientific financier is bound to discuss them.

" The doctrines of this report may be summed up thus : —

" 1. The value of an inconvertible currency depends on its *amount* relatively to the needs of the country for circulating medium (only to a very subordinate degree on the security on which it is based or the credit of the issuer).

" 2. If gold is at a premium in paper, the paper is redundant and depreciated. The premium measures the depreciation.[1]

" On a system of even nominal convertibility, the motives of speculation and of price fluctuations lie outside of the currency in industrial and commercial circumstances. Speculation, in the widest and best sense, controls the amount of the currency. On an inconvertible system, the amount of the currency controls speculation. If it is not redundant, its effect is slight; if it is very excessive, it ' floats ' every thing, and becomes the controlling consideration. No one believes that an inconvertible currency suspends the operation of any of the economic laws which govern prices; but, if it is redundant, it decides whether the fluctuations in price of a unit of a given commodity shall be above and below $1, or above and below $2. Every contraction or expansion alters this general level.[2]

" Of the three questions involved in the report, as stated above : — Is the paper depreciated ? why are the exchanges adverse ? how ought the Bank to regulate its issues ? — the first and third have no great importance for us. No one denies that our paper is depreciated, unless it be those who think that we have ' grown up ' to the currency, though that notion seems to have gone out of fashion again. The question of regulating an inconvertible Bank paper is not our question, because our paper is fixed in amount. But the second question of the Bullion Committee has great im-

[1] History of American Currency, pp. 245-249.
[2] Ibid., pp. 253, 254.

portance. It is the one in regard to which doctrines opposed to those of the Bullion Report are most frequently affirmed and most profoundly believed amongst us, and there is no hope of any exit from our circumstances until we get to understand the laws which govern the distribution of the precious metals, and those laws of currency which are connected therewith. It will be remembered, as stated above, that the question about the exchanges is really this question : If the exchanges are adverse to such a degree as to produce a serious and prolonged outflow of the precious metals, where must we look for the cause ? Is it due to the balance of payments, or to some deterioration of the currency ? Or, to put the same question in another form : If we desire to produce an influx of gold, to what force must we look to cause it ? Must we look to the ' balance of trade,' or can we do any thing in the matter save sit still and wait for the balance of trade to turn ? Can we bring it about by correcting some error in the currency ?

" The answer to these questions given in the report, and by those who supported it, is, that the balance of imports and exports never can move the exchanges, either above or below par, more than just enough to start a movement of bullion. On a specie system, any outflow of bullion would bring down prices, and immediately make a remittance of goods more profitable than one of bullion ; and, if the exportation of bullion was artificially continued (as, for instance, to pay the expenses of a foreign war), it would reduce prices until a counter current would set in and restore the former relative distribution all the world over. . . . If, therefore, there is an outflow of gold, serious and long continued, accompanied by an unfavorable exchange, it is a sign that there is an inferior currency behind the gold, which is displacing it. The surplus of imports of goods above the exports of goods is nothing but the return payment for this export of gold, and is not a cause, but a consequence. If, finally, we want to turn this tide and produce an influx, there is only one way to do it ; and that is simply to remove the inferior currency. As for waiting for the balance of trade to turn and bring gold into a country which has a depreciated paper currency, one might as well take his stand at the foot of a hill, and wait for it to change into a declivity before climbing it.

" The authorities of the Bank strenuously denied that their issues, so long as they were made at five per cent on bills representing real transactions, at three months' date, could become excessive. The Committee and their supporters held that this rule would not be a guarantee against inflation, but that, if the exchanges were adverse, and bullion was being exported, it was a sign that the paper was excessive, and that the Bank should check its issues. The Bank maintained that it had nothing to do with the exchanges, and could not govern its issues by any reference to them. The bullionists maintained that while the paper was inconvertible, the adverse exchange and the premium on gold were the only signs by which the Bank could judge when its issues were excessive. Thus the real issue was, whether, in case of a drain of specie, we must look at the ratio of imports to exports, or at the ratio of paper currency to requirement, for the explanation of it and the means of checking it."[1]

" There is no such thing or condition," says Mr. Sumner, " as balance of trade. If it means equilibrium, it may be used correctly to denote the equality of exports and imports; but then it regulates itself, and no power can control it. If it means remainder, and suggests analogies of book-keeping, it is a mere myth, to which no fact corresponds, and is to be entirely rejected." If a country export gold, it receives, he says in common with the Economists, an equal value of merchandise. If it import it, it exports an equal value of merchandise. Where is the "balance of trade" in transactions that mutually balance the one the other? they triumphantly ask, as if that were an end of the whole question. But is it certain that countries, in parting with their gold, always receive an equivalent, and are no worse off therefor? Suppose an individual possessed of a thousand dollars in coin to expend it in the purchase of the necessaries of life even, his means are reduced in like ratio. If he would reinstate his former condition, he must forego future expenditures to an equal amount. So, if a person run into debt to his shopkeeper to the amount of a thousand dollars, if he would pay it, he must forego a like amount of his future earnings. His indebtedness until paid would very properly be termed a balance of trade against him. So with a nation. If it import more in value of ordinary merchandise than it exports, its specie will have to go to make up the deficit. Now, no nation not producing gold can part with any considerable amount of it without causing embarrassment to its industries and trade ; for the reason that that which it possessed and exported was a part of the machinery by which these were carried on. The tendency of the precious metals the world over is to distribute themselves according to the means and needs of those using them. If there be no movement in any direction, it is assumed that they are in proper equilibrium. If this be disturbed in any country, it must be restored. If England, for example, from any cause, lose £10,000,000 in coin, she must bring the amount back again, in order to prosecute her industries on their wonted scale. Now the imports that are made by an export of gold

---

[1] History of American Currency, pp. 262–266.

will always embrace a large number of articles which the nation might as well be without as with. The export of a large amount of coin is usually due to a vicious paper currency, and such a currency is always attended with wasteful expenditure. So far, the position of a nation is relatively weakened; for she has parted with that which is essential to her welfare, and must be reclaimed by future accumulations. Mr. Sumner admits that the condition of things described may exist, but says that no " balance of trade " has resulted: only that from an inferior currency an excess of a particular commodity has been exported, to be brought back by the re-exportation of that received for it, or its equivalent; and that, as soon as the inferior currency is removed, the equilibrium will restore itself. Admitting the cause, has not the export of coin resulted in a loss? and, if so, may not the loss as well be described as an " unfavorable balance of trade " as by any other term? Nor is there any want of scientific accuracy in that ordinarily used. The condition is something more than mere myth, Mr. Sumner's flippant assertions to the contrary. A nation that has parted with its coin, which has to be brought back again, would have been much better off had it never parted with it. That which has been received will never suffice to bring it back; and, if it would, the charges of transportation and interest would involve a large loss; so that, after all, " balance of trade " is a veritable fact, and always exists to a greater or less extent in commerce between nations, and must always exist until human affairs reach the accuracy and certainty of natural laws.

But what is an " inferior currency "? One kind is the inconvertible notes of government, issued not for the purpose of loaning capital, but to supply the lack of it. The demand for merchandise must increase in ratio to its amount; for it is always superadded to the existing currencies. As such notes are always made legal tender, they not only drive coin out of the country, but keep it out till they are retired. Such a currency admits of no corrective by the laws of trade. Another " inferior " currency is that issued by Banks, without a constituent. This exerts, in the outset and to the amount of its issue, precisely the same effects as the notes of government. Both equally tend to drive coin out of the country, from the consumption of foreign fabrics to which they lead. But, as their paper is convertible into coin, the Banks must supply the gold to meet the expenditures that have been made. The remedy, therefore, is speedily applied by the laws of trade. They must pay for the excess of imports over exports from their reserves. It is impossible, however, for them to tell whether all the bills discounted by them have their proper constituent: they can only determine the fact by the result. If they see gold beginning to move, they understand at once that improper bills have been discounted; that the currency has been issued in excess, and must so far be taken in by a reduction of their line of discounts. The movement of gold, therefore, is an indication of the state of the currency, as infallible as is that of the mercury of meteoric conditions. It is the thing of all others upon which an issuer of currency, at the great centres of trade, must keep his eye steadily fixed, and by which he must daily adjust all his operations.

Mr. Sumner's test of an "inferior currency" is very different from that which has been described. With him, it is not a question of quality, but of quantity. It is never "inferior," so long as its amount does not exceed that required by a country in its exchanges, even if it be not backed by a single dollar of coin. The conclusion of the Bullion Committee was, to use his own words, " that the value of an inconvertible currency depends upon its amount, relatively to the needs of a country for a circulating medium; and only to a very subordinate degree upon the security on which it is based, or the credit of the issuer." Their conclusions, he tells us, that the value of money depends upon its quantity, not upon the provision made for its convertibility, " are not matters of opinion, but of demonstration." If so, then it is a matter of demonstration that one and one make four. It has been shown over and over again, in this discussion, that the real or estimated value of articles, whether they be merchandise or money, is their exchangeable value. To assume otherwise, would be to say that the exchangeable value of a piece of silver having the weight and insignia of a sovereign equals the value of a sovereign. Humanity is not yet brought to so low a pitch as this. Even the Economists are by no means the simple race their theories would make them. In spite of the conclusions of the Bullion Committee, which, with Mr. Sumner, are the very acme of financial wisdom, he would be the last man to take a bank or government note without especial reference to the provision made for its discharge. If their creed were their law, a few days would suffice for the Economists to fool away whatever they possessed.

The following extracts from a work entitled " The Elements of Political Economy," by Mr. A. R. Perry, Professor of Political Economy in Williams College, are given as an additional evidence of the kind of *pabulum* which is dealt out to the young men in our colleges. He has all the incoherence of Bonamy Price, though somewhat less of his rant. The reader can make his own criticisms.

" There is no use in saying that money is such a mysterious and complicated agent that nobody can understand it. That is the language of indolence. Money is wholly a matter of man's device : it was invented, just as any other instrument is invented, to accomplish a certain purpose ; and it would be strange if men cannot comprehend what men themselves have devised.[1]

" The word ' money,' a medium of exchange, is to be taken in its etymological and strict sense, as something that comes between two extremes, and serves also to relate them to each other. Money is only a medium of exchange, and not a real subject of exchange : it is a very great help in exchanging all other things, but is never exchanged for itself in an ultimate transaction.[2]

" Probably the ratio of one to forty is below, rather than above, the true ratio of the aggregate money of the commercial nations to the money value of their products, reckoned only once, which their money helps to exchange. Therefore we see that the hub and spokes and rim of the wheel of exchange consist of services and commodities of every description ; while, to borrow the famous comparison of Hume, money is but the grease which makes the wheel turn easier. It is a vast mistake to suppose that the grease is the wheel itself.[3]

" The difference between money as a medium and money as a measure is one that should be clearly delineated and perfectly apprehended, because there is no such thing as adequately understanding the subject of money, unless the two functions be kept distinct in the mind, as well in their single as in their commingled action. There is the same difference between money as a medium and money as a measure that there is between a bushel of wheat and that round vessel by which we determine that there is a bushel :

[1] Elements of Political Economy, p. 188.
[2] Ibid., p. 193.
[3] Ibid., pp. 195, 196.

dollars and cents perform their duties as a medium by virtue of their being commodities; they perform their duties as a measure by virtue of their being denominations. . . . The distinction between denominations and those things themselves which are reckoned by denominations seems a very obvious distinction, and one would suppose not likely to be confounded; but, the truth is, the two are perpetually confounded, even in some of the most recent and approved works on money. Indeed, the grand difficulty and source of error in discussions on money heretofore has been that this distinction has rarely, if ever, been consistently attended to; and I flatter myself that I am doing the science a service at this point by calling attention to this confusion, by explaining how it arises, and by clearing up, so far forth, a vexed portion of the subject. . . .

"It may be asked, Why cannot this source of error be obviated? I reply that the error may be obviated, but the source of it cannot be obviated, from the nature of the case. It was shown in our chapter on Value, that to find an invariable measure of value is a natural impossibility. Money, as it is the medium of exchange, is also the best attainable measure of value, and is used throughout the civilized world to compare with each other all values except its own; but since value in general, and the value of money as well, is a thing of relation, and varies with every change affecting either of the things exchanged, as much by changes affecting the things it exchanges for as by changes affecting itself, — the value of a hat, for instance, as estimated in gloves, increasing by any cheapened process in glove-making, though no change at all take place in the cost of hat-making, — a perfect measure of value is impossible. Therefore the denominations of money, which is the best attainable measure, can never have a meaning absolutely fixed, but slide up and down the scale along which the purchasing power of money as a medium is moving, and they are consequently useless as a standard to detect any changes in the medium itself; while, the medium remaining uniform, they instantly detect the changes in all other purchasing powers.[1]

" Society is so constituted that a want is felt in it of some medium of purchase; this want cannot be supplied without an effort; whoever makes the effort will demand a corresponding effort made for him. When it comes to the exchange of the medium for the wheat, for example, there stand face to face, as in every other instance of exchange, two desires and two efforts. There is then, as always, a reciprocal estimation of the two services about to be exchanged, and the estimation agreed on is the *value* of the medium expressed in wheat. If the want of any medium of exchange is less felt in any community, or if the effort required to secure it be for any reason less, other things remaining the same, the value of the money will be less; that is to say, it will purchase less of other things. If the demand for money as an instrument of purchase be greater, or the obstacles in the way of its supply be increased, other things remaining as before, the value of the money

---

[1] Elements of Political Economy, pp. 203–207.

will be more. It is the old circuit over again of wants, efforts, estimations, satisfactions. The value of money arises under the same conditions as every other value, and is variable by every change in any one of the four elements which alone can vary the value of any thing. Two desires and two efforts invariably precede every exchange. A change in any one of these, the rest unchanged, can vary value, and nothing else can vary it; and, as it seems to me, no person has ever shown, or can show, that the value of money is in any respect, save the superficial one already noticed, exceptional and peculiar. And it also seems to me that nothing more is needed, in order to remove the last vestige of the dark cloud which has so long overhung this subject, than to familiarize one's self, first of all, with the true doctrine of value in general, and then hold fast the truth, exemplified on every side, that the value of money is just like any other value.[1]

"The earlier period of the suspension proves this important point, that when a government possesses the monopoly of issuing paper money, and carefully limits the quantity issued, and both receives it and pays it out as legal tender, it may keep an inconvertible paper at par, and even, by sufficiently limiting its quantity, carry it above par. But this truth does not make an inconvertible paper a good money; because it does not make it a self-regulating money, and because no one is wise enough, nor ever will be, to issue just enough, and no more, of such money."[2]

NOTE. — The following extracts, taken from a reprint in pamphlet form of an article written by Hon. David A. Wells, which appeared in the "New York Herald," of Feb. 13, 1875, "The Cremation Theory of Specie Resumption," show the flippant nonsense which parades itself as oracular wisdom in the newspapers of the day : —

"In the first place, I do not believe that any man can affirm how much currency a country wants or will use, so long as that currency is restricted to an exclusively local circulation. A three-cent piece, if it could be divided into a sufficient number of pieces, with each piece capable of being handled, would undoubtedly suffice for doing all the business of the country in the way of facilitating exchanges if no other better instrumentality was available. . . . What specific amount of contraction of the legal tender would be necessary, no one can tell with certainty. But, speaking generally, we can affirm with absolute certainty that, to just the extent to which our present volume of currency, supposing it to be exclusively coin, would, by the laws of trade, be diminished by exportation, to just that same extent the volume of our existing paper currency needs to be contracted to equalize its value with coin. If the present average premium on gold represents and measures the excess of currency, and we assume the amount of currency in active circulation at $750,000,000, then a contraction of from $80,000,000 to $90,000,000, and a period of less than four years, would suffice to restore our currency to a specie basis. But if, on the other hand, the excess of currency over and above what is required to do the business of the country on a gold basis is greater than is indicated by the present average gold premium (a point concerning which opinions differ) then a longer period would be required. But, sooner or later, if the contraction was continued, the desired correspondence would be effected.

"Again, a definite policy of contraction, once agreed and entered upon, it does not seem to me that there need be a single further legislative provision, other than to provide the means necessary to furnish the requisite supply of

[1] Elements of Political Economy, pp. 211, 212.   [2] Ibid., p. 264.

The object of the second part of this work has been, not only to trace the History of Monetary Theories, but to illustrate the correctness of the laws or principles previously laid down. So firmly had become riveted in the public mind the ideas, the teachings, and the traditions of the past, — so inveterate the tendency to accept the phenomenal for the real, — that it is doubtful whether any statement of principles, no matter how authoritative or conclusive, could secure acceptance, unless it could be shown at the same time that they successfully disproved the dogmas or theories set out in the books. For twenty-two

notes for cremation. *There is no necessity of talking of redemption in the sense of exchanging gold for notes on presentation and demand by holders of the latter across the counter of the Treasury.*"

A three-cent piece could hardly be cut up so fine as to represent all the notes and checks as well as coin now used in the exchanges of the country. But as a value, according to Mr. Wells, equal to that of a three-cent piece would be all that would be required in the exchanges, why not do the next best thing, and use paper? The cost of a thousand-dollar note would not equal one cent. What other kind of material, taking cost and portability into account, could be so appropriate? By its use the whole cost of a currency for the United States could not, indeed, be brought to Mr. Wells's minimum; but would come pretty near it, considering the vast amount required. By the use of paper, our currency ought not to cost over $100,000 annually, — a sum hardly more to be thought of than a three-cent piece. Mr. Wells, in fact, advocates the use of a government currency, only with limitations, — the quantity not to exceed that required for the exchanges of the country. We should be all right, he says, if our paper money did not exceed the amount of coin which but for it would be in circulation. We are afraid, if he would reduce the amount of paper to that of the coin which otherwise would be in circulation, he would reduce it far below $650,000,000, or $350,000,000 even; as, but for its use, by far the greater number of transactions in which it is used would never take place. They are rendered possible only by the use of paper money. As the premium on gold when he wrote equalled about 12 per cent (the amount of paper in circulation at the time equalling about $750,000,000), a reduction of the currency equal to $80,000,000 or $90,000,000 would, he estimates, be sufficient to raise the whole value of that remaining outstanding to par. This could be done in less than four years, by " cremating " $500,000 weekly. The premium has now fallen to five per cent; reducing the amount necessary to be cremated to less than $200,000 weekly, or to $37,500,000 for the four years. Certainly, the nation should make no great ado about such a paltry sum as this. The necessary amount might be raised by subscription in twenty-four hours. However, if the question be simply one of quantity, and as with the progress of our population and commerce the amount of our currency should increase at least at the rate of five per cent annually, the far better way, admitting the correctness of Mr. Wells' assumption that the question is simply one of quantity, would be to do nothing but wait till the nation has grown up to the present volume of currency. As it is now within five per cent of it, a year at least should suffice to bring our two kinds of money upon a level. A process so natural and healthy should not be disturbed by any kind of empiricism.

hundred years, the more important Laws of Money have been assumed to be settled beyond cavil or dispute. These laws are still accepted, in their original integrity, with the same confidence as are accepted the demonstrations of Newton of the laws which control the motion of the heavenly bodies. To declare the old ideas to be not only inadequate, but wholly opposed to the fact, would have been to be open to the charge of unwarrantable presumption, unless followed by demonstrations which should conclusively establish the correctness of such an assumption. That no such charge might be made, the whole question of money has been carefully reconsidered, and subjected to a process of rigid analysis. This has shown that its laws as laid down in the books have from the outset been wholly without warrant, and that the confusion which has prevailed in reference to them has been the necessary result. The science in its present form is the work of Aristotle, accepted by the Schoolmen, and transmitted by them to modern times, without having, in any single instance, challenged or received any thing like a critical examination. It still remains a striking example of the method which assumes to solve by dialectics every question coming within the range of human inquiry. In this science, its founder still reigns supreme, — a most signal illustration of the permanence of opinions after their correctness has been once accepted, and the easy immunity secured to them after hoary antiquity shall have rendered impious all attempt to inquire as to their right to rule.

The whole subject turns upon the question, whether or not value be an essential attribute of money. That it was a convenient attribute, few, perhaps, would deny. But such attribute was held to be useful chiefly in providing a way for the retirement of whatever might exist, or be issued, in excess of the amount required in the exchanges ; and if such excess could be used, or converted into that which could be used, for other purposes, then the currency was self-regulating, and so far value would be a useful attribute. But it was of no use so long as the money did not exceed the public want : so long would its real equal its nominal value, from the necessity of its use ; and so long it was indifferent of what material it was composed, or whether or not it had a constituent, or carried any obligation. Such assumptions are laid down as fundamental principles by every writer upon the subject. They have been shown, it is believed, to be wholly opposed to natural laws, as well as to the common experience of mankind. The appeal to the empirical has fully sustained the conclusions of induction. Such a result being established, there should be an end to this branch of the discussion, — not only from its superfluousness, but to spare the reader a repetition which might exhaust his patience, but which could add nothing to the force of his convictions.

CURRENCY AND BANKING IN THE UNITED STATES.

THAT which has preceded will have prepared the way to an intelligible discussion of the financial and monetary systems of the United States. It was useless to undertake any thing of the kind till the whole subject of money had been reconsidered, its laws determined, and applied to every proposition which the ingenuity of the Economists could suggest. Till then, any isolated essay, or statement of principles, without detailing the process by which they were reached, would have only added to the confusion which prevailed. Every proposition to be found in the books in reference to money, especially paper money, is exactly opposed to the fact. Although all writers upon it agree in the main, it is always with some qualification, in order to show some degree of independence and originality ; so that error itself takes a thousand different shapes. The debates in Congress are simply the roar of chaos. The laws of paper money have, it is believed, been placed, in what has preceded, upon impregnable foundations ; and their application made palpable to the most ordinary understanding. We can now see exactly where we stand, and correctly estimate the nature and effect of our circulation, and the methods or steps to be taken to relieve ourselves of it, and to provide one which, by being capital, or the representative of capital, will promote in the highest possible degree, the welfare of the nation. As our present legal-tender currency is the second one of the kind, — for the existing government is to be considered only as a continuation and part of that instituted at the outbreak of the War of Independence, — it becomes important to give a brief sketch of the first, in illustration of the reasons for the issue of the second, and of the influence exerted by it upon the operations of government, as well as upon those of production and trade.

Our government as first organized was vested in a Congress, or body of delegates, representing the thirteen original States. As it did not spring directly from the people, it lacked that representative character considered under our own system as well as that of England as indispensable to the exercise of the right or power of taxation. It could make requisitions upon the States, but was utterly powerless to enforce them. The latter still remained independent communities, united in a voluntary confederation for the prosecution of the war. As the central Government, as the chief Executive, was compelled to act at once in reference to the necessities imposed upon it, it must itself provide the means as best it could. Without the power of taxation, the mode obviously suggesting itself was an issue of notes to serve as money. All the colonies, in similar necessities, had issued greater or less amounts of such notes; although, for some time preceding the outbreak of the war, they had been greatly reduced, not only from a general sense of their mischievous effect, but from an Act of Parliament forbidding their continued issue. Though the results of their issue had, without exception, been most disastrous, yet there is nothing in which a community so soon forgets the lessons of the past. The first effect of paper money always seems beneficent; for it always creates activity in all the departments of industry and trade, in ratio to its amount. If this be small, it will for a considerable time circulate at only a very slight discount, from the use that can be made of it by indebted parties, for whom it will have the value of gold. Its issue, therefore, in the outset is always welcome to the great mass; as in the present enjoyment and satisfaction, both past and future are alike forgotten; or, if some uneasiness and apprehension be felt, they are quieted by the assumption that the amount will be small, and that whatever may be issued will speedily be taken in.

The first Continental Congress assembled on the 10th of May, 1775. On the 30th of that month, the colony of New York, through its delegates, submitted that as from the inability of the National and State Governments to raise money, either by loans or taxation, notes of one or the other, to serve as money, would have to be resorted to, they should be issued by the General Government, from the greater credit that would be attached to them, representing, as they would, the whole country; the greater ease and certainty with which their amount could be regulated; and the wider circulation which could be secured. It was also urged that as the State of New York would, from its central position, be that in which a large proportion of expenditures would be made, unless the notes were issued by the central Government, that State would soon be flooded with those of other States, upon whose issues there would be no check, and for which there would be no sufficient vent, greatly to the public detriment. If notes were to be issued, the reasons urged by the New York delegates appeared to have more force than they really deserved, as the provisional Government might cease at any moment to exist, while those of the States would, in any event, be continued. Their representations, however, prevailed; and on the 22d of June, 1775, an issue of $3,000,000 was authorized to be made as occasion required. Such was the beginning of the Continental money, — as humble and insignificant, in the outset, as the Genie of the Arabian Tales, whom a small bottle at first sufficed to hold, but who, freed from its imprisonment, swelled into proportions so vast as to enfold both sea and land. But the Genie could contract as well as expand. In a freak of vanity, to show his power, he crept back again into his bottle, which the fisherman who had unwittingly set him free instantly closed, and so escaped with his life. Here the parallel ends: for the Genie of the printing press, from an equally insignificant beginning, swelled into proportions still vaster than those of his prototype, which no power, not even his own, could reduce; and could be got rid of only by his death, but not till a whole nation was very nearly brought to the same desperate pass.

The following is a copy of the notes first issued: —

"CONTINENTAL CURRENCY.

"No.———   ———Dollars.

"This bill entitles the bearer to receive" (from one to twenty) "Spanish milled dollars, or the value thereof in gold or silver, according to the resolution of the Congress held at Philadelphia on the 10th day of May, A. D. 1775."

The first issue of notes was apportioned among the several States in ratio to their population, as their proper quota to the expenses of government, which were, in theory at least, to be borne by them by virtue of their power of taxation, — a power which the central Government did not possess. The notes issued were to be returned for cancellation to the latter, in ratio to the amount received, in four annual instalments, — the first one to be paid before the last day of November, 1779; and the last, on or before the last day of November, 1782. The smallness of their amount, and the provision made for their repayment, show how little was foreseen of the long and dreary struggle upon which the country had already entered.[1]

No sooner had these issues been made, than the States made the notes their own. The first one to act was Rhode Island, which declared every person who refused to take them to be a public enemy. Other States followed with laws to a similar effect.

On the 29th day of November, 1775, a second issue of $3,000,000 was authorized, with similar provisions for their retirement as for that of the first. This issue was strongly opposed by Franklin, who urged that an attempt should be made to borrow back the notes first issued. He had also urged that all the notes should bear interest. Neither of his recommendations prevailed.

The necessities of the government still continuing, a third issue of $4,000,000 was made on Feb. 17, 1776. Before the close of 1775, however, and when only $6,000,000 of notes had been authorized, an unwillingness to take them began to show itself. The first hesitation appeared among the Quakers, not from any alleged want of their value, but from conscien-

---

[1] The apportionment among the States was as follows : —

New Hampshire	$124,069¼
Massachusetts Bay	434,244
Rhode Island	71,959½
Connecticut	248,139
New York	248,139
New Jersey	161,290½
Pennsylvania	372,208½
Delaware	87,219½
Maryland	310,174½
Virginia	496,278
North Carolina	248,139
South Carolina	248,139
Total	$3,000,000

Georgia was not included in the apportionment, as she was not represented in Congress.

tious scruples which forbade them to take, even indirectly, any part in war. The real cause was undoubtedly distrust, as they afterwards showed no hesitation in taking them at their market value. The year closed disastrously for the American cause. Canada was lost: public confidence was no little shaken. Rumors constantly reached Congress of an unwillingness to receive its notes; in consequence of which, on the 11th of January, 1776, only a little more than six months after the first issue, and only a little more than three after they got into circulation, it put forth the following preamble and resolution: —

" *Whereas*, It appears to this Congress that several evil-disposed persons, in order to obstruct and defeat the efforts of the United Colonies in defence of their just rights, have attempted to depreciate the bills of credit emitted by the authority of this Congress,
" *Resolved*, Therefore, that any person who shall hereafter be so lost to all virtue and regard for his country as to refuse to receive said bills in payment, or obstruct and discourage the currency or circulation thereof, and shall be duly convicted by the committee of the city, county, or district, or, in case of appeal from their decision, by the Assembly, convention, council, or committee of safety of the Colony where he shall reside; such person shall be deemed, published, and treated as an enemy of his country, and precluded from all trade or intercourse with the inhabitants of these Colonies." [1]

The States did their best to sustain the action of the general government. They denounced all recusants, and remitted them for punishment to committees of safety, which in many

[1] Would it not have been well for the Economists, who assert that the only cause of the depreciation of government notes is their excess of issue, to explain the cause of the early decline in value of the Continental money? Evidences of such decline in value manifested themselves by the time that only a little more than $3,000,000 had got into circulation, the issue authorized Nov. 29, 1775, not being actually made until after the close of that year. The coin in circulation at the outbreak of the war was variously estimated as from $12,000,000 to $30,000,000. Considering the largely increased expenditures of government, an addition to the currency of $6,000,000 of notes could certainly not be regarded as excessive, if that kind of money were to be resorted to. Professor Fawcett assumes that a country engaged in war may issue, in addition to the currency in circulation, its own notes to serve as money, in ratio to its increased expenditures without affecting prices, or what is the same thing, without causing a depreciation of their value. Is it not astonishing that the Economists should have gone on repeating Adam Smith for a century, without once stopping to interrogate history, or to investigate the conditions upon which the value of all currencies must rest?

cases had hardly any more sense of justice than infuriated mobs. Newspapers were by no means wanting in the same direction.

" When paper money," says a writer of the time, in one of them, " circulates in the common course of trade, its value gradually rises and falls in proportion to its quantity, when relatively considered with the value of the real effects of a country, such as houses, lands, provisions, gold, silver, and merchandise of every kind ; for though paper merely has not any significant value in itself, and has only such value as we place upon it, a single dollar bill being as large as an eight dollar bill, yet, as by general consent we agree to receive and pass *this* as *one* and *that* as *eight*, so long as this mutual confidence and resolution continues, they are to all intents and purposes of as much real worth as so much actual gold and silver, which are of themselves of no other absolute value than what mankind have been pleased to fix on them.[1] . . .

" It is a grand continental experiment we are trying, and nothing but the experiment itself can determine the expediency: we are not to look on our present situation as a matter of choice, but of necessity ; we have got into a labyrinth, and must get out of it as well as we can. If, by giving a general credit to our money and forcing a trade, we should weary out Great Britain, or involve her

---

[1] This brief paragraph, written before the publication of the " Wealth of Nations," embodies the substance of all that was ever written upon the subject of paper money ; and, compared with the loose and incoherent treatise of Adam Smith, is a model of conciseness both in thought and style. It shows the absurdity of any claim for him for originality upon the subject of money. All he did was to obscure and perplex, by irrelevant illustrations and unmeaning verbiage, a subject which had been most perfectly stated — that is, according to his views, if he had any — by those who preceded him, but which he neither investigated nor understood.

" The American paper money," says John Adams, " is nothing but bills of credit, by which the public, the community, promises to pay the possessor a certain sum in a certain limited time. In a country where there is no coin, or not enough in circulation, these bills may be emitted to a certain amount, and they will pass at par; but as soon as the quantity exceeds the value of the ordinary business of the people, it will depreciate, and continue to fall in its value in proportion to the augmentation of the quantity." — Adams's Works, vol. vii. p. 296.

The writer who at the time best appreciated the nature and effect of paper money was Pelatiah Webster, who published a series of essays, the first under date of the 5th of October, 1776, which were continued during the war. He early presented, with great clearness and force, the danger that was being incurred from the issue of government notes, and constantly urged the retirement of the " superfluity," in order to avoid the catastrophe which he predicted and subsequently described. His essays are to be thoroughly studied, if one would gain any thing like an adequate picture of the time. He, however, by no means grasped the whole subject. It was the " excess " that he wished to get rid of, forgetting that every dollar of the kind is always in excess.

in a war with some of her European neighbors, we may then take our own time to pay off the debt we have been contracting, and every year will restore the currency nearer to its original value. To what extent a country may venture to run itself in debt is a question beyond my abilities to solve. Whether a community and an individual may with propriety be compared, I cannot pretend to determine; but, if the comparison would hold, I should say that as an individual has a right to spend or run in debt to the exact amount of what he is worth, without injury to his creditors, so may a community; if this be true, it may be easy to determine how much farther we may safely go." [1]

The arguments presented in the preceding paragraphs undoubtedly appeared conclusive enough to their writers when they were not immediately engaged in paying or receiving money; but when they came to act, they were governed by a law far more potent than that which their feeble natures attempted to set up. The loudest advocates of the doctrine that the value of money depended upon convention — upon its quantity, not upon its quality — are not in the least degree influenced by their arguments. They never became parties to a convention to accept a note for $10, utterly worthless in itself, for merchandise equalling its nominal value in coin. Nor is there the slightest evidence or probability that the notes then issued ever circulated at any other than their estimated value; while it was inevitable that confidence in them should decline in ratio to the extraordinary efforts made to sustain their price. The writer also forgot that the money of a country represents the proper amount of its consuming power, which equals only its annual product, not its lands, machinery, public works, and the like, which are to form the basis of production, and are not the proper subjects of consumption.

The necessities of the government still continuing, with no other resource than its notes, it authorized, on the 6th day of May, 1776, a further issue of $5,000,000; one-half of which was to be made in June, and the other half in July of that year. A serious decline in the value of the notes followed. This was increased by a further issue of $5,000,000 in November. Gov-

---

[1] In illustration of the intense patriotic feeling which prevailed at the time, it may be stated that, early in 1776, some American privateers, who brought into Philadelphia $22,000 in specie captured from the enemy, offered that entire sum to Congress in exchange for its notes, and received the thanks of that body for their generous conduct.

ernment, to check the decline, directed General Putnam, then in command of the army at Philadelphia, to issue an order, under date of Dec. 14, 1776, that if any one refused to take the government notes in payment for goods, the goods should be forfeited, and the person so refusing should be thrown into prison.[1] These orders produced no other effect than to increase the decline. The state of things near the close of the year will be best shown by a letter written by Robert Morris to one of the government agents in Europe, under date of 21st of December, 1776 : —

. . . . "I must add," he says, "to this gloomy picture one circumstance more distressing than all the rest, because it threatens instant and total ruin to the *American* cause, unless some radical cure is applied and that speedily : I mean the depreciation of the Continental currency. The enormous pay of our army, the enormous expenses at which they are supplied with provisions, clothing, and other necessaries, and, in short, the extravagance that has prevailed in most departments of the public service, have called forth prodigious emissions of paper money, both Continental and colonial. Our internal enemies — who, alas ! are numerous and rich — have always been undermining its value by various artifices ; and, now that our distresses are wrought to a pitch by the successes and near approach of the enemy, they speak plainly, and many persons peremptorily refuse to take it at any rate. Those that do receive it, do it with fear and trembling ; and you may judge of its value even amongst those, when I tell you that £250 Continental currency, or 666⅔ dollars, is given for a bill of exchange of £100 sterling, sixteen dollars for a half-johannes, two paper dollars for one of silver, three dollars for a pair of shoes, twelve dollars for a hat, and so on. A common laborer asks two dollars a day for his work, and idles half his time.

" All this amounts to real depreciation of the money. The war must be carried on at an expense proportional to this value, which must inevitably call for immense emissions, and of course still further depreciations must ensue. This can only be prevented by borrowing in the money now in circulation. The attempt is made, and I hope will succeed by loan or lottery. The present

---

[1] "PHILADELPHIA, Dec. 14, 1776.

. . . . " The General commanding, to his great astonishment, has been informed that several of the inhabitants of this city have refused to take the Continental currency in payment of goods. In future, should any of the inhabitants be so lost to public virtue and the welfare of their country as to presume to refuse the currency of the American States in payment for any commodities they may have for sale, the goods shall be forfeited, and the person or persons so refusing shall be kept in close confinement.

"ISRAEL PUTNAM,
" *Major General.*"

troubles interrupt these measures here, and as yet I am not informed how they go on in other States. But something more is necessary: force must inevitably be employed, and I dread to see that day. We have already calamities sufficient for any country, and the measure will be full when one part of the *American* people is obliged to dragoon another, at the same time that they are opposing a most powerful external foe."

In a letter to the President of Congress, under date of Dec. 23, 1776, he speaks in a similar strain: —

"It is very mortifying to me when I am obliged to tell you disagreeable things; but I am compelled to inform Congress that the Continental currency keeps losing in credit. Many refuse openly and avowedly to receive it; and several citizens that retired into the country must have starved, if their own private credit had not procured them the common necessaries of life when nothing could be got for your money. Some effectual remedy should be speedily applied to this evil, or the game will be up. Mr. Commissary Wharton has told the General that the mills refuse to grind for him, either from disaffection, or dislike to the money. Be that as it may, the consequences are terrible; for I do suppose the army will not consent to starve."

As the alarm and apprehension for the future increased, Congress, in order to allay them, adopted, on the 14th of January, 1777, the following preamble and resolution: —

"*Whereas*, The Continental money ought to be supported at the full value expressed in the respective bills, by the inhabitants of these States, for whose benefit they were issued, and who stand bound to redeem the same according to the like value; and the pernicious artifices of the enemies of American liberty to impair the credit of the said bills, by raising the nominal value of gold and silver, or any other species of money whatsoever, ought to be guarded against and prevented:

"*Resolved*, That all bills of credit emitted by the authority of Congress ought to pass current in all payments, trade, and dealings in these States, and be deemed in value equal to the same nominal sums in Spanish milled dollars; and that whosoever shall offer, ask, or receive more in the said bills, for any gold or silver coins, bullion, or any other species of money whatsoever, than the nominal sum or amount thereof in Spanish milled dollars, or more in the said bills, for any lands, houses, goods, or commodities whatsoever, than the same could be purchased at of the same person or persons in gold, silver, or any other species of money whatsoever; or shall offer to sell any goods or commodities for gold and silver, or any other species of money whatsoever, and refuse to sell the same for the said Continental bills, — every such a person ought to be deemed an enemy to the liberties of these United States, and to forfeit the value of the money so exchanged, or house, land, or commodity so sold or offered to sale. And it is recommended to the legislatures of the respective States to enact laws inflicting such forfeitures and other penalties on offenders, as aforesaid, as will prevent such pernicious practices.

"That it be recommended to the legislatures of the United States to pass laws to make the bills of credit issued by Congress a lawful tender in payment of public and private debts; and a refusal thereof an extinguishment of such debts; that debts payable in sterling money be dischargeable in Continental dollars at the rate of 4s. 6d. sterling per dollar; and that, in discharge of all other debts and contracts, Continental dollars pass at the rate fixed by the respective States for the value of Spanish milled dollars; that it be recommended to the legislatures of the several States to pass resolutions that they will make provisions for drawing in and sinking their respective quotas of the bills emitted by Congress at the several periods fixed, or that shall be fixed, by Congress. That it be recommended to the legislatures of the several States to raise by taxation in the course of the ensuing year, and remit to the treasury, such sums of money as they shall think will be most proper in the present situation of the inhabitants; which sums shall be carried to their credit, and accounted in the settlement of their proportion of the public expenses and debts, for which the United States are jointly bound."

The situation was indeed most critical. Congress was without means, except those raised through its notes, which were already largely depreciated, and becoming more so day by day, as no one would longer receive them at their nominal value. It passed, 27th of December, 1776, a resolution empowering Washington to raise forces, and take whatever could be found necessary for their subsistence or clothing; and if the owner would not sell at a fair price, to be paid in Continental money, he might be arrested, and kept in confinement. The Committee of Safety of Pennsylvania were, at the same time, requested to take speedy and rigorous measures to punish all who refused to receive the government notes. It acted with commendable promptness; and, on the 31st of December, of the same year, it resolved, — and its resolution at such time had all the force of a legal enactment, — that if any person should refuse to receive government notes offered to him in payment for goods, he should forfeit, for the first offence, the goods to the party seeking their purchase; and, in addition, be liable to a penalty of £5, where the amount to be purchased was under that sum; and to a penalty equal in amount to that of the purchase, when it was above it. One-fourth part of the penalty was to be paid to the informer, and three-fourths to the State. For a second offence, in addition to the above penalties, the offending party was rendered liable to banishment from the State to any place the Committee might designate. The result was that shop and inn keepers took down their signs, and refused to expose their goods or premises for sale or use. It was the reign of anarchy as well as tyranny. That the nation did not speedily succumb, and its cause utterly collapse, was due to the fact, that the greater part of the people were cultivators of the soil, and in the possession of an abundance of fertile land, which, with very little labor, brought forth abundant crops. The bounty and forces of nature more than compensated for the poverty and weakness of man.

The total amount of notes issued in 1776 equalled $19,000,000; and, for 1775 and 1776, $25,000,000. To meet the increasing unwillingness on the part of the public or malcontents to receive them, the States established tariffs of prices, by which all goods were to be sold. The four New England States met, by their delegates, at Providence, on the 25th of January, 1777, and formed a tariff of prices, by which a bushel of wheat was made the equivalent of 7s. 6d. in notes; one of rye, 5s.; a pound of wool, 2s.; a bushel of salt, from 10s. to 12s.; a gallon of rum, 6s. 8d.; a pound of raw cotton, 33s.; and so on, through the whole list of articles ordinarily consumed. Congress immediately passed an approving vote, and recommended other States to follow the example; that the delegates from Virginia and other Middle States should meet at Yorktown, on the third Monday of the ensuing March, and those from the Southern States, at Charleston, on the first Monday of the ensuing May, to concert and adopt similar measures. Congress, at the same time, earnestly entreated the States to cease the issue of their own notes, and to forbid the circulation of those issued previous to April 19, 1775. These had been issued in immense amounts in nearly all of the States, and very seriously interfered with the operations of the Central Government. As the State Governments possessed the power of taxation, which the Central Government did not, their notes began to be preferred, and were hoarded in large amounts.[1]

---

[1] As all government currencies are the same in kind, a sketch of that issued by the central one will suffice for all issued at the time. All were issued from

Meanwhile the embarrassments of the government were no little increased by the immense amount of spurious notes thrown into circulation, — a matter of very little difficulty, from the inartistic manner in which its own were printed or engraved. These counterfeits were held to be the tricks of the enemy. The results of the war, during the whole year of 1776, continued adverse, which greatly increased the confidence and influence of the Tories, who were especially numerous and powerful in the State of New York. Congress had still little other resource than its notes. In the latter part of 1776, Benjamin Franklin was sent to France, in the hope of securing the co-operation of that country. Although, for some time, he could not obtain any open recognition of the cause of the patriots, he was enabled to secure loans to the amount of 3,000,000 livres, which were expended chiefly in the purchase of arms and supplies, all of which safely reached their destination. In this way he was of great service, although he could do but little to relieve the pressure upon the Home Government. The cause of the patriots at the time was at its lowest ebb. France, though desirous of doing all in her power in their aid, was not willing to take any step likely to embroil her in war, till their success was better assured. This assurance came from the capture of Burgoyne, in the latter part of 1777. That was properly regarded as an achievement of the first magnitude; and her government, on the 6th of February, 1778, entered into a treaty of alliance and commerce with the United States; made their cause her own; dispatched powerful fleets, with considerable bodies of troops, to America; and from time to time made considerable loans of money.[1] For the present, however, Congress had no other resource than its notes; and on the 26th of February, 1777, it made a further issue of $5,000,000; on the 27th of May, of the same year, an issue to an equal amount; on the 15th of August, one of $1,000,000; on the 7th of November, $1,000,000, and the

the same necessity; all produced precisely the same results; and all, in great measure, met the same fate. Such of the State issues as were redeemed, were taken in at very low rates. Of the loss and suffering which were caused by them all, no pen or pencil can present any thing like an adequate picture.

[1] The total amount of money borrowed by the United States from France, during the War of the Revolution, as recognized by the United States after the adoption of the Constitution, equalled 34,532,864 livres. The arrears of interest due up to the first day of January, 1790, equalled 8,967,912 livres; making a total of 43,500,276 livres, or $7,895,800.

same amount on the 3d of December, 1777 : the total issue
for the year being $13,000,000. The amount outstanding at
the close of 1777 was $38,000,000. The value of the notes at
that time was reduced in ratio of four to one. At the date
last named, Congress made a requisition upon the States to the
amount of $5,000,000.[1] The amounts called for were not con-
sidered as the proper proportions for each State ; but were
made rather with reference to the present abilities of each,
the territories of several of them being largely held by the
enemy.   The proceeds were to be put to the credit of their
States, which were to be allowed interest at the rate of six
per cent on their respective amounts, until the proper quotas
were adjusted for each by the the final action of Congress.
The excess of payments or contributions was to take the form
of a debt against the government.   If a deficit should be
found against any State, this was to be made good by further
requisitions.   Congress again urged the withdrawal of the
currencies of the States, and still invoked their aid in securing
the circulation of the government notes, and in continuing
the tariff regulating prices.

The year 1778 was comparatively an uneventful one.   The
nation, however, was greatly buoyed up by the success achieved
at the close of the previous one, and attempted to make large
loans in Europe, in the expectation of which its own financial
affairs were greatly neglected.   Congress again attempted,
without success, to compel the States to take in their notes
issued previous to the outbreak of the war.   It still had little

[1] The apportionment among the several States was as follows : —

New Hampshire	$200,000
Rhode Island and Providence Plantations	100,000
New York	200,000
Pennsylvania	620,000
Maryland	520,000
North Carolina	250,000
South Carolina	500,000
Virginia	800,000
Delaware	60,000
New Jersey	270,000
Connecticut	600,000
Massachusetts Bay	820,000
Georgia	60,000
Total	$5,000,000

other resource than its own ; and on the 8th of January, 1778, was driven to issue $1,000,000, and $2,000,000 on the 22d of the same month. The winter of 1777–78 was passed by the army at Valley Forge in a condition of the greatest want and suffering. It was literally without food or clothing. As supplies could not be had for the notes of the government, commissaries were authorized to seize whatever they could lay their hands upon, paying therefor in government certificates. But even such harsh measures availed little in a country a prey alike to the enemy's troops and its own. As notes were still the only resource, these were issued, in the months of February, March, and April, 1778, to the extent of $10,500,000. At the end of April, their value had fallen as low as six to one of specie ; the amount then outstanding equalling $51,000,000. In May came the news of the French alliance, in consequence of which the price of the notes rose to one-fourth their nominal value. Encouraged by the improved aspect of affairs, Congress, on the 8th of that month, issued an address to the nation, which was read in all the pulpits, as the best mode, at the time, of bringing it to the attention of the people. From this the following extracts are given : —

"After the unremitting efforts of our enemies, we are stronger than before. Nor can the wicked emissaries, who so assiduously labor to promote their cause, point out any one reason to suppose that we shall not receive daily accessions of strength. They tell you, it is true, that your money is of no value, and your debts so enormous that they can never be paid. . . .

"Surely there is no man so absurd as to suppose that the least shadow of liberty can be preserved in a dependent connection with Britain. . . .

"And this mad, this impious system, they would lead you to adopt, because of the derangement of your finances.

"It becomes you deeply to reflect on this subject. Is there a country upon earth which hath such resources for the payment of her debts as America ? such an extensive territory ? so fertile, so blessed in its climate and productions ? Surely there is none ; neither is there any to which the wise Europeans will sooner confide their property. What, then, are the reasons that your money hath depreciated ? Because no taxes have been imposed to carry on the war ; because your commerce hath been interrupted by your enemy's fleet ; because their armies have ravaged and desolated a part of your country ; because their agents have villainously counterfeited your bills ; because extortioners among you, inflamed with the lust of gain, have added to the price of every article of life ; and because weak men have been artfully led to believe that it is of no value. How is this dangerous disease to be remedied ? Let those among you who have leisure and opportunity collect the money which individuals in their neighborhood are desirous of placing in the public funds. Let the several legislatures sink their respective issues ; that so, there being but one kind of bills, there may be less danger of counterfeit. Refrain a little while from purchasing those things which are not absolutely necessary ; so that those who have engrossed commodities may suffer (as they de-servedly will) the loss of their ill-gotten hoards, by reason of the commerce with foreign nations, which fleets will protect."

The new alliance paved the way for considerable loans ; a portion of which was used for the payment of interest on the certificates of indebtedness, which had now been issued in considerable amounts, in the purchase of supplies for the army. The tariff of prices was suspended ; as it was believed that, through the aid of the French fleet, the foreign commerce of the country would revive, and that means for the future prosecution of the war could be provided largely by loans. The people were buoyed up for a time by a belief that the war was soon to be brought to a close. Congress, actuated by a similar feeling, made little or no attempt for the restoration of the finances. It still continued to meet the demands that were constantly made upon it by issues of notes ; which, from April to January, 1779, equalled $50,500,000, making the whole amount outstanding at the close of that year $101,500,000. At that time, their value had fallen to about eight to one of coin. The military operations for the year were, on the whole, unfavorable. The French fleet came too late in the season to carry out those which had been planned in connection with it, and the war seemed as far from an end as ever. Despondency again succeeded to the hope which had been raised so high.[1] Congress, in view of the situation, was at last forced to act, which it did by the appointment of a Committee, consisting of Robert Morris, Elbridge Gerry, Richard H. Lee, Francis

[1] The following letter from William Hosmer to Governor Trumbull well illustrates the state of feeling at the time : —

"I wish I could with truth assure your excellency that, in my view, our affairs are in a happy train ; and that Congress has adopted wise and effectual measures to restore our wounded public credit, and to establish the United States, their liberty, union, and happiness, upon a solid and permanent founda-tion. I dare not do it while my heart is overwhelmed with the most melancholy presages. The idleness and captiousness of some gentlemen, maugre the wishes and endeavors of an honest and industrious majority, in my apprehension threaten the worst consequences." — Letters to Washington, vol. ii. p. 196.

Witherspoon, and Gouverneur Morris, to consider the financial situation. The Committee made its report to Congress on
the 15th of September, 1778. It was not, however, acted
upon till the 8th of October following.

The first question that came up for consideration was the
recommendation of the Committee to take off the limitation
of the price of gold; that is, to repeal the law which had
attempted to make the notes equal in value to a corresponding
amount of the former. They had now become so depreciated
that the absurdity of the law was too manifest to allow it
to remain on the statute-book. The recommendation was
adopted; and by it the first direct blow to the credit of the
notes was dealt by the very party issuing them. It was an
acknowledgment of a difference in value between them and
coin, although payable in coin on their face. The whole
question of their value was now opened up for discussion. If
they were not worth their face, what were they worth? The
people at once saw the abyss over which they stood. That
which they had acquired with so much labor and toil might
become utterly worthless. It was charged that the Act meant
repudiation. This was indignantly denied. Congress, as
usual, protested its good faith, and that every dollar of the
notes would be eventually discharged. The time in which
such protests and assurances could have much effect had long
since passed. The notes, however, continued to be issued in
greater sums, and to decline more rapidly than ever in value.
That they did not go at once out of circulation was due to the
fact, that every issue served to pay old debts at a reduced cost
to the debtor. There were always plenty to take them, provided they could be had at a sufficient discount. Swindling was
at once reduced to a system, Congress all the time abetting it,
by issues which were always put upon the market, each at a
less rate than the previous one. All could run into debt, with
a certainty of making money by the operation.[1]

[1] The following quotation from Sparks' "Life of Washington" will show
the use made of the notes, as well as what the latter thought of it: —

"When the army was at Morristown, a man of respectable standing lived in
the neighborhood, who was assiduous in his civilities to Washington, which were
kindly received and reciprocated. Unluckily, this man paid his debts in the depreciated currency. Some time afterward, he called at head-quarters, and was
introduced as usual to the General's apartment, where he was then conversing
with some of his officers. He bestowed very little attention upon the visitor.

Although at this day a retrospect would seem to discover nothing but imbecility and folly in the financial operations of the Revolutionary Government, and would show it to be chargeable with no small part of the want of success of the military operations of the country, and the impoverishment and distress which followed, it was not, considering its organization, properly liable to any such censure. It was simply a government upon which the gravest duties were imposed, but which was wholly without the power for their execution. Such a government, like an individual, — assuming every thing, and capable of nothing, — speedily falls into utter contempt. It could represent and implore, but not command. It derived its power from thirteen distinct peoples, all foreign to and jealous of each other ; and each fearing that it should do more than its share in the struggle in which all were engaged. Their only tie was hatred of the common enemy. Apart from this, there was hardly more resemblance, sympathy, or cohesion between Massachusetts and Virginia — the two leading States in the contest — than between England and France. They were as antagonistic as was possible for two States having a common parentage. It was a common parentage which rendered the antagonism between them all the more irreconcilable. Had they not belonged to the same race, their differences would have been held to be constitutional, and therefore to be respected. Where the difference is one between members of the same race, the assumption is that one must be wrong, and that that one must yield. To yield may be to give up whatever a people holds most dear. Opinion, where its defeat involves such consequence, is of all things that most worth fighting for. The history of this country is the history of two great tendencies which are as old as humanity, and which, since its settlement, have divided its people into two hostile camps, — that which seeks to subject all, high and low, to the restraints of a common rule ; and that which refuses such subjection. It is the difference between government and no

---

The same thing occurred a second time, when he was more reserved than before. This was so different from his customary manner that Lafayette, who was present on both occasions, could not help remarking it ; and he said, after the man was gone, 'General, this man seems to be much devoted to you, and yet you have scarcely noticed him.' Washington replied, smiling, 'I know I have not been cordial: I tried hard to be civil, and attempted to speak to him two or three times; but that Continental money stopped my mouth.'" — Life and Writings of Washington, vol. i. p. 333.

government, order and anarchy, progress and decay.   The
North, engaging from necessity in commerce and manufactures,
sought the world for a market, and immunity wherever their people or products could go.   The South, devoted to agriculture,
with their markets mostly in Europe, and with institutions
founded on force, would take counsel only of their necessities
and fears.   To commit themselves to the guidance of ideas, or to
the people of the North, would be to court the overthrow of
the very conditions upon which all their prosperity was supposed
to rest.   The history of this country is but a history of the
struggle for the mastery of opposing tendencies and ideas,
growing out of conditions differing radically in kind.   Hence
the importance of studying well the period from the formation of the Provisional Government in 1775 to the adoption of the Constitution in 1788.   It is the only mode by
which we get at the motives that led to the formation and
adoption of the Constitution, and the different constructions
given to its provisions.   The great question then, as it has
ever since been, was whether the second government only
repeated the loose confederation which preceded it, — a government without purposes or powers; or whether it was an
autonomy within itself, paramount to all, and responsible to
nothing but its own will, controlled and guided, to a certain extent, by that provision by which the competency of its
acts was to be decided by a tribunal provided by the Constitution itself.   That instrument was but the result of the reaction
against the anarchy and barbarism toward which the country
was then rapidly tending.   He who did the most to secure its
adoption understood best the incompetency and worthlessness
of the government it superseded.[1]

[1] So loose were the ties by which the confederacy was bound together, so
limited was the control exercised by Congress over the States, and so little inclined were the parts to unite in a consolidated whole, that, from imbecility on
the one hand and public apathy on the other, Washington became more and
more fearful of the consequences. "The great business of war," said he, "can
never be well conducted, if it be conducted at all, while the powers of Congress
are only recommendatory.   While one State yields obedience, and another
refuses it, while a third mutilates and adopts the measure in part only, and all
vary in time and manner, it is scarcely possible that our affairs should prosper,
or that any thing but disappointment can follow the best-concerted plans.   The
willing States are almost ruined by their exertions; distrust and jealousy ensue.
Hence proceed neglect and ill-timed compliances; one State waiting to see what
another will do.   This thwarts all our measures, after a heavy though ineffectual

The country continuing to suffer greatly from the spurious notes put upon the market,[1] Congress was compelled to call in those issued on May 22, 1777, and April 11, 1778, which had been more extensively counterfeited than any others. The order for calling them in excited great complaints. No one would take them in trade, as the government was not immediately prepared to issue new notes for the old. The loss and inconvenience caused, as well as the distress prevailing at the time, will be seen by the following letter, preserved in the Pennsylvania archives : —

"How comes it that Congress, by their resolve relative to the two emissions of May, 1777, and April, 1778, have set the country in such a ferment, and given room for a set of speculating people who are enemies to the real good of their country to take occasion from it to depreciate the value of these two emissions in the manner they have done, and are now daily doing ? There are a set of them here very busy in this matter ; that by their management within this day or two it is rendered twenty-five per cent worse than the other emissions ; which, God knows, were sunk low enough before. Our butchers, bakers, and farmers begin to refuse it entirely, owing to the stories propagated about it. Must people who have this money either lose a fourth of it or starve ? And when the time comes for exchanging it, must they spend half the value of the little they have in taking it to Philadelphia to place it in the office ? and after that wait sixty days, and attend a second time for payment ? Indeed, I think the resolve is not one of the wisest, and wish to see these evils speedily remedied. The merchants, or rather hucksters, of Philadelphia are playing the same there. Surely Congress can call in these or any other emissions in a manner less injurious to the country. I am so angry at this affair that I hardly know what I write, and so vexed at the daily schemes

expense is incurred." And he adds, on the point of vesting Congress with competent powers, "Our independence, our respectability and consequence in Europe, our greatness as a nation hereafter, depend upon it. The fear of giving sufficient powers to Congress, for the purposes I have mentioned, is futile. A nominal head, which at present is but another name for Congress, will no longer do. That honorable body, after hearing the interests and views of the several States fairly discussed and explained by their representatives, must dictate, and not merely recommend and leave it to the States to do afterwards as they please ; which, as I have observed before, is in many cases to do nothing at all." — Life and Writings of Washington, vol. i. pp. 349–350.

[1] The hopes of the enemy were largely fed on the probable failure of the Continental currency. General McDougal, writing from Peekskill to General Joseph Reed, says, "The enemy is confident our currency will fail us, . . . and that, whenever the supplies for the army fail, the people will return to their allegiance. He is now counterfeiting another emission, which will soon be out." — Life of President Reed, vol. ii. p. 57.

for depreciating of our currency, that I sometimes think we don't deserve the liberty we have been contending for, while such miscreants are suffered to breathe among us. And, indeed, I can't help thinking that the Congress's own servants, such as quartermasters, commissaries of purchase, &c., do as much injury to it as any other speculators; for the more they lay out or charge for articles which themselves have engrossed, the more are their commissions."

The following letter, written from Albany to the " Philadelphia Packet," furnishes another illustration of the manner in which the assumed " hucksters and forestallers " were dealt with : —

" Last week, two transgressors who sold rum for more than the regulated price were publicly cried through the city, by order of the committee, as having incurred the just indignation of the people. The inhabitants ordered them immediately to appear before them, being met at the market-place; where, by falling on their knees on a scaffold, they acknowledged themselves guilty, and promised to abide by and assist the orders of the committee: upon which they were discharged. *Hard money is not to pass here any longer:* we have lately hung up and burned in effigy a dealer in hard money."

One of the greatest alleged grievances during the war was the conduct of a class who were assumed to have purchased merchandise for the very purpose of forestalling the market and growing rich out of the necessities of consumers. They were loaded with every opprobrious epithet, and were not unfrequently thrown into prison and plundered of whatever they possessed. With a currency steadily declining in value, all holders of merchandise appear in effect to be forestallers, by refusing to sell except at an advance necessary not only to meet the present, but the future decline, likely to take place before they can use the money they receive. They must, in addition to a fair profit, charge a considerable advance to cover the risks of the future. What with them is only an exercise of ordinary prudence, is by those who (from a constant decline in the value of the notes they hold) suffer a heavy loss, often treated as a conspiracy to defraud and injure them, to be punished by the severest penalties. With the public, it is always that prices are advanced, not that the money has declined in value. The great majority of holders of merchandise at such periods have not only no design to defraud or oppress, but would gladly sacrifice all profit could they be protected against loss. It is impossible that it should be otherwise; for the greatest amount of profit, in the long run, is to be gained under a currency uniform in volume and value. The manner in which this class are often treated shows how completely an irredeemable currency subverts the sense of those using it. Another class, who are real offenders, but who often escape all annoyance and censure, are those who are able to monopolize such large amounts of this money as to control the market on a grand scale, and, by alternately raising and depressing prices, often make a profit equal to the degree of the fluctuation they can cause. A legal-tender currency always tends to flow to the great centres of trade, for the reason that it cannot distribute itself, like gold, or be absorbed in the arts, or retired by the operations of production and trade. It is always upon the market in full volume, its amount bearing no relation to the quantity of merchandise to be moved by it. It is wholly unlike a convertible currency, which is always disappearing, to reappear only. to symbolize new creations of merchandise. The latter, as soon as it has served its purpose by reaching for consumption that which it represents, becomes *functus officio*. Such a currency, consequently, bears an exact relation to that which is to be moved by it. In addition to the monopoly of money which a government currency always serves to create, those who hold it are always able to increase or diminish its purchasing power, by increasing or diminishing its apparent value ; that is, the credit of the government issuing it. This credit, therefore, becomes at once the great object of attack by a large and powerful class. So far as they can affect its value, it is the same as if they could, upon the occasion, create the instruments by which is to be measured the extent or quantity of whatever they buy or sell. The credit of all governments, and with it the prices of their securities, is constantly fluctuating ; but none so much so as that of governments issuing legal-tender notes, as these are regarded as the last resort of incompetency and exhaustion. The credit of such governments, and with it the standards of value, are in the hands of the rich and unscrupulous ; who, as far as its subsistence is concerned, may have a whole community in their power. A legal-tender currency, therefore, in whatever light viewed, is the crowning blunder and injustice of a State. It corrupts the morals ; arrays class against class ; exposes the unoffending to the fury of merciless mobs, impelled by a sense of wrong and suffering, the cause of which they cannot understand; creates the most odious of all monopolies, — that of money; and saps the very foundation of material prosperity, by reducing all industry and enterprise to the mere hazards of games of chance. It tends directly to reduce society to a condition of barbarism; for the reason that, from the want of an accurate measure of value, almost every act becomes more or less tainted with injustice and fraud.

At the close of 1778, the total amount of notes authorized and issued equalled $101,500,000: of which $6,000,000 were authorized in 1775; $19,000,000, in 1776; $13,000,000, in 1777; and $63,500,000, in 1778. Their value at the close of the last year was reduced to about eight to one of coin. The military operations for the year were on the whole unfavorable. Great distrust and despondency were the natural results. By this time, the most potent enemy with which the nation had to contend was its money. Very little coin was in circulation. Its notes were the common measure of value, — a measure enormously depreciated, and never two days the same; which no honest man dared trust or use; but which could, at its face, legally discharge debts contracted to be paid in coin. No wonder the anarchy and distress which prevailed, the hand of every man being against his neighbor; or the impotence of Government, and the impossibility of carrying out any plan of operations which the Commander-in-chief might propose. Almost every thing that was undertaken came to nothing, from the lack of money to raise and pay troops, to provide military supplies and means of transportation. In vain did Congress invest Washington with dictatorial powers. He could urge and entreat the States to act; but was as incapable of compelling obedience as was Congress itself. The soldiers, whose pay was at best a pittance, saw that even this was fast losing all its value. The discontent, occasioned as much by the depreciation of what they held as by the non-payment of what was due them, ended, in the winter of 1778–79, in a mutiny in the army stationed at Morristown, which at one time threatened the gravest consequences. These were only averted by the address and influence of Washington. While the army was unable, for want of means, to achieve any thing worthy of itself, and was filled with discontent bordering upon insubordination, the operations of commerce and trade were almost completely paralyzed. Never was there a more wretched picture than that presented by the United States for the four years beginning with 1776 and ending with 1779. Any one reading this sketch may well wonder that the cause of the patriots did not utterly fail. One reason was the imbecility and incapacity with which it was opposed. With the exception of Lord Cornwallis, there does not appear to have been a single officer high in command in the British army possessing any capacity for military or civil affairs. Another was the vast extent of country to be overrun and occupied, if the rebellion were to be put down. Although the colonists had been most loyal subjects of the crown, such was the injustice with which they were treated, and the sufferings they had endured, that, after the war had been waged a few years, no concession made by the Home Government could ever have brought them back to their former allegiance. They could have been held in subjection only by an armed force in every little community, far beyond the ability of the enemy to maintain. If finally worsted in the field, great numbers would have taken to the forests, from which they would have carried on a guerilla warfare, which would never have allowed him to be weak in force or off his guard. It is well-known that it was the purpose of Washington, had the final result been against him, to have crossed the Alleghanies for a home in the vast solitudes of the Mississippi Valley. Another reason was the independent condition of the people. Nine out of every ten were cultivators of the soil. Nearly all that was consumed by a family was produced by its own labor, so that the interruption of trade and the destruction of the foreign commerce of the country did not, after all, weigh so heavily upon the nation. The accounts that we get of the time come from the cities, the inhabitants of which, chiefly concerned in trade and manufactures, suffered severely. The first effect of the government notes was to create a general inflation in prices and great activity in all business operations, to be soon followed by a corresponding depression and inactivity ; which, as their cause was not understood, produced great complaints, without leading to the adoption of any remedy. For the enemy to over-run the country was a mere waste of time and means, unless it could be filled with troops, for which all that England could have put into the field would by no means have sufficed. The Home Government wholly misconceived the nature of the struggle in which it engaged, and the extent of the natural obstacles opposed to its arms, which were more formidable than any which could be opposed by the hand of man.

The financial position becoming daily more and more critical, Congress resolved to reduce the amount of its notes, in order to raise the credit of those outstanding. On the 1st of January, 1779, it passed a resolution calling upon the States to pay in $15,000,000 in notes for the current year, and $6,000,000 a year for the next eighteen years. It also declared, that if any were issued in the year ensuing, they should, in the manner and within the period prescribed for the other notes, be taken in, to be first applied to the payment of interest; next, to that of the principal of the loans outstanding, and made prior to Jan. 1, 1780; and that all not necessary for the above purposes were to be destroyed. It was hoped that such measures would prevent any further decline. All such expedients proved unavailing, for the reason that no one supposed the requisitions would be complied with. The notes could not be got in; and Congress was compelled to make further issues, which it did to the amount of $10,000,000 in the following month. Matters continued to go rapidly from bad to worse. Early in May, 1779, the President of the Council for Pennsylvania and others were admitted upon the floor of Congress, to state the dilemma in which they were placed, and solicit its interposition to avert a popular movement which was apprehended. A meeting of the citizens of Philadelphia was to be held, and violence was feared from an excited and suffering populace. Congress could only issue one of its manifestoes, that the country had been forced into a cruel war, that it had resorted to notes as its only resource, that ultimate success was certain, that all its obligations would be. faithfully respected, that the great cause of high prices was the conduct of forestallers and monopolizers, and that these must be looked after and severely punished; all to end, however, with a further issue of notes. The Philadelphia meeting was held, and resolved : —

"That, whereas prices of goods and provisions have, within the last six months, risen to an enormous height, far beyond what they ought to be in proportion to the quantity of money; and, whereas the prices of rum, sugar, flour, coffee, and tea have greatly risen within the past week, without any real or apparent cause: and, as it is our determination not to be eaten up by monopolizers and forestallers, therefore we unconditionally insist and demand that the advanced or monopolized price of the present month be instantly taken off, and that prices be immediately reduced to what they were on the first day of May, instant." [1]

Committees of safety were at that time almost supreme powers in the land; and one, as a matter of course, was appointed at the meeting referred to, charged with full authority to carry out its objects; to regulate the value of property, of rentals, of labor, and, in fact, of almost every act of society. The people, sensible only of their sufferings, and ignorant of the cause, clamored fiercely for a reduction in the price of food. Congress promised to give ear to their complaints; but constantly aggravated them by new issues of paper, at the same time urging the States to establish tariffs of prices, and denouncing to the severest punishments all who should violate them. In all such measures, it was certain to have the sympathy of the great mass of the people, who still believed that prices could be regulated by law. In illustration, the following extract is given, from a communication which appeared at the time in the " Philadelphia Packet : " —

"I am one who thinks," says the writer, " a limitation of prices is absolutely necessary. I am sure every man must wish it as the only means to get rich. We have all been wrong in our notions of getting rich. It is true we have got money. I have more money than I ever had; but I am poorer than I ever was. I had money enough some time ago to buy a hogshead of sugar. I sold it again, and got a great deal more money for it than what it cost me; yet what I sold it for, when I went to market again, would buy but a tierce.

[1] What some of these prices were on the first day of May will be seen by the following statement : —

West India Rum, per gallon	£6 15s.
Country ,, ,, ,, ...	5 0
Brandy ,, ,, ...	7 0
Tea, per pound	4 10
Salt, per bushel	10 0
Flour, per cwt.	20 0
Molasses, per gallon	4 12

I sold that tierce for a great deal of profit; yet the whole of what I sold it for would afterwards buy but a barrel. I have now more money than ever I had; yet I am not so rich as when I had less. This is what I have experienced myself; and I believe every man in town and country feels the same. I am sure we shall all grow poorer and poorer, unless we all fall on some method to lower our prices; and then the money we have to spare will be worth something. I am glad to see the affair begun upon. May God give it success; and let all the people say AMEN."

Among the expedients resorted to at the time, for the purpose of maintaining the value of paper money, were associations organized for the purpose of driving hard money out of circulation, in the hope that, by confining all the operations of society to paper money, its decline, at least, could be prevented. The following copy of a handbill placarded at the time in Boston will give a good idea of the mode by which such a result was sought to be accomplished: —

" SONS OF BOSTON!   SLEEP NO LONGER!

" Wednesday, June 16, 1779.

" You are requested to meet on the floor of the *Old South Meeting-House* to-morrow morning, at 9 o'clock, at which time the bells will ring.

" Rouse and catch the Philadelphia spirit; rid the community of those monopolizers and extortioners, who, like canker-worms, are gnawing upon your vitals. They are reducing the currency to waste paper, by refusing to take it for many articles. The infection is dangerous. We have borne with such wretches; but will bear no longer. Public examples at this time would be public benefits. You, then, that have articles to sell, lower your prices; you that have houses to let, refuse not the currency for rent; for, inspired with the spirit of those heroes and patriots who have struggled and bled for their country, and moved with the cries and distresses of the widow, the orphan, and the necessitous, Boston shall no longer be your place of security. Ye inhabitants of Nantucket, who first introduced the accursed crime of refusing paper money, quit the place, or destruction shall attend your property, and your persons be the object of

" VENGEANCE.

" N. B. Lawyers, keep yourselves to yourselves.
" It is our determination to support the reputable merchant and fair trader "

Congress, still having little other resource than its notes, continued their issue on a larger scale than ever, to meet their more rapid and excessive decline. On the 26th of August, the amount issued equalled $161,500,000. Of this sum, $100,000,000 had been issued during the year. The value was then reduced to eighteen for one. Congress still attempted to arrest a further decline, by an address in which it promised, " if possible," not to exceed the amount already outstanding; and to inspire confidence by the method so often resorted to in similar cases, of depreciating the magnitude of present burdens by showing the vastly increased number of shoulders upon which they must soon rest ; for, peace established, crowds of emigrants would flee from oppressed Europe to this land of liberty. A country so rich by nature, and soon to be so populous, could easily bear all the burdens likely to be imposed upon her by the war : —

" Let us suppose," it said, " for the sake of argument, that at the conclusion of the war the emissions should amount to $200,000,000; that, exclusive of supplies from taxes, which will not be inconsiderable, the loans should amount to $100,000,000, — then the whole national debt of the United States would be $300,000,000. There are at present 3,000,000 of inhabitants in the thirteen States; $300,000,000, divided among 3,000,000 of people, would give to each person $100; and is there an individual in America unable, in the course of eighteen or twenty years, to pay it again? Suppose the whole debt assessed, as it ought to be, on the inhabitants in proportion to their respective estates, what would then be the share of the poorer people? Perhaps not $10. Besides, as this debt will not be payable immediately, but probably twenty years allotted for it, the number of inhabitants by that time in America will be far more than double their present amount. It is well known that the inhabitants of this country increased almost in the ratio of compound interest. By natural population they doubled almost every twenty years, and how great may be the host of emigrants from other countries cannot be ascertained. We have the highest reason to believe the number will be immense. Suppose that only ten thousand should arrive the first year after the war, what will those ten thousand, with their families, count in twenty years time? Probably double the number. This observation applies with proportionable force to the emigrants of every successive year. Thus you see a great part of your debt will be payable, not merely by the present number of inhabitants, but by that number swelled and increased by the natural population of the present inhabitants, by multitudes of emigrants daily arriving from other countries, and by the natural population of those successive emigrants; so that every person's share of the debt will be constantly diminishing by others coming in to pay a proportion of it." [1]

The injustice of being compelled to accept the government notes in the payment of debts previously contracted had now become so great as to be no longer tolerated. Even Washington would no longer receive them in the payment of old debts, but at their value. In a letter to the manager of his estate, Lund Washington, written under date of the 17th of August, 1779, he said : —

" Some time ago you applied to me to know if you should receive payment of General M ——'s bonds, and of the bond due from the deceased Mr. M ——'s estate to me ; and you were, after animadverting a little upon the subject, authorized to do so. Of course, I presume the money has been received. I have since considered the matter in every point of view in which my judgment enables me to place it ; and am resolved to receive no more old debts (such, I mean, as were contracted and ought to have been paid before the war) at the present nominal value of the money, unless compelled to do it, or it is the practice of others to do it. Neither justice,

[1] The amount of the public debt incurred in the prosecution of the war, in addition to that incurred by the several States, was given in the address from which the preceding extract was made, as follows : —

Notes issued	$159,948,880
Money borrowed in France	7,545,196
Money borrowed at home, for which government certificates were chiefly given	26,188,909
Money borrowed in Europe, and not yet received	4,000,000
Total	$197,682,985

At that time the whole amount received from taxation, through requisitions upon the States, amounted only to $3,027,560. The whole amount supplied by the people up to the date of the address, other than that furnished on the notes, equalled $29,216,469. The domestic debt was chiefly in the form of certificates, or acknowledgments of the government of supplies furnished it, which were given largely by commissaries in payment of articles seized by them, and represented the estimated value of such as were taken.

The following statement of expenditures of the government for 1778, and the proportions of paper and metallic money used, will show the extremities to which it was reduced : —

Notes	$62,156,842
Specie	78,666
Livres	28,525

The amount of specie amidst such a vast mass of paper was very like the wit of Gratiano in the play.

reason, nor policy requires it. The law, undoubtedly, was well designed. It was intended to stamp a value upon, and to give a free circulation to, the paper bills of credit; but it never was nor could have been intended to make a man take a shilling or sixpence in the pound for a just debt which his debtor is well able to pay, and thereby involve himself in ruin. I am as willing now as I ever was to take paper money for every kind of debt, and at its present depreciated value for those debts which have been contracted since the money became so; but I will not in future receive the nominal sum for such old debts as come under the above description, except as before specified. No man has gone, and no man will go, further to serve the republic than myself. If sacrificing my whole estate would effect any valuable purpose, I would not hesitate one moment in doing it; but my submitting in matters of this kind, unless the same is done by others, is no more than a drop in the bucket." [1]

And in a letter of the 22d August, to the President of Congress, Mr. Reed, he says: —

" The sponge, which you say some gentlemen have talked of using, unless there can be a discrimination and proper saving clauses provided (and how far this is practicable I know not), would be unjust and impolitic in the extreme. Perhaps I don't understand what they mean by using the sponge. If it be to sink the money in the hands of the holders of it, and at their loss, it cannot in my opinion stand justified upon any principles of common policy, common sense, or common honesty. But how far a man, for instance, who had possessed himself of twenty paper dollars by means of one or the value of one in specie, has a just claim upon the public for more than one of the latter in redemption, and in that ratio according to the periods of depreciation, I leave to those who are better acquainted with the nature of the subject, and have more leisure than I have, to discuss." [2]

The solution of this matter had now come to transcend the forecast of even Washington himself. He would not repudiate the notes; but, certainly, a person who had contracted to pay $10 in coin, had no right to discharge the debt by a note which cost him only $1 in coin; nor had the holder of a note for $10, which cost him only $1, a right to be paid its full amount. No solution was, in fact, possible; for matters had now reached such a pass that the proper one was to let the money die in the hands of its holders. Less suffering and less injustice would result from this mode of disposing of the problem, than any other. ' Justice could never have been done by any attempts

[1] Life and Writings of Washington, vol. vi. p. 321.
[2] Ibid. p. 332.

to take in the money at any equitable scale. If it were to be taken in, it could only be done by raising the necessary amount by a tax, which would have to be assessed somewhat in ratio to the amount held by each. To retire it, therefore, by taxation or payment would be to employ a useless machinery to accomplish that which could be better accomplished, with the same justice, by really doing nothing.

As no argument urged by Congress had any effect whatever in raising the value of its notes, its only course was to make the most of its power of issue while any thing could be had for them. The amount issued between Aug. 26 and Nov. 29, 1779, the date of the last one, equalled $40,000,000; the total amount up to the last date being $241,552,280.[1] At the close of the year, the notes had fallen to about forty for one of coin. With such a depreciation, any further issue would have been regarded as too absurd to be attempted. Congress, however, was by no means at the end of its expedients. On the 18th of March, 1781, it issued an address, which, after reciting the necessities which had driven it to the issue of a large amount of notes, and their great decline in value, declared it to be expedient to reduce the amount outstanding: and for that purpose it made a requisition upon the States for $15,000,000 of notes per month, to continue up to April, 1781;

---

[1] Statement showing the dates of issue, and amounts of Continental money issued, during the War of Independence : —

Dates authorizing issues.		Amounts authorized.	Dates authorizing issues.		Amounts authorized.
1775	June 22d	$2,000,000	Amount brought forward		$61,500,000
"	July 25th	1,000,000	1778	July 30th	5,000,000
"	Nov. 29th	3,000,000	"	Sept. 5th	5,000,000
1776	Feb. 17th	4,000,000	"	" 26th	10,000,000
"	May 9th and 27th . .	5,000,000	"	Nov. 4th	10,000,000
"	July 22d and Aug. 13th	5,000,000	"	Dec. 14th	10,000,000
"	Nov. 2d and Dec. 28th	5,000,000	1779	Feb. 3d	5,000,160
1777	Feb. 26th	5,000,000	"	" 19th	5,000,160
"	May 20th	5,000,000	"	April 1st	5,000,160
"	Aug. 15th	1,000,000	"	May 5th	10,000,100
"	Nov. 7th	1,000,000	"	Jan. 4th and May 7th .	50,000,100
"	Dec. 3d	1,000,000	"	June 4th	10,000,100
1778	Jan. 8th	1,000,000	"	July 17th	5,000,180
"	" 22d	2,000,000	"	" "	10,000,100
"	Feb. 16th	2,000,000	"	Sept. 17th	5,000,180
"	March 5th	2,000,000	"	" "	10,000,180
"	April 4th	1,000,000	"	Oct. 14th	5,000,180
"	" 11th	5,000,000	"	Nov. 17th	5,000,040
"	" 18th	500,000	"	" "	5,050,500
"	May 22d	5,000,000	"	Nov. 29th	10,000,140
"	June 20th	5,000,000			
"	Amount carried forward	61,500,000	Total		$241,552,280

and that the amounts so taken in were to be cancelled, except those issued the preceding January and February, which would be necessary for the operations of government. In lieu, however, of the payment of notes, gold and silver were receivable in payment of such requisitions, at the rate of $1 for $40 of paper. As fast as the notes were brought in and cancelled, new notes were to be issued, at the rate of $1 to $20 taken in, redeemable in specie in six years ; and to bear interest at the rate of 5 per ceht per annum, also payable in specie at the redemption of the notes, or annually, at the election of the holder : the notes to be issued on the funds or security of the several States ; for the payment of which, however, the faith of the United States was to be pledged. Of such notes, six-tenths were to go to the States, and four-tenths to the United States, to be credited to the States on whose funds or security they were issued ; the new notes to be receivable in payment of the monthly quotas, at the same rate as specie. These notes, however, were no better received than the old ones ; nor does it appear that any considerable amounts of them ever got into circulation.[1] The public had so often been deceived and imposed upon that it turned a deaf ear to all propositions of the kind. The days of the Continental paper money, in whatever form issued, were numbered. Congress did not attempt to press the circulation of its new notes. While the

---

[1] "Our new paper money," says Josiah Quincy in a letter to Washington, "issued by recommendation of Congress, no sooner began to circulate than two dollars of it were given for one hard one (that is the rate of the old). To restore the credit of the paper by making it a legal tender, by regulating acts or by taxes, are political manœuvres that have already proved abortive ; and for this obvious reason, that, in the same proportion as ideal money is forced into currency, it must, from the nature of every thing fraudulent, be forced out of credit. I am firmly of the opinion, and think it entirely defensible, that there never was a paper pound, a paper dollar, or a paper promise of any kind, that ever yet obtained a general currency but by force or fraud, — generally by both." — Letters to Washington, vol. iii. p. 157.

"The people of the States at that time had been so worried and fretted, disappointed and put out of humor, by so many tender-acts, limitations of prices, and other compulsory methods to force value into paper money, and compel the circulation of it; and by so many vain funding schemes, declarations, and promises, all of which issued from Congress, but died under the most zealous efforts to put them into operation and effect, — that their patience was all exhausted. I say, these irritations and disappointments had so destroyed the courage and confidence of these people, that they appeared heartless and almost stupid when their attention was called to. any new proposition." — Webster's Essays, p. 116.

old steadily declined in value, they were actively dealt in, till their price fell so low that even their holders had no interest in seeking to dispose of them. Their activity, even when they fell as low as 500 to 1, excited the wonder of writers at the time. There always appeared to be a plenty of parties ready to take them, till they fell below this rate, against the chance that some provision might be made for their ultimate redemption.

The cessation of issue was a practical demonetization of the Continental paper, although, for some time thereafter, it remained on the statute books, not only of Congress but of the several States, as lawful money. Early in 1781, however, the former recommended the total repeal of all laws making its notes money. The States, one after another, adopted the recommendation. No sooner, however, had it been seen that the notes, from their worthlessness, were to go out of circulation, than the people began to take measures to provide themselves with a currency of coin. The process was so noiseless and natural as to attract no attention whatever. Metallic money seemed to be improvised by the necessity for its use. All that was wanting was to leave the people free to act solely with a view to their own welfare. It is with money as with every other help by which the operations of society are carried on. It may be that the best cannot be immediately had ; but it will always be sought until it is secured. Its realization will be free from disturbance in ratio as the people are emancipated from the control of government. No sooner had the occasion or necessity arisen for it, than coin appeared. Large amounts were brought into the country from the subsistence and payment of the British troops. The foreign loans were paid in coin. Considerable amounts of silver were, during the war, constantly received from Spain and Mexico, through Havana. From the beginning of 1780, hard money, as it was termed, began to show itself in large amounts. Indeed, from that time there appears to have been no lack of specie in the country. "Gold and silver," says Paine,[1] "that for a while seemed to have retreated again into the bowels of the earth, have once more risen into circulation, and every day adds a new strength to trade, commerce, and agriculture."

[1] The Crisis, p. 209.

It was not possible but that the effect of the government notes should, during the whole period of their use, have been most mischievous. For the little time their credit was maintained, they relieved Government of a duty which should have been assumed at the very outset, of providing, in some adequate manner, for the expenses of the war. It would have been far easier to have done this in 1775, before the notes were issued, than in 1780, after they ceased to be available. It was inevitable that the time should come in which they would be no longer used, from the total discredit of the government, — caused, in great measure, by their use. The testimony of contemporaneous writers, as to the baleful influence they exerted over the moral and material welfare of the people, is as emphatic as it is unanimous. Ramsay, in his "History of the War of the Revolution," in which he was actively engaged, says of it: —

"The aged who had retired from the scenes of active business to enjoy the fruits of their industry found their substance melting away to a mere pittance, insufficient for their support. The widow who lived comfortably on the bequests of a deceased husband experienced a frustration of all his well-meant tenderness. The laws of the country interposed, and compelled her to receive a shilling where a pound was her due. The blooming virgin who had grown up with an unquestionable title to her patrimony was legally stripped of every thing but her personal charms and virtues. The hapless orphan, instead of receiving from the hands of an executor a competency to set out in business, was obliged to give a final discharge on the payment of 6d. on the pound. In many instances, the earnings of a long life of care and diligence were, in the space of a few years, reduced to a trifling sum. . . . That the helpless part of the community were legislatively deprived of their property was among the lesser evils which resulted from the legal tender of the depreciated bills of credit: the iniquity of the laws estranged the minds of many of the citizens from the habits and love of justice. The nature of obligations was so far changed that he was reckoned the honest man who, from principle, delayed to pay his debts. The mounds which government had erected to secure the observance of honesty in the commercial intercourse of man with man were broken down. *Truth, honor, and justice were swept away* by the overflowing deluge of legal iniquity; nor have they yet assumed their ancient and accustomed seats."[1]

The testimony of another contemporaneous writer and accurate observer is equally to the point: —

[1] History of the American Revolution, vol. ii. p. 134 *et seq.*

CURRENCY OF THE REVOLUTION.

"It has," said Pelatiah Webster, a most trustworthy authority, "polluted the equity of our laws, turned them into engines of oppression and wrong; corrupted the justice of our public administrations; destroyed the fortunes of thousands who had the most confidence in it; enervated the trade, husbandry, and manufactures of the country; and went far to destroy the morality of our people."[1] "We have suffered more," says Webster, in another place, "from this cause than from any other cause or calamity. It has killed more men, pervaded and corrupted the choicest interests of our country more, and done more injustice, than even the arms and artifice of the enemy." "Old debts," says another, "were paid when paper money was more than seventy for one. Brothers defrauded brothers, children parents, and parents children. Widows, orphans, and others were paid for money lent in specie with depreciated paper, which they were compelled to receive. A person who had been supplied with specie in the jail of Philadelphia while the British were in possession of that city repaid it in paper at a tenth part of its value."[2] "That the army," said Josiah Quincy, in a letter to Washington, "has been grossly cheated; that creditors have been infamously defrauded; that the widow and the fatherless have been oppressively wronged and beggared; that the gray hairs of the aged and the innocent, for want of their just dues, have gone down with sorrow to their graves, in consequence of our disgraceful, depreciated paper currency — may now be affirmed without hazard of refutation; and I wish it could be said with truth that the war has not thereby been protracted. May it not, therefore, be safely concluded, that no kind of paper currency is adequate to the purpose of collecting and combining the forces of these United States for their common defence?"[3]

As no notes were issued after 1779, Congress thereafter had to sustain itself, as best it could, by loans, by purchases made in exchange for its certificates, by seizures by commissaries, and by aid of moneys and troops raised by the States. The war dragged along through 1780, without any decisive advantage on either side. Its prolongation, however, tended to exhaust the enemy more than the people of the States. Early in 1781, Louis XVI. presented Congress with 6,000,000 livres. A loan to the amount of 10,000,000 livres was also obtained from the French government. Before these could be made available, Congress was reduced to the greatest straits. Early in 1781, a very important step was taken toward reorganizing and systematizing the finances of the country, by the creation of the office of Financier-General, to which Robert Morris was

[1] Webster's Essays, p. 174.
[2] Breck.
[3] Letters to Washington, vol. iii. p. 157.

appointed. He brought to his position great capacity, great industry, untiring devotion to the cause; and, as he was possessed of large means, he often raised upon his own credit considerable sums to meet pressing emergencies.

Had such an office been erected at the outset, and Mr. Morris, or some equally competent person, been appointed to it, the war might have been brought to a close in a comparatively short time, instead of dragging (as it did) through eight weary years. The government by which it was waged had neither an executive, nor departments, nor control over the revenues of the country. Perhaps no better one was possible at the time. So intense were the local jealousies, so different the institutions, pursuits, habits, and ideas of the various sections, and so firmly were they wedded to their local governments, — that years of anarchy and suffering were still necessary to teach the necessity of, and reconcile them to, one of paramount authority, if they would escape the barbarism to which the nation was already rapidly tending.

Among the expedients devised in 1780 for the support of the war was a voluntary association of citizens of Philadelphia, formed on the 17th of June of that year, for the purpose of opening a "security subscription to the amount of £300,000, Pennsylvania currency, in real money," to be expended, or the greater portion of it, in sending three million of rations, and three hundred hogsheads of rum, to the army, then reduced to the greatest distress for the want of food and clothing. The organization was termed a "Bank." Congress warmly seconded the movement, and appointed a Committee to confer with those having it in charge. The Committee made their report on the 21st of June, and, on the same day, Congress resolved that: —

" *Whereas*, a number of the patriotic citizens of Pennsylvania have communicated to Congress a liberal offer on their own credit, and by their own exertions, to supply and transport three millions of rations and three hundred hogsheads of rum, for the use of the army, and have established a Bank for the sole purpose of obtaining and transporting the said supplies with greater fidelity and dispatch; and *whereas*, on the one hand, the associators animated to this laudable exertion by a desire to relieve the public necessities mean not to derive from it the least pecuniary advantage, so, on the other, it is just and reasonable that they should be fully reimbursed and indemnified:

Resolved, That the Board of Treasury be directed to deposit in the said Bank bills of exchange in favor of the directors thereof, on the ministers of these United States in Europe, or any of them, and in such sums as shall be thought convenient, but not to exceed, in the whole, £150,000 sterling ; that the said bills are to be considered not only as a support of the credit of the said Bank, but as an indemnity to the subscribers for all deficiencies, losses, and expenses which they may sustain on account of their said engagements, and which shall not, within six months from the date thereof, be made good to them out of the public treasury."

So valuable was the aid furnished by the " Bank," that Mr. Morris determined to secure for it a legal organization, and applied to Congress therefor.[1] The application was referred to a committee, consisting of Messrs. Clymer, Smith, Sullivan, and Witherspoon, who reported favorably thereon ; and Congress, on the 26th of May, 1781, resolved that : —

" Congress do approve of the plan for establishing a National Bank, in these United States, submitted to their consideration by

[1] " One of the first acts of the Superintendent of Finance was to propose the plan of a Bank, which was incorporated by Congress under the name of the Bank of North America. Mr. Gouverneur Morris says, in a letter to a friend, written not long before his death, ' The first Bank in this country was planned by your humble servant.' By this he probably meant that he drew up the plan of the Bank, and the observations accompanying it, which were presented to Congress, and not that he, individually, originated the scheme. This was doubtless matured in conjunction with the superintendent. A warm friendship had subsisted between them for some time, which, it may be presumed, was increased by a similarity in their turn of mind for financial pursuits. To Hamilton, also, may properly be ascribed a portion of the merit in forming this Bank. About two weeks before the plan was sent to Congress, Hamilton wrote a letter to Robert Morris, enclosing an elaborate project for a Bank. In a letter acknowledging the reception of this paper, the financier speaks of it with commendation. He says, ' I have read your performance with that attention which it justly deserves ; and, finding many parts of it to coincide with my own opinions on the subject, it naturally strengthened that confidence which every man ought to possess, to a certain degree, in his own judgment.' He then tells him that he shall communicate it to the Directors of the Bank, to aid them in their deliberation on certain points, which it was not thought expedient to embrace in the plan itself, — particularly that of interweaving a security with the capital.

" This Bank had an extraordinary effect in restoring public and private credit in the country, and was of immense utility in aiding the future operations of the financier, although it was begun with the small capital of $400,000. Hamilton's project contemplated a vastly larger sum, in which Mr. Morris agreed with him : but its immediate success on so large a scale was doubtful, and, if it failed in the outset, it could not be revived ; whereas, by beginning with a small capital, and. establishing a credit with the public gradually, it would be easy afterwards to increase the amount, and, in the end, all needful advantages might be derived, to the utmost extent of banking facilities." — Sparks' Life of Gouverneur Morris, vol. i. p. 325.

R. Morris, on the 17th May, 1781; and that they will promote and support the same, by such ways and means from time to time as may appear necessary for the institution, and consistent with the public good.

"That the subscribers to the said Bank shall be incorporated, agreeably to the principles and terms of the plan, under the name of the 'President, Directors, and Company of the Bank of North America,' so soon as the subscription shall be filled, the Directors and President chosen, and application for that purpose made to Congress by the President and Directors elected."

The plan of organization having been matured, Congress, on the 31st of December, 1781, granted to the association an Act incorporating them under the name of the " Bank of North America." The Act conferred the usual and proper powers, and named the first Board of Directors and their President. It provided that the share capital might equal $10,000,000. The amount, however, with which the bank was to begin operations was fixed at $400,000. Of this sum, Congress agreed to subscribe $250,000. It, however, found itself able to pay in but $50,000. The citizens of Philadelphia subscribed $85,000. The balance, $265,000, was furnished from abroad, — chiefly from Holland. The Bank opened its doors for business on the 7th of January, 1782. Accompanying the Act of Incorporation was a resolution of Congress recommending to the State Legislatures to pass such laws as might be necessary to give effect to its Act. Such recommendation, and its adoption by most, if not all the States, affords a striking illustration of the idea which prevailed as to the limited powers and functions of the Central Government. Its constituents were the States, not the people; and for every Act of the kind it was deemed necessary to ask their concurrence, in order to give it the force and validity of a law of the land.[1]

The Act incorporating the Bank was an event of first-rate importance in the history of the country. It was the first adequate attempt of the kind to symbolize its merchandise, so

---

[1] Much valuable information for this account of the paper money of the Revolution has been obtained from Mr. Henry Phillips' "Historical Sketches of American Paper Money." In addition to this, he has published several sketches in relation to the paper currencies of the different States. They are all painstaking and creditable works, and contrast most favorably with the loose and slipshod manner in which books upon this and kindred subjects are usually made in this country.

that it could be made available, and transferred from hand to hand, without the interposition of coin. As proof of what was gained, the Bank, within six months after its organization, loaned $400,000 to Congress, and $80,000 to the State of Pennsylvania. What Congress chiefly wanted was food and clothing for the army. Had it been possessed of coin, it would have expended it in their purchase. If such articles could be had by means of the notes of the Bank, these were equally serviceable with coin. All that a person possessed of merchandise, and who wished to render it available to government, had to do, was to lend to the latter the proceeds of the discount of the bills taken in its sale. These would be returned to the Bank in payment of the bills discounted. The operation would be the same as that which has been so often described. In this way, the means of a government may be increased in ratio to the whole amount of those of its people, not absolutely necessary to their subsistence. In order to avail itself of such merchandise it need not be possessed of a dollar in coin. All the coin necessary for a Bank to maintain would be that required to make good its losses. With coin to the amount of $100,000, it may safely put in circulation notes equalling ten times that amount. In no other way than by the use of Banks has it been found possible to supply, on a sufficient scale, adequate instruments of distribution in the place of coin, which, so long as they serve as such, may be properly termed "money." The difference to a country, therefore, between a symbolic currency and the lack of it, may be a difference in its available means, equal, or nearly equal, to the whole amount of its merchandise proper to be symbolized. Added to the positive gain is that resulting from the greater convenience of the use of a currency of symbols over one of coin.

No sooner was peace established, and the people relieved from the pressure of a necessity which, while it lasted, gave to the country a semblance at least of unity, than Congress lost even the little respect and authority it had once enjoyed. With peace came duties graver and more difficult to discharge than those imposed by the war. Provision was to be made for carrying out the treaty with Great Britain, for opening relations with other powers, establishing internal order, and adjusting, and if possible discharging, the enormous debts that had been contracted.   The terms of the treaty were not carried out: internal order was disturbed: no adequate provision was made for the discharge of interest on the domestic or foreign loans.   Local jealousies and rivalries began to manifest themselves on every hand.   The revenues, if any were to be raised, were to come from imposts on foreign merchandise.   Each State sought to increase its own importance by regulations which should attract the commerce of the country to its own ports.   In place of being united against a common enemy, each State threatened to become the enemy of all others.   All that had been won with so much blood and treasure seemed in danger of being wholly lost.   The condition of things is well described in a letter from General Washington to Mr. Jay, under date of Aug. 1, 1786: —

"Your sentiments, that our affairs are drawing rapidly to a crisis, accord with my own.   What the event will be is also beyond the reach of my foresight.   We have errors to correct.   We have probably had too good an opinion of human nature in forming our confederation.   Experience has taught us that men will not adopt and carry into execution measures the best calculated for their own good, without the intervention of a coercive power.   I do not conceive we can exist long as a nation without having lodged somewhere a power that will pervade the whole Union in as energetic a manner as the authority of the State governments extends over the several States.   To be fearful of investing Congress, constituted as that body is, with ample authorities for national purposes, appears to me the very climax of popular absurdity and madness.   Could Congress exert them for the detriment of the public, without injuring themselves in an equal or greater proportion?   Are not their interests inseparably connected with those of their constituents?   By the rotation of appointment, must they not mingle frequently with the mass of citizens?   Is it not rather to be apprehended, if they were possessed of the powers before described, that the individual members would be induced to use them, on many occasions, very timidly and inefficaciously, for fear of losing their popularity and future election?   We must take human nature as we find it.   Perfection falls not to the share of mortals.   Many are of opinion that Congress have too frequently made use of the humble, suppliant, tone of requisition in applications to the States, when they had a right to assert their imperial dignity and command obedience.   Be that as it may, requisitions are a perfect nullity where thirteen sovereign, independent, disunited States are in the habit of discussing and refusing compliance with them, at their option.   Requisitions are actually little better than a jest and a byword through the land.   If you tell the legislatures they have violated the treaty of peace, and invaded the prerogatives of the confederacy, they will laugh in

your face. What, then, is to be done? Things cannot go on in the
same train for ever. It is much to be feared, as you observe, that
the better kind of people, being disgusted with the circumstances,
will have their minds prepared for any revolution whatever. We
are apt to run from one extreme to another. To anticipate and
prevent disastrous contingencies would be the part of wisdom and
patriotism.

  " What astonishing changes a few years are capable of producing!
I am told, that even respectable characters speak of a monarchical
form of government without horror. From thinking proceeds
speaking ; thence to acting is but a single step, — but irrevocable
and tremendous ! What a triumph for the advocates of despotism,
to find that we are incapable of governing ourselves, and that systems
founded on the basis of equal liberty are merely ideal and fallacious !
Would to God that wise measures may be taken in time to avert
the consequences we have but too much reason to apprehend ! " [1]

  From the condition of anarchy so graphically and feelingly
described, the nation was rescued by the genius and patriotism of Washington, Hamilton, Madison, Franklin, Jay, and a
few other exalted natures, in the formation of the Federal
Government. This was a task far more formidable and difficult
than the severance of the political relations which had bound
the colonists to the mother country. That was one which
might have been accomplished, had the people been wholly
incapable of political organization and subjection to one common rule. The Mexican and South American colonies were
able to defy the utmost power of Spain. Acquiring political
independence, they have never been able to establish social
order, or to form themselves into any thing deserving the name
of a State.

  There can be no doubt that the Constitution of the United
States was a conception far in advance of the ideas and sentiments prevailing at the time of its adoption, and that it
was carried by personal influence, rather than from any well-
grounded conviction of the people in its favor. All had implicit faith in the great chieftain who had brought the war to a
triumphant conclusion, and whose moral and civic qualities,
displayed during its prosecution, had excited still greater admiration than his military achievements. If he would again lead,
the people would again commit their cause and their welfare
wholly to his keeping. But for his transcendent influence the
adoption of the Constitution, which he contributed so largely

---

[1] Life and Writings of Washington, vol. vi. p. 187.

to frame, could not have been secured.   It was natural that most of the leading actors in the War of the Revolution should be advocates of a strong government, from an experience of the limited powers and imbecility of the old.   The notable exceptions were Patrick Henry and Samuel Adams.   Jefferson, its great future enemy, was, fortunately, out of the country at the time.   The same good fortune that placed Washington in command of the armies of the Revolution committed the new government to the guidance of his matchless wisdom and prudence, till it had in a measure become consolidated; till sufficient time had elapsed to illustrate its advantages, and to secure to it the confidence and affection of the people, before it passed into the hands of others less firm, patriotic and sagacious.   The strength it acquired under his administration enabled it to meet and overcome the shocks to which it was exposed, till the maturing and widening of the wholly irreconcilable tendencies existing at the time, and which were the great obstacles to its formation, left no other solution but the final arbitrament of the sword.   ·

The government formed, Mr. Hamilton was placed in charge of the Department of the Treasury, — the one upon which, of all others, was imposed the burden of restoring the financial and material condition of the country, reduced to its lowest ebb by the late war, and the disturbances and distrust which followed.   Whether or not he had a consciousness of his great mission, he could not have been actuated by broader views, or have taken measures better adapted to lay firm the foundations of a great empire, — the greatest, should it continue another hundred years, that the world has yet seen.   He saw what all such men see, that, to use the words of Washington, "influence is not government," and that no nation can become truly great that is not possessed of powers capable of subordinating all conflicting and refractory elements to the authority of a common rule.   Political unity is a product of conditions either natural or enforced.   When enforced, its achievement is the crowning work of the statesman.

The first step to be taken was a recognition and payment, as far as possible, by the new government, of the debts contracted in the late war.   Hamilton would have the new State signalize its beginning by an act of justice, which should not only stand as a guarantee and promise of the future, but secure for it, at the very outset, an honorable place among the nations. He well understood that private, cannot long survive the neglect or decay of public morals; and he determined to re-enforce the former by a scrupulous observance of the latter. The debt adjusted upon an equitable basis, the next step was provision for the payment of its annual charge, as well as the current expenses of the government. These were provided for by imposts upon foreign merchandise, as the most efficient, and the least oppressive and expensive mode; and as affording at the same time encouragement and protection to domestic industries. His third great measure was the provision, by means of a Bank, of a symbolic currency alike adapted to the wants of the government and of the people.[1]

All these measures excited great opposition. That which was the chief object of attack was the Bank. For its creation the Constitution contained no provision in terms. The authority to charter it was derived from that clause which gave Congress " the power to pass all laws necessary and proper to carry into execution the preceding powers." It was assumed that the Bank was " necessary and proper " for the execution of " the power to levy and collect taxes, and pay the debts, and provide for the common defence and general welfare." Mr. Hamiltŏn, in his argument in support of its constitutionality, maintained that " every power vested in a government is in its nature SOVEREIGN; and includes, by force of the term, a right to employ all the means requisite and fairly applicable to the attainment of the ends of such power, and which are

---

[1] The debt of the old government, assumed by the new, equalled $72,775,895, as follows : —

Foreign debt	$12,556,874
Domestic debt	40,256,802
Debt of the States assumed	19,962,219
Total	$72,775,895

The foreign debt was paid in full; so was the domestic debt, for which an equivalent was received, or was assumed to have been received. The claims of the States for advances made on account of the war, were adjusted upon what was assumed to be an equitable basis. The Continental money was "cut off with a shilling." No person desired its recognition. To show, however, that it was not forgotten, it was allowed to be funded at the rate of 100 to 1. Of the whole amount, it appears that the holders of $168,280,219 took advantage of the provision for funding it, receiving therefor $1,682,802.

not precluded by restrictions and exceptions specified in the Constitution, or not immoral, or not contrary to the essential ends of political society ; " and that the Bank was one of the means that might be properly employed to such ends. Mr. Jefferson, in opposition, maintained that " the Constitution allows only the means which are ' necessary,' not those which are merely convenient for effecting the enumerated powers. If such a latitude of construction be allowed to this phrase, ' the power to make all laws necessary and proper for carrying into execution the enumerated powers,' as to give any non-enumerated power, it will go to every one ; for there is no one which ingenuity may not torture into a convenience in some way or other to some one of the long list of enumerated powers : it would swallow up all the delegated powers, and reduce the whole to one phrase, as before observed. Therefore it was that the Constitution restrained Congress to the necessary means ; that is to say, to those means without which the grant of the power would be nugatory."

Such were the opposing constructions as to the nature and effect of its organic law upon which have turned, through its whole career, the legislation and history of the nation. Their authors stood as types of American ideas and life. Whatever followed, and a library would hardly suffice to hold all that has been written on one side or the other of this question, has been but an elaboration and application of their respective arguments or positions, which are sufficiently stated in the preceding brief paragraph. Their different constructions grew out of differences radical in kind. There is no record of the division in the Senate upon the passage of the bill creating the Bank; but in the House only one member from the North voted against the bill, and only six from the South in its favor. The members of the Cabinet, as well as Congress, were divided geographically : Mr. Jefferson, Secretary of State, and Mr. Randolph, Attorney-General, both from Virginia, giving opinions adverse to the constitutionality of the proposed measure ; and Mr. Hamilton of New York, Secretary of the Treasury, and Mr. Knox of Massachusetts, Secretary of War, giving opinions in its favor. General Washington, after having given the subject the most careful consideration, signed the bill.

The formation of the Constitution was nothing less, in fact, than an unsuccessful attempt to fuse into one two distinct nations. The result has demonstrated the utter impossibility of such an attempt, without some more potent force than commercial considerations, or legal enactments or ties. All sagacious men at the time recognized the magnitude of the refractory element, — Slavery ; but all, at the North at least, confidently looked for its disappearance through the operation of moral and industrial causes. The result showed how greatly they were mistaken. They forgot that slavery was not permeable or subject to the influences upon which they counted so much. The North, addicted to commerce and manufactures, welcomed all the helps that government could bestow. They saw in a Bank a useful instrument in facilitating its operations, in alleviating its burdens, and at the same time one that would greatly promote individual welfare. To such a people, Hamilton's construction appeared wholly reasonable. They were willing to make convenience law, and to commit themselves to the guidance of ideas, no matter the conclusions to which they might lead. The South could take nothing on trust. Every thing must be determined and settled at the start. To commit themselves to the guidance of ideas might be to court the overthrow of the very institutions upon which their welfare was assumed to rest. Slavery was forbidden by public as well as by moral law. A convenient or liberal construction might question its propriety, restrain it within its original limits, or, without any aggressive act, render its continuance impossible. Hence the necessity of a "strict construction," not only where slavery was directly concerned, but upon every subject touching the material welfare of the nation. The South could derive no advantage from the adoption of measures "tending to promote the general welfare." Such measures were those designed for the encouragement of domestic industries and trade. Their policy was to blindfold labor, as a means of keeping it contented, or in ignorance of its lot. With them, the encouragement of the industries of the nation meant an increase of the preponderance of their rivals; which, as soon as it gained sufficient strength, might turn upon and crush them. The necessities of the South made them good seers of the final catastrophe of 1860, of the possibility of which they never lost sight.

The preceding remarks have been submitted, for the reason that without an accurate knowledge of the grounds upon which the country divided as to the nature of its Constitution, the controversies in reference to Banks and money which have so convulsed it throughout its history would seem to be mere riddles, — contests having no more sense or meaning than those which make up the experience of barbarous life. The question involved was not a financial or monetary, but a political one. No one distinguished person among all the actors in the grand drama ever denied the importance of Banks. They were created in all the States as a matter of common necessity. The only question was as to the competency of the United States to create them. The consequences were infinitely wider and more disastrous than if the contest had turned upon the principles involved in the nature of metallic or paper money. Had this been the question, no more heat might have been generated than that belonging to the consideration of any question in science or philosophy. As it was presented, its solution might involve, on one side at least, the destruction of the institutions of a whole people. It was, therefore, the question of all others most fitted to excite to the highest pitch of frenzy some of the strongest passions of the race. It was the signal for the division of the country into two great political parties ; the theme which has convulsed it from the formation of the government, and which could be put to rest only by the triumph by arms of one or the other of the opposing parties.

The Act establishing the Bank was finally passed on the 25th of February, 1791. The amount of its capital was fixed at \$10,000,000, divided into shares of \$400 each. Of this sum, \$2,000,000 was to be subscribed on behalf of the United States, to be paid in ten equal annual instalments. The balance of the share capital, \$8,000,000, to be taken by private parties, was to be paid in six equal annual instalments : one-fourth part of which was to be in gold and silver coin ; the remaining three-fourths, in evidences of the public debt. The Board of Directors was to consist of twenty-five members, all of them citizens of the United States, who were to choose one of their number President. The Bank was not to owe, over and above its deposits, a larger sum than its capital. It was allowed to sell any part of the securities of which its capital was composed, but was not allowed to purchase any kind of public debt whatever. Its notes were not made legal tender, but were receivable in the payment of the revenues, of which it was at the same time made the depository. The Act also provided that " said corporation shall not, directly or indirectly, deal or trade in any thing except bills of exchange, gold or silver bullion, or in the sale of goods really and truly pledged for money lent, and not redeemed in due time, or of goods which shall be the produce of its lands ; neither shall the said corporation take more than at the rate of six per centum per annum for or upon account of its loans or discounts. No loan shall be made by said corporation for the use, or on account, of the government of the United States, to an amount exceeding $100,000 ; or of any particular State to an amount exceeding $50,000 ; or of any foreign prince or State, unless previously authorized by a law of the United States." Provision was made in the bill for the establishment of eight branches : one at Boston, with a capital of $700,000 ; one at New York, with a capital of $1,800,000 ; one at Baltimore, with a capital of $600,000 ; one at Washington, with a capital of $200,000 ; one at Norfolk, with a capital of $600,000 ; one at Charleston, with a capital of $600,000 ; one at Savannah, with a capital of $500,000 ; and one at New Orleans, with a capital of $300,000. The balance of the capital, $4,700,000, was assigned to Philadelphia, where the Bank was to have its chief office.

The Act, like every thing that came from the hand of its author, was a masterpiece of its kind. It might, indeed, serve as a model for all countries and all times. All its provisions were perfectly adapted to their object, — the creation of a symbolic currency, by means of which the revenues of the government. could be collected and disbursed, and the exchanges effected, without the interposition of coin. The notes of a government made receivable in the payment of the revenues, and bearing a proper proportion thereto, might, without any other provision for their redemption, maintain themselves at a high value for the uses they would serve. The taxes to be paid in them would be the constituent provided for their discharge. As, however, such notes would always be without a constituent in merchandise, and as there would always be a tendency to issue them in excess of the revenues presently falling due, they might, and often would, become disturbing elements in the business operations of the country. The notes of a Bank symbolizing merchandise could be liable to no such objection. There could be no excess, while the use of such notes in the payment of the revenues would greatly strengthen the institution issuing them. A panic affecting the general credit could exert very little influence in causing the notes receivable for revenues to be returned for coin ; for the reason that, whatever the value of their constituent either in coin or merchandise, so long as they were so receivable their holders would, as a rule, have no inducement to return them. There is the same reason that the revenues of government should be paid in symbolic money as that the exchanges of the public should be made by means of it. The parties to whom it is paid will, as a rule, wish to use it as money; and, if it represent what they have occasion to purchase and consume, it will be preferred to coin. The interest payable on the public debt should, so far as the government is concerned, be always paid or provided for in symbolic money. If payable abroad, it will, in fact, be paid in great measure in merchandise. Those who are to receive it, if paid in coin, will immediately seek to expend it for merchandise, — perhaps of the very kind which the paper money of the indebted nation symbolized. For such payments, therefore, merchandise will serve as well as coin. Those made by nations not producing gold and silver must, from necessity, be paid in it ; the mode of payment by government being the use of merchants' or bankers' bills representing merchandise. The exports of a people, therefore, not producing metallic money, must exceed their imports by the amount of the annual payments they are compelled to make not arising out of commercial transactions. All that a government indebted abroad has to do is to provide itself with symbolic money, as its issuers must supply to it whatever will discharge its indebtedness wherever it may exist.

Such were the financial measures provided for the nation at the very beginning of its career, — measures as perfect as could be provided by the hand of man, and equally adapted to all conditions and all times ; and such are some of the services Hamilton rendered to his country. With the Bank of England as an example, that created by him was a vast improvement upon the model. The latter, in theory at least, cannot convert that part of its capital represented by the public debt. A large portion of its means, consequently, are not available when most needed. If, instead of this stock, it held a corresponding amount of good bills, it would be absolutely beyond the reach of harm ; the causes or occasions of the monetary crises now so frequently happening could not exist. They did not exist until after the Bank got into the clutches of the government, — an embrace, unfortunately, as advantageous to it as it is disastrous to the general welfare. The government is too good a customer not to be preferred to the public. The Bank of the United States was wholly free from such an entangling alliance. After its organization, it speedily converted its government debt into money, and consequently had at all times its capital in hand. As a consequence, the period of its existence was the brightest one in the whole financial or monetary history of the country. It was the Golden Age, soon to be overwhelmed by one of barbarism, which in its ignorance, intolerance and ferocity, carries us back a thousand years.

At the time the first Bank went into operation, there were only three State Banks, — the Bank of North America, at Philadelphia ; the Massachusetts Bank, at Boston ; and the Bank of New York, at New York City. The aggregate capital of these, when organized, equalled $1,650,000. In 1792, the number of State Banks had increased to eleven, with an aggregate capital of $8,935,000. In 1801, the number had increased to thirty-two, whose joint capital equalled $23,500,000. In 1805, there were seventy-five State Banks, with a capital of $40,493,000, — an amount exceeding four times the capital of the United States Bank. The excellence of the system of Hamilton was, that while it created a Bank whose operations extended to every part of the country, and by means of which the revenues were collected and disbursed, it allowed the creation of State or local Banks, by means of whose issues the greater part of the exchanges must always be effected. The system was ideally as well as practically perfect in all its parts. A currency adapted to local exchanges must be locally supplied, for the reason that it can be properly issued only by parties possessing a competent knowledge of the means and character of the applicants for loans. It will yet be found that the only possible mode of retrieving our condition, and securing a currency uniform in amount and value, will be a return to the financial system of Hamilton; just as a return to the maxims and policy of Washington will be the only safe guarantee for the domestic peace and order of the country.

The approval of the Bank by all the departments of government, and by the Supreme Court as soon as the question could be presented to that tribunal, only served to increase and imbitter the hostility of Jefferson to a construction so opposed to all his theories, and, in his estimation, so fraught with danger to that portion of the country with which, not only as a citizen, but from his training, habits, and ideas, he was so closely identified. The Bank, indeed, seemed beyond his reach. To claim such a measure as this to be sufficient ground for breaking up the government would only expose him to ridicule and contempt; and he patiently bided his time. This was not long in coming. Washington in due time was succeeded by Mr. Adams, whose great personal unpopularity exposed him to constant and virulent attacks from newspapers and foreigners in the interest of France. To protect him, as well as the government, were passed the famous "Alien and Sedition Laws," enacted to punish libellers, and foreigners who used the asylum offered by the country for the purpose of embroiling it in war. The laws were very probably ill-advised and inopportune, although Washington did not so regard them. They were Jefferson's great occasion. In opposition to them, he immediately drafted the celebrated resolutions which were passed by the legislature of the State of Virginia in 1798, and by that of Kentucky in 1799; and which, among other things, declared: —

"That the several States composing the United States of America are not united on the principle of unlimited submission to their general government, but that, by a compact under the style and title of the Constitution of the United States, and of amendments thereto, they constituted a general government for special purposes; delegated to that government certain definite powers; reserving, each State to itself, the residuary measure of right to their own self-government; and that, whensoever the general government assumes undelegated powers, its acts are unauthoritative, void, and of no force; that to this compact each State acceded as a State, and is an integral party: that the government created by this compact was not made the exclusive or final judge of the extent of the powers delegated to itself, since that would have made its discretion, and not the Constitution, the measure of its powers; but that, as in all other cases of compact among parties having no common judge, each party has an equal right to judge for itself, as well of infractions, as of the mode and measure of redress, . . . and that a nullification by those sovereignties of all unauthorized acts done under the color of that instrument is the rightful remedy."

These resolutions embodied in a most complete and perfect form Jefferson's construction of the Constitution as opposed to that of Hamilton, who insisted that it united the people not as a confederacy, but as a nation. They took the whole question out of the arena of the National Legislature and of the courts, and submitted it to the opinions and judgment of the whole people; by whom, or by a great majority of whom, at least so far as their decision could be gathered from the expressions of their popular assemblies, they were accepted as the cardinal rule for the construction of the Constitution, and as justifying the destruction of the government, whenever it should suit the interest or caprice of any member of it.

It will be proper in this connection to consider further the opinions upon government, and upon the nature of our own, of this extraordinary man, who exerted such a paramount and baleful influence over the nation for the first hundred years of its existence. He was, in fact, opposed to all governments worthy the name. No one had the natural right to bind any generation not a party to it.

"Can," he said, "one generation bind another, and all others, in succession for ever? I think not. The Creator has made the earth for the living, not the dead. Rights and powers can only belong to persons, not to things, — not to mere matter, unendowed with will. The dead are not even things. The particles of matter which composed their bodies make part now of the bodies of other animals, vegetables, or minerals, of a thousand forms. To what, then, are attached the rights and powers they held while in the form of men? A generation may bind itself as long as its majority continues in life; when that has disappeared, another majority is in place, holds all the rights and powers their predecessors once held, and may change their laws and institutions to suit themselves. Nothing is unchangeable but the inherent and inalienable rights of men."[1]

[1] Letter to Major Cartwright, Jefferson's Works, vol. vii. p. 859.

" The earth belongs to the living, not to the dead. The will and
the power of man expire with his life, by nature's law. Some societies give it an artificial continuance for the encouragement of
industry ; some refuse it, as our aboriginal neighbors, whom we call
barbarians. The generations of men may be considered as bodies
or corporations. Each generation has the usufruct of the earth
during the period of its continuance. When it ceases to exist, the
usufruct passes on to the succeeding generation, free and unencumbered ; and so on, successively, from one generation to another for
ever. We may consider each generation as a distinct nation, with
a right, by the will of its majority, to bind themselves, but none
to bind the succeeding generation more than the inhabitants of
another country. Or the case may be likened to the ordinary one of
a tenant for life, who may hypothecate the land for his debts during
the continuance of his usufruct; but at his death the reversioner
(who is for life only) receives it exonerated from all burden. The
period of a generation, or the term of its life, is determined by the
laws of mortality, which, varying a little only in different climates,
offer a general average to be found by observation.[1]

Jefferson's notions of the nature of what little government
we had in this country were well set out in the letter to Major
Cartwright, above quoted : —

" With respect to our State and Federal governments, I do not
think their relations correctly understood by foreigners. They
generally suppose the former subordinate to the latter. This is not
the case. They are co-ordinate departments of a single and integral whole. To the State governments are reserved all legislation
and administration in affairs which concern their own citizens only,
and to the Federal Government is given whatever concerns foreigners, or the citizens of other States ; these functions alone being
made federal. The one is the domestic, the other the foreign,
branch of the same government ; neither having control over the
other, but within its own department. There are one or two exceptions only to this partition of power. But, you may ask, if the
two departments should claim the same subject of power, where is
the common umpire to decide ultimately between them ? In cases
of little importance or urgency, the prudence of both parties will
keep them aloof from the questionable ground ; but, if neither can
be avoided nor compromised, a convention of the States must be
called to ascribe the doubtful power to that department which
they may think best." [2]

His hostility to the present Constitution was early proclaimed. Writing from Paris, under date of Nov. 13, 1787,
he says, —

[1] Letter to J. W. Eppes, Jefferson's Works, vol. vi. p. 136.
[2] Jefferson's Works, vol. vii. p. 358.

"Indeed, I think all the good of this new Constitution might have been couched in three or four new articles, to be added to the good, old, and venerable fabric, which should have been preserved even as a religious relique."[1]

From the preceding extracts, it will be seen that Jefferson completely ignored the Supreme Court of the United States as the authorized expounder of the Constitution. In reference to this tribunal, he says:—

"The judiciary of the United States is the subtle corps of sappers and miners constantly working under ground to undermine the foundations of our constitutional fabric. They are construing our Constitution from a co-ordination of a general and special government to a general and supreme one alone. This will lay all things at their feet; and they are too well versed in English law to forget the maxim, *Boni judicis est ampliare jurisdictionem.* We shall see if they are bold enough to take the daring stride these five lawyers" (judges) "have lately taken. Having found, from experience, that impeachment is an impracticable thing, a mere scarecrow, they consider themselves secure for life; they skulk from responsibility to public opinion,—the only remaining hold upon them,— under a practice first introduced into England by Lord Mansfield. An opinion is huddled up in conclave (perhaps by a majority of one), delivered as if unanimous, and with the silent acquiescence of lazy or timid associates, by a *crafty chief judge*" (Marshall), "who sophisticates the law to his mind by the turn of his own reasoning.[2] A judiciary law was once reported by the Attorney-General to Congress, requiring each judge to deliver his opinion *seriatim* and openly, and then to give it in writing to the clerk to be entered on the record. A judiciary independent of a king or executive alone, is a good thing; but independence of the will of the nation is a solecism, at least in a republican government."[3]

Jefferson would have no government capable of binding the future, and no courts as the final arbiters of disputes. His remedy for misgovernment and political oppression was rebellion:—

"Wonderful is the effect of impudent and persevering lying. The British ministry have so long hired their gazetteers to repeat, and model into every form, lies about our being in anarchy, that the world has at length believed them, the English nation has believed

[1] Letter to John Adams, Jefferson's Works, vol. ii. p. 317.
[2] The case referred to was McCulloch v. The State of Maryland, in which Judge Marshall made his famous argument in support of the constitutionality of the Bank.
[3] Letter to Thomas Ritchie, Jefferson's Works, vol. vii. p. 192.

them, the ministers themselves have come to believe them, and, what is more wonderful, we have believed them ourselves. Yet where does this anarchy exist? Where did it ever exist, except in the single instance of Massachusetts? And can history produce an instance of rebellion so honorably conducted? I say nothing of its motives. They were founded in ignorance, not wickedness. God forbid we should ever be twenty years without such a rebellion! The people cannot be all and always well informed. The part which is wrong will be discontented in proportion to the importance of the facts they misconceive. If they remain quiet under such misconceptions, it is a lethargy, — the forerunner of death to the public liberty. We have had thirteen States independent for eleven years. There has been one rebellion. That comes to one rebellion in a century and a half for each State. What country before ever existed a century and a half without a rebellion? And what country can preserve its liberties, if its rulers are not warned from time to time that their people preserve the spirit of resistance? Let them take arms. The remedy is to set them right as to facts, pardon and pacify them. What signify a few lives lost in a century or two? The tree of liberty must be refreshed from time to time with the blood of patriots and tyrants. It is its natural manure." [1]

Jefferson not only most earnestly opposed Washington's principles of government, but he claimed to have been, by his election to the Presidency, the instrument for their complete overthrow. Writing to Judge Roane, under date of September 6, 1819, soon after the famous decision of Judge Marshall affirming the constitutionality of the United States Bank, he said : [2] —

" The Revolution of 1800 was as complete a revolution in the principles of our government as that of 1776 was in its form; not effected, indeed, by the sword, as that, but by the rational and peaceable instrument of reform, — the suffrage of the people. The nation declared its will by dismissing functionaries of one principle, and electing those of another, in the two branches — executive and legislative — submitted to their election. Over the judiciary department the Constitution had deposed them of their control. That, therefore, has continued the *reprobated* system."

The preceding extracts, which might be multiplied in kind, so as to fill a volume, furnish the key, and the only one, by means of which the political as well as the financial history of this country can be made intelligible, not only to foreigners, but to ourselves. Up to 1860, Jefferson was the patron saint of the nation. His teachings in reference to the

[1] Letter to Colonel Smith, Jefferson's Works, vol. ii. pp. 318, 319.
[2] Ibid. vol. vii. p. 133.

nature of our government were held to be the sum of political wisdom.   Taught only too well, a part of the nation, in antici- pation of any overt act or grievance, withdrew from the Union. From opinion, which up to that time had been the arbiter of events, the North took an appeal to a still higher tribunal, — that of the sword.   Then flowed like a flood the blood which, with Mr. Jefferson, was "the natural manure of the tree of liberty."   In this final appeal he was again overruled, and an emphatic judgment reaffirmed for his great rival.   The over- throw of Jefferson was a revolution as much in the literature as in the politics of the country.   If his teachings were false, then the works which sought to base upon them its institu- tions were equally so.   Hence the desperate attempt, so late as 1865, of our great historian to impose upon the ignorance and credulity of the nation, that Jefferson was the champion of whatever centralizing tendency our Constitution contained, and that "no man ever contributed so much toward the con- solidation of the Union: " —

"When John Adams," says Mr. Bancroft, "was elected Presi- dent, before any overt act, before any other cause of alarm than his election, the legislature of Virginia took steps for an armed organization of the State, and old and long-cherished sentiments adverse to union were renewed.   The continuance of the Union was in peril.   It was then that the great Virginia statesman, now per- fectly satisfied with the amended Constitution, came to the rescue. . . . The thought never crossed the mind of Jefferson that the general government had not proper powers of coercion. . . . No one man did so much as he towards consolidating the Union." [1]

As Jefferson was the very person through whose influence "the legislature of Virginia took steps for an armed organiza- tion of the State," and was himself the author of those "old and long-cherished sentiments hostile to the Union," the as- sertion, that at the moment when, under the elder Adams, the stability of the government was threatened, — and all know how seriously it was threatened, — "he rushed to the rescue," may well excite astonishment.   He was the person who, far in advance of all others, developed and proclaimed, in all their length and breadth, the doctrines of nullification.   But for him, they might not have been heard of for a half century.   So

[1] Place of Abraham Lincoln in History, by George Bancroft, Atlantic Monthly, June, 1865.

alarming were the consequences of his teachings, and so insidious and untiring his efforts to undermine the government, that
Washington, who had wholly retired from public life, which
he hoped never again to enter, was forced to forego his determination, and appear once more in the political arena. The
Virginia Resolutions were passed in the latter part of December, 1798. No sooner had the knowledge of this reached him,
than he made an earnest appeal to Patrick Henry, who had
now become a supporter of the Constitution, to consent to
become a member of the State legislature, in order to be in a
position in which he could exert his great influence to defeat
a movement aimed at the very life of the nation : —

"It would be a waste of time," said Washington, " to attempt to
bring to the view of a person of your observation and discernment
the endeavors of a certain party (referring to Jefferson) among us,
to disquiet the public mind with unfounded alarms, to arraign
every act of the administration, to set the people at variance with
their government, and to embarrass all its measures. Equally useless would it be to predict what must be the inevitable consequences
of such a policy, if it cannot be arrested.

"Unfortunately, and extremely do I regret it, the State of Virginia has taken the lead in this opposition. I have said the State,
because the conduct of its legislature in the eyes of the world will
authorize the expression ; and because it is an incontrovertible fact,
that the principal leaders of the opposition dwell in it, and that,
with the help of the chiefs in other States, all the plans are arranged
and systematically pursued by their followers in other parts of the
Union ; though in no State except Kentucky, that I have heard of,
has legislative countenance been obtained beyond Virginia. . . .
At such a crisis as this, when every thing dear and valuable to us is
assailed ; when this party hangs upon the wheels of government as a
dead weight, opposing every measure that is calculated for defence
and self-preservation ; when measures are systematically and perti-
naciously pursued which must eventually DISSOLVE THE UNION, OR
PRODUCE COERCION, — I say, when these things have become so obvious, ought characters (like yourself), who are best able to rescue
the country from the pending evil, to remain at home ? Rather
ought they not to come forward, and by their talents and influence
stand in the breach which such conduct has made on the peace and
happiness of this country, and oppose the widening of it?

"Vain will it be to look for peace and happiness, or for the
security of liberty or property, if civil discord should ensue. And
what else can result from the policy of those among us who, by all
the measures in their power, are driving matters to extremity, if
they cannot be counteracted effectually? . . . If their conduct is
viewed with indifference,—if there are activity and misrepresentation
on one side, and supineness on the.other, — their numbers accumu-

lated by intriguing and discontented foreigners under proscription, who are at war with their own governments, and the greater part of them with all governments, they will increase, and nothing short of Omniscience can foretell the consequences. . . . Your weight of character and influence in the House of Representatives would be a bulwark against such dangerous sentiments as are delivered there at present. It would be a rallying-point for the timid, and an attraction to the wavering. In a word, I conceive it to be of immense importance at this crisis that you should be there; and I would fain hope that all minor considerations will be made to yield to the measure.

" If I have erroneously supposed that your sentiments on these subjects are in unison with mine, or if I have assumed a liberty which the occasion does not warrant, I must conclude, as I began, with praying that my motives may be received as an apology. My fear that the tranquillity of the Union, and of this State in particular, is hastening to an awful crisis, has extorted them from me." [1]

Which of the two came to the rescue when the " legislature of Virginia took steps for an armed organization of the State, and old and long-cherished sentiments adverse to the Union were renewed," — the author of these hostile steps and sentiments, or he who saw in them a meaning of such terrible import ; who exerted himself so strenuously for their defeat, and who foresaw, if they could not be arrested by an appeal to public opinion, the terrible catastrophe of the civil war, — in which, when it did come, half a million of lives and ten thousand millions of property were sacrificed? The amazing untruthfulness with which history has been written in this country is in itself a most striking illustration of the hold which Jefferson has had upon the public mind.

The charter of the Bank expired on the 4th of March, 1811. In view of such expiration, its stockholders, in 1808, memorialized Congress for its renewal. The bill for this purpose, although strongly supported by Mr. Gallatin, then Secretary of the Treasury, was defeated in the House by a single vote, and in the Senate by the casting vote of its President. The ground on which the extension of the charter of the Bank was refused was the unconstitutionality of the measure ; in other words, the grounds upon which Jefferson opposed the first Bank, and to which he clung with unyielding

---

[1] Letter to Patrick Henry, Sparks' Life of Washington, vol. xi. pp. 388-91.

tenacity.   The Bank having ceased to exist, the government. was, from necessity, driven to the employment of State Banks. It used them as depositories of the revenues, and received their notes in payment.   No sooner, however, was it seen that the charter of the United States Bank was not to be renewed, than all the States vied with each other in the rage for the creation of local Banks.[1]   In 1812, the nation found itself involved in a war with Great Britain.   In 1814, all the Banks of the country, with the exception of those of New England, suspended payment.   The government was speedily reduced to a most mortifying and dangerous position.   The expenses of the war could only be met by loans made payable in bank-notes greatly depreciated and rapidly sinking in value.   Specie was not to be had.   Their decline was much more rapid in the outset than that of the Revolutionary currency.   For the former, the whole wealth of the nation was assumed to be pledged, and it derived an additional value from being made legal-tender. The notes of the State Banks had no such support.   They might be, and a great many of them were, issued without any provision for their redemption.   The amount of their notes outstanding in 1811, as estimated by Mr. Gallatin, equalled $22,700,000 ; those of the Bank of the United States, $5,400,000: making a total of $28,100,000.   The amount of notes of the State Banks outstanding in 1816 was estimated by Mr. Crawford, Secretary of the Treasury, at the time of his report upon the " currency," under date of Feb. 12, 1820, made in obedience to a resolution of the House of Representatives passed March 1st, 1819, at $110,000,000.[2]   These notes were

---

[1] "A Committee of the Senate of Pennsylvania, appointed in December, 1819, to inquire into the extent and causes of the present general distress, ascribed it to the improvident creation of so many Banks, as will appear from the following extract from their report: —

" ' At the following session, the subject was renewed with increased ardor ; and a bill authorizing the incorporation of forty-one banking institutions, with capitals amounting to upwards of $17,000,000, was passed by a large majority.   This bill was also returned by the Governor, with additional objections ; but, two-thirds of both houses (many members of which were pledged to their constituents to that effect) agreeing on its passage, it became a law on the 21st of March, 1814; *and thus was inflicted upon the Commonwealth an evil of a more disastrous nature than has ever been experienced by its citizens.*   Under this law, thirty-seven Banks, four of which were established in Philadelphia, actually went into operation.' " — Considsiderations on the Currency, by Albert Gallatin, p. 50.

[2] Mr. Gallatin, in his " Considerations upon the Currency," written in 1830,

depreciated all the way from 10 to 30 per cent, and were constantly declining in value. No wonder that the nation stood appalled at the thought of the volcano beneath its feet, which might at any moment burst forth and overwhelm government and people in a common ruin. By universal consent, the only mode of escape was another Bank of the United States. The memory of the advantages secured by the former was still fresh in the minds of all. For the instant, in the face of a supreme necessity, Jefferson and his construction were wholly forgotten. Hamilton was again in the ascendent. With the approbation of Mr. Madison, then President of the United States, who had been one of the most determined opponents, upon constitutional grounds, of the old Bank, and who delivered in Congress the ablest argument made on his side of the question, a bill was brought in. This was vetoed by him, not from the unconstitutionality of the proposed measure, — that, he said, having been finally disposed of by repeated precedents of the government, and of the tribunal of last resort in the interpretation of the Constitution (the Supreme Court of the United States), — but for the reason that it was not properly adapted to its objects. The bill was vetoed too late in the session to allow time for maturing another. At the following session, one was brought in and passed ; receiving the signature of the President on the 10th of April, 1816. The capital of the Bank was increased to $35,000,000. Like that of the previous one, its charter was to run for twenty years. When the first Bank was chartered, there were but three State Banks in operation, whose joint capital did not exceed $2,000,000. They had been prudently conducted, and the currency was in a sound condition. This, at the time, consisted chiefly of specie. The new Bank, consequently, was only an additional instrument in advancing the general prosperity. As its loans were confined to the discount of bills, they could not be made in excess. New State Banks were created from time to time, as called for by the wants and the increasing business operations of the country. There does not appear to have been any excessive issue or speculative movement of any considerable magnitude during

estimates the amount of the notes of the State Banks in circulation in 1816 at $68,000,000. He gives no reason for differing so widely from Mr. Crawford, who certainly was in a position to be the better informed of the two.

the whole period of the existence of the first Bank.   This was the brightest and most satisfactory one in the financial history of the nation.   The system in operation was based upon the soundest principles, and conducted in the most prudent and competent manner.   When the second Bank went into operation, the fountains of the great deep had been broken up. In the frenzy for paper money, it was as if a vast mob, guided by the most lawless impulses, had taken possession of the land, had subverted all law and order, and well-nigh its moral and material prosperity.   Such was the condition of affairs which the second Bank was created to remedy.   It went manfully to work ; but the very foundations for a proper system of currency had to be laid.   The paper money of the State Banks had driven the greater part of the specie out of the country. As speedily as possible, and in less than two years, the Bank brought back $7,311,750 from Europe, to serve as its reserves, — at a loss, including interest, of $525,247.   It could not, however, hope for permanent success, unless the monetary condition was in a measure restored.   For that purpose, it undertook to help such Banks as were deserving of aid.   One great obstacle in the way of resumption by the State Banks was their indebtedness to the government, arising out of a deposit of the public money and unpaid proceeds of loans, the only means for the discharge of which was their depreciated paper. The United States Bank assumed such debts to the amount of $10,807,410 ; of which, $3,336,491 were in the form of special deposits, giving a credit to the State Banks sufficient for the realization of their assets.   By such measures, progress was steadily made ; so that by 1820 most of the Banks in the Eastern States had resumed.   The United States Bank, at the same time, undertook to extend large accommodations to Southern and Western States which were without any adequate system of their own ; in consequence of which it made very heavy losses.   It also made a loss, soon after it went into operation, of $1,671,221, by the mismanagement of the Baltimore branch.   The total losses made within two years after it went into operation were estimated at $3,500,000.   These, together with the extensions of loans it was compelled to make, so very seriously crippled it that grave apprehensions were at one time felt that it would be compelled to suspend. It, however, weathered the storm, and gradually worked itself into a satisfactory position. In no single instance, either at the Bank or at any one of its branches, was specie ever refused upon notes or deposits. It could, however, by no means arrest the passion for new Banks, — particularly in the Southern and Western States, which still continued to create them by scores, only to disappear after an ephemeral existence, but not till after they had flooded the country with worthless paper. The consequences of such inflation, with the necessary contraction, were sought to be met by the States with stay-laws, and other expedients to prevent the seizure by law, and the sacrifice of property. A brief sketch of the banking system or operations of the State of Kentucky will suffice for the whole. In 1802, that State chartered a Bank at Lexington, with a capital of $150,000. In 1803, this was followed by the Bank of Kentucky, with a capital of $1,000,000. These Banks appear to have been well-managed and prosperous. In 1815, the State caught the prevailing mania, and increased the capital of the Bank of Kentucky to $3,000,000, with power to create thirteen branches, of which seven went speedily into operation. In 1818, forty-three new Banks were chartered, the greater part of which went into operation. These, for some time, made a show of paying specie ; but soon they all suspended, as well as the Bank of Kentucky, which again undertook to resume in 1819, and continued nominally to pay specie for about a year. In the general crash which followed, the common expedient, "stay-laws," was resorted to. To its credit, the Court of Appeals — the highest legal tribunal in the State — pronounced these laws unconstitutional. The people, however, were by no means to be balked. Through the legislature, which they controlled, they established a new Court of Appeals, composed of judges known to be in favor of sustaining the laws. The State at once divided into two most rancorous parties. That favorable to the stay-laws and the new Court remained dominant until 1826, when the opposing party got the upper hand, reversing the action of the one preceding it ; but not until almost infinite mischief had been done, both to the moral and material welfare of the State. By the time that reason had resumed its sway, the Banks had almost wholly disappeared. Not a trace of them was to be found in 1830. Mr. Gallatin, in his pamphlet on the currency, puts the number of Banks which failed in this State between 1811 and

1830, at forty-three.   He was able to ascertain the capital of only nineteen, which amounted in the aggregate to $6,297,730. The total capital of all the Banks probably equalled $10,000,000. Their circulation and deposits at one time probably equalled their capital.   Such was the paper-money debauch in that State.   A corresponding exhaustion followed.   In all this, Kentucky only stood for an example of Western and Southern States; and shows the perilous sea upon which the second Bank of the United States was launched, and from which it barely escaped complete shipwreck.

In estimating the causes of financial disturbance in the United States, the condition of affairs and the influences at work in other countries are always to be carefully considered. During the whole period, from 1791 to 1811, Europe was convulsed by wars, which created a market at high rates for all the more important products of this country, and gave active employment to her merchant shipping.   The "balance of trade," for almost the whole period, continued largely in its favor, and brought into it plentiful supplies of coin.   In 1816, peace was restored to Europe, in consequence of which the factitious advantages previously enjoyed by the United States were almost wholly lost.   Thenceforth the financial and commercial condition of the country was greatly affected by that of others.   The period in England from 1816 to 1826 was the most disturbed and unsatisfactory in her financial history. Resumption there, as in the United States, caused an excessive contraction, to be followed by great speculative movements, which culminated in 1826, — a year alike memorable in both countries for great commercial disasters.   The Bank of England resumed in 1821.   At that time it seemed sufficiently strong to defy all assault.   The resumption of specie payment, and the apparent restoration of its material interests, was followed in that country by a mania for Banks, as widespread and intense as any that ever prevailed in the United States.   The consequences were the same in that country as in this.   Great numbers of Banks failed, and the Bank of England itself appeared to be brought to the very brink of ruin.   As the greatest achievement of society is the effecting of its exchanges by symbols, — by the representatives of the articles exchanged, — so the greatest wrong it can do to itself is to sever the symbol from the constituent, or to accept that as money which has none, either in merchandise or coin. With such a currency, society is in the condition of one whose will exerts no control over his acts. The more violent his action, the greater the harm to which he inevitably comes. Experience has shown that ten years is a very short period in which to recover from the effects of an excessive and long-continued indulgence in the use of paper money which is severed from capital. Hence the criminality of those who wantonly tamper with the currency, or who are instrumental in the imposition of a fictitious one.

The nation had hardly recovered from the disasters consequent upon the refusal to recharter the old Bank, than came the announcement of General Jackson, in his first Annual Message, that : —

" Both the constitutionality and the expediency of the law creating this Bank are well questioned by a large portion of our fellow-citizens, and it must be admitted by all that it has failed in the great end of establishing a uniform and sound currency.

" Under these circumstances, if such an institution is deemed essential to the fiscal operations of the government, I submit to the wisdom of the legislature whether a national one, founded upon the credit of the government and its revenues, might not be devised, which would avoid all constitutional difficulties, and, at the same time, secure all the advantages to the government and country that were expected to result from the present Bank."

This announcement created all the astonishment of a clap of thunder in a cloudless sky. It was received with mingled feelings of indignation, ridicule, and contempt. The Bank had never stood higher in popular estimation. The question of its constitutionality was supposed to have been for ever set at rest. The attack did not excite alarm, as it was believed that it would be utterly futile, in view of the experience and precedent of the past. By the usual courtesy, that part of the message relating to the Bank was referred to the Committee of Ways and Means of the House ; consisting of Mr. McDuffie, of South Carolina, the chairman, Mr. Verplanck, of New York, Mr. Dwight, of Massachusetts, Mr. Smyth, of Virginia, Mr. Ingersoll, of Connecticut, Mr. Gilmore, of Pennsylvania, and Mr. Overton, of Louisiana. A large majority of

the Committee was friendly to the administration, as were
two-thirds of the House. As the greater number of which
the Committee was composed were .personally familiar with
the operations of both Banks, of the period between the two,
and with all the political and material questions involved;
and as these were discussed with a fulness, ability, and conclusiveness never surpassed in the discussion of a similar subject in this or any other country ; and as we must yet return
to a National Bank, founded on the model of Hamilton, before
we can hope to restore the financial condition of the country, —
copious extracts are given from the report of the Committee,
not only for the information they contain, but for the reason
that they carry much more force than would any summary or
abstract.

" There are few subjects," says the report, " having reference to
the policy of an established government, so vitally connected
with the health of the body politic, or in which the pecuniary interests of society are so extensively and deeply involved. No one
of the attributes of sovereignty carries with it a more solemn
responsibility, or calls in requisition a higher degree of wisdom,
than the power of regulating the common currency, and thus fixing
the general standard of value for a great commercial community
composed of confederated States.

" Such being, in the opinion of the Committee, the high and
delicate trust exclusively committed to Congress by the Federal
Constitution, they have proceeded to discharge the duty assigned
to them, with a corresponding sense of its magnitude and difficulty.

" The most simple and obvious analysis of the subject, as it is
presented by the Message of the President, exhibits the following
questions for the decision of the National Legislature : —

" 1. Has Congress the constitutional power to incorporate a
Bank, such as that of the United States ?

" 2. Is it expedient to establish and maintain such an institution ?

" 3. Is it expedient to establish a National Bank, founded upon
the credit of the government and its revenues ?

" If the concurrence of all the departments of the government
at different periods of our history, under every administration, and
during the ascendency of both the great political parties into which
the country was divided, soon after the adoption of the present
constitution, shall be regarded as having the authority ascribed to
such sanctions by the common consent of all well-regulated communities, the constitutional power of Congress to incorporate a
Bank may be assumed as a postulate no longer open to controversy.
In little more than two years after the government went into operation, and at a period when most of the distinguished members of the
Federal Convention were either in the executive or legislative
councils, the Act incorporating the first Bank of the United States

passed both branches of Congress by large majorities, and received the deliberate sanction of President Washington, who had then recently presided over the deliberations of the Convention. The constitutional power of Congress to pass the Act of Incorporation was thoroughly investigated, both in the executive cabinet and in Congress, under circumstances in all respects propitious to a dispassionate decision. There was, at that time, no organization of political parties; and the question was, therefore, decided by those who, from their knowledge and experience, were peculiarly qualified to decide correctly, and who were entirely free from the influence of that party excitement and prejudice which would justly impair, in the estimation of posterity, the authority of a legislative interpretation of the constitutional charter. No persons can be more competent to give a just construction to the Constitution than those who had a principal agency in framing it; and no administration can claim a more perfect exemption from all those influences which sometimes pervert the judgments even of the most wise and patriotic, than that of the Father of his Country during the first term of his service.

" Such were the circumstances under which all the branches of the National Legislature solemnly determined that the power of creating a National Bank was vested in Congress by the Constitution. The Bank, thus created, continued its operations for twenty years, — the period for which its charter was granted; during which time public and private credit were raised from a prostrate to a very elevated condition, and the finances of the nation were placed upon the most solid foundation.

" When the charter expired, in 1811, Congress refused to renew it; principally owing, as the Committee believe, to the then existing state of political parties. Soon after the Bank was chartered, the two great parties that have since divided the country began to assume an organized existence. Mr. Jefferson and Mr. Madison, the former in the executive cabinet and the latter in Congress, had been opposed to the establishment of the Bank, on constitutional grounds; and, being placed at the head of the party most unfavorable to the extension of the powers of the government by implication, the bank question came to be regarded as in some degree the test of political principles.

" When Mr. Jefferson came into power, upon the strong tide of a political revolution, the odium of the Alien and Sedition Laws was in part communicated to the Bank of the United States; and, although he gave his official sanction to an Act creating a new branch of that institution at New Orleans, and to another to punish the counterfeiting of its bills, yet, when the question of renewing the charter came before Congress, it was discussed as a party question. And, though some of the most distinguished Republicans — including Mr. Gallatin, then Secretary of the Treasury, and Mr. Crawford, then a member of the Senate — were decidedly in favor of the renewal, sustaining the measure by able arguments, the votes in both branches of Congress were distinctly marked as party votes. . . .

" In less than two years after the expiration of the charter, — the war with Great Britain having taken place in the mean time, — the circulating medium became so disordered, the public finances so deranged, and the public credit so impaired, that the enlightened patriot, Mr. Dallas, who then presided over the Treasury Department, with the sanction of Mr. Madison, and as it is believed every member of the Cabinet, recommended to Congress the establishment of a National Bank, as the only measure by which the public credit could be revived and the fiscal resources of the government redeemed from a ruinous and otherwise incurable embarrassment ; and such had been the impressive lesson taught by a very brief but fatal experience, that the very institution which had been so recently denounced and rejected by the Republican " [Democratic] " party, being now recommended by a Republican " [Democratic] " administration, was carried through both branches of Congress, as a Republican " [Democratic] " measure, by an overwhelming majority of the Republican party. It is true that Mr. Madison did not approve and sign the bill which passed the two Houses, because it was not such a bill as had been recommended by the Secretary of the Treasury, and because the Bank it proposed to create was not calculated, in the opinion of the President, to relieve the necessities of the country. But he premised his objections to the measure ' by waiving the constitutional authority of the legislature to establish an incorporated Bank, as being precluded, in his opinion, by repeated recognitions, under varied circumstances, of the validity of such an institution, in Acts of the legislative, executive, and judicial branches of the government, accompanied by indications, in different modes, of a concurrence of the general will of the nation.' Another bill was immediately introduced ; and would, in all probability, have become a law, had not the news of peace, by doing away the pressure of the emergency, induced Congress to suspend further proceedings on the subject until the ensuing session.   At the commencement of that session, Mr. Madison invited the attention of Congress to the subject ; and Mr. Dallas again urged the necessity of establishing a Bank, to restore the currency, and facilitate the collection and disbursement of the public revenue ; and so deep and solemn was the conviction upon the minds of the public functionaries that such an institution was the only practicable means of restoring the circulating medium to a state of soundness, that, notwithstanding the decided opposition of all the State Banks and their debtors, — and, indeed, the whole debtor class of the community, — the Act incorporating the present Bank of the United States was passed by considerable majorities in both branches of Congress, and approved by Mr. Madison.

" This brief history of the former and present Bank forcibly suggests a few practical reflections. It is to be remarked, in the first place, that, since the adoption of the Constitution, a Bank has existed, under the authority of the Federal Government, for thirty-three out of forty years ; during which time, public and private credit have been maintained at an elevation fully equal to what has existed in any nation in the world: whereas, in the two short intervals during which no National Bank existed, public and private credit were greatly impaired, and, in the latter instance, the fiscal operations of the government were almost entirely arrested. In the second place, it is worthy of special notice, that, in both the instances in which Congress has created a Bank, it has been done under circumstances calculated to give the highest authority to the decision. The first instance, as has already been remarked, was in the primitive days of the Republic, when the patriots of the Revolution and the sages of the Federal Convention were the leading members both of the executive and legislative councils, and when General Washington, who at the head of her armies had conducted his country to independence, and at the head of the Convention had presided over those deliberations which resulted in the establishment of the present Constitution, was the acknowledged President of a people undistracted by party divisions. The second instance was under circumstances of a very different, but equally decisive, character. We find the very party which had so recently defeated the proposition to renew the charter of the old Bank, severely schooled both by adversity and experience, magnanimously sacrificing the pride of consistency and the prejudices of party at the shrine of patriotism. It may be said, without disparagement, that an assembly of higher talent and purer patriotism has never existed since the days of the Revolution than the Congress by which the present Bank was incorporated. If ever a political party existed, of which it might be truly said that 'all the ends they aimed at were their country's,' it was the Republican " [Democratic] " party of that day. They had just conducted the country through the perils of a war waged in defence of her rights and honor; and, elevating their views far above the narrow and miserable ends of party strife, sought only to advance the permanent happiness of the people. It was to this great end that they established the present Bank.

" In this review, it will be no less instructive than curious to notice some of the changes made in the opinions of prominent men, yielding to the authority of experience. Mr. Madison, who was the leading opponent of the Bank created in 1791, recommended and sanctioned the Bank created in 1816; and Mr. Clay, who strenuously opposed the renewal of the charter in 1811, as strenuously supported the proposition to grant the charter in 1816.

" That may be said of the Bank charter which can be said of few contested questions of constitutional power. Both the great political parties that have so long directed the country have declared it to be constitutional, and there are but very few of the prominent men of either party who do not stand committed in its favor. When to this imposing array of authorities the Committee add the solemn and unanimous decision of the Supreme Court, in a case which fully and distinctly submitted the constitutional question to their cognizance, may they not ask, in the language of Mr. Dallas, ' Can it be deemed a violation of the right of private opinion to consider the constitutionality of a National Bank as a question for ever settled and at rest?' . . .

" The earliest and the principal objection urged against the constitutionality of a National Bank was that Congress had not the
power to create corporations. That Congress has a distinct and
substantive power to create corporations, without reference to the
objects intrusted to its jurisdiction, is a proposition which never
has been maintained, within the knowledge of the Committee; but
that any one of the powers expressly conferred upon Congress is
subject to. the limitation, that it shall not be carried into effect by
the agency of a corporation, is a proposition which cannot be maintained, in the opinion of the Committee.

" If Congress, under the authority to pass *all laws* necessary and
proper for carrying into effect the powers vested in all or any of
the departments of the government, may rightfully pass a law
inflicting the punishment of death, *without any other authority*, it
is difficult to perceive why it may not pass a law, under the same
authority, for the more humble purpose of creating a corporation.
The power of creating a corporation is one of the lowest attributes,
or, more properly speaking, incidents of sovereign power. The
chartering of a Bank, for example, does not authorize the corporation to do any thing which the individuals composing it might not
do without the charter. It is the right of every individual of the
Union to give credit to whom he chooses, and to obtain credit where
he can get it. It is not the policy of any commercial country to
restrict the free circulation of credit, whether in the form of promissory notes, bills of exchange, or bank-notes. The charter of the
Bank of the United States, therefore, merely enables the corporation to do in an artificial capacity, and with more convenience,
what it would be lawful for the individual corporators to do without
incorporation. . . .

" But the question really presented for their determination is
not between a metallic and a paper currency, but between a paper
currency of uniform value, and subject to the control of the only
power competent to its regulation, and a paper currency of varying and fluctuating value, and subject to no common or adequate
control whatever. On this question, it would seem that there could
hardly exist a difference of opinion; and that this is substantially
the question involved in considering the expediency of a National
Bank, will satisfactorily appear by a comparison of the state of the
currency previous to the establishment of the present Bank and its
condition for the last ten years.

" Soon after the expiration of the charter of the first Bank of the
United States, an immense number of local Banks sprung up under
the pecuniary exigencies produced by the withdrawal of so large
an amount of bank credit as necessarily resulted from the winding
up of its concerns, — an amount falling very little short of fifteen
millions of dollars. These Banks, being entirely free from the salutary control which the Bank of the United States had recently
exercised over the local institutions, commenced that system of
imprudent trading and excessive issues which speedily involved the
country in all the embarrassments of a disordered currency. The
extraordinary stimulus of a heavy war expenditure derived prin-

cipally from loans, and a corresponding multiplication of local Banks, chartered by the double-score in some of the States, hastened the catastrophe; which must have occurred, at no distant period, without those extraordinary causes. The last year of the war presented the singular and melancholy spectacle of a nation abounding in resources, a people abounding in self-devoted patriotism, and a government reduced to the very brink of avowed bankruptcy solely for the want of a national institution, which, at the same time that it would have facilitated the government loans and other treasury operations, would have furnished a circulating medium of general credit in every part of the Union. In this view of the subject, the Committee are fully sustained by the opinion of Mr. Dallas, then Secretary of the Treasury, and by the concurring and almost unanimous opinion of all parties in Congress; for, whatever diversity of opinion prevailed as to the proper basis and organization of a Bank, almost every one agreed that a National Bank of some sort was indispensably necessary to rescue the country from the greatest of financial calamities.

"The Committee will now present a brief exposition of the state of currency at the close of the war; of the injury which resulted from it, as well to the government as to the community; and their reasons for believing that it could not have been restored to a sound condition, and cannot now be preserved in that condition, without the agency of an institution such as the Bank of the United States.

"The price current appended to this report will exhibit a scale of depreciation in the local currency, ranging through various degrees to 20, and even to 25, per cent. Among the principal Eastern cities, Washington and Baltimore were the points at which the depreciation was greatest. The paper of the Banks in those places was from 20 to 22 per cent below par. At Philadelphia, the depreciation was considerably less; though even there it was from 17 to 18 per cent. In New York and Charleston, it was from 7 to 10 per cent. But, in the interior of the country where Banks were established, the depreciation was even greater than at Washington and Baltimore. In the Western part of Pennsylvania, and particularly at Pittsburgh, it was 25 per cent. These statements, however, of the relative depreciation of bank paper at various places, as compared with specie, give a very inadequate idea of the enormous evil inflicted upon the community by the excessive issues of bank paper. . . .

"A very serious evil, already hinted at, which grew out of the relative depreciation of bank paper at the different points of importation, was its inevitable tendency to draw all the importations of foreign merchandise to the cities where the depreciation was greatest, and divert them from those where the currency was comparatively sound. If the Bank of the United States had not been established, and the government had been left without any alternative but to receive the depreciated local currency, it is difficult to imagine the extent to which the evasion of the revenue laws would have been carried. Every State would have had an interest to encourage the excessive issues of its Banks and increase the degradation of its currency, with a view to attract foreign commerce. Even in the condition which the currency had reached in 1816, Boston and New York and Charleston would have found it advantageous to derive the supplies of foreign merchandise through Baltimore; and commerce would, undoubtedly, have taken that direction, had not the currency been corrected. To avoid this injurious diversion of foreign imports, Massachusetts and New York and South Carolina would have been driven, by all motives of self-defence and self-interest, to degrade their respective currencies, at least to a par with the currency of Baltimore; and thus a rivalry in the career of depreciation would have sprung up to which no limit can be assigned. As the tendency of this state of things would have been to cause the largest of the revenue to be collected at a few places, and in the most depreciated of the local currency, it would have followed that a very small part of that revenue would have been disbursed at the points where it was collected. The government would consequently have been compelled to sustain a heavy loss upon the transfer of its funds to the points of expenditure. The annual loss which would have resulted from these causes alone cannot be estimated at a less sum than $2,000,000.

" But the principal loss which resulted from the relative depreciation of bank paper at different places, and its want of general credit, was that sustained by the community in the great operations of commercial exchange. The extent of these operations, annually, may be safely estimated at $60,000,000. Upon this sum, the loss sustained by the merchants and planters and farmers and manufacturers was probably not less than an average of 10 per cent, being the excess of the rate of exchange between its natural rate in a sound state of the currency, and beyond the rate to which it has been actually reduced by the operations of the Bank of the United States. It will be thus perceived that an annual tax of $6,000,000 was levied from the industrious and productive classes, by the large moneyed capitalists in our commercial cities who were engaged in the business of brokerage. . . .

" But no adequate conception can be formed of the evils of a depreciated currency, without looking beyond the relative depreciation at different places to the general depreciation of the entire mass. It appears from the report of Mr. Crawford, the Secretary of the Treasury, in 1820, that, during the general suspension of specie payments by the local Banks in the years 1815 and 1816, the circulating medium of the United States had reached the aggregate amount of $110,000,000, and that in the year 1819 it had been reduced to $45,000,000, being a reduction of 59 per cent in the short period of four years. The Committee are inclined to the opinion, that the severe and distressing operation of restoring a vicious currency to a sound state, by the calling in of bank paper and the curtailment of bank discounts, had carried the reduction of the currency, in 1819, to a point somewhat lower than was consistent with the just requirements of the community for a circulating medium; and that the bank discounts have been gradually enlarged since that time, so as to satisfy those requirements. It will be assumed, therefore, that the circulating medium of the United States has been $55,000,000 for the last ten years, taking the average.

" Even upon this assumption, it will follow that the national currency has been 100 per cent more valuable for the last ten years than it was in 1816. In other words, two dollars would purchase no more of any commodity in 1816 than one dollar has been capable of purchasing at any time since 1817. . . .

" The Committee have given this part of the subject an attentive and careful examination ; and they cannot estimate the pecuniary losses of the government, sustained exclusively for the want of a sound currency and an efficient system of finance, at a sum less than $46,000,000. If they shall make this apparent, the House will have something like a standard for estimating the individual losses of the community.

" The government borrowed, during the short period of the war, $80,000,000, at an average discount of 15 per cent ; giving certificates of stock amounting to $80,000,000 in exchange for $68,000,000 in such bank paper as could be obtained. In this statement, treasury notes are considered as stock at 20 per cent discount. Upon the very face of the transaction, therefore, there was a loss of $12,000,000, which would in all probability have been saved if the treasury had been aided by such an institution as the Bank of the United States. But the sum of $68,000,000 received by the government was in a depreciated currency, not more than half as valuable as that in which the stock given in exchange for it has been and will be redeemed. Here, then, is another loss of $34,000,000, resulting incontestably and exclusively from the depreciation of the currency, and making, with the sum lost by the discount, $46,000,000. While, then, the government sustained this great pecuniary loss in less than three years of war, amounting annually to more than the current expenses of the government in time of peace, it is worth while to inquire who were the persons who profited to this enormous amount by the derangement of the currency? It will be found that the whole benefit of this speculation upon the necessities of the government was realized by stock-jobbers and money brokers, by the very same class of persons who profited so largely by the business of commercial exchanges in consequence of the disorders of the currency, and who have the same interest in the recurrence of those disorders as lawyers have in litigation, or physicians in the diseases of the human frame. Having presented these general views of the evils which existed previous to the establishment of the Bank of the United States, it remains for the Committee to inquire how far this institution has effected a remedy of those evils. . . .

" It has been already stated that it has saved the community from the immense losses resulting from a high and fluctuating state of the exchanges. It now remains to show its effect in equalizing the currency. In this respect, it has been productive of results more salutary than were anticipated by the most sanguine advocates of the policy of establishing the Bank. *It has actually furnished a circulating medium more uniform than specie.* This proposition is susceptible of the clearest demonstration. If the whole circulating medium were specie, a planter of Louisiana who should desire to purchase merchandise in Philadelphia would be obliged to pay one per cent either for a bill of exchange on this latter place, or for the transportation and insurance of his specie. His specie at New Orleans, where he had no present use for it, would be worth one per cent less to him than it would be in Philadelphia, where he had a demand for it. But, by the aid of the Bank of the United States, one-half of the expense of transporting specie is now saved to him. The Bank, for one-half of one per cent, will give him a draft upon the mother Bank at Philadelphia, with which he can draw either the bills of that Bank or specie, at his pleasure. . . .

"For all the purposes of the revenue, it gives to the national currency that perfect uniformity, that ideal perfection, to which a currency of gold and silver in so extensive a country could have no pretensions. A bill issued at Missouri is of equal value with specie at Boston, in payment of duties; and the same is true of all places, however distant, where the Bank issues bills and the government collects its revenue. When it is, moreover, considered that the Bank performs, with the most scrupulous punctuality, the stipulation to transfer the funds of the government to whatever point they may be wanted, free of expense, it must be apparent that the Committee are correct to the very letter in stating that the Bank has furnished, both to the government and to the people, *a currency of absolutely uniform value in all places, for the purposes of paying the public contributions and disbursing the public revenue.* And, when it is recollected that the government annually collects and disburses more than $23,000,000, those who are at all familiar with the subject will at once perceive that bills, which are of absolutely uniform value for this vast operation, must be very nearly so for all the purposes of general commerce. . . .

"But the salutary agency of the Bank of the United States, in furnishing a sound and uniform currency, is not confined to that portion of the currency which consists of its own bills. One of the most important purposes which the Bank was designed to accomplish, and which, it is confidently believed, no other human agency could have effected under our federative system of government, was the enforcement of specie payments on the part of numerous local Banks deriving their charters from the several States, and whose paper, irredeemable in specie and illimitable in its quantity, constituted the almost entire currency of the country. Amidst a combination of the greatest difficulties, the Bank has almost completely succeeded in the performance of this arduous, delicate, and painful duty. With exceptions too inconsiderable to merit notice, all the State Banks in the Union have resumed specie payment. Their bills, in the respective spheres of their circulation, are of equal value with gold and silver; while, for all the operations of commerce beyond that sphere, the bills or the checks of the Bank of the United States are even more valuable than specie. And even in the very few instances in which the paper of State Banks is depreciated, these Banks are winding up their concerns; and it may be safely said that no citizen of the Union is under the necessity of taking depreciated paper, because a sound currency cannot be obtained.   North Carolina is believed to be the only State where paper of the local Banks is irredeemable in specie, and consequently depreciated.   Even there the depreciation is only one or two per cent; and, what is more important, the paper of the Bank of the United States can be obtained by all those who desire it, and have an equivalent to give for it.

"The Committee are aware that the opinion is entertained by some that the local Banks would, at some time or other, either voluntarily, or by the coercion of the State legislatures, have resumed specie payments.   In the very nature of things, this would seem an impossibility.   It must be remembered that no Banks ever made such large dividends as were realized by the local institutions during the suspension of specie payments.   A rich and abundant harvest of profit was opened to them, which the resumption of specie payments must inevitably blast.   While permitted to give their own notes, bearing no interest and not redeemable in specie, in exchange for better notes bearing interest, it is obvious that, the more paper they issued, the higher would be their profits.   The most powerful motive that can operate upon moneyed corporations would have existed to prevent the State Banks from putting an end to the very state of things from which their excessive profits proceeded.   Their very nature must have been changed, therefore, before they could have been induced to co-operate voluntarily in the restoration of the currency.   It is quite as improbable that the State legislatures would have compelled the Banks to do their duty.   It has already been stated that the tendency of a depreciated currency to attract importations to the points of greatest depreciation, and to lighten the relative burdens of federal taxation, would naturally produce among the States a rivalry in the business of excessive bank issues.   But there remains to be stated a cause of more general operation, which would have prevented the interposition of the State legislatures to correct those issues.

"The Banks were, directly and indirectly, the creditors of the whole community; and the resumption of specie payments necessarily involved a general curtailment of discounts and withdrawal of credit, which would produce a general and distressing pressure upon the higher class of debtors.   These constituted the largest portion of the population of all the States where specie payments were suspended and Bank issues excessive.   Those, therefore, who controlled public opinion in the States where the depreciation of the local paper was greatest were interested in the perpetuation of the evil.   Deep and deleterious, therefore, as the disease evidently was in many of the States, their legislatures could not have been expected to apply a remedy so painful as the compulsion of specie payments would have been, without the aid of the Bank of the United States.   And here it is worthy of special remark, that, while that Bank has compelled the local Banks to resume specie payments, it has most materially contributed, by its direct aid and liberal arrangements, to enable them to do so, and that with the least possible embarrassment to themselves and distress to the community.   If the State legislatures had been ever so anxious to compel the Banks to resume specie payments, and the Banks ever so willing to make the effort, the Committee are decidedly of the opinion that they could not have done it, unaided by the Bank of the United States, without producing a degree of distress incomparably greater than has been actually experienced. They will conclude their remarks on this branch of the subject by the obvious reflection, that if Congress, at the close of the war, had left it to the States to restore the disordered currency, this important function of sovereignty would have been left with those from whom the Constitution had expressly taken it, and by whom it could not be beneficially or effectually exercised.   But another idea, of considerable plausibility, is not without its advocates.   It is said that this government, by making the resumption and continuance of specie payment the condition upon which State Banks should receive the government deposits, might have restored the currency to a state of uniformity.   Without stopping to give their reasons for believing that specie payments could not have been restored in this way, and that, even if they could, a uniform currency of general credit, throughout the Union, would not have been provided, the Committee will proceed to give their reasons for thinking that such a connection between the Federal Government and the State Banks would be exceedingly dangerous to the purity of both. While there is a National Bank, bound by its charter to perform certain stipulated duties, and entitled to receive the government deposits as a compensation fixed by the law containing the charter, and only to be forfeited by the failure to perform those duties, there is nothing in the connection at all inconsistent with the independence of the Bank and the purity of the government.   The country has a deep interest that the Bank should maintain specie payments, and the government an additional interest that it should keep the public funds safely, and transfer them, free of expense, wherever they may be wanted.   The government, therefore, has no power over the Bank, but the salutary power of enforcing a compliance with the terms of its charter.   Every thing is fixed by the law, and nothing is left to arbitrary discretion.   It is true that the Secretary of the Treasury, with the sanction of Congress, would have the power to prevent the Bank from using its power unjustly and oppressively, and to punish any attempt, on the part of the Directors, to bring the pecuniary influence of the institution to bear upon the politics of the country, by withdrawing the government deposits from the offending branches.   But this power would not be lightly exercised by the treasury, as its exercise would necessarily be subject to be reviewed by Congress : it is in its nature a salutary corrective, creating no undue dependence on the part of the Bank.

" But the state of things would be widely different if there was no National Bank, and it was left to the discretion of the Secretary of the Treasury to select the local Banks in which the government deposits should be made.   All the State Banks would, in that case, be competitors for the favor of the Treasury; and no one who will duly consider the nature of this sort of patronage can fail to perceive, that, in the hands of an ambitious man not possessed of perfect purity and unbending integrity, it would be imminently dangerous to the public liberty. The State Banks would enter the lists of political controversy, with a view to obtain this patronage; and very little sagacity is required to foresee, that, if there should ever happen to be an administration disposed to use its patronage to perpetuate its power, the public funds would be put in jeopardy by being deposited in Banks unworthy of confidence, and the most extensive corruption brought to bear upon the elections throughout the Union. A state of things more adverse to the purity of the government, a power more liable to be abused, can scarcely be imagined. If five millions of dollars were annually placed in the hands of the Secretary of the Treasury, to be distributed, at his discretion, for the purposes of internal improvement, it would not invest him with a more dangerous and corrupting power. . . .

"A very grave and solemn question will be presented to Congress, when they come to decide upon the expediency of renewing the charter of the present Bank. That institution has succeeded in carrying the country through the painful process necessary to cure a deep-seated disease in the national currency. The nation, after having suffered the almost convulsive agonies of this necessary remedy, is now restored to perfect health. In this state of things, it will be for Congress to decide whether it is the part of wisdom to expose the country to a degree of suffering almost equal to that which it has already suffered, for the purpose of bringing back that very derangement of the currency which has been remedied by a process as necessary as it was distressing.

"If the Bank of the United States were destroyed, and the local institutions left without its restraining influence, the currency would almost certainly relapse into a state of unsoundness. The very pressure which the present Bank, in winding up its concerns, would make upon the local institutions, would compel them either to curtail their discounts, when most needed, or to suspend specie payments. It is not difficult to predict which of these alternatives they would adopt, under the circumstances in which they would be placed. The imperious wants of a suffering community would call for discounts, in language which could not be disregarded. The public necessities would demand, and public opinion would sanction, the suspension, or at least an evasion, of specie payments.

"But, even if this desperate resort could be avoided in a period of peace and general prosperity, neither reason nor experience will permit us to doubt that a state of war would speedily bring about all the evils which so fatally affected the credit of the government and the national currency during the late war with Great Britain. We should be again driven to the same miserable round of financial expedients, which, in little more than two years, brought a wealthy community almost to the very brink of a declared national bankruptcy, and placed the government completely at the mercy of speculating stock-jobbers.

" The Committee feel warranted, by the past experience of the country, in expressing it as their deliberate opinion, that, in a period of war, the financial resources of the country could not be drawn into efficient operation, without the aid of a National Bank, and that the local Banks would certainly resort to a suspension of specie payments. The maxim is eminently true, in modern times, that money is the sinew of military power. In this view of the subject, it does appear to the Committee that no one of the institutions of the country, not excepting the Army or Navy, is of more vital importance than a National Bank. It has this decided advantage over the Army and Navy: while they are of scarcely any value except in war, the Bank is not less useful than either of them in war, and is also eminently useful in peace. It has another advantage, still greater. If, like the Army or Navy, it should cost the nation millions annually to sustain it, the expediency of the expenditure might be doubted. But when it actually saves to the government and to the country, as the Committee have heretofore attempted to show, more millions annually than are expended in supporting both the Army and Navy, it would seem that, if there were any one measure of national policy, upon which all the political parties of the country should be brought to unite, by the impressive lessons of experience, it is that of maintaining a National Bank."

The preceding extracts present, succinctly and intelligibly, the reasons for the creation of both of the Banks; the constitutional objections that were urged; the final abandonment of these in 1816; the services that each Bank rendered both to the government and the people; and the tremendous disasters that were suffered in the interregnum between them. In the four years, the government in its operations made a loss of $54,000,000, from the depreciation of the currency, and in the cost of transfers which had been previously made by the Bank without charge. It had no alternative but to use the notes of the State Banks, no matter the degree of their depreciation. It was only too happy to obtain them at any rate in payment of loans. Coin was not to be had. In the dilemma in which all — government and people — were alike placed, a new United States Bank seemed the only escape from utter ruin. If the former, with expenditures equalling only about $25,000,000 yearly, suffered a loss of $54,000,000 from a depreciated currency, how vast must have been that of the people whose transactions were tenfold greater! Those of the former were restricted in time to about three years; while nearly fifteen were required to restore the financial condition of the country to that existing at the expiration of the charter of the first

Bank. The reduction of the currency from $110,000,000, according to Mr. Crawford, to $45,000,000, in the short period of three years, is sufficient evidence of the terrible waste and destruction which all contemporaneous writers describe. In spite of all the efforts that the Bank could exert, vast numbers of State Banks were, for a long time after its organization, constantly coming into and going out of existence. It was not till after 1826 that the financial condition of the country seemed fully restored.

The report of the House Committee was generally accepted as effectually disposing of the attack by the President upon the Bank. Its friends, however, counted wholly without their host. They knew little of the man with whom they had to deal, and as little of the causes already at work which were to produce an outburst of fanaticism that was to sweep with resistless fury over the nation. Jefferson, who had carried the doctrine of nullification to the extremest limits short of an overt act,[1] was followed by Presidents, who, from their characters rather than from purpose, tended to restore the government to the model of Washington and Hamilton. Madison — who earnestly opposed, on constitutional grounds, the chartering of the first Bank; and who, as a member of the Legislature of Virginia, wrote an elaborate report in vindication of the Resolutions of 1798 — wholly abandoned his former position, by recommending, and affixing his signature to, the Act incorporating, in 1816, the second Bank. His reasons were those which should influence and control the judgment of every right-minded man, — the uniform precedents, through a long series of years, of the National Legislature, and of the legal tribunal of last resort. Monroe followed by the approval of the Bill making provision for elaborate surveys, with a view to the construction of extended lines of public works. Under such administrations, which accepted the precedents of the past as their guide, and which left the articulations of the people almost wholly free, the nation entered upon a period of natural and orderly development, inferring the functions of government from the advantages resulting from their exercise. Such is the inference of every people capable of order and progress.

[1] After his accession to the Presidency, he discharged from custody parties held under the Alien and Sedition Laws, on the ground that such laws were void from their unconstitutionality.

This tendency, thoroughly pronounced, caused the greatest consternation on the part of Jefferson, who lost not a moment in sounding the alarm that the country, under the loose construction of the Constitution which was everywhere prevailing, was tending toward consolidation and monarchy, — all, however, for a time to very little purpose. So long as Virginians occupied the presidential chair, it was very difficult to revive the old, or divide the country upon new, issues. During the latter part of Mr. Monroe's administration, political parties seemed to have wholly disappeared. He had returned to the sentiments and practice of one, without seeming to have deserted those of the other. To him succeeded the second Adams, not by the choice of the people, but by that of Congress. His election was the signal for the immediate revival of the old parties, with all their former bitterness. In place of Virginians, the laxity of whose political morals could be overlooked out of respect to their citizenship, services, and character, came a Puritan of the Puritans, — severe in his manners and life, of all men the most obnoxious to the South ; and who, to crown all, was far more free in the construction of the Constitution than Hamilton himself.[1] His election was an insult to the ideas, institutions, and dignity of the South. It was an accident resulting from want of proper precaution and organization, and was by no means to be allowed to happen a second time.

The unanimity and earnestness with which Mr. Adams was opposed at the South, and the ease with which, by the help of Northern allies, he was defeated when he ran for a second

[1] " The question of the power of Congress to authorize the making of internal improvements is, in other words, a question whether the people of this Union, in forming their common social compact, as avowedly for the purpose of promoting their general welfare, have performed their work in a manner so ineffably stupid as to deny themselves the means of bettering their own condition. I have too much respect for the intellect of my country to believe it. The first object of human association is the improvement of the condition of the associated. Roads and canals are among the essential means of improving the condition of nations; and a people which should deliberately, by the organization of its authorized power, deprive itself of the faculty of multiplying its own blessings, would be as wise as a creator who should undertake to constitute a human being without a head."—Letter of John Quincy Adams, Niles' Register, vol. xxvi. p. 251.

Nothing could excite greater alarm and opposition at the South than such sentiments as these. Their adoption would be nothing less than a government of the majority, which might know no other law than the promotion of its real or fancied welfare.

term, taught a lesson which was only too well heeded ; which was, to form a party based upon Southern ideas, which could undergo no change so long as their chief institution remained. Never, apparently, was there a firmer foundation upon which to build, and never a combination which promised to yield to both parties more satisfactory results. The South was content, as a means of preserving slavery, with the construction of the Constitution, and with the privilege of defining the nature of the general government. All this their Northern allies freely conceded, for the possession of the public patronage. " The South was to be secured by going with the South, and the North by party machinery," was a maxim in politics which grew out of this combination for a partition of the government and its patronage. At the time of which we are speaking, " strict construction " was felt to be of far more importance to the South than in 1791. Time had only served to increase the differences between the two great sections of the country, — two nations from the beginning. During the early part of Mr. Adams' administration took place the famous experiment on the Stockton and Darlington Railway, in England, — the most important event in modern times, as it demonstrated the practicability of the use of steam as a locomotive power. The preceding half century had been greatly distinguished by the prodigious progress made in the useful arts. The North caught, in full measure, the spirit abroad in other lands, and welcomed the new helps which the inventive genius of the race had brought to its aid, many of which possessed a peculiar value in a country like their own. One great want was public highways, to give a value to the products of the soil. To encourage manufactures, protective tariffs were enacted. In all such measures to be undertaken by the general government, the South, which blindfolded labor in order to keep it in ignorance and contented with its lot, saw no advantage but to their rivals ; who were to increase in numbers and strength at their cost, from the use of contrivances and methods for which they were to be taxed, but in the benefits resulting from which they could have little share. Hence the redoubled earnestness with which they pressed the doctrine of " strict construction," and the unconstitutionality of the Bank. The Northern wing of the party readily yielded to all demands in this direction, not only as the price of the emoluments conceded to it, but from sheer incredulity as to the consequences. What were stern realities with one, were mere metaphysical abstractions with the other. What harm could come, reasoned the Northern wing, of the most extravagant popular harangues, or the extremest language in political addresses and resolutions? Every thing went on just as well after as before. The government continued in the orderly discharge of its wonted functions, although every attribute of power conflicting with the sovereignty of the States was denied it. The consequences were all the more fatal, the less they were perceived. Constant iteration begat in time a conviction, in both wings of the party, that the government was one without powers, unless it were those necessary to uphold and extend slavery; so that when the inevitable crisis came, those administering it denied to it the power of attempting to put down an armed insurrection aimed at its very life. The great majority at the North well knew that it had ceased to represent them and the better and higher sentiments of the nation; but how to attack and overthrow a party so intrenched in office, and so sustained by the precedents of the past, was for a long time a problem that seemed to defy solution. Foreigners, who could not see beneath the surface, inferred, and very properly, the manners of the nation from the brutalities practised at the national capital and in the halls of Congress; and its morals, from the chicanery and intrigue which, from the example set in the national politics, invaded and polluted the public service, not only of the Nation and States, but often of the most insignificant municipality. Along with all this demoralization went a mighty moral and material development; so that when the North seized the reins of the government, and when nothing was expected of it but incoherency and imbecility, the world was electrified by a display of intelligence and power which not only triumphed over the most formidable obstacles, but for the first time in its history placed the institutions of the country upon the basis not of force, but of right, — scattering to the winds Jefferson's and Jackson's construction of the Constitution, by the overthrow of the very institution whose necessities gave it birth.

In vain did Congress, with all the most sagacious and patriotic of all parties, earnestly protest against the position taken

by the President, which appeared so wanton and ill-advised.
Two men were then living, who of all others, were best fitted
to counsel and guide the nation. These were Mr. Madison
and Mr. Gallatin, — alike venerable for their age, but far more
so for the eminent services that each had rendered to the
nation. Next to Washington and Hamilton, no one contributed
so much as Madison toward the formation of its government.
Secretary of State for the whole period of Jefferson's administration, he was President for the eight succeeding years, discharging all the duties of his exalted station with singular
disinterestedness and success. He earnestly opposed the first
Bank, upon constitutional grounds. Its charter expired under
his administration. He was witness of the terrible disasters
which followed the refusal to extend it. As the only means
of escaping from them, he recommended the creation of a new
Bank, waiving his constitutional scruples as having been overruled by competent precedents of the past. The reasons for
the change in his opinions were fully set out in a letter, designed for publication, in reply to General Jackson's attack,
in which he said : —

"The charge of inconsistency between my objection to the constitutionality of such a Bank in 1791 and my assent in 1817 turns
on the question, how far legislative precedents, expounding the
Constitution, ought to guide succeeding legislatures, and to overrule
individual opinions.

"Some obscurity has been thrown over the question, by con-
founding it with the respect due from one legislature to laws
passed by preceding legislatures. But the two cases are essentially different. A constitution, being derived from a superior
authority, is to be expounded and obeyed, not controlled or varied,
by the subordinate authority of a legislature. A law, on the other
hand, resting on no higher authority than that possessed by every
successive legislature, its expediency as well as its meaning is
within the scope of the latter.

"The case in question has its true analogy in the obligations
arising from judicial expositions of the law on succeeding judges ;
the constitution being a law to the legislator, as the law is a rule
of decision to the judge.

"And why are judicial precedents, when formed on due discussion and deliberately sanctioned by reviews and repetitions,
regarded as of binding influence, or rather of authoritative force,
in settling the meaning of a law? It must be answered, 1st, Because it is a reasonable and established axiom, that the good of
society requires that the rules of conduct of its members should
be certain and known, which would not be the case if any judge,

disregarding the decisions of his predecessors should vary the rule of law according to his individual interpretation of it: " Misera est servitus ubi jus est aut vagum aut incognitum." 2d, Because an exposition of the law, publicly made, and repeatedly confirmed by the constituted authority, carries with it, by fair inference, the sanction of those who, having made the law through their legislative organ, appear under such circumstances to have determined its meaning through their judiciary organ.

" Can it be of less consequence that the meaning of a constitution should be fixed and known than that the meaning of a law should be so ?   Can, indeed, a law be fixed in its meaning and operation, unless the constitution be so ?   On the contrary, if a particular legislature, differing in the construction of the constitution from a series of preceding constructions, proceed to act on that difference, they not only introduce uncertainty and instability in the constitution, but in the laws themselves ; inasmuch as all laws preceding the new construction, and inconsistent with it, are not only annulled for the future, but virtually pronounced nullities from the beginning.

" But it is said that the legislator, having sworn to support the constitution, must support it in his own construction of it, however different from that put on it by his predecessors, or whatever be the consequences of the construction.   And is not the judge under the same oath to support the law ?   Yet, has it ever been supposed that he was required or at liberty to disregard all precedents, however solemnly repeated and regularly observed ; and, by giving effect to his own abstract and individual opinions, to disturb the established course of practice in the business of the community ?   Has the wisest and most conscientious judge ever scrupled to acquiesce in decisions in which he has been overruled by the matured opinions of the majority of his colleagues ; and subsequently to conform himself thereto, as to authoritative expositions of the law ?   And is it not reasonable to suppose that the same view of the official oath should be taken by a legislature acting under the constitution, which is his guide, as is taken by a judge acting under the law, which is his ?

" There is, in fact, and in common understanding, a necessity of regarding a course of practice, as above characterized, in the light of a legal rule of interpreting a law ; and there is a like necessity of considering it a constitutional rule of interpreting a constitution.

" That there may be extraordinary and peculiar circumstances controlling the rule in both cases, may be admitted ; but, with such exceptions, the rule will force itself on the practical judgment of the most ardent theorist.   He will find it impossible to adhere to, and act officially upon, his solitary opinions as to the meaning of the law or constitution, in opposition to a construction reduced to practice during a reasonable period of time ; more especially where no prospect existed of a change of construction by the public or its agents.   And if a reasonable period of time, marked with the usual sanctions, would not bar the individual prerogative, there could be no limitation to its exercise, although the danger of error must increase with the increasing oblivion of explanatory circumstances, and with the continual changes in the import of words and phrases.

"Let it, then, be left to the decision of every intelligent and candid judge, which, on the whole, is most to be relied on for the true and safe construction of a constitution : that which has the uniform sanction of successive legislative bodies, through a period of years, and under the varied ascendency of parties ; or that which depends on the opinions of every new legislature, heated as it may be by the spirit of party, eager in the pursuit of some favorite object, or led astray by the eloquence and address of popular statesmen, themselves perhaps under the influence of the same misleading causes."[1]

To these words of moderation and wisdom, to a construction necessary to the maintenance of government even under a despotism, — for, unless the past be in great measure the guide for the immediate future, chaos usurps the place of order and law, — General Jackson replied, in his veto of the bill extending the charter of the Bank that : —

"The Supreme Court ought not to control the co-ordinate authorities of this government. The Congress, the executive, and the court must each for itself be guided by its own opinion of the Constitution. Each public officer who takes an oath to support the Constitution swears that he will support it as he understands it, and not as it is understood by others. It is as much the duty of the House of Representatives, of the Senate, and of the President, to decide upon the constitutionality of any bill or resolution which may be presented to them for passage or approval, as it is of the supreme judges, when it may be brought before them for judicial decision. The opinion of the judges has no more authority over Congress than the opinion of Congress has over the judges ; and on that point the President is independent of both. The authority of the Supreme Court must not, therefore, be permitted to control the Congress or the Executive, when acting. in their respective capacities ; but to have only such influence as the force of their reasoning may deserve."

In the preceding extract, every one now sees the beginning of the end : Jackson completed the work of Jefferson. The latter denied to our government the powers necessary to its very existence ; the former, by making the will or caprice of the individual the rule of his conduct, inaugurated the reign of anarchy and barbarism.[2]

[1] History of the Bank, p. 778.

[2] Jackson has usually been regarded as deserving great praise for upholding the Constitution at the first attempt of South Carolina to put into practice Jeffer-

Next to Mr. Madison, the person best entitled to be heard
and to counsel the nation in such a crisis was Mr. Gallatin.

son's theory of the nature of our government. Never was praise more unde-
served. There was hardly a shade of difference in the political principles of the
two. South Carolina was personated in Calhoun, — a man of boundless ambition,
whose place Jackson had secured. Defeated, Calhoun, partly in revenge, brought
forward his nullification doctrines, — the pretext being the tariff. Jackson,
enraged against his rival for seeking his place, attacked him with the utmost
fury, and always regretted that he had not hanged him, as a proper and summary
mode of dealing with such an antagonist. In reply to the Ordinance of Secession,
Jackson did utter some fine things about the Constitution, and the obligations it
imposed, — far too fine for his Southern friends, who in turn assailed him with as
much fury as he had assailed Calhoun. Finding that he had gone too far, that
he had been wholly misunderstood, he authorized a full recantation of the doctrines contained in the proclamation, planting himself squarely on the resolutions
of 1798, the very grounds upon which South Carolina threatened to secede : —

"The proclamation, then, in the passages objected to, has merely spoken
the facts of *history*, — *the language of the Constitution*, and of the *Declaration of
Independence*. There is no speculative opinion advanced, no theory proposed.
And we have endeavored to show that nothing in these generalities tended in the
slightest degree to justify the inferences drawn from them, and which have been
substituted as the principles of the proclamation. But we are authorized to be
more explicit, and to say positively that no part of the proclamation was meant
to countenance the consolidating principles which have been ascribed to it. On
the contrary, its doctrines, if construed in the sense they were intended, and
carried out, inculcate that the Constitution of the United States is founded in
compact, — that this compact derives its obligation from the agreement entered
into by the people of each of the States, in their political capacity, with the people
of the other States ; that the Constitution, which is the offspring of this compact,
has its sanction in the ratification of the people of the several States, acting in the
capacity of separate communities ; that the majority of the people of the United
States, in the aggregate, have no power to alter the Constitution of the general
government, but that change or amendment can only be proposed in the mode
pointed out in the Constitution, and can never become obligatory unless ratified
by the people of three-fourths of the States, through their respective legislatures or State conventions ; that, inasmuch as the sovereign power of the people
in each State has imparted to the Constitution of the United States, and the laws
made in pursuance thereof, paramount obligation over State legislation, or any constitution or form of State government which may be instituted by the people of
such State ; and inasmuch as the people of each State have bound themselves,
by compact with the rest, to abide by one paramount authority until changed
according to the provisions of the Constitution, so declared to be paramount, — no
constitution, law, or ordinance of any one State is valid to defeat the Constitution
and laws of the States, or to sever the mutual obligations which bind the States
together ; — *that, in the case of a violation of the Constitution of the United States, and
the usurpation of powers not granted by it on the part of the functionaries of the general
government, the State governments have the right to interpose to arrest the evil,* UPON
THE PRINCIPLES WHICH ARE SET FORTH IN THE VIRGINIA RESOLUTIONS OF 1798,
AGAINST THE ALIEN AND SEDITION LAWS." — Washington Globe, Sept. 21, 1833.

There is not a word in all this to which Calhoun would not have fully subscribed. So long as a State remained in the Union, and did not question the

A Senator from Pennsylvania, he was appointed Secretary of
the Treasury by Mr. Jefferson, soon after his inauguration,
— a position which he held till April, 1813 ; serving through
the whole period of Jefferson's Presidency, and through four
years of that of Mr. Madison.   No other man ever held a place
in the cabinet for so long a time.   Certainly, no man, with one
single exception, discharged the duties of his office with equal
ability.   He was one of those rare men as capable in affairs as
in political life.   No one ever had so favorable an opportunity
of estimating the services rendered by the Bank to the nation,
and the importance, at all times, of such an institution.   In
his "Considerations on Currency,"— a work of remarkable
insight into the laws of money, and expressed in a style of
conciseness and elegance rare among writers on the subject, —
he bears the following testimony to the constitutionality of
both Banks, and to the services rendered by them : —

"It is our deliberate opinion that the suspension might have been
prevented at the time when it took place, had the former Bank of
the United States been still in existence.   The exaggerated increase
of State Banks, occasioned by the dissolution of that institution,
would not have occurred.   That Bank would, as before, have restrained within proper bounds, and checked their issues; and, through
the means of its offices, it would have been in possession of the
earliest symptoms of the approaching danger. . . .

"It will be found, by reference to the report of the Secretary of
the Treasury of December, 1815, that his recommendation to establish a National Bank was, in express terms, called 'a proposition
relating to the national circulating medium,' and was exclusively
founded on the necessity of restoring specie payments and the national currency.   He states it as a fact, incontestably proved, that
the State Banks could not at that time be successfully employed to
furnish an uniform national currency.   He mentions the failure of
one attempt to associate them with that view ; that another attempt

constitutionality of any act complained of, it must submit. So, if it sought to
change the Constitution, it must proceed according to the appointed methods. It
had, however, according to General Jackson, always reserved to itself the right to
peaceably withdraw from the Union, when it should judge a further continuance
in it to be opposed to its interests, its ideas, or its rights, "according to the principles laid down in the Resolutions of 1798 ; " which provided that each State
was a judge as well of the infraction (of the Constitution), as of the mode and
measure of redress ; and that a nullification, by such sovereignty, of all unauthorized acts done under the color of that instrument, is the rightful remedy.   The
whole contest between Jackson and Calhoun grew out of political rivalries, and,
so far as the former was concerned, never rose above the dignity of a squabble
for spoils.

by their agency in circulating treasury notes, to overcome the in-
equalities of the exchange, has only been partially successful; that a
plan recently proposed, with the design to curtail the issues of bank-
notes, to fix the public confidence in the administration of the affairs
of the Banks, and to give to each Bank a legitimate share in the
circulation, is not likely to receive the general sanction of the
Banks; and that a recurrence to the national authority is indispensable for the restoration of a national currency. Such was the
contemporaneous and deliberate opinion of the officers of the government, who had to struggle against the difficulties of a paper
currency, not only depreciated, but varying in value from day to
day and from place to place.

"It was not till after the organization of the Bank of the United
States, in the latter part of January, 1817, that delegates from the
Banks of New York, Philadelphia, Baltimore, and Virginia assembled in Philadelphia for the purpose of agreeing to a general and
simultaneous resumption of specie payments. A compact proposed
by the Bank of the United States, acceded to by the State Banks,
and ratified by the Secretary of the Treasury, was the result of that
convention. The State Banks engaged to commence and continue
specie payments, on various conditions relative to the transfer and
payment of the public balances on their books, to the Bank of the
United States, and to the sum which it engaged previously to discount for individuals, or, under certain contingencies, for the said
Banks; and also with the express stipulation, that the Bank of the
United States, upon any emergency which might menace the credit of
any of the said Banks, would contribute its resources to any reasonable
extent in support thereof, confiding in the justice and discretion of
the Banks respectively to circumscribe their affairs within the just
limits indicated by their respective capitals, as soon as the interest
and convenience of the community would admit. To that compact,
which was carried into complete effect, and to the importation of
more than $7,000,000 in specie from abroad by the Bank of the
United States, the community is indebted for the universal restoration of specie payments, and for their having been sustained during
the period of great difficulty, and of unexampled exportation of
specie to China, which immediately ensued. . . .

"Both those advantages were anticipated in the establishment of
the Bank of the United States; and it appears to us that the Bank
fulfils both these conditions. As respects the past, it is a matter of
fact that specie payments were restored, and have been maintained
through the instrumentality of that institution. It gives a complete
guarantee that, under any circumstances, its notes will preserve the
same uniformity which they now possess. Placed under the control
of the General Government; relying for its existence on the correctness, prudence, and skill with which it shall be administered; perpetually watched and occasionally checked by both the Treasury
Department and rival institutions; and without a monopoly, yet
with a capital and resources adequate to the object for which it was
established, — the Bank also affords the strongest security which can
be given with respect to paper, not only for its ultimate solvency,

but also for the uninterrupted soundness of its currency. The statements we have given of its progressive and present situation show how far these expectations have hitherto been realized.

"Those statements also show that the Bank of the United States, wherever its operations have been extended, has effectually checked excessive issues on the part of the State Banks, if not in every instance, certainly in the aggregate. They had been reduced, before the year 1820, from $66,000,000 to less than $40,000,000. At that time, those of the Bank of the United States fell short of $4,000,000. The increased amount required by the increase of population and wealth during the ten ensuing years has been supplied in a much greater proportion by that Bank than by those of the States. With a treble capital, they have added little more than $8,000,000 to their issues. Those of the Bank of the United States were nominally $12,000,000 — in reality about $11,000,000 — greater in November, 1829, than in November, 1819. The whole amount of the paper currency has, during those ten years, increased about 45, and that portion which is issued by the State Banks, only $22\frac{1}{2}$ per cent. We have indeed a proof, not very acceptable perhaps to the Bank, but conclusive of the fact that it has performed the office required of it in that respect. The general complaints, on the part of many of the State Banks, that they are checked and controlled in their operations by the Bank of the United States, — that, to use a common expression, 'it operates as a screw,' — is the best evidence that its general operation is such as had been intended. It was for that very purpose that the Bank was established. We are not, however, aware that a single solvent Bank has been injured by that of the United States, though many have undoubtedly been restrained in the extent of their operations much more than was desirable to them. This is certainly inconvenient to some of the Banks, but in its general effects is a public benefit to the community. . . .

"The manner in which the Bank checks the issue of the State Banks is equally simple and obvious. It consists in receiving the notes of all those which are solvent, and requiring payment from time to time, without suffering the balance due by any to become too large. Those notes on hand, taking the average of the three and a half last years, amount always to about $1,500,000; and the balances due by the Banks in account current (deducting balances due to some), to about $900,000. We think we may say that, on this operation, which requires particular attention and vigilance, and must be carried on with great firmness and due forbearance, depends almost exclusively the stability of the currency of the country."[1]

To overcome the force of the arguments of Mr. Madison and Mr. Gallatin, which carried with them the intelligence and the better sense of the nation, Jackson was driven to a new issue. In the first, the Bank was unconstitutional, and did not accom-

[1] Considerations on the Currency and Banking System of the United States.

plish its objects, — the creation of a currency uniform in value. It was now an institution wholly incompatible with our form of government, the liberties and the moral and material welfare of the people ; and he appealed to them, at the price of every thing they held dear, to come to his aid in putting down " the monster," as he was accustomed to term the Bank. His indictment against it is fully set forth in his final legacy, — his farewell address, — which, in imitation of Washington, he delivered to the country at the close of his official life, a year after the charter of the Bank expired, and passion had time to cool. In this he said, —

" Recent events have proved that the paper-money system of this country may be used as an engine to undermine your free institutions; and those who desire to engross all power in the hands of the few, and to govern by corruption or force, are aware of its power, and prepared to employ it. Your Banks now furnish your only circulating medium, and money is plenty or scarce according to the quantity of notes issued by them. While they have capitals not greatly disproportioned to each other, they are competitors in business, and no one of them can exercise dominion over the rest : and although, in the present state of the currency, these Banks may and do operate injuriously upon the habits of business, the pecuniary concerns, and the moral tone of society, yet, from their number and dispersed situation, they cannot combine for the purposes of political influence ; and, whatever may be the disposition of some of them, their power of mischief must necessarily be confined to a narrow space, and felt only in their immediate neighborhoods.

" But when the charter for the Bank of the United States was obtained from Congress, it perfected the schemes of the paper system, and gave to its advocates the position they have struggled to obtain, from the commencement of the Federal Government to the present hour. The immense capital and peculiar privileges bestowed upon it enabled it to exercise despotic sway over the other Banks in every part of the country. From its superior strength, it could seriously injure, if not destroy, the business of any one of them which might incur its resentment ; and it openly claimed for itself the power of regulating the currency throughout the United States. . . .

" The result of the ill-advised legislation which established this great monopoly was to concentrate the whole moneyed power of the Union, with its boundless means of corruption and its numerous dependents, under the direction and command of one acknowledged head : thus organizing this particular interest as one body, and securing to it unity and concert of action throughout the United States ; and enabling it to bring forward, upon any occasion, its entire and undivided strength to support or defeat any measure of the government. In the hands of this formidable power, thus perfectly organized, was also placed unlimited dominion over the amount of the circulating medium; giving it the power to regulate the value of property and the fruits of labor in every city of the Union, and to bestow property or bring ruin upon any city or section of the country, as might best comport with its own interest or policy.

"We are not left to conjecture how the moneyed power, thus organized, and with such a weapon in its hands, would be likely to use it. The distress and alarm which pervaded and agitated the whole country when the Bank of the United States waged war upon the people, in order to compel them to submit to its demands, cannot yet be forgotten. The ruthless and unsparing temper with which whole cities and communities were oppressed, individuals impoverished and ruined, and a scene of cheerful prosperity suddenly changed into one of gloom and despondency, ought to be indelibly impressed on the memory of the people of the United States. If such was its power in a time of peace, what would it not have been in a season of war, with an enemy at your doors? No nation but the freemen of the United States could have come out victorious from such a contest: yet, if you had not conquered, the government would have passed from the hands of the many to the hands of the few; and this organized money power, from its secret conclave, would have dictated the choice of your highest officers, and compelled you to make peace or war as best suited their own wishes. The forms of your government might, for a time, have remained; but its living spirit would have departed from it. . . .

"It is one of the serious evils of our present system of banking, that it enables one class of society, and that by no means a numerous one, by its control over the currency, to act injuriously upon the interests of all the others, and to exercise more than its just proportion of influence in political affairs. The agricultural, the mechanical, and the laboring classes have little or no share in the direction of the great moneyed corporations; and, from their habits and the nature of their pursuits, they are incapable of forming expensive combinations to act together with united force. Such concert of action may sometimes be produced in a single city, or in a small district of country, by means of personal communications with each other: but they have no regular or active correspondence with those who are engaged in similar pursuits in distant places; they have but little patronage to give to the press, and exercise but a small share of influence over it; they have no crowd of dependents about them, who hope to grow rich without labor, by their countenance and favor, and who are, therefore, always ready to execute their wishes. The planter, the farmer, the mechanic, and the laborer, all know that their success depends upon their own industry and economy, and that they must not expect to become suddenly rich by the fruits of their toil. Yet these classes of society form the great body of the people of the United States; they are the bone and sinew of the country; men who love liberty, and desire nothing but equal rights and equal laws, and who, moreover, hold the great mass of our national wealth, although it is distributed in moderate amounts among the million of freemen who possess it. But, with overwhelming numbers and wealth on their side, they are in constant danger of losing their fair influence in the government, and with difficulty maintain their just rights against the incessant efforts daily made to encroach upon them. The mischief springs from the power which the moneyed interest derives from a paper currency which they are able to control; from the multitude of corporations with exclusive privileges, which they have succeeded in obtaining in the different States, and which are employed altogether for their benefit; and, unless you become more watchful in your States, and check this spirit of monopoly and thirst for exclusive privileges, you will, in the end, find that the most important powers of government have been given or bartered away, and the control over your dearest interests has passed into the hands of these corporations.

"The paper-money system, and its natural associations, — monopoly and exclusive privileges, — have already struck their roots too deep in the soil; and it will require all your efforts to check its further growth, and to eradicate the evil. The men who profit by the abuses, and desire to perpetuate them, will continue to besiege the halls of legislation in the general government, as well as in the States, and will seek, by every artifice, to mislead and deceive the public servants. It is to yourselves that you must look for safety and the means of guarding and perpetuating your free institutions. In your hands is rightfully placed the sovereignty of the country, and to you every one placed in authority is ultimately responsible. It is always in your power to see that the wishes of the people are carried into faithful execution; and their will, when once made known, must sooner or later be obeyed. And while the people remain, as I trust they ever will, uncorrupted and incorruptible, and continue watchful and jealous of their rights, the government is safe, and the cause of freedom will continue to triumph over all its enemies.

"But it will require steady and persevering exertions on your part to rid yourselves of the iniquities and mischiefs of the paper system, and to check the spirit of monopoly and other abuses which have sprung up with it, and of which it is the main support. So many interests are united to resist all reform on this subject, that you must not hope the conflict will be a short one, nor success easy. My humble efforts have not been spared, during my administration of the government, to restore the constitutional currency of gold and silver; and something, I trust, has been done towards the accomplishment of this most desirable object. But enough yet remains to require all your energy and perseverance. The power, however, is in your hands; and the remedy must and will be applied, if you determine upon it."

This was the first deliberate and successful attempt in this country to arouse local and sectional jealousies, to array the agricultural against the manufacturing and commercial classes, labor against capital, and the poor against the rich. Against a demagogue so adroit and unscrupulous, and who in his mastery over the baser instincts of the race has never been excelled, it was perhaps at the time impossible to make headway. His prodigious untruthfulness and falsifications of history would, at the present day, defeat themselves. No assertion could have been more false than that the commercial and manufacturing classes, the managers of its Banks, had, from the foundation of our government, been in desperate league to overthrow the liberties of the nation, and erect an unscrupulous oligarchy upon their ruins, — classes who of all others had the most at stake in their preservation. The success which followed Jackson's attack upon the Bank enables us to understand fully that which followed Jefferson's attack upon Hamilton, as having for his whole purpose the supplanting by a monarchy, of the Republic which, with the single exception of Washington, he contributed most to establish. Hamilton told the people that they required a strong government, as a means of dealing with the refractory elements which existed on every side, — that their lawless instincts were not their proper guide. His eye took in the vast continent upon which only a lodgement had then been made ; and his polity was framed in view of its possession by a people whose sectional jealousies and peculiarities were to be controlled by laws of universal application, supported by adequate provision for their vigorous enforcement. In his presence every indolent, indifferent, incapable, and lawless nature stood rebuked, and instinctively rallied itself around the banner of his great enemy and rival. All excellence that rises much above the ordinary level is a dangerous possession, especially when it assumes to direct and control weaker or baser natures than its own. By dextrous appeals to the passions and prejudices of the people, Jefferson persuaded them that Hamilton, by opposing license, was an enemy of civil liberty. Under such a charge, which came to be considered as proved, — under such a load of obloquy, his memory rested till the War of the Rebellion. Till then Jefferson was the demigod of the nation. By that event was he completely dethroned. Then for the first time had Hamilton a standing in the court of the nation, a right even to be heard. Jefferson then took the place of Hamilton, to receive in full measure, from being all the more deserved, the obloquy and disgrace which he had heaped upon the latter.   The event of the war has been equally fatal to Jackson.   Jefferson, typifying ideas, held his place so long as these remained in the ascendant. Jackson's attack upon the Banks, and upon the commercial classes, was simply an outburst of passion and hate, hardly fitted to survive the moment of its expression.   The political reputation which he enjoyed, he derived largely from the founder of the dynasty of which he was a conspicuous member, — a dynasty which, it is to be hoped, is for ever overthrown.

Who are, or rather who were, the dangerous classes in this country, — those most to be feared during the epoch of Jacksonism?   The whites of the South and South-west, whose moral sense had been subverted by their "peculiar institution;" who, drawing their subsistence chiefly from the soil they occupied, had the least at stake in the maintenance of social and political order; whose vanity and sectional jealousies had, from the foundation of the government, been so flattered by demagogues that they came to regard their lawless instincts as the highest expression of political and social wisdom; who, from their isolation, could see nothing better in the world than their own experience; who regarded the least restraint imposed by others to be tyranny, to be resisted by the extremest means, and who stood ready to renounce their allegiance to the general government the moment it came to be administered by those entertaining sentiments different from their own.   The fate of such a people, unless rescued from their condition, is either to become the victims of despotism, or, like those of Mexico, to lose the coherence necessary to the existence of any efficient and stable form of government. Such, down to the close of the war of the Rebellion, were the dangerous classes in the United States.   We are now in a position to take a retrospect of the past, and to determine accurately the relation of Jefferson and Jackson, and the political school of which they were the most conspicuous representatives, to the great crisis, the result of which is to effect a radical change in the policy of our government and the character of our people.   We have passed through a great revolution, in which social order was overturned, the industries and commerce of the country for a time destroyed, and innumerable lives sacrificed, upon pretexts no more to be justified than resistance to restraints imposed upon any lawless passion or act.

Who, at the time of which we are speaking, were the least dangerous classes, — in other words, who were the great conservators of the peace and order of society ? Merchants, manufacturers and bankers, who always had the greater part of what they possessed in the hands of the public, and who suffered from the slightest social or political disturbance. A commercial people are necessarily pacific and orderly. Such have been throughout history the upholders of freedom, as production and trade are in ratio to the degree in which this is enjoyed.

The preceding remarks will find complete confirmation in an examination of the methods and operations of the Bank of the United States. It established branches in all the more important towns of the country. · Wherever established, they received the notes and credits of all the State Banks in good standing, both on deposit and in the payment of their bills, as a means of increasing the amount of their loanable capital. Without such deposits, there would be no inducement to their establishment, as without them their profits would not equal the ordinary rates of interest on their own capital employed. The greater the degree of the general welfare, the greater would be the amount of their deposits, the greater their loans, and the greater the certainty of their payment. The healthier the condition of production and trade, the greater the profit, has come to be an axiom among men of affairs. · It is for the interest of great institutions, like the Bank of England and the Bank of the United States, to sustain all smaller ones. They cannot oppress them, so long as the latter are adequately managed. A Bank with a capital of $100,000 may be just as strong in ratio to its liabilities as a Bank of $100,000,000. Each are equally independent and each equally at the mercy of the other. As the money in which the Bank of the United States dealt was largely created by smaller Banks and bankers, it was always for its interest that it should have an actual equal to its nominal value : otherwise it might directly lose by taking it. It was for its interest that every Bank should remain in a sound condition. If any became embarrassed, the bills of merchants would be less promptly paid. These merchants might be the customers of the United States Bank, which might have a portion of the bills that would not be paid under discount. Merchants, manufacturers, and bankers, in fact, constitute one great firm. The loss of one is the loss of all. The loss suffered by any one member will be in ratio to the extent of his operations. As those of the United States, or of its branch, wherever it had one, were usually greater than those of any State Bank, where the former was established, it took the largest share of any loss that might be sustained. It would, consequently, have the same motive for sustaining State Banks as it would for sustaining one of its own customers, and would do all that it could properly do to keep them from failing. If it erred at all, it would, as toward its own customers, always err on the side of leniency. With it, duty, inclination and self-interest would always go together. It would always desire to see an improvement in the morals of a community, as the welfare of the nation would always be in ratio to its good conduct. It would always desire to see it become more intelligent, that its labor might be more profitably employed. It would always desire to see freedom promoted, as the essential condition of production and trade. General Jackson could charge that underwriters would insure rotten ships, or put in command of their risks ignorant, drunken, and dishonest captains and crews, — nay, would set them on fire, knowing that they themselves would have to pay the losses, — with the same reason that he asserted that the managers of the Bank were in conspiracy to destroy the well-being and morality of society. So far from this being the case, there is no morality, using the word in its broadest sense, so high as that of merchants, bankers, and manufacturers, for the reason that, from the elevated positions they occupy, they can see more clearly than others the consequences of any immoral act; and, from the magnitude of their transactions, have vastly more at stake than others in the result.

Early in 1832, four years before it was to expire, the Bank memorialized Congress for an extension of its charter. This application at once brought the controversy to a direct issue. General Jackson not only declared the Bank to be unconstitutional, that its existence was incompatible with the liberties of the country, but that it was insolvent, and an unsafe depository of the public moneys. To these charges, the House of Representatives, in which the administration had a very large majority on other matters, replied, by a vote of 110 to 46, that the public moneys were safe in the Bank; and by a vote of 106 to 84 extending its charter for twenty years. The Senate concurred in the last measure by a vote of 28 to 20. It was promptly vetoed by the President.

As the re-election of General Jackson, with a largely increased majority of the House in his favor, for a second term, which would not expire until after the termination of the charter of the Bank, precluded all expectation of its renewal, the necessity of filling up the vacuum which was so soon to be created by the withdrawal of $35,000,000 of banking capital, of $21,355,724 of notes, and $22,671,431 of deposits, making a total circulation of $44,027,155, — equalling fully one-third of the amount of that of all the Banks in the country, — necessarily attracted the attention of the legislatures of the several States. It was natural that each one should feel called upon to make provision for a portion of the capital and circulation that were so soon to be withdrawn. In this way, without perception of its process, a sentiment in favor of the creation of Banks got hold of the community, — a sentiment of all others the most to be dreaded, for the reason that their creation to supply an anticipated deficiency of the currency, and not for the purpose of loaning capital, is always attended by the most disastrous consequences. After a people have for a long time been habituated to a sound currency, they are in a condition most favorable for the imposition of an unsound one. The precedents of the past are accepted as a guide for the present, so that adventurers who in such a state of the public mind can obtain authority for the issue of paper money are likely to reap a rich harvest. The currency, from 1826 to 1830, whether furnished by the National or State institutions, had suffered so few fluctuations that its value was assumed as a matter of course. In 1830, there were 329 Banks, including the National one, in operation in the country, having a share capital equalling $145,192,268. Their note circulation, at the time, equalled $61,328,898 ; their deposits, $55,559,928 : making a total circulation of $116,888,826. The number of Banks in the United States on the 1st of January,

1820, equalled 307; their share capital $137,110,641; their note circulation, $44,863,344; their deposits, $35,950,479: making a total circulation of $80,813,823. The rate of increase of the number of Banks in the ten years equalled 7 per cent; that of their capital, 6 per cent; that of their circulation, including notes and deposits, 47 per cent. The rate of increase of the circulation undoubtedly corresponded very nearly to that of the production and trade of the country. It is a significant fact in favor of the general soundness, that this increase was not accompanied by any considerable increase in the number of Banks, or in the amount of their nominal capital. The increased demand for money was met by the existing institutions, by an increase of their reserves. So long as this is the case, the money market will always be in great measure free from disturbance. Those who supply the banking accommodations, so long as they are not distracted or interfered with by any new or hostile elements, will always proportion their operations to their means. Their nominal may have no relation whatever to their available capital. The rapid creation of new Banks is always followed by great monetary disturbances, for the reason that their issues do not proceed regularly and normally, bearing a proper relation to the wants of the public, but to the real or fancied interests of those who control them.

There are no means of ascertaining the rate of increase of the number, capital, and operations of the Banks from Jan. 1, 1830, to Jan. 1, 1834. We are indebted to Mr. Gallatin's "Considerations on the Currency" for their number, capital, and circulation, at the former date. His estimates, which were made with great care, are probably very near the mark. In 1832, Congress directed the Secretary of the Treasury to procure and publish, annually, statements of the number of Banks in each State, with the amount of their capital, and of the nature and extent of their operations. The returns first obtained and published were those which represented their number and condition on the 1st of January, 1834. Since that time, similar statements have been annually made. At the date last named, the number of Banks in operation equalled 506, against 329 on the 1st day of January, 1830, — the time that General Jackson began his attack upon the United States Bank, and his "experiments for the reformation of the currency." The rate of increase in their number during the four years equalled 53 per cent. The amount of their capital increased, in the same time, from $145,192,268 to $200,005,944, or at the rate of 37.7 per cent. Their circulation increased from $61,328,878 to $94,839,570, or at the rate of 54.6 ; their deposits, from $55,559,928 to $75,666,986, or at the rate of 36.2 per cent. The increase of their circulation, including notes and deposits, equalled 45.2 per cent. The preceding statements show the magnitude of the inflation which had taken place so early as Jan. 1, 1834. The period from 1830 to 1834 was distinguished by no remarkable advance in the industries or commerce of the country. It is not probable that any greater rate was required from 1830 to 1834 than from 1820 to 1830. At the rate of increase during the latter period, the number of Banks which would have been in operation on the 1st day of January, 1834, would have been 338 ; their share capital, $151,190,380 ; their note circulation, $70,330,348 ; their deposits, $63,404,856. The excess of increase in the number of the Banks equalled 168 ; of their capital, $48,815,664 ; of their note circulation, $24,509,222 ; of their deposits, $12,262,130. It will be seen that the excess of circulation was in great part made up of notes. The inflation must in a great measure have been caused by new Banks, which were set on foot mostly in small towns. The circulation of such necessarily consisted of notes.

The inflation, which began so soon as it was seen that the attack upon the Bank might succeed, became excessive in the early part of 1833. It was then in a condition to be greatly affected by any untoward event. This speedily came, in October of that year, in the order for the removal of the public moneys then held by the Bank, on deposit, to the amount of about $10,000,000. The transfer at that time of so large a sum from one institution to others could not have taken place without creating great disturbance, even had the act been a perfectly legal and proper one. As it was considered highly revolutionary as well as injurious, a great shock was given to public confidence, and great monetary stringency was the necessary result. People did not dare to lend, or Banks to discount, till matters assumed a more satisfactory shape. The act was strongly opposed by the best men of the President's own party. Both Mr. Van Buren and Mr. Wright believed it was ill-advised, and doubted its legality. Mr. Duane, then

Secretary of the Treasury, refused to execute the order of the President. He was removed, and his place filled by a more supple tool, who was in time further rewarded for his servility, by being made Chief Justice of the Supreme Court of the United States. This appointment was undoubtedly made in view of the reversal, should occasion offer, of the decisions of Judge Marshall affirming the constitutionality of the Bank; and of the establishment, by judicial authority, of the doctrines of Mr. Jefferson as to the nature of our government.

As great distress everywhere followed the removal of the deposits, delegation after delegation, representing the various interests of the country, waited upon the President, to state their condition, and solicit his favorable action. As the removal was his act, the distress complained of was in a measure charged upon him; and as he was influenced in all he had done by no higher motive than to gratify an old pique, or to revenge himself upon the Bank for having stood in the way of rewarding his partisans,[1] he could not conceive these delegations to

[1] To find places for the hungry crew that followed in his train, General Jackson, soon after his accession, sought to procure the removal of Mr. Jeremiah Mason from the presidency of the branch Bank at Portsmouth, New Hampshire. The charges made against Mr. Mason were that " small and safe loans had been refused to business men in Portsmouth, while at the same time large sums were located out of the State at greater risks." These charges were examined into by the parent Bank, and found to be utterly groundless. The evidence seemed entirely satisfactory to the Secretary of the Treasury. Not so to General Jackson : he was determined upon revenge. Mason was an " old Federalist," for whom Isaac Hill, a famous New Hampshire politician holding an important office under government, and one of General Jackson's most trusted advisers, entertained the greatest hatred. He inflamed the mind of the President with artful representations that the action of the Bank in this matter was evidence of a great combination of capitalists, headed by the Bank, in opposition to him : —

" That the reader," says Parton, " may see the movements of this gentleman," [Isaac Hill] " as they appeared to General Jackson, and that he may fully understand the process by which the administration were brought into collision with the parent Bank, I will present here a brief condensation of the papers and letters relating to the Portsmouth affair, in the order in which they were produced. The correspondence began in June, and ended in October. I believe myself warranted in the positive assertion, that this correspondence relating to the desired removal of Jeremiah Mason was the direct and real cause of the destruction of the Bank. If the Bank had been complaisant enough to remove a faithful servant, General Jackson, I am convinced, would never have opposed the rechartering of the institution." — Life of General Jackson, by James Parton, vol. iii. p. 260.

An earlier affront, undoubtedly, still rankled in General Jackson's bosom : —

" An incident," to quote further from Parton, " occurred during the stay of General Jackson at New Orleans, which was afterwards supposed to have made

be governed by any higher motives than his own. He regarded all presentations of the conditions of the country as insults to himself, and was prompt to repay them in kind. Among the delegations was one representing the bankers and merchants of New York, having upon it six thousand names, asking that the deposits might be restored. This delegation was headed by Mr. James G. King, of New York, — a man of the highest respectability and character, and of stately manners; whose consequence was not a little increased by being a son of the celebrated Rufus King, — one of the most honored in the catalogue of our great names. The following description of the reception with which this delegation met is taken from Parton's Life of Jackson : —

" The adventures of one of these deputations, a friendly inform-ant, who witnessed their interview with the President, enables me to relate. The petition of the New York merchants, bearing six thousand signatures, was intrusted to the care of a deputation of great bankers and great merchants, headed by Mr. James G. King. When these worthy gentlemen entered the office of the President, at the White House, they discovered him seated at a table writing, with a long pipe in his mouth, which rested on the table, and re-vealed the intensity of the President's interest in his work by the volumes of smoke which gushed from its blackened bowl.

"'Excuse me a moment, gentlemen,' said the President, half rising, and bowing to the group. ' Have the goodness to be seated.'

"In a few minutes he pushed back his paper, rose, and said, —

"' Now, gentlemen, what is your pleasure with me?'

"The members of the deputation were introduced to the Presi-dent by the gentleman whose recollections of the scene I am now recording. Mr. King then began, in his usual deliberate and dig-

a lasting impression upon his mind, and to have been a remote cause of import-ant events. He came into collision with the Bank of the United States. Desir-ing to take with him to Florida a sum of money, with which to defray the first expenses of organizing his government, he sent an aid-de-camp to the branch of the United States Bank at New Orleans to learn whether the Bank would ad-vance ten or fifteen thousand dollars on a draft to be drawn by General Jackson upon the Department of State. The messenger returned with the reply, that the branch Bank had no authority to advance money upon drafts. The mother Bank, said the cashier, had expressly forbidden him to negotiate drafts. The aide-de-camp remonstrated, and pointed out the inconvenience that might result from the refusal ; but the cashier was immovable, as he was bound to be." — Life of Andrew Jackson, vol. ii. p. 596.

Such were the causes, or rather the occasion, which led to General Jackson's famous war upon the Bank of the United States, which aroused the fiercest personal and political animosities, and which was so disastrous in its conse-quences to the whole nation. It could never have become such a potent element of strife, but from its relation to the great questions which concerned the nature and powers of the central government.

nified manner, to state the object of the interview; which was to inform the President of the embarrassment under which the merchants of New York were laboring, and to ask such relief as the executive alone was supposed to be able to afford. Mr. King had uttered only a few sentences of the address which he had meditated, when the president interrupted him with an irrelevant question :

"'Mr. King, you are the son of Rufus King, I believe?'

"'I am, sir,' was the reply.

"Whereupon the President broke into a harangue which astonished the grave and reverend seigniors to whom it was addressed.

"'Well, sir,' said the President, 'Rufus King was always a Federalist, and I suppose you take after him. Insolvent, do you say? What do you come to me for, then? Go to Nicholas Biddle. We have no money here, gentlemen. Biddle has all the money. He has millions of specie in his vaults at this moment lying idle, and yet you come to me to save you from breaking. I tell you, gentlemen, it's all politics.'

"He continued to speak in a strain like this for fifteen minutes, denouncing Biddle and the Bank in the manner usual to him, and gradually working himself up to a high degree of excitement. He laid down his pipe; he gesticulated wildly; he walked up and down the room; and finished by declaring, in respectful but unmistakable language, that his purpose was unchangeable, not to restore the deposits. He ceased at length. The deputation, correctly surmising that their mission was a failure, rose to retire, and were dismissed by the President with the utmost politeness. The gentleman who had introduced the deputation left the apartment with them; but was overtaken by a messenger, as he was descending the stairs, who informed him that the President wished him to return. He accordingly went back to the office, where he found the President exulting over the result of the interview. 'Oh! didn't I manage them well?' he exclaimed. The only object of the President in calling him back was to enjoy a chuckle with him over the scene that had transpired."[1]

Such was the manner in which were received delegations composed of the most distinguished and most honored citizens of the republic. Was it strange that other nations should regard our government with disgust and wonder, ignorant of the cause of such brutalities, and of the good which still existed and grew strong by their side?

As the stringency of 1833–34 was not followed by the suspension of specie payments, there was no lack of money so soon as confidence was in a measure restored. After a slight check, a spirit of speculation again seized upon the nation, the

---

[1] Life of Andrew Jackson, vol. iii. pp. 549, 550.

strength of which was strikingly illustrated by the creation, in 1834, of 198 new Banks, whose aggregate capital equalled $31,144,393. The aggregate note circulation of the country increased, during the year, from $94,839,570 to $103,692,495; the deposits, from $75,666,986 to $83,180,365. All this was but a prelude to the mighty movement which was to follow. On the first day of January, 1836, the note circulation of the Banks had reached $140,301,038, and their deposits $115,104,440; making the total increase of circulation $68,632,618 in a single year, — the rate of increase for the year equalling 36.6 per cent. The inflation continued, although with less force, during the following year. On the first day of January, 1837, the number of Banks had increased to 788; their paid-up share capital, to $290,772,091; their note circulation, to $149,185,890; their deposits, to $127,397,185: making the total circulation $276,583,075, against $116,888,826 in · ?30, — the rate of increase in the seven years equalling 1. ? per cent.

The result of this enormous increase of paper money was an extravagance of expenditure never before seen in this country; nor in any other, with the exception of England during the existence of the South Sea Bubble, and of France during that of the Mississippi Scheme. There were, literally, not sufficient objects of expenditure within reach of the people. To provide them, vast importations of foreign goods were made; the amount of these increasing from $108,118,310, in 1833, to $189,980,035, in 1836. After speculation had raised the price of all kinds of merchandise to an extraordinary pitch, it was turned toward landed property, which, throughout the whole country, was carried to prices often exceeding many times its value. There was at the time one great holder of this kind of property, — the United States, — which continued to sell at the old rate of $1.25 the acre. Here seemed to be opened an inexhaustible mine. All that had to be done to realize immediate wealth was to buy at this rate, and sell at prices five or ten fold greater. The consequence was that the sales of land rose from 3,856,227 acres, realizing the sum of $4,972,284, in 1833, to 20,074,870, realizing $25,167,833, in 1836. The receipts from the public lands in 1835 and 1836 equalled the sum of $41,167,637. These immense sales were apparently the only thing that attracted the attention or the apprehensions of the government. In order to check them, it issued, on the 11th of July, 1836, the famous "Specie Circular," which required all payments for lands to be made in specie. This circular had little effect so long as the Banks continued to pay coin, but was one of the potent causes in producing the catastrophe which was already near at hand.[1]

The sales of land and the excessive importations of foreign merchandise increased the revenues of government to an extraordinary degree, although the rates of imposts had been largely reduced in 1832, to induce South Carolina to recede from her threats of nullification, or as a concession for receding from them. The result of this movement was a complete victory on her part. Her grievance was the tariff; to redress which she threatened to draw the sword. Government, instead of enforcing obedience, yielded to her demands, setting the example which proved so fatal when the next great crisis came. From the excess of revenues, derived chiefly from the sale of lands, government found itself in possession of an enormous sum for which it had no use. The public debt had been paid. It was against the ideas and genius of the people to allow large sums to remain idle in the Treasury. These arose chiefly from property belonging to the whole nation. They should be restored to its rightful owners. An Act was accordingly passed, in June, 1836, providing that, after deducting therefrom the sum of $5,000,000, the money that should be found in the Treasury of the United States on the first day of January, 1837, should be deposited with the several States, in ratio to the number of their Senators and Representatives in

---

[1] *Statement showing the Number of Acres of Public Lands sold, and the Amounts received therefor, each Year, from 1829 to 1847, inclusive.*

Years.	Acres.	Amount received.	Years.	Acres.	Amount received.
1829 . . .	1,244,860	$1,572,863	1839 . . .	4,976,382	6,464,556
1830 . . .	1,929,733	2,433,432	1840 . . .	2,236,889	2,789,637
1831 . . .	2,777,856	3,557,023	1841 . . .	1,164,796	1,463,364
1832 . . .	2,462,342	3,115,376	1842 . . .	1,129,217	1,417,972
1833 . . .	3,856,227	4,972,284	1843 . . .	1,605,246	2,016,644
1834 . . .	4,658,218	6,099,981	1844 . . .	1,754,763	2,207,678
1835 . . .	12,864,478	15,999,804	1845 . . .	1,843,527	2,470,308
1836 . . .	20,074,870	25,167,833	1846 . . .	2,263,730	2,969,637
1837 . . .	5,601,103	7,007,523	1847 . . .	2,521,305	3,296,404
1838 . . .	3,414,907	4,305,564			

Congress. The money was nominally deposited for safe-keeping, to be returned whenever it was wanted to defray the expenses of the general government, although no one at the time supposed a dollar of it would ever be. returned. The amount to be deposited was ascertained to be $37,468,859. The deposits were to be made in four equal instalments, — the first on Jan. 1, the second on April 1, the third on June 1, and the last on Oct. 1, 1837. They were all to be made in specie, or its equivalent; and to be paid from the reserves of the deposit Banks, or by the calling in of loans. This Act helped to complete the work begun by the Specie Circular. The Banks were now placed between two fires, — one from specu-lators in the public lands, the other from the States which were to have their proceeds. The demands of both were to be paid in coin. As the deposits received by the States were largely distributed direct to the people, *per capita*, the money paid them was for a long time wholly taken out of the channels of commerce and trade. By desperate efforts, the Banks paid the first two instalments, amounting to $18,735,430. They were by this time exposed to calls from another quarter, — the demands of the foreign trade. The imports for 1836 exceeded the exports by $61,314,975. According to the Economists, the nation was all the richer by this amount. Foreigners, unfortu-nately, found themselves all the poorer by it, and demanded something in return, which the Banks were called upon to provide. The result was, that by the time the second instal-ment of the public revenues was paid, the means of the Banks were so thoroughly exhausted that, in view of the third instalment which was soon due, nothing was left to those of the city of New York, upon whom the whole brunt fell, but to suspend specie payments; which they did on the 10th of May, 1837. All the other Banks in the country followed their example.

As the Banks of the State of New York were the first to suspend, they were, with those of the New England States, the first to resume. As their suspension was a violation of their charters, the legislature relieved them of the penalty by allowing them a year for this purpose. They so diligently improved their time, that they found no difficulty in resum-ing within the period prescribed. The Banks of New England resumed at the same time (May 10, 1838). Those of New Jersey, Pennsylvania, and the States to the South and West, followed their example later in the season ; the United States Bank of the State of Pennsylvania leading the way, by resuming on Aug. 13. Events showed, however, that the resumption of all except those of New York and New England was premature, as they all suspended again in October, 1839, — the Bank of Pennsylvania again leading the way. This Bank resumed, for a short time, early in 1841. Those of New Jersey, Pennsylvania, and the Southern and Western States, resumed gradually, without concert, as they could provide the means. It was not till the beginning of 1843 that the Banks of the country might be said to be fairly upon a specie basis. This was not accomplished, however, until their liabilities were reduced considerably below what those of the Banks were in 1830, thirteen years before ! This fact shows most strikingly the degree of exhaustion to which the country was reduced. The note circulation of the Banks on the first of January, 1843, equalled only $58,563,608; their deposits, $56,168,628 : making a total of $114,732,236, against an aggregate of $276,583,070 in 1836, $170,506,556 in 1833, and $116,883,826 in 1830, when General Jackson began his famous experiments for the reformation of the currency. Had the rate of increase of the circulation from 1820 to 1830 been maintained from 1830 to 1843, the total at the last date would have equalled $197,761,749. There can be no doubt that the rate should have been far greater from 1830 to 1843 than from 1820 to 1830. Had the currency not been interfered with, the amount outstanding Jan. 1, 1843, including deposits, must have been $250,000,000, — an amount more than twice greater than that actually in circulation, and the whole of it the equivalent of coin. What a prodigious perturbation and loss must have resulted from the reduction of the currency, from $276,583,070 to $114,732,236, in the short period of six years ! Thousands of millions would not have sufficed to make it good. The condition of the foreign commerce of the country reflected, in a striking degree, that of its domestic industries and trade. Its imports in 1836 equalled $189,980,035. In 1843, the year after the Banks finally resumed, they equalled only $86,333,398 : the reduction in this period being $103,646,637, or considerably more than one-half. The imports for the decade ending with 1839, during which General Jackson's experiments were going on and the Banks were under suspension, equalled $1,196,410,483; the exports, $1,034,105,475: the excess of exports equalling in value $162,305,008. In the next decade, which was that of the recovery from Jackson's experiments and the disasters which followed, the imports equalled $1,218,341,575; the exports, $1,266,881,619: the excess of exports over imports for this decade equalling $48,540,044. At the close of the last decade, the nation was better off, so far as its foreign commerce was concerned, than it was at the close of the previous one, by $210,845,052! We know that the Economists will assert that it was the worse off by this amount, for the reason that, during the first decade, we got from foreigners merchandise having a value of $162,305,008 greater than we sent them (the difference was our profit); while, during the second decade, we sent them merchandise having a value of $48,540,044 greater than that we received in exchange from them.[1]

When General Jackson came to the Presidency, the currency of the country, as well as its industries and trade, was in an eminently sound and healthy condition. Its paper or sym-

---

[1] *Statement showing the amount of Loans and Discounts, Note Circulation, and Deposits of the Banks, the amount of Imports and Exports of the United States, from 1833 to 1847, inclusive.*

YEARS.	Loans and Discounts.	Note Circulation.	Deposits.	Imports.	Exports.
1833	$324,119,499	$94,839,570	$75,666,986	$108,118,311	$90,140,133
1834	365,163,834	103,692,445	83,081,365	126,521,332	104,336,973
1835	457,506,080	140,301,038	115,104,440	140,897,742	121,693,577
1836	525,115,702	149,185,890	127,397,185	189,980,035	128,663,046
1837	485,631,687	116,338,910	84,691,184	140,989,217	117,419,376
1838	492,278,015	135,170,995	90,240,146	113,717,404	108,486,616
1839	462,896,523	106,968,572	75,696,857	162,092,132	121,028,416
1840	386,487,662	107,290,214	64,890,101	107,141,519	132,085,946
1841	323,957,569	83,734,011	62,408,870	127,946,177	121,851,803
1842	254,544,937	58,563,608	56,168,628	100,162,087	104,691,534
1843	264,905,814	75,167,646	84,550,785	86,338,398	112,461,973
1844	288,617,131	89,608,711	88,020,646	108,435,035	111,200,146
1845	312,114,404	105,552,427	96,913,070	117,254,564	114,654,606
1846	311,282,945	105,519,766	91,792,533	121,691,797	113,648,622
1847	344,476,542	128,506,091	103,226,157	154,998,928	158,648,622

The returns for the Banks made under date of *January* are those for the preceding years. In the above table, they are set down for the year to which they relate, in order to correspond with the years for which the imports and exports are given.

bolic money equalled about $9 per head of its population. The ratio of the coin reserves of its Banks to their liabilities equalled nearly 20 per cent. During his administration, the number of the Banks was increased from 339 to 788. Their issues rose from $9 per head of population to $19 per head, while the coin reserves of the Banks fell from about 20 to about 13 per cent of their liabilities ; the latter being the lowest point reached in the history of the Banks of the country. In assuming to reform the currency, for which he was about as competent as was Attila to write a treatise upon Roman Law, or a critique upon Greek Art, he erected one of the most stupendous, and at the same time one of the most rotten and unsubstantial systems of paper money that the world has yet seen ; upon which, as his perfect work, only two months before its fall, which was to involve a nation in ruin, he pronounced his benediction; craving that, as a faithful public servant having accomplished the mission assigned him, he might now be allowed to pass on in peace to his final rest. After the explosion, eight long years were required to restore the condition of the country to the financial soundness, but by no means to the degree of prosperity, in which he found it. Before specie payment could be wholly resumed, the currency, which when he became President equalled $9 per head of population, had to be reduced to $4.50 per head. In a period of profound peace, he brought upon the country all the waste incident to a prolonged war ; and still greater evils in setting the first example of prostituting the patronage of government as the reward of political partisanship. The nation has long since recovered from the material injury inflicted upon it, but it has as yet made very little progress in restoring the standard of political purity and decorum, which had been maintained from the formation of the government down to his accession to the Presidency.[1]

[1] " From his home in Tennessee," says Bancroft, " Jackson came to the Presidency, resolved to lift American legislation out of the forms of English legislation, and to place our laws on the currency in harmony with the principles of the Republic. He came to the Presidency of the United States determined to deliver the government from the Bank of the United States, and to restore the regulation of exchanges to the rightful depository of that power, — the commerce of the country."* No doubt, Jackson came, resolved to lift American legislation out of the forms of English legislation ; and he did it most effectually, by substi-

* Bancroft's Miscellaneous Works (Eulogy on General Jackson), p. 471.

The most melancholy part of this retrospect is, that the loss and suffering brought upon the nation, by ignorance, passion and brutality, have not taught a single lesson that has been heeded, nor, so far, produced a single valuable result. The nation is more deeply involved in the meshes of paper money, from which there is no apparent escape, than it has been at any time since the foundation of the government. The very party, or the greater portion of it, that abetted General Jackson in his attack upon the paper-money system of the country are now the chief supporters of that with which the nation is cursed. That we should have learned nothing and gained nothing, or rather that we should be in a more perilous condi-

tuting for the deliberate and decorous forms of that country the pistol, the bludgeon, and the bowie knife. In 1832, Sam Houston, who had previously been Governor of the State of Tennessee, and Representative in Congress from that State, and who was subsequently President of the Republic of Texas and for a long time a United States Senator from that State, was in Washington; and reference having been made to him in the House of Representatives by a member, Mr. William Stanberry of Ohio, as being mixed up with contracts for supplying the Indian rations, he addressed a note to Mr. Stanberry, asking whether the allusion to him had been correctly reported. Mr. Stanberry replied that he would not be called to account for words spoken in his place in the House. Thereupon Houston, who was a man of colossal proportions, waylaid Stanberry, who was a small and feeble man, knocked him down with a bludgeon, and, after beating him to his heart's content, left him, as a United States Senator who was standing by and in sympathy with the act testified, motionless, and he feared, dead. For this act Houston was summoned to the bar of the House for a breach of the privilege of its members. He was zealously defended by Mr. Polk, afterwards President of the United States, on the ground that it was no breach of privilege to waylay and knock down a member of the House for words spoken in debate, provided such act caused no interruption of its proceedings! Mr. Houston was allowed to defend himself in person before the whole House; which he did, not by denying the act, but by maintaining the inalienable right of every freeborn American, where he imagines his honor is assailed, to take the law into his own hands; that to deny this right would be to take away every thing that rendered life dear and valuable. The following are the two last paragraphs of his defence: —

"Sir, when you shall have destroyed the pride of American character, you will have destroyed the brightest jewel that Heaven ever made. You will have drained the purest and the holiest drop which visits the heart of your sages in council, and your heroes in the field. You will have annihilated the principle that must sustain that emblem of the nation's glory, and elevate that emblem above your own exalted seat. These massy columns, with yonder lofty dome, shall sink into one crumbling ruin. Yes, sir, though corruption may have done something, and luxury may have added her seductive powers in endangering the perpetuity of our nation's fair fame, it is these privileges which still induce every American citizen to cling to the institutions of his country, and to look to the assembled representatives of his native land as their best and only safeguard.

"But, sir, so long as that flag shall bear aloft its glittering stars — bearing them amidst the din of battle, and waving them triumphantly above the storms

tion, and understand less than ever the laws of money, after all the experience we have gone through, affords very little comfort or hope for the future.

A few days before the expiration of their charter, the stock-

of the ocean, so long, I trust, shall the rights of American citizens be preserved safe and unimpaired, and transmitted as a sacred legacy from one generation to another, till discord shall wreck the spheres, — the grand march of all time shall cease, — and not one fragment of all creation be left to chafe on the bosom of eternity's waves!"*

In spite of Houston's defence, the House voted by a small majority that a breach had been committed; and he was sentenced to a reprimand, which was administered by the speaker, Mr. Andrew Stevenson of Virginia, in a manner which showed that he applauded, rather than censured, the assault.   Jackson highly approved of it; remarking that, "after a few more examples of the same kind, members of Congress would learn to keep civil tongues in their heads." Although the House voted that Houston deserved censure, they refused to exclude him from a seat on their floor, to which he was entitled as having previously been a member.

Stanberry, who was not killed, only shockingly bruised, not getting much satisfaction from the House, a large number of whose members regarded him as rightly served, had the matter brought before the courts of the district, by which Houston was mulcted in the sum of $500, and ordered into confinement till that sum was paid.   Thereupon Jackson, as President, instantly interposed, remitted the fine, and ordered Houston to be released from custody!†   And this was the man who, Bancroft says in his eulogy, "was imbued with all the great ideas which constitute the moral force of the country"!

So far from coming to Washington, as Bancroft alleges, "for the purpose of restoring the regulation of the exchanges to the rightful depository of their power, — the commerce of the country," — he had about as much idea of this as he had of devoting his presidential term to writing a treatise upon the Talmud. Bancroft applauded Jackson to the echo for his attack upon, and overthrow of, the United States Bank; although, only a short time after the war upon it began, he used the following language in reference to it, in an elaborate article upon Mr. McDuffie's report, published in the "North American Review," of January, 1831: —

"The course pursued by the United States Bank since its incorporation, entitles it to the fairest hearing.   With some exceptions in the earlier part of its career, it has conducted its affairs strictly according to the received principles by which the best Banks in the country are regulated.   It has adopted among its officers many who had acquired experience and established a reputation in the service of older corporations.   It has been supported in its career by the basis of a solid capital; its modes of doing business have been exact, gentlemanly, and accommodating; it has not perverted its excessive and almost irresponsible powers to any purpose of a grasping cupidity, but has rather used them with irreprehensible moderation.   Towards many of the Banks in the West, it has exhibited a fostering kindness; and although it has ample resources to crush any inconsiderable rival, and wreak its vengeance on a feeble enemy, yet it has never, as far as our knowledge extends, attempted to subvert the credit, or even impair the rightful action, of any local institution."

---

* Debates in Congress, 1831–32, vol. viii. part ii. p. 2821.
† This whole affair is fully detailed in Parton's Life of Jackson, vol. iii. p. 388 *et seq.*

holders of the Bank were incorporated by the State of Pennsylvania, under the name of the United States Bank of Pennsylvania. The act was simply a continuation of the Bank under a State, instead of a National, organization. The new Bank suspended specie payment, with the New York Banks, on the 10th of May, 1837. It did not resume with the latter; alleging as a reason the necessity it was under of consulting the interests of the weaker institutions of its State. The true reason, undoubtedly, was its own financial weakness. It contracted to pay the State $5,775,000 for its charter. This was sufficient evidence of the incompetency of its management at the time. The following is the explanation for not resuming with the New York Banks, given by Mr. Biddle, its President, in a letter to John Quincy Adams, under date of April 5, 1838: —

" The credit system of the United States and the exclusively metallic system are now fairly in the field, face to face with each other. One or other must fall. There can be no other issue. It is not a question of correcting errors or reforming abuses, but of absolute destruction; not which shall conquer, but which shall survive. The present struggle, too, must be final. If the Banks resume, and are able by sacrificing the community to continue for a few months, it will be conclusively employed at the next elections to show that the schemes of the Executive are not as destructive as they will prove hereafter. But if they resume, and again are compelled to suspend, the Executive will rejoice at this new triumph, and they will fall in the midst of a universal outcry against their weakness. This is perfectly understood; and accordingly all the influence of the Executive is directed to drive the Banks, by popular outrage and clamor, into a premature resumption, — not a business resumption, general and permanent, but a political and forced resumption, which may place them at the mercy of those in power. They who have special charge of these interests must then beware of being decoyed from their present position. They are now safe and strong, and they should not venture beyond their intrenchments while the enemy is in the plain before them. If they resume, one of two things will happen — their notes will not be received by the government, or they will be received. If they are not received, the government, to the extent of the revenue, will force the holders of the notes to draw specie from the Banks, to be deposited with the collectors of the revenue. For the difference between the revenue and the expenses, the government will issue treasury notes to be sold for bank-notes, and converted into specie; and as the disbursements are made at points on the frontiers remote from the places of collection, it will not return to the Banks issuing it except circuitously. But if the notes are received, they will not as formerly be deposited in Banks, and drawn out again so as to enter into the circulation, leaving the public creditor his choice of specie or notes, but they will be left on special deposit with the receivers. When warrants are drawn on these receivers, they will call on the Banks for specie to pay the favored public creditor, selecting of course the Bank on whom they will draw according to its servility or opposition to the Executive, and thus placing them all under his control. Now, under such circumstances, is it wise for the Banks to disarm themselves in the presence of their enemy ? " [1]

The man who could write such stuff as this had wholly lost his senses, if he ever had any. If the Bank had been as strong as it should have been, it could have defied the hostility of government as well as that of everybody else. All that government could do would be to compel it to discharge the obligations of which it became possessed. It could not come into possession of these without paying the full equivalent therefor. The greater their value, the greater the price to be paid. To refuse to resume for the reason that an enemy was lying in wait, was to refuse to resume from an inability to meet him. Mr. Biddle was never a strong man. He made a competent President until the breaking out of his quarrel with General Jackson. The Bank was then in an eminently sound and healthy condition. But for this quarrel, there is no reason why it should not have remained so. In ordinary times, great abilities were not required of its President. The quality chiefly wanted was good judgment as to the paper offered for discount. Mr. Biddle could not have propitiated General Jackson without a loss of self-respect. Had he yielded to his demands in one instance, he would have been compelled to yield in all; for nothing less than the whole patronage of the Bank would have satisfied the President, and the greedy and remorseless crew that followed in his train. The reasons of the attack were so groundless and absurd that Mr. Biddle believed himself to be wholly master of the situation ; and he was by no means indisposed to measure swords with his great antagonist. The airs he put on were turned most effectively against him. An elegant and unimpressive man was opposed to one who had the most consummate mastery over the passions of his fellows. It was a pigmy in the lists against a giant.

[1] Financial Register, April 5, 1838.

The result was that Biddle daily grew weaker, while his antagonist grew stronger. There was one way, and only one, in which he could have secured the victory : and that was, to tell the country that he had no quarrel in hand ; that he should continue the discharge of his duties as he had discharged them ; and that, if the people did not want the Bank, he should wind it up at the expiration of its charter, return the stockholders their money, and await the wishes of the country. Instead of taking a course so simple, and at the same time so effective, he descended to a personal controversy, in which Jackson could throw more and dirtier mud in an hour than he could throw in a lifetime. The consequence was, that he was speedily driven from the field with a soiled reputation, a soured temper, and a perverted judgment. He was determined that the Bank should not be put down : so he took a charter from the State of Pennsylvania, paying therefor a sum equalling one-sixth of its capital, when he should not have paid a dollar. If the charter had cost him nothing, he would have made a failure in accepting it, from the impossibility of finding in Philadelphia, to which his operations were chiefly to be confined, adequate employment for so large a capital. The total amount of banking capital in that city now equals only $17,135,000, — not one-half that of the United States Bank. As an inevitable result, he was driven into speculations, which took the direction of cotton. The market went heavily against him. Suspending in 1837, the losses he had made in speculations, including the bonus paid the State, had so crippled the resources of the Bank that it was in no condition to resume, which it undertook to do August 15, 1838. This attempt at resumption was only the opportunity of its creditors. They so exhausted its means that it was again compelled to suspend in October of the following year. In obedience to the requirements of the legislature of Pennsylvania, it again attempted to resume on the 15th of January, 1841. A run immediately set in upon it ; and, after losing $6,000,000 of specie, it again suspended, and finally, on the 4th of February, 1841. It was, or rather its assignees were, able to take in its notes and pay off its depositors. Its stock was wholly lost. It by no means fell alone. Elliot, in his " Funding System," gives a tabular statement of 55 Banks, having an aggregate capital of $67,036,265, and a note circulation of $23,577,752, which failed the same year, whose capitals were wholly lost, and whose notes were in great measure a loss to their holders.

One of the most striking illustrations of the monetary history of the time, as well as of the character of the people whom General Jackson led so gallantly to the attack of the United States Bank, is that afforded by the State of Mississippi. That young but ambitious member of the Confederacy, aroused by the General's attack, thought it becoming her interest and dignity to provide a system of her own. In 1830, she chartered the Planters' Bank of Mississippi; which, however, did not get into operation before 1832. In 1833, desirous of giving the Bank the means of making a respectable show in the world, and to enable it to aid in "developing the resources of the State," she issued bonds to it to the amount of $2,000,000, bearing interest at the rate of 6 per cent. These were sold in New York at a premium of 13.25 per cent; realizing an advance of about $250,000, of which the State prudently invested $212,740 in the Bank, increasing her interest in it to $2,212,740. Great success appeared to attend this operation; for, with the money obtained on the bonds, the Bank was for a time enabled to pay the interest accruing on them and mag- nificent dividends. On the 1st of January, 1834, its paid-up capital was reported to be $2,666,805; of which, it appears, the public held $464,065. Its loans and discounts, at that time, equalled $5,461,464; its circulation, $1,510,426; its deposits, $545,353; its specie, $113,220. Encouraged by all this, nine new Banks were chartered that year, which, with the Planters' Bank, reported on the first day of January, 1835, a paid-up capital of $5,890,162; loans and discounts to the amount of $10,379,651; circulation, $2,418,475; deposits, $1,888,762; specie, $359,302. There was a rapid increase in the number and operations of the Banks until 1838, when the State, unwilling to allow the people, individually, to bear off all the emoluments and honors, again entered the field, and chartered the "Union Bank of Mississippi," with a capital of $15,500,000, subscribing thereto $5,000,000; for the payment of which she issued her bonds for a like amount, bearing interest at the rate of 5 per cent. These bonds were sold in Europe, chiefly in Holland, through the agency of the United States Bank, by which the payment of the interest accruing thereon was guaranteed. The bonds realized their par value, which was paid over to the Union Bank, bringing into the State a sum of money of which the like was never before heard of. The Genie of the fable was again let loose. All the Banks of the State did their best to rival the young giant rising in their midst. At the close of 1839, the amount of paid-up capital of the State, including that of the Union Bank, was reported at $30,379,403; the loans and discounts, at $48,333,728; note circulation, at $15,171,639; deposits, at $8,691,601; specie, at $867,977. The free white population of the State at that time numbered about 170,000. The paid-up capital per head of population equalled $180; loans and discounts, $285; circulation, including deposits, $140. Had all been gold, the touch of Midas could hardly have effected more.[1]

While all were gazing in silent wonder upon this meteor, which swept with dazzling brilliancy across the horizon, came a sudden crash, and, for the moment, total darkness. A few

[1] The following statement will show the extent of the banking operations in this State, on Jan. 1, 1840, compared with those of the States of New York, Massachusetts, and Pennsylvania.

STATES.	Free Popul'n	No. of Banks.	Share Capital.	Loans and Discounts.	Note Circulati'n.	Deposits.	Specie.
Mississippi	170,000	26	$30,379,403	$48,333,728	$15,171,639	$8,691,601	$867,977
New York	2,400,000	98	37,101,460	79,313,188	24,198,000	30,883,179	6,857,020
Massachusetts	730,000	117	34,478,110	56,643,172	10,892,249	8,784,516	1,455,230
Pennsylvania	1,700,000	49	23,750,338	44,601,930	13,749,014	12,902,250	3,113,990

The amount of loans and discounts of the Banks of Mississippi equalled $285 per head of free population; their circulation, including deposits, $140 per head. Those of the Banks of the State of New York equalled $30 per head; their circulation, including deposits, equalled $23 per head.

The following statement will show the number, amount of paid-up capital, loans and discounts, note circulation, deposits and specie, of the Banks of the State of Mississippi, from Jan. 1, 1834, to Jan. 1, 1840, inclusive: —

YEARS.	No. of Banks.	Share Capital.	Loans and Discounts.	Note Circulation.	Deposits.	Specie.
1834	1	$2,666,805	$5,461,464	$1,510,426	$545,353	$113.220
1835	10	5,890,162	10,379,651	2,418,475	1,888,762	359,302
1836	13	8,764,550	19,124,977	4,490,521	6,401,518	659,470
1837	18	12,872,815	24,351,414	5,073,425	5.345,384	1,369,457
1838	26	19,231,123	28,999,984	7,472,334	4,638,669	766,360
1840	26	30,379,403	48,333,728	15,171,639	8,691,601	867,977

No returns for 1839 appear to have been made.

fragments, a few pieces of scoria picked up here and there, were all that remained.   The nucleus which was provided by the State bonds served for hardly a mouthful for the rapacious and barbarous crew by which it was seized.   That which appeared to the public was the merest shadow, as vapory and unsubstantial as the trail of a comet.   The $30,000,000 of reported paid-up capital was, with the exception of that borrowed on the bonds of the State, paid in in "stock notes," which were discounted by the Banks, — the proceeds going to pay up their stock subscriptions.   The operation was simply a change in the form of the credits; so that, after the money borrowed on the State bonds was exhausted, nothing remained but entries upon the books and papers, representing indebtedness, from which hardly a dollar was ever realized.   The $48,000,000 of loans were never paid; the $23,000,000 of notes and deposits never redeemed.   The whole system fell, a huge and shapeless wreck, leaving the people of the State very much as they came into the world.   Their condition at the time beggars description. Society was broken up from its very foundations.   Everybody was in debt, without any possible means of payment.   Lands became worthless, for the reason that no one had any money to pay for them.   The only personal property left was slaves, to save which, such numbers of people fled with them from the State, that the common return upon legal processes against debtors was in the very abbreviated form of "G. T. T.," *gone to Texas,* — a State which in this way received a mighty accession to her population.

The interest of the bonds issued to the Planters' Bank was paid by it up to 1840.   That of those issued to the Union Bank were paid by that institution, or by the United States Bank, by which their payment was guaranteed, up to and including Nov. 1, 1840.   That falling due on May 1, 1841, not being paid by either Bank, Messrs. Hope & Company, of Amsterdam, as agents of the bondholders, addressed, on the 22d of May, 1841, a courteous communication to the Governor of the State; calling the delinquencies to his attention, and respectfully urging him to take proper action in the premises. This communication received from him a prompt and characteristic reply; informing Messrs. Hope & Company that his State, in her sovereign capacity, had repudiated payment of her bonds!

The bondholders were not silenced by this communication, for the reason that it was not believed that the action of the Governor would be sanctioned by the people. To get rid of their importunities, which were as annoying as they were urgent, the legislature, in 1841, formally took up the matter, and referred it to a Committee of its own body ; which reported, on the 10th of February, 1842, the payment of the bonds to be incompatible with the honor and dignity of the State. We have room here to give only the last paragraph of the Committee's report : —

"The Committee, in coming to the foregoing conclusion, are aware that they differ from many worthy men in opinion. But they cannot believe that if this subject be examined free from all party influences, and determined by an application of law and morals to the facts, any other conclusions can be arrived at than those which they have adopted. Entertaining, as we believe, mistaken views as to the true principles of this government, as well as of the facts in this case, men have taken the liberty of slandering the State, both at home and abroad, on account of the stand she has taken. It was so at the memorable era when our fathers leagued together and pledged " their lives, their fortunes, and their sacred honor " to resist an unconstitutional invasion of their rights as British subjects. They, also, were slandered. Every opprobrious epithet was heaped upon them that the ingenuity or malice of their enemies could invent. Many of *their* fellow-citizens, under mistaken views of the principles upon which they acted, denounced them as disorganizers, agrarians, and rebels, and joined their enemies to force them into submission to an unconstitutional law. The result of the memorable and eventful contest that ensued is now known. The decision of the civilized world has been had as to the correctness of the principles and conduct of that much abused and slandered, but noble race of men. Through scenes of toil and blood they maintained the position they assumed, and have transmitted to their posterity their principles, together with the rich inheritance of liberty, secured by a well-regulated and constitutional government. Their names are stamped on the page of immortality, and their memory is embalmed in the hearts and affections of a grateful people ; and distant generations will pronounce with exultation the names of Washington, Jefferson, Madison, Hancock, Franklin, and a host of worthies who struggled together through that gloomy period in our history. The people of Mississippi have taken a similar stand. They are not controlled by selfish or mercenary motives. The low and grovelling consideration of dollars and cents has nothing to do with the merits of this question. Their honest obligations they will fulfil, should they have to divest themselves of the comforts and necessaries of life to do so. Higher and holier motives than mere pecuniary acquisitions actuate them. They have determined that they never will submit to an invasion of their Constitution by either foreign or domestic foes. The rights secured to them under that sacred instrument they will maintain at all hazards; and, relying on the correctness of their principles and the justness of their cause, they will with confidence and cheerfulness submit to the verdict of posterity."

Glowing as was the eloquence of this Report, it was fairly eclipsed in a speech delivered in the halls of Congress by Mississippi's favorite son, Mr. Jacob Thompson, then a member of the House, — a man whom his people delighted to honor, and who, from one elevation after another, became under Buchanan, as Secretary of the Interior, one of his cabinet, and serving during his whole term, and till the outbreak of the Rebellion, as one of the chief administrators of the affairs of the nation. In 1842, it became convenient for the United States to borrow a few millions. The question was as to the mode. In the debate which took place in the House upon the subject, the firm of Prime, Ward, & King, of New York, was referred to (Mr. King, one of its members, being the gentleman whom General Jackson so successfully bullied in 1833) as having expressed opinions unfavorable to the negotiation of a loan in Europe, in consequence of the discredit thrown upon American securities by the action of the State of Mississippi. This insinuation brought her gallant son to his feet. He gloried in the act of repudiation, and indignantly hurled back upon its authors the foul stigma sought to be cast upon the fair fame of his State : —

"From the late action of the State of Mississippi," he said, "I feel a renewed, a deeper confidence in the intelligence, the honor, the firmness, and patriotism of that people. Frowned upon at home by those who denied their power to inquire into their rights, denounced and misrepresented by their enemies from abroad, they have gone on in the even tenor of their way, seeking truth and asserting right. And I am now prepared to say to the friends of liberty, of the rights of freemen, of constitutional government, everywhere, Stand firm! be of good cheer! Here is a people who will extend to you sympathy and succor and effective aid. Doubt not their courage, their honor, or their willingness. Let the hour and the necessity come, and Mississippi will go forward, and take as bold a stand in asserting the rights of mankind, in resisting oppression, in vindicating the integrity of constitutions, as any other State in the Union. . . .

"Mississippi has passed through some severe trials. While the credit system was considered a blessing, and others were sipping of its delicious and intoxicating poison, she slaked her thirst with eager haste, and drained the cup to its very dregs. Exhilaration followed; for the hour there was 'the feast of reason and the flow of soul.' The hectic flush upon her cheek was mistaken for the rich crimson of health and beauty. The life currents coursed rapidly through her veins, and gave a charm to being, which cast its rainbow tints on all surrounding nature. She walked in grandeur, — the wonder, the admiration, the envy of all. The excitement grew higher and higher. Flattered and caressed on all sides, she was deemed the fairest of the fair, the loveliest of the lovely, the proudest of the proud. Wherever her citizens travelled abroad, they were the 'observed of all observers.' Each one was considered a hero of princely fortune and princely liberality. The *dealer* in the cities hasted to make his acquaintance, laughed at his wit, aided and connived at him in his prodigality and irregularity, and *quailed* at his frown. But the fatal hour came, — foretold and foreseen, indeed, by some of the wise and considerate, but well-nigh forgotten by all in the general intoxication. Her overstrained nerves gave way, and prostration ensued. Then were seen the awful contortions of the limbs and the wild flushings of the eye, which betokened madness and presaged death. The alarmed executive called together the legislative doctors, and bade them in their wisdom consult, and speedily administer the healing balm, or dissolution was inevitable. They did consult, and they determined that, as the patient was sinking, more stimulant must be procured and speedily applied. The Constitution, the bulwark of the freedom of the citizen, intended to guard his rights in this hour of trial and temptation, stood in the way! With more benevolence than wisdom, they leaped its barriers, and drenched the sufferer with a copious draught of the noxious poison. The disease grew worse, the pains increased, and the writhings were more distressing. At last, the physician's skill and the physician's medicine were exhausted, and no further reliance was placed on artificial means. The patient was told that she must trust for recovery to the strength and vigor of her constitution and natural resources. From that hour she felt more calm and easy, and recovery commenced. The improvement has been slow, but progressive, — still she feels debilitated and enfeebled; but all look forward to an early and complete restoration. The only precaution required in her condition is a total abstinence from that intoxicating poison which caused her disaster. In recurring to the past, she feels mortified and chagrined at her excesses; and, in returning to a state of soundness, her first and highest duty is to herself. Restore a bleeding, prostrate Constitution, which has been trampled under feet. She will

> " ' To her own self be true ;
> And it will follow, as the night the day,
> She cannot then be false to any man.'

"I said I felt prouder of Mississippi this day than I ever felt before. I have seen her people tried, and I know them. Too proud to acknowledge themselves insolvent, too firm and too proud to submit to a violation of their rights, regardless of the strokes of calumniators, they take their stand, and appeal, as our ancestors did, to a candid world and an impartial posterity for support. Every true-hearted Mississippian feels proud of his State. She has forty thousand freemen who are ready to risk all, to sacrifice every thing, for her honor and her rights. Warmed by a Southern sun, fanned by a Southern breeze, fed upon a generous soil, our hearts are entwined around our noble State, and we 'grapple her to our bosom with hooks of steel.' We love Mississippi, our sovereign mistress, to whom we owe fealty and obedience; for her we would live, and for her sake we would not refuse to die. It is praise enough to satisfy the ambition of a common man, tread where he may, to feel and to say, 'Mississippi is my home.'"

But the end was not yet. The holders of the bonds issued to the Union Bank, by dint of importunity obtained authority to try the question of their constitutionality in the highest legal tribunal of the State. This court affirmed the constitutionality of the Act issuing them, and that they were binding obligations on the State. As no execution could issue against her, all that the bondholders took by their proceedings was a bootless decision in their favor. The holders of the bonds issued by the Planter's Bank, the constitutionality of the issue of which was never questioned, were equally persistent in their efforts for redress. They obtained from the legislature of the State so late as 1853, twelve years after default in payment of interest, an Act referring the question of their payment to the people. These "rose in their majesty," to quote the language which reported their great achievement, and voted that the bonds should not be paid! Having exhausted all remedies open to them in the legislature of the State, as well as in the courts of conscience and law, the unlucky holders of both classes of bonds, seeing nothing in store for them but continued losses and insults, slowly and sullenly retired from the contest.

As all the States chartered Banks, there were as many systems — if such a word may be used — in the country as there were States. There was, however, nothing deserving the name, with the exception of that of the Suffolk Bank. Charters were to be had in nearly all the States, upon the application of proper parties. In most of them, no provision was made for the security of their note-holders, other than their share capital. A greater or less proportion of this was held as reserves, according to the

1 Cong. Globe, Appendix, 3d sess. 27 Cong., p. 177.

location of the Bank, and the kind of business which it transacted. The first attempt at any thing like a system, provided
by the legislature of Massachusetts, was the passage, in 1829,
of a law which provided that no Bank should go into operation
unless 50 per cent of its capital were paid in in coin; and
that no Bank should issue notes exceeding in amount 25 per
cent of its share capital. Its liabilities of all kinds, excepting
deposits, were not to exceed twice the amount of its capital.
Such provisions, however, amounted to little, for the reason
that, a considerable portion of their loans being in the form of
credits, the Banks had no motive to issue larger amounts of
notes than their capital. As no provision was made for the
amount of reserves to be held, the coin to set a Bank in motion
could be purchased, and sold immediately after it got into
operation. The guarantee for the proper management of the
• Banks of this State, as well as the New England States, whose
laws were largely copied from those of the former, was the
(Suffolk Bank) system of redemption which has already been
sufficiently described. This system provided the safest and
best currency of the kind ever issued.

The State of New York, from time to time, had created
Banks by special charters. These were established almost
wholly in New York City, and in the leading towns upon the
Hudson. To meet the necessity for new Banks in the interior,
the State, in 1829, established what was called the " safety-
fund system," which authorized to the Banks created under it
the issue of notes equalling twice the amount of their paid-up
capital, and allowed them to make loans to twice and a half its
amount. As security for the holders of the notes, every Bank
which was to be organized thereafter, or whose charter was to
be extended (a large number expiring in 1829), was required
to pay, annually, to the treasurer of the State a sum equal to
one-half of 1 per cent upon its share capital, — these payments
to continue till each Bank had paid a sum equalling 3 per cent
upon its share capital; the amounts so paid to be held as a
common fund for the discharge of notes or other liabilities of
any Bank included in the system. If this fund, from any
cause, became diminished, it was to be made good in manner
already described. In 1841–42, 11 of the safety-fund Banks
failed; making a loss to their creditors of $2,558,933. The

fund at this time equalled only $86,274.   The whole amount contributed to it up to Sept. 30, 1848, equalled only $1,876,063. The balance of the loss was provided for by the State, which was to be reimbursed by further additions to the fund.   In 1842, the Act was so amended that the fund became chargeable only with the losses to the public on the note circulation, which greatly reduced the present or prospective charge upon it. In 1838, this State established what was called the "free-banking system," by which banking associations could be formed without application to the legislature. These associations were required to deposit with the Comptroller of the State stocks of the United States, or of the several States, which should be equivalent, in interest, to a 5 per cent stock; or bonds and mortgages upon improved real estate having a value of twice the sum secured, equal in amount to their note circulation.   Upon such deposit the Comptroller was to issue a corresponding amount of notes.   This was nothing less than a system founded upon securities or real property.   The result was, that previous to 1843, 29 of these Banks failed, having an aggregate circulation of $1,233,374.   The nominal value of the securities deposited for their circulation amounted to $1,555,338.   They produced, on their sale, in winding up the Banks, only $953,371, — a sum equalling only 74 per cent of their circulation.   The law was thereupon amended so as to exclude all stocks except those of the United States and of the State of New York, which were required to be the equivalent of 6 per cent stocks.   A wiser provision had been adopted in 1840, requiring all the Banks of the State to redeem their notes, either in New York City, Albany, or Troy, at a discount of one-half of 1 per cent.   In 1851, this discount was reduced to one-quarter of 1 per cent.   After the passage of the Act of 1851, two of the principal Banks of the City of New York undertook to establish for the State a system somewhat similar to the Suffolk Bank system of New England.   The notes of such of the country Banks as kept deposits with them were returned, — the redeeming Banks dividing the discount between themselves and the issuers.   This system, though by no means perfect, exerted a very salutary influence by forcing constant redemption of issues, and in keeping the currency down to the necessities and wants of the people.   After 1838, no more safety-fund Banks were chartered, and that system went gradually out of existence. In 1846, the amended constitution of the State took away from the legislature " all power to pass any Act granting any special charter for banking purposes," and provided that corporations or associations might be formed for such purposes under general laws. The amended constitution also provided, that, after the year 1850, stockholders of Banks should be liable to the amount of their shares for all debts and liabilities of every kind ; and that, in case of insolvency, the holders of notes should have a preference in payment over all other creditors.

The State of Ohio affords another pertinent illustration of the system, or want of system, which has prevailed in this country, in the creation and management of Banks. In 1808, she chartered a Bank at Marietta, with a capital of $500,000, and another at Chillicothe, with a capital of $100,000. From 1809 to 1816, 4 more Banks were chartered. In 1816, 6 Banks were chartered, having an aggregate capital of $1,600,000. From 1811 to 1832, 11 Banks were chartered, with an aggregate capital of $2,700,000. In 1833, the Franklin Bank at Cincinnati, with a capital of $1,000,000, was chartered ; and in 1834, the Ohio Life and Trust Company, with a capital of $1,000,000. Only a part of these Banks went into operation. There does not appear to have been any special provision made to secure their circulation. The number of them in operation on the 1st of January, 1835, was 24. Their aggregate share capital equalled $5,819,692 ; their circulation, $5,221,520 ; their deposits, $2,090,065; their loans and discounts, $9,751,973. From this time they increased rapidly, in consequence of the mania created by General Jackson's attack upon the United States Bank. In 1837, there were 32 in operation having a share capital of $9,247,296 ; circulation, $8,326,974 ; deposits, $7,590,933 ; loans and discounts, $18,178,699. They all suspended in May, 1837. The system had so little real foundation that most of the Banks went out of existence, — the number in 1844, the year after the Banks of the country resumed, being only 8, — their share capital being reduced to $2,167,628 ; their note circulation, to $2,246,999 ; their deposits, $505,430; their loans and discounts, $2,968,441 ! The reduction of their loans and discounts, equalling $15,210,258 in a period of seven years, shows the enormous inflation under

Jackson's experiment, and the tremendous penalty that was paid, in the almost total annihilation of the proper instruments of distribution. Ohio recovered but little till after 1845, when she established the State Bank, with a capital of $6,150,000, with authority to establish 63 branches, — the whole to be managed by a Board of Control of one member from each branch. The capital for each was to be supplied where it was established. The system was made liable for the losses of all. To provide therefor each branch was to deposit with the Board of Control a sum equalling 10 per cent of the notes issued to it, in stocks of the State, or the United States ; or bonds and mortgages upon productive real estate, having a value of twice the amount secured thereby, and payable on demand to the board. In case of failure, the stock and bonds of the insolvent Bank were first to be applied to the discharge of its notes, before any of the fund contributed by the other Banks could be called upon. The capital was allotted to various parts of the State, which, for this purpose, was divided into twelve districts. The five Banks previously chartered, and then in operation in this State, were allowed to avail themselves of the privileges of the Act. The notes for circulation were to be issued by the Board of Control, and were limited to double the amount of capital on the first $100,000 ; to one and one-half the amount on the second $100,000, or any part thereof ; and to one and one-quarter the amount upon the third $100,000, or any part thereof. Of these Banks, 36 were in operation in 1856, having a capital of $4,034,524, and a circulation of $7,112,320. At that time, the Ohio Life and Trust Company was the only one of the old Banks remaining in operation. The Act of 1845 also authorized the formation of Banks independent of the State Bank. These, however, were to secure their circulation by deposits of the stock of the United States or of the State. Of these Banks, 9 were in operation in 1856, — having a capital of $587,500, and a circulation of $893,839.

In 1851, a system of free banking was authorized, whose circulation was to be secured by a pledge of the United States, or Ohio State bonds. Of these, 10 were in operation in 1856 ; having a capital of $738,050, and a circulation of $769,397. In 1852, the revised Constitution of the State provided that no new Banks should be created by the legislature, unless sanctioned by the people at the next general election. In 1854, there were in operation in Ohio, four distinct classes of Banks: those incorporated prior to 1845, having a capital of $1,550,000; the State Bank and its branches, having a capital of $4,100,000; the independent Banks, created under the safety-fund system, having a capital of $720,000; and the free Banks, created under the Act of 1851, having a capital of $695,000. Most of the Banks organized under the Act of 1851 were gradually driven out of existence by excessive taxation. In 1856, the Act of 1845, incorporating the State Bank and branches, was extended to May, 1877. That Act forbade any higher rate of taxation upon banking than upon any other kind of capital.

The creation of the State Bank and its branches contributed greatly to restore the finances of the State and the people, although all safety-fund systems are radically vicious. No Bank, except, perhaps, a National Bank, should be required to hold securities against its circulation. Whatever means Banks possess over and above that provided by their bills, should always be in the form of coin, or the equivalent of coin, to be held as reserves. The provision for the retirement of the notes and credits should be their bills. Where other provision is made, the inference is unavoidable, that notes may be properly issued upon it, and will circulate by virtue thereof, — an inference fatal to all sound banking.

In contrast with the safety-fund system of Ohio, and in fact with all systems of the kind, was that which, for a long time, prevailed in the adjoining State, Indiana. That State, in 1834, established the State Bank of Indiana, the capital of which was almost wholly borrowed from abroad, chiefly on the bonds of the State. The Bank, starting with adequate means, fortunately fell into competent and upright hands. It enjoyed, for the twenty years of its existence, uninterrupted success. It did not even suspend specie payments in the great crisis of 1837. Owing government, as one of the deposit Banks, at the time, something over $1,000,000, it promptly paid the amount in coin. During the whole trying period of the suspension, which in the West lasted several years, with a capital of only about $2,500,000, it usually maintained coin reserves equalling $1,000,000. These, for several years after the Bank went into operation, equalled 60 per cent of its note circulation. It was for a long time a bright spot in a vast desert of incompetency and ruin. Had it been a safety-fund Bank, with its means locked up in securities, for the alleged protection of its note holders, it would necessarily have followed in the wake of all the Western systems, and ended, perhaps, in bankruptcy; involving an enormous loss to the holders of its notes, even if they had been finally redeemed. As it was, it always had its means in hand for any emergency; securing, at the same time, the confidence of the public, which prevented any runs upon it for coin. The management of this Bank is probably the best subject for study of any instance of the kind in the country. It was in a new State, in which a high degree of mercantile training and experience is not to be expected, and in which it is always difficult for Banks to resist the importunities of their customers. Conducting its operations on strictly business principles, discounting no paper but such as represented actual transactions in merchandise, it supplied, during the whole period of its existence, and without embarrassment, a currency very nearly uniform in amount, and always of the value of coin. In the great contraction which took place between 1837 and 1843, the loans and discounts of the Banks of Ohio fell off from $18,178,699 to $2,968,441; while those of the Banks of Indiana, chiefly of the State Bank and its branches, only fell off from $3,179,271 to $2,677,530. In the same period, the note circulation of the Ohio Banks fell off from $8,329,974 to $1,911,983, while that of those of the State of Indiana only fell off from $1,970,595 to $1,828,371. The operations of her State Bank are a striking illustration of the correctness of the principles laid down in this work, and are carefully to be considered in the provision of any system for the country in the future. Its charter expired in 1854. It was then wound up, returning to the shareholders their capital, with a very large addition in accumulated profits. A new State Bank was created in its place, with a capital of $6,000,000, with the right to establish numerous branches. It was managed with the same ability as was the old Bank, and did not suspend specie payments in 1857, as the old one did not in 1837. In 1862, when it became a National Bank, its capital equalled $3,354,200; its circulation, $5,559,467; its deposits, $1,723,624; its loans and discounts, $4,007,990; its specie,

$3,284,696. It was then, probably, in a stronger position than any other Bank in the country.

There is another side to the picture of the management of Banks in this State, by no means so agreeable. In 1851, the new Constitution forbade the creation of Banks except by general laws. In 1852, an Act was passed, providing for the issue, by the proper authorities, on the deposit by any banking association of the stock of the United States, or of the several States, of notes for circulation equal to 95 per cent of such stocks, which were, in the matter of interest, to be made equal to 6 per cent stocks. The law did not require either the stockholders or boards of directors to reside in the State. In 1854, 86 of these safety-fund Banks had been established. The returns from 67 of them for that year showed an authorized capital of $32,900,000, and a note circulation of $7,425,000. In 1856, there were 94 of these Banks nominally in existence, of which 53 had failed, their notes selling all the way from 25 to 75 per cent of their nominal value. By these failures, the banking capital of the State was reduced from $7,281,935, in 1855, to $4,045,325, in 1856; the note circulation, from $8,165,856 to $4,516,422. Little was left but the State Bank. The whole safety-fund system gradually went out of existence; not, however, until the people had suffered enormous embarrassment and loss from its operation. The securities deposited, were those of States which were in default, or which speedily were to make default, and which either remained for a long time at a large discount, or proved wholly valueless. The manner in which these Banks were got up and managed is well shown by the following extract from the message of the Governor to the legislature, in 1853 : —

" The speculator comes to Indianapolis with a bundle of bank-notes in one hand and the stock in the other; in twenty-four hours he is on the way to some distant point of the Union, to circulate what he denominates a legal currency authorized by the legislature of Indiana. He has nominally located his Bank in some remote part of the State, difficult of access, where he knows no banking facilities are required, and intends that his notes shall go into the hands of persons who will have no means of demanding their redemption."

The State of Michigan had a similar system, to describe which would be only to repeat the description already given of that of the State of Indiana. In reference to this, the Governor of that State, in his message to the legislature of 1853, says : —

" At present we are giving charters to the issues of Banks about which we actually know nothing, in whose management we have no participation; and are thus literally paying a large tribute for what generally in the end proves to be a great curse."

The States of Illinois and Wisconsin, and in fact many others, had similar systems, followed by similar results. The country was for several years deluged with safety-fund money ; which, from the inflations and consequent contractions which were caused, exerted a most potent influence in bringing about the panic in 1857, and the general suspension of the Banks throughout the country.

As the suspension of specie payments cut the government wholly off from its resources, other than the notes and credits of the deposit Banks, and as these might prove to be in a measure valueless, Congress was called together, with all practicable speed, to consider the situation and provide for the future. An issue of Treasury notes was ordered to be made receivable in payment of the revenues. The collectors and receivers were directed to hold their collections to be drawn against directly by the Treasury. Drafts upon the deposit Banks, in case of their non-payment, were also made receivable in the payment of the revenues. This provision made their negotiation, at a very small discount, comparatively easy. The whole community was in the same condition ; and as creditors were, as a rule, willing to accept the money in circulation, government did not experience any considerable difficulty from the suspension. The third instalment of the public moneys to be deposited with the States, July 1, 1837, was paid in the notes of the suspended Banks. As soon as Congress assembled, the fourth payment, due in October, was directed to be withheld. The most singular feature of this great drama or farce was the instantaneous change of front by the government the moment suspension took place. For eight long years, the great theme which had engrossed its attention and labors was the " reformation of the currency," by measures which called into existence an immense number of State Banks, to be used by adventurers and speculators as the instruments of flooding the country with paper money. Nearly $100,000,000 of worthless stuff was created and thrown upon the market in the short period of four years. No sooner did the whole fabric tumble to the ground, than those who reared it discovered that the only money known to the Constitution was gold and silver. Thenceforth the operations of the government must be wholly severed from Banks of all kinds. It was to consider its own interests, leaving the people to take care of theirs as best they could. The paternal character which it had so long assumed was thrown off with all the ease of a mask. The proposition for the separation of the government from the Banks, again brought the Southern leaders, whose fidelity had been somewhat shaken by the quarrel between Jackson and Calhoun, into full accord with the administration. The new attitude assumed in reference to the Banks was regarded as another step to remove it still further from all consideration of the public welfare. In 1840, the Act creating the Independent Treasury, as it was termed, was passed. By this Act, all the revenues of the government were to be collected into the Treasury in coin, and disbursed from it in coin. In 1842, from a change in the administration, the Act of 1840 was repealed. In 1846, the old party having been restored to power, the Act of 1840 was re-established. This has been continued till the present time. The same Congress that repealed, in 1842, the Act creating the Independent Treasury, also passed a bill for the creation of another — a third Bank of the United States. This bill was vetoed by Mr. Tyler, who succeeded to the Presidency upon the demise of General Harrison. The new President belonged to the most rigid school of "strict" constructionists. The Act establishing the Subtreasury possesses an additional interest, from the relation it bears to the present financial condition of the country. As Mr. Chase found it in operation when he became Secretary of the Treasury under Mr. Lincoln, he, from a singular perversity of temper or judgment, continued it in operation, although especially authorized to dispense with its provisions. By attempting to carry on the enormous expenditures of the War of the Rebellion by means of specie alone, he speedily compelled the Banks that were to furnish it to suspend payment ; leaving government, as he contended, no other alternative than the issue of its notes. By this act, an irredeemable currency became a permanent feature in the monetary system of the country.

As already seen, the greatest depreciation in the operations of the Banks was not reached until 1843. They could resume only by an unprecedented reduction of these liabilities. From that year, a rapid improvement took place. By the first of January, 1847, their loans and discounts had reached $310,282,945; an increase of $55,738,008, in a period of four years. Their note circulation increased to $105,519,766; an increase of $46,956,158. Their deposits reached $91,797,533; an increase of $35,628,905: the aggregate increase of both kinds of circulation equalling $82,585,063. The most favorable feature of this exhibit was a reduction of the share capital of the Banks from $228,861,948 to $203,070,622; showing, after resumption, a constant weeding out of weak institutions. The nominal banking capital of the country was in fact less in 1851 than in 1843: although within the eight years the circulation of the Banks rose from $58,563,608 to $155,165,251; their deposits, from $56,168,628 to $128,957,712; the aggregate increase of the two equalling $169,390,726. Their loans and discounts in the same period arose from $254,444,937 to $413,756,799. The money market is always in the soundest state when the increase of currency is supplied by Banks in existence, — by institutions possessed of capital, training, and experience, which increase their loans to meet the increasing wants of commerce, and increase their reserves as they increase their loans. Their conduct for the present is governed by the precedents of the past. The increase of their operations is perfectly natural, and for this reason excites no attention. Their operations are most carefully directed, as they are more solicitous about the preservation of their capital than about their dividends. A rapid increase in the number of Banks is always to be regarded as a signal of danger; as a part of them will always be got up for the purpose of imposing a worthless currency upon the public, while another part, though managed with integrity, are liable for a time to be managed improvidently.

The year 1847, from the potato blight in Ireland and the failure of crops in England, brought unprecedented amounts of specie into the country, and gave a great impulse to its affairs. The people were then just entering upon the construction of railways, which now cover the whole country like a net-work, and which, while absorbing vast amounts of capital, contributed enormously to its wealth. In 1848 came the great discoveries in California, which at once placed this country in the first rank among the gold-producing nations of the world. In 1854, the banking movement received an extraordinary impulse, 458 new Banks having been created that year, the increase of their share capital equalling $93,467,552; that of their circulation, $58,616,427; of their deposits, $42,634,868; of their loans and discounts, $148,454,021. This upward movement was followed by a considerable reduction in the circulation the following year. The check, however, was only temporary. On the first day of January, 1857, the note circulation of the Banks reached the enormous sum of $214,778,822; their deposits, $230,351,312. The inflation was excessive; and the Banks, by the necessary recoil, were compelled, on the 13th of October of that year, to suspend specie payments. Various expedients were resorted to, to alleviate the pressure. The legislature of the State of Pennsylvania authorized her Banks to continue in suspension till the following May. The Secretary of the United States Treasury ordered the purchase of considerable amounts of bonds, in order to throw money into circulation. The legislature of the State of New York refused to grant any indulgence to her Banks. The judges of her Supreme Court, however, upon consultation, decided that they would not issue injunctions against any Bank in default, except at the suggestion of insolvency or fraud. The means of the Banks of New York City were so little impaired, that they resumed specie payments on the 14th of December of the same year. Their notes upon the day following the suspension were at hardly any discount. No difficulty was found in obtaining all the gold that was wanted. The New England Banks resumed simultaneously with those of New York City. Those of the rest of the country followed as they could provide the means. Resumption, however, was not accomplished without an enormous reduction in the liabilities of the Banks. Their note circulation, on the first day of January, 1858, equalled only $155,208,344, against $214,778,822, on the first day of January of the preceding year. Their deposits fell off to $185,932,049, against $230,351,312. The aggregate reduction in their circulation and deposits during the year equalled $103,987,741; the reduction being nearly twenty-five per cent. Their great strength, however, was shown by the rapidity with which they recovered their position; the aggregate of their notes and deposits for 1859 equalling $452,875,196, against an aggregate of $445,130,134 in 1857. In 1860, their notes and deposits equalled $460,904,606. This was the highest point which had been reached. In November of that year occurred the election of Mr. Lincoln to the Presidency; an event which was the first substantial triumph in the country of Northern over Southern ideas as to the nature of our government, since the administration of Washington. His accession to the Presidency was the signal for the immediate outbreak of the civil war. The new administration succeeded to one which was itself in virtual conspiracy against the life of the nation. It found the Treasury empty, and the Army deeply tainted with seditious sentiments. The Navy, representing the commercial spirit of the North, was almost unanimous on the side of freedom. One of the last acts of the previous Congress, it having been purged by the secession of most of the Southern members, was to authorize a loan of $10,000,000. This sum sufficed for the immediate necessities of the new administration. The new Congress, which had been elected at the same time with the President, was speedily called together; and, on the 17th of July, authorized the negotiation of large loans. In the mean time the disastrous battle of Bull Run had taken place, causing great depression at the North, which made it evident that the only mode in which loans could be negotiated was for the Banks of the country to combine by their advances, to relieve the pressing necessities of the administration; and by their example, to inspire public confidence to a degree that would render possible the negotiation of the government loans. The manner in which the Banks combined, and the success achieved, are fully set out in the following extracts from a statement prepared by one largely instrumental in promoting their union for the purposes described : —

"After the disastrous battle of Bull Run, and when Washington was closely beleaguered and the avenue thence to New York through Baltimore was intercepted by the enemy, Mr. Chase, then Secretary of the Treasury, came to this city *via* Annapolis, and immediately invited all persons in this community who were supposed to possess or to control capital to meet him on the evening of August 9th, at the house of John J. Cisco, Esq., then Assistant Treasurer of the United States in New York. This invitation drew together a large number of gentlemen of various occupations and circumstances. During the discussion which ensued, I suggested the practicability of uniting the Banks of the North by some organization that would combine them into an efficient and inseparable body, for the purpose of advancing the capital of the country upon government bonds in large amounts ; and, through their clearing-house facilities and other well-known expedients, to distribute them in smaller sums among the people in a manner that would secure active co-operation among the members in this special work, while in all other respects each Bank could pursue its independent business. This suggestion met the hearty approbation of the assembled company, and arrested the earnest attention of the Secretary. At his request, it was presented to the consideration of the Banks, at a meeting called for that purpose at the American Exchange Bank on the following day ; and was so far entertained as to secure the appointment of a Committee of ten bank officers, to give it form and coherence. The Committee convened at the Bank of Commerce, whose officers zealously united in the effort, and a plan was reported unanimously. Their report was cordially accepted and adopted by the Banks in New York ; those in Boston and Philadelphia being represented at the meeting, and as zealously and cordially united in the organization. . . .

" It was at once unanimously agreed that the Associated Banks of the three cities would take fifty millions of 7 3·10 notes at par, with the privilege of an additional fifty millions in sixty days, and a further amount of fifty millions in sixty days more, making one hundred and fifty millions in all, and offer them for sale to the people of the country at the same price, without change. In this great undertaking, the Banks of New York assumed more than their relative proportion. To insure full co-operation and success, the expedient of issuing clearing-house certificates, and of appropriating and averaging all the coin in the various Banks as a common fund, which had been invented but the year before, was applied to this special object with good effect. . . .

" The capitals of the Banks thus associated made an aggregate of one hundred and twenty millions, — an amount greater than the Bank of England and the Bank of France combined, each of which institutions had been found sufficient for the gigantic struggles of those great nations, from time to time, in conflict with all Europe. . . .

" The following figures also show that the financial condition of the Banks at the time was one of great strength : —

	Liabilities.		Assets in
	Deposits.	Circulation.	Coin.
Banks in New York . . .	$92,046,308	. . . $8,521,426	. . . $49,733,990
„ Boston	18,235,061	. . . 6,366,466	. . . 6,665,929
„ Philadelphia . .	15,335,838	. . . 2,076,857	. . . 6,765,120
	$125,617,207	$16,964,749	
		125,617,207	
Total		. $142,581,956,	against $63,165,039

coin on hand, equal to 45 per cent of all liabilities. Surely, such conditions as these, with judicious administration, were adequate

to the work which the country required. A great merit of this
bank combination at that critical moment, when the life of the
nation hung in the balance, consisted in the fact that it fully committed the hitherto hesitating moneyed capital of the North and
East to the support of the government. The bank officers and
directors who thus counselled and consented were deeply sensible of the momentous responsibility which they assumed; but all
doubt and hesitation were instantly removed, and perfect unanimity was secured by the question, ' *What if we do not unite?* '
And acting as guardians of a great trust exposed to imminent
danger, they fearlessly elected the alternative best calculated. to
protect it.

" The problem to be practically resolved by the Banks was this :
How can the available capital be best drawn from the people,
and devoted to the support of government, with the least disturbance to the country? and by what means can arms, clothing, and
subsistence for the army be best secured in exchange for government credit? These were simple questions of domestic exchange,
and most naturally suggested the use of the ordinary methods of
bank-checks, deposits, and transfers, that the experience of all
civilized nations had found most efficient for the purpose ; and that
this should be accomplished by the Associated Banks, in a manner
best calculated to prolong their useful agency and to preserve the
specie standard, it was indispensable that their coin reserves remain
with the least possible change. Accordingly, it was at once proposed to the Secretary that he should suspend the operations of
the Sub-Treasury Act in respect to these transactions, and, following the course of commercial business, that he should draw checks
upon some one Bank in each city representing the Association, in
small sums as required, in disbursing the money thus advanced.
By this means his checks would serve the purpose of a circulating medium, continually redeemed, and the exchanges of capital
and industry would be best promoted. This was the more important in a period of public agitation, when the disbursement of these
large sums exclusively in coin rendered the reserves of the Banks
all the more liable to be wasted by hoarding. To the astonishment of the Committee, Mr. Chase refused ; notwithstanding the
Act of Congress of August 5th, which it seemed to us was passed
for the very object then presented, but which he declared upon his
authority as finance minister, and from his personal knowledge of
its purpose, had no such meaning or intent. This issue was discussed from time to time with much zeal; but always with the
same result. It was seen by the most experienced bank officers
to be vital to the success of their undertaking. To draw from
the Banks in coin the large sums involved in these loans, and to
transfer them to the Treasury, thence to be widely scattered over
the country at a moment when war had excited fear and distrust,
was to be pulling out continually the foundations upon which the
whole structure rested. And inasmuch as this money was loaned
to the government, and was in no sense a trust reposed in the
Banks, there appeared to them no reason why it should not be
drawn by checks in favor of government contractors and creditors,

who would require to exchange them for other values in commerce and trade, through the process of the clearing-house. And this consideration was greatly strengthened by the fact, that these advances were made, and the money publicly disbursed, a long time before the treasury notes were ready for delivery to the Banks which had paid for them. In the light which has since been shed upon the Act of Congress referred to, it is evident that undue weight was given to the views of the Secretary, and that the Banks would have conferred an incalculable benefit upon the country, had they adhered inflexibly to their own opinions. . . . It soon became manifest that, in consenting to have their hands tied and their most efficient powers restricted, while engaged in these great operations, and in allowing their coin reserves to be wasted by pouring them out upon the community in a manner so unnecessary and exceptional, the Banks deprived themselves and the government of the ability of long continuing, as they otherwise could have done, to negotiate the National loans upon a specie standard.

" This first great error, if it did not create a necessity for the legal-tender notes, it certainly precipitated the adoption of that most unhappy expedient, and thereby committed the nation at an earlier day to the most expensive of all methods of financiering.

" One other subject of discussion between the Secretary and the Associated Banks at the same time arose, which led in the same direction. Congress by its Act of 17th July had authorized loans to the amount of two hundred and fifty millions. This could be issued either in bonds running twenty years at not over seven per cent interest — 7-30 notes running three years, or fifty millions of the amount could, at the discretion of the Secretary, be made in currency notes payable on demand without interest. As the undertaking of the Associated Banks covered one hundred and fifty millions of this sum, and it was desired that they continue the work thus auspiciously begun, a question of the expediency of putting out the circulating notes was immediately raised by one of its members. A very small amount had been emitted. The Treasury was empty of coin to redeem them, and could only be replenished by the proceeds of the bank loans. It was evident to the bank officers that they could not sustain coin payments, if the transfers from their vaults to that of the Treasury were subject to be intercepted and absorbed by these notes of government. Nor could the Banks receive them upon deposit from the public as money, while they were responding to the government and to their own dealers in coin. It was an inflation of the currency in the form most embarrassing to the enterprise they had commenced. Accordingly, the Secretary was urgently solicited to refrain from exercising the discretionary powers given him of creating the Treasury currency, until all other means were exhausted. In response to a resolution to that effect, the Secretary assured the bank officers of his acquiescence in their suggestion; but at the same time insisted that it was improper for a public officer to openly pledge himself *not* to exercise a power conferred by the law. With this understanding the Banks began their work; paying into the Treasury, in coin, one hundred and fifty millions, in sums at the rate of about five millions, at intervals of six days. Even with all these unfavorable circumstances surrounding them, it was an encouraging fact, observed by those who were anxiously watching the practical operation of this great and novel experiment, that, while the circulating notes in the country were restricted, the disbursements of the government for the war were so rapid, and the consequent internal trade movement was so intense, that the coin paid out upon each instalment of the loan came back to the Banks, through the community, in about one week; the natural effect of this general commercial activity upon the circulating medium being simply to quicken its flow. ·

"After taking the third amount of fifty millions by the Associated Banks, those in New York, who had at that time paid in of their proportion over eighty millions in all, found themselves in this position : —

Their aggregate coin, which on the 17th August, before the
  first payment into the Treasury, was $49,733,990
Was in December 7th   42,318,610

A reduction of only $7,415,380

and the other two cities in like proportion.

"In the mean time the 7-30 notes taken by the Banks had been purchased by the people to the extent of some fifty millions, notwithstanding a prolonged and vexatious delay in issuing them by the Treasury Department. The popular feeling was all that could have been desired for continuing that method of distribution. It may be confidently affirmed, that, had the Banks been permitted to exercise their own methods of exchanging the bonds for the varied products of industry required by the government, they could have continued their advances in sums of fifty millions for an indefinite period, and until the available resources of the people had been all gathered in. It is to be borne in mind that these resources were all existing at home, and that the increased industry which the war excited was daily increasing new means for investment. . . .

"But at this time the demand notes were paid out freely by the Treasury, and began to appear as a cause of embarrassment among the Banks which were pressed to receive them upon deposit; and while they could not decline them without diminishing public confidence in the government credit, they could not give them currency without impairing their own specie strength. In fact, the notes became at once a substitute for coin withdrawn from circulation, and their emission expressed a purpose of resorting to government paper issues to carry on the war. So soon as these notes thus appeared, the reflux of coin to the Banks at once sensibly diminished. During three weeks from the 7th December, the reserves of the Banks in New York fell to $29,357,712, — a loss of thirteen millions within that short period ; and on the 28th December, after conference with the Secretary, in which he still adhered to the views before expressed, it was decided as expedient for the Banks to suspend specie payments.

"At that moment the Associated Banks yet held over forty millions in coin, and it was still possible for them to continue their advances to the government but for the two obstacles thus interposed. Before entering into this last conference with the Associated Banks, some of the members expressed to the Secretary the importance of continuing his relation to an organization which combined so much of experience, capital, and financial resource, and which was yet capable of rendering the government invaluable service ; and that if an irredeemable paper currency was the inevitable resort, it would be more expedient and economical for the government not to become involved in its dangers, but to impose the duty and responsibility of issuing the notes upon the Banks, who would naturally be compelled to keep the day of redemption continually in view. Thus, as a suspension of coin payment was about to be declared, it was practicable to preserve from distribution and set aside the forty millions of coin then owned by the Banks, together with one hundred and fifty or sixty millions of government bonds, which could be taken by them as a special security for two hundred millions of notes, which could then be immediately issued by the Associated Banks from their own plates, and be verified and made National by the stamp and signature of a government officer. And that such an issue, so supported by coin and bonds, at once simple and expeditious, would serve the temporary purpose required, with little if any deterioration below coin value ; and that it would be then practicable for the Banks to continue, without further agitation, their advances. But the Secretary declined to entertain this suggestion ; preferring the system of National Banks, which he had already conceived.

"Looking back over events that have since transpired, it must be admitted that this suggestion possessed true merit. It would have preserved a coin basis for the currency, prevented the destructive expansion, relieved the government from its almost inextricable entanglement with the circulating notes, and compelled an early restoration of coin payments. And with a proper use of the expedients and machinery of Banks, by utilizing their power of affecting exchanges, which was substantially applied by the Secretary in the National Banking system without reserve, this amount would have been found sufficient. When we review the excessive cost of the war, the vast increase of the National debt, and the public and private evils which a profuse currency has entailed upon the country, it must appear evident that, in failing early to use and to exhaust all those means and appliances of commerce and banking that the experience of other civilized nations has proved most effective, a great and irreparable mistake was made. . . .

"This forcible entry of the government into the private affairs of the people, so utterly at variance with the fundamental principles of our system, so great an abridgment of personal liberty, and operating as a tax so unequal in its effects, was a rigorous measure of war, and as such was vindicated only as a temporary act of dire necessity. In enforcing this unequal burden, Congress did not leave the holders of the notes without some measure of relief; but it gave to all the option of converting them at pleasure into a six per cent gold-interest-bearing bond, payable in twenty years. By this means, the notes became equal in value to the bonds for which they were made exchangeable; and while, during the war, the payments of gold interest continually operated to produce a curtailment of the volume of the notes in circulation, the return of peace opened a market abroad for the bonds, which would have insured the early and entire absorption of the war currency, and thus clear the way for specie payments.

" But, in an evil hour for the country, other counsel obtained possession of the good judgment of the Secretary; and, yielding to it, he consented and urged Congress to withdraw this privilege of converting the notes, so that thenceforth all issues were made without it. All notes emitted consequently became an unmitigated burden upon commerce, of indefinite duration, from which there was no escape. A new currency was created, utterly at variance with all economic laws, and in conflict with all recognized rules of commerce and exchange. It did not, like all sound currency, naturally spring out of industry, production, and trade; but it was an enforced result of exhaustion and necessity. It did not come and go, following the beneficent courses of commerce, expanding and contracting with the times and seasons that required it; but it remained an unyielding, inflexible mass, subject only to the chances and vicissitudes of war. As the war progressed and the country became poorer, this currency increased, giving new instruments and facilities to expend just in proportion as the means of payment were consumed. With a compulsory currency thus made the measure of prices, and daily deteriorating yet still increasing, is it strange that all other property was eagerly sought for in preference to this, and that prodigal expenditure became the law of the land?"[1]

Such were the financial operations of the new administration, up to the 30th of December, 1861, — to the suspension of specie payment, and the issue of government notes. Without means, without sufficient credit or faculty to provide them, the results of the military operations of the government in great measure disastrous, Mr. Chase, in his extremity, appealed to the Banks. This appeal was most patriotically responded to. In view of his necessities and of the employment of the Banks in his operations, the provisions of the Act creating the Independent Treasury had been so far modified as to allow the use of their circulation, and to make them the depositories of the public moneys. Pending the negotiations, the Banks earnestly pressed upon Mr. Chase the importance of his dealing with them as their own customers dealt with them, and of availing himself of the proceeds of their loans; by drawing

[1] Financial History of the War, by George S. Coe, President of the American Exchange Bank. See Bankers' Magazine, January, 1876.

upon them in the ordinary course of business, and allowing them to pay his drafts in whatever manner their holders might designate. The Banks assumed that, as the ordinary operations of the public had no tendency to withdraw their coin, those of government, if conducted in a similar manner, would exert no such tendency; that in this way the war might be carried on by the use of their paper, symbolizing merchandise at the value of coin. To a request and to reasons so pertinent and judicious, Mr. Chase turned a deaf ear. He would take nothing in payment of his loans but coin. The result is the present condition of the country. Had he taken the course pressed upon him, the specie in the Banks must have constantly increased, not only from the products of our mines, but from importations which were being made in very large amounts. The exports of specie from the country the year preceding the war, exceeded the imports by $57,996,154. During the first year of the war, and before the Banks had suspended, the imports over exports equalled $22,558,791; making in a single year a change in favor of the country of $80,554,945. No sooner was trouble with the South apprehended, than the Northern Banks began instinctively to strengthen themselves. On the 1st of January, 1860, before any suspicion or distrust was excited, and when the country was in an eminently sound and prosperous condition, the coin reserves of the Banks of the three great cities, New York, Boston, and Philadelphia, equalled $29,822,320; of which the Banks of New York held $20,119,779; those of Boston, $4,796,000; those of Philadelphia, $4,906,541. On the 1st of January, 1861, when the disruption of the country seemed imminent, they had increased their reserves to $43,849,628; and on the 9th of August, 1861, when they undertook to aid the government, to $63,165,039. There was no concert or method in all this; only ordinary prudence. Even so late as 1862, after the Banks had suspended, and Mr. Chase had drawn from them $150,000,000, they held $44,887,093 in coin; a sum greater, by $15,000,000, than that held on the 1st of January, 1860. Had he acceded to their request at the outset, he might have availed himself, at the value of coin, of every dollar of capital in the country which could have been spared for the war. No sooner did the Banks enter upon their undertaking, than they brought into action the most efficient method ever devised for its object. They employed all the Banks in the loyal States, numbering some twelve hundred, to become their brokers; and to peddle out, over their own counters, the obligations of the government, which were of denominations to suit every class of purchasers, — the capitalist with his millions, and the day-laborer who had accumulated a few months' wages. Such was the intense spirit of patriotism aroused at the North that every man was prepared to lay down his last dollar for the cause. Starting with ample reserves, the Banks were certain of having these re-enforced from the mines of the country, at the rate of a million dollars each week, in addition to the receipts from abroad. With their constantly increasing strength, the public securities would steadily have advanced in demand and price, so as to have commanded at least their par value in coin ; and at the close of the war, when the debts incurred in its prosecution came to be paid, they would be paid in a currency of the same value as that in which they were contracted, instead of one twice as valuable. As it was, the National Debt was more than doubled, the war prolonged to twice its necessary length, the public service thoroughly demoralized, the morals of the country debauched, and innumerable and valuable lives sacrificed, merely to gratify the whim or selfish purpose of a man ignorant as a Hottentot upon the matters in reference to which he acted with such reckless levity. More than fifteen years have elapsed since his scheme for the " reformation of the currency " was set on foot, during which the people have hardly handled or seen a dollar of gold ; while they have now a far more difficult task before them, in the restoration of the currency from the condition in which he placed it, than they had in providing the means of putting down the Rebellion.

While the Banks were supplying the government with money (coin) at the rate of more than a million dollars daily, a potent element of mischief — one which caused and precipitated their suspension, and at the same time that of the government, and led to the issue of legal-tender notes — was an issue by Mr. Chase of demand notes, payable in coin (authority having been given him therefor, to the extent of $50,000,000, afterwards increased to $60,000,000). Against their issue the Banks earnestly remonstrated. The government had not a dollar for their payment but what these supplied.

It was, in effect, the exhaustion of their means to an equal amount. For the loans made directly by the Banks they received government securities, by means of the sale of which they were speedily reimbursed their advances. The process was perfectly natural and healthy. They had nothing to fear so long as they could sell securities as fast as they contracted to supply money. The result showed that they could do this, at the outset, at the rate of more than a million dollars in coin daily, and, when confidence was at its lowest ebb, without seriously impairing their reserves. Every sale they made prepared the way for new ones. For 1863 their advances could have equalled, if necessary, a million and a half a day, if such an amount had been required, — certainly if they had been made in their own paper, having the value of coin. It is well known that the customs revenues have been collected in gold to the amount of two hundred millions annually, by the use of less than one-fifth of that sum, by the constant return of that collected into circulation. When Mr. Chase came into the field, it was not to sell bonds ; not to get that in hand for which he had years to pay ; but to issue his own promises payable on demand, and which were to be paid by some one almost as soon as issued. For their payment he did not attempt to provide a dollar. He threw them upon the market as money. The Banks were compelled to receive them, in order to protect the credit of the government. By receiving them on deposit, they contracted and were speedily compelled to discharge them in coin. For these notes they received no bonds. Their only mode of providing the means therefor was to call in their loans. To do this would create a disturbance in the money market, which, equally with the discredit of the government, would defeat altogether their great undertaking. They appealed to Mr. Chase to desist; but he refused. As the notes he had authority to issue nearly equalled their reserves, and had to be paid out of them, they were quite enough to break the Banks, into which they constantly tended to flow ; although, with the methods employed and the equivalents received, the latter had been enabled to advance to the government nearly three times the amount of such notes, without seriously reducing their reserves. As he persisted in his course, and as the event sooner or later was inevitable, the Banks thought it wise to anticipate it by suspending with comparatively full coffers. They held at the time the extraordinarily large sum of $44,887,893. In their relation to the government, they should have acted simply as brokers, to turn its securities, if possible, with sufficient rapidity to supply its necessities, — at least as fast as customers could be found for their purchase. Mr. Chase's chief care should have been not to have drawn a dollar in coin from them; and not, permanently, a dollar of their capital. All he wanted was that which would purchase articles necessary for the support of the war. His object was accomplished so long as the paper of the Banks would do this as cheaply as coin. The stronger their position, the better could they dispose of his securities. Their aggregate share capital was far less than the amount with which they supplied him, in the short period of five months. In order to sell his securities, the money market was to be kept in an easy condition. For such purpose, the whole capital of the Banks with which he dealt should have been held. In ordinary times Banks cannot, nor should they, part with a dollar of their reserves. To part with them is always a sign of weakness, — that losses or bad debts have been made. At the time of the suspension of the Banks, Dec. 30, 1861, the amount of demand notes outstanding equalled $33,460,000, mostly held by the Banks, and for which they had been compelled to part with a corresponding, or at least with a large amount of gold. The process seemed a perfectly simple, but proved to be a thoroughly fatal one. Mr. Chase undertook to become an issuer of a convertible currency, without the provision of any means for its redemption. His defeat was only another, but a crowning example of an undertaking which can have but one issue. From it should have been learned a lesson which, if well heeded, would have helped to unlock all the mysteries of paper money. The government, for the time, was wholly without means. The coin which the Banks had paid it had been expended. It had no bank-notes, nor could it get any. Its wants in money equalled a million and a quarter daily. Its revenues did not equal one-tenth that amount. Now, if the doctrine of every writer upon the subject of money, that worthless bits of paper, by calling them money, may, from the necessity of their use, be maintained at the par value of coin; or that of most writers, that they may, by limiting their amount, be raised to any possible pitch of value ; or that of Mr. Fawcett, of the most moderate school of the Economists, that a government engaged in war may issue its own inconvertible paper, equal to its increased expenditures, which will be maintained at the par of coin from the necessity of its use, — be true, why was it that the United States notes, issued to meet the expenditures of the War of the Rebellion, and equalling the paltry sum of only $33,460,000, should, at the moment that five times that amount was required, fall to a discount so soon as government suspended ; selling in the market, like all other kinds of property or securities, only at their estimated value ? Till this question be answered, how absurd for writers to repeat stale assertions, as impossible in realization as that heavy bodies should fly from instead of to the earth ! and how ridiculous for our present Secretary of the Treasury to prate about the ease with which some four hundred millions of government notes may be maintained at the par value of coin, without any adequate provision for their conversion into coin or merchandise, at the very time that the commercial currency of the country is probably inflated to the extent of $300,000,000 !

The position of the demand notes was indeed most anomalous. Government could not pay them. They bore no interest. The Treasury notes, bearing interest at the rate of 6 per cent and receivable in payment of the revenues, were at a discount of about 1 and one-half per cent. These could be absorbed — taken out of the market — from the interest they bore. No one wanted non-interest-bearing notes, when interest-bearing ones could be had. The Banks were no longer willing to receive them, and got rid of them as fast as possible by paying them out over their counters to such of their customers as were willing to take them. In all business and monetary circles they were unwelcome intruders, — an incongruous element, the nature of which no one understood, and which all wished to avoid. No one could be compelled to receive them. They would not have been taken on any terms, but for the fact that they were receivable for the revenues. In every transaction in which they were used, they were the unpleasant reminders of the poverty and broken faith of the government. It was as if the dishonored check of a merchant were hawked about the streets till it found a purchaser, at a discount, in some one indebted to the drawer, and who could use it by way of offset. No one would take them as money, in the proper sense of that word. Government saw at once that it could not get along with such expedients as these : that the only way in which it could make its notes circulate as money was to *compel* their circulation, by making them competent to discharge all contracts ; for so far they were to indebted parties the equivalent of gold.

As the suspension of the Banks was a precautionary meas- ure, rather than the result of any immediate necessity, they would undoubtedly have speedily resumed, but for the imme- diate provision for the issue of legal-tender notes. They were sufficiently strong, and proposed to Mr. Chase a plan by which the war could still be carried on by the use of their paper at the value of coin, or at only a slight discount from coin. Upon their suspension, from the apprehension naturally created, gold rose in January to a premium of about 3 per cent, to fall off by the middle of March to about 1 per cent. Mr. Chase, however, was wholly averse to any arrangement with them. The object nearest his heart was not money so much as the breaking down of the financial system which he found in existence on his accession to office, — which was in a thoroughly healthy and strong condition, and by means of which alone the war could be conducted on a specie basis ; and to substitute in its place his own, from which the proper constituent for conversion was to be wholly eliminated ; and that, too, in the very face of the tremendous struggle in which the nation was already engaged. At the very moment when the Banks were advancing him $150,000,000, he declared them to be unworthy of credit ; that " their currency was incongru- ous, unequal, and unsafe." Their failure, which was his own work, was his first great triumph.

Such is a brief account of the early financial operations of the government, of the suspension of payment by the Banks, and of the reasons for the issue of the government notes. Never did consequences more momentous hang upon questions apparently more insignificant in themselves, — whether the notes of the Banks of the three great cities should be used, and whether Mr. Chase would deal with them on the same footing as other customers, or demand payment of all his loans in coin. They were questions, however, which lay at the very

root of the most important functions and operations of society, — the modes by which its means can be best transferred
and utilized. Could the consequences have been foreseen, the
Banks would undoubtedly have stood upon their convictions.
As their objections were vital, they should have been insisted
upon. The disasters that resulted should have been inferred
from the violation of so obvious a duty or rule. Had they
persisted, Mr. Chase would in the end have yielded, or, what
was far better, would have been compelled to give up his place.
One would have supposed that, after he had been lifted out of
his embarrassments by the Banks, and had had such proof of
their patriotism and financial strength, he would most readily
have deferred to their suggestions, in matters coming so peculiarly within their own experience, and in which he must have
known them to be far better fitted to advise and direct than
himself. Among the managers of the hundred and twenty
Banks which formed the association, were men of the most
eminent weight and influence, in social as well as in monetary
circles, — men who were uninfluenced by party ties or animosities, whose experience could be confidently appealed to, and
who had no purpose apart from the general welfare. If results
be the test, certainly no conduct could have been more criminal than to refuse to give ear to persons so well fitted to
counsel and guide.[1]

The Banks having suspended, and with them the government, what was Mr. Chase to do? The following extracts
from his Second Annual Report will give his answer: —

" The Banks of New York suspended on the 30th of December,
1861. Their example was followed by most of the Banks through-

---

[1] The following is the section of the Act authorizing a National Loan, providing for a modification of the Independent Treasury: —

" Section 6. *And be it further enacted:* That the provisions of the Act entitled, ' An act to provide for the better organization of the Treasury, and for
the collection, safe-keeping, transfer and disbursements of the public revenues,'
passed August 6, 1846, be and the same are hereby suspended, so far as to allow
the Secretary of the Treasury to deposit any of the moneys obtained on any of
the loans now authorized by law, to the credit of the Treasurer of the United
States, in such solvent specie-paying Banks as he may select; and the said
moneys, so deposited, may be withdrawn from such deposit for deposit with the
regular authorized depositories, or for the payment of public dues, or paid in
redemption of the notes authorized to be issued under this Act, or the Act to
which this is supplementary, payable on demand, as may seem expedient to, or
be directed by, the Secretary of the Treasury." *

* Appendix Congressional Globe, 1st Session 37th Congress, p. 41.

out the country; and government yielded to the same necessity in respect to the United States notes then in circulation.

" These changed circumstances required a change of measures. The expenditures had already reached an average of nearly a million and a quarter of dollars each secular day, while the revenues from all sources hardly exceeded one-tenth of that sum. It was necessary, therefore, to raise by loans in some form about thirty millions a month, or sixty millions for every sixty days.

" Careful inquiries satisfied the Secretary that the first $60,000,000 could not be had, in coin, at better rates than a dollar in bonds for eighty cents in money; and that each succeeding loan would involve submission to increasingly disadvantageous terms. To obtain the first $60,000,000 would require, therefore, an issue of bonds to the amount of $75,000,000, and, of course, an increase of the public debt by the same sum; the next $60,000,000 would require, perhaps, $90,000,000 in bonds and debt; and the next $60,000,000, if obtainable at all, would require perhaps $120,000,000. It was easy to see that, on this road, utter discredit and paralysis would soon be reached. The adoption of a plan of finance involving such consequences was not compatible with the Secretary's ideas of public duty.

" There remained but one other possible way of raising money by the negotiation of bonds in the usual mode. That way was to receive in payment of loans the notes or credits of the Banks in suspension.

" To ascertain what would have been the consequences of a resort to this expedient, it is necessary to remember that the Bank circulation of the loyal States amounted, on the 1st day of January, 1861, to $150,000,000; that it had been reduced to $130,000,000 on the 1st day of January, 1862; and that this circulation was diffused throughout the country in all the channels of business. In these circumstances, the collection by loans of sufficient amounts to meet the demands upon the Treasury in season for prompt payments would be extremely difficult. The negotiation of such loans to the extent required by the public exigencies would create a demand for the notes, which would involve the necessity at first of sacrifices not greatly inferior to those attendant on coin loans. If subsequent negotiations should become practicable at seemingly better rates, it would be because the government demand had stimulated the making and issuing of bank-notes to an extent far beyond the ordinary needs of business. The increase of circulation thus stimulated would be unlimited, except by the possibility of obtaining interest on loans of it; or, in other words, by the possibility of obtaining credit for it with the community and the government. This limit, certain to be finally reached by all Banks improvidently managed, would not, however, be reached immediately or at the same time by all institutions, or by the same rate of progress in all parts of the country. But an excessive circulation would surely be thrust upon the community; forming a currency the business of the people, and to embarrass, if not arrest, the operations of the government. Loans negotiated in this circulation would be simply exchanges of the debts of the nation, bearing interest and certain to be paid, for the debts of a multitude of corporations, bearing no interest, and certain, in part, never to be paid." [1]

As Mr. Chase assumed that he could borrow neither coin nor bank-notes, and as he could not, without full provision for their payment, make plain notes circulate as money, he bent all his energies, as the only alternative, to secure an issue of legal-tender notes.   In a letter addressed, under date of Jan. 29, 1862, to Mr. Stevens, Chairman of the Committee of Ways and Means of the House, he said : —

"The provision making United States notes a legal tender has doubtless been well considered by the Committee, and their conclusion needs no support from any observations of mine.   I think it my duty, however, to say that, in respect to this provision, my reflections have conducted me to the same conclusions they have reached." [2]

On the 7th of June, 1862, Mr. Chase addressed a communication to the Committee of Ways and Means (accompanied by a bill of his own drafting providing therefor), asking for a further issue of $150,000,000 of legal-tender notes.   In his communication he said : —

"He proposed that authority be given to the Secretary of the Treasury to issue $150,000,000 in United States notes, in addition to the issue already authorized, *and that these be a made legal tender for debts.*" [3]

In reference to the issue of notes after it was made, he said : —

"No other mode of providing, with any tolerable degree of promptitude, for the wants of the army and the necessities of other branches of the public service, seemed likely to effect the object with so little public inconvenience and so considerable public advantage as the issue of United States notes, adapted to circulation as money, and available therefor immediately in government payments. . . . The choice was now to be made between a currency furnished by numerous and unconnected Banks, in various States, and a currency furnished by the government, which the government could and would, except in a very improbable, not to say impossible, contingency, amply provide for and protect.   With these alternatives before him, the Secretary had already declared his unhesitating preference for a circulation authorized and issued by national authority.[4]

"The recommendations now submitted, of a limited " (further)

---

[1] Report of the Sectretary of the Treasury, for 1862, pp. 7, 8.
[2] Spaulding's Financial History of the War of the Rebellion, p. 45.
[3] Ibid. p. 155.
[4] Report of the Secretary of the Treasury, for 1862, pp. 8, 9.

" issue of United States notes, as a wise expedient for the present time, and as an occasional expedient in future times, . . . are prompted by no favor to excessive issues of any description of credit money." [1]

" In former reports, the Secretary has stated his convictions, and the grounds of them, respecting the necessity and the utility of putting a large part of the debt in the form of United States notes, without interest, and adapted to circulation as money. These convictions remain unchanged, and seem now to be shared by the people. For the first time in our history has a real approach to a uniform currency been made ; and the benefits of it, though still far from the best attainable condition, are felt by all. The circulation has been distributed throughout the country, and is everywhere acceptable. It is a gratification to know that a tribunal so distinguished by the learning and virtues of its members as the Supreme Court of New York has given the sanction of its judgment to the constitutional validity of the law." [2]

Upon the suspension of the Banks due solely to his folly and obstinacy, and that of the government, which necessarily followed in their train, Mr. Chase could see but one course open for him. The government suspended upon its demand notes, equalling in amount only $33,460,000 ; although these were equally receivable with coin in payment of the revenues. What folly could have been greater than to allow government to break for such a paltry sum ? As the notes were receivable, and were constantly being paid into the Treasury, in the collection of the revenues, a few millions of dollars would have been sufficient to have maintained them at par, — to have taken in such as were not returned through the revenues. What was the result, at least in Mr. Chase's estimation ? That its suspension had so far destroyed the credit of the government that he could not hope to borrow from the public, coin which the Banks had paid him in exchange for its securities at par, on any better terms than 100 of the former to 80 of the latter ; and at this rate, for only $60,000,000, to be supplied in sixty days. For the second $60,000,000, to be supplied within four months, he would have to give $90,000,000 in bonds ; and for the third, $120,000,000. Certainly, money was not to be borrowed on such terms as these ! He forced the government to suspend, and then proclaimed to the world that no one would trust it. In turning in the direction of the

---

[1] Report of the Secretary of the Treasury, for 1862, p. 21.
[2] Report of the Secretary of the Treasury, for 1863, p. 15.

Banks, the prospect was equally discouraging. The circulation of those of the Northern States had fallen from $150,000,000, at the beginning of the year, to $130,000,000 near its close; and this, he said, was so distributed in the channels of commerce, that it could not be reached on any better terms than coin, if an attempt were made. If it were made, the notes would be supplied in such abundance as to very speedily become worthless; so that the process of borrowing would be simply an exchange of the debts of the nation, bearing interest and certain to be paid, for debts of a multitude of corporations, bearing no interest, and certain, in part, never to be paid. Mr. Chase held Banks to be a sort of " confidence " concerns, and their managers a set of shysters, always seeking to impose their worthless issues upon every feeble and derelict subject with whom they came in contact. It is to be remembered, that he dealt only with those of New York, Boston, and Philadelphia: it was not necessary, nor was it proposed, that he should deal with any others. The former had relations with all the other Banks in the United States, and could avail themselves of all the aid these could furnish. Had he been told that they dealt in solid capital, supplying to every borrower the full amount of his loan, either in coin or its equivalent, he would have been as incredulous as if he had been told that money grew on trees.

The statement was omitted in its proper place, that, immediately upon the passage of the first legal-tender Act, this paving the way, Congress, upon the application of Mr. Chase, passed a bill making the notes issued under that of July, 1861, and the amended Act of February 12, 1862, legal tender in the discharge of all contracts; the professed object being to raise their value by enlarging the sphere of their use. They were previously at a considerable discount, as they would only pay debts due to the government. The Banks in the leading cities would not receive them as money. Their value was raised by their being made receivable in the payment of debts to individuals as well as to the government. They still remained at a discount from gold, for the reason that they could not, as legal tender, serve all the uses of gold. The whole question of value was one of uses. The law which regulated their value could have been comprehended by a child. Its simple statement, properly attended to, would have unlocked to Mr. Chase all the mysteries of money. That neither he nor

those who followed him should have made so simple a discovery, is another evidence of the complete mastery which the
groundless dogmas laid down in the books have obtained over
the public mind.

Mr. Chase would not attempt to borrow coin or bank-notes,
from the excessive rate of interest he would be compelled to
pay, by the low price of government bonds. But did an issue
of his own notes enable him to come at that which he wished
to purchase, at any more favorable rate? He had already
asserted government to be unworthy of credit; that, should
he attempt to borrow on its bonds, they would not bring fifty
cents on the dollar. He now demonstrated his assertion by
issuing a forced loan. Could he resort to such an extraordinary expedient without paying a higher rate of interest, or,
what is the same thing, a higher rate for what he wished to
purchase, than he would have been compelled to pay by borrowing in the ordinary mode? The legal-tender notes gave
him no authority to seize what he wanted at his own price.
He must still go into the market with a broken credit, and
with expedients the last resort of imbecility and exhaustion,
and sell them for what they would bring. What would be
thought of a merchant who should resort to similar, or to any
extraordinary expedients for the purpose of supporting his
credit, and of supplying himself with means? Would not such
action wholly destroy what little he had remaining? A government is in a position precisely similar. In its relation to capital,
it is subject, like individuals, to all the laws that control it or
its use. It has indeed, or is assumed to have, a power not
possessed by individuals, — that of giving to its promises, payable at its pleasure and perhaps never to be paid, a competency to discharge debts at the value of coin. No sooner,
therefore, does it issue its notes, than it finds plenty of parties
eager to accept them, and supply it with whatever it wants,
provided they can use such promises as a means of paying their
own debts at the value of coin. From the first, however, the
holders of merchandise have the government in their power,
as it must always yield to them in the matter of price. But
as soon as contracts in existence at the time of the issue of
government notes, are discharged, these will speedily fall in
price to their estimated value. This was not long in happening to the United States notes. By the 15th of October, 1862,
when the second batch began to get into circulation, gold had

risen to a premium, payable in them, of 37⅜ per cent. The public ascribed this advance to an inflation of the currency. Mr. Chase denied the assertion. The currency was not inflated. To use his own language, —

"It is true that gold commands a premium in notes; in other words, that to purchase a given amount of gold a greater amount in notes is required. But it is also true that, on the suspension of specie payments and the substitution for coin of United States notes, convertible into six per cent specie bonds as the legal standard of value, gold became an article of merchandise, subject to the ordinary fluctuations of supply and demand, and to the extraordinary fluctuations of mere speculation. The ignorant fears of foreign investers in national and State bonds and other American securities, and the timid alarms of numerous nervous individuals in our own country, prompted large sacrifices upon evidences of public and corporate indebtedness in our markets, and large purchases of coin for remittance abroad or hoarding at home. Taking advantage of these and other circumstances tending to an advance of gold, speculators employed all the arts of the market to stimulate that tendency and carry it to the highest point. This point was reached on the 15th day of October. Gold sold in the market at a premium of 37½ per cent.

"That this remarkable rise is not due wholly, or even in greatest part, to the increase of the currency, is established beyond reasonable doubt by considerations now to be stated : —

"First. The whole quantity of circulation did not, at the time, greatly if at all exceed the legitimate demands of payments. On the 1st day of November, 1861, the circulation of United States notes, including credits to disbursing officers and to the Treasurer of the United States, was $15,140,000. On the 1st day of November, 1862, it was, with like inclusions, $210,104,000. Of corporate notes, on the 1st of November, 1861, the circulation in the loyal States was, according to the best estimates, $130,000,000 ; on the 1st of November, 1862, it was $167,000,000. The coin in circulation, including the coin in Banks, was probably not less on the 1st of November, 1861, than $210,000,000. On the 1st of November, 1862, the coin had been practically demonetized and withdrawn from use as currency, or as a basis for currency, and is therefore not estimated. The aggregate circulation of the loyal States, therefore, was, at the first date, $355,140,000 ; and at the second, only $377,104,000.

"Secondly. The whole, or nearly the whole, increase in the volume of the currency which has taken place was, it is believed, legitimately demanded by the changed condition of the country in the year between the two dates. The activity in business which, at the close of that year, had taken place of the general stagnation which marked its beginning ; and the military and naval preparations and movements which had vastly augmented the number and amounts of payments to be made in money, have, it is believed, legitimately demanded nearly or quite the whole of it. . . .

" Thirdly. It is perhaps still more conclusive against the theory of great redundancy, that, on the 15th day of October, when the aggregate actual circulation, national and corporate, was about $360,000,000, the premium on gold was 37⅛; whereas, on the 29th of November, when the circulation had increased by more than twenty millions, the premium on gold was 20 to 30 per cent." [1]

An inflated currency, no matter by whom issued, is that which has no proper constituent in merchandise for its conversion. This covers the whole ground. Such was Mr. Chase's currency. Instead of there being, as he stated, no inflation, on or near the 1st of November, 1862, it is demonstrable that it was inflated to the extent of nearly $250,000,000. The liabilities of the Banks, their notes and deposits, increased from November, 1861, to November, 1862, from $480,114,487 to $632,363,444; the amount of increase being $152,248,957. The increase of government notes during the year equalled $194,964,000; the total increase of paper money being $347,-212,957. The amount of coin in the country on the 1st of November, 1861, was estimated by Mr. Chase at $210,000,000. Of this sum, $102,146,215 were held by the Banks as reserves. The amount of coin held in reserve on November 1, 1862, equalled $101,227,369. Mr. Chase claimed that the whole amount of coin in the country on the 1st of November, 1861, had been demonetized previous to the 1st of November, 1862. But the coin held by the Banks in 1861 was no more in circulation at that time than that held by them in 1862. It was no more demonetized at one period than another. In every return which the Banks have made, from suspension of specie payments to the present time, all the specie held by them has been claimed, and allowed by the government, as a part of their reserves. Deducting the difference between Mr. Chase's estimate (which was merely conjectural) of the amount in circulation, and that held as reserves by the Banks, the amount demonetized during the year equalled $108,772,631; the increase of the currency, consequently, equalled $238,440,326. As it is demonstrable that it was inflated to that degree, it is useless to follow out Mr. Chase's explanation, when the cause can be referred to its proper law, which he wholly ignored.

[1] Report of the Secretary of the Treasury, for 1863.

A suspension of Banks, when they have no relation to governments, is always a temporary expedient or measure. The strong resume as speedily as possible, for the purpose of self-protection. The weak have at once to go into liquidation. In this way the ground is soon cleared. The strong Banks well know that the only way in which they can preserve themselves from loss is to compel the payment of their bills in coin or its equivalent. To do this, they must set the example. Banks can no more carry on their operations without paying their liabilities than can merchants. A merchant, temporarily embarrassed, may be allowed to remain in the management of his affairs, as the best means of securing the most favorable results. If, however, it be feared that he is neither capable nor upright, he has speedily to give place to his creditors. So with Banks. If it be assumed that they will speedily get out of their difficulties, they are allowed to do so, as the most competent for the management of their own affairs. There is nothing that a well-managed Bank dreads so much as prolonged suspension. This resorted to, it is compelled for the future to sail without compass or chart, in constant fear of making shipwreck. Upon suspension, its first thought is resumption. It never dreams that such a measure is to become permanent. The Bank of England, after its suspension in 1797, restored its affairs with such wonderful celerity as to be able to resume within three years ; and would have resumed, could permission have been obtained from the government.

Mr. Chase claimed the issue of the government notes to be among the most brilliant and successful acts of his administration. He pointed with pride to the decision of the Supreme Court of the State of New York, the leading State of the Union, affirming its constitutionality. After leaving the department of the Treasury, he was made Chief Justice of the Supreme Court of the United States. He had not been long in his new place before the question of the constitutionality of the notes issued by him came before him for adjudication. He now believed that they were likely to become as unpopular as they had been popular ; and he washed his hands of all connection with them, denying that he ever even suggested the expediency of their issue.

" It was," he said, "my fortune at the time that the United States legal-tender clause was inserted in the bill to authorize the issue of United States notes, and received the sanction of Congress, to be charged with the anxious and responsible duties of procuring funds for the prosecution of the war. In no report made by me to Congress was the expedient of making the notes of the United States a legal tender *suggested*." [1]

There have been a plenty of corrupt and servile judges; but it is doubtful whether history affords another example of such absurd untruthfulness. Congress passed three bills authorizing the issue of plain legal-tender notes. Of these, Mr. Chase certainly drew one with his own hand. In the decision in the case referred to, he speaks of the legal-tender clause as a sort of accident, "inserted in the *bill* to authorize the issue of United States notes." There was no "insertion," for the reason that the sole object of all the bills was to create an irredeemable legal-tender currency; and Mr. Chase urged the passage of all, from their alleged necessity, with all the force of which he was capable. The facility with which, in this country, such men reach the most exalted and responsible stations, is little fitted to excite our national pride.

One advantage of a currency of depreciated bank-notes over the depreciated notes of a government is the uniformity in value of the former. The "books" of a Bank tell what its notes are worth, and at that price they remain. Those familiar with its affairs are always ready to take them at their value. All understand that a Bank whose notes are depreciated will either speedily resume or be wound up; and that in either case the holders of its notes will soon receive their value in coin. By what book is the value of the depreciated notes of a government to be ascertained, and who is to administer upon and wind up its affairs? In the month of September, 1864, the price of those of the United States fluctuated between 187 and 254⅛; a difference of 67¼ per cent in a few days, due almost wholly to the varying fortunes of the war. A great disaster would send up the price of gold all the way from 10 to 20 per cent. A great victory would reduce its price in equal ratio. The crowning attribute of a competent currency is that its value is wholly independent of

[1] Knox *v.* Lee, 12 Wallace's Reports.

all such influences. A currency depreciated from its nominal value is by no means an intolerable one. Where government does not interpose, it will pass only at its real value, as does the silver coin of the United States at the present time. A bank-note, where its constituent is worth 50 per cent of its par value, will pass at that price. No one is deceived or injured in taking it. It will not rise or fall much above or below its value. Its price has always' close reference to its actual worth. The mischief comes with a currency the value of which there is no possible means of determining, but to which a potency is sought to be given equal to that of coin ; and may be given, as far as debtors are concerned, although it may prove to be utterly worthless in their hands. It is this attribute of discharging debts, without reference to their value, which renders all government currencies so intolerable. In the two great historical examples, the currencies became worthless, although having at one time the price of coin. It is a currency mischievous from the very beginning, and terribly so where the issues are large. Those who issue it will always, in the end, be able to supply their necessities far better without than with it. Its issue is a crime ; and, if those issuing it be not criminals, it is only from ignorance of its nature and effect.

The currency of government notes having been secured, Mr. Chase returned to the work of establishing a system of banking, to be created by the United States ; its notes to be provided for by the deposit of bonds. The following presentation of the subject is taken from his first report, under date of December 5th, 1861 : —

" To enable the government to obtain the necessary means for prosecuting the war to a successful issue, without unnecessary cost, is a problem which must engage the most careful attention of the legislature. The Secretary has given to this problem the best consideration in his power, and now begs leave to submit to Congress the result of his reflections.

" The circulation of the Banks of the United States on the 1st day of January, 1861, was computed to be $202,000,767. Of this circulation, $150,000,000, in round numbers, was in the States now loyal, including Western Virginia, and $50,000,000 in the rebellious States. *The whole of this circulation constitutes a loan, without interest, from the people to the Banks,* costing them nothing except the expense of issue and redemption, and the interest on the specie kept on hand for the latter purpose ; and it deserves consideration whether sound policy does not require that the advantages of this loan be transferred, in part at least, from the Banks, representing only the interests of the stockholders, to the government, representing the aggregate interests of the whole people.

" It has been well questioned by the most eminent statesmen whether a currency of bank-notes, issued by local institutions under State laws, is not, in fact, prohibited by the National Constitution. Such emissions certainly fall within the spirit, if not within the letter, of the Constitutional prohibition of the emission of " bills of credit " by the States, and of the making by them of any thing except gold and silver coin a legal tender in payment of debts.

" However this may be, it is too clear to be reasonably disputed that Congress, under its constitutional powers to lay taxes, to regulate commerce, and to regulate the value of coin, possesses ample authority to control the credit circulation which enters so largely into the transactions of commerce, and affects in so many ways the value of coin. In the judgment of the Secretary, the time has arrived when Congress should exercise this authority. The ....g bank-note circulation depends on the laws of thirty-four States, and the character of some sixteen hundred private corporations. It is usually furnished in greatest proportions by institutions of least actual capital: circulation, commonly, is in the inverse ratio of solvency. Well-founded institutions, of large and solid capital, have, in general, comparatively little circulation; while weak corporations almost invariably seek to sustain themselves by obtaining from the people the largest possible credit in this form. . . .

" The Secretary thinks it possible to combine with this protection a provision for circulation, safe to the community and convenient for the government.

" Two plans for effecting this object are suggested. The first contemplates the gradual withdrawal from circulation of the notes of private corporations, and for the issue, in their stead, of United States notes, payable in coin on demand, in amounts sufficient for the useful ends of a representative currency. The second contemplates the preparation and delivery, to institutions and associations, of notes prepared for circulation under national direction, and to be secured as to prompt convertibility into coin by the pledge of United States bonds and other needful regulations.

" 1. *The first* of these plans was partially adopted at the last session of Congress, in the provision authorizing the Secretary to issue United States notes, payable in coin, to an amount not exceeding $50,000,000. That provision may be so extended as to reach the average circulation of the country, while a moderate tax, gradually augmented, on bank-notes, will relieve the national from the competition of local circulation. It has been already suggested, that the substitution of a National for a State currency, upon this plan, would be equivalent to a loan to the government without interest, except on the fund to be kept in coin, and without expense, except the cost of preparation, issue, and redemption; while the people would gain the additional advantage of a uniform currency, and

relief from a considerable burden in the form of interest on debt.
These advantages are, doubtless, considerable; and if a scheme
can be devised by which such a circulation will be certainly and
strictly confined to the real needs of the people, and kept constantly equivalent to specie by prompt and certain redemption in
coin, it will hardly fail of legislative sanction. . . .

" 2. *The second* plan suggested remains for examination. Its
principal features are : first, a circulation of notes bearing a common
impression, and authenticated by a common authority; second, the
redemption of these notes by the associations and institutions to
which they may be delivered for issue; and, third, the security of
that redemption by the pledge of United States stocks, and an
adequate provision of specie.

" In this plan, the people in their ordinary business would find
the advantages of uniformity in currency; of uniformity in security; of effectual safeguard, if effectual safeguard is possible, against
depreciation; and of protection from losses in discounts and exchanges : while, in the operations of the government, the people
would find the further advantages of a large demand for government securities; of increased facilities for obtaining the loans
required by the war; and of some alleviation of the burdens on
industry, through a diminution in the rate of interest, or a participation in the profit of circulation, without risking the perils of a
great money monopoly.

" A further and important advantage to the people may be reasonably expected in the increased security of the Union, springing
from the common interest in its preservation, created by the distribution of its stocks to associations throughout the country, as the
basis of their circulation.

" The Secretary entertains the opinion, that, if a credit circulation
in any form be desirable, it is most desirable in this. The notes
thus issued and secured would, in his judgment, form the safest
currency which this country has ever enjoyed; while their receiv-
ability for all government dues, except customs, would make them,
wherever payable, of equal value as a currency in every part of the
Union. The large amount of specie now in the United States,
reaching a total of not less than $275,000,000, will easily support
payments of duties in coin, while these payments and ordinary demands will aid in retaining this specie in the country as a solid
basis both of circulation and loans.

" The whole circulation of the country, except a limited amount
of foreign coin, would, after the lapse of two or three years, bear
the impress of the nation, whether in coin or notes; while the
amount of the latter, always easily ascertainable, and, of course,
always generally known, would not be likely to be increased beyond
the real wants of business. . . .

" It only remains to add that the plan is recommended by one
other consideration, which, in the judgment of the Secretary, is
entitled to much influence. It avoids, almost, if not altogether,
the evils of a great and sudden change in the currency, by offering
inducements to solvent existing institutions to withdraw the circu-

lation issued under State authority and substitute that provided by the authority of the Union. Thus, through the voluntary action of the existing institutions, aided by wise legislation, the great transition from a currency heterogeneous, unequal, and unsafe, to one uniform, equal, and safe, may be speedily and almost imperceptibly accomplished."

It may be replied, to invert a little the order of Mr. Chase's statement, that it never "has been well questioned by the most eminent statesmen, whether a currency of bank-notes, issued by local institutions under State laws, is not in fact prohibited by the National Constitution." No competent authority had ever maintained that the notes of a State Bank are the " bills of credit" contemplated and forbidden by the Constitution ; nor has any one worth listening to ever questioned the authority or power of the States to charter Banks for the purpose of issuing notes, as the representatives of capital, to serve as money. Previous to the formation of the Constitution, all the States had issued their own notes to serve as money. Having no capital, these were termed " bills of credit." Immediately upon the formation of the Constitution, and before the United States Bank was created, Banks were chartered by the several States, without a suggestion of their unconstitutionality from any quarter. On the contrary, it was claimed by the strict constructionists, in the debates upon the bill creating the first United States Bank, that the right to charter Banks was among those reserved to the States, and was never conferred upon the general government. Mr. Chase's assertion was not only a pure fiction, but was opposed to the whole experience of the country and the theory of our government. It might, with some reason, be claimed, as it was claimed, that, the central government having no express authority therefor, the power to create Banks resided only in the States. It is the common trick with those who have a selfish or personal scheme on foot to begin by invoking the Constitution. Underneath this covert they stalk for game. Jackson appealed to the Constitution against the creation of a United States Bank, and in favor of State Banks. Mr. Chase's appeal was against State Banks, and in favor of United States Banks. Between the two, who were simply types of American politicians, the country has had no Constitution, by having as many constructions of it as there were demagogues seeking plunder and place. Neither does the "whole circulation of Banks constitute a loan, without interest, from the people to the Banks, costing them nothing except the expense of issue and redemption, and the interest on the specie kept on hand for the latter purpose." Every issue of the Banks, to be convertible, must be founded on solid capital; and, if they make more than the ordinary rates of interest, it is because they are intrusted with large sums, for safe keeping, which they are allowed to loan. Every borrower at a solvent Bank receives the command and use of capital equal in value to the amount of his loan. Neither did " the value of the existing bank-note circulation depend on the laws of thirty-four States, and the character of some sixteen hundred different corporations." Its value was almost wholly independent of legislation. It is probable that, at the date of Mr. Chase's report, the currency of the country would have been more valuable than it was, had there been no legislation whatever in reference to it. A currency may exist as well without legislation as may any method employed in the operations of production and trade. A great deal more harm than good came of all the safety-fund systems. Neither is it true that " the greatest amount of circulation is furnished by the weaker Banks." Deposits are circulation as well as notes. The former constitute the circulation and means of strong Banks. If amount of circulation be evidence of weakness, then those Banks which Mr. Chase would consider to be the strongest are the weakest. A " credit circulation " is never desirable, nor can it long be maintained unless it be made legal tender. When a suspension takes place, the public will for a time use the notes of the suspended Banks, but always in the expectation that they will speedily resume. The moment it is seen that they will not resume, or that any one will not, its notes will no longer be taken as money. Mr. Chase had not the trace of an idea of the principles upon which the notes of Banks circulate. He assumed that they would remain at par, the capital to redeem them being locked up in Washington. He might as well have assumed that a steamer could cross the Atlantic with its coal locked up in the same place. Every note issued by a Bank must, to maintain itself at par, be convertible into coin or its equivalent, at the will of the holder. The power to convert on demand is that which gives it value. If convertible in terms in ten years from date, it might be worth 50 per cent of its nominal value.   If not convertible at all, and bearing no interest, it will be worth nothing.   If a Bank accumulate a sufficient amount of means to carry on its business in addition to the bonds held for the redemption of its notes, it may treat the former as so much surplus or invested capital, and be well content not to disturb it.   Few Banks, however, can afford to lock up an amount of means equal to their circulation.   When called upon to resume, they must reclaim their bonds, or wind up their affairs.   It is, however, after the démonstrations in the preceding pages, useless to reply further to Mr. Chase.   Wholly ignorant of the laws of money, his financial policy, like that of General Jackson, was simply a means of securing political power.   Jackson became mighty and famous in consequence of his attack upon and overthrow of the United States Bank.   Why might not Mr. Chase become equally so by overthrowing the State Banks, and substituting United States Banks in their place?   Mr. Chase, however, while attempting a similar *rôle*, was wholly without those qualities which enabled General Jackson to play with such success upon the passions and prejudices of the nation. He did, indeed, succeed in breaking up the State Banks.   In face of the chaos which was threatened by the secession of the South, the North were prepared to accept almost any measure that promised to unite by closer ties the States still remaining faithful to the government.   What, at first sight, could seem better calculated to this end than a uniform currency, supported and sustained by the public credit?   Plying with such arguments the derelict minds of the members of Congress, Mr. Chase at last succeeded in carrying his scheme, by which associations to be formed under general laws were to receive, upon a deposit of United States bonds, notes for circulation, equalling 90 per cent of the nominal value of the former.   The new Banks were required to hold reserves in irredeemable United States notes, equalling 25 per cent of their liabilities. Such reserves, however, were only required of the Banks of the leading cities.   Those of country banks might be very largely made up of the notes and credits of the former.   Specie was carefully and thoroughly eliminated from the whole system.   The notes of the Banks were made redeemable, not in coin, not in that which had a higher value, but in that which had an inferior value to themselves.   This is the reason why they are never returned for redemption. The value of the notes of the government depends solely upon its will or solvency. They may never be paid. In such case, they would be utterly worthless. The government is above and beyond law. In addition to the bonds which the Banks put up, exceeding their circulation 10 per cent in amount, and which now command a high premium, they hold means equal, in theory at least, to the amount of such circulation; so that, should the government fail to pay either its notes or bonds, the holders of the notes of the Banks would receive a respectable dividend.

But the question of chief concern is not so much the manner in which the nation got into its present dilemma, as how it is to get out of it. Fortunately, we are not left to opinion or sentiment for the method. We can, if we will, have demonstration for our guide. All agree that paper is to constitute the greater portion of the currency, both for the government and the people; and that this paper must, at all times, be the equivalent in value of coin. What is the kind of paper money that is always the equivalent in value of coin? That which can be converted on demand into coin, or into merchandise of the value of coin. It is plain that the notes of a government cannot be this kind of money. It never issues notes or symbols as instruments for the loaning of capital, but always to supply the lack of it. No government possessed of the means for its redemption ever thought of issuing paper money. When it could not borrow by contracting to pay interest, it issued its notes without interest; making them a legal tender, by means of which they have a high value for those in debt, who, by the rise of that which they possess, consequent on their issue, can get them at a price far less than their value in coin, and pay them away at the value of coin: in other words, government gets its notes into circulation by helping the debtor to swindle the creditor classes. The retribution comes when the notes are to be paid.

Until governments can borrow without interest, the evidences of their indebtedness, which call for none, will always remain at a discount, no matter what their form. Their notes, payable at a future day, without interest, can never equal in value a similar nominal amount of capital in hand. Such notes must be wholly demonetized; that is, must cease to be currency before specie payment can be resumed. We are aware that the public will reply that, "if Banks maintain large amounts of notes in circulation, holding very little coin, why cannot governments do the same? Governments can do the same by becoming bankers, and discounting bills given for merchandise. Their notes, in such case, will circulate as money; and will return to them, provided no bad loans are made, in the payment of their bills. It is not the gold they hold which secures the return and convertibility of their notes, but the merchandise these bills represent. Possessed of this in sufficient quantity, their notes will be returned to them for conversion without effort on their part, if they did not hold a dollar of coin. These taken in, they might make new issues; which would, if based on merchandise, return in the same way as those previously put in circulation. An issue of currency by Banks and bankers is always, as already shown, accompanied by a mutual exchange of obligations, — of those of the borrower, that he will pay a certain sum at a future day, for those of the lender or issuer, that the former can have on demand an amount of coin or merchandise equal in value to the notes issued. The notes are the instrument by which the borrower secures the use of such coin or merchandise. He may pay his bills by returning to the Bank the obligations issued by it, in which case those created on either side are mutually discharged; or in coin, with which the Bank will discharge its notes which have fallen into other hands. When a government issues a currency, no such proceedings take place: it alone contracts to retire it. When Banks issue a currency, the receiver as well as the issuer contracts to provide the means for its redemption. The wide difference in the modes of issue of the two currencies will show their difference in kind. Unless governments are at all times prepared to discharge their obligations in the same way that those of bankers are discharged, they can never issue one of the kind that the nation is now seeking to establish.

Governments are not to turn bankers by discounting bills and providing adequate reserves for the discharge of their liabilities. Mr. Chase attempted the *rôle* of a banker, without any provision for his issues; and soon found himself broken, with the whole government at his back. He had outstanding, when he suspended, $33,460,000 of notes, which immediately fell to a discount for gold, although equally receivable with it in the payment of the revenues.   Why did they fall to a discount?   Simply for the reason that they could be used at their face for one purpose only, — the payment of the revenues.   Those to whom they might be offered who had other uses for their money would not pay the par of coin for that which would not serve them in its place.   If they wanted the latter, the only way to get it would be to sell, in the open market, for what they would bring, the notes they might hold or receive.   Such a process would of itself involve an inconvenience which would reduce their value below that of coin. Those first issued got into circulation only for the reason that they were supposed to be convertible into coin.   So soon as .this could not be had for them, they were reduced in value by being restricted to one use.   They did not fall very largely in price, for the reason that it was seen that they would speedily be taken in in the payment of the revenues.   No more of the kind were attempted to be issued, for the reason that government had no means for their payment.   To attempt the issue of notes payable on demand, without any provision of means therefor, would be to break down its credit altogether. Hence the issue of legal-tender notes, which had a competency (which plain notes did not have) of discharging contracts. By virtue of this attribute they would serve as money, at some value, in almost unlimited amounts.   Although they had a competency to discharge contracts, which plain notes had not, they fell, after they had been issued in considerable sums, to prices far below those which the plain notes commanded; for the reason that definite provision was made for the retirement of the latter, while no such provision was made for the former. The value of one could be pretty accurately estimated ; that of the other was a mere matter of conjecture.   So long as it is believed that the notes will be paid, the legal-tender clause adds to their value.   When it is believed that they will not be paid, no one will contract to receive them, although creditors may be still compelled to do so after they become wholly valueless.   As they can never serve all the uses of coin, they can never have its value until they are actually exchangeable therefor.   To resume, therefore, the government must be prepared to take in, and must take in and retire permanently, all its notes now circulating as money. Till such provision be made, they will remain at a discount. This proposition is as demonstrable as that an acute angle cannot equal a right angle.

The demand notes first issued by Mr. Chase, after their dishonor were only at a small discount, for the reason that they were receivable in payment of the revenues. Now, assuming that those annually collected in the United States equal $300,000,000, should the government issue its notes receivable in their payment, without interest, it is probable that at least $100,000,000 of these would at all times be outstanding, and in the hands of the public for the purposes they would serve. These notes would be current as money, at a discount equalling the interest that would accrue, at a low rate, on their amounts, from the time of their issue till they were returned to the Treasury. If they bore an interest at the rate of, say 2 per cent, they would circulate as money at their par value. In this way, and in this way only, might a government issue a convertible currency; which, except in extraordinary emergencies, would be maintained at the par of coin. As the proper constituent for its retirement would be provided, it would exert no effect to inflate prices. The objection to such a currency would be the constant liability to its excessive issue. Its proper amount would soon come to be measured by the necessities of government. This of itself is sufficient reason against its use. Another reason, not so conclusive, but still sufficiently so, is that by the use of its notes bearing no interest, government could not, on their issue, realize their par value; while, if they bore interest, it could not get them in at their par value. In either case, the notes would be in the nature of a loan, upon which interest would have to be paid, either directly, or by selling them below their face. The ordinary operations of government should never be carried on by borrowing, but by capital in hand, or the symbol of capital. They should, in great measure, be carried on by the latter, precisely as the ordinary operations of society are carried on, for the purpose of allowing gold and silver to serve as reserves rather than as currency.

Payments abroad, as far as the government was concerned, would, even if the country were on a specie basis, be made by the use of symbols rather than of coin. It would make its remittances in bills, leaving it to the drawers to send forward their proper constituent. To meet them, it might not be necessary to send forward a dollar of coin. If this were required at all, it would only be to make good any balance growing out of the ordinary operations of trade. All such balances must, in the long run, be paid in merchandise by countries that are not producers of the precious metals. This country, as it is a producer, would, after resumption, be a large exporter of them as merchandise. Even in such case, government would never become the direct exporter of them. In the purchase of bills, the notes and credits of a specie-paying Bank would serve to it all the uses of coin; and, from their greater convenience, would be preferred thereto, precisely for the reason that they are preferred to coin by the commercial public. The sellers of bills, producers of merchandise, would prefer, for their own convenience, to be paid in symbols rather than coin. With very large payments to be nominally made in it, years might elapse without the export of a dollar of it. When the work of redemption is fairly entered upon, this country will for some time be a large importer of coin from the very countries to which it is now most indebted. These will not only be wholly paid in merchandise, but they will be compelled to send us large amounts of coin, in discharge of the balances arising against them in the course of trade. Ours will then, for a time, become the creditor instead of the debtor nation. Resumption is to inaugurate an era of economy; an excess of exports of merchandise over imports; a " balance of trade " in our favor, to be paid in coin. If government can discharge all foreign obligations by the use of symbols, still better can it discharge by their use all domestic ones.

A currency of the kind described must be issued by Banks, or a Bank. Private bankers, no matter the extent of their means, and however competent they might be to issue a currency, could not give sufficient guarantees for its uniformity and stability, nor could they perform for government all the duties required in its operations. The Bank whose currency government is to use should be created by it, that it may be in a position to impose and enforce conditions necessary to its own protection as well as to that of the public. Such currency could not be furnished by Banks generally, for the reason that conditions necessary to be imposed would be too onerous to be borne by them, and could be borne only by the Bank which was to become the depository of the revenues of the government, and which, for this reason, would attract to itself very large deposits from the commercial and mercantile classes. The Bank to be created should be required to deposit with the government the bonds of the latter, to the extent of at least $100,000,000 (with provision, if proper, for their increase), the interest of which should not exceed $3\frac{1}{2}$ per cent, as security for the public deposits, and as ultimate security for its creditors. It should be required to establish branches in every State in the Union, and in every city having a population exceeding 50,000; and to transfer, without charge, the public revenues from place to place. In providing for its capital, the Banks, wherever the parent Bank or a branch was to be established, should for this purpose be allowed to combine their own capitals. In this way, that for a National Bank might be provided, without any increase for the country, and without supplanting or invading the rights of those already in existence. Assuming the coin in the National Treasury to equal $100,000,000, this sum, transferred to the Bank, would form adequate reserves for an issue of convertible currency the amount of $300,000,000, as at least one-third that sum would be maintained in circulation in the collection and disbursements of the revenues. For such an amount of notes, only a small amount of reserves would be required. A panic in Great Britain has no tendency to send home the notes of the Bank of England for coin; nor would it, in this country, have a tendency to send home the notes of a Bank receivable in the revenues; for, whether valuable or not, they would always in the end serve to the holders in the place of coin. That transferred to the Bank, consequently, could be made the basis for an issue, in addition to that required in the operations of the government, of $200,000,000 of convertible notes, to serve for the purposes of production and trade. In this way the government could immediately place itself on a specie basis, as could individuals who had sufficient means therefor. The Bank would at once become the depository of all the specie in the country, and whatever was imported, or produced from the mines: so that its means of making loans upon a specie basis would undoubtedly increase much faster than suitable paper could be found for discount. Every person that was able to resume would open an account with it, and would conduct his operations in the currency issued by it; and this process, like all healthy and natural ones, would steadily gain strength till all unhealthy and unnatural ones were completely superseded.

But provision for resumption, and the creation of a currency by means of which the operations of the government, and in time those of the whole country, could be carried on, would be by no means the only or chief advantage resulting from a Bank of the United States. No matter the extent of its operations, the greater part of the currency is always to be furnished by other and local institutions. To render a currency furnished by such safe and adequate to the wants of the country, provision must be made for the constant redemption of their issues. The tendency of money of every kind is always to the centres of capital and trade. When, however, the notes and credits of Banks are issued in the discount of bills representing merchandise, they will as a rule remain in circulation till they have served for its distribution. Where issues are made on accommodation paper, these, having no proper constituent for their employment, tend immediately toward the commercial centres. The tendency of all the issues of the New England States was constantly toward Boston. With daily redemptions in that city, of all the Banks within the territory dependent upon it, there could be no considerable excess of issue by any Bank, as such excess had to be taken in almost as soon as it was made. By the system peculiar to that section of the country, and which has already been described, a currency uniform in quantity and value, or one reflecting the means and wants of the people, was secured. This system, which was purely voluntary, and which imposed upon all the members to it the duty of redeeming their notes at their own cost, at the point to which they constantly tended to flow, never obtained in any other part of the country, chiefly for the reason that no other section formed such a complete geographical and commercial unit. By means of the United States Bank and its branches, and by these alone, will a similar system, or rather series of systems with similar results, be formed for the whole country. A branch of this

Bank established at Chicago would, as a means of increasing its loanable capital and its business, receive in payment of its bills, and on deposit, the notes and credits of all solvent specie-paying Banks within the territory of which that city is the commercial centre. It would, however, require all such Banks, whose notes and credits it received, to make them "good," daily, at its own counter. It would be equally for the interest of all solvent Banks to make such an arrangement, as a means of securing for their notes and credits the widest circulation. A good reputation would do for them what it does for a merchant ; and they would, as a rule, seek to deserve it. The managers of Banks, if they are not influenced by higher motives, are subject to much fewer temptations than merchants to deviate from their proper path. By means of a United States Bank and branches, the system of redemption which so long prevailed in the New England States would, as far as specie payments were resumed, be created for the whole country, and would be enforced by the most potent of all laws, — that of self-interest. If the notes of a Bank in Minnesota, for example, were "good" at the branch Bank in Chicago, they would be equally so in every other part of the country, less the rate of exchange between that city and the point at which they might be offered ; or they might have a higher value than coin in certain sections from which remittances to that city were to be made. A branch at Louisville would, in the same way, receive the notes and credits of all the Banks in good standing within the territory dependent upon that city ; imposing, however, the conditions described. Another system of redemption would thus be created for another and important section of the country. These systems would be repeated, so as to apply to every portion of it. Wherever a branch was established, the local Banks would be forced to come up to its standard ; and as the notes and credits of the Bank and its branches, less in each case the rate of exchange, would be of uniform value throughout the country, the notes and credits of all the Banks in good standing within it would everywhere possess a similar value. A safe, homogeneous and convertible currency would thus be created by the operation, as it were, of natural laws. Its use, like that of bills of exchange, would necessarily involve occasional losses ; but such losses are no argument against the use. The possibility of loss, in every operation or investment, would teach the necessity of providing every safeguard against it. The great danger in the matter of currency is that such safeguards will not be provided. A notice by the Suffolk Bank, while that system was in operation, that the notes and credits of any Bank were "not good" at its counter, was always received by the public as a valuable warning. Experience proved that in almost every case it was not seasonably given ; not from the fault of the Bank, but for the reason that every one redeeming at it would naturally make every sacrifice to prevent an exposure of its own affairs. There never was a charge made against the former that it ever acted in any case from improper motives, or unadvisedly. Never was there a well-founded charge made against either Bank of the United States that it treated any Bank otherwise than with the greatest forbearance and consideration. If it erred at all, it always erred on the side of too great leniency. Every Bank should be held to the strictest account. No injustice can be done it in compelling it to make all its issues the equivalent of coin. The public, who are the holders of the greater part of its notes and credits, have no means of determining their value. Hence the importance of a system which shall disclose, at the earliest moment, the weakness or improper conduct of every issuer of currency. No injustice can be done a Bank, should all its liabilities be demanded for immediate payment. It contracts to pay them all on demand. They will not be presented for immediate payment so long as its loans are properly made. No Bank will collect the notes and credits of another Bank, for the purpose of making a run upon it, and thereby injuring its credit, as it would be liable to create in this way distrust and disturbance which might weaken its own position, its own liabilities being always payable on demand. As it is for the interest of merchants to deal fairly with their customers and the public, as the best means of promoting their own welfare, so it is for the interest of Banks to treat each other in a similar manner. Their interest becomes the rule of their conduct ; and this interest always coincides with duty.

It is needless to remark that the results predicated of an United States Bank to be created are precisely those which followed the establishment of the second Bank in 1816. The nation then was in a desperate condition in reference to its currency, and was restored mainly through the instrumentality of the Bank, by methods which have been fully set forth in the extracts given from Mr. McDuffie's Report of 1832.

Adequate provision for the future having been made, so that government, and individuals as far as they are able, can conduct their operations upon a specie basis, the next question is the mode of getting rid of our present inconvertible currency. That having relation to the government notes can be easily disposed of. The only provision to be made for their retirement is to fund them at a low rate of interest. That done, the duty of government will be at an end. They are to be wholly and finally retired. The degree of rapidity of their retirement is to be left with their holders. With provision for funding them, the notes should be demonetized, except in the discharge of contracts entered into in them. In their retirement not a dollar of coin should be used. If the notes, as is so generally claimed, be good money, they will continue to circulate as money. If not, it will be for the interest of their holders to get rid of them as soon as possible. As they will have a great deal of work to do in discharging the contracts that are still outstanding, they will be funded only in an easy state of the money market, and when no embarrassment would be created thereby. It would be a great misfortune to have resumption proceed too rapidly at the outset. The retirement of the notes will create the least disturbance when their holders are left to act as their interest may dictate. The process will be a healthy, for the reason that it will be a natural one. Taken in connection with the provision of a Bank, it will be a most rapid one, for the reason that a new currency will constantly be provided to take the place of the old. The old will disappear so soon as the new can be created. Nothing could be more absurd than for government to attempt to pay off its notes in coin. This would involve the employment of a cumbersome and expensive machinery to effect that which could be accomplished far more easily without than with it. To pay off the notes in coin, government would be compelled to provide a sum equal to a million dollars in coin, weekly, for a period of more than seven years. No provision for a new currency having been made, it could proceed only a few weeks in this direction without creating the greatest alarm and embarrassment.

The plan proposed by government is as if an army should burn all its ships, and all the material necessary to build new ones, before attempting to cross a river that obstructs its way. It imagines, in fact, that it has no river to cross ; that resumption is a mere ceremony, not a radical revolution in the monetary system of the country. Were the method it proposes practicable, the time required for its accomplishment would be a sufficient reason against its adoption. Instead of a little more than one year within which resumption is now to be had, ten years would not suffice ; while the country would suffer more in the process of resumption in coin, than it has suffered from the first issue of the notes to the present time. The plan proposed is as unjust as it is impracticable. No one has paid coin, or their value in coin, for the notes. Why should the holders receive more than their value in coin ? If they are paid in it, who are to be its fortunate receivers ? Only a small amount can be paid off at any one time. The coin paid out would not go into circulation, for the reason that the notes remaining outstanding would still be at a discount. Whoever received the coin for them would immediately sell it, as do the Banks at the present time, in order to make the premium. The attempt to retire the notes by payment in coin would be worse than the labor of Sisyphus. If the government were to announce that it would immediately begin the payment of its notes in gold, at the rate of a million dollars in a week, and that it would continue such payments for three hundred and sixty weeks consecutively, that is, until the whole were taken in, they would fall to a discount far greater than that at present existing. Their value could then be pretty accurately estimated, and they would only command their value. If the whole were to be retired within an average period of three and a quarter years, they would probably fall to a discount of twenty-two, instead of six or seven per cent. The impression now prevails that they are to be retired by the first day of January, 1879. It is this idea that controls their present price. They can no more be retired by payment in coin, or brought to their par value by 1879, than the waters of Lake Superior can before that time be pumped into the ocean. The exact period of resumption can no more be foretold than can the state of the weather on the first day of January, 1879. Nothing but mischief can come from fixing a certain day upon which the event is to take place, especially when every step now taken tends to postpone instead of to advance it. When every thing is done that can be done by way of preparation, the nation must quietly await the event.

Provision having been made for the creation, by a Bank, of a convertible currency, to serve as well in production and trade as in the operations of the government, and for the demonetization of the legal-tender notes, the next step to be taken is the repeal of the law imposing a tax upon the notes of State Banks. That step taken, such of the latter as were able would immediately begin the issue of convertible currency. There are now some six hundred of these institutions in existence in the country, having an aggregate capital of $80,000,000; loans and discounts to the amount of $178,000,000; and deposits to the amount of $158,000,000. Among these are some of the strongest Banks in the country. Their means, whatever they are, are in hand, not (like those of most of the National Banks) tied up in Washington They would be compelled to issue convertible notes, or none at all. The public will never take an inconvertible currency when they can get a convertible one ; and this they could get in the notes and credits of the United States Bank. To issue a currency, the State Banks would have to provide reserves in coin, as it is assumed that the United States legal-tender notes have been demonetized. The tax on their notes being removed, great numbers of the National Banks would immediately reorganize themselves as local or State institutions. Such as had no considerable part of their means in governments could very speedily become the issuers of notes for circulation. They could, for the reasons stated, issue no other than convertible ones. Resumption by the National Banks which received their full quota of notes would necessarily be a much more gradual process, unless government should consent to return to any Bank its bonds, upon the deposit of a corresponding amount of National bank-notes which might not be its own. Government could compel the various Banks to redeem their notes so returned in its own notes, to be cancelled if advisable. As the Banks in receiving their securities would presently, as State institutions, become the issuers of money, no great or necessary stringency would result from the retirement of one kind of currency, as it would speedily be followed by the issue of another. The return of their bonds would enable them to provide coin reserves, far exceeding in amount any that would be required in their operations. The bonds held as security for their notes, equalled, according to the last annual report of the Comptroller of the Currency, the sum of $337,170,400. There were held by them, in addition, at the same time, securities of the United States to the amount of $47,840,150 ; the total amount equalling nearly $400,000,000. The coin value of their securities largely exceeded that sum.

Assuming the Banks to resume with total liabilities of $800,000,000, and that they should hold at the time, in coin, a sum equalling 25 per cent of this amount, one-half their government securities would provide all the reserves required. Why should they not be allowed to become possessed of their capital as fast as it can be reclaimed, even if they remain national institutions? As it is, not a dollar of the whole $400,000,000, or at least of that portion of it held for their circulation, is available as banking capital! The Banks cannot resume, for the reason that that which is to enable them to do so is out of their possession, and must always be so, so long as they issue notes. As long as they are deprived of it, they must remain at a dead lock, so far as resumption is concerned. But if the present system be abolished, what, it is inquired, is to become of the people, — the poor, ignorant, and innocent note-holders? What has become of them for the past fifteen years, and what has been the result of the paternal action of government during the whole of this period? During the whole of it, their measure of value and instrument of exchange has fluctuated all the way from thirty-five to ninety-five per cent of its par value ; in consequence of which, all ideas of relation of cost to value have been well nigh lost, and all the operations of society brought, as it were, to a dead stand. Would the people, could they have had their own way, have for fifteen long years put up with the currency which has been imposed upon them? With Banks alone to furnish it, it is impossible that an inconvertible currency should long remain in circulation. Strong Banks will always be speedily compelled to resume ; weak ones, to go out of existence. Government officials are certainly, of all parties, the last to be intrusted with the direction of the business operations of the country. Who, but these, brought her into her present dilemma? The beauty and excellence of Mr. Chase's measures have been their theme from their adoption to the present time. They successively repeat the same story, parrot-like, from year to year. Their iterations, however absurd they may be, tend to confirm the general delusion. Would the people, left to themselves, make use of weights or measures to be selected by lot or chance; no two of which, though nominally the same, were alike; and which could not fail to involve in loss, often excessive, one, and perhaps both parties to their use? And yet this is precisely the condition of the country in reference to her paper money. She cannot get out of her dilemma, as her hands are fast tied. Why not, for the future, let the note-holders take care of themselves? Has not experience shown that they are as competent to do this as the government? They would not be compelled to receive the notes of a single Bank. They could always demand to be paid in coin at the rate of bank-notes. They would always demand to be paid in it, were there any cause for distrust. They should always be encouraged to exercise a distrust of bank-notes, precisely as the managers of Banks should be encouraged to exercise it in reference to bills offered for discount. Neither notes nor bills should be accepted until a case had been made out in their favor. Mutual distrust, or caution rather, is the essential condition of all sound banking, as of all the business operations of society. If note-holders understand that they have no protection but the capital of Banks and their competent management, there will be very few unsound ones. Why does not government interfere in all the transactions of society? Why does it not say to a builder of ships, that he shall not begin the construction of one till he has deposited in the Treasury a sum equalling the value of the ship he is to build, as a guarantee that he will discharge all obligations contracted in its construction? How many ships would be built under such provisions as these? Would not the parties who were to deal with the builder protest against them, for the reason that they would destroy his power of purchasing their materials or labor? And would they not demand that he should be left with his means, for their advantage as well as his own? Would any one purchase a bill of exchange, were he told that it might not be paid on its presentation, but that the equivalent therefor had been provided by the drawer on its return, not in merchandise but in securities? Bills are used in foreign trade to serve as money. They will not be purchased if they will not serve as such. To remit one that might not be paid might involve a loss far greater than its amount. The operations of commerce and trade can no more than those relating to real property be carried on by instruments severed from their proper constituents. The purchaser wants the specific thing contracted for, not some other which may have no relation to it. To require drawers of bills to put up securities for their payment, in addition to the merchandise represented by them, would be to abridge commerce, between nations or countries widely separated, to one-tenth its present proportions. Purchasers would be the last to require such deposits, as they would very properly infer that, to make them, drawers had been compelled to divert some portion of that which should provide for their bills. So with the notes of Banks. These represent their bills. By means of the former, their holder can obtain the proportion of merchandise for which they call. He does not want an interest in securities locked up in Washington; but that which he can eat, drink, and wear. So far as the bills discounted do not represent merchandise, the Banks must make up the deficit in coin. All safety-fund Banks are constantly liable to make issues which do not represent capital, as a means of supplying the place of that with which they parted in order to purchase their securities. They are taught to regard the notes delivered to them with so much ceremony and formality, as money to be used in any way they choose. Not the first attribute of money has been given to them. It can only be given by their being made to represent, in the discount of bills, merchandise which will be certain to retire them in its purchase for consumption. It is impossible sufficiently to impress this fact upon the issuers of a currency created by safety-fund Banks. Hence the constant disturbance and disasters arising from their operations. The issuers of a currency without any special provision for its redemption are not liable to similar temptations and mistakes. They see that the only way in which they can secure circulation for their issues, and bring them back without loss to themselves, is to base them upon capital that must soon be taken for consumption. An unsecured currency, therefore, is much more uniform in amount and value than a secured one, and consequently far preferable. The losses of the holders of the unsecured notes of the New England Banks during the continuance of the Suffolk system did not, in ratio to their amount, equal one-tenth those of the holders of the notes of the New York safety-fund Banks. Under the former, from its efficiency in enforcing constant redemptions, it was hardly possible that any Bank should become so embarrassed as not to be able to provide for its liabilities out of its means. If these were not sufficient, the stockholders of the Banks were liable to an amount equal to that of the shares held by them. No safety-fund system assumes to provide security for deposits, which are currency equally with notes, and by means of which Banks are much more liable to become embarrassed than by means of their notes. The principle of security, if it be worth any thing, and if it would produce its proper results, should apply to both kinds of currency. It is not, however, either from notes or deposits that the greater part of the losses incident to banking operations arise. The Bank of England has paid specie on all its liabilities for fifty years past; yet its action may have been instrumental in promoting enormous inflations, to be followed by excessive contractions, in consequence of which losses have been caused equalling many times its own circulation. The moment the issues of a Bank cease to represent merchandise speedily to enter into consumption, it is exerting a disturbing influence on affairs, in ratio to the extent of its operations. If the ordinary instruments of distribution were suddenly destroyed, the loss that would be caused would exceed tenfold their value. If these be the notes and credits of Banks, a great inflation and subsequent contraction of them will often result in losses many times greater than the whole circulation issued. It is in this way that nine-tenths of all the losses incident to or caused by Banks arise. The chief care, consequently, in their administration, and in legislating in reference to them, is to guard, not so much against losses occasioned by their inability to meet their obligations, as against the disastrous influence they may exert over prices, and over production and trade. They may be instruments of immense mischief at the same time that they possess means amply sufficient to discharge all their liabilities. The remedy

can come only from systems of redemption which shall immediately return upon all the Banks every issue that is not
employed in the distribution of its proper constituents. So far
as the public is concerned, a note issued by a Bank, based
upon an United States bond, produces precisely the same effect
as a note issued in the discount of a fictitious bill. It serves
not as the instrument of distribution for a corresponding
amount of merchandise, but as one for the consumption of
an equal amount of accumulated capital. As capital so symbolized is not, as a rule, made the basis of reproduction, there
has been an excess of expenditure equal to its amount, with a
contraction usually far more excessive than was the inflation.

A safety-fund system, in whatever light viewed, is radically
vicious. It is impossible that it should be established throughout the United States, and at the same time provide a currency
that will not be either deficient in amount, or inconvertible
and depreciated. Our present national system would never
have been established, had Mr. Chase possessed a competent
knowledge of the laws and functions of money. His great
theme was a " credit circulation," — a circulation sustained by
faith, not by works. When any one took a note of a Bank
created by his system, he was told to look confidingly toward
Washington, and believe that locked up in the vaults of the
Treasury was a security which possessed a value in coin equal
to all the notes the Bank might issue. Suppose the holder
did not want a government security, but food. Could he avail
himself of the former, he would still have to convert it into
money, which could only be effected at an expense and loss of
time, involving a loss of interest, equalling perhaps two-
thirds the value of his note. At one time, since the safety-
fund notes have been issued, they were worth, in coin, only
about one-third of their nominal value. It is little consolation
to be told that Mr. Chase was as wise as his time. The misfortune is that he was as reckless and unscrupulous as he was
ignorant. He could not rest till he had hopelessly involved
the whole country in the meshes of paper money. His first
achievement was the establishment of an inconvertible currency of United States notes. Upon this superstructure he
erected his safety-fund system. But for one, he could not
have established the other. By means of the former, the

Banks were practically relieved of all responsibility, so far as concerned their note circulation. In consideration of taking away their means, he provided that they should never need them. The only way, consequently, in which they can provide for their liabilities is by the return to them of their means. To insist upon the continuance of his system, is to insist upon continued suspension. The Banks of such States as Iowa and Minnesota cannot be permanent lenders to government, at 6 per cent, to an amount equalling their entire capital, and have any thing left to be loaned to the public. The idea is preposterous. It will appear so to every one who has emancipated himself from the idea that money is a fiction, not a substance; or that its value in exchange depends upon its amount, not upon any provision by merchandise or coin for its retirement.

By allowing Banks to reclaim their bonds, and to issue notes for the future without any further provision for them but their capital and bills, they would, for the first time since they went into operation, be in a position in which they could resume. They would then eagerly avail themselves of the opportunity, as absolutely necessary to the preservation of their means. All of them must see, by this time, that every day passed without resumption is seriously impairing their value. Every day is the number of their bad debts increasing. Under the present system, time alone is wanting to complete their ruin. The great majority of them are now indifferent or opposed to any change, only for the reason that they see no way out of their present condition. Let it be known that they can get back their securities, become State organizations, or issue notes as National Banks without any deposit therefor, and the great majority will earnestly set their face toward resumption. Until they move, the most effective step in this direction will remain to be taken. The national system should be got rid of as fast as possible. The greater part of the currency is always to be furnished by local institutions, and all such should be under local supervision and control. The work of the central government, as far as the currency is concerned, should be at an end when it has created an United States Bank.

It is easy to point out, even to demonstrate the way. Will those see and follow it who are charged with the work? Here

lies the real difficulty.   Mr. Sherman, now at the head of the
Treasury Department, sees in it nothing but a ceremony.   He
has only to " salute the flag," and the thing is done : —

" Nor are we to decide whether our paper money shall be issued
directly by the government or by Banks created by the government; nor whether at a future time the legal-tender quality of
United States notes shall continue.   I am one of those who believe
that a United States note issued directly by the government, and
convertible on demand into gold coin, or a government bond equal
in value to gold, is the best currency we can adopt; that it is to be
the currency of the future, not only in the United States, but in
Great Britain as well; and that such a currency might properly
continue to be a legal tender, except when coin is specifically stipulated for. . . .

" In my judgment, the real solution of specie resumption will
thus come through the voluntary act of National Banks, each acting for itself, under the general direction of the law, precisely as
the Bank of England, the Bank of France, and the New York
Banks brought about and maintained resumption.   I have never
regarded with solicitude the amount of United States notes outstanding, for, as I will show, they can be easily maintained at par
in gold; but the agency of the Banks in securing resumption, and
the effect of resumption upon their customers, were matters of
solicitude.   This I no longer doubt or fear.   The whole problem
consists in a partial and limited transfer of capital, now invested by
National Banks in United States bonds, to individuals.   The high
price of these bonds, and the idle capital that seeks investment in
them, will enable each Bank to strengthen itself by a sale of bonds,
without in the least impairing its ability to discount or loan, and,
in fact, to increase its power to do so ; and the bonds will be absorbed by the increasing demand for such securities.   Strong Banks
in cities do not need the currency, for their currency is certified
checks.   Their currency is largely held by them; or, if in circulation,
it can be retired and cancelled without impairing in the least their
ability to loan or discount.   The Bank currency being thus diminished, as the time for resumption approaches, the United States
notes, supported by a gold reserve and the power of the Secretary
to sell bonds, will easily be maintained at the gold standard, and
the problem is solved.

" This partial contraction of Bank currency will unlock and dis-
sipate a greater contraction which has gone on since the panic, and
will go on until the public mind rests assured that the day of
resumption is not only promised, but rendered certain by the course
of events.   An increase of currency will follow resumption.   Great
masses of notes now lie idle in bank-vaults and in the Treasury, and
are hoarded in homesteads all over the land.   There is deposited in
the Treasury, without interest and belonging to Banks, $31,005,000,
represented by currency certificates.   There are now in the vaults
of the National Banks $73,626,100 United States notes and frac-

tional currency, $17,166,190 bank-notes, in all $90,792,290; and in the Savings-Banks, State Banks, and other Banks that have made returns to the Comptroller of the Currency, the sum of $48,431,409: in all making $170,228,699, and this is far more than the reserve required by law. The practice of hoarding currency has greatly increased from the day of the panic; and it may be safely said, that there is among the people, and in Savings-Banks and trust companies, not less than $200,000,000 of currency idle. Nothing but the best of security will tempt it from its hiding-places; but, that security offered, it can be had for a less rate of interest than ever before. Capital met its periodical shock in September, 1873; and great masses of it (some say one thousand millions) vanished as a dream, and are now represented by worthless bonds, bills, notes, and certificates of stock, worth but little more than the paper on which they are printed. This panic came upon us when the paper god was lord of the ascendant; when corner lots, at fictitious prices, were the par of exchange; when unproductive railroads were the El Dorados of visionaries, and wild schemes of improvement, both in this city and in all the cities of the Union, increased municipal debts to an unexampled degree. This reckless inflation of credits collapsed long before this law was passed. Money, the agent of capital, and, when idle, capital itself, was hoarded, and still remains inactive, or is loaned on call or unquestioned security. *This* is the contraction of which so many complain. It is not caused by the Resumption Act, but by a want of confidence in investments that offer. Confidence cannot be restored by a repeal, or by issuing more paper money. But the occasion does offer you an opportunity of withdrawing a portion of this idle money, and thus reaching a specie standard. The Banks can freely surrender a portion of their circulation, and thus be strong for resumption; while frightened and timid capital will gladly float into United States bonds when sold by the Banks. Nothing is wanted but confidence, faith, and time, to secure the closing triumph of our war policy, by the redemption of the only promise we then made that has not been honestly redeemed. . . .

" The amount of United States notes outstanding to-day is $370,943,392, less those lost and destroyed. Now, many who fear resumption suppose the whole mass of United States notes will then be presented for the gold; and they have counted up the number of tons of gold that will be required to do it. They figure up the interest at 5 per cent on the whole sum, and state that as an addition to our annual interest account. It is not necessary to reply to such exaggerations; nor is it possible to state with precision what amount of United States notes would circulate at par in coin. They could then be made receivable for customs dues, without a violation of the public faith. They will always be the reserve of National Banks. They could then be made receivable for bonds of the United States. They could be supported by the power to sell bonds to redeem them. They would, as a matter of course, be supported by the whole gold reserve in the Treasury. They would take the place of certificates of deposit, and be used in clearing-house exchanges. . . .

" With all these advantages, with the growing wealth and credit of our country, I do not believe the present volume of United States notes need be largely if any reduced, to keep them at par in coin. We have now a gold balance in the Treasury of $37,120,772.73, and a currency balance of $9,529,404 over and above our currency and coin certificates. It is true this balance is subject to overdue and accruing demands, fully stated in a recent letter of the Secretary of the Treasury; but a certain amount of these demands always remain uncalled for, and when presented are met by accruing revenue. Suppose (what I regard as an extreme case) that we add to this reserve $100,000,000, — fifty million in coin certificates, and fifty million in coin, — does anybody doubt but it will be ample to redeem any note that is presented? Confidence being once established in their redemption, and who will want the gold for them? They can be and no doubt will be reissued, without or with the legal-tender clause, as the law may hereafter provide; and with their credit secured, established at par in coin, they will not only circulate in Texas and on the Pacific slope, as well as in other parts of the United States, but, like the Bank of England note, in all countries that have commercial relations with us."[1]

Had Mr. Sherman remained in the Senate, such remarks would have been passed over as but a repetition, after the fashion of the speaker, of the incoherent and meaningless talk which is the burden of all. The Senator has now become the Minister of Finance, charged with the duty of conducting the nation out of the perils which beset it. Upon him depends, very largely, whether it shall be carried through them, or whether it shall, by the inadequacy and absurdity of the method to be adopted, make disastrous shipwreck of all its dearest interests. The question before him is not, as he persistently and on all occasions asserts, the maintenance, with some slight modifications, of the financial system of the country, but a revolution as radical as that made by the issue of the legal-tender notes. This is the question. It is not one that will brook delay. Upon the answer, if he be to remain Minister of Finance, depends whether the administration shall be a success, or make an utter and disastrous failure, in a matter by far the most important of those that are to engage its attention. " We are not to decide," he says, " whether our paper money shall be issued directly by the government or by Banks created by the government; nor

---

[1] Speech of Hon. John Sherman, in the United States Senate, March 6, 1876. Pamphlet edition, pp. 4, 16, 17, 20, 21.

whether at any future time the legal-tender quality of United States notes shall continue." The only question for decision is, whether government or Banks shall issue our paper money. Governments can never, or will never, issue a convertible one. This has been demonstrated over and over again. Banks, when governments do not enter the field, will issue no other. They require to be paid in coin, as the only mode of preserving their capital. Their note-holders, for the same reason, require to be paid in coin or its equivalent. For either not to require that which may be due them in coin or its equivalent is to court the total destruction of all their material interests. Governments, from necessity, make their issues inconvertible : Banks, from necessity, make theirs convertible. The difference between the two is as wide as the poles. They are as unlike as is light to darkness, truth to untruth, something to nothing. If nothing be equal to something, then we are not called upon to decide whether government or Banks issue our paper money. If nothing cannot equal something, then the first question to be decided is, who is to issue this money? Neither," continues Mr. Sherman, "are we called upon to determine whether our currency shall be plain or legal-tender notes. Both," he assumes, "may equally be made to circulate as money." It has been already shown that plain notes, not convertible into coin, cannot be got into circulation, much less maintained in it. Mr. Chase's attempt to issue demand notes, to serve as money, was almost the only one in history ; and the suddenness with which that great charlatan was brought to grief should stand as a warning for all time. Legal-tender notes, by being made competent to the discharge of contracts, can be made to circulate, though possessing no intrinsic value. If governments issue a currency, as they will never provide the means for its conversion previous to its issue, the kind to be issued is not a matter of choice. It is a foregone conclusion. The Secretary "believes that a United States note issued directly by the government, and convertible on demand into gold coin, or a government bond equal in value to coin, is the best currency we can adopt ; that it is the currency of the future." Suppose the government notes now outstanding, equalling $360,000,000, which are now at a discount of about seven per cent, be made convertible into bonds having for the present a value equal to that of coin, what would be the result? In place of the notes rising to par, the bonds would fall, say to 95 per cent. The effect of the provision, making depreciated notes convertible into bonds, would be to sink the value of the latter much more than to raise that of the former. It would be simply a question of supply and demand. With the supply, the demand would fall off. The notes might, and if they were not legal tender would, be converted into the bonds, and so disappear; but while they remained in circulation they would be at the same discount as the bonds. In ratio as they disappeared, both bonds and notes would rise in value. If they were plain notes, no matter the price to which the bonds fell, they would still be converted, for the reason that an interest-bearing security would always be preferred to a non-interest-bearing one. If the notes were in the usual form of those serving as money, this fact would have no influence whatever in causing them to serve as such. Their price would be their real or estimated value. If the bonds into which the notes were convertible were at a premium for coin, the notes would be at a corresponding one. The latter would derive all their value from the former. As the bonds issued by the most stable governments are always fluctuating in price, and frequently excessively, that of the notes made convertible into them would be subject to precisely the same fluctuations. The price of the bonds, consequently, would become the standard by which all the transactions of a nation would be measured. It would not only, in the ordinary course of events, fluctuate largely, but it could be made to fluctuate excessively, by those who were strong enough to affect the credit of the issuer. The standard of value, consequently, might depend upon the success of the machinations or intrigues of the unscrupulous and powerful, who would never hesitate to sacrifice the public welfare to advance their own selfish ends. It would be the same as if they had the making of the weights and measures for every transaction to which they were a party. Mr. Sherman's best currency, consequently, is the worst one that could possibly be created. The alternative is that established by Providence, the quality and value of which can never be impugned by any artifice or contrivance. No one of ordinary sense has ever lived who could be made to believe that it was unsafe to hold the precious metals; while the fears or apprehensions of the most sagacious are often so worked upon that they eagerly part with all their government securities, for fear that some accident or event may weaken or destroy their value ; perhaps soon to lament their folly. Mr. Sherman might at any moment find his bonds, created for the purpose of funding his notes at par, at a discount of from ten to twenty per cent. What, in such case, becomes of his scheme for maintaining government notes, at all times, at the value of coin? " An increased currency," he says, " will follow resumption." How? By bringing into circulation $200,000,000 of currency now hoarded by the people, or idle in Savings-Banks and trust companies; $31,005,000, deposited in the Treasury and represented by certificates of indebtedness; $90,792,290 of National Bank and fractional currency now held, and largely as reserves, by the Banks, and which will go into circulation when specie payments are resumed (for gold and silver will then take their place); and a part of $48,431,409, now held by Savings, State, and other Banks. Deducting from this last sum $20,000,000, as held by the Savings-Banks, which in Mr. Sherman's estimate are counted twice, the sum which is to come into circulation, in addition to the present amount, is to equal $350,228,699! And at what cost is this vast sum to be liberated and added to the circulation? By the provision of $50,000,000 of coin, in addition to that in the Treasury, which when his speech was made equalled $37,120,772. He would indeed add, by borrowing, $40,000,000 of gold, for which he would be authorized to issue coin certificates, payable on demand, to the amount of $50,000,000; that is, for $10,000,000 more than the coin borrowed. The amount necessary to be provided for resumption, consequently, would equal only $40,000,000; as the coin which was borrowed, payable on demand or coin certificates, could not be made available therefor. The $37,112,699 in the Treasury could not be made so available, for the reason that the whole amount would be required for the payment of interest on the government indebtedness, unless the Independent Treasury were abolished, and a United States Bank created to take its place. The United States notes, after resumption on Mr. Sherman's plan, " could be made receivable for customs dues, without a breach of the public faith. They would always be the reserves of the National Banks." What kind of notes? Not plain notes, certainly, as these could not be got into nor maintained in circulation. Plain notes, if made convertible into them, would be simply orders for bonds, which would be executed as soon as issued. Such notes would exert no influence over prices, as they would not serve as money. Bonds would fall in ratio to the amount of notes issued. If the public should be found indifferent whether they held interest or non-interest bearing securities, the sooner government should stop the payment of interest the better. It is assumed, however, that the historic preference for interest-bearing securities is founded in reason, and must be still respected. If the notes were legal tender, then they would be at a discount, for the reason that they would be instruments in excess of the means of expenditure. As they would not be convertible into coin, how could government provide itself with the latter, wherewith to pay the interest on its indebtedness? By selling its legal-tender notes, in which its revenues would be collected, in the market, to the highest bidder. With one or two sales of the kind it would find its notes at fifty per cent of their nominal value. How could they serve as reserves of the Banks, as Mr. Sherman asserts they always would? There would be no plain notes to serve as such, as they would not be money, only orders for bonds. The latter could not serve as reserves, especially after resumption, as these would have to be in that form of capital whose value was uniform and absolute. If the notes were legal tender, their reserves would be in that which would always be at a discount compared with coin. In other words, so long as this kind of reserves was used, the Banks would not have resumed. All this is plain enough, if any distinction is to be made between things which possess value and those which do not. Upon this distinction turns the whole question of money. Mr. Sherman declares, in substance, that there is no difference between reality and fiction. His great factor in resumption is " confidence "! That secured, " who," he triumphantly asks, " will want gold for the notes?" That secured, "the present volume of United States notes need not be largely, if any, reduced. . . . They can then, and no doubt will, be reissued, without or with the legal-tender clause; and, with their credit secured and established at par for coin, they will not only circulate in Texas and on the Pacific slope, as well as in other parts of the United States, but, like the Bank of England notes, in all other countries having relations with us." There is the same sense in all this as to say, that people will no longer want food, when they know they can have it for the asking. But would resumption bring an additional amount of some $350,000,000, now claimed by him to be in great part hoarded, into circulation? What do men hoard, and why do they hoard? They hoard only the highest kind of property, — that which is the universal equivalent, — not the lowest kind, as government notes often are, and as our own threaten to be. They hoard when great social or political convulsions are immi- nent. Why do not the holders of the government notes invest them in good securities, as Mr. Sherman assumes they will do after resumption? The latter are as valuable now as they will be then. This talk about hoarding is the idlest of tales. Resumption would not bring an additional dollar of currency into circulation. It is, however, in view of what has preceded, useless to comment further. His assumptions and arguments are too puerile and absurd to deserve the least notice. They would receive none but for the fact that they show the method by which, as Minister of Finance, he proposes to conduct the country to specie payments. The alternatives are a complete and radical change in his views and policy, or certain and terrible disasters to the country, if he remain in his present position. To resume, every dollar of government notes is to be taken in as the condition precedent thereto. The currency furnished by Banks, including deposits, will have to be retired by an amount equalling probably $300,000,000. The notes of the National Banks now in circulation equal that sum in round numbers; their deposits, $650,000,000; the deposits of the State Banks, $159,000,000: making an aggregate of $1,100,000,000. It is very doubtful whether resumption can be had with a circulation exceeding $800,000,000. This sum is nearly twice as great as that outstanding on January 1, 1860; and probably equals the amount which would now be outstand- ing, at a normal rate of increase since that time.

If, as is demonstrable, the condition of resumption be the previous retirement of currency to the amount of $650,000,000, is there any mode by which the vacuum can be so well filled as by the creation of a National Bank, to become possessed of the specie now in the Treasury, to serve as reserves for its issues, — these to be further supported by being made receivable in the payments and disbursements of the revenues? Is there any other mode by which even the first step can be taken, preserving the present fabric till another can be provided in its place? If such mode be not adopted, the new can only arise out of the ruins of the old. There are now (June, 1877) in the Independent Treasury $108,137,083 in coin or bullion, — a sum sufficient for the issue of a convertible currency equalling three times its amount. Why should not this sum be allowed to repeat itself three times its amount? for with the creation of a Bank, that portion of it represented by coin certificates, as well as that belonging to the government, will alike go into it, and serve as reserves. Would not every one, government and people, be equally benefited? It may be urged that a Bank with a capital of $100,000,000 would be a great and dangerous monopoly. There could be no monopoly, no matter the extent of its operations, as it would supply only a small proportion of the currency. The Bank of England, which enjoys privileges which would by no means be granted to a Bank of the United States, does not, including deposits, supply one-tenth that in use in that country. Where the issue of a currency is perfectly free, it can no more be monopolized by one institution than can the entire capital of the country. Currency is but a symbol of capital, and will always have in this country, as at present, thousands of issuers. But suppose all the currency in circulation in the United States, amounting to, say, $1,000,000,000, were issued by a single institution, would the public safety and welfare be imperilled? What would be its position? It would be liable to be called upon at any moment to take in all its liabilities in coin, while it could not get in its means in a less time than three or four months. As any disturbance or distrust might drive it into suspension or bankruptcy, it would be compelled to observe the most scrupulous moderation and justice in all its dealings. Its advantage would be promoted in the degree of the morality, social order, and intelligence which prevailed. It would seek to promote the general welfare, as the surest means of advancing its own. Suppose such a Bank should undertake, as General Jackson asserted the old Bank undertook, to subvert the liberties of the country. This could not be done without a revolution which would involve all interests — those of the Bank, as well as of the country — in common ruin. Is it credible that it would court its own destruction ? The greater its issues, the greater the guarantees it would give for good conduct. Should it be alleged that such a Bank might become the instrument of oppression, by exacting excessive rates on its loans, it may be replied that exorbitant charges would greatly reduce its operations and profits. It would be as much for its advantage to make loans as it would be for that of the public to borrow. It would, like merchants, from a wise self-interest, always adopt a broad and liberal policy. The most effectual mode by which the latter increase their operations and profits is an equitable rule of conduct toward their customers. None so fully appreciate the fact that the highest material result from the highest moral conditions. The Bank would be governed by merchants, and by their methods and rules. With all its power, the Bank of England was never charged with demanding exorbitant rates with a view to profit. No similar charge was ever made against the Bank of France, the sole issuer of notes in that kingdom. But a monopoly of issue in such a country as the United States is impossible. If it were possible, as the borrower would always receive the value of his loan, the only oppression could come from being compelled to make payment according to its terms. The assumption of oppression arises from the idea that Banks, in making loans, do not part with capital, but demand it in their payment. It is from such an assumption that the prejudice against Banks and bankers has chiefly arisen. As in making their loans they lend coin or its equivalent in merchandise, they will take nothing in exchange that does not represent coin or its equivalent in merchandise. They will discount no bills the means for the payment of which are not provided before their creation. The victims of a " moneyed monopoly " are borrowers of small local capitalists, not issuers, who may and often do oppress their debtors. Banks always steer clear of such borrowers as these. They not only cannot oppress, advancing as they do capital equalling the nominal amount of their loans, but they are the most lenient of all lenders, for the reason that the failure of their customers may so disturb public confidence as to imperil their own condition ; and that their managers, who are usually merchants, have always a deep sympathy in the misfortunes of their fellows, and always stand ready to do what they properly can for their relief. Monopoly or oppression, therefore, either by national or local institutions, is the last thing to be feared. The assertion of Jackson, Benton, Hill and others, that the Banks and bankers of the country were in league against its liberties and welfare, was the natural expression of the hatred cherished by ignorant, jealous, and vindictive natures against those of whose superiority they were painfully conscious, and in whose overthrow they found some compensation for their wounded vanity. It is to be hoped that the era of such men is for ever passed ; and that the subject of a National Bank can now be discussed as a financial, not as a political or personal, question. Virginia very earnestly and very naturally opposed the old Bank, for the reason that the grounds upon which it was created might serve as a precedent for an attack upon her cherished institution, to which, while it existed, she was prepared to sacrifice every other consideration. The question involved in the creation of the Bank — the powers of the central government — brought on the war of the Rebellion, in which her territory was devastated by contending armies, her cities sacked and burned, her domain dismembered, her great institution wholly overthrown, and her " Ancient Dominion " reduced, from the proud pre-eminence it had so long enjoyed, to the rank of a second-class State. For doctrines alike subversive of all welfare and order, she wholly turned her back upon the teachings and example of Washington ; to which not only she, but the nation, must return, if they would establish on this continent an empire worthy the opportunity. Virginia, stripped, as she is, not only of wealth but of means for acquiring it at all commensurate with her resources, will welcome an institution which is to supply the place of the banking capital so indispensable to her welfare, and so ruthlessly swept away. What is true of Virginia is true of the whole South. One hundred years have elapsed since we were a nation, and that section of the country has hardly taken the first step toward the promotion of her real welfare. Up to the outbreak of the Rebellion, every step she took was directly opposed to it. She is only beginning to enter upon a period in which her policy is to be in harmony with her highest interests. To this end she will, as fast as possible, seek to rid herself not only of the precedents, but of the memories, of the past.

The object of this work, however, is not so much to pre-scribe methods for the future, as to state the laws of money in a manner so plain that every person of ordinary intelligence may act understandingly in reference to any measure that may be proposed, — to show the beneficent influence of Banks; that those entrusted with their management are the most zealous upholders of a free and upright government; that there can never be a monopoly of capital, so long as it is the product of industry and trade; and that merchants and manufacturers may safely be left to the guidance of an enlightened self-interest, with the certainty that the manner in which their ends are sought will always be in harmony with the public good. When such a degree of intelligence is reached, it may safely be left to the people to decide upon the methods or institutions they will summon to their aid.

APPENDIX.

THE QUESTION OF A DOUBLE STANDARD.

THE principles established in the preceding pages afford an easy solution of the question of a double standard.

As all currencies circulate only at their value, the cost of the standard to be adopted, whether of gold or silver, will always be the same. Should it be decided to establish one of gold, such silver as the country or government may become possessed of is to be converted, at its cost and value, into gold. The silver will always be convertible into gold at its value as currency. If silver is to be the standard, then the gold that is to come into possession of the country or the government is to be exchanged, at its value as currency, for a corresponding value of silver. The only question to be considered, therefore, is the relative convenience of the two standards : —

First : Gold will be the most convenient standard, as its value, in ratio to its weight, is at least sixteen times greater than that of silver.

Second : As the greater number of commercial countries have adopted gold as the standard, and as the tendency of all is in the same direction, the United States must follow. As nearly all exports of coin from this country are made to England, — to London, as the clearing-house of the world; — as the English standard is gold, and as all shipments of silver, as money, to that country, must be monetized in it, — that is, converted into gold before it can be used, — all foreign nations have practically, for us, adopted the gold standard. Gold, therefore, is the standard indispensable for us to adopt in our foreign commerce; if so, its adoption is equally indispensable in our domestic commerce.

Third : The adoption of a double standard will end in a single one, unless the cost and value of the two metals remain permanently uniform. There is no probability that they will remain uniform. The value of silver, from the excess of its production over that of gold, has largely fallen within a few years. The tendency is still in the same direction. Should it, as well as gold, be made a standard at the present value of each, and should it fall in value, the effect would be to drive the more valuable standard out of the market, precisely as the legal-tender notes drove out metallic money, leaving the country with but one standard, and that, as far as regards other nations, a debased one.

So far as this country is concerned, therefore, the question is no longer an open one. There being no difference in the cost of the standards, whether gold or silver, the most convenient should be the one adopted. Gold is the most convenient, in domestic as well as in foreign commerce. It is the only one in which foreign debts and balances can be paid. By adopting gold as the sole standard, in all sums exceeding, say one hundred dollars, our reserves will always be in that form in which they will discharge our balances by direct exchange, and place our industries and trade on an equality with those of other nations. Otherwise we shall have to convert our standard, depreciated, for the reason that it is exceptional, into that common to other nations with which we come in contact, upon their own soil, at their own terms, and often greatly to our injury. No possible advantage, but great disadvantage must result from the use of silver as a standard. This being demonstrable, the question, as already remarked, is not even open for discussion.

It is to be borne in mind that in commercial countries the standard of value is no longer the instrument by which exchanges are effected, symbols in great measure taking its place. In England, the currency, including deposits, equals nearly $3,000,000,000, against which the reserves held — the standard of value — do not exceed $200,000,000. Upon resumption in this country, the proportion of reserves — the standard of value — will be about the same to the currency issued. Whatever the standard adopted, exchanges will not be made by its use, but at its value, through the instrumentality of symbols. The amount required will not perceptibly affect the price or value of the vast mass which forms the stock of the world.

METHOD OF RESUMPTION. — AMOUNT OF SPECIE REQUIRED.

It has been assumed, in the preceding pages, that the United States notes, after provision of a Bank, and the return to the National Banks of their securities, are to be demonetized except in the discharge of contracts entered into in them; and are to be retired, not by payment in coin, but by funding. This mode of getting rid of them will relieve government of the necessity of providing a dollar of coin on their account, other than that necessary to meet the interest annually accruing on the funding bond.

Neither would the government have to provide a dollar of coin, other than that in its treasury, to place itself at once on a specie basis in all its future operations. It never can, or rather never will issue a convertible currency, for the reason that it never can, or never will make provision for its conversion — the necessary condition of all convertible currencies — previous to its issue. If it would conduct its operations on a specie basis, using paper money, it must use that which is the symbol of merchandise. The issue of such a currency is never one of its functions. It is to aid in its creation by depositing in the Bank to be established by it the coin of which it may be possessed; by making such Bank the depository of the public moneys, and by using its notes in the collection and disbursement of the revenues. Should the coin in its possession not prove adequate for the reserve of the Bank, the stockholders could readily supply what was wanting. By such means provision could at once be made for the issue of a convertible currency to the amount of $300,000,000, a portion of which should be got into circulation as the first step in the process of resumption. The government, as a necessary condition thereto, must unite its financial operations with those of the people. It must abolish the Independent Treasury, or so much of it as provides for the collection and disbursement of the revenues in coin. This institution was established as an act of hostility to the commercial classes; and to destroy, as far as possible, the paternal character of our government. If a Bank could be created to exist for twenty years, the necessary inference was that the government erecting it should at least exist twenty years, to give the proper efficacy to its act. If the government, as was the theory of those administering it, could be dissolved at any moment by the secession of any member of it, — that is, of any one of the States, —nothing could be more absurd than an act wholly opposed to such a

theory. It was to have no entanglements that could not be resolved
at an hour's notice. If the necessity, or reason, that led to the creation
of the Independent Treasury has ceased, the thing itself should
cease. The British government, using nothing but paper in its
operations, which far exceed in amount those of our own, is on a
specie basis by means of Bank of England notes, in which all its
revenues are collected and disbursed. Whatever coin it wants, it
draws from the Bank. Our mode of collecting the revenues in coin
is worthy only of such countries as Turkey or Morocco, in which
no form of money but that of coin is trusted. If the people, by
supplementing coin by symbols, make a saving equal to the interest
on a corresponding sum, — conducting their operations, at the same
time, with vastly greater convenience and safety, — then government
would, by imitating their example, make a similar saving, with
equally increased convenience and safety in its own.

It is assumed that the government is to retire its notes by funding. At what price or rate? At that, in each case if possible, at
which all outstanding contracts were entered into. This is not
possible. It must adopt one rate for all ; and that must be the one
at which the greatest number were entered into. Such a rate can
be sufficiently approximated to do substantial justice, not in all
cases, but in the aggregate. The creditor classes earnestly objected
to the issue of the legal-tender notes, for the reason that they were
compelled thereby to receive, in the payment of their debts, a less
value than was contracted to be paid. Great numbers were paid in
notes whose value did not equal one-half their nominal amounts.
Their remonstrances were treated with contempt. They received
no sympathy in their losses, as it was assumed they had a plenty left.
It is equally a hardship for debtors to be compelled, by an advance
in the value of the currency, to pay a greater value or sum than
was contracted to be paid, as it was for creditors to be compelled to
receive less. As the creditor must accept the notes, whatever their
value, so a debtor, after they have driven coin out of circulation,
can contract in no other currency. The value at which contracts
are entered into is always assumed by both parties to be the value
at which they are to be discharged. So accustomed have the race
become to regard uniformity of value as a necessary attribute of
money that it never occurs at the time, to parties to contracts, that
they are to receive or pay any other than the present value of
money, any more than it does that the scales or weights by which
they buy are to differ from those by which they are to sell. Were
the measures of extension or quantity liable to be different in

every transaction, it would not be long before society would be thoroughly demoralized, morally as well as materially. By the use of measures of value — United States notes — which fluctuate constantly, and often excessively, the people are in the same position that they would be were the former never two days alike. They are demoralized morally as well as materially. Recovery can only come from the substitution of the true for the false, — of the measures of value established by Providence in place of those established by man.

Relief, so far as it can be administered, must be general, not particular. If varying measures of extension were in use, and it were attempted to bring all outstanding transactions to one standard, the only equitable mode would be to ascertain the length, (the denomination being the same), of that by which the greater number of engagements were entered into, and adopt that as the standard for all. So with varying measures of value. That which is to be adopted for all must be the one at which the greater number of outstanding transactions were entered into. Great injustice will be done by any plan; but the lesser good must be sacrificed to the greater. The issue of the notes at the outset was an immeasurable crime, for which the appropriate penalty had to be paid, — and has, in part, been paid the present year, in the terrible strikes upon our railroads, and in the frightful loss of life and property which they involved. These are warnings that the reformation of our currency is not to be postponed a moment longer. Not only is its reformation the prime condition of the material recovery of the country, but of the maintenance of domestic order; of the public faith in engagements other than the government notes; — nay, of the existence of government itself. Fortunately, the period immediately preceding the present has been the longest in which the value of the legal-tender notes has, since their issue, continued very nearly uniform. Such value, consequently, is the one in which the greater number of outstanding contracts were intended to be paid. It must be adopted as the one at which all are to be paid. Commercial undertakings, which always make up a considerable portion of those outstanding, are entered into and run off, at least three times each year: these, consequently, are upon the present basis of value of the notes. If they can be carried out in the spirit in which they were entered into, resumption will be attended with comparatively little loss or disturbance.

The value of the currency at which contracts are to be discharged being determined, either by assuming its value as it stood on the first day of July, 1877, or by taking the average for the year preceding, then provision is to be made for funding at such value ; the equivalent being a bond having a long time to run, and bearing interest, in coin, at the rate of, say, 4 per cent. Such a mode of adjustment would be equitable, and satisfactory to creditors, as it would secure to them all to which they were entitled. It would wholly relieve government of the burden pressing upon it. It would be just and satisfactory to the indebted classes, as it would compel them to pay no more than they contracted to pay. It would silence the only objection to resumption which is well founded. While government or society may outrage the creditor classes with impunity, they cannot the debtor. The despoiling of the former excites little sympathy, for the reason that they are assumed to be above want : that of the poor may take away their very means of existence. However much may be taken from the rich, they still have enough left to render indispensable the maintenance of social order : its maintenance by those who have nothing to lose may become a matter of indifference. Hence, the complaints of the latter must be listened to, and their grievances redressed, although a deaf ear may be turned with impunity to those, equally well founded, of the rich. The latter will be well content with the plan proposed, as the alternative might leave them wholly without remedy, so far as the debts due them are concerned. By the mode of adjustment indicated, the government would be liable to no charge of bad faith, for the reason that it is impossible to reduce its faith, depending upon its " pleasure," to any definite quantity or value. It may execute its " pleasure " whenever it chooses : the holder of the notes must fix his own time at which it will be executed. If his estimate as to time be wrong, he has no one to blame but himself. It was expected, when the notes were issued, that the " pleasure " of the government would be speedily executed ; the notes, consequently, bore a high price. Fifteen years have elapsed, and government is still awaiting the time at which it may find itself able, or find it convenient, to pay them. No one charges it with bad faith ; although, had it been known at the time of issue that fifteen years would elapse before they were paid, they would not have produced one quarter their nominal value. Government will not be properly chargeable with bad faith, if it does not pay them within fifteen years from the present time. It is this uncertainty as to the value of the notes, dependent upon the " pleasure " of the government, that causes them to fluctuate so constantly in value. Should it declare its " pleasure " by providing for their funding into bonds having one hundred years to run, bearing a certain rate of interest, then a value which was before wholly conjectural becomes ascertainable and measurably uniform. The notes would have the value of that into which they would be convertible, whatever that might be. At any rate, government would have done all in its power to give its notes, so long as they remained outstanding, the attribute of uniformity; and all, in fact, that it can undertake to do.

Were the government to undertake to discharge its notes in coin, it could not resume till they were wholly provided for. They would go out of circulation as fast as provision was made therefor. As only a comparatively small amount of the coin by which they were taken in would go into circulation, the country, by their retirement by payment in coin, would, for a time at least, be virtually without a currency. By provision for the retirement of the notes by funding, government would have in effect resumed at the same time that they, or the greater portion of them, would still be in circulation, by virtue of being money — legal-tender — so far as all outstanding contracts were concerned. They would be money to a part of the community; and capital, for funding, to another. Those not in debt, and who preferred an interest to a non-interest bearing security, would fund. But funding would not go on long before the notes, as money, would produce to their holders a greater rate of interest, on loans of them, than that of the funding bonds. Funding would then cease, till money became easy by the running off of outstanding contracts; when it would again begin, to be again checked in the manner already stated. In this way, the notes would go out of circulation only very gradually, and as the new convertible currency came in to take the place of the old. The public would never be without a sufficient amount of currency in some form, wherewith to carry forward its operations; and would escape, as far as possible, those convulsions almost inseparable from all great changes in financial or monetary conditions.

It is assumed that the $100,000,000 of coin to constitute the reserves of an United States Bank could be readily provided, by means of which the government, and such of the public as were able, could place themselves immediately upon a specie basis. It is also assumed that the securities of the Banks composing the present safety-fund system are to be returned to them, for the purpose of providing the means for resumption; that they are to remain National or become State Banks, at their option; and that no other than the ordinary restrictions are to be imposed upon their issues.

Such provisions would not only give the greater part of them the means of resumption, but very large amounts in addition. It is also assumed that the whole amount of circulation, including deposits outstanding upon resumption, will not exceed $800,000,000; requiring reserves of say $200,000,000, of which one half will be held by the United States Bank. As already remarked, the convertible currency of the Banks, as it comes into circulation, will for a considerable time be largely supplemented by the government notes, which, being still legal tender in the discharge of outstanding contracts, will go out of circulation only as such contracts are run off. The rapidity with which the notes are funded will depend largely upon that with which the new convertible money will come into circulation : the removal of all apprehension on the score of the lack of circulation will go far toward carrying the country in safety from one system to the other.

But to resume upon any thing like an adequate basis for the whole country, vastly more is required than what appears to be ample reserves for the Banks. There is the same reason why the public — consumers of merchandise — should hold reserves in coin as that Banks should. The latter are little more than instruments arising out of production and distribution. Should their reserves prove inadequate, or be too largely drawn upon, as in case of a heavy export demand, they must strengthen themselves by drawing coin from the public, whose excessive expenditures have been the cause of the export. They may have no other mode of strengthening themselves, and at the same time of checking a prevailing extravagance, but by compelling the public to pay their bills in coin, which they can do by ceasing to make loans. As their issues, by means of which their bills were ordinarily paid, ceased, the latter would, in part at least, have to be paid in coin. Banks are never in a secure position, unless they have a large fund to draw upon other than that in their vaults. The public are never in a safe condition unless such fund exists, which is to make good, on their part, any deficit of products, the ordinary subjects of consumption. A perfect equilibrium between production and consumption is impossible. Balances will be constantly arising to be discharged in coin, for which Banks should not be called upon, or, if called upon, should be able to reimburse themselves from those against whom, from extravagance, or want of production, they were found. To resume with safety, an amount of coin, chiefly gold, should be in the hands of the public equal to that in the hands of the Bank, or, say, $400,000,000 in all. With the means that will come into the possession of the Banks, and with the products of our industries, the necessary amount of coin for resumption could be provided ' with all the dispatch consistent with our highest welfare : for it should be our aim to resume without causing any disturbance in those countries which are the great consumers of our products, which, and not our public securities, should supply the means. When our people move, the danger will be that they will move with too great, instead of with too little emphasis. The haste should be in adopting a competent method. The moment it is entered upon, there will be no complaint that it is not sufficiently rapid. It is far better to take time, to proceed slowly and methodically ; to rest occasionally on what is achieved, than to run the risk, by inconsiderate haste, of losing all.

Cambridge : Press of John Wilson & Son.